LUNHENG 論衡

The Complete Essays of Wang Chong 王充

Vol. 3

Appendices, Notes, Index

Quirin Pinyin Updated Editions (QPUE)

Dedicated to re-issuing classic works in the field of Asian Studies, these Revised Editions offer the full original text with the following features:

🐟 Older Wade-Giles transliteration fully updated and revised to Pinyin.
🐟 Fully re-typeset and proofed for typographical errors and inconsistencies.
🐟 Expanded index. 🐟 Paperback books designed to be a pleasure to hold and easy on the reading eye.

Series Titles Include the Following Revised Editions:

🐟 *The Poetry of the Early Tang*, by Stephen Owen
ISBN: 978-1-922169-02-0 (2012)

🐟 *The Great Age of Chinese Poetry: The High Tang*, by Stephen Owen
ISBN: 978-1-922169-06-8 (2013)

🐟 *Taoism and Chinese Religion*, by Henri Maspero
ISBN: 978-1-922169-04-4 (2014)

🐟 *Zen Dust: The History of the Koan and Koan Study in Rinzai (Linji) Zen*
by Isshū Miura and Ruth Fuller Sasaki   ISBN: 978-1-922169-12-9 (2015)

🐟 *Yin-Yang and the Nature of Correlative Thinking*, by A. C. Graham
ISBN: 978-1-922169-18-1 (2016)

🐟 *Poems on Poetry: Literary Criticism by Yuan Haowen* 元好問 *(1190-1257)*,
by John Timothy Wixted   ISBN: 978-1-922169-34-1 (2019)

🐟 *Poetics and Prosody in Early Mediaeval China: A Study and Translation of Kūkai's* 空海 *Bunkyō Hifuron* 文鏡秘府論, by Richard Wainwright Bodman
ISBN: 978-1-922169-36-5 (2020)

🐟 *Methods of "Nourishing the Vital Principle" in the Ancient Daoist Religion*
by Henri Maspero   ISBN: 978-1-922169-20-4 (2020)

🐟 *Reason and Spontaneity: A New Solution to the Problem of Fact and Value*
by A. C. Graham   ISBN: 978-1-922169-38-9 (2021)

🐟 *Ikkyū and the Crazy Cloud Anthology: A Zen Poet of Medieval Japan*
by Sonja Arntzen   ISBN: 978-1-922169-40-2 (2022)

🐟 *Lunheng: The Complete Essays of Wang Chong*,
Translated & annotated by Alfred Forke
Vol. I, Chapters 1–38   ISBN: 978-1-922169-14-3 (2023)
Vol. II, Chapters 39–85   ISBN: 978-1-922169-16-7 (2023)
Vol. III, Appendices, Notes, Index   ISBN: 978-1-922169-24-2 (2023)

For further details visit: www.quirinpress.com
Twitter: @QuirinPress

QUIRIN PRESS
P.O. Box 4226, Melbourne University, Vic. 3052, Australia

LUNHENG 論衡

The Complete Essays of Wang Chong 王充

Revised and Updated

Vol. III

Appendices, Notes, Index

**Translated and annotated
by
†ALFRED FORKE**

QUIRIN PRESS
Melbourne & Basel
2023

Published by Quirin Press
P.O. Box 4226, Melbourne University, Vic. 3052, Australia
E-mail: enquiries@quirinpress.com
http://www.quirinpress.com

The National Library of Australia Cataloging-in-Publication entry:

Wang, Chong 王充, 27–ca. 97, author.
Lunheng 論衡: The Complete Essays of Wang Chong 王充
Translated and annotated by †Alfred Forke

3 volumes, contents:
Volume I. Preface, Introduction, Chapters 1–38.
xviii + 437pp (ISBN: 9781922169143 paperback)
Volume II. Chapters 39–85.
ix + 427pp (ISBN: 9781922169167 paperback)
Volume III. Appendices, Notes, Finding List, Chinese Works Quoted, Index.
x + 401pp (ISBN: 9781922169242 paperback)

Wang, Chong; Alfred Forke (translator & editor).
Revised & Updated edition.
ISBN: 9781922169242 (paperback)
Quirin Pinyin Updated Editions (QPUE)
Includes bibliographical references and index (Vol. III)

Philosophy—Chinese.

Forke, Alfred, 1867–1944 - translator & editor.
181.1

Contents

Appendix I   The Theory of the Five Elements and the
            Classifications Based Thereon   865
            i   Various Terms for the Elements   887
            ii   What Are the Five Elements?   888
            iii   Fluids, Substances, and Seasons   893
            iv   Transformations of the Elements   895
            v   Local and Numerical Relations of the
              Elements   900
            vi   The Different Modes of Enumerating
              the Five Elements   904
            vii   The Regular Changes of the Elements
              during the Seasons   908
            viii   The Element Earth and Its Season   910
            ix   The Five Elements under Their Religious
              and Metaphysical Aspect   910
            x   Wrong Analogies   913

Appendix II   The Cycle of the Twelve Animals   915

Appendix III   On Some Implements Mentioned by Wang
            Chong   926
            i   Fans   926
            ii   Chopsticks   931
            iii   Burning Glasses and Moon Mirrors   932

Notes   935
    Notes to Introduction   937
    Notes to Chapters 1–85   938
    Notes to Appendix I   1146
    Notes to Appendix II   1153
    Notes to Appendix III   1156
Finding List   1159
Quotations   1165
Chinese Works Quoted   1173
Additional Note to the 1907 Edition   1175
Postscript to the 1911 Edition   1176
Index   1181

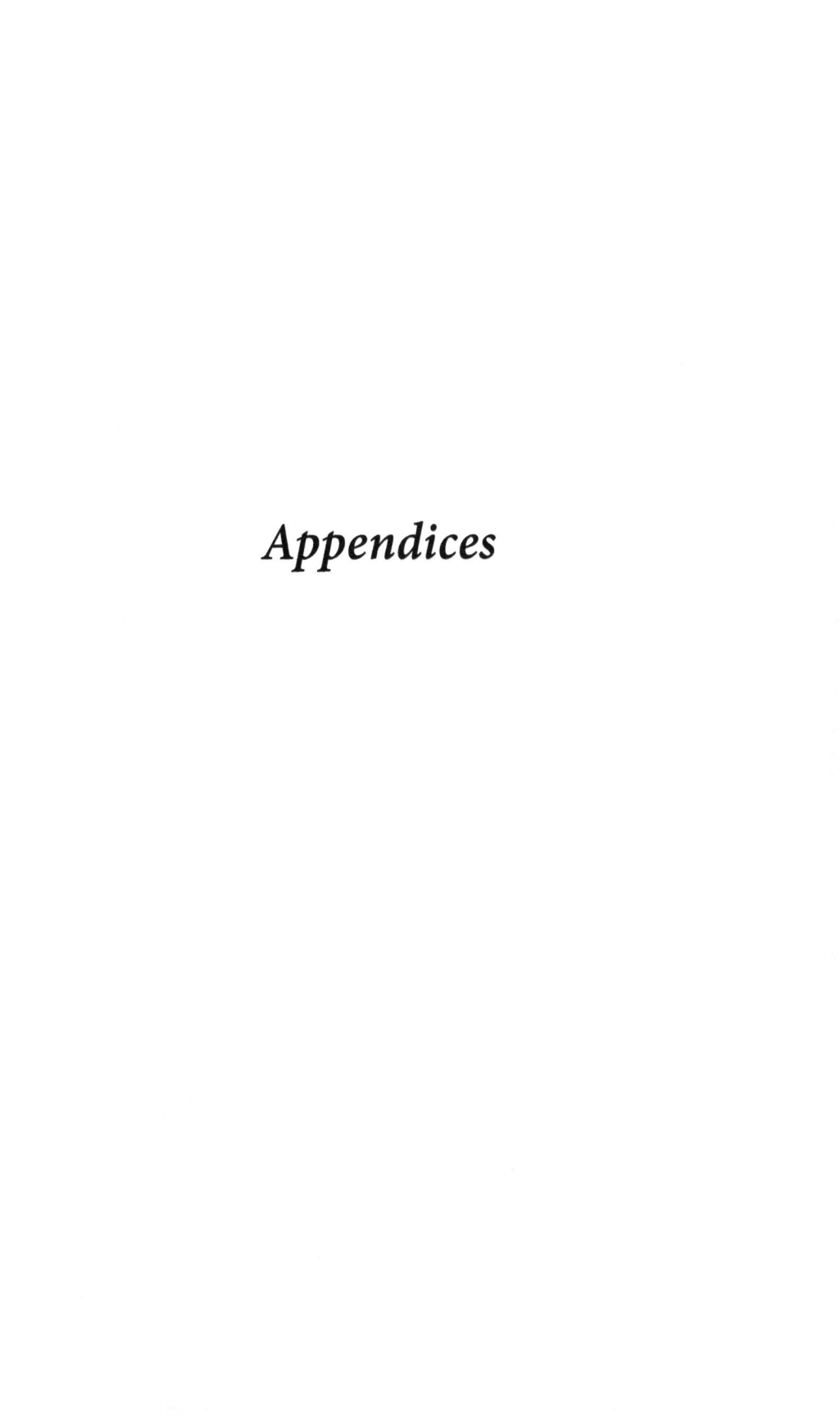

Appendices

APPENDIX I

The Theory of the Five Elements and the Classifications Based Thereon

A Sketch of Chinese Natural Philosophy

The theory of the Five Elements is no doubt of Chinese origin and its existence in ancient times proved by many old documents. We read in one of the first books of the *Shangshu* 尚書, the "Counsels of the Great Yu 禹," 大禹謨:

"Yu 禹 said,[1] 'Well! may Your Majesty think of it. Virtue implies good government, and government consists in nourishing the people. *Water, fire, metal, wood, earth*, and *grain* must be attended to. The rectification of virtue, the supply of all useful things, and ample provision for the necessaries of life must be well balanced. These nine achievements succeed each other, and the nine successive steps are praised in songs.—Caution the people with kindness, govern them with majesty, and incite them with the nine songs, in order that there may be nothing amiss.'

The emperor[2] said, 'Yes,[3] the earth is undisturbed now, heaven is in perfect order, and the six treasuries and three affairs properly managed. Ten thousand generations may perpetually rely on them. All this is your doing.'" (Legge, *Classics* Vol. III, Part I, p. 55 seq.)

What does it mean that the Five Elements: *water, fire, metal, wood,* and *earth* must be controlled by the Emperor? How can he exercise any power on nature?—By regulating his administration on the natural sequence of the elements, doing only those things which are in harmony with the element ruling for the time being. Natural phenomena are thus affected by the actions of the son of Heaven, being either disturbed or kept in their regular course. The *Liji* 禮記 will give us the necessary details.

The elements are here enumerated in the series in which they overcome or destroy one another, for which the terms 勝 or 克, are used. This part of the theory of the Five Elements seems to have been known to the compilers of the *Shangshu.*

The above passage is quoted and explained by the *Zuozhuan* 左氏傳, Duke Wen 文 7th year, and its genuineness thus firmly established. The corresponding passage of the *Zuozhuan* reads thus:

"The book of Xia 夏[4] says, 'Caution the people with kindness, govern them with majesty, and incite them with the nine songs, that there may be nothing amiss.' The virtues of the nine achievements may be sung, and are called the nine songs. The six treasuries and the three affairs are called the nine achievements. *Water, fire, metal, wood, earth,* and *grain* are called the six treasuries. The rectification of virtue, the supply of all useful things, and ample provision for the necessaries of life are called the three affairs."[5] (Cf. Legge, *Classics* Vol. V, Part I, p. 247.)

In another book of the Xia dynasty, entitled "the Speech at Gan" 甘誓, the following words are attributed to the Emperor Qi 啟, who is supposed to have spoken them in 2194 BCE:

"The Lord of Hu 扈 offers violence and insult to the *Five Elements,* and neglects and discards the three commencements (of the seasons). Therefore Heaven employs me to destroy and cancel his appointment. Now I merely reverently mete out the punishment of Heaven."[6] (Legge, *Classics* Vol. III, Part I, p. 153.)

Legge rightly observes that the crime of the Lord of Hu is stated in a somewhat obscure and mystical language. The Five Elements are not to be taken in the simple physical sense, for then they could not be outraged by a sovereign, but are metaphysical terms, equivalent almost to the four seasons 四時, as one commentator points out. The seasons are nothing else than the result of the revolutions of the Five Elements, and a ruler commits a crime, if for his administrative acts he does not choose the proper time, neglecting the seasons. At all events there is some theory at the bottom of the very concise expression.

Another criminal of this sort is introduced to us in the chapter *Hongfan* 洪範 (The Great Plan) of the *Shangshu*, where the Viscount of Ji 箕子 says: "I have heard that of old Gun 鯀 by damming up the Great Flood *threw the Five Elements into confusion*. God was highly incensed at him, and did not grant him the Great Plan with the nine divisions."[7] (Legge, *Classics* Vol. III, Part II, p. 323.)

I suppose that the imaginary guilt of Gun did not so much consist in his illtreating the element water as in not observing the propitious time for his draining work, thereby disturbing the Five Elements *i.e.*, the Five Seasons and thus bringing down calamities upon his people.

Further on the *Hongfan* informs us of the nature of the Five Elements, the fullest description to be found in the *Shangshu*:

"First the Five Elements: the first is termed *water*; the second, *fire*; the third, *wood*; the fourth, *metal*; the fifth, *earth*. Water is described as soaking and descending; fire as blazing and rising; wood as crooked and straight; metal as yielding and changing, whereas the nature of earth appears from sowing and reaping. That which is soaking and descending becomes *salt*; that which is blazing and rising becomes *bitter*; that which is crooked and straight becomes *sour*; that which is yielding and changing becomes *acrid*; and the produce of sowing and reaping becomes *sweet*."[8] (Legge, *Classics* Vol. III, Part II, p. 325.)

The sequence of the Five Elements is different from that in the *Xiashu* 夏書 insomuch as here wood precedes metal. It is the sequence in which originally the elements were created. This at least is the opinion of Zhu Xi 朱熹, which we shall examine later on. The nature of the *Five Elements* is described, and another category, that of the *Five Tastes*: *salt, bitter, sour, acrid*, and *sweet* connected therewith *i.e.*, we have here the first classification based on the Five Elements. From this one to the others there is only one step. It is just this book of the *Shangshu* which shows us the great partiality of the ancient Chinese to numerical categories and classifications. We find already the 五事 *Five Businesses*: 貌言視聽思 *demeanour, speech, seeing, hearing*, and *thinking*, immediately following upon the Five Elements, and further on the 五徵 *Five Manifestations*, or 五氣 *Five Atmospheric Influences* as they are now called, *viz.* 雨暘燠寒風 *rain, sunshine, heat, cold*, and *wind* (Legge, *loc. cit.* p. 339) which subsequently were combined with the Five Elements. The love of symbolism, and the tendency of discovering analogies between natural and moral phenomena appears already in what the *Hongfan* has to say on the *Five Manifestations*:

"There are the auspicious manifestations:—self-possession is related to seasonable rain; orderliness, to seasonable sunshine; judiciousness, to seasonable heat; discretion, to seasonable cold; and sageness, to seasonable wind. There are likewise the evil manifestations:—excitement is related to incessant rain; confusion, to incessant sunshine; fickleness, to incessant heat; impetuosity, to incessant cold; and dullness, to incessant wind.

It is said that the emperor pays attention to the year; his ministers and high officers, to the months, and the petty officials, to the single days. When, during a year, a month, or a day, the seasonableness does not change, then all the crops ripen, the administration is enlightened, excellent persons become illustrious, and the people enjoy peace and happiness. But, when during a day, a month, or a year, the seasonableness changes, then the crops do not ripen, the administration is beclouded and unenlightened, excellent persons remain in obscurity, and the people do not enjoy quietude."[9] (Legge, *loc. cit.* p. 340 seq.)

Already at the beginning of the Zhou 周 dynasty, in the 11th century BCE, the Chinese had discovered some resemblance between heaven and earth, and the four seasons with the six ministries, which appears from the names of these departments recorded in the *Zhouli* 周禮. There is the prime minister, the chief of the Civil Office 冢宰 or 天官 Officer of Heaven; the minister of the interior and of revenue 司徒 or 土官 Officer of Earth; the minister of ceremonies 宗伯 or 春官 Officer of Spring; the minister of war 司馬 or 夏官 Officer of Summer; the minister of punishments 司寇 or 秋官 Officer of Autumn; and the minister of works 司空 or 冬官 Officer of Winter.

We learn from the same source that the vice-president of the Board of Ceremonies "erected altars to the *Five Emperors* in the four suburbs:" 兆五帝於四郊 (Cf. *Le Tcheou-li* par E. Biot. Vol. I, p. 421, 441 and Vol. II, p. 324). These Five Emperors were five old rulers subsequently deified and venerated as the deities of the *Five Points*.

These are two more corner stones added to the system of the Five Elements. We have no literary evidence to show that this was done already at the commencement of the Zhou epoch, although there is nothing against such a supposition. At all events this step had been taken some centuries later, for in the *Zuozhuan* we see the theory pretty well evolved from the nucleus observed in the older sources.

We read under Zhaogong 昭公 29th year: "Therefore there were the *officers of the Five Elements*, who accordingly were called the Five Officers. They, in fact, received their family and clan names, and were appointed high dignitaries. As divine spirits they were sacrificed to, and honoured, and venerated at the altars of the Spirits of the Land and Grain and the Five Sacrifices. The ruler of wood was called Gou Mang 勾芒, that of fire Zhu Rong 祝融, of metal Ru Shou 蓐收, of water Xuan Ming 玄冥, and of earth Hou Tu 后土 ... Viscount Xian 獻 inquired of which families were these Five Officers partaking of the oblations to the Spirits of the Land and Grain and the Five Sacrifices. Cai Mo 蔡墨 replied: 'At the time of Shao Hao 少昊 there were four men: Zhong 重, Gai 該, Xiu 脩, and Xi 熙, who were able to regulate metal, wood, and water. Zhong 重 was made Gou Mang, Gai 該 was made Ru Shou, and Xiu 脩 and Xi 熙, Xuan Ming. They never were remiss in discharging their duties and in assisting Qiong Sang 窮桑 (Shao Hao 少昊). For these are the Three Sacrifices. Zhuan Xu 顓頊 had a son named Li 犁, who become Zhu Rong; Gong Gong 共工 had a son named Gou Long 勾龍, who became Hou Tu. For these are the Two Sacrifices. Hou Tu became Spirit of the Land and Grain and director of the fields.'"

Here we have five sons of old legendary rulers raised to the dignity of spirits of the Five Elements after their deaths. They partake of the Five Sacrifices offered to the Five Emperors in the four suburbs and the centre *i.e.*, they are assistant deities of the Five Points. That they were, moreover, regarded as genii of the seasons appears from their names, for Gou Mang "Curling fronds and spikelets" evidently points to spring, and Ru Shou "Sprouts gathered" designates autumn. Zhu Rong referring to heat may well denote summer, and Xuan Ming "Dark and obscure," winter. Thus we have the *Five Elements* and their deities connected with the *Five Points* and the *Five Seasons*. See also p. II.757–58. The Five Sacrifices of Wang Chong 王充 (p. II.757) are others than those of the *Zhouli*, here referred to.

But the most important testimony of the *Zuozhuan* is to be found in the following passage, Duke Zhao 昭 25th year:

"Jian Zi 簡子 said, 'I venture to ask what is meant by propriety?' — Zi Tai Shu 子大叔 replied, 'I heard the former great officer Zi Chan

子產 say: Propriety is the principle of Heaven, the rule of Earth, and the basis of human conduct. This principle of Heaven and Earth is imitated by the people conforming to the luminaries of Heaven and agreeing with the nature of Earth. The *Six Fluids* are produced and the *Five Elements* made use of. The fluids become the *Five Tastes*, manifest themselves as the *Five Colours*, and appear as the *Five Sounds*.'"[10]

And farther on we read: "People feel love and hatred, pleasure and anger, sorrow and joy, which feelings are produced from the *Six Fluids*. Therefore one carefully imitates relations and analogies, in order to regulate these *Six Impulses*."[11]

By the Six Fluids or atmospherical influences are understood 陰陽 風雨晦明 the *Yin* 陰 principle, the *Yang* 陽 principle, *wind*, *rain*, *darkness*, and *light*, a classification somewhat different from that of the Five Fluids of the *Shangshu*.

In the above quoted passage the Five Elements are combined with the Five Tastes, the Five Colours, and the Five Sounds on the one side, and with the Six Fluids and the Six Impulses on the other. After all, there are but five entities which appear to us under different forms, either as substances or as atmospherical fluids, or as tastes, colours or sounds. And even human feelings are nothing else but manifestations of these fluids.

Elsewhere the *Zuozhuan* informs us that "the former kings constituted the *five tastes* and harmonized the *five sounds*. It is by these that they made their minds equable and regulated their administration. Sounds are nearly related to tastes."[12] (*Zuozhuan*, Duke Zhao 昭 20th year.)

That the antagonism of the elements was well known at the time of the *Zuozhuan* we infer from the following passages: "Water overcomes fire"[13] (Duke Ai 哀 9th year), and "Fire overcomes metal"[14] (Duke Zhao, 31st year). The meeting of two opposed elements is compared to a marriage, and the stronger element subduing the weaker, called the husband, the weaker being looked upon as the wife. "Water is the husband of fire"[15] (Duke Zhao, 17th year), and "fire is the wife of water"[16] (Duke Zhao, 9th year).

Finally the Five Elements are connected with the cyclical signs of the Ten Stems and the Twelve Branches. A disaster is predicted on a *Bingzi* 丙子 or a *Renwu* 壬午 day, because on these there is a meeting of water and fire,[17] *bing* 丙 corresponding to fire, and *zi* 子 to water, *ren*

壬 to water, and *wu* 午 to fire. Since these cyclical signs serve to denote the points of the compass, the Five Elements must be referred to them also. So we read that "*zi* is the position of water"[18] (Duke Ai, 9th year) *i.e.*, that water is placed in the North.

The *Zuozhuan* states that the Five Elements manifest themselves as the Five Colours, but does not assign the different colours to the various elements. This is done in the *Jizhong zhoushu* 汲冢周書, a collection of ancient texts excluded by Confucius from the *Shangshu*, and consequently prior in time to the 6th century BCE. (Cf. Chavannes, *Mem. Hist.* Vol. V, p. 457). There we read: "Among the Five Elements the first, the *black* one, is water; the second, the *red* one, is fire; the third, the *green* one, is wood; the fourth, the *white* one, is metal; and the fifth, the *yellow* one, is earth."[19]

Resuming the adduced old testimonies, we may assert that, at the time of Confucius and before, the theory of the Five Elements was known and developed in all its chief features. The elements are roughly described and conceived as partly physical, partly metaphysical entities. They vanquish one another in a certain order already given in the *Shangshu*. The weaker element in such a contest is termed the wife, the stronger, the husband. The atmospherical fluids, closely connected with the elements, affect mankind, in so far as they are believed to produce impulses and sensations, and, conversely, human actions may influence these fluids. The sovereign especially regulates the elements by the virtue displayed in his administration. There are five officers or deities presiding over the elements and, at the same time, venerated as genii of the seasons, in the five directions, together with the Five Emperors, ruling over the five points of the compass. Thus we have a link between the elements, the seasons, and the five directions. Moreover, the fluids and the elements manifest themselves under the form of the five tastes, the five colours, and the five sounds. Tastes and colours are enumerated and assigned to the respective elements, and we may assume that the same was done with the five sounds, although we have no literary evidence to prove it. By their combination with the signs of the denary and duodenary cycles, the Five Elements were again located in those points of the compass to which these signs correspond.

In the Appendix to Couvreur's Dictionary there is a table of the Five Elements and their corresponding categories, altogether 12 columns.

Of these we have so far traced nine, only the five heavenly Emperors, the five planets, and the five viscera have not yet been mentioned. But these also were referred to the elements in the Zhou dynasty, as we shall see from the *Liji* and other works.

A short sketch of a natural philosophy is given in the chapter *Liyun* 禮運 of the *Liji* (Legge, *Sacred Books* Vol. XXVII p. 380 seq.), in which the Five Elements play a part. Man is said to be the product of the forces of Heaven and Earth, by the interaction of the *Yin* and the *Yang*, the union of the animal and intelligent spirits, and the finest matter of the Five Elements.[20] This, of course, would account for the many relations existing between the elements and the human body as well as human actions. Moreover, the Five Elements are distributed over the Four Seasons.[21] They are in constant movement and alternately exhaust one another. Each of them becomes in its turn the fundamental one just like the Four Seasons and the Twelve Months.[22] It is not expressly stated that the five sounds, the five tastes, and the five colours are identical with the Five Elements, but they are mentioned in close connexion with the elements and declared to undergo similar regular revolutions by which each sound, taste, and colour for a certain time becomes the principal one. Throughout the whole treatise we notice the intimate relation of human life to all the forces of nature, the elements included.

The chapter *Liyun* is by some attributed to Zi You 子游, a disciple of Confucius or to his disciples and regarded as one of the most valuable parts of the *Liji*. I do not share Legge's view that the ideas about elements, numbers, colours, &c. are Daoistic admixtures to the commonsense of Confucianism, for we have met them all in the Confucian Classics. (Cf. Legge's *Liji*, Introduction p. 24.)

How the elements and their correlates were distributed over the twelve months we learn from another book of the *Liji*, the *Yueling* 月令 (Legge, *eod.* p. 249 seq.) embodying the fullest scheme of this theory in classical literature. It is a sort of a calendar clearly showing us how much the doctrine of the Five Elements was interwoven with the life of the ancient Chinese. For each of the four seasons it is stated that the Grand Annalist informed the Son of Heaven of the day on which the season began and of the element ruling over the three months composing the season. The element earth alone had no proper season.

About the first month of spring we learn that its days are *jia* 甲 and *yi* 乙,[23] its *divine ruler* is Tai Hao 太昊, and the attending *spirit* Gou Mang. Its *creatures* are the *scaly*, its *musical note* is *jue* 角, its *number* 8,[24] its *taste* is *sour*, its *smell* is *rank*. Its *sacrifice* is that at the *inner door*,[25] and for this the *spleen* of the victim is essential. The *east* winds resolve the cold. The Son of Heaven occupies the apartment on the left of the Qingyang 青陽 Fane,[26] and rides in a carriage drawn by *green dragon* horses, carrying a *green* flag and wearing *green* robes and pieces of *green* jade. His food consists in *wheat* and *mutton*. At the head of his ministers and the feudal princes, the emperor meets the spring in the *eastern* suburb. The inspectors of the fields are ordered to reside in the lands having an *eastward* exposure. They instruct the people, and see that all the necessary measures for cultivating the fields be taken. Prohibitions are issued against cutting down trees and the killing of young animals, birds, or insects. No fortifications are to be erected, no warlike operations to be undertaken, for they would be sure to be followed by the calamities from Heaven. I refrain from quoting all the other prescriptions and defences and would only draw attention to the characteristical last paragraph of this section which has its counterpart in all the other months:

"If in the first month of spring the governmental proceedings proper to summer were carried out, the rain would fall unseasonably, plants and trees would decay prematurely, and the states would be kept in continual fear. If the proceedings proper to autumn were carried out, there would be great pestilence among the people; boisterous winds would work their violence; rain would descend in torrents; orach, fescue, darnel, and southernwood would grow up together. If the proceedings proper to winter were carried out, pools of water would produce their destructive effects, snow and frost would prove very injurious, and the first sown seeds would not enter the ground."

In a similar way the other months are described. We abstract therefrom the following Table (p. III.874).

The *Yueling* is now universally ascribed to Lü Buwei 呂不韋 of the 3rd century BCE (Legge, *Liji*, Introduction p. 20), but there is no reason to suppose that it was invented by him and that it is not a calendar of the Zhou period, for its contents accords very well with other sources and was, at all events, regarded as a genuine record of old customs by the compilers of the *Liji*.

Table of the Five Elements, the Four Seasons and other correspondencies according to the *Liji* 禮記

Five Elements 五行	Four Seasons 四時	Five Emperors 五帝	Five Spirits 五神	Five Sacrifices 五祀	Five Animals 五牲	Five Grains[a] 五穀	Five Intestines 五臟	Five Numbers (五數)	Ten Stems 天干	Five Colours 五色	Five Sounds 五音	Five Tastes 五味	Five Smells 五臭	Five Points 五方	Five Creatures 五蟲
wood	spring	Tai Hao 太昊	Gou Mang 勾芒	inner door	sheep	wheat	spleen	8	*jia yi* 甲乙	green	*jue* 角	sour	goatish	east	scaly
fire	summer	Yan Di 炎帝	Zhu Rong 祝融	hearth	fowl	beans	lungs	7	*bing ding* 丙丁	red	*zhi* 徵	bitter	burning	south	feathered
earth		Huang Di 黄帝	Hou Tu 后土	inner court	ox	panicled millet	heart	5	*wu ji* 戊己	yellow	*gong* 宮	sweet	fragrant	centre	naked
metal	autumn	Shao Hao 少昊	Ru Shou 蓐收	outer door	dog	hemp	liver	9	*geng xin* 庚辛	white	*shang* 商	acrid	rank	west	hairy
water	winter	Zhuan Xu 顓頊	Xuan Ming 玄冥	well	pig	millet	kidneys	6	*ren gui* 壬癸	black	*yu* 羽	salt	rotten	north	shell-covered

[a] The correspondencies of the Five Grains do not quite agree with those given in Mayers' Manual p. 316 inasfar as he combines *beans* with water, and *millet* with fire. His translation of 稷 by rice instead of "panicled millet," which I have followed in p. 1.118, is not quite correct. It is also better to render 稗 by "spleen," for which in p. II.628, note 6 [QP 1911 Ed. seems to have a typographical error: "Vol. 1, p. 105" should read "Vol. 1, p. 195"] I have written "stomach" as Mayers does.

The literary evidence of ancient texts collected above is more than sufficient, I trust, to establish the fact that the theory of the Five Elements is of Chinese origin. This has been contested by no less an authority than Ed. Chavannes, who is of opinion that the Chinese have borrowed it from the Turks (cf. Ed. Chavannes, "Le cycle turc des douze animaux," *T'oung-pao*, Serie II Vol. VII No. 1 p. 96–98). His view can hardly be upheld against the old texts. L. de Saussure ("Les origines de l'astronomie chinoise," *T'oung-pao* 1910, Vol. XI p. 265–288) has already disposed of it. To his counter-arguments, with which I concur in general, some more may be added. It is rather surprising that of all the Chinese authors who have written on the Five Elements almost nobody refers to Zou Yan 鄒衍 whom Chavannes believes to have been the first exponent of the Turkish theory in China. They all go back to the old Chinese sources quoted above. In the fourth or the fifth centuries BCE when the Turkish theory must have found its way into China, the Turkish tribes, Xiongnu 匈奴 or Scythians bordering on the Chinese empire were practically barbarians from whom the Chinese could not learn much. In the *Shiji* 史記 chap. 110 they are described as nomads without cities who could not write and did not care for the moral laws. The accounts found in *Herodotus* Book IV seem to confirm that, at that early age, the Turkish tribes lived in a very primitive state of culture, and it is highly improbable that the theory of the interaction of the elements, supposing a mystical sympathy of all the forces of nature, an attempt at a natural philosophy, should have been devised by an uncivilised people like the early Turks. To the Chinese mind such sorts of speculations have been familiar from time immemorial. In ancient times the Turks most likely received the little culture they had from their neighbours, the Chinese, and when, subsequently, the Çakas made their incursions into Bactria and India, from the Greeks and Indians. When, many centuries later, they went over from Buddhism to the Islam, their language as well as their civilisation fell under the influence of the Arabs and Persians. They possessed very little originality, wherefore the invention of the theory of the Five Elements cannot well be set down to their credit.

I strongly doubt that at the time of Zou Yan the Xiongnu already possessed any notion of the elements, which require a more advanced state of civilisation than theirs was. Their descendants, the Uigurs, know 4 elements, but which? *Fire, wind, water,* and *earth* (*Kudatku Bilik* by H. Vámbéry, p. 75 and 78). They are the same as those of the Greeks and Indians, and they evidently learned them from these directly or through the Arabs, as they must have borrowed the seven planets and the twelve signs of the zodiac from the same source. After deducting these foreign loans, there remains nothing originally Turkish.

Even if the 4 elements: *fire, wind, water,* and *earth* were of Turkish invention, it would not help us much, for the 4 elements of the *soi-disant* semi-Turkish Qin 秦 dynasty, according to Chavannes, must have been: *fire, wood, metal,* and *earth, i.e.,* besides two elements occurring in Europe as well, they embrace two characteristically Chinese elements: *wood* and *metal* unknown in Europe and India.

I should say that the principal passage on which Chavannes bases his belief in the Turkish origin of the theory of the Five Elements, admits of a totally different interpretation than that of the eminent sinologist. The Emperor Han Gao Zu 漢高祖 expressed his astonishment that in Qin only four heavenly emperors were sacrificed to, since he had heard that there were five in heaven. (*Mem. Hist.* Vol. III, p. 449.) In my opinion this means to say that the emperor knew that before the Qin epoch there were five emperors worshipped under the Zhou, and that he simply reverted to the old custom, changed by the Qin, by instituting a sacrifice to the black emperor, the representative of *water.*

At first sight the theory of the Five Elements and the classifications ingrafted thereon may seem strange to us, and one of the many Chinese peculiarities, but sociology teaches us that similar classifications, though based on other principles of division, are common all over the world and among people not connected with one another. Such classifications must, therefore, be a product of human nature which is more or less the same everywhere. Consequently, we need not look for a foreign origin of the Chinese theory.

Most Australian natives divide up the things of the world conformably to their clans and fraternities, which, each of them, have their special totems. All things belonging to the same group are allied and, so to say, the same reality under different forms. Animals of the same class must not be eaten by their kindred. (E. Durkheim and

M. Mauss, *De quelques formes primitives de classifications*, in *L'Année Sociologique*, Paris 1901–02, Vol. 6 p. 17.) The totems are not only animals but also plants, fruits and other objects. They may be natural phenomena as well, such as *wind, water*, the *sun, clouds* amongst the Aruntas (p. 28 Note 2). With the totem *fire* are connected the branches of eucalyptus, the red leaves of the eremophile, the sounds of trumpets, warmth, love (p. 31).

A tribe of the Sioux in North America has grouped all objects according to the position occupied by their clans in their camp *viz. right, left*, in the *front*, and in the *rear* (p. 47).

Another tribe of the North American Indians, the Zuñis, have taken the seven directions: *north, south, west, east*, the *zenith*, the *nadir*, and the *centre* as the basis for their classifications, and filled them up with all the things in which they are specially interested. Thus they have the following equations:

North: wind, winter, the pelican, the crane, the green oak, strength, destruction, yellow
West: water, spring, moist wind, the bear, the wild dog, vernal herbs, peace, hunting, blue
South: fire, summer, agriculture, medicine, red
East: earth, seeds, frost, the buck, the antelope, the turkey, magic, religion, white, &c. (p. 35 seq.).

The Dacotahs have a similar division, but they have lost their clans. The Australian Wotjoballuk have distributed their clans and their correlates over thirteen points of the compass (p. 51).

The classifications according to clans and totems appear to be the more primitive; and those starting from the points of the compass are probably derived from the grouping of the clans in the camp.

It is owing to the preponderance of astrology amongst the Chaldeans that with them and their successors, Greeks and Romans, the planets have become the corner stones of very similar classifications. The Chaldeans have attributed the following colours to the planets: Saturn = *black*, Jupiter = *light red*, Mars = *purple*, the Sun = *golden*, Venus = *white*, and Mercury = *blue*.

Ptolemy gives them somewhat different colours: Saturn = *a livid grey*, Jupiter = *white*, Mars = *red*, the Sun = *golden*, Venus = *yellow*, and Mercury = *changing colours.* The scholiasts also differ and only agree in the colours of Mars (*red*) and the Sun (*golden*) (A. Bouche Leclercq, *L'Astrologie Grecque*, Paris 1899 p. 313, 314).

In addition to colours, *metals*, *plants*, and *animals* are also classified under these planets. Thus mercury is the metal of the homonymous planet; dragons, snakes, foxes, cats, night birds, donkeys, and hares resort from Saturn; wild beasts, monkeys, pigs, from Mars (p. 317, 318). Moreover Ptolemy has distributed the *parts of the body* and the *senses* among the seven planets according to the following scheme:

> *Saturn*: the right ear, the bladder, the spleen, the phlegm, the bones.
> *Jupiter*: the sense of touch, the lungs, the arteries, the semen.
> *Mars*: the left ear, the kidneys, the veins, the testicles.
> *Sun*: the eyes, the brain, the heart, the nerves—all the chief organs.
> *Venus*: the smells exciting love, the liver, the seat of prophecy, the flesh.
> *Mercury*: the tongue, the gall.
> *Moon*: the taste, the stomach, the womb (p. 321).

This system has undergone a great many modifications at the hands of later authors, for instance Demophilus and Hermippus.

Proclus teaches that the different spheres of the human spirit correspond to the spheres of the stars: *Fixed stars* = intellectual life, *Saturn* = contemplation, *Jupiter* = political and social instincts, *Mars* = passionateness, *Sun* = perceptive faculties, *Venus* = desires, *Mercury* = faculty of speech, *Moon* = vegetative life (p. 325).

In the middle-ages the *Kabbala* sets forth various systems of classification simultaneously. According to the *Sepher Iezirah* (9th-10th cent, CE) the world has been built up by the *Three Elements* named the Three Mothers: *fire* is the substance of heaven, *water* that from which the earth was produced, and both antagonistic elements are separated by the third element, *air*. These Three Elements govern the *Three Seasons*:—*summer*, the *rainy season*, and the *cool season* and the *Three Parts of the Body*:—the *head*, the *breast*, and the *belly*. This gives the following table:

3 Elements	3 Seasons	3 Parts of the World	3 Parts of the Body
fire	summer	heaven	head
water	rainy season	earth	breast
air	cool season	void	belly

Besides there are the "*Seven Double Ones*" being partly good and partly wicked. These are the *Seven Planets* and corresponding to them the *Seven Days* and the *Seven Nights* of a week, and the *Seven Orifices of the Head*.

The "*Twelve Single Ones*" are the *Twelve Months* combined with the *Twelve Signs of the Zodiac* and the *Twelve Human Activities*: sight, hearing, smell, touch, speech, nutrition, generation, motion, anger, laughing, thought, and sleep. (A. Lehmann, *Aberglauben und Zauberei*, 2nd ed., translated by Petersen, Stuttgart 1908 p. 145 seq.)

At the end of the middle-ages, these classifications received their highest development in Europe by the mystic Agrippa von Nettesheim (1456–1535 CE) who in his great work "De occulta philosophia" combined the Physics of Aristotle, the astronomy of Ptolemy, the New Platonism, and the *Kabbala* with his own observations and fanciful ideas. His works and those of his contemporaries show us that in the beginning of the 16th century people in Europe were not a whit farther advanced in natural science than the Chinese philosophers of the Song 宋 epoch or those of to-day. Many of the arguments of Agrippa remind us of similar ones of the Chinese theorists of the Five Elements.

Agrippa maintains that everything is subject to a planet or a constellation. Thus fire and blood are *solar*, and the same is said of gold, and of the precious stones:—pyrope, heliotrope, jasper, emerald, ruby, the sun-flower, the lotus flower, and the big and audacious animals:— the lion, the crocodile, the rain, the bull, the phœnix, the eagle, the cock, the raven. Similar lists are given for all the planets.

Everything on earth is classified according to fixed numbers. Agrippa has established groups and classes of 1–12 links each, and combined them to systems, following perhaps the precedent of the *Kabbala*. As a specimen I give his table of the Seven Planets:

AShRAHIH = Asher Eheie

	Zaphkiel	Zadkiel	Chamael	Raphael	Haniel	Michael	Gabriel	God's name in 7 letters
In the world of archetypes								
In the world of ideas	Zaphkiel	Zadkiel	Chamael	Raphael	Haniel	Michael	Gabriel	7 angels before God's face
In the heavenly world	Saturn	Jupiter	Mars	Sun	Venus	Mercury	Moon	7 planets
In the elementary world	whoop	eagle	vulture	swan	pigeon	stork	night-owl	7 planetary birds
	cuttle-fish	dolphin	pike	seal	shad-fish	blenny	sea-cat	7 planetary fish
	mole	stag	wolf	lion	ram	monkey	cat	7 planetary animals
	lead	tin	iron	gold	copper	mercury	silver	7 planetary metals
	onyx	sapphire	diamond	pyrope	emerald	agate	crystal	7 planetary stones
In the world of men	right foot	head	right hand	heart	pudenda	left hand	left foot	7 members
	right ear	left ear	right nostril	right eye	left nostril	mouth	left eye	7 orifices of the head
In the infernal world	Gehenna	gate of death	shadow of death	well of death	slough	perdition	abyss	7 dwellings of the damned

After this historical and sociological excursion we return to the Zhou period where we left the subject. We possess still more sources dating from that time, though not classical ones, proving that already then the table derived from the *Liji* was still further developed:

The Daoist writer He Guan Zi 鶡冠子 (4th cent BCE) arranges the Five Elements according to the position taken by soldiers in a camp, referring them to the human body, and not to the four quarters. "In choosing a position, he says, one must take advantage of the ground and select it according to the Five Elements. Wood is on the *left* side, metal on the *right*, fire in *front*, water in the *rear*, and earth in the *centre*. In army camps, and in marshalling troops this order must be observed. These five divisions being well defined, everything may be undertaken with safety."[27] This arrangement of the elements agrees with their positions in the four quarters, if the observer turns his face to the chief quarter, which for the Chinese is the south. Then fire is in the front or in the south, water in the rear or in the north, wood on the left side or in the east, metal on the right side or in the west, and earth, in both cases, remains in the centre.

The *Huangdi suwen* 黃帝素問, the oldest work on Chinese medicine—which Wylie places several centuries before Christ, so that it would be a relic of the Zhou time—devotes several chapters to the theory of the Five Elements. This theory has remained the basis of all Chinese medicine up to the present day. As appears from the title of the work, it consists of questions addressed by Huang Di 黃帝 to his assistant Qi Bo 岐伯. This, of course, is fiction.

"Huang Di asked in what manner cold and heat, dryness and moisture, wind and fire operated on man, and how they produced the transformations of all things."[28] Qi Bo replied about the operation of these six atmospherical influences in the five quarters. For our purpose it suffices to consider what he says about heat and cold, and their derivates. A strict parallelism goes through all his deductions:—"The south produces heat, heat produces fire, fire produces bitterness, bitterness the heart, the heart blood, and blood the spleen. In heaven it is heat, on earth it is fire, and in the body, the veins. As a breath it respires, and among the viscera, it is the heart. Its nature is hot, its quality effulgence, its manifestation drying up. Its colour is red, its transformation luxuriance, its creatures the feathered ones, its government enlightenment, its weather sultry, its sudden change burning, its calamity a conflagration. Its taste is bitter, its sentiment joy. Joy injures the heart, but fear overcomes joy. Heat injures the breath, but cold overcomes heat, and bitterness injures the breath, but salt overcomes bitterness."[29]

"The north produces cold, cold produces water, water produces salt, salt the kidneys, the kidneys produce bones and marrow, the marrow produces the liver. In heaven it is cold, on earth it is water, and in the body, the bones. As a breath it is hard, and among the viscera it is the kidneys. Its nature is glacial, its quality cold, and its manifestation.......[30] Its colour is black, its transformation frost, its creatures are the shell-covered, its government is quiet, its weather......, its sudden change is freezing, its calamity ice and hailstones. Its taste is salt, its sentiment fear. Fear injures the kidneys, but desire overcomes fear. Cold injures the blood, but dryness overcomes cold. Salt injures the blood, but sweetness overcomes salt."[31]

Qi Bo winds up by saying, "The Five Fluids come forward in turn, and each of them takes precedence once. When they do not keep in their proper spheres, there is disaster; when they do, everything is well ordered."[32]

The *Huangdi suwen* adds some more categories to those given by the *Liji*: the 5 styles of government 五政:—*Relaxation, enlightenment, carefulness, energy,* and *quietude*,[33] the 5 impulses 五志:—*anger, joy, desire, sorrow,* and *fear*,[34] and the 5 constituent parts of the body 五體:—*muscles, veins, flesh, skin* and *hair,* and *bones*.[35] The 5 intestines or viscera are the same as those of the *Liji*, but their sequence is different, and in each class, in addition to the principal intestine, a secondary one is introduced, *viz.* every secondary one is the principal intestine of the next class.

As to the theory of the Five Elements, the medical work agrees with the *Shangshu* and the *Zuozhuan* whose general hints it specifies. It distinguishes three spheres of the elements, which in each of them appear in different forms, the spheres of heaven, of earth, and of man, just as Agrippa has seven spheres. The original form of the elements is that of the Six Fluids or atmospheric influences:—*cold* and *heat, dryness* and *moisture, wind* and *fire*.[36] They produce the Five Elements on earth, but in combining each element with a fluid the author drops *fire*. All the other diverse forms of the elements are the result of constant transformations, which to us appear very strange. How can fire produce bitterness, bitterness the heart, the heart blood, and blood the spleen? The qualities and manifestations of the elements described in the work are more in accordance with nature.

But what does it mean that "fear injures the kidneys, but desire overcomes fear. Cold injures the blood, but dryness overcomes cold. Salt injures the blood, but sweetness overcomes salt," and the like passages under the other heads? These are merely equations deducted from the theory of the antagonism of the elements, and seem to be the basis for the medical treatment of the parts of the body. We know that fear may affect the kidneys, and that a strong desire may vanquish fear. The last conclusion, however, the Chinese theorist probably did not draw from practice, but from the premises that desire corresponds to earth, and fear to water. Consequently, earth overcoming water, desire must vanquish fear likewise. In the same manner cold (water) injures the blood (fire), and dryness (metal) again overcomes cold (water), not directly, it is true, but indirectly, for metal overcomes wood, wood earth, and earth water. Moreover salt (water) injures the blood (fire), but sweetness (earth) vanquishes salt (water).

The new classes of the *Huangdi suwen* are thus grouped:

5 Fluids 五氣	5 Elements 五行	5 Parts of Body 五體	5 Intestines 五臟	5 Impulses 五志	5 Styles of Government 五政
wind	wood	muscles	liver (heart)	anger	relaxation
heat	fire	veins (blood)	heart (spleen)	joy	enlightenment
moisture	earth	flesh	spleen (lungs)	desire	carefulness
dryness	metal	skin and hair	lungs (kidneys)	sorrow	energy
cold	water	bones (marrow)	kidneys (liver)	fear	quietude

Each element preponderates during one season, and, while so doing, it may be well balanced and have its proper quantity, it may be excessive or deficient. Excess and deficiency both entail calamities affecting the vegetation and human body. In the latter case we have all kinds of diseases and maladies. All these states are minutely described, and still more categories added. Each element in its proper state of equilibrium is said to be governed by a part of the body different from those already mentioned: the eye, the tongue, the mouth, &c. Moreover it is connected with two sorts of fruit, a fleshy and a not fleshy—wood for instance with a plum and a nut—and with a domestic animal like the dog, the horse, &c. Even in its felicitous state each element has a special sickness assigned to it:—palpitations and convulsions belong to fire, coughing to metal, constipation to earth. The classes of the *Liji* are again ascribed to the elements well balanced, but not in the proper order. Thus *e.g.* wood is combined with hemp, the hairy creatures, and the liver; fire has as correlates:— wheat, feathered creatures, and the heart.

In case a ruling element be excessive or insufficient, two or more things of the same sort are made to correspond to it, whereas as a rule there is only one. There may be two fruits, two animals, two colours, two tastes corresponding to one element; even three are combined, probably to show the irregularity of the ruling element. At the same time the Five Planets are introduced as correlates of the elements, mostly two or three connected with one element. Thus we find Jupiter and Venus in connection with excessive wood, Mars and Mercury combined with excessive fire, Venus and Mars together with insufficient wood, and Mars, Mercury, and Saturn together with insufficient fire.

All irregularities of the elements entail a great variety of diseases. Whenever wood is superabundant, earth and the spleen have to suffer. This leads to pains in the limbs, flatulency, diarhœa, and vomiting. A scarcity of wood is accompanied by pains of the ribs and the stomach, by coughs and catarrhs, eruptions, scarlatina, sores and ulcers. A scarcity of fire causes pains in the breast, the back, the shoulders, the arms, the heart, rhumatism, cramps, paralysis of the legs, dumbness, swooning, &c.

Whereas the *Huangdi suwen* insists upon the effects of the irregularities of the elements upon man, the philosopher Guan Zi 管子 of the 5th century BCE attempts to show how natural events, connected with the elements, are influenced by the government of the emperor. We must bear in mind that the work passing under Guan Zi's name and forming part of the collection of the Ten Philosophers 十子, contains many later additions and is only partly genuine. But the style of the chapters on the Four Seasons 四時 and the Five Elements 五行 which interest us most, is rather archaic, and they may well be old.

"*Yin* and *Yang*" says Guan Zi, "are the great principles of heaven and earth, and the Four Seasons are the warp in the web of *Yin* and *Yang*. Punishments and rewards are the correlates of the Four Seasons.[37] Their conformity to the seasons brings about happiness, their discrepancy leads to misfortune."[38] (*Guanzi* 管子 XIV, 7 r.) Then Guan Zi proceeds to describe the seasons in a similar way as the *Liji* does, but, whereas the *Liji* distinguishes but *Four Seasons*, earth having no special one and belonging to all, Guan Zi gives Five Seasons,[39] each lasting 72 days. Besides he joins a special heavenly body to every quarter:—the centre corresponds to the *earth*, the south to the *sun*, the north to the *moon*, the east to the *stars*, and the west to the *zodiacal signs*.[40] For each of the Four Seasons five administrative measures 五政 are prescribed, the carrying out of which ensures felicity, whereas their omission or change is fraught with disaster. In the opinion of one commentator each season would have counted 90 days, and to each of the five administrative measures 18 days would have been allotted. Thus our author says in regard to winter:

"In the three winter months, on the *rengui* 壬癸[41] days five administrative measures are carried out. The first is providing for orphans and destitute persons and succouring the old and the aged; the second is conforming to the *Yin*, preparing the sacrifices for the spirits, bestowing titles and emoluments, and conferring ranks; the third is verifying accounts, and not to exploit the treasures of mountains and rivers; the fourth is rewarding those who seize runaway criminals and arrest robbers and thieves; the fifth is prohibiting the moving about of the people, stopping their wanderings, and preventing their settling in other parts of the empire.[42] If these five measures are taken at the proper time, so that the affairs of winter are not disregarded, one obtains one's wishes, and that which one dislikes does not take place."[43]

Guan Zi then proceeds to show how an emperor should act conformably to the Four Seasons:

"If plants wither in spring and blossom in autumn, if it thunders in winter, and there is frost and snow in summer, all this is harm caused by the fluids. If regarding rewards and punishments the periods are changed, and the natural order is confounded, then injurious fluids quickly arrive, and, upon their arrival, the State is visited with many disasters. Therefore a wise emperor observes the seasons and accordingly regulates his administration. He provides education and makes his warlike preparations, offers sacrifices and thereby establishes virtue. It is by these three things that a wise emperor puts himself into harmony with the movement of heaven and earth."[44]

"The sun governs the *Yang*, the moon the *Yin*, the stars govern harmony. *Yang* produces rewards, *Yin* punishments,[45] and harmony makes business possible. Consequently when there is an eclipse of the sun,[46] a State that has failed in its rewards is to be blamed for it. When there is an eclipse of the moon,[47] a State that has failed in its punishments is responsible. When a comet puts in an appearance, a State that has lost harmony is guilty, and when wind fights with the sun for brightness, a State that has failed in productiveness is answerable.[48] Wherefore, at an eclipse of the sun, a wise emperor improves rewards; at an eclipse of the moon, he improves punishments; when a comet becomes visible, he improves harmony, and when wind and sun fight together, he improves production. By these four measures the wise emperor avoids the punishments of heaven and earth."[49]

The disasters which may befall a sovereign not conforming to the seasons in his administration are thus described:

"When we see the cyclical sign *jiazi* 甲子[50] arrive, the element wood begins its reign. If the son of heaven does not bestow favours or grant rewards and, contrariwise, extensively allows cutting, destroying, and wounding,[51] then the sovereign is in danger, and should he not be killed, then the heir-apparent would be in danger, and some one of his family or his consort would die, or else his eldest son would lose his life. After 72 days this period is over. When we see the cyclical sign *bingzi* 丙子 arrive, the element fire begins its reign. In case the son of heaven be anxious to take hurried and hasty measures,[52] an epidemic would be caused by a drought,[53] plants would die, and the people perish by it. After 72 days this period is over. When we see the sign *wuzi* 戊子 arrive, the element earth begins its reign. If the son of heaven builds palaces or constructs kiosques, the sovereign is in danger, and if without city walls are built,[54] his ministers die. After 72 days this period is over. When we see the sign *gengzi* 庚子 arrive, the element metal begins its reign.

Should the son of heaven attack the mountains and beat the stones,[55] his troops would be defeated in war, and his soldiers die, and he would lose his sway. After 72 days this period is over. When we see the sign *renzi* 壬子 arrive, the element water begins its reign. If the son of heaven cuts the dykes and sets the great floods in motion, his empress or his consort die, or else the eggs of birds become addled, the hairy young are miscarried, and pregnant women have an abortion. Plants and trees are spoiled in the roots. After 72 days this period is over."[56]

Among the authors of the Han 漢 time Huai Nan Zi 淮南子 and Dong Zhongshu 董仲舒, both of the 2nd century BCE, have written more or less systematically on the theory of the Five Elements, to which several chapters of their chief works are devoted. Liu Xiang 劉向 in the 1st century BCE emposed the *Wuxingzhi* 五行志, a treatise on the Five Elements which has not come down to us. Ban Gu 班固 of the 1st century CE discourses at some length on the subject in his *Baihutong* 白虎通. Afterwards it was taken up by a great many writers and forms an important part of the disquisitions of the philosophers of the Song 宋 dynasty.

We are now going to consider the results at which these writers and their predecessors have arrived.

i. Various Terms for the Elements

The modern work *Zhanghuang tushubian* 章潢圖書編 states that in the *Yijing* 易經 the Five Elements are named 五位 *Wuwei, Five Positions,*[57] in historical works 五材 *Wucai, Five Materials,* in chronicles or essays 五物 *Wuwu, Five Things,* and in medical works 五運 *Wuyun, Five Revolutions.* Mayers (Manual p. 313) gives some more terms: 五節 *Wujie, Five Sections,* 五美 *Wumei, Five Excellencies,* and 五氣 *Wuqi, Five Fluids.* They are descriptive of the elements under various aspects, as substances formed of matter, as fluids or vapours, as moving and revolving, or as keeping certain positions. But by far the commonest expression is 五行 *Wuxing,* on the meaning of which the Chinese and foreign authorities are agreed. 行 *xing* is "to act" and "to move," the *Wuxing* are, therefore, the five essences which are always active and in motion. Mayers (*loc. cit.*) calls them the primordial essences or per-petually active principles of nature. The term is all but equivalent to 五 運 *Wuyun*, the *Five Revolutions*.

ii. What Are the Five Elements?

The designation *Wuxing* goes back to the *Shangshu* and implies that at these remote times the elements were conceived already as ever active essences, which again supposes the existence of some sort of a theory devised to explain the phenomena of nature. In the most ancient description of the elements contained in the *Shangshu* (cf. above p. III.867) they are considered from the physical point of view as natural substances:—water has the tendency of descending and soaking other stuffs, fire that of rising and blazing; wood is char-acterised as crooked and straight, which seems to refer to the ap-pearance of the branches of trees; metal is said to be yielding and changing, which is only true of metal in a liquid state; earth is not described any further, and its nature found in its generative and pro-ductive power. At all events, the authors of the Classic had not some metaphysical entities in view, but the substances usually understood by the names:—water, fire, wood, metal, and earth.

As to the impressions produced by these elements upon our sens-es and resulting in the categories of *colours*, *sounds*, *tastes*, and *smells*, the *Shangshu* concerns itself with tastes only:—Water becomes salt, fire bitter, wood sour, metal acrid, and cereals, the produce of earth, sweet. Of course pure water is not salt, but tasteless, yet, as the com-mentators remark, it becomes salt in the ocean, a wrong notion. Fire we would rather describe as burning than bitter, and wood as bitter instead of sour. The acrid taste of metals and the sweet one of cereals, such as rice and millet, may pass. It is difficult now to say which con-siderations led the ancient Chinese to attribute just these tastes to the Five Elements. Since the five tastes are always given in the Series:— *salt*, *bitter*, *sour*, *acrid*, *sweet*, it is not impossible that the ancients merely coupled them with the Five Elements of the *Shangshu* in the same order, without any regard to their natural relations.

In the same superficial manner the five colours:—*black*, *red*, *green*, *white*, and *yellow* may have been connected with the Five Elements, although the correspondencies have been explained:—Fire may well be described as red, though yellow would seem more appropriate. Wood appears green at least outwardly in plants and trees, whereas inwardly it is mostly white or yellow. The colours of metals are manifold, only their glittering may be said to be white. Earth is not yellow in most countries, but it was so in the *loess* regions in Henan 河南 and Shanxi 山西 where the Chinese were first settled. How can water be called black, however, a colour it almost never shows? It seems to refer to the *Yin* fluid preponderating in winter, the time of the element water. *Yang* is light and sunshine, *Yin* darkness, *Yang*, day-time, and *Yin*, night. These correspondencies are universally accepted, but I met with one exception in the 'Family Sayings of Confucius' 孔子家語[58] chap. VI p. 1, from which we learn that the Xia dynasty reigned by the virtue of *metal* and of the colours most appreciated *black*, the Yin dynasty reigned by *water* and appreciated *white*, the Zhou by *wood* with the *red* colour. Yao's 堯 element was *fire*, and his colour *yellow*, Shun's 舜 element *earth*, and his colour *green*. These different combinations of elements and colours show the arbitrariness of the whole scheme. It is impossible to find one colour for each element, because each embraces many species with different colours:—Water may appear pellucid, white, green, blue, red, yellow, grey, black; earth may be black, brown, yellow, red, blue, white, &c.;[59] and so different substances burn with different lights. Therefore to ascribe one colour to each element cannot but be arbitrary.

The Zuñis of North America have no elements,[60] but they have attributed certain colours to their seven points of the compass. Their reasons for doing so are not very convincing either:—The *North* is yellow, because at sunrise and sunset the sunlight appears yellow. The *West* is blue, the colour of the evening light. The *East* is white, the colour of day, the *South* red, because it is the seat of summer and of the red fire. The *Zenith* is multicoloured like the clouds, the *Nadir* black, and the *Centre* has all colours. (*Année Sociologique* Vol. VI, p. 35 seq.)

Of the *Five Smells* only *burning* and *fragrant* seem to refer to the corresponding elements fire and earth (cereals). *Goatish*, *rank*, and *rotten* have nothing to do with wood, metal, and water. They probably apply to the Five Animals joined to these elements:—the *sheep* (goat), *dog*, and *pig*.

On the principle by which the *Five Sounds* have been combined with the elements I am unable to express any opinion.

Guan Yin Zi 關尹子[61] has amplified the statement of the *Shangshu* about the rising and descending of fire and water:—"That which rises, he says, is fire; that which descends, water. That which would like to rise, but cannot, is wood; and that which would like to descend, but cannot, is metal."[62] This depicts fairly well the tendency of plants of growing up and that of metals of sinking down. These tendencies, however, are restricted and less free than those of fire and water which, endowed with a greater agility as air and fluid, can follow their propensities and rise and fall.

The *Zhanghuang tushubian* makes an attempt to distinguish between the different *forms* of the elements:—water is level, fire is pointed, earth round, wood crooked and straight, and metal square.[63] These are indeed the forms under which these substances often appear to us. Whereas water shows a level surface, a flame rises and seems pointed. Clods of earth are more or less round, and ore has often angular and square shapes. The description of wood as crooked and straight is taken from the *Shangshu*.

It is but natural that the Chinese should have connected their Five Elements with the two principles of nature established by their old philosophers, the *Yin* and *Yang*, and derived them therefrom. Dong Zhongshu says in his *Chunqiu fanlu* 春秋繁露 XIII, 5 v. that the fluid of Heaven and Earth united is one. But it splits into *Yin* and *Yang*, becomes divided into the Four Seasons, and separated into the Five Elements.[64] *Yin* and *Yang*, which we may here translate by *cold* and *heat*, are the primogenial essences from which the Five Elements are produced in the following way:—Water has its seat in the north which is governed by the *Yin* fluid. Wood is placed in the east which is likewise under the sway of the *Yin*, but the *Yang* begins to move already. Fire occupies the south where the *Yang* reaches its climax. Metal rests in the west, and is governed by the *Yang*, but the *Yin* begins to stir. Consequently "Fire is *Yang*, it is noble and therefore rises; water is *Yin*, it is mean and therefore goes down; wood is a scanty *Yang*, and metal a scanty *Yin*."[65] (Ban Gu's 班固 *Baihutong* 白虎通 II, 1.) The idea is quite clear, if we take into consideration the Four Seasons with which the elements are combined. In summer ruled by fire, *Yang* = heat prevails, in winter ruled by water, *Yin* = cold. In spring and autumn when wood and metal are paramount, *Yin* and *Yang*, heat and cold fight together, so that one may speak of a scanty *Yang* or an incomplete *Yin*. The element earth which does not well agree with the Four Seasons is left out by Ban Gu.

Later authors have gone more into details. Zi Huazi 子華子 (Song dynasty) characterises fire as an abundant Yang 太陽, and water as an abundant Yin 太陰, wood as a scanty Yang 少陽, metal as a scanty Yin 少陰, and earth as sometimes *Yin* and sometimes *Yang*.

"The *Yang* in the *Yang* is fire, he says, the *Yin* in the *Yin* is water, the *Yin* in the ᵧₐₙg is wood, the *Yang* in the *Yin* is metal. Earth keeps in the middle between the two essences and thus governs the four quarters:—in the *Yin* it is *Yin*, and in the *Yang* it is *Yang*."[66] (*Zihuazi* 子華子 II, 11 v.)

"In the north the extreme *Yin* resides. It produces cold, and cold engenders water. In the south the extreme *Yang* resides, which produces heat, and heat produces fire. In the east the *Yang* is set in motion. It disperses and calls forth wind, which again produces wood. In the west the *Yin* stops and gathers. It thus causes dryness, which produces metal. In the centre the *Yin* and the *Yang* mix and produce moisture which engenders earth."[67]

In other words fire is considered to be *Yang* throughout, *Yang* in *Yang*, i.e., an unalloyed *Yang*; water, a pure and genuine *Yin*. Wood is also *Yang*, but with an admixture of *Yin*; metal is *Yin*, but with an alloy of *Yang*. Earth may be both.

Zhu Xi 朱熹 and his school take a somewhat different view. They look upon the Five Elements as created by Heaven and Earth alternately, Heaven and Earth thus taking the place of the *Yin* and the *Yang*. "Heaven first creates water. Earth secondly creates fire, Heaven thirdly creates wood, Earth fourthly creates metal."[68] This idea seems to have originated from an obscure passage of the *Yijing* believed to refer to the Five Elements.[69] Zhu Xi quotes the famous Su Dongpo 蘇東坡 (1036–1101 CE) as his authority, who says that water is the extreme *Yin*, but it requires Heaven to co-operate before it can be produced. *Yin* alone without *Yang* cannot produce it. Fire is the extreme *Yang*, but it likewise requires the co-operation of Earth to come into existence. And so it is with all the Five Elements, they all cannot be created, unless the *Yin* and the *Yang* are both at work. When the *Yang* is added to the *Yin*, water, wood, and earth come forth, and when the *Yin* is added to the *Yang*, fire and metal are produced.[70]

About the creation of the elements and their nature Zhu Xi further asserts that by the joint action of *Yin* and *Yang* water and fire are first produced. Both are fluids flowing, moving, flashing, and burning. Their bodies are still vague and empty, and they have no fixed shape. Wood and metal come afterwards. They have a solid body. Water and fire are produced independently, wood and metal need earth as a substratum from which they issue.[71] Heaven and Earth first generate the light and pure essences, water and fire, afterwards the heavy and turbid ones, wood, metal and earth. The last is the heaviest of all. As to their density, water and fire are shapeless and unsubstantial fluids, fire, hot air in the atmosphere, wood is a soft substance, metal a hard one.

Zhou Zi 周子, a predecessor of Zhu Xi, gives still another formula for the elements:—water is the moist fluid in the *Yang*, fire, the dry fluid in the *Yin*, wood, the moist fluid in the *Yang*, but expanded, metal, the dry fluid in the *Yin* contracted, earth the *Yin* and the *Yang* blended and condensed, so as to become a substance. *Yang* and *Yin*, heat and cold are allotted to the Five Elements in the same manner as by Zhu Xi, but as a secondary constituent we have moisture and dryness. These are the same principles from which Aristotle has evolved his Four Elements:—earth, water, fire, and air. The Chinese have become acquainted with his theory by the geographical work *Kunyu tushuo* 坤輿圖說 written by the Jesuit lather Verbiest about the end of the 17th century and cited by the *Tushu jicheng* 圖書集成. According to the Aristotelian theory dryness and cold produce earth, moisture and cold produce water, moisture and heat give air, and dryness and heat give fire.[72] The result arrived at by Zhou Zi is different, he only composes earth similarly namely by heat and cold (*Yin* and *Yang*). His water consists of moisture and heat (*Yang*) instead of cold, and his fire, of dryness and cold (*Yin*) instead of heat. The Aristotelian view appears more natural than that of Zhou Zi who is under the spell of the *Yijing*. Perhaps Zi Huazi 子華子 agrees with the Greek philosopher, for his above mentioned dictum that fire is the *Yang* in the *Yang*, and water the *Yin* in the *Yin* may be understood to mean that fire is dryness in heat, and water, moisture in the cold, *Yang* denoting heat as well as dryness and *Yin* cold and moisture.

iii. Fluids, Substances, and Seasons

Originally the elements were not combined with the Seasons. The fact that there always have been Five Elements, but Four Seasons, and that our oldest sources do not allude to such a connexion, tells against it. On the other side, the term *"Wuxing"* makes it plain that the Five Elements were conceived already in times immemorial as something more than simple substances. From the passage of the *Zuozhuan* where the elements are mentioned together with the heavenly fluids, which become the Five Tastes, the Five Colours and the Five Sounds, and even manifest themselves in human affections (cf. p. III.870) we may gather that, at a very early date, the elements were identified with the heavenly fluids or atmospherical influences. These are in the *Shangshu*:—*rain, sunshine, heat, cold,* and *wind.* They again, I presume, formed the link with the Four Seasons, which in the opinion of the Chinese, who did not know the real cause of the seasons, are the result of the regular changes of the heavenly fluids. In the *Liji* elements and seasons are linked together already. *Guanzi* 管子, XIV, 7 seq. asserts that *wind* produces *wood*, the *Yang* fluid *fire*, the *Yin* fluid *metal*, and *cold, water.* Earth has no special fluid.

The Song philosophers were the first clearly to point out the difference of *substances* 質 and *fluids* 氣. Substances are produced, says Zhou Zi, by the interaction and coagulation of the *Yin* and the *Yang*, whereas the Fluids are the regular revolutions of these two primary essences.[73] Cai Shen 蔡沈, a disciple of Zhu Xi, holds that in heaven the Five Elements are the Five Fluids:—rain, sunshine, heat, cold, and wind, and on earth the Five Substances:—water, wood, fire, metal, earth. Of the Five Heavenly Fluids rain and sunshine are the substances, which seems to imply that they are more substantial than heat, cold, and wind—and of the Five Substances of Earth water and fire are the fluids—possessing more the nature of fluids than of substances, a view held by Zhu Xi also, as we have seen above.[74] Another writer maintains that the substances adhere to and have their roots in the earth, and that the fluids revolve in heaven. The latter generate, the former complete all organisms,[75] *i.e.*, the fluids give the first impulse to every new creation and the substances complete it. It may not be out of place to point out that the afore-mentioned Agrippa puts forward quite similar ideas. The elements in the lower worlds he declares to be coarser and more material, whereas in the higher spheres they appear only as forces or qualities. (Lehmann, *Aberglaube* p. 198.)

This view has again been modified, all elements being held to be compounded of substance and fluid. There is a difference between the various elements insomuch as they are more substantial or more etherial. "Fire and water have much fluid and little substance, wherefore they were produced first. Metal and wood have much substance and little fluid, and for this reason were created later. In earth substance and fluid are equally balanced, consequently it came after water and fire, but preceded metal and wood."[76]

"The fluid of water is *Yang*, its substance *Yin*. The nature of *Yin* is procreative, therefore water produces wood. The fluid of fire is *Yin*, its substance *Yang*. Since the nature of *Yang* is burning and destructive, fire cannot produce metal. As regards earth, its fluid is *Yang* and its substance *Yin*. Consequently it makes use of the *Yang* of fire to produce the *Yin* of metal."[77] Here we have again the mysticism of the *Yijing*.

Fire and earth together produce metal, and water and earth combined produce wood. In both cases earth is indispensable. When wood produces fire, and metal, water, earth is not required.

Regarded as the ultimate causes of the seasons the elements were also invested with the qualities which, properly speaking, belong to the seasons alone. These characteristic features of the seasons are, according to Ban Gu's *Baihutong* 白虎通:—*generating, growing, reaping*, and *hiding*.[78] Dong Zhongshu already gave similar attributes to the elements. Wood, said he, is the generative nature of spring and the basis of agriculture. Fire is the growing of summer, earth the maturing of the seeds in mid-summer, metal the deadly breath of autumn, and water the hiding in winter and the extreme *Yin*.[79]

iv. Transformations of the Elements

a) In Heaven:—the Celestial Bodies and the Five Planets

The whole universe, the material as well as the intellectual world are nothing else than transformations of the Five Elements. The world has been evolved from the primary essences the *Yin* and the *Yang*, of which the elements are derivates or compounds.

We have seen that Guan Zi (p. III.885) joined the heavenly bodies to the different quarters:—the earth to the centre, the sun to the south, the moon to the north, the stars to the east, and the zodiacal signs to the west. It is natural that the earth should be regarded as the centre of the universe and the sun be connected with the south, the seat of heat and light. The moon then had to go to the opposite direction, the north, where cold and darkness reign. Then the stars had to take the two remaining quarters, the east and west. We learn from Wang Chong that in his time not only the sun was regarded as fire, but that the moon also was believed to consist of water (cf. p. I.373–74 and p. I.243). Fire being the element of the south and water that of the north, the celestial bodies were believed to be formed of the element belonging to their quarter. The Earth consists of earth, the element of the centre. Then the stars must be of wood and the zodiacal constellations, of metal.

But the combination of the Five Planets with the Five Quarters or the Five Elements is much more common than that of the celestial bodies in general. *Huainanzi* 淮南子 III, 3 r. seq. declares the *Five Planets:—Jupiter, Mars, Saturn, Venus,* and *Mercury*[80] to be the spirits 神 of the Five Quarters. The *Shiji* 史記 chap. 27 says that the Five Planets are the elements of the Five Quarters ruling over the Seasons, *e.g.*, "Mars is said to be the fire of the south and governs summer"[81] (*eod.* p. 18v.). Of course one may translate that Mars *corresponds* to the fire, but the literal translation seems to me preferable and more in accordance with the materialistic views of the Chinese to whom Mars, the Fire Star 火星, is made of fire, and Jupiter, the Wood Star

木星, is made of wood. These characteristic terms of the Planets are frequently used in the *Shiji*. The *Jinshi* 金史 (14th cent. CE) distinctly states that in heaven the fluid of the essence of the Five Elements becomes the Five Planets, on earth, the Five Substances and in man the Five Virtues and the Five Businesses.[82] From another modern treatise we learn that looking up to the Five Planets at dusk we see their five colours quite clearly, without the least confusion, because they are the essences of the Five Elements.[83] Here again we notice quite analogous conceptions in Agrippa (*loc. cit.* p. 198), who likewise takes the planets for products of the elements. Mars and the Sun he pronounces to be fiery, Jupiter and Venus to be airy, Saturn and Mercury to be watery, and the Moon to be earthy.

We do not know which consideration led to the connexion of each element with each planet. Probably it was in the different colours of the planets that the Chinese imagined they recognised the five colours:—green, red, yellow, white, and black of the elements. That at dusk we see the five colours quite distinctly, without the least confusion, as the above quoted Chinese author would have us believe, is out of the question. The ancients as well as the moderns are at variance in regard to the colours of the planets (see above, p. III.877–78). There only seems to be some unanimity about the red colour of Mars and the white one of Venus.

Valens goes so far as to give the reasons why the planets logically must have the colours which he assigns to them:—Saturn, he says, is black, because it is Time or Kronos which obscures everything. Jupiter is radiant, because he cares for glory and honour. Venus shows various colours owing to the various passions which she excites, and Mercury is yellow, for he governs the gall which is yellow.[84] These arguments are very queer, but quite in the Chinese way of reasoning, and it would not be surprising to find them slightly modified, in an ancient Chinese writer.

As we have learned from *Huainanzi* in the Zhou epoch already the Five Planets were regarded as the spirits of the Five Quarters. As such they were venerated and named the *"Five Emperors."* They were distinguished by their colours as the Green Emperor = Jupiter, the Red Emperor = Mars, the Yellow Emperor = Saturn, the White Emperor = Venus, and the Black Emperor = Mercury. (Cf. *Shiji* chap. XXVIII, Chavannes, *Mem. Hist.* Vol. III, p. 449).

b) On Earth:—the Inorganic and the Organic Kingdom; Man.

The element earth embraces all kinds of earth and stones; metal, the various metals; so the entire inorganic kingdom is the outcome of these two elements. Of water different kinds are distinguished according to their origin, such as spring water, rain water, water from ditches, lakes, the sea, &c. Fire may take its origin from wood, from oil, from stones or other substances, from lightning, or it may be the glowing of insects, or a will-o'-the-wisp. The whole flora belongs to the element wood which includes trees, plants, and flowers. But here we meet with a difficulty. If all plants are produced by the element wood, how is it that in the *Liji* the five kinds of grain:—wheat, beans, millet, &c. are connected with the Five Elements, and not with wood alone, so that beans correspond to fire, and millet to water? A Chinese philosopher would probably reply that all these cereals issue from the element wood, but have an admixture of one of the other elements. So wheat would be wood in wood, beans fire in wood, and millet water in wood.

It would be logical, if the whole animal kingdom were classed under one chief element also, but they are distributed among the Five Elements, and it is difficult to understand the plan of this division:—The scaly creatures, fishes, and reptiles *e.g.*, snakes and dragons belong to the element wood, the shell-covered or crustaceous animals:—turtles, crabs, oysters, &c. to the element water. The element earth embraces all naked creatures, among which are found toads, earthworms, silkworms, spiders, eels, and man. Fire is the element of all feathered animals or birds, and metal, that of all hairy ones or beasts.[85] Consequently the Five Sacrificial Animals:—sheep, cock, ox, dog, and pig should be looked upon as transformations of the element metal save the cock corresponding to fire, but the *Liji* makes them correspond to all the Five Elements, and we would again have combinations of two elements:—metal and wood = sheep, metal and earth = ox, &c.

Here the views of Agrippa von Nettesheim (*loc. cit.* p. 198) are very instructive. He teaches us that from the Four Elements of Aristotle issue the four principal divisions of nature:—stones, metals, plants, and animals. Each of these groups consists of all the elements combined, but one predominates. Stones are earthy, metals watery, because they can be liquified and by the Alchimists are declared to be the products of living metallic water (mercury), plants depend upon air, and animals upon fire, their vital force.

Among stones which as such are earthy, the opaque ones are earthy, the pellucid ones and crystal which have been secreted from water, are watery, those swimming on water like sponges are airy, and those produced by fire like flints and asbestus are fiery. Lead and silver are earthy, mercury is watery, copper and tin are airy, and iron and gold are fiery.

As regards animals, vermin and reptiles belong to earth, fish to water, and birds to the air. All animals with great warmth or with a fiery colour such as pigeons, ostriches, lions and those breathing fire, belong to this element. But in each animal the different parts of its body belong to different elements:—the legs belong to earth, the flesh to air, the vital breath to fire, and the humours to earth.

Man is treated in the same manner by the Chinese. As the foremost among the three hundred and sixty naked creatures (cf. Ch. 72 n. 7) he belongs to the element earth, but the parts of his body and his moral qualities are connected with the different elements and produced by them. From the *Liji* and the *Huangdi suwen* (p. III.882–83) we have learned the correspondencies of the Five Constituent Parts of the body:—muscles, veins, flesh, skin and hair, and bones, and of the Five Intestines with the elements. An inner reason for this classification is difficult to discover, but there has certainly been one, although it may not tally with our ideas of a scientific classification.

The transition of the Five Elements from the material into the spiritual world is by some writers believed to be a direct one, whereas others see in the parts of the human body the connecting links. Chu Yong 儲泳 of the Song period informs us that the Five Elements are the Five Organs of the human body, and that the fluids correspond to the Five Intestines.[86] The Five Organs are the ear, the eye, the nose, the mouth, and the body serving to produce the five sensations. Wang Chong (p. II.628–29 and p. I.118) is of opinion that the Five Virtues are closely connected with the Five Intestines which are their necessary substrata. By a destruction of these inner parts of the body the moral qualities of man are destroyed as well. According to this view the elements appear as moral qualities only after having been transmuted into parts of the human body. Other writers assume a direct process of transformation. We have seen the *Jinshi* maintaining that in heaven the fluid of the Five Elements becomes the Five Planets, on earth the Five Substances, and in man the Five Virtues and the Five Businesses (above, p. III.896). The Daoist Tan Qiao 譚峭 (10th cent.) also merely states that the Five Virtues are the Five Elements, setting forth the following classification:—"Benevolence is equivalent to fostering and growing, therefore it rules through wood. Justice means assistance of those in need, therefore it rules through metal. Propriety is enlightenment, whence it rules through fire. Wisdom denotes pliability, whence it rules through water, and faith is the same as uprightness, wherefore it rules through earth."[87] The reasoning is rather weak, but we find the same distribution of the Five Virtues in the following list of the Song 宋 school of thought.[88] That its classification does not quite agree with that of the *Liji* and the *Huangdi suwen* given above is not to be wondered at, since in reality the elements have nothing to do with moral qualities, and the supposed relations are pure imagination:

5 Elements	5 Parts of Body	5 Intestines	5 Souls[a]	5 Senses[b]	5 Impulses	5 Virtues
wood	muscles	liver	mind	smell	joy	benevolence
fire	hair	heart	spirit	vision	gaity	propriety
earth	flesh	spleen	reason	touch	desire	faith
metal	bones	lungs	animal soul	taste	anger	justice
water	skin	kidneys	vitality	hearing	sorrow	wisdom

[a] 魂神意魄精   [b] 臭色形味聲

We have seen above (p. III.877–78) how Ptolemy joined the parts of the body and the senses to the seven planets, and how Proclus made the different spheres of the human mind correspond to the spheres of the stars. In this respect they were only the successors of the Chaldeans and Egyptians, who first connected the parts of the human body with the twelve signs of the zodiac. A human body was thought extended over the vault of heaven, its head resting on Aries. Then its neck lay on Taurus, its shoulders and arms on Gemini, the breast on Cancer, the flanks on Leo, the stomach and the bladder on Virgo, the buttocks on Libra, the genitals on Scorpio, the thighs on Sagittarius, the knees on Capricorn, the legs on Aquarius, and the feet on Pisces. In the *Kabbala* the three elements, fire, water, and air were combined with the three parts of the body:—the head, the breast, and the belly. The Seven Planets correspond to the Seven Orifices of the Head, and the Twelve Signs of the Zodiac to the Twelve Human Activities (p. III.879). These ideas were taken up by Agrippa as appears from his table (p. III.880). A similar scheme was in vogue among the Central American Mayas. (Cf. P. Carus, *Chinese Thought*, 1907, p. 87.) The Chinese do not lay much stress upon the relation between the parts of the human body and the planets, but it exists, since the planets are nothing else than manifestations of the Five Elements in the celestial sphere, the parts of the body, its sensations, feelings, and moral qualities being manifestations of the same elements in the human sphere.

v. Local and Numerical Relations of the Elements

It has been shown that at a very early date the Five Elements were referred to the Four Seasons, a fact evidenced by the *Zuozhuan* and the *Liji*. It is not difficult to guess—strict proofs we have not—how the elements were assigned to the seasons. Fire could only be joined to the hottest time of the year, when the sun sends its fiery rays, summer. Conversely, water, considered as the extreme *Yin* and the product of cold, had to be combined with the coldest and darkest season, winter. Wood could serve to symbolise the new growing of the vegetation in spring, and metal the cutting of the cereals and other plants, used by man, in autumn. For earth there was no special season first.

The obvious analogy between the Four Seasons and the Four Quarters then led to the connexion of the elements with the Four Points of the Compass. Within the space of a Year the four seasons: spring, summer, autumn, and winter follow one another, and during one day the sun successively passes from the east through the south and the west to the north, to begin the same course on the following morning. What more natural than the equation:

wood,	*fire,*	*metal,*	*water*		
spring	summer	autumn	winter	=	*east, south, west, north.*

With spring the new year begins, as in the east the sun begins its course; in summer, and in the south the sun is hottest, summer being the season, and the south the region of the greatest heat; in autumn, and when the sun is in the west its heat decreases; in winter, and in the north the heat is gone, and we then arrive at the cold season and the region of cold. Here we have a seat for earth also *viz.* the centre, so that the Five Elements correspond to the Five Points. Our point of observation is the centre, and we have earth under our feet. The south is filled with the element fire, the north with water, whereas wood permeates the east, and metal the west. Facing the south, the chief direction according to the Chinese view, we have fire in the *front* and water in the *rear*, wood on our *left*, metal on our *right side*, and earth in the *centre* where we stand. These positions, first assigned, to the elements by He Guan Zi (p. III.881) are merely derived from their combinations with the Five Points.

The Four Quarters or, more correctly speaking, the Four Quadrants of Heaven, 四宮 *Sigong*, have been symbolised by four fancy animals:— the *Green Dragon* in the east, the *Scarlet Bird* in the south, the *White Tiger* in the west, and the *Black Warrior* or the *Black Tortoise* in the north, to which *Huainanzi* 淮南子 still adds the *Yellow Dragon* corresponding to the centre.[89] Each of these four animals embraces seven of the twenty-eight Constellations or Solar Mansions. We find the same names in the *Shiji* 史記 chap. 27 (Chavannes, *Mem. Hist.* Vol. III, p. 343 seq.) and in the *Lunheng*, p. I.159 and p. II.745.[90] Wang Chong seems to regard them as heavenly spirits formed of the fluids of the Five Elements and as constellations at the same time. Ban Gu likewise speaks of the essence of these animals, but instead of the Scarlet Bird he gives the Yellow Thrush and the Phoenix.[91] It is not improbable that the ancient Chinese really saw the shapes of animals in these constellations and took them for celestial animals imbued with the fluids of the four elements:—wood, fire, metal, and water, for the Yellow Dragon of *Huainanzi* belongs to the earth and is no constellation. The classes as well as the colours of these four animals harmonise with those of the *Liji*. The dragon is a scaly animal, the scarlet bird feathered, the tiger hairy, and the tortoise shell-covered, and their colours are green, red, white, and black like wood, fire, metal, and water. The yellow colour of the thrush and that of the phœnix or argus pheasant though not red, would still accord more or less with the colour of fire.

From the *Zuozhuan* and the *Liji* onward the Ten Stems or cyclical signs of the cycle of ten have been combined with the elements. The principle has been explained above (p. III.1149, n. 50). To distinguish each of the Five Seasons of 72 days governed by one element, a couple of these signs, as they follow one another in the regular series, are used. The days are numbered by means of the sexagenary cycle, and each Season or element is designated by the two Stems beginning the compound number of the first and second day of the season. The two first days of spring are *jiazi* 甲子 and *yichou* 乙丑, therefore the whole season and its element wood have the cyclical signs *jia* 甲 and *yi* 乙. The first and the second days of summer are after the sexagenary cycle a *bingzi* 丙子 and a *dingchou* 丁丑 day, therefore the whole season of summer and its element fire are connected with the Stems *bing* 丙 and *ding* 丁. The second characters of the component numbers belonging to the Twelve Branches, *zi* 子 and *chou* 丑, are left out of account. So the Ten Stems:—*jia* 甲 *yi* 乙 (wood-spring), *bing* 丙 *ding* 丁 (tire-summer), *wu* 戊 *ji* 己 (earth- latter part of summer), *geng* 庚 *xin* 辛 (metal-autumn), *ren* 壬 *gui* 癸 (water-winter) serve to denote the commencements of the seasons or the periods when each element begins its reign; they are time marks so to say.

In the *Liji* only the *Ten Stems* are thus used, *Huainanzi*, moreover, conformably to the method alluded to in the *Zuozhuan*, joins a couple of the *Twelve Branches* to the Five Elements. Their meaning is quite different, they are local marks showing the point of the compass where the respective element is located, for the Chinese denote the Four Quarters and their subdivisions by means of these Branches. According to the position of the elements, the Branches designating the east, south, west, and north points and the intermediary points nearest to these, are added to them. So we have:

> wood = *yin* 寅 *mao* 卯, E.N.E and East;
> fire = *si* 巳 *wu* 午, S.S.E and South;
> metal = *shen* 申 *you* 酉, W.S.W and West;
> water = *hai* 亥 *zi* 子, N.N.W and North.

With good reason *Huainanzi* III, 17 v. leaves out earth, on the ground that it belongs to all the four seasons. Earth being in the centre cannot well be combined with a sign connoting a point of the compass on the periphery. Later authors have done it all the same. Dai Ting Huai 戴廷槐[92] attributes to earth the four remaining cyclical signs:— *chen* 辰, *xu* 戌, *chou* 丑, and *wei* 未[93] *viz*. E.S.E, W.N.W, N.N.E, S.S.W. If this has any sense at all, it can only mean that earth is to be found in every direction, approximately denoted by the four characters. In Couvreur's Table only the signs *chou* and *wei* are assigned to earth.

It is well known that the Twelve Branches also serve to mark the twelve double-hours of the day, but I doubt whether all sinologists are aware of the reason of this peculiar use. Even when denoting the hours of day and night, the Branches have no temporal, but only a local value, marking the direction where the sun stands during a certain hour. In spring and autumn, when day and night are nearly of equal length, between 5–7 a. m. the sun stands in, or passes through *mao* 卯 = East, whence the hour from 5–7 a. m. is called the *mao* hour 卯時. At noon, 11–1 p. m. it passes through *wu* 午 = South, between 5–7 p. m. through *you* 酉 = West, and at midnight from 11–1 a. m. the sun, though not seen by us, traverses *zi* 子 = North. Originally the Twelve Branches merely mark the points of the compass, their designation of the twelve hours is only a secondary use based on the course of the sun through these points.

The *ordinary numerals* attached to the elements in the *Liji*: earth = 5, water = 6, fire = 7, wood = 8, and metal = 9 are said to refer to the 10 stages or turns in which originally the Five Elements were evolved from *Yin* and *Yang*, or Heaven and Earth. This is again in accordance with the above mentioned obscure passage of the *Yijing*. Dai Ting Huai 戴廷槐[94] states that

> 1st Heaven engendered water,
> 2ndly Earth engendered fire,
> 3rdly Heaven engendered wood,
> 4thly Earth engendered metal,
> 5thly Heaven engendered earth,
> 6thly Earth completed water,
> 7thly Heaven completed fire,
> 8thly Earth completed wood,
> 9thly Heaven completed metal,
> 10thly Earth completed earth.

Now all elements are given the number of their completion: water = 6, fire = 7, wood = 8, metal = 9 except earth which bears the number of its generation, because, says a commentator, generation is the principal thing for earth.[95] This reason is as singular as the whole theory of this creation in ten stages.

vi. The Different Modes of Enumerating the Five Elements

There are at least four different ways of enumerating the elements, each series having its special meaning:

a) The order in which the elements are believed to have originally been created: *Water, fire, wood, metal, earth.*

We found this series in the *Shangshu* (p. III.867) and the *Jizhong zhoushu* 汲冢周書 (p. III.871–72). Whether it really has the meaning disclosed by the Song 宋 philosophers, is open to doubt. According to the *Taijitu* 太極圖 this series refers to the substances, showing the order in which they were produced, in contradistinction to the fluids whose successive revolutions are expressed by series b):—*wood, fire, earth, metal, water.*[96] Zhu Xi speaks of the order in which the Five Elements were first created by Heaven and Earth.[97] He holds that the vague and shapeless elements water and fire came first and were followed by the solid substances wood and metal which required earth as a substratum from which they issued. But in this case earth ought to take the third place in the series and not the last.

b) The order in which the elements or their fluids follow and produce each other in the course of the seasons:—*Wood, fire, earth, metal, water.*

This is the order of the *Liji.* During each season one element predominates. The others are not completely destroyed, but they have dwindled away and have no power until their turn comes, when they are resuscitated and become preponderant. The elements thus succeeding each other are said to produce one another. Both *Huainanzi* III, 17 v. and *Dong Zhongshu* 董仲舒 XI, 2 v. expressly state that wood produces fire, fire produces earth, earth produces metal, metal water, and water wood. The former regards each element producing another as its *mother*, the latter as is *father*, and the element thus generated as the *son* or child. According to this terminology wood for example would be the mother or the father of fire, and metal the son of earth. This analogy has induced both authors to judge the relations of the elements by the moral and the family laws, which leads to strange consequences. As men under given circumstances act in a certain way, the elements are believed to affect each other in a similar manner. This view has been adopted by other writers as will appear from some instances given *ad* c).

The theory that the Five Elements produce each other in the order of this series is to a certain extent based on natural laws. One may say that wood produces fire, and fire leaves ashes or earth. In the interior of the earth metal grows, but how can metal produce water? Here is a hitch. The Chinese try to avoid it by asserting that metal may become liquefied or watery, and in this respect they are at one with Agrippa who likewise, as we saw, looks upon all metals as watery. But liquid metal is not real water, and it can never be transformed into water in the same way as wood becomes ashes or earth metal. Moreover, water alone cannot become wood, there must be earth besides—not to speak of the necessity of a germ—and to produce metal, earth and fire must co-operate. This has been pointed out in the *Xingli huitong* 性理會通 stating that, for the production of metal, fire and earth, and for that of wood, water and earth are wanted, so that in both cases earth cannot be dispensed with.

c) The order in which the elements subdue or overcome each other:—*Water, fire, metal, wood, earth.*

This series occurs in the *Shangshu* and the *Zuozhuan* (p. III.866), and the author of the latter work knows its principle, for he informs us that water overcomes fire and fire, metal, and calls the stronger element the husband, the weaker the wife. The full list of the antagonistic elements is given by *Huainanzi* IV, 8 v.[98] *Dong Zhongshu* XIII, 5 v. remarks that of the elements in series b) those placed together produce one another, whereas those separated by one place vanquish each other.[99] If we take the series:—*wood, fire, earth, metal, water,* then wood subdues earth and earth, water; fire subdues metal, and metal wood, &c. The series must be regarded as an infinite ring; from the last link one returns to the first.

How this mutual antagonism of the elements is to be understood we best learn from the *Huangdi suwen*:—"Wood brought together with metal is felled; fire brought together with water is extinguished; earth meeting with wood is pierced; metal meeting with fire is dissolved; and water meeting with earth is stopped."[100]

In other words:—water extinguishes fire, fire melts metal, metal cuts wood. That growing wood perforates the surrounding soil, and that earth stops the course of water, when there is an inundation for example, seems a little far-fetched, but we must bear in mind that the Chinese reasoning is not always as strict and logical as we would like to have it. The explanation given in the *Huangdi suwen* most likely completely satisfies the Chinese mind. I would prefer the explanation of de Saussure, *T'oung-pao* 1909, p. 259 that earth vanquishes water by absorbing it; and the same thing may be said of the relation of wood and earth, in so far as growing plants draw from the soil all the substances necessary for their development. This may be looked upon as a destruction of earth by wood.

In connexion with this theory some writers make interesting observations on the way in which the elements affect each other. Wood, says Guan Yin Zi, when bored, gives fire, when pressed, gives water. Metal is such a substance that, when struck, it produces fire, and when melted it becomes water.[101] The *Zhanghuang tushubian* points out the following changes undergone by the elements, when operated upon by one another:—Earth becomes softened by water and hardened by fire. Metal becomes liquid by fire and continues unchanged by water. Wood grows by water and is consumed by fire. Fire grows by wood and dies by water. Water is cooled by metal and warmed by fire.[102] In Chu Yong's *Quyishuo* 祛疑說 the action of some elements is spoken of in a way, that a tacit reproof may be read between the lines:—Fire is produced by wood, but it consumes it; metal grows in earth, but it hoes it *i.e.,* both elements show a very unfilial behaviour towards their parents. Wood subdues earth, but earth nourishes wood; earth subdues water, but water irrigates earth[103] *i.e.,* earth and water requite the maltreatment by their inimical elements with kindness. Dai Ting Huai is quite outspoken on this subject and sets forth the curious law that, when an element is vanquished by another, its son always will revenge the wrong inflicted upon its mother element upon the aggressor and subdue him in his turn.[104] *E.g.,* when water overcomes fire, earth, the son of fire, will subdue water, and when fire overcomes metal, water, the son of metal, will subdue fire. There really is such a relation between the various elements according to the Chinese theory of their mutual production and destruction. This destruction is considered a natural rebuff, after an element has been produced and exceeded a certain limit, or it may have been brought about by men on purpose, in order to shape or transform certain substances, or avert calamities. Thus fire is employed to melt metal and cast vessels and utensils, and earth is formed into dikes and embankments to check inundations.

In the occult arts of the middle ages the sympathies and antipathies of the elements play an important part. Agrippa (*loc. cit.* p. 229) contends that fire is hostile to water, and air to earth. A sympathetic action is exercised by a magnet attracting iron, an emerald procuring riches and health, a jasper influencing birth, and an agate furthering eloquence. Contrariwise, a sapphire is believed to repel plague ulcers, fever, and eye diseases, amethyst acts against drunkenness, jasper against evil spirits, emerald against wantonness, agate against poison. The panther dreads the hyena so much, that, if the skin of a panther be suspended opposite to the skin of a hyena, its hair fall out. In accordance with this doctrine of Agrippa the famous physician Theophrastus Bombastus Paracelsus, 1493–1541 CE, based his cures on the sympathetic action of the elements. Since every part of the body pertained to a planet, all the substances belonging to the same star were considered to be efficacious antidotes against all ailments of the part in question. Gold *e.g.*, passed for a specific against heart diseases, because gold and the heart both pertain to the sun (*eod.* p. 232). Even animals have recourse to this sort of cures. Agrippa relates that a lion suffering from fever cures itself by eating the flesh of a monkey, and that stags, when hit by an arrow, eat white dittany (Eschenwurz) which extracts the arrow.

d) The order in which the elements are usually enumerated at present:—*Metal, wood, water, fire, earth.* This series seems to be used for the first time by Ban Gu in his *Baihutong* II, 1 r. I found only one attempt at explaining this order by Zhu Xi, which is very unsatisfactory. Metal, he says, is the mother of all fluids, and the body of Heaven is dry metal.[105] Because all things begin to grow after they have received the fluid, therefore wood follows metal, &c.

Perhaps the principle underlying this series may be that first the two substantial elements are given, secondly their two transformations, and thirdly one second transformation. Metal and wood are transmuted into water and fire, and fire again is changed into earth (embers).

Accordingly the above four orders of the elements may briefly be thus characterised:

    a) series of the creation of the elements
    b) series of their mutual production
    c) series of their mutual destruction
    d) series of their transformation.

vii. The Regular Changes of the Elements during the Seasons

Apart from the transformations which the elements undergo when meeting, they are subject to regular modifications during the seasons, which repeat themselves every year. In the course of a year, they grow, reach their climax, and decline again. While one element is at its height, another has fallen off, and a third is still growing. The times are usually denoted by the Twelve Branches, which, as a rule, are merely local marks. Here they are almost equivalent to the twelve months, for the sun stays about a month in each of the twelve constellations or branches which, therefore, serve to designate the months.

Huainanzi III, 16 r. gives us the following comparative table:[106]

Wood is born in *hai* 亥 (N.N.W.—10th moon)
Wood is full-grown in *mao* 卯 (E.—2nd moon)
Wood dies in *wei* 未 (S.S.W.—6th moon)
Fire is born in *yin* 寅 (E.N.E.—1st moon)
Fire is full-grown in *wu* 午 (S.—5th moon)
Fire dies in *xu* 戌 (W.N.W.—9th moon)
Earth is born in *wu* 午 (S.—5th moon)
Earth is full-grown in *xu* 戌 (W.N.W.—9th moon)
Earth dies in *yin* 寅 (E.N.E.—1st moon)
Metal is born in *si* 巳 (S.S.E.—4th moon)
Metal is full-grown in *you* 酉 (W.—8th moon)
Metal dies in *chou* 丑 (N.N.E.—12th moon)
Water is born in *shen* 申 (W.S.W.—7th moon)
Water is full-grown in *zi* 子 (N.—11th moon)
Water dies in *chen* 辰 (E.S.E.—3rd moon).

After this scheme each element is alive nine months, and dead three months. Its body then still exists, but it is lifeless *i.e.*, inactive. In the next year it is revived again, and the same process, its growing and decaying begins afresh. Each element is full-grown and shows its greatest development in the second or the middle month of the season over which it rules, wood in the second month of spring, and fire in the second month of summer, or the fifth month. The position assigned to earth is peculiar. It is just one month behind metal, consequently earth would govern a season almost falling together with autumn, but a little later.

Elsewhere *Huainanzi* makes the elements pass through five different stages, adding to those given above "old age" and "imprisonment." Thus we have the following comparative list:[107]

	strong	old	born	imprisoned	dead
Spring	wood	water	fire	metal	earth
Summer	fire	wood	earth	water	metal
	earth	fire	metal	wood	water
Autumn	metal	earth	water	fire	wood
Winter	water	metal	wood	earth	fire

Later authors go still more into details. Sun Zhao 孫昭 of the Ming 明 dynasty informs us that the "Classic of Huang Di"[108] distinguishes twelve changes undergone by each element during a year. He treats the elements like human beings and therefore takes the names of these changes from human life. They are:—birth, bathing, being an official, a minister, a sovereign, decline, sickness, death, burial, cessation, stirring up, and growing as an embryo.[109] Sun Zhao characterises the twelve stages which follow the Twelve Branches a little differently:—1) Water exists as a sperm in *si* 巳, 2) in an embryonic state in *wu* 午, 3) develops in *wei* 未, 4) is born in *shen* 申, 5) is washed and bathed in *you* 酉, 6) receives the cap and the girdle in *xu* 戌, 7) begins its official career in *hai* 亥, 8) obtains imperial glory in *zi* 子, 9) becomes old and decrepid in *chou* 丑, 10) sick in *yin* 寅, 11) dies in *mao* 卯, 12) and is buried in *chen* 辰.[110] The life of each element, its development, its acme, and its decline, in all their phases are compared to the life of man. It is washed like a baby, capped like a youth, must become an official—the ambition of every Chinaman—becomes even an emperor, and then gradually declines. The same list holds good for the other elements likewise, but the cyclical signs indicating the months change. Thus fire exists in a spermatic state in *hai*, wood in *shen* and metal in *yin*.

viii. The Element Earth and Its Season

When the Five Elements were joined to the Four Seasons, there was one element too much which could not be combined with a season. This element was earth. Why was just this one left out? Perhaps simply because in the two oldest series a) and c) of the *Shangshu* earth came last. The Chinese give other reasons. Both *Dong Zhongshu* X, 10 r. and *Ban Gu* II, 1 r. urge that earth is the noblest of the elements. Earth (the element) 土, says the latter, is but another name of the Earth 地. As such it governs the other elements and cannot be classed with them. This is true in so far as Heaven and Earth are held to have produced the elements. Besides we saw that wood and metal are believed to be products of earth, so that this element must be ranked as a sort of primary element. Though it did not produce water arid fire, it supports them as it does wood and metal.

But although there was no season left for earth, the Chinese did not like to drop this element altogether in their calendars. Since locally it was placed in the centre, they also inserted it into the middle of the Four Seasons, between summer and autumn, without attributing a special season to it. This was done in the *Liji*.[111] Subsequently earth was conceived as the element of "late summer" 季夏. The next step was to make Five Seasons instead of Four, each of 72 days, and to assign the third, "late summer," to earth. This step was taken by Guan Zi (see above, p. III.885) by *Huainanzi* III, 9 v. and by Dong Zhongshu, *Chunqiu fanlu*, XIII, 9 v.

ix. The Five Elements under Their Religious and Metaphysical Aspect

The veneration of the Five Elements or properly speaking of the deities presiding over the elements reaches back to the commencement of the Zhou dynasty. In the *Zhouli* we met with the Five Sacrifices offered to the Five Heavenly Emperors, the deities of the five directions whose altars were erected in the four suburbs and the centre. They were old legendary rulers deified as the spirits of the Five Points and the Five Elements. Subsequently, they received five assistant spirits, also sons of old emperors, credited with the power of mastering the elements, and therefore revered as the spirits of the Five Elements and the Four Seasons. The Spirit of Earth alone had no special season. They partook of the sacrifices made to the Five Emperors (p. III.868). In the *Liji* each season has a couple of these deities, a Heavenly Emperor or divine ruler and his attendant spirit.

The Five Sacrifices to these deities of the elements were performed by the emperor and the princes in the proper season. The Five Sacrifices of the house *viz.* the outer and the inner door, the hearth, the inner court, and the well were likewise referred to the Five Elements (cf. p. III.1147, n. 25). They were offered by the great officers, scholars and common people performing only one or two of them.[112] At the sacrifice the part of the victim which is supposed to correspond to the respective element was essential. Besides, the entire ceremonial to be observed by the emperor at these religious functions was more or less connected with the theory of the Five Elements. The hall occupied by the emperor was situated so as to be turned towards the quarter ruled by the predominating element. The colour of his horses, his flag, his robes, and his jade ornaments had to correspond to the colour of the worshipped element. His food, meat as well as vegetables, was similarly determined.

But not the religious life of the ancient Chinese alone, their political life is also overshadowed by the elements. In the *Shangshu* already we found the statement that the good qualities of the sovereign:—self possession, orderliness, judiciousness, discretion, and sageness are related to the seasonable atmospheric influences *i.e.*, to the fluids of the elements proper to the season, whereas their vices:—excitement, confusion, fickleness, impetuosity, and dullness are the correlates of such fluids as are out of season. Seasonable fluids produce rich harvests, call forth a good government, and make people happy; unseasonable ones have the opposite result (p. III.868).

On the other hand, the actions of the sovereign and his administration have an influence upon the seasons and the weather, and thereby may bring down calamities upon his subjects. The *Liji* enumerates all proceedings which may be done during each season and which may not. The latter are not wicked in themselves, but they do not harmonise with the imaginary nature of the ruling element. In spring everything favourable to the cultivation of the fields must be done, and all destructive measures are forbidden. Trees must not be cut, young animals, birds, or insects not be killed. No warlike operations aiming at the destruction of human life are to be undertaken. The *Liji* points out all the natural calamities:—heavy rainfalls, storms, pestilence, &c. caused by unseasonable administrative acts (p. III.873).

Guan Zi prescribes five administrative measures for each season, the observation of which secures happiness and the accomplishment of one's desires, whereas its disregard entails misfortune. Even an eclipse of the sun and the moon and the appearance of a comet are the upshot of unseasonable government. Since malpractices in the rewarding of meritorious actions are the cause of an eclipse of the sun, and since unjust punishments and a want of harmony have brought about the eclipse of the moon and the appearance of the comet, by removing these causes the effects are removed also (p. III.886).

According to the *Huangdi suwen* there is felicity only in the case that the element governing a season has its proper quantity, being neither excessive nor defective. That means to say that in summer, for instance, it must not be too hot, but not too cool either, and that in winter it must not be too cold, but, on the other side, not too warm. A cool summer and a warm winter are fraught with all kinds of evils. The vegetation suffers, and especially man is attacked by diseases (p. III.884-885).

Dong Zhongshu, who more than others looks upon the elements as moral entities, puts forward a great variety of cases, in which the principal element of a season comes into collision with the other elements. The terminology sounds very abstract and profound, but the meaning is very simple. Dong Zhongshu wants to show the effect of extraordinary changes of the character of the seasons, one season assuming that of another and losing its own nature:

"When (in autumn) metal meets with water, fish become torpid; when it meets with wood, plants and trees sprout again; when it meets with fire, plants and trees blossom in autumn; and when it meets with earth the Five Grains do not mature.[113] When (in winter) water meets with wood, the hibernating insects do not hide; when it meets with earth, the insects that ought to become torpid come out in winter; when it meets with fire, a star falls down; and when metal meets with water, winter becomes very cold."[114]

Like Guan Zi, Dong Zhongshu maintains that natural calamities, the result of irregularities of the elements and the seasons, must be laid to the charge of the sovereign and his administration, and that they will cease, as soon as the latter are reformed. Thus he says of spring and summer:—"When wood undergoes an extraordinary change, spring withers, and autumn blossoms; there are great floods in autumn, and there is too much rain in spring. This has its cause in excessive personal services. Taxes and imposts are too heavy; the people become impoverished, revolt, and leave the path of virtue, and many starve. This may be remedied by a decrease of the services and a reduction of imposts and taxes, by taking the grain from the granaries and distributing it among the distressed."

"When *fire* undergoes an extraordinary change, winter becomes warm, and summer cool. This is because the ruler is not enlightened:—Excellent men are not rewarded, bad characters not removed; unworthy persons occupy the places of honour, and Worthies live in obscurity. Therefore heat and cold are out of order, and the people visited with diseases and epidemies. This state of affairs may be helped by raising good and wise men, rewarding merit and appointing the virtuous."[115]

These ideas may seem odd, but they are not illogical. If the virtues of the ruler are manifestations of the Five Elements, an axiom laid down by the old Classics and contested by nobody, then there must be fixed relations between the two, and a change on one side affect the other. Irregularities of the elements and the seasons must also manifest themselves in the conduct of the sovereign and his government, and any deviations of the latter, have an influence on the seasons and the weather, with which the happiness of the people living on agriculture was closely connected.

x. Wrong Analogies

The theory of the Five Elements is to a great extent built up on wrong analogies, but few Chinese scholars seem to have become aware of the impossible consequences to which they were led by it. Wang Chong does not reject the theory altogether, but very often points out the wrong analogies, *e.g.*, in the chapter on the Nature of Things (p. I.158 seq.), where he says that there ought to be an internicine strife between the inner organs of man just as there is between the elements, and that the Twelve Animals corresponding to the twelve points of the compass ought to behave quite differently from the way how they do, if they were at all influenced by the elements, and in p. II.741 seq.

In addition to this theory of the Five Elements the Chinese possess still another somewhat similar, derived from the *Yijing* and based on the Eight Diagrams. It is much less known and less developed than that of the Five Elements, and the correspondences are quite different. The principal ones are enumerated by De Groot, *Relig. System* Vol. III, p. 964.

The Cycle of the Twelve Animals

This cycle is common to the people of Eastern Asia and used by them for the numeration and designation of years. Chavannes gives a list of the corresponding cycles of the Chinese, Annanese, Cambodgians, Siamese, Chams, Japanese, Turks, Persians, Mongols, Mandshus, and Tibetans.[1]

In China this cycle is a correlate of the duodenary cycle of the Twelve Branches arranged as follow:

1. 子 *zi*, 鼠 the Rat,
2. 丑 *chou*, 牛 the Ox,
3. 寅 *yin*, 虎 the Tiger,
4. 卯 *mao*, 兔 the Hare,
5. 辰 *chen*, 龍 the Dragon,
6. 巳 *si*, 蛇 the Serpent,
7. 午 *wu*, 馬 the Horse,
8. 未 *wei*, 羊 the Goat,
9. 申 *shen*, 猴 the Monkey,
10. 酉 *you*, 雞 the Cock,
11. 戌 *xu*, 犬 the Dog,
12. 亥 *hai*, 猪 the Pig.

Wang Chong (p. I.158 seq. and p. II.680) is perhaps our oldest source testifying to the use of this cycle among the Chinese. Since Wang Chong speaks of these animals as universally known, we may safely assume that the Chinese were already acquainted with this cycle some time before Wang Chong; say the first or second centuries BCE. (Chavannes *loc. cit.* p. 84). If we could trust a passage of the *Wu Yue chunqiu* 吳越春秋, written in the 1st century CE, it would establish the fact that the cycle was already in use about 500 BCE. The passage is plain and reasonable, but the *Wu Yue chunqiu*, as a whole contains so many fictions, that its testimony is of doubtful value. The statement may be reliable, but we cannot be quite sure of it.

The cycle of the Twelve Animals cannot have been invented independently by all the nations making use of it, but must have been derived from one common source. The majority of sinologists seems to be inclined to regard it as of Turkish origin. This is the opinion of Remusat, Klaproth, Wylie, Mayers, and Chavannes, whereas Schlegel and de Saussure have maintained its Chinese origin. Hirth advises us to be careful in asserting the non-Chinese origin.[2] The Chinese critics are also divided in their opinions, some look upon the Turks as the inventors, others claim the cycle for the Chinese.

Originally Remusat and Klaproth were induced to assume a Turkish origin by their incomplete knowledge of the Chinese texts proving the existence of the cycle. They believed that it was first mentioned in the *Tangshu* 唐書 chap. 217c, p. 7v., where it is said that the Kirghis (a Turkish tribe) were in the habit of numbering their years by means of the twelve animals. Consequently the Kirghis were credited with the invention of this cycle which the Chinese would have learned from them. But Schuyler[3] informs us that it was introduced to the Kirghis from China by the Mongols; a statement for which he must have had some foundation, probably some native tradition. In that case the Kirghis themselves would decline the honour of having been the teachers of the Chinese.

Both Schlegel and de Saussure vindicate the twelve animals for China on grounds taken from old Chinese astronomy. Schlegel contends that six of the twelve animals are the well known Six Domestic Animals 六畜:—the horse, the ox, the goat, the pig, the dog, the cock, and the other six have astronomical functions.[4] The arguments of de Saussure are not always easy to grasp, since they suppose a certain amount of astronomical knowledge which most people do not posses. He attempts to show the various astronomical, symbolical, and religious associations attached to the twelve animals by the ancient Chinese.[5]

Before entering more fully into the question we must point out a fundamental difference between the Chinese and the other nations. The latter all use the cycle of the twelve animals when numbering years, whereas the Chinese merely employ it for divination, denoting years by their duodenary cycle mentioned above. Now there are three possibilities:—either this duodenary cycle and the cycle of animals are independent of one another, or the Chinese derived the cycle of animals from the Turks, or the Turks got it directly or indirectly from China.

Both cycles exactly coincide:—any year bearing the first cyclical sign *zi* 子 is by the Turks invariably connected with the *rat*, and every Turkish *dog* year has in China the cyclical sign *xu* 戌. It is highly improbable that two independent cycles should fall together, so that every new cycle begins with the same year. Such a thing is not impossible, it is true, but very improbable; the improbability would be 1 to 12. Therefore we are compelled to admit an inner connection of the two cycles.

Now the Chinese duodenary cycle of the Twelve Branches reaches back to the dawn of Chinese civilisation, for we find it referred to in the most ancient literature. For the designation of years it was already used under the Zhou 周 dynasty. We have literary evidence showing that as far back as the 7th century BCE. the Chinese marked their years according to the position of the planet Jupiter passing through twelve constellations in the course of twelve years, the time in which this planet completes one revolution round the sun. Each year was designated by the duodenary sign denoting that part of the horizon in which the planet stayed during the year. Originally not the duodenary signs themselves but twelve other synonymous names or the Twelve Divisions of the Ecliptic 十二宮 were used for this purpose.[6] But already in the *Erya* 爾雅 of the 5th century BCE the position of Jupiter, the year-star is marked by the duodenary cycle.[7] The *Erya* being a dictionary explaining expressions of the Classics and ancient authors, its method of denoting the cycle of Jupiter must have been known prior to the 5th century, say in the 6th or the 7th. At this early time the Turks did not yet exist, not even their predecessors the Xiongnu 匈奴; the application of the duodenary cycle to years, therefore, cannot have been derived from them. Besides it requires much more astronomical knowledge than the Turks, who have not produced a culture of their own, ever possessed. In Chinese history the Turks do not appear before the 6th century CE. The cycle of the Twelve Animals is only a corollary of the duodenary cycle involving no small amount of astronomical observations. Since the Chinese did not learn it from the Turks, these must have received it from the Chinese.

The Babylonians already knew the cycle of Jupiter, and used it as early as the 3rd century BCE.[8] The Hindoos also made use of it in their chronology, but there is no evidence to show that this was done before the 4th century CE.[9]

All chronological cycles have a beginning. They usually commence from some memorable event in the history of the people employing it.

Ulugh Beg in his treatise on the well known chronological epochs speaks of those of the Arabs, the Greeks, the Persians, the Seljuks, the Chinese and Uigurs.[10] The Arabs date their epoch from the Hegira, the flight of Muhammed, the Greeks from the death of Alexander, the Persians from the reign of Yezdejerd, the Seljuks from the sultan Melikshāh Arslān Seljūq, the Chinese — says Ulugh Beg — from the creation of the world, in reality from the year 2637 BCE when the sexagesimal cycle is said to have been invented by Da Nao 大撓 the minister of Huang Di 黃帝. Only in regard to the cycle of the Twelve Animals of the Uigurs Ulugh Beg states that "with the aforementioned duodenary cycle the Turks deal in a shorter way. But the length of their epoch is unknown to me."[11] This cannot mean anything else than that Ulugh Beg was in the dark as to the commencement of the cycle, for else he would have known its length. Ulugh Beg was himself a Turkish prince and a great scholar.[12] If anybody among his countrymen had been informed about this fact, he would have known it. But the Turks were not cognizant of the beginning of their own cycle or its principle. From this we infer that the cycle was not of Turkish invention, but, imported from abroad. The Turks adopted it without knowing why it was applied to the years and the twelve double hours of the day. It never quite lost its foreign character.

The Chinese have always been very slow in borrowing from other nations especially from those less civilised. *Primâ facie* it is much more likely that the Turks borrowed the cycle of the Twelve Animals from the Chinese than *vice versa*. Moreover, the combination of a number of animals with cyclical signs is quite in accordance with the Chinese way of thinking. They have symbolised the *Four Quadrants* or *Four*

Palaces 四宮 into which they divide the vault of heaven, by four animals:—the green dragon, the black tortoise, the scarlet bird, and the white tiger, and among the numerous categories joined to the *Five Elements* we found the *Five Sacrificial Animals* 五牲:—the ox, the goat, the pig, the dog, the cock (cf. p. III.874), one less than the *Six Animals* mentioned above, which comprise the horse. The Twelve Animals of the cycle either may have only a symbolical and allegorical meaning, such as are usual in divination, or they may have been another old Zodiac of which no traces are left in literature. This view has been held several scholars who saw in these animals old designations of the signs of the ecliptic. Ideler objects that then it would be incomprehensible how from these signs a cycle of years could have been evolved.[13] By no means, the cycle of Jupiter explains it most satisfactorily. Under this supposition the ancient Chinese would have been in possession of four cycles serving to denote the hours of the day by the course of the sun, to mark the months by the course of the moon, and to designate the years by the course of Jupiter. The sun passes through each sign of these cycles in two hours, the moon in a month, and Jupiter in a year. One cycle is that of the Twelve Divisions of the Ecliptic especially in vogue during the Zhou dynasty, the second that of Shetige 攝提格 mostly used in the Han 漢 time, the third the duodenary cycle now universally used, and the fourth the cycle of the Twelve Animals perhaps the oldest of all. There may be small differences between these cycles, in so far as they were referred to the heavenly equator, the ecliptic, or the horizon, but this requires further investigations by some one well versed in astronomy.

With regard to the Turkish list of the Twelve Animals we have to make the following remarks:

The Chinese *Tiger* is replaced by the *Panther* or the *Cheetah*, the hunting leopard = پارْس *pârs* or *bârs*. Now, if the Chinese had borrowed the list from the Turks, there is no reason why they should have changed the panther into the tiger, both animals being equally well known to them. Contrariwise, the tiger is very little known in Central Asia where the Turks were originally settled, though occasionally a tiger is found even there. But its home is the warmer south, India and the southern China. Consequently it would be but natural that the Turks should have replaced the tiger by the panther or cheetah better known to them, and in that case the cycle of the Twelve Animals would be of Chinese origin. Even with the panther the ancient Turks must not have been thoroughly acquainted, for their word *pârs* seems to be borrowed from the Persian and be the same as the Greek πάρδος [*párdos*] and the English *pard*.

Vambery calls attention to the fact that for all the ideas referring to the higher North and its attributes, such as winter, cold, wind, snowshoes, elk the Turks have genuine words, whereas for animals coming from the south like the goat, the *panther*, and others they use Persian words. By etymology he finds the regions near the sources and the upper courses of the Angara, the Jenissei, Ob, and Irtish to be the primitive seats of the Turks.[14]

Again, in the list of the Twelve Animals we have the *Monkey*, in Turkish *bičin* or *pîčîn*. There are no monkeys on the table-lands of Central Asia and, if the cycle were of Turkish invention, they would most likely not have chosen an animal alien to their own country. Being a southern animal, the monkey, likewise, was given a Persian name, for according to Klaproth *pîčîn* would be the Persian بوزينه *pûjinah*.[15]

Chavannes meets these objections against the Turkish origin of the cycle by the supposition that it was invented by Turkish tribes in Gandhâra and Cashmere, referring to the Indoscythian King Kanishka of the first century of our era (p. 122). But, as we have seen, the cycle must have been known to the Chinese before this time already. Moreover, it is very doubtful whether the Indoscythians really were Turks. The language of their descendants, the Tochari, recently discovered and deciphered rather points to an Aryan people.[16] Chavannes seems to think of the Çakas as well, who are said to have conquered the south in the 2nd century BCE. They may have been Turks, although this is not beyond doubt,[17] but if Chavannes supposes that the cycle of animals was known to the Turks more than 8 centuries before its first mention in the inscriptions of the Orkhon, we may make the same conjecture for the Chinese, going back 8 centuries from Wang Chong's time, our earliest authority on the cycle in China. That would bring us back to the 8th century BCE, a time for which the Çakas are out of the question.

But the animal which in my opinion turns the balance to the Chinese side is the *Dragon*. The ancient Turks neither had the idea of this fabulous animal so intimately interwoven with Chinese mythology nor a name for it, and therefore simply adopted the Chinese name. All authorities are agreed to see in *lui* or *lu* the Chinese *long* 龍.[18] The Turks of Constantinople like the Persians replace the dragon by the crocodile نهنگ *neheng*, and other Turkish dialects, by fish بالِغ *baligh*. The Chinese dragon is a saurian somewhat resembling a crocodile, living in the water, but also able to fly and to ride on the clouds. The fact that the Turks borrowed from the Chinese the notion as well as the name of the dragon, an animal which plays no rôle in their life except in the cycle, this fact makes it highly probable that the Turks took the word from the Chinese while adopting the whole cycle of animals.

Ulugh Beg in his chronological work describes 5 different systems, one of them is that of the Chinese and Uigurs. The latter were, as is well known, the most civilised of the Eastern Turks. This Chinese-Uigur chronology is completely Chinese, the cycle of the Twelve Animals forms part of it, consequently the Uigurs must have borrowed it from the Chinese, as they adopted the whole chronological system.

As a peculiarity of the Chinese and Uigur astronomers Ulugh Beg mentions that they count their civil day from midnight to midnight,[19] whereas the Arabs, Persians, and Europeans calculate differently. Moreover, the Chinese and Uigur astronomers divide their civil day into twelve parts each of which they call چاغ *chāgh*, and to each *chāgh* they give a special name according to a series.[20] Then follow side by side the duodenary cycle and the cycle of the Twelve Animals.

Chāgh originally means a time, a period, in this special sense a double-hour, exactly corresponding to the Chinese *shi* 時.

The astronomers again divide each *chāgh* into eight parts which they call *keh*.[21]

This, of course, is the Chinese *ke* 刻, a quarter of an hour.

The wise men of China and Turkestan have established a cycle consisting of twelve signs for the days and the years like the parts of day and night, and have given it the names before mentioned[22] *i.e.*, those of the duodenary cycle and the cycle of the Twelve animals. Consequently these cycles were not only used for the notation of the double hours, but for that of the days and the years as well, and also for the months as Albiruni informs us.[23] In addition, Ulugh Beg proceeds, the Chinese have a cycle of ten combined with the former to a cycle of sixty, but the Turks merely use the duodenary cycle.

This shows that the cycle of the Twelve animals was a true chronological series exactly fulfilling the functions of the Chinese duodenary cycle.

If we had no other evidence, the adoption of the Chinese names for double-hour and quarter of an hour, to which must be added the expression "intercalary" شون *shûn* = *run* 閏 e.g. ماه شون *māh shûn* "intercalary month" and سال شون *sāl shûn* "intercalary year," would prove that the Turks owe their chronology to the Chinese, and in this chronology just the cycle takes a prominent place.

From a study of the Turkish inscriptions Hirth (p. 126) comes to the conclusion that the calendar of the ancient Turks coincides with the Chinese and consequently, we continue, must be derived from it.

How the Turks received the Chinese calendar we learn from the *Suishu* 隋書, the official history of the Sui 隋 dynasty, when the Turks became first better known to the Chinese. Under the reign of the founder of this dynasty Gao Zu 高祖 the intercourse with the Turks must have been very lively, for during his first years they are very frequently mentioned, several times during the same year:

581 CE in the 8th month the Turkish *kagan* A Bo 阿波可汗 sent an envoy and tribute. In the 9th month the Turkish *kagan* Shabolüe 沙鉢略可汗 did the same.[24]

582 CE in the 4th month the great general Han Seng Shou 韓僧壽 defeated the Turks on the Jitou mountain 雞頭山, and the minister Li Chong 李充 vanquished them on the Hebei 河北 mountain. In the 5th month the Turks passed through the Great Wall. In the 6th month the minister Li Chong defeated the Turks at Mayi 馬邑[25] in Shanxi 山西.

583 CE in the 2nd month the Turks committed robberies at the frontier. In the 4th month the Prince of Wei 衛, Shuang 爽, vanquished the Turks at Baidao 白道. In the same month the Turks sent an envoy and appeared at court. In the 5th month again the generalissimo Li Huang 李晃 routed the Turks at Mona dukou 摩那渡口, and in the same month the commander-in-chief Dou Rong Ding 竇榮定 defeated the Turks together with the Tuyuhun 吐谷渾 at Liangzhou 涼州 in Gansu 甘肅. In the 6th month the Turks sent envoys and sued for peace.[26]

584 CE *in the 1st month a new calendar was published*. In the 2nd month the Turkish Suni 蘇尼 tribe, more than ten thousand people, male and female, arrived and offered their submission, and the Turkish *kagan* Ashina Dian 阿史那玷 with all his people did

the same about the same time. In the 4th month the envoys of the Turks, the Koreans, and the Tuyuhun were entertained at a banquet in the Daxing hall 大興殿.[27]

585 CE in the 5th month the great general Yuan Qi 元契 was sent as envoy to the Turkish *kagan* A Bo. In the 7th month Shabolüe sent a letter to the emperor in which he styled himself a minister, and in the following month he sent his son Kuhanzhen tele 庫合眞特勒 to court.[28] The text of the letter of the *kagan* has been preserved. The emperor was highly gratified by it. In his reply he said that although China entertained friendly relations with the Turks, heretofore they were two States, now there being a sovereign and a minister they were united into one. How he appreciated the new friendship appears from the fact that he had it announced in the temple to Heaven and promulgated throughout the empire. As a special honour to the *kagan* he resolved that in future edicts his name should not be mentioned, as the personal name of the emperor is avoided in official papers. The wife of the *kagan*, the *kagatun*,[29] was a Chinese princess of the house of the Northern Zhou 北周, called Qianjin gongzhu 千金公主. She was received by the emperor into his own family and given the imperial family name of the Sui, Yang 楊, and her title was changed into Dayi gongzhu 大義公主. The son of the *kagan*, Kuhanzhen 窟含眞, was appointed a duke of the empire with the title Zhuguo fengan guogong 柱國封安國公. He was feasted in the inner palace, presented to the empress, and granted rich presents in recognition of his efforts for cementing the friendship with China. The *kagan*, on his side, sent the yearly tribute by his son. He asked to be allowed to hunt upon Chinese territory in a certain district. Not only was this privilege granted him, but the emperor sent him wine and food for the hunt. On one day the *kagan* killed eighteen stags with his own hand and presented their tails and tongs as trophies to the emperor.[30] After all there was an intimate friendship between the two nations for the time being. Under these circumstances we are not surprised to read that in:

586 CE *in the 1st month the calendar was communicated to the Turks.*[31]

The *Tongjian gangmu* 通鑑綱目 chap. 36 p. 9 remarks that this was the first instance of China issuing her calendar to foreign barbarians.[32] From that time the Chinese have always regarded the acceptance of their calendar as a sign of submission.

The cycle of the Twelve Animals forms part of the official calendar. So we find in the calendar for 1904 at the end the preceding 120 years, all with their cyclical signs and corresponding animals, and the number of years elapsed up to 1904. Every one may look up in this list the year of his birth with all necessary particulars *e.g.*:

Guangxu 光緒 30th year, *jiachen* 甲辰, fire, one year, *dragon*, male 6th mansion, female 9th.[33]

Guangxu 29th year, *guimao* 癸卯, metal, two years, *hare*, male 7th mansion, female 8th, 5th intercalary month,[34] &c.

I suppose that the calendar of the Sui dynasty was similarly arranged and that at all events the Twelve Animals were mentioned, which for every one are of great importance, being believed to influence his destiny. Then in 586 CE the Turks would have received the cycle of the Twelve Animals with the Chinese calendar.

It is possible that the ancestors of the Turks obtained a knowledge of Chinese chronology at a much earlier date, for we learn from the *Shiji* 史記 chap. 26 p. 3 v. that "after You 幽 and Li 厲 the house of Zhou begin declining:—ministers of tributary States controlled the government, the astronomers did not record the seasons, and the sovereigns did not announce the first day of the month. *Therefore the descendants of the astronomers*[35] *dispersed, some in China, others among the Yi* 夷 *and Di* 狄."[36] From these mathematicians or astronomers the northern barbarians may have learned something about the Chinese calendar, in the 8th or 7th century BCE and perhaps at that time already they became acquainted with the cycle of animals which subsequently became the basis of their own chronology.

That the other neighbours of the Chinese all derived the cycle of animals from China can easily be shown by the way in which they adopted the denary cycle of the Ten Stems:

The Manchus use the cycle of animals instead of the duodenary cycle like the Turks, and for the Ten Stems they make use of the Five Colours in their correct sequence, doubling each colour:—green, greenish; red, reddish; yellow, yellowish; white, whitish; and black, blackish. By the combination of these two cycles they form the sexagenary cycle. So they call the 11th year the green dog and the 25th, the yellow mouse.[37]

The Mongols either use the Chinese Ten Stems as denary cycle, having translated them phonetically, or the Five Chinese Elements, adding either the word male or female—the Chinese *yin* 陰 and *yang* 陽 of course—or the Five Colours with a male or a female suffix.[38]

The Tibetans do the same, but do not employ the Five Colours.[39]

The Japanese have recourse to the two Chinese cycles written with Chinese characters, but for the denary cycle they also may use the Five Elements which by the division into male and female are brought to the number of ten.[40]

Now, what historical evidence is there proving that the Chinese received the cycle of the Twelve Animals or other astronomical knowledge from the Turks? None. A Turkish inscription of the year 692 CE. is the first monument dated by means of the cycle, whereas in Chinese literature we find it universally known in the 1st century CE. The ancient Turks were uncivilised and could not write; the culture which they afterwards possessed they had acquired from their neighbours. Consequently they have no ancient literature, and we cannot expect any information on the origin of the *soi-disant* Turkish cycle from this side.

The only argument of E. Chavannes in support of the Turkish origin of the cycle which has some weight is that the cycle of animals has been much more in vogue among the Turks and Mongols than among the Chinese, being the base of chronology of the former. It must have been invented by them, being much more inherent to their mind than to that of the Chinese who never quite assimilated it, and therefore, says Chavannes, must have borrowed it from the Turks.[41] De Saussure has well answered this objection.[42] The Chinese duodenary cycle was too abstruse for those people which, therefore, adopted it under its more popular form, the cycle of the Twelve Animals, which after all is nothing else than a category corresponding to the twelve cyclical signs. With the twelve animals they could connect some ideas, with the technical signs not. It is for the same reason that the Manchus, Mongols, and Tibetans replaced the denary cycle by the Five Colours or the Five Elements divided into male and female, *Yin* and *Yang*. It cannot be said that the Chinese have never assimilated the twelve animals so as to use them in chronology, because they did not require them for that purpose, having three other cycles at their disposal. They always used them and still use them in divination, as they do most of those categories attached to the Five Elements.

APPENDIX III

On Some Implements Mentioned by Wang Chong

i. Fans

Wang Chong speaks of fans in two places (p. I.75 and p. II.540), calling them by the two different names which they have in Chinese:—扇 *shan* and 箑 *sha*. The dictionary *Fangyan* 方言 ascribed by many to Yang Xiong 揚雄 of the 1st century BCE states that the expression *shan* was in use in the regions west from the Pass, which probably means Dong-guan 東關 where the three provinces Shanxi 山西, Shanxi 陝西, and Henan 河南 meet, and the expression *sha*, east of it.[1]

The *Bencao gangmu* 本草綱目 infers from the character 扇 that in ancient times fans were made of feathers 羽, and that only later on people also used paper and bamboo for their fabrication, whence the combination with 竹 "bamboo" in the character 箑. The first conclusion seems to be wrong, for the primary signification of 扇 is not a fan, but the fold or the leaf of a folding door, a "Thür-*Flügel*," "*l'aile* d'une porte." The character is a logical aggregate 會意 in which 戶, not 羽 is the chief meaning.[2] The meaning *fan* is a derivate. It is something resembling the fold of a door in so far as it may be moved to and fro, and thereby causes wind.

In Chinese literature, and in the modern language the word 扇 *shan* is by far the commoner of the two.

The use of fans must have been common in China in the Zhou 周 dynasty, for our literary evidence reaches to that period. We read in

Guanzi 管子 XIV, 9 r. about a prohibition of fans and straw hats.[3] That would carry us back to the 7th century BCE. Baopuzi 抱朴子 of the 4th century BCE says that as long as the wind does not abate, fans are of no use, and that while the sun does not appear, candles cannot be extinguished[4] *Huainanzi* 淮南子 XVIII, 16 r. compares certain people to those digging a well after a fire and using a fan, while wearing a fur-coat.[5] Dong Zhongshu 董仲舒 (2nd cent. BCE) in his *Chunqiu fanlu* 春秋繁露 states that the dragon attracts rain, and that the fan expels heat.[6]

In poetry the fan has been sung of many a time, and the *Tushu jicheng* 圖書集成 and other encyclopedias contain quite a collection of such poems. The oldest and the best perhaps is the famous one on a silk fan round as the full moon by Ban Jieyu 班婕妤,[7] aunt to the historian Ban Gu 班固, who himself wrote some fine verses on bamboo fans.[8]

The material fans were made of was *feathers*, especially those of *pheasants, peacocks, kingfishers, swans, &c., bamboo splints, rush-leaves, palm-leaves,*[9] *silk, paper, bark,* and *ivory.* I doubt whether the first fans were really made of feathers as some authors maintain. *A priori* it is more likely that the leaves of the fan-palm were first used as fans, and that artificial fans came later.

Of the celebrated Zhuge Liang 諸葛亮 it has been recorded that at a battle he gave his signals with a fan of white feathers, and that his army advanced or stopped accordingly.[10]

Fans were often *ornamented* with *precious things* such as mother-of-pearl. Zhao Feiyan 趙飛燕, the successful rival of the afore-mentioned Ban Jieyu 班婕妤, who was raised to the rank of an empress by the Han 漢 Emperor Cheng Di 成帝, is said to have been in possession of fans of mother-of-pearl, of kingfisher feathers, and of peacock feathers.[11]

Sometimes the handle of a fan was made of jade or precious stones. In 477 CE the empress-dowager presented the vicious Emperor Fei Di 廢帝 or Cangwu Wang 蒼梧王 of the Liu Song 劉宋 dynasty, a mere boy, with a fan made of feathers with a jade handle. The emperor was so much displeased with this gift, because the feathers and the handle were not ornamented, that he resolved to have the donor poisoned. He had already ordered his chief physician to prepare the poison, when he was prevented by his attendants from carrying out his wicked design.[12]

Silk and paper fans were often *inscribed* with *poetry*, or some *picture*, especially landscapes, was painted upon them. This custom prevails up to the present day. Persons proficient in calligraphy are often requested by their friends to write some lines on a fan. The *Nanshi* 南史 relates a characteristic anecdote:—Zheng Xin 正信, the son of Prince Hong 宏 of Linchuan 臨川, did not study as a boy. He used to carry a white round fan. The Prince of Xiangdong 湘東 wrote eight characters on the fan making fun of its bearer, who did not understand the meaning and used his fan as before.[13]

The usual forms of fans were *round* like a disc, *quadrangular*, *hexagonal*, or shaped *like a wing*. The people of Wu 吳 are believed to have been the first who cut off the wings of birds and used them as fans.

In some old sources the term 腰扇 "*waist fan*" occurs, *e.g.* in the History of the Southern Qi 南齊 dynasty,[14] 479–501 CE. This seems to mean a fan hung up at the girdle. Pfizmaier calls it a "Lendenfächer," a rather clumsy expression. This fan cannot be a folding fan as some commentator suggested, for in the 5th century folding fans were not yet known in China.

The common name for a *folding fan* is 摺扇 *zheshan* or 摺叠扇 *zhedie shan*, a fan that may be folded together. Another name is 撒扇 *sashan*, a fan that may be opened. The old name is said to have been 聚頭扇 *jutoushan*, a fan the heads of whose ribs may be joined together. This variety of fan seems not to have been invented in China, but to be of foreign origin. All authorities are unanimous in stating that the Chinese first became acquainted with folding fans by a Korean embassy, opinions differ only about the time.[15] The 游宦記聞 *Youhuan jiwen*, a reliable source of the 13th century, records that in the 9th month of the 6th year Xuanhe 宣和 = 1124, Korea sent two envoys, Li Zide 李資德 and Jin Fuzhe 金富轍, to the Chinese court, who at a private audience brought with them three boxes of pinewood fans and two folding fans.[16] A verse of the famous Su Dongpo 蘇東坡, 1036–1101, and some other poems of the same epoch prove that from the beginning of the Song 宋 dynasty in 960 CE. folding fans were at least known in China.

Su Dongpo says that "the Korean fans of white pine wood, when spread out, cover more than a foot, and folded up, they only measure two fingers."[17]

But though known, folding fans were not yet in vogue at this early date, and it was not before the reign of the Ming 明 Emperor Yong Le 永樂 (1403–1405) that their use became common, and they soon supplanted the stiff fans. Yong Le, delighted with the handiness of the fans, brought by the Koreans as tribute, ordered Chinese artisans to imitate them. At first it was not fashionable to use this new kind of fan, and only courtesans liked to carry them, but after some time honest women also discarded the round fan in favour of the more convenient folding fan.

It is mentioned that these folding fans are manufactured by the Japanese likewise, who make the ribs of black bamboo and bespatter the paper with gold. The author of the 蓬窗續綠 *Pengchuang xulü* tells us that the foreign missionary Matteo Ricci 外國道人利馬竇 presented him with four Japanese folding fans, measuring not more than a finger when folded, very light, but strong and beautiful, and causing much wind.

In the first place the Chinese use their fans as we do for creating a light draught to cool themselves, but they also employ them as shades, holding them up towards the sun, and to protect themselves from wind and dust. In China, not only women make use of fans, but even soldiers and officers may be seen with them, and Europeans in China soon learn to follow their example.

Fans are often given by friends as a present, notably those with autographs or paintings by their own hand, a custom even followed by the emperor who may honour some subject by the gift of a fan. Some instances are given in the Yuhai 玉海. The *Yunxian zaji* 雲仙雜記 mentions the fact that the people of Luoyang 洛陽 would at the dragon-boat festival present each other with fans supposed to avert sickness.[18]

At certain times the use of certain kinds of fans was forbidden by sumptuary laws, or at least subject to some regulations. We learn that the Han very much appreciated quadrangular bamboo fans,[19] and that according to their ordinances the emperor took a feather fan in summer, and a silk fan in winter.[20] The latter was probably merely decorative, whereas the feather fan produces much wind. In the time of Han Wu Di 漢武帝, princes and marquises were not allowed to use fans made of pheasant feathers, and all below a duke had to use round fans.[21] In 402 CE the Jin 晉 Emperor An Di 安帝 forbade the use of silk fans and gambling.[22]

There are some fan-like contrivances also called fans by the Chinese. The *Zhouli* 周禮 already mentions great State fans or flabelli, and so does the *Liji* 禮記. They were used in the 10th century BCE. and they may still be seen to-day especially at funeral processions. The Chinese name of these flabelli is 翣 *sha*. Couvreur has a drawing under this character. In ancient times they were carried in one of the carriages of the empress to protect her from wind and dust, and at funeral processions. In the Han time they were made of a wooden frame, three feet broad and 2½ feet high, and covered with a white stuff on which were embroidered clouds, vapours, or hatchets. At the funeral of an emperor eight big fans were used, for a great dignitary six, for a prefect four, and for a scholar two (*Tschcou Li* par E. *Biot* Vol. II pp. 126, 232). The modern flabelli are made of feathers, of painted cloth, or of wood and provided with a long stick. They are carried by the side of a coffin or a princely carriage, and after the funeral stuck into the ground round the grave.

The *punkah*, in Chinese 風扇 *Fengshan* "Wind fan," of which the Europeans living in China make an extensive use, is not much appreciated by the Chinese, who seldom have it in their houses. But some kind of a punkah seems to have been known in China at a very early date. We learn from the *Xijing zaji* 西京雜記, a work of the 6th century, that a clever artisan of Chang'an 長安 connected seven fans shaped like big wheels, each having a diameter of ten feet. When they were moved by a man, the whole room became cool.[23]

Another instance is given of a fan used for evaporating water and thus reducing the hot temperature. In the house of a certain Wang Yuanbao 王元寶 there was a very strong skin fan. When during the hot season some guest was invited to dinner, this fan was placed in front of his seat and sprinkled with fresh water. Forthwith a cool breeze came up. As soon as the guest, while the wine was circulating, looked refreshed, the fan was removed. The emperor sent some officer to fetch this fan and have a look at it, but, though it pleased him very much, he did not keep it. He said that this fan was made of dragon skin.[24]

This invention, now often used in our modern houses with radiators, was not utilised by the Chinese either. It was one of those good ideas they often had, but which they failed to develop and take advantage of.

ii. Chopsticks

The use of forks at meals is a sign of higher civilisation. Not only savages, but also highly cultured people have been accustomed to take their meals with their natural forks, their fingers. The ancient Greeks and Romans had only spoons at their banquets, but no forks. These are first mentioned by Petrus Damianus, who died in 1072 CE. He reports that a Byzantine princess introduced this innovation in Venice. For many centuries forks were regarded as an instrument of sinful effeminacy, and it was not before the 17th and 18th centuries that their use became general in Europe.

In China chopsticks have always taken the place of forks. Both are, so to say, artificial prolongations of the fingers, invented to keep the latter clean; forks are stiff, chopsticks moveable fingers. The early use of chopsticks testifies to the old age of Chinese civilisation.

If we can believe a notice in the *Shiji* 史記, chopsticks were already known under the Yin 殷 dynasty, for their last emperor is said to have employed ivory chopsticks. (*Shiji* chap. 14 and 38, Chavannes *Mem. Hist.* Vol. III, p. 16 Note 3 and Vol. IV, p. 216.) Wang Chong relates the same fact in two places, Vol. I, p. 354 and Vol. II, p. 117. Sima Zhen 司馬貞 proposes to explain the expression 象箸 occurring in the *Shiji* by *ivory cups*, which might perhaps agree better with the context, but 箸 *zhu* cannot mean a cup.[25] It is the usual sign for chopsticks, for which 筯 and 櫡 are also written.

For the Zhou 周 epoch the use of chopsticks is quite certain. *Xunzi* 荀子 XV, 11 r. says that trees a hundred feet high seen from a mountain appear like chopsticks.[26] The philosopher Xun Zi 荀子 lived in the 4th century BCE. *Huainanzi* 淮南子 XI, 2 r. connects ivory chopsticks with mounds of dregs,[27] referring, as the commentator says, to the extravagance of the last emperor of the Yin 殷 dynasty, Zhou 紂.

In the *Hanshu* 漢書 chap. 40 p. 6 r. Zhang Liang 張良 arrived when the emperor was at dinner. In order to demonstrate his ideas Zhang Liang 張良 begged to borrow the chopsticks of the emperor. Another passage of the same historical work, *Hanshu* chap. 40 p. 29 r. narrates an adventure of general Zhou Ya Fu 周亞夫 who died in 152 BCE. As a joke the emperor offered him a big piece of meat to eat, but uncut, and without chopsticks. Zhou Ya Fu became uneasy, and asked for some chopsticks from the emperor's table.[28]

The *Feiyan waizhuan* 飛燕外傳 says of Zhao Feiyan 趙飛燕 that, when she was raised to the rank of an empress, Ban Jieyu 班婕妤 congratulated her and presented her with various objects. Amongst these was a pair of chopsticks made of rhinoceros horn to avoid poison.[29] The Chinese believe that this horn indicates whether a dish is poisonous. The new empress was very capricious. When she felt the slightest suffering, she did not eat or drink alone, and the emperor was obliged to hold the spoon and the chopsticks for her.[30]

The *Liji* 禮記 tells us when chopsticks may be used and when not:—"Do not use chopsticks in eating millet,"[31] and "If the soup be made of vegetables, chopsticks should be used; but not if there be no vegetables."[32] (Legge, *Sacred Books* Vol. XXVII p. 80 and 82.) The meaning seems to be that chopsticks are only to be used for solid food, whereas for soup and liquid food the spoon is the proper implement.

From the characters used for chopsticks it seems that in ancient times they were mostly made of *bamboo*. Subsequently common *wood* was employed as well as *bone* and *ivory*. *Tutenague* 白銅 is also said to be a suitable material, but gold and jade are regarded as unfit. These are the chief materials of which chopsticks are still made.

iii. Burning Glasses and Moon Mirrors

We read in the *Zhouli* 周禮 that the officials in charge of light 司烜氏 received the brilliant light from the sun with the *Fusui* 夫遂, and the clear water from the moon with a mirror.[33] (*Le Tscheou-li* par *E. Biot.* Vol. II p. 381.) The commentators say that *Fusui* is equivalent to *Yang-sui* 陽遂 or 陽燧 a *burning glass* or a *burning mirror*.

Wang Chong speaks of burning glasses in p. I.115 and p. II.499–500 where he informs us that they were made by liquefying five stones on the *bingwu* 丙午 day of the 5th moon. If this be true, the material must have been a sort of glass, for otherwise it could not possess the qualities of a burning glass. Just flint glass of which optical instruments are now made consists of five stony and earthy substances:—silica, lead oxide, potash, lime, and clay. The Daoists in their alchemistical researches may have discovered such a mixture.

Other authors maintain that the *Yangsui* as well as the *Fangzhu* 方諸 were both metal mirrors. The *Bencao gangmu* 本草綱目 describes the *Yangsui* as follows: "It is a fire mirror made of cast copper. Its face is concave. Rubbing it warm and holding it towards the sun, one obtains fire by bringing some artemisia near it. This is what the *Zhouli* says about the comptroller of light receiving the brilliant light from the sun by his fire speculum."[34]

According to the same authority the *Kaogongji* 考工記 states that both mirrors are made of an alloy of copper and tin.[35] Other writers describe this alloy as 金錫 "gold and tin" or "bronze and tin." The fire mirror must be cast in the 5th month on a *bingwu* day at noon, the moon mirror in the eleventh month on a *renzi* 壬子 day at midnight.[36] These times, the middle of summer and of winter are in harmony with the theory of the Five Elements.

The secondary names of the two mirrors show that they are looked upon as correlates and opposites, one connected with the *Yang* fluid or fire, the other with the *Yin* fluid or water. The *Yangsui* 陽燧 is also called 陽符, and the *Yinsui* (moon-mirror) 陰燧, 陰符.

It is possible that the ancient Chinese also knew burning glasses to which Wang Chong refers, as well as burning mirrors. *Huainanzi* III, 2 r. mentions both burning glasses (mirrors) and moon mirrors. "When the burning glass sees the sun, it burns, and there is fire; and when the *Fangzhu* sees the moon, there is moisture and water."[37]

We learn from the *Liji* (Legge, *Sacred Books* Vol. XXVII, p. 449) that in the Zhou period the use of the fire mirror was quite common among the people, for among other articles a son serving his parents should hang on the left side of his girdle was the metal speculum for drawing fire from the sun, and on the right, the borer for obtaining fire from wood.[38] The commentator remarks that the son used his metal speculum to obtain fire when there was sunshine, and his borer when the sky was covered.

The *Fangzhu* attracting water from the moon is differently described by various authors quoted by the *Bencao gangmu* under the head 明水釋名. One writer holds that it is a big oyster 大蚌 which, when rubbed and held up towards the moon, draws some drops of water from it, resembling dew in the morning. Another regards it as a stone, others as a mixture of five stones. We find also the explanation that 方 means a stone 石, and 諸 a pearl 珠. The *Bencao gangmu* rejects all these explanations contending that the *Fangzhu* was a mirror like the burning speculum, and similarly manufactured. This view is supported by the above quoted passage of the *Zhouli*, which expressly speaks of a mirror employed to obtain water from the moon. This very pure water was perhaps used at sacrifices.

According to the Chinese theory the moon is water, consequently water can be drawn from it. As a matter of fact this is an illusion, and, if the Chinese have discovered some drops upon their moon-mirrors, they were probably dew drops.

Burning reflectors were known to the Greeks. Euclid about 300 BCE mentions them in his works, and Archimedes is believed to have burned the Roman fleet at Syracuse in 214 BCE with these reflectors, probably a myth. Plutarchus in his life of Numa relates that the Vestals used to light the sacred fire with a burning speculum. As the *Zhouli* dates from the 11th century BCE it is not unlikely that the Chinese invented the burning reflector independently and knew it long before the Greeks.

Notes

Introduction

1 http://data.perseus.org/citations/urn:cts:latinLit:phi0550.phi001.per-seus-engl:5.449-5.494

2 http://data.perseus.org/citations/urn:cts:latinLit:phi0550.phi001.per-seus-engl:5.495-5.508

3 http://data.perseus.org/citations/urn:cts:latinLit:phi0550.phi001.per-seus-engl:1.238-1.328

4 http://data.perseus.org/citations/urn:cts:latinLit:phi0550.phi001.per-seus-engl:2.991-2.1047

5 http://data.perseus.org/citations/urn:cts:greekLit:tlg0004.tlg001.perseus-engl:10.1

6 http://data.perseus.org/citations/urn:cts:greekLit:tlg0094.tlg003.perseus-engl:4.3

7 http://data.perseus.org/citations/urn:cts:latinLit:phi0550.phi001.per-seus-engl:2.142-2.183

8 http://data.perseus.org/texts/urn:cts:greekLit:tlg0004.tlg001.perseus-engl

9 Ibid.

10 http://data.perseus.org/citations/urn:cts:latinLit:phi0550.phi001.per-seus-engl:3.445-3.486

11 http://data.perseus.org/citations/urn:cts:latinLit:phi0550.phi001.per-seus-engl:3.445-3.486

12 http://data.perseus.org/citations/urn:cts:latinLit:phi0550.phi001.per-seus-engl:3.548-3.591

13 http://data.perseus.org/citations/urn:cts:latinLit:phi0550.phi001.per-seus-engl:3.776-3.818

14 http://www.perseus.tufts.edu/hopper/text?doc=Perseus:text:1999.04.0057:entry=sfo/ndulos

15 http://data.perseus.org/citations/urn:cts:latinLit:phi0550.phi001.per-seus-engl:6.379-6.422

CHAPTER 1

Success and Luck

Fengyu 逢遇

(*Lunheng* Book I, Chap. i)

1   At different times different qualities are appreciated, and scholars use different methods for obtaining advancement.

2   Jie 桀, the last Emperor of the Xia 夏 dynasty, as usual the representative of bad government, and Yao 堯 a synonym for an excellent ruler.

3   Cf. Ch. 6 n. 19.

4   First minister of Fu Chai 夫差, King of Wu 吳, 495–473 BCE. The text has 帛喜, but we are informed by a note that in lieu of 喜 we should read 嚭. The *Shiji* 史記 writes the name: 伯嚭. See Chavannes, *Mem. Hist.* Vol. IV, p. 523.

5   Minister of Cheng Tang 成湯, the founder of the Shang 商 dynasty.

6   On Viscount Ji 箕 see p. I.241 and Ch. 22 n. 12. He was thrown into prison for having remonstrated against the excesses of his master Zhou Xin 紂辛, the last Emperor of the Shang 商 dynasty.

7   Cf. Ch. 42 n. 26.

8   The two States where the philosopher passed a great deal of his life.

9   驥騄, two of the eight famous steeds of King Mu 穆.

10   A famous charioteer.

11   Cf. Ch. 12 n. 3.

12   A horse running a thousand Li a day, an impossible task, the quickest couriers making but 5–600 Li with many relays.

13   A hermit, see Ch. 29 n. 16.

14   *Viz.* Yao 堯, Prince of Tang 唐.

15   Cf. Ch. 21 n. 23.

16   Observe the gradation: 皇, 帝, 王 rendered by emperor, ruler, king. Wang Chong wishes to express by these terms three different degrees of sagehood.

17   This statement in the mouth of a Chinese is little short of blasphemy, for the four men thus described are universally held to be China's greatest Sages, even superior to Confucius. But we must refer it to what has been said above on the different degrees of virtue, which may be more or less

pure and more or less refined. The highest degree is ascribed to Xu You 許由 and Bo Yi 伯夷 only, compared to whom even Yao 堯 and Shun 舜 appear coarse and vulgar.

18 Zhuang Zi 莊子 makes Bei Ren Wu Ze 北人無擇 a friend of Shun who wished to resign the empire to him, but the former declined and drowned himself. (Cf. Giles, *Zhuangzi* 莊子 p. 382.)

19 According to Zhuang Zi, Bo Cheng Zi Gao 伯成子高 had been a vassal of Yao and Shun, but disliked Yu's 禹 system of government. (Giles *eod.* p. 142.)

20 On Shang Yang 商鞅 see Ch. 21 n. 37.

21 The groom of Confucius who spoke to the country people who had taken away his master's horse. Cf. p. II.853 and *Huainanzi* 淮南子 XVIII, 19r.

22 A general of Chu 楚 who died in 575 BCE. The story here alluded is told in *Huainanzi* XII, 15r.

    There was a clever thief much esteemed by Zi Fan 子反, who had a *faible* for all kinds of skill. When the army of Chu 楚 under Zi Fan's command was pressed hard by the outnumbering forces of Qi 齊, the thief in three consecutive nights entered the camp of the enemies and stole a cap, a pillow, and a hair-pin. The soldiers of Qi became nervous, and said that unless they retreated the thief would steal their heads next night. Then the army of Qi went home.—Huai Nan Zi 淮南子 calls the general Zi Fa 子發.

23 Tian Wen 田文 of Qi, Prince of Meng Chang 孟嘗. The story of the cock-crowing will be found on p. II.793.

24 籍孺 the correct form found in the *Shiji* 史記 chap. 125. In p. I.96 it was transcribed Jie Ru from 藉孺.

25 On the final downfall of this minion see p. I.139.

26 A wife of Huang Di 黃帝. Cf. Ch. 56 n. 6.

27 Properly speaking, Wu Yan 無鹽 is not the name of the lady in question who was a native of a place Wuyan in Shandong 山東. Her name is 鍾離春 Zhongli Chun. At the age of forty years, she was still unmarried, but so impressed King Xuan 宣 of Qi, 342–323 BCE, by her intelligence, that he made her his wife in spite of her ugliness. See Giles, *Biogr. Dict.* No. 519. The *Lienüzhuan* 列女傳 (quoted in the *Peiwen yunfu* 佩文韻府) relates that she herself offered her services as a palace servant to the king, who afterwards married her.

28 The *Taiping yulan* 太平御覽 chap. 488, p. 4r., quotes this passage.

29 Qin Xi 禽息 recommended a friend to Duke Mu 穆 of Qin and committed suicide when his advice was not accepted. His death impressed the duke so much, that he took the protege of Qin Xi 禽息 into his service.

This story is told in p. I.293.

Of Bao Shu 鮑叔 we know that he recommended his friend Guan Zhong 管仲 to Duke Huan 桓 of Qi.

CHAPTER 2
Annoyances and Vexations
Leihai 累害

(*Lunheng* Book I, Chap. ii)

1   Fatalism pure and simple.

2   累.

3   害. The two Chinese terms are synonymous and might be interchanged like their English equivalents.

4   Quarrel of friends.

5   Here again our author forgets his own theory that honour and happiness are not won by excellent qualities, but are the free gift of fate.

6   Envy of less successful rivals.

7   Strife through roughness of character.

8   Unfair competition among officials. There is no great difference with the second annoyance which, however, refers more to private life.

9   Natural antipathy of the vicious against honest men.

10   Favouritism.

11   All metaphors denoting the insidious attacks of backbiters.

12   Calumniation must be a very frequent trait of the Chinese character, since in all the six cases those dissatisfied resort to it.

13   A verse quoted in somewhat altered form from the *Shiji* 史記 chap. 84, p. 6r. where it is spoken by Qu Yuan 屈原 before his death. 邑犬羣吠兮吠所怪也誹俊疑桀兮固庸能也. Our text omits the finals 兮 and writes: 非俊 and 庸能.

14   Cf. p. II.805.

15 A famous lute-player of old who played so well, that a friend of his actually could see the scenes which he put into music, such as hills and water.

16 See Ch. 1 n. 9.

17 A Queen of Chu 楚, 4th cent. BCE.

18 鼻 for 劓. The King of Wei 魏 had sent the King of Chu a beautiful girl whom the latter liked very much. His consort Zheng Xiu 鄭袖, in order to destroy her rival, told her that the king loved her, but disliked her nose, and that she had better cover it with a kerchief. The unhappy girl followed this advice. When the king expressed his astonishment the queen informed him that the girl could not endure the smell of the king's breath. This enraged the king so much, that he ordered the girl to have her nose cut off. Han Feizi 韓非子 (*Taiping yulan* 太平御覽 chap. 367, p.3v.).

19 An officer of Cai 蔡.

20 A Prince of Wei 魏, died 244 BCE.

21 戚施.

22 蘧除, which should be written 籧篨.

23 Common people are not exposed to the dust of envious slander or to hurricanes caused by their rivals.

24 Cf. Ch. 1 n. 3.

25 Since the drowning in the Yangzi 江 seems to refer to Wu Zixu 伍子胥, whose body was thrown into the Qiantang river 錢塘江 or the Yangzi 江, the jumping into the Yellow River must be said of the violent death of Deng Xi 鄧析, of whom we merely know that he was put to death, but not how.

26 A sophist of the 6th cent. BCE, on whom see my article "The Chinese Sophists" p. 11 (*Journal of China Branch, R. Asiat. Society* Vol. XXXIV, 1901–02).

27 Cf. Ch. 10 n. 1.

28 方心.

29 Cf. Ch. 10 n. 39.

30 Ed. A. here and elsewhere has the peculiar sign 㐀 for 丘 not to be found in *Kangxi* 康熙.

31 The smallest defects are thus magnified.

32 A place in Henan 河南. Cf. Ch. 9 n. 44.

33 One of the nine circuits of Yu 禹 comprising parts of Zhili 直隸 and Shandong 山東.

34 刺史.

35 Figuratively said of men.

CHAPTER 3
On Destiny and Fortune
Minglu 命祿
(*Lunheng* Book I, Chap. iii)

1   Passing the examinations, which is mere luck.

2   The god of cereals (cf. p. I.144).

3   The wise minister of Shun 舜 (cf. Ch. 25).

4   This was the name assumed by the famous minister of the Yue 越 State Fan Li 范蠡, when, having retired from public life, he lived incognito in Qi 齊. Under this name he amassed a large fortune so, that Tao Zhu Gong 陶朱公 has become a synonym for a "millionaire." (Cf. Giles, *Bibl. Dict.* No. 540.)

5   King Cheng 成 of the Zhou 周 dynasty (cf. Ch. 20).

6   Huan 桓, Duke of Qi 齊 (cf. p. I.123).

7   A keen business man, who flourished under the Marquis Wen 文 of Wei 魏 in the 5th cent. BCE.

8   A disciple of Confucius, who became very rich.

9   Zhu Fu Yan 主父偃 lived in the 2nd cent. BCE. He was an enemy of Dong Zhongshu 董仲舒 (cf. p. II.841).

10   Who could explain a book, and solve knotty questions in the presence of the sovereign.

11   Cf. p. II.473.

12   Cf. Ch. 11.

13   Because Cai Ze 蔡澤 was not a native of Qin 秦, but of Yan 燕. King Zhao 昭 of Qin (305–250 BCE) made him his minister on the recommendation of Fan Ju 范雎.

14   Cf. p. I.95.

15   See Ch. 30.

16   A scholar of the 2nd cent., who wrote the *Xinshu* 新書 and some poetry.

17   The King of Huainan 淮南, who had revolted.

18   A celebrated physician.

19   The passage is quoted from the *Shiji* 史記, chap. 8 (Chavannes, *Mem. Hist.* Vol. II, p. 400).

20 One of the Three Heroes who helped Han Gao Zu 漢高祖 to win the throne.

21 Cf. p. II.463.

22 According to Chinese customs executions of criminals take place in autumn.

23 The fifth son of the Emperor Gao Zu 高祖. The Empress Lü Hou 呂后 wished to leave the empire to one of the Lü 呂 princes, her own kinsmen.

24 179–157 BCE.

25 Chief minister of Han Wen Di 漢文帝 (cf. Ch. 11).

26 30 catties.

27 A swift horse supposed to make a thousand Li in one day.

28 He was assassinated by his younger brother in 376 BCE (Chavannes, *Mem. Hist.* Vol. IV, p. 433, Note 5).

CHAPTER 4
Long Life and Vital Fluid
Qishou 氣壽
(*Lunheng* Book I, Chap. iv)

1 What has been received as fate is the vital fluid or life. The length of life depends on the quality of this fluid, but it can be shortened by accidents, such as war, fire, etc. coming from abroad, before vitality is exhausted, and death would ensue under normal conditions.—The Chinese word used here, 命 means "fate" as well as "life."

2 And this nature becomes manifest by the way in which the new-borns cry. Strong babies have strong voices, weak ones give only a whine.

3 On the Chinese foot see Ch. 15 n. 19.

4 Wang Chong explains the term *zhangfu* 丈夫 "young man" as originally meaning a man of ten feet=*zhang* 丈.

5 丈人. A husband thus addresses his father and mother-in-law.

6 Quotation from the *Shangshu* 尚書 Pt. I, chap. III, 12 (Legge, *Classics* Vol. III, Pt. I, p. 25).

7   The *Shiji* 史記 chap. 1, p. 20 (Chavannes, *Mem. Hist.* Vol. I, p. 69) writes twenty years.

8   In that case Shun 舜 cannot have reigned for him longer than 20 years, for 70+20+8=98.

9   Quotation from the *Shangshu* (*Shundian* 舜典) Pt. II, Bk. I, chap. VI, 28 (Legge, *Classics* Vol. III, Pt. I, p. 51).

10   The computation gives 110 not 100 years. We should read "he was tried twenty years" instead of thirty, the reading adopted in the *Shiji* and defended by several old commentators. Cf. Legge's notes to the passage and Chavannes *loc. cit.* p. 91 Note 2.

11   Quoted from the *Liji* 禮記, Wen Wang shizi 文王世子 (Legge, *Sacred Books* Vol. XXVII, p. 344). The commentators are at a loss how to explain that Wen Wang 文王 was only ten years older than his son, Wu Wang 武王, and how he could give him some of his years.

12   1078–1053 BCE.

13   Sima Qian 司馬遷 mentions this report in his biography of Lao Zi 老子 (*Shiji*, chap. 63, p. 3). Some said that Lao Zi became over 160 years old, others that he lived over 200 years, prolonging his life by the practice of virtue.

14   The *Shangshu* Pt. V, Bk. XV, 5 (Legge, *Classics* Vol. III, Pt. II, p. 467) expressly states that Gao Zong 高宗 = Wu Ding 武丁 enjoyed the throne for fifty and nine years, not for a hundred. He reigned from 1324–1266 BCE.

15   Thus the *Shangshu* (Lüxing 呂刑) Pt. V, Bk. XXVII, 1 (Legge, *Classics* Vol. III, Pt. II, p. 588) as Wang Chong and others understand the passage (On Legge's different view cf. his notes). According to the *Shiji* King Mu's 穆 reign lasted but 55 years. It is usually reckoned from 1001–947 BCE.

CHAPTER 5
On Chance and Luck
Xing'ou 幸偶

(*Lunheng* Book II, Chap. i)

1 Another disciple of Confucius. On his sickness cf. *Analects* VI, 8 and p. I.231.

2 *Analects* VI, 17.

3 The meaning is that the successes of superior men are due to their own excellence, not to mere chance, but that they are often visited with misfortune. With common people it is different. Their happiness is never their own work, but luck, which often favours them.

4 *Zhongyong* 中庸 (Doctrine of the Mean) chap. XV.

5 Two minions of the emperors Han Gao Zu 漢高祖 (206–194 BCE) and Hui Di 惠帝 (194–187 BCE).

6 *Shiji* 史記 chap. 125.

7 An old State in modern Shanxi 山西, where the Marquis Wen 文 reigned from 779–744 BCE.

8 The name of a State, whose lords were viscounts, in modern Anhui 安徽.

9 An old feudal State in Shandong 山東.

10 Higher titles used to be given to those feudal princes than they were entitled to.

11 *Zhuangzi* 莊子 XIV, 25v. (Tianyun 天運) informs us that the traces of Confucius were obliterated in Wei 衛. Confucius spent there many years of his life, but without gaining any influence on its prince, and therefore left no trace.

12 When Confucius was travelling from the Chen 陳 State to Cai 蔡, his provisions became exhausted, and Confucius with his followers had to suffer hunger. *Analects* XV, 1. Chen and Cai were situated in southeastern Henan 河南.

CHAPTER 6
What Is Meant by Destiny?
Mingyi 命義

(*Lunheng* Book II, Chap. ii)

1   The followers of Mo Di 墨子.
2   A disciple of Confucius.
3   *Analects* XII, 5.
4   A city in Anhui 安徽.
5   A city in Shanxi 山西.
6   This massacre took place in 260 BCE (Cf. *Mayers Reader's Manual* N. 544.)
7   722–481 BCE.
8   The founder of the former Han 漢 dynasty, a native of Pei 沛 in Jiangsu 江蘇. Feng 豐 was another region in the neighbourhood.
9   This great fire, which on the same day broke out in the capitals of the four States, is recorded in the *Chunqiu* 春秋 Book X, 18 (Duke Zhao 昭) as happening in 529 BCE. It is believed to have been foreshadowed by a comet, which appeared in winter of the preceding year.—These four States were comprised in Henan 河南, except Song 宋 which occupied the northern part of modern Jiangsu.
10 The rival of Han Gao Zu 漢高祖, before the latter ascended the throne.
11 Wang Chong puts a construction upon the words of Zi Xia 子夏, of which he probably never thought. Zi Xia used Destiny and Heaven as synonyms, as we do.
12 Namely the stars.
13 The first legendary rulers of Chinese history.
14 Two famous charioteers of old, the latter the driver of the eight celebrated steeds of King Mu 穆 of Zhou 周.
15 *Mencius*, Book VII, Pt. I, chap. 3
16 Two famous robbers of antiquity, especially the former, to whom a chapter is devoted in *Zhuangzi* 莊子.
17 The same as Yan Hui 顏囘, the favourite disciple of Confucius.
18 He worked too hard, and died at the age of thirty-two. His hair had turned

quite white already. (Cf. Legge, *Analects*, Prolegomena p. 113.)

19　Qu Yuan 屈原 or Qu Ping 屈平, a faithful counsellor of Prince Huai 懷 of Chu 楚 in the 4th century BCE, committed suicide by drowning himself, because his admonitions were disregarded. The dragon-boat festival is celebrated in commemoration thereof. Wu Yuan 伍員 or Wu Yun 伍員, a minister of the last King of Wu 吳 circa 520 BCE was sentenced to perish by his own hand. His body was afterwards sewn into a leather wine-sack, and cast into the river near Suzhou 蘇州, where he has been deified as the spirit of the water like Qu Ping. This is the common tradition. (Cf. *Mayers Manual* N. 879 and Giles, *Biogr. Dict.* N. 2358. According to Wang Chong the body of Wu Yuan was cooked.)

20　The term *nature* is used in the sense of spiritual nature, disposition, as well as for constitution, *i.e.* physical qualities.

21　The *Yueling* 月令 is the Book III, N. 6 of the *Liji* 禮記, the *Book of Rites*. The "same month" referred to in the passage, quoted from the *Yueling*, is the second month of spring. Wang Chong seems to have had in view the final paragraph as well, which says that, if in the last month of winter the spring ceremonies were observed, the embryos would suffer many disasters. (Cf. Legge, *Liji*, Book IV, p. 260 and 310 [*Sacred Books of the East*, Vol. XXVII].)

22　A native of Jin 晉, 6th cent. BCE.

23　The unworthy son of the Emperor Yao 堯 2357 BCE.

24　The degenerated son of the Emperor Shun 舜 2255 BCE.

25　Cf. *Dadaili* 大戴禮 chap. 3, p. 6v (*Han Wei congshu* 漢魏叢書).

26　The first emperor, a mythical personage.

27　The founder of the Shang 商 dynasty, who was imprisoned by the last emperors of the Xia 夏.

28　The ancestor of the house of Zhou 周. He was incarcerated at Youli 羑里 by the last emperor of the Shang dynasty.

29　Under Yan Zi 晏子, Yan Ying 晏嬰, a celebrated statesman of the dukes of Qi 齊, is usually understood. Since Yan Ying was very successful in his career, no misfortune whatever being recorded of him, I would suggest to alter 晏子 into 顏子, abbreviated for 顏回 Yan Hui, the name of the ill-fated disciple of Confucius, whose misfortune, his untimely death, is mentioned p. II. 843, Ch. 84 n.10 and elsewhere [QP *see* index entry].

30　See p. I.95.

31　In addition to good luck, according to our author, he who seeks employment requires a contingency, he must find some one who appreciates him.

CHAPTER 7
Unfounded Assertions
Wuxing 無形

(*Lunheng* Book II, Chap. iii)

1   *Liji* 禮記 chap. I, No. 1 (Quli 曲禮), p. 20v. (Legge's translation Vol. I, p. 84.) Various reasons have been assigned by the commentators for this rule. They say, in opposition to Wang Chong, that during heavy rain-falls fish are so easily got as not to be valuable, or that then they are muddy and not fit for eating. This last reason seems the most plausible.

2   To become like a quail or a crab.

3   Quoted from *Huainanzi* 淮南子, who adds that the tiger devoured his brother, when he opened the door.

4   A legendary minister of Yao 堯 and father to Great Yu 禹.

5   An adherent of the founder of the Han 漢 dynasty. The Daoists have claimed him as one of their patriarchs and mystics. See p. II.665.

6   The Yellow River.

7   This event in told in detail on p. II.663.

8   Posthumous name of the Shang 商 Emperor Wu Ding 武丁, 1324–1265 BCE.

9   A paper mulberry tree grew in the court of the Emperor, which had two spans of circumference on the second day already. This was, of course, regarded as a portent. Cf. *Lunheng, Yixu* 異虛 (Ch. 18, p. I.195) where the legend is told in full.

10   According to the *Shangshu* 尚書 Pt. V, Bk. XV (Legge, *Classics* Vol. III, Pt. II, p. 467) Gao Zong 高宗 reigned 59 years.

11   515–451 BCE.

12   This story is told in full in *Lunheng* Ch. 17, p. I.186 which seems quoted from *Huainanzi* XII, 11v. The planet Mars being in the constellation of the "Heart," the astrologer Zi Wei 子韋 informed the duke that Heaven was going to inflict a punishment upon him, advising him, however, to shift this misfortune on his prime minister, or on his people, or on the year. The prince thrice declined to allow others to suffer in his stead, giving his reasons for each refusal. These are the three good maxims of our text. Zi Wei then changed and congratulated

the duke, saying that Heaven had heard the three excellent sentiments uttered by him, that the same night it would cause Mars to pass through three solar mansions, and that it would add twenty-one years to his life, each mansion consisting of seven stars and each star representing one year.

13 658–619 BCE.

14 Shang Di 上帝, the supreme being, God.

15 A magician of the time of Shen Nong 神農.

16 A Prince of Jin 晉 571 BCE, who became a Daoist and an immortal. He was seen riding through the air upon a white cane. Mayers, No. 801.

17 The meaning is, as summer is preceded by spring, thus the body exists, before it is informed by the vital force.

18 This verse does not occur in the *Liji* 禮記, but in the *Shijing* 詩經 Pt. IV, Bk. III, Ode II (Legge, *Classics* Vol. IV, Pt. II, p. 635): "He (the ancestor) will bless us with the eyebrows of longevity.—We will have yellow hair and wizened faces indefinitely."

19 For more details see the *Shanhaijing* 山海經.

20 Great Yu 禹 2205–2197 BCE.

21 A minister of Yu 禹.

22 A Daoist goddess. Cf. my article "Mu Wang und die Königin von Saba" in the *Mitteilungen des Seminars für Orientalische Sprachen zu Berlin* Vol. VII, 1904.

CHAPTER 8
The Forming of Characters
Shuaixing 率性

(*Lunheng* Book II, Chap. iv)

1 *Shangshu* 尚書, The Announcement of Shao 邵 V, Bk. XII, 18–19. Wang Chong reads 於戲 "alas!" instead of 嗚呼.

2 *Shijing* 詩經 I, Bk. IV, Ode IX, 2 where we read now 何以予之 "what can he give?" instead of 與之 "what can he be compared to?"

3 Yang Zhu 楊朱, the philosopher of egoism. The story referred to here is

told in *Liezi* 列子 VIII, 10v. A sheep had been lost on by-roads. When Yang Zhu heard of it, he became thoughtful and changed countenance. No mention is made of his having wept. Wang Chong seems to have quoted from *Huainanzi* 淮南子 XVII, 25v, who expressly mentions Yang Zi's 楊子 weeping.

4   Mo Di 墨翟, the philosopher of altruism. We read in his works: *Mozi* 墨子 chap. 3, p. 4 (What colours) and in the *Lüshi chunqiu* 呂氏春秋 chap. 2, No. 4, p. 8 (Colouring) that Mo Zi 墨子 witnessing the dying of silk said, heaving a sigh, "Dyed blue, it turns blue, and dyed yellow, it turns yellow" and then he goes on to explain, how man also takes the colour of his environments, especially of those with whom he has intercourse, wherefore "colouring" is a very serious affair. Nothing is said about his having shed tears.

5   So excellent were they all.

6   The last emperors of the Xia 夏 and Shang 商 dynasties, type of tyrants.

7   Bo Yi 伯夷 and Shu Qi 叔齊, two brothers famous for their disinterestedness in refusing to ascend the throne of their father, lest the other should be deprived of it. Mayers No. 543.

8   An official of the State of Lu 魯 famous for honesty and upright character, often mentioned by Confucius.

9   The four classes, into which the ten principal followers of Confucius were divided. Cf. *Analects* XI, 2.

10 A disciple of Confucius, whose full name was Duanmu Ci 端木賜 alias Zi Gong 子貢, possessed of great abilities. He became a high official.

11 The name of the ancient copper coins, which first were called 金 "metal," not "gold," as may be seen from the works on coinage.

12 This sword is said to have been fabricated by the famous blade-smith Mo Ye 莫邪 in the kingdom of Yue 越.

13 A place in Henan 河南.

14 This sword is the work of Mo Ye of Yue and Gan Jiang 干將 of Wu 吳, both celebrated sword-cutlers, who wrought it for the King of Chu 楚.

15 A place most likely in Zhejiang 浙江, called 劍川 "Sword river" under the Song 宋 dynasty. Playfair, *Cities* No. 4650.

16 The Tribute of Yu 禹, *Yugong* 禹貢, is also the name of a book of the *Shangshu*.

17 Cf. *Shangshu* Pt. III, Book I (Legge, *Classics* Vol. III, Pt. I, p. 127).

18 A principality in Hubei 湖北.

19 The time of this Marquis of Sui 隨 is unknown. His pearls are very famous in Chinese literature. According to one tradition the marquis found

a wounded snake, and cured it. Out of gratitude the snake presented him with a precious pearl, which shone at night. Wang Chong makes the marquis produce artificial pearls himself.

20　A number of the sexagenary cycle used for the designation of years, months, and days.

21　Yan Di 炎帝 is usually identified with Shen Nong 神農 and said to have been his predecessor, but we do not learn that he fought with Huang Di 黃帝 for the empire.

22　According to Kang Xi 康熙, Gun = 鮌 would be the same as 鯀 Gun, Yao's 堯 Minister of Works, who in vain endeavoured to drain the waters of the great flood. His son Yu 禹, who subsequently became emperor, succeeded at last in regulating the water courses. Here we seem to have a different tradition.

23　Six kinds of horses were distinguished in the studs of the Zhou 周 emperors, according to their height. *Tcheou Li* (*Zhou Li* 周禮), trad. par *Biot*, Vol. II, p. 262.

24　There are many myths illustrative of the power of music. Hu Ba, 瓠芭, played the guitar, so that the fish came out to listen, and Bo Ya, 伯牙, played the lute in such an admirable way, that the horses forgot their fodder, and looked up to harken. *Hanshi waizhuan* 韓詩外傳, quoted by the *Peiwen yunfu* 佩文韻府 chap. 96 under 仰秣.

25　The aborigines of China.

26　They were settled in modern Huguang 湖廣 and Zhejiang 浙江.

27　An allusion to *Mencius* Bk. III, Pt. II, chap. 6, where the difference of the dialects of Qi 齊 and Chu 楚 is pointed out. Zhuang 莊 and Yue 嶽 were two quarters in the capital of Qi.

28　The Qi State was in northern Shandong 山東, Qin 秦 in Shanxi 陝西, and Yan 燕 in Zhili 直隸. The characteristic of the inhabitants of these provinces is partly still true to-day.

29　King of the Wu 吳 State, 514–496 BCE.

30　Another name of the Taihu lake 太湖 in Jiangsu 江蘇, which consisted of five lakes, or five connected sheets of water.

31　The ruler of the Yue 越 State, 496 BCE, who overthrew the kingdom of Wu 吳.

32　A hero of enormous strength in the Zhou 周 epoch.

33　An official of great power under Han Gao Zu 漢高祖, who subdued the arrogance and superciliousness of the princes and nobles by the ceremonial they were made to undergo at an audience before the new emperor. *Shiji* 史記 chap. 99, p. 7v.

34 Hemp, millet, rice, wheat, and beans.

35 The Five Cardinal Virtues: benevolence, justice, propriety, knowledge, and truth.

36 The heart, the liver, the stomach, the lungs, and the kidneys.

37 Human character, to wit the Five Qualities, depends on the volumen of the original fluid, the vital force, which shapes the Five Organs. According as they are bigger or smaller, the nature of the individual is different. This idea finds expression in the Chinese language. A man with a big heart, 心厚, is generous and liberal, with a small heart, 心薄, mean. The fluid of the stomach, 脾氣, is equivalent to anger.

38 Cf. p. II.462.

39 In both cases the belt or girdle is the same indispensible part of a gentleman's toilet, but the use made of it, and the results achieved, are quite different. The same may be said of human nature.

40 Human nature is like those houses. They are all houses, and serve the same purpose, but some are in good repair, others in a wretched state.

41 An ancient State in North Henan 河南 and South Zhili 直隸.

42 The modern Zhangdefu 彰德府.

43 A large tributary of the river Wei 衛 in Henan, near Zhangdefu.

44 A Zhong 鍾, an ancient measure equal to 4 pecks = 1 bushel, as some say. According to others it would be as much as 34 pecks.

45 The capital of the Zhou dynasty in Henan, the modern Henanfu 河南府.

46 Probably with pump-works.

47 The excellent man is like the river Luo 洛. Streams of kindness and justice part from him.

48 She changed her domicile for the purpose of saving her son from the bad influences of the neighbourhood.

49 Zhao Tuo 趙他 went to Yue 越, modern Guangdong 廣東, as general of Qin Shi Huangdi 秦始皇, and subsequently became king of the southern barbarians, whose customs he adopted. Lu Jia 陸賈 was sent to him by the first emperor of the Han 漢 dynasty to receive his declaration of allegiance.

CHAPTER 9

Auspicious Portents
Jiyan 吉驗

(*Lunheng* Book II, Chap. v)

1   The harsh and unfeeling father of the virtuous Shun 舜.
2   Shun's wicked brother.
3   Cf. *Mencius* Book V, Pt. I, chap. II (Legge p. 222–223) and *Shiji* 史記 chap. I, p. 23.
4   *Vid. Shangshu* 尚書 Pt. II, Book I, chap. II.
5   A mythical personage, the "Lord of the Grain," said to have been Director of Husbandry under Yao 堯 and Shun.
6   The word mother, required by the context, must be supplemented in the original.
7   A legendary emperor prior to Yao, Hou Ji's 后稷 father, after one tradition.
8   A Kirghis tribe settled in the N. E. of Ferghana in the 2nd cent. BCE (*Shiji* chap. 123, p. 4).
9   The powerful Turkish tribes, which were China's northern neighbours during the Han 漢 time, perhaps the Huns. Long wars were waged between the Chinese and the Xiongnu 匈奴.
10   The title of the chieftain of the Xiongnu.
11   This passage is taken almost literally from the *Shiji* chap. 123, p.9v. The *Shiji* still adds that Kun Mo 昆莫 was suckled by a she-wolf.
12   A State in northern Korea, *Ma Duanlin* 馬端臨 chap. 324, p. 14v., where our passage is quoted.
13   Barbarous, non Chinese tribes in the east.
14   In Liaodong 遼東.
15   The chief minister of Tang 湯, the founder of the Shang 商 dynasty 1766 BCE. Many legends are current about his origin.
16   In ancient times holes in the earth were used as mortars.
17   Namely the underground water.
18   Cf. p. I.95.

19 In 686 BCE Duke Xiang 襄 was assassinated by his nephew Wu Zhi 無知 (*Chunqiu* 春秋 III, 8). Zi Jiu 子糾 was a brother of Duke Huan 桓.

20 Guan Zhong 管仲 and Bao Shu Ya 鮑叔牙 were bosom-friends. At the recommendation of Bao Shu Ya, Guan Zhong, later on, entered into the service of Duke Huan, whom he had first opposed.

21 The ancient Chinese foot was much smaller than ours.

22 589–558 BCE.

23 558–543 BCE.

24 539–527 BCE.

25 The *Shiji* chap. 40, p. 14 tells this story with nearly the same words, and has taken it from the *Zuozhuan* 左氏傳, Duke Zhao 昭 13th year. *Vid.* Legge, *Chinese Classics* Vol. V, p. 650, 1st col. and Chavannes, *Mem. Hist.* Vol. IV, p. 367.

26 A minister of the State of Jin 晉 597 BCE.

27 Also a minister of Jin and rival of Tu An Gu 屠岸賈.

28 Likewise slain by Tu An Gu.

29 Zhao Shuo's 趙朔 widow, being a daughter of the ducal house of Jin, had sought refuge in the palace.

30 A faithful adherent of Zhao Shuo.

31 598–579 BCE.

32 Cf. the detailed account given in Ch. 64.

33 The Mang 芒 Mountains were situated in Henan 河南, the Dang 碭 Mountains in Gansu 甘肅.

34 These myths about the first emperor of the Han dynasty are related in almost the same words in the *Shiji* chap. 8, p. 1v.

35 The famous counsellor of Gao Zu's 高祖 rival, Xiang Yu 項羽.

36 The title of Fan Zeng 范增.

37 The story is told more in detail in the *Shiji* chap.7, p. 14v.

38 Partisans of Gao Zu, whose success is to a great extent due to their efforts.

39 The wife of the Emperor Wen Di 文帝, 179–156 BCE, and the mother of Jing Di 景帝, 156–140 BCE.

40 A district in Henanfu 河南府.

41 The capital under the former Han dynasty.

42 Qinghe 清河, a State in Henan 河南, the present prefecture of Kaifengfu 開封府, of which Guanjin 觀津 formed a district.

43 Probably a misprint for Wu Di 武帝; for Wu Di 武帝, not Wen Di 文帝 succeeded Jing Di 景帝.

44 In Kaifengfu 開封府 (Henan).

45 The *Taiping yulan* 太平御覽 quoting this passage writes Tang Wen Bo

唐文伯. Nothing more is to be learned about this person from the cyclo-pedias.

46　The modern Puzhou 蒲州 in Shanxi 山西.

47　Literally: the country east of the (Yellow) River.

48　An ancient name of the region about Chengdu 成都 and Tongchuan 潼川 in Sichuan 四川.

49　The first number of the sexagenary cycle.

50　6–2 BCE.

51　This palace, once used by the Emperor Han Wu Di 漢武帝 as a travelling lodge, had been closed. Guang Wu Di's 光武帝 father finding his yamen too wet to live in, had moved into the old palace, and installed himself in the halls at the back.

52　The modern Caozhoufu 曹州府 in Shandong 山東.

53　Cf. *Taiping yulan* (Guang Wu Di 光武帝) where the *Dongguan hanji* 東觀漢記 is quoted.

54　Han Yuan Di 漢元帝 48–32 BCE. The *Dongguan hanji* relates that the phœnix came down at the birth of Guang Wu Di, 6 BCE.

55　An old name of Tai'anxian 泰安縣 in Shandong.

56　A city in Henan.

57　Under the Han a district "north of the Yellow River," corresponding to the modem Pingluxian 平魯縣 in Shanxi.

58　In case of a great political revolution.

59　In case of regular succession, the son following the father.

60　Both founders of new dynasties.

CHAPTER 10

Coincidences
Ouhui 偶會

(*Lunheng* Book III, Chap. i)

1   Wu Zixu 伍子胥 or Wu Yuan 伍員.
2   On Wu Zixu 伍子胥 and Qu Yuan 屈原 see Ch. 6 n. 19.
3   King Huai 懷 of Chu 楚, 327–294 BCE.
4   Fu Chai 夫差, King of Wu 吳, 495–473 BCE.
5   I presume that the two chances are good and bad chances, and the three
     coincidences, the meeting of a king, a virtuous minister, and a slanderer.
6   Two ancient dynasties.
7   The founders of the last named dynasties.
8   Minister to the tyrant Jie 桀.
9   Cf. Ch. 1 n. 6.
10   A nobleman put to death by the Emperor Zhou 紂.
11   Cf. Ch. 1 n. 5.
12   The counsellor of King Wu 武, more generally known by the name of
     Tai Gong 太公, his surname being Lü Shang 呂尚 (Giles, *Biogr. Dict.* No.
     1862).
13   Gao Zong 高宗 = Wu Ding 武丁, an Emperor of the Shang 商 dynasty. Cf.
     Ch. 4 n. 14.
14   Fu Yue 傅說, originally a poor man, became minister of the Emperor Gao
     Zong.
15   Sovereign and minister both doing their duty.
16   Yan Yuan 顏淵 = Yan Hui 顏回, a disciple of Confucius. See p. I.94–95.
17   Quotation from *Analects* XI, 8.
18   The story is told in full p. I.164–65 and on p. I.197.
19   The cocks of two nobles of Lu 魯 were in the habit of fighting. The one
     noble sheathed the head of his cock, and the other gave metal spurs to his.
     This cockfight increased the enmity of the two gentlemen who were instru-
     mental in bringing about the dethronement of Duke Zhao 昭 of Lu. See
     Zuozhuan 左氏傳, Duke Zhao 昭 25th year (Legge, *Classics* Vol. V, p. 710).

20 The mainah or mino bird—Legge calls it the mino-grackle—is a kind of thrush or starling which uses to breed in holes of walls and banks. The fact that in the 25th year of Duke Zhao of Lu it was seen building its nest in a tree, was interpreted as a bad augury for the duke, who in the same year was compelled to leave his State and flee to Qi 齊. For more details see *Zuozhuan*, Duke Zhao 25th year (Legge, *Classics* Vol. V, p. 709, Par. 3).

21 Shun's 舜 territory 虞 Yu.

22 The Emperor Yu 禹.

23 Mars is called the "Fire Star" 火星.

24 魁 Kui is the constellation α, β, γ, δ of Ursa major, the other three stars: ε, ζ, η being called 杓 Shao, the "handle" of the Dipper *i.e.*, the Tail of the Great Bear. From time immemorial the Chinese have determined the seasons and the month by the revolution of the Great Bear, regarding its Tail as the hand of a natural clock. In the beginning of the first Chinese moon it points to the cyclical sign *yin* 寅 *viz.* E.N.E. 月令曰正月之節...斗建寅位之初 (*Taiping yulan* 太平御覽 chap. 18, 1v. The *Yueling* 月令 here quoted is not that of the *Liji* 禮記). See also: *Astronomy of the Ancient Chinese* by Chalmers in Legge's *Shangshu* 尚書, Prolegomena p. 93.

    I have translated 破 by "opposed to." Shen 申 W.S.W. is exactly opposite to *yin* 寅 = E.N.E. The expression seems to refer to the supposed antagonism of the cyclical signs and their attributes. Cf. p. I.158 and Ch. 73.

25 As long as her mother-in-law is alive, the daughter-in-law who lives in the same family with her husband has to obey her commands like her own daughter, and does not become her own mistress before the death of the mother-in-law, when she succeeds to her position.

26 Again the usual symbolism supposing a mysterious sympathy between the moon representing the liquid element and the animals living in the water. *Huainanzi* 淮南子 III, 2r. says that when the moon, the ruler of the *Yin* 陰, fades, the brains of fish decrease, and when it dies shells and oysters shrivel. The moon, says the *Lüshi chunqiu* 呂氏春秋, is the source of all *Yin* 陰. It being bright, all oysters are full, and the *Yin* is exuberant; when it is dark oysters are empty, and all *Yin* shrinks together. The moon appears in the sky, and all the *Yin* creatures undergo their transformations in the deep. (*Taiping yulan* chap. 942, p. 1v.)

27 Cf. Ch. 41 n. 3.

28 In Zhejiang 浙江 province.

29 A mountain on the north shore of the gulf of Beizhili 北直隸, in the prefecture of Yongping 永平.

30   The tilling was accidental.

31   A place in Hunan 湖南 in the Ningyuan 寧遠 district.

32   This tradition is mentioned in the 帝王世紀 *Diwang shiji* quoted by the
     Taiping yulan chap. 81, p. 2v. and chap. 82, p. 2r. where it is said that below
     the grave of Yu 禹 crows weeded the land: 羣烏耘田. No further explana-
     tion of these rather obscure passages is given. How did those animals till
     the burial ground of the old emperors, and what does it mean?

33   Cf. p. I.137.

34   This story is told in full in p. I.137–38.

35   All the three editions of the *Lunheng* have 䅎, a character not found in any
     dictionary, instead of 穀 = grain. It comes near a variant in the *Shanhai-
     jing* 山海經 = 䅎 mentioned in the *Zhengzitong* 正字通.

36   These subjects will be found thoroughly discussed in Ch. 69–73.

37   A relative of the ducal house of Lu.

38   A member of one of the three powerful families of Lu.

39   See *Analects* XIV, 38 and Ch. 53 n. 6.

40   A favourite of Duke Ping 平 of Lu.

41   Cf. p. I.348.

42   Regions in the province of Jiangsu 江蘇, where the founder of the Han 漢
     dynasty, a native of Pei 沛, began his career.

43   Cf. p. II.658 and p. I.137–38.

44   The relations between Han Anguo 韓安國 and Ni Kuan 倪寬 are related
     in p. I.139–40.

45   The famous "Orphan of Zhao 趙" who later on became the hero of the
     well known drama translated by Stanislas Julien, which is not a mere copy
     of the "Mysterious Box," as v. Gottschall (*Das Theater und Drama der
     Chinesen*, Breslau 1887, p. 108) seems to intimate, the subject being much
     older and semi-historical. For more details see p. I.124.

46   Others remain uninjured.

47   Because they are doomed to die.

CHAPTER 11

On Anthroposcopy
Guxiang 骨相

(*Lunheng* Book III, Chap. ii)

1 Huang Di 黃帝, Zhuan Xu 顓頊, Di Ku 帝嚳, Yao 堯, Shun 舜, and Yu 禹 are mythical or half legendary rulers of old China.

2 Tang 湯, Wen Wang 文王, and Wu Wang 武王 are the founders of the Shang 商 and Zhou 周 dynasties.

3 Dan 旦, Duke of Zhou 周公, a younger brother of Wu Wang, whom he helped to win the throne.

4 A minister of Shun.

5 Like the wings of a bird.

6 Chong Er 重耳 reigned as Marquis of Jin 晉 from 634–626 BCE.

7 A famous statesman who in 333 BCE succeeded in forming a league of the Six States: Yan 燕, Zhao 趙, Han 韓, Wei 魏, Qi 齊, and Chu 楚 against Qin 秦.

8 A celebrated politician of the 4th century BCE, in early life a fellow-student of Su Qin 蘇秦.

9 A partisan of the founder of the Han 漢 dynasty, Gao Zu 高祖, one of the Three Heroes, who in early youth lived in great poverty and subsequently rose to the highest honours.

10 Another adherent of Han Gao Zu 漢高祖, also one of the Three Heroes, the third being Zhang Liang 張良. He was to be executed for treason, but was pardoned.

11 As anomalous features.

12 This passage occurs in the *Shiji* 史記 chap. 8, p. 2, which treats of Han Gao Zu.

13 A place in Shandong 山東.

14 He succeeded his father Gao Zu in 194 BCE.

15 A river in Shandong.

16 Cf. *Shiji* 史記 *loc. cit.* which slightly differs.

17 A city in Shandong; Playfair No. 1642.

18 73–48 BCE.

19 48–32 BCE.

20 32–6 BCE.

21 Huang Ci Gong 黃次公 was prime minister of the Emperor Xuan Di 宣
帝, died 51 BCE.

22 In Henan 河南.

23 A parallel passage occurs in the *Hanshu* 漢書, quoted in the *Taiping yulan*
太平御覽 729 p. 4.

24 516–457 BCE.

25 457–425 BCE. Cf. p. II.658 and *Shiji* chap. 43, p. 8 *seq.*

26 A military adventurer of the 2nd century BCE. His surname was originally
Ying Bu 英布. It was changed into the sobriquet Qing Bu 黥布 "Branded
Bu 布," after he had been branded in his early life. He made his escape,
joined in the rebellions which led to the rise of the Han dynasty, and was
rewarded with the title and the fief of a "Prince of Jiujiang 九江." *Mayers
Reader's Manual* No. 926.

27 Quotation from *Shiji* chap. 91, p. 1.

28 Cf. p. I.234.

29 Quoted from the *Shiji* chap. 111, p. 1 v.

30 Cf. Giles *Biogr. Dict.* No. 426, where the end of Zhou Ya Fu 周亞夫 is told
a little differently.

31 The capital of the Jin 晉 State in Shanxi 山西, the modern Jiangzhou 絳州.

32 Han Wen Di 漢文帝 179–156 BCE.

33 Another ancient city in Shanxi not far from Jiang 絳.

34 Han Jing Di 漢景帝 156–140 BCE.

35 Quotation in a abridged form from *Shiji* chap. 57, p. 6v. seq.

36 Deng Tong 鄧通 was a minion of the Emperor Wen Di 文帝.

37 Cf. Deng Tong's biography in *Shiji* chap. 125, p. 2.

38 Han Anguo 韓安國, 2nd cent. BCE.

39 Died 112 BCE.

40 A native of the Yue 越 State, and minister of King Gou Jian 勾踐 of Yue,
in modern Zhejiang 浙江, 5th cent. BCE.

41 An old State in Shandong 山東.

42 Quoted from the *Shiji* chap. 41, p.6v. The last clause is abridged.

43 Wei Liao 尉繚 wrote a work on the art of war.

44 An ancient name of Kaifengfu 開封府.

45 The first emperor of the Qin 秦 dynasty 221–209 BCE.

46 Shi Huangdi's 始皇帝 kingdom in Shanxi 陝西.

47 Quoted in an abridged form from the *Shiji* chap. 6, p. 6 seq.

48 A disciple of Confucius, extremely ugly, but very talented. Cf. *Analects* VI, 12.

49 A famous physiognomist 3rd cent. BCE.

50 A native of Yan 燕, who first studied physiognomy with Tang Ju 唐舉 and later on was appointed minister by King Zhao Xiang 昭襄 of Qin (305–249 BCE).

51 In Henan.

52 A disciple of Confucius.

53 The appellation of Gongsun Qiao 公孫僑, a famous minister of the Zheng 鄭 State in the 6th cent. BCE.

54 A quotation from *Shiji* chap. 47, p. 12v. Cf. Legge, *Analects*, Prolegomena p.78.

55 One of the disciples of Confucius, whose character was not quite on a level with his fluency of speech, wherefore the Master said of him, "In choosing a man for his gift of speech, I have failed as regards Zai Yu 宰予."

CHAPTER 12
Heaven's Original Gift
Chubing 初稟
(*Lunheng* Book III, Chap. iii)

1 Cf. *Shiji* 史記, chap. 4, p. 8 (Chavannes, *Mem. Hist.* Vol. I, p. 216 Note 1, and p. 226).

2 Wen Wang 文王 did not yet attain the imperial dignity, which subsequently devolved upon his son, Wu Wang 武王.

3 The ancestor of the Zhou 周 dynasty.

4 Tai 邰 and Bin 邠 were both situated in Shanxi 陜西.

5 The *Shiji* chap. 4, p. 4 relates that Tai Bo 太伯 as well as Zhong Yong 仲雍, whom the *Shiji* styles Yu Zhong 虞仲, retired to the barbarians out of regard for their younger brother Ji Li 季歷.

6 The kingdom of Wu 吳, the modern province of Jiangsu 江蘇, at that

time still inhabited by aborigines, hence the tattooing.

7   Chamberlains of the Palace Guard.

8   These offices are mentioned by *Mencius* Bk. V, Pt. II, chap. 2, who informs us that a chief minister had four times as much income as a *dafu* 大夫, and a *dafu* twice as much as a *yuanshi* 元士. Legge translates "great officer" and "scholar of the first class," which does not say much. I would like to say "Director of a Department" and "First Clerk."

9   Two renowned physiognomists, cf. Ch. 11.

10   A peculiarity of Wen Wang, cf. Ch. 11.

11   See p. I.124.

12   The first emperor of the Later Han 漢 Dynasty, 25–58 CE.

13   Cf. p. I.126.

14   Old coins.

15   Guan Zhong 管仲 and Bao Shu Ya 鮑叔牙 lived in the 6th cent. BCE. They were intimate friends, and are the Chinese Damon and Pythias.

16   The *Shiji* chap. 62 p. 1v, Biography of Guan Zhong, states that Guan Zhong cheated his friend. He there admits himself that in doing business with Bao Shu Ya, he took more than his share of the gain, but that he did it, because he was very poor, and not out of greed.

17   Guan Zhong took more than his share not on purpose, out of greed, but unintentionally.

18   The empire falls to the share of the Sage, he takes it as a matter of course, but does not long for it.

19   His actions are like those of intimate friends: natural, unpremeditated, and spontaneous.

20   This incident is told more fully on p. I.124.

21   The imperial house of Qin 秦, which was dethroned by Han Gao Zu 漢高祖.

22   Xiang Yu 項羽 committed suicide, when defeated by Han Gao Zu.

23   *Shangshu* 尚書 Pt. V, Book IX, 4.

24   *Shijing* 詩經 Pt. III, Book I, Ode VII, 1.

25   Quotation from the *Yijing* 易經, Qian 乾 Hexagram (N.1). The commentator says that the Sage and Heaven are always in accordance, no matter who acts first, because they both follow the same principles.

26   *Analects* VIII, 12.

27   *Shiji* chap. 4, p. 8.

28   A famous teacher and in later years a minister, of the 1st cent. CE.

29   A native of Henan 河南, died 57 BCE. Giles, *Biogr. Dict.* N. 1323.

30   A city in Henan.

CHAPTER 13

On Original Nature
Benxing 本性

(*Lunheng* Book III, Chap. iv)

1　His full name is Shi Shi 世碩. He was one of the seventy disciples of Confucius and a writer. The Catalogue of the *Hanshu* 漢書 chap. 30 mentions twenty-one chapters of his pen. Faber in his Doctrines of Confucius p. 29 states that the title of the lost work of *Shi Shi* was "*yangshu*" 養書, and that he is said to have been a disciple of Qi Diao Kai 漆雕開, whom vide.

2　All disciples of Confucius, whose writings were still extant during the Han 漢 dynasty, but are now lost. According to Liu Xin's 劉歆 Catalogue Fu Zi Jian 宓子賤 alias Fu Bu Qi 宓不齊 wrote 16 chapters, Qi Diao Kai 12, and Gongsun Nizi 公孫尼子 28.

3　*Mencius* Bk. VI, Pt. I.

4　The Viscount of Wei 微, a kinsman of Prince Zhou 紂 *i.e.* Zhou Xin 紂辛, the last emperor of the Shang 商 dynasty, who lost the throne through his wickedness and tyranny (1154–1122 BCE).

5　The Yangshe 羊舌 family was very powerful in the Jin 晉 State. Lady Shu 叔姬 had married one Yangshe 羊舌 and was thus related to Yangshe Shiwo 羊舌食我.

6　This took place in the Jin State in 513 BCE.

7　*Mencius* Bk. IV, Pt. I, chap. XV.

8　The spiritual nature may be transformed, but not the physical one. Human nature is so wonderful, that even originally bad people may by much training become benevolent and just. Mencius seeing these wonderful results was misled into the belief that human nature was originally good.

9　*Mencius* Bk. VI, Pt. I, chap. II.

10　Either good or bad, not partly good and partly bad.

11　*Analects* II, 19.

12　*Analects* XVII, 2.

13　*Analects* XVII, 3.

14　*Shijing* 詩經 I, Bk. IV, Ode IX, 2. *Vid.* above p. I.112.

15 One of the Ten Philosophers, whose work has come down to us. He lived in the 3rd cent. BCE. His original surname Xun 荀 — hence Xun Zi 荀子 — 荀 was changed into Sun 孫 under the reign of the Emperor Xuan Di 宣帝 of the Han 漢 dynasty, 73–48 BCE, whose personal name was Xun 詢. Cf. Edkins, "Siün King the Philosopher" in *Journal of the Royal Asiatic Society*, Shanghai Vol. XXXIII, p. 46.

16 *Viz.* of Yao 堯 who reigned at Tang 唐, in Zhili 直隸.

17 A famous author, more generally known by the name Liu Xiang 劉向, 80–9 BCE, whose works we still possess.

18 A politician and scholar of the 3rd and 2nd cent. BCE, author of the "New Words" 新語, the same as mentioned above p. I.119 as envoy to the king of the southern Yue 南越.

19 Cf. p. I.102.

20 Another outlaw.

21 An author of the 2nd cent. BCE who wrote the "Dew of the Spring and Autumn" 春秋繁露 which is still extant.

22 A quotation from *Analects*, IV, 5, where we read that the superior man always cleaves to benevolence.

23 Who maintain that human nature is partly good and partly bad.

24 The text has 酆文茂記 which looks like a name: the *Record of Feng Wen Mao*. The fact, however, that a philosopher of the name of Feng Wen Mao 酆文茂 is unknown, and the symmetry of the context leads me to the conclusion that instead of 酆 we should read 豐 and translate, as I have done.

25 In prehistoric times China was divided into nine provinces, hence the term the Nine Provinces has become a synonym of China.

26 Cf. Ch. 8 n. 35.

27 The last sentences are repeated from p. I.151.

CHAPTER 14

The Nature of Things
Wushi 物勢

(*Lunheng* Book III, Chap. v)

1　The meaning is that, if the creation of man by Heaven and Earth be compared to the melting of copper or the burning of earthenware, these latter processes must be taken in their entirety like a body or an organism. Touching one member, one affects the whole organism. One cannot single out some constituent parts of the process, such as the moulding or the firing. Then "purpose" is comprised in the image, which thereby becomes distorted.

2　The completion of a work done by man on purpose, depends on conditions and circumstances over which he has not always control. Man acts with a purpose, but the forces of nature which he sets in motion, and which bring about the final result, have no purpose.

3　The Five Elements of Chinese natural philosophy: metal, wood, water, fire, and earth.

4　In the ancient, so called natural philosophy of the Chinese, a cyclical character, such as Xu 戌, Chou 丑, Wei 未, etc., and a certain animal are supposed to correspond to each of the Five Elements. From the relations between the elements one has drawn conclusions concerning their attributes. The greatest Chinese scholars have indulged in these plays, and mistaken them for natural science.

5　To wit the horse is hurt by the rat, because fire, the element of the horse, is quenched by water, which corresponds to the rat.

6　The points of the compass, the stars, hours, days, months, and years, colours, grains, etc. have all been incorporated into the afore-mentioned scheme, based on the interaction of the elements.

7　These Four Constellations are the Four Quadrants into which the Twenty-eight Stellar Mansions are divided. (Cf. *Mayers Manual*, Pt. II, N. 91 and 313.)

8　Those four constellations are stars, but not animals, though they bear the names of animals. How then could Heaven produce animals from their essence?

9   The Twelve Horary Characters are the Twelve Branches or Twelve Cyclical Signs applied to the twelve double hours of the day. They as well as their corresponding animals have been enumerated above, though not in their regular sequence. The Twelve Animals are: Rat, ox, tiger, hare, dragon, serpent, horse, sheep, monkey, cock, dog, boar. (*Vid.* Giles, *Dict.* p. 1383.)

10 Metal is stronger than wood, as we were told above.

11 Yang Hu 陽虎 was the principal minister of the Ji 季 family, one of the three leading families in the Lu 魯 State, Confucius' country. Yang Hu being an usurper, scheming to arrogate the whole authority of the Lu State to himself, Confucius refused to see him. (Cf. *Analects* XVII, 1.)

12 White overcomes blue.

13 Because the south is supposed to be stronger than the west.

CHAPTER 15
Miracles
Qiguai 奇怪
(*Lunheng* Book III, Chap. vi)

1   薏苡.

2   This legend is mentioned in the *Wu Yue Chunqiu* 吳越春秋, the Chronicle of Wu 吳 and Yue 越, by Zhao Ye 趙曄 of the 1st cent. CE

3   Cf. Ch. 83. The *Shijing* 詩經 Pt. IV, Bk. III, Ode 3 only says that Heaven commissioned the swallow to descend and give birth to Xie 契 (Legge, *Classics* Vol. IV, Pt. II, p. 636).

4   子, which also may signify an egg.

5   跡.

6   Jiang Yuan 姜原, the mother of Hou Ji 后稷 "trod on the toe-print made by God" says the *Shijing*, Pt. III, Bk. II, Ode 1 (Legge, *Classics* Vol. IV, Pt. II, p. 415).

7　姬 Yu 禹, Xie 契, and Hou Ji 后稷 are the ancestors of the Three Dynas-
　　ties: Xia 夏, Yin 殷, and Zhou 周. The *Shuowen* 說文 observes that be-
　　cause the mothers of these Sages were moved by Heaven, Son of Heaven
　　became a term for a Holy Emperor.

8　*Shijing* Pt. III, Bk. II, Ode I, 2.

9　The last emperors of the Xia 夏 and the Yin 殷 dynasties.

10　The last reigning emperor of the house of Zhou 周 (314–256 BCE), who in
　　256 BCE had to surrender 36 cities to the King of Qin 秦 and in the same
　　year died as a prisoner of Qin.

11　A book of prophecies wrongly ascribed to Confucius.

12　*Shiji* 史記 chap. 8, p. 2.

13　The father of Gao Zu 高祖.

14　The son-in-law of the powerful eunuch Zhao Gao 趙高, who contrived
　　the death of the emperor. Cf. Chavannes, *Mem. Hist.* Vol. II, p. 213 seq.

15　The Emperor Ershi Huangdi 二世皇帝, son of Qin Shi Huangdi 秦始皇,
　　209–206 BCE.

16　Cf. p. I.124-25.

17　A child which occupied the throne 65 days only.

18　The forester of the Emperor Shun 舜.

19　Man measures seven feet according to the measurement of the Zhou 周
　　epoch, when 1 foot was like 20 cm, and 7 feet = 1.40 m.

20　The *Shijing loc. cit.* explicitly states that the foot-prints were made by God.

21　The name of Hou Ji's mother.

22　For details cf. *Shiji* chap. 4, p. 25 (Chavannes, *Mem. Hist.* Vol. I, p. 281) which
　　quotes a passage from the *Guoyu* 國語, and *Lunheng, Yixu* 異虚 (Ch. 18).

23　781–771 BCE.

24　The famous favourite of King You 幽, who ruined the empire by her ex-
　　travagance.

25　With two dragons.

26　See p. II.657, where this story is told in detail.

27　Cf. p. I.107.

28　Cf. p. I.135.

29　For this legend *vid.* p. I.258.

30　A minister of Huang Di 黃帝 cf. p. II.673.

31　The surname Ji = 姬 does not point to the foot-prints which Jiang Yuan 姜
　　原 in believed to have walked upon.

32　Cf. p. I.126.

33　Chap. 2–4 of the *Shiji.*

34　Chap. 13 of the *Shiji.*

35   As the mother of Xie 契 did, when she swallowed the egg, cf. Ch. 83.

36   We learn from *Lunheng* Ch. 70 that it was against the custom to make music on the anniversaries of the downfall of the Xia and Yin dynasties, as one did not write on the death day of Cang Jie 蒼頡 the inventor of writing. I infer from this that the last emperors of the Xia and Yin dynasties were famous for their music, and that Confucius feeling in himself a talent for music imagined that he was a descendant of the Yin emperors.

37   Shun had double pupils as well, *vid.* p. I.135.

CHAPTER 16
Falsehoods in Books
Shuxu 書虛

(*Lunheng* Book IV, Chap. i)

1   短書.

2   A Prince of Wu 吳, Ch. 77 n. 46.

3   See *eod.*, Ch. 77 n. 47.

4   This coat was probably the only garment which the man possessed, who seems to have been a sort of a hermit not caring for changes of temperature or worldly affairs.

5   Notice the modern construction 取彼地金來. Cf. Ch. 38 n. 33.

6   So far the *Peiwen yunfu* 佩文韻府 under 裘 quotes this story from the *Gaoshizhuan* 高士傳 of Huangfu Mi 皇甫謐, 3rd cent. CE.

7   A hermit. See Ch. 29 n. 16 [QP original refers back Ch. 1 n. 13].

8   *Huainanzi* 淮南子 XIII, 19r. says the same of Confucius: 孔子辭廩邱終不盜刀鉤 "Confucius refused Linqiu 廩邱 (a town which the Duke of Qi 齊 had offered him as fief) and did not steal a crooked blade." The crooked sword is perhaps used here as an emblem for a feudal lord.

9   See p. II.761.

10   In Suzhou 蘇州 of the province of Jiangsu 江蘇 where the capital of the ancient kingdom of Wu was.

11 At the age of 29, the hair of Yan Yuan 顏淵 had turned white, and at 32 he died. Cf. p. I.421.

12 A man of very keen sight of the time of Huang Di 黃帝, whose eyes were so good, that he could see the tip of a spikelet at a hundred paces distance. Giles, *Bibl. Dict.* No. 1116.

13 Another name for the afore-mentioned Li Zhu 離朱.

14 Cf. Ch. 37 n. 18.

15 *Shijing* 詩經, Part II, Book V, Ode III, 2 (Legge, *Classics* Vol. IV, Part II, p. 337).

16 A place in Hunan 湖南 province. The *Shiji* 史記 likewise mentions it as the place where Shun 舜 died. Chavannes, *Mem. Hist.* Vol. I, p. 91, Note 3.

17 *Loc. cit.* p. 162, Note 4. Guiji 會稽 in the province of Zhejiang 浙江.

18 Chapter of the *Shangshu* 尚書. Shun's 舜 tour of inspection, however, is not related in the *Yaodian* 堯典, but in the next chapter, the *Shundian* 舜典 (Legge, *Classics* Vol. III, Part I, p. 35).

19 Another name for the Taishan 太山 in Shandong 山東.

20 The mountains are not named in the *Shangshu*, except the first, and generally explained as the Hengshan 衡山 in Hunan, the Huashan 華山 in Shanxi 陝西, and the Hengshan 恆山 in Shanxi 山西, the so-called Four Sacred Mountains. Huoshan 霍山 is but another name for the Hengshan in Hunan.

21 These tours of the emperor took place every five years.

22 In Wang Chong's opinion these places were too distant from the capital and not reached by the emperors.

23 See p. II.838.

24 會計.

25 This statement is too sweeping. Many local names can be explained.

26 These are the names of the ancient kingdoms to which Guiji may have belonged, but not names of a city.

27 Chavannes in his list of the circuits of the Han 漢 dynasty (*Mem. Hist.* Vol. II, p. 534 seq.) enumerates 108.

28 See p. I.131.

29 One of the Nine Provinces of Yu 禹, comprising Zhili 直隸, Shanxi 山西, and parts of Henan 河南 and Manchuria.

30 In Yongdinxian 永定縣, Hunan.

31 This may have been the case in prehistoric times, but now-a-days there are no more elephants in Hunan.

32 The Poyang 鄱陽 Lake in Jiangxi 江西.

33 The *Shangshu* writes: 豬, Ed. A and B: 瀦, Ed. C: 潴.

34 *Shangshu* Part III, Book I, 38–39 (Legge, *Classics* Vol. III, Part I, p. 108). Our author seems to imply that in Guiji there were as many birds as on the Poyang 鄱陽 Lake.

35 Probably a place in Jiangsu 江蘇, see Playfair No. 2022.

36 According to the popular tradition adduced by our author, a deer seems to have tilled the graves of the two emperors. I could not find any other reference to this story.

37 Cf. Ch. 6 n. 19.

38 18 Li south-east of the district of the same name forming the prefectural city of Zhenjiang 鎮江 in Jiangsu.

39 See Ch. 85 n. 5.

40 The common tradition is that Qu Yuan 屈原 drowned himself in the Mi-luo river 汨羅 (see Biography of Qu Yuan, *Shiji* chap. 84, p. 7r.). The Mi-luo 汨羅 is an affluent of the Xiang 湘, cf. 讀史方輿紀要 *Dushi fangyu jiyao* chap. 80, p. 16v.

41 See *Shiji* chap. 83, p. 11v. where the commentator says that Shen Tu Di 申徒狄 lived at the end of the Yin 殷 dynasty. Zhuangzi 莊子 (Giles p. 394) relates of him that, no heed being paid to his counsels, he jumped into the river with a stone on his back.

42 Cf. Ch. 63 n. 67.

43 Both Shanyin 山陰 and Shangyu 上虞 are cities in Shaoxingfu 紹興府 (Zhejiang).

44 Part of the present prefecture of Shaoxing 紹興 in Zhejiang.

45 The modern Xiaoshanxian 蕭山縣 in Hangzhoufu 杭州府, Zhejiang.

46 District in Shaoxingfu.

47 精魂. Ed. A has the bad reading 魂魂.

48 Cf. p. II.636.

49 Wang Chong seems to intimate that there were such pictures representing Wu Zixu's 伍子胥 wrath in the waves.

50 This is only true of rivers near the sea, where the influence of the tide makes itself felt.

51 Quoted from the *Shangshu* Part III, Book I, 47 (Legge, *Classics* Vol. III, Part I, p. 113).

52 The above named three rivers of Qiantang 錢唐, Shanyin 山陰, and Shangyu 上虞 which have big waves.

53 A place in Jiangsu.

54 Quoted by the *Peiwen yunfu* chap. 22b. under 浩洋.

55 If the high waves of a river must be the work of an angry spirit, then those of the Qu 曲 near Guangling 廣陵 might likewise be caused by Wu Zixu,

but it would be senseless to cause floods in a place where he did not suffer any wrong.

56 This refers to the famous spring-tide or Hangzhou 杭州 Bore occurring at regular intervals and entering the Qiantang river.

57 The ancient Romans already had a vague idea of the cause of the tides. Cœsar observed that at full moon the tide used to be higher than usual, and Pliny distinctly ascribes this phenomenon to the influences of the sun and the moon. Kepler was the first who based it on attraction.

58 An absurdity, therefore the said spring-tide and the usual tides as well are caused by the moon and not by Wu Zixu.

59 揚疾. Ed. A has the misprint 疾 = 知.

60 This story is told in the *Shiji* chap. 6, p. 18r. (Chavannes, *Mem. Hist.* Vol. II, p. 154 seq.). Instead of 赭 which Chavannes renders by "painting in red," Wang Chong writes 履 "to trample upon."

61 See p. II.665.

62 Ch. 28 n. 53.

63 According to Chinese ideas the Five Emperors rank above Confucius.

64 The *Taiping yulan* 太平御覽 quotes this passage.

65 This explanation is not very satisfactory, there being a great difference between flowing backwards and taking a new course. Perhaps Wang Chong wanted to say that some natural obstacle forced the Si 泗 to meander and eventually revert to its channel.

66 685–643 BCE.

67 "One must not marry a wife of the same surname" says the *Liji* 禮記, Quli 曲禮 (Legge, *Sacred Books* Vol. XXVII, p. 78). This prohibition is still in force to-day.

68 As the leading prince.

69 Our text has 郜, the reading of Gongyang 公羊, instead of 祥.

70 Legge, *Classics* Vol. V, Part I, p. 74.

71 On this episode cf. *Shiji* chap. 32, p. 12v. (Chavannes, *Mem. Hist.* Vol. IV, p. 58 seq.).

72 Ed. A has 計 instead of 訃. According to the *Shiji loc. cit.* the corpse of the duke was left sixty-seven days on his death-bed, before it was placed into a coffin, so that the vermin crept through the door.

73 This meeting was held in 651 BCE. Cf. Legge, *Classics* Vol. V, Part I, p. 152 and Chavannes, *Mem. Hist.* Vol. IV, p. 55.

74 In the smallest hamlets.

75 Confucius in his modesty says so himself, *Analects* V, 27, but it is evident that not every hamlet possesses a Confucius.

76 Cf. p. I.128–29.

77 Bi Gan 比干 was the son of King Tai Ding 太丁, 1194–1192 BCE and an uncle of his murderer, King Zhou 紂. Chavannes, *Mem. Hist.* Vol. I, p. 199, Note 1.

78 534–493 BCE.

79 九九之人. A short reference to this fact is found in the *Hanshu* 漢書, Biography of Mei Fu 梅福 chap. 67, p. 9v.

80 A poor cart-driver, who was heard singing and beating the time on the horns of his oxen by Duke Huan 桓. He took him into his service, and subsequently made him Privy Councillor. Giles, *Bibl. Dict.* No. 1568.

81 This expedition took place in 656 BCE.

82 綏. Ed. A has 授.

83 To be appreciated by the Chinese, music must be melancholy. Light music appears to them frivolous and licentious.

84 調樂如夔一足矣.

85 This explication is ingenious, but not sufficiently grounded. It seems to be derived from *Huainanzi* 淮南子: "Duke Ai 哀 of Lu 魯 asked Confucius saying, 'Is it credible that Kui 夔 had only one leg?' 'Kui', replied Confucius, 'was a man and in no way different from others but in his knowledge of tunes. Yao 堯 said 'Kui alone suffices', 夔一足矣, and he made him director of music. There can be no question of one leg.'" A fuller version of this story is to be found in the *Lüshi chunqiu* 呂氏春秋 XXII, 6v.

   A simpler explanation is that 夔 Kui originally is the name of some one-legged monster, and that this peculiarity was ascribed to the bearer of this name as well. Giles would identify it with the walrus and accordingly translates a passage of *Zhuangzi* 莊子 chap. VI, p. 14r. "The walrus said to the centipede, 'I hop about on one leg, but not very successfully. How do you manage all these legs you have?'" (Giles, *Zhuangzi* p. 211.)

86 Quotation from the *Shangshu* Part II, Book I, 23 (Legge, *Classics* Vol. III, Part I, p. 47).

87 秩宗卿.

88 As another reading Dongmo 東莫 is given. Neither name seems to be mentioned elsewhere. The *Lüshi chunqiu* VI, 2v., from which this story appears to be taken, writes: 東陽贊山 [QP some Ed. give 東陽簣山] "the Pin 贊 mountain of Dongyang 東陽," a region at the frontier of Zhili 直隸 and Henan.

89 Ed. B: 后來之子. Ed. A and C write 後來. The fuller text of the *Lüshi chunqiu* 呂氏春秋 has 后來.

90　Cf. Ch. 30 n. 60.

91　As a rule a cripple cannot become an official in China.

92　Of the 11th or 10th cent. BCE.

93　曰得一人之作.

94　宋丁公鑿井得一人.

95　This interpretation is much too far-fetched and not convincing. The story was probably believed, when it had been invented, and no further philological or psychological arguments are required to explain this simple fact.

　　The *Lüshi chunqiu* XXII, 6v. gives a variation of this story: "Mr. Ding 丁 of Song 宋 had no well in his compound, and there was always a man employed in fetching water from outside, until he himself bored a well. Then he said to others: 'I have bored a well, and got a man.' This report spread and reached the Prince of Song 宋, who summoned him and asked for an explanation. Then the man replied: 'I obtained a man's service, but not a man in the well.'"

96　A famous bravo in Henan, who died in 397 BCE.

97　Better known as Yan Zhong Zi 嚴仲子, an officer of Han 韓 and an enemy of Xia Lei 俠累.

98　399–387 BCE.

99　In 397 BCE.

100　This number, of course, is wrong. We must read ten years.

101　The *Shiji* chap. 86, p. 8r. in the biography of Nie Zheng 聶政 only speaks of his assassination of Xia Lei 俠累, but the Zhanguoce 戰國策 says that, while stabbing Xia Lei, the assassin also struck the Marquis Ai 哀, who reigned from 376–370 BCE.

102　See Ch. 26 n. 42.

103　A native of Yan 燕 and friend of Jing Ke 荊軻. After the execution of the latter, he changed his name and, for a time, lived as a poor man and unknown, until his musical talent was found out. Qin Shi Huangdi 秦始皇 pardoned his former connexion with Jing Ke and wished to hear him.

104　The *Shiji* chap. 86, p. 18v. narrates the event, but says that Gao Jianli 高漸麗 failed to hit the emperor and was put to death.

105　All these details are to be found in the *Shiji* chap. 6.

106　This is a mistake. This journey was made in the 37th year = 211 BCE. Cf. *Shiji* chap. 6, p. 26v. (Chavannes, *Mem. Hist.* Vol. II, p. 184). In his 27th year the emperor made another journey.

107　*Vid.* p. II.662 and p. II.663.

108　Ch. 15 n. 11.

CHAPTER 17
Fictitious Phenomena
Bianxu 變虛
(*Lunheng* Book IV, Chap. ii)

1   This phenomenon happened after 480 and before Duke Jing's 景 death in 451 BCE.

2   The astrologer of the court, cf. Ch. 20 n. 2.

3   Ed. B: 耳甲. Ed. A and C, *Huainanzi* 淮南子, and the *Shiji* 史記: 聽甲.

4   三善. *Huainanzi* repeats: 君人之言三 "three maxims of a superior man."

5   三徙行七星. *Huainanzi*: 舍行七里 "through each mansion it will move seven Li."

6   殿下. *Huainanzi*: 陛下.

7   Quoted with some few alterations from *Huainanzi* XII, 11v. See also Ch. 7 n. 12.

8   The same story is related in the *Shiji* chap. 38, p. 15v. (Chavannes, *Mem. Hist.* Vol. IV, p. 245), but more condensed, and the end is omitted. The planet passes through three degrees: 三度.

9   In the year 516 BCE.

10 A counselor of the Duke of Qi 齊.

11 彗.

12 *Shijing* 詩經 Part III, Bk. I, Ode II (Legge, *Classics* Vol. IV, Part II, p. 433).

13 A lost Ode.

14 Quotation from the *Zuozhuan* 左氏傳, Duke Zhao 昭 26th year (Legge, *Classics* Vol. V, Part II, p. 718). This event is also recorded in the *Shiji* chap. 32, p. 19v. (Chavannes, *Mem. Hist.* Vol. IV, p. 76), but in quite a different way, especially Yan Zi 晏子 uses other arguments.

15 Cf. p. I.195.

16 Their wisdom and sageness did not enable them to understand foreign languages.

17 The small foot of the Zhou 周 time.

18 Man.

19 They are not bad, but not very good.

20 方伯.

21 In the later Zhou epoch the king was much too weak to punish feudal lords either himself or by deputy.

22 The exceptional phenomenon was either due to luck or merit, but not to the duke's listening to the counsel of Zi Wei 子韋.

23 天人同道. Ed A. erroneously writes 夫人.

24 This great fire took place in 524 BCE, and is described in the *Zuozhuan*, Duke Zhao 18th year.

25 A great officer of Lu 魯.

26 Sincerity and earnestness of purpose are supposed to move Heaven and cause phenomenal changes.

27 Quotation from *Huainanzi* XII, 22r. See also p. II.471.

CHAPTER 18

Fictitious Prodigies
Yixu 異虛

(*Lunheng* Book V, Chap. i)

1 桑穀. For the last character, Giles No. 6229, 穀 (Giles 6228) = *Broussonetia papyrifera* should be written.

2 Cf. Ch. 7 n. 8 and 9.

3 They were non-Chinese States requiring interpreters to offer their submission.

4 The same legend is referred to in the Preface to the *Shangshu* 尚書, 22 (Legge, *Classics* Vol. III, Part I, p. 6), in the *Bamboo Annals*, and in the *Shiji* 史記 chap. 3, p. 7r. and chap. 28, p. 2r. But in all these texts the phenomenon is said to have happened under the reign of Tai Wu 太戊, 1637–1563 BCE who consulted his minister 伊陟 Yi Zhi. In the *Shiji* the two trees got a circumference of two spans in one evening.

5 Ed. B.: 政, ed. A. and C. have: 改.

6 Which is fixed beforehand.

7   See Ch. 10 n. 20.

8   The queer ditty portending the duke's disaster had developed, so to speak, and become realised as naturally as leaves blossom, and water flowing from a spring swells and grows.

9   This seems to be a mistake. The *Shiji* writes King Li 厲 (Chavannes, *Mem. Hist.* Vol. I, p. 282). He reigned from 878–828 BCE, King You 幽 from 781–771 BCE.

10   Cf. p. I.164–65.

11   This must be King You, whose favourite Bao Si 褒姒 became.

12   That is not quite correct. The Xia 夏 dynasty came to a close in 1766 BCE.

13   See Ch. 64 n. 55.

14   The Five Sages 五聖 are: Yao 堯, Shun 舜, Yu 禹, Tang 湯, and Wen Wang 文王.

15   Ten Worthies 十賢 are mentioned in Chinese literature but for more recent times, and we do not know whom Wang Chong had in view.

16   The last ruler of the Xia dynasty.

17   Cf. Ch. 51.

18   See Ch. 51.

19   Pheasants cannot be looked upon as inauspicious because they hide among wild plants, as men do not become so, by living in a cottage and in the country.

20   They are not to be taken for bad omens.

21   Cf. Ch. 25 n. 35.

22   Wild tribes in the West and the North.

23   Cf. Ch. 78 n. 50. The homage of this chieftain to the Duke of Lu 魯 was, on the contrary, bYi elieved to be a good augury.

24   See Ch. 26 n. 47, where this people is called 越裳 instead of 越嘗.

25   There being no resemblance of shape, Wang Chong presumably means to say that the two phonetics 矢 and 士, both = *shi* 4th tone, are similar.

26   A Han 漢 general of the 1st cent. BCE who conquered Sichuan 四川 and proclaimed himself Emperor of Shu 蜀, and took white as his imperial colour.

27   This theory is explained and combatted in the chapter "On Reprimands" in p. II.459 seq.

28   Five harvests being foreboding the ruin of a State, the not ripening of cereals ought to be a lucky augury; conversely, an impending calamity affects the grain, so that is does not ripen. Then its not ripening is a bad augury as well. Such contradictions should have shown Wang Chong the futility of such researches.

29 書記 (Ed. B.) better than 善記 (Ed. C.).

30 See p. II.673, Ch. 65 n. 17. The passage is quoted from *Huainanzi* 淮南子 VIII, 5r.

31 All these plants pass for auspicious portents.

32 576–559 BCE.

33 This story is referred to in the *Xinxu* 新序 of Liu Xiang 劉向 (*Taiping yulan* 太平御覽).

34 五色無主.

35 Quoted from *Huainanzi* VII, 8v. See also Ch. 22 n. 4. *Huainanzi* has the following conclusion: 顏色不變龍乃弭耳掉尾而逃 "He did not change countenance. Then the dragon dropped its ears, wagged its tail, and fled."

36 The site is not certain. It was either in the prefecture of Kaifengfu 開封府 (Henan 河南) or in Caozhoufu 曹州府 (Shandong 山東). The battle took place in 632 BCE. Cf. *Chunqiu* 春秋, Duke Xi 僖 28th year.

37 彗星, a comet.

38 I. e., the stick or the tail of the comet was turned towards the kingdom of Chu 楚.

39 An officer of Jin 晉.

40 Cf. Ch. 71 n. 25.

CHAPTER 19
Fictitious Influences
Ganxu 感虛

(*Lunheng* **Book V, Chap. ii**)

1 See Ch. 32 n. 40.

2 Wang Chong reckons the distance at 60,000 Li. p. I.379.

3 精誠. We are not told how this is possible.

4 Wang Chong conceives heaven as something solid, a firmament, p. I.363 and p. II.750.

5 Cf. Ch. 18.

6   In Henan 河南, west of Huaiqingfu 懷慶府.

7   The commentary to *Huainanzi* 淮南子 says that Yanghou 陽侯 means the Marquis of Yang 陽 *viz.* of Lingyang 陵陽, whose territory was contiguous to the river and whose spirit could cause big waves, the marquis having been drowned in the river.

8   It is derived from *Huainanzi* VI, 1v.

9   Quotation from *Huainanzi* VI, 1v. See also Ch. 84 n. 35.

10   A chapter of the *Shangshu* 尚書.

11   Cf. Ch. 32 n. 58.

12   *Viz.* their penchant for wind or rain, which only manifests itself when the moon approaches them.

13   See p. I.363.

14   Taking the character 舍 in the acceptation of degree, not of solar mansion.

15   See above, p. I.186 seq.

16   Which according to the view of many scholars may work wonders.

17   Like Duke Jing 景 of Song 宋 who is believed to have caused Mars to pass through three solar mansions.

18   The east point.

19   Whereas in fact it was rising. This conjecture is not very plausible.

20   Cf. *Shiji* 史記 chap. 83, p. 9v. and p. II.475.

21   Ch. 43 n. 38 and 39.

22   The *Peiwen yunfu* 佩文韻府 cites this passage. See also Ch. 43 n. 28.

23   Ch. 6 n. 27 and 28.

24   Sima Qian 司馬遷 makes this remark at the end of *Shiji* chap. 86, but in our text he does not say: 大抵皆虛言也, but simply 大過 "it is a great exaggeration."

     In *Shiji* chap. 34, p. 9r. we read that Prince Dan 丹 was kept a hostage in Qin 秦, but in 232 BCE contrived to escape to Yan 燕.

25   Cf. p. II.474 and p. II.475.

26   A general of Qi 齊 of the 3rd cent. BCE. See Ch. 43 n. 29.

27   於邑 which seems to stand for 歔唈, the two words used by *Huainanzi* 淮南子 VI, 2r. where he speaks of Yong Men Zi 雍門子. The commentator remarks that this man was famous as a guitar-player and for his weeping, by which he touched the hearts of others. He wished to obtain something from Meng Chang Jun 孟嘗君.

28   See Ch. 41 n. 9.

29   Zeng Zi 曾子 having been all but killed by his wicked father for some small inadvertence, played the guitar and sang when he had recovered consciousness. *Kongzi jiayu* 孔子家語 IV, 3r.

30 Few will be willing to admit this.

31 Heir-apparent of Jin 晉 who committed suicide, having been deposed and calumniated by the intrigues of the wife of Duke Xian 獻. He was not put to death as stated in Ch. 65 n. 31.

32 A faithful minister of Wu 吳 who in 485 BCE received a sword from his sovereign to kill himself. Cf. Ch. 6 n. 19.

33 See p. II.462.

34 According to the old Chinese symbolism the note A = 角 corresponds to wood 木, which again is supposed to cause wind, a confusion of cause and effect, for the branches of trees are agitated by wind, but do not produce it.

35 The guitar.

36 A famous lute-player of primitive times.

37 A quotation from Xun Zi 荀子 who, however, says 遊魚 in lieu of 淵魚. Lie Zi 列子 observes 瓠巴鼓琴而鳥舞魚躍. "While Hu Ba 瓠芭 was playing the guitar, the birds danced and the fish jumped." *Huainanzi* 淮南子 XVI, 1v. writes 瓠巴鼓瑟而淫魚出聽伯牙鼓琴駟馬仰秣, ascribing to Bo Ya 伯牙 what our author says of Kuang 曠.

38 Ch. 8 n. 24.

39 Ch. 8 n. 24.

40 *Shangshu* Part II, Bk. I, 24 (Legge, *Classics* Vol. III, Part I, p. 49).

41 A remarkable statement. Heaven here is treated as a being superior to God = *Shang Di* 上帝, who has to obey its commands.

42 See p. II.564.

43 *Analects* VII, 34.

44 Quotation from the *Yijing*: 周易程傳, ed. 1880, chap. I, p. 7v., not to be found in Legge's translation.

45 He would not have been the Sage he was.

46 We cannot cure the diseases within the small compass of our body; how could immense Heaven do it, Heaven taken as the empyrean?

47 See above p. I.200. Quotation from *Huainanzi* VIII, 5r.

48 Ch. 23 n. 18, and Ch. 23 n. 19.

49 Cf. p. I.381.

50 In the year 55 CE.

51 In the province of Henan 河南.

52 Baron Yi 益, the forester of Shun 舜 and assistant of Yu 禹. See p. I.360.

53 Quoted from *Huainanzi* VIII, 5r.

54 The tutelary deity of agriculture, a legendary emperor.

55 *Vide* p. I.240–41 and p. I.243–44.

56 The *Peiwen yunfu* quotes a similar passage from the *Diwang shiji* 帝王世紀.

57 Cf. p. I.241–42.

58 The various kinds of existing spirits.

59 A mountain in the province of Shanxi 陝西, 90 Li north-east of Hanchengxian 韓城縣.

60 An officer of Jin 晉.

61 The *Shiji* chap. 39, p. 31r (Chavannes, *Mem. Hist.* Vol. IV, p. 322) informs us that this mountain collapsed in 586 BCE. Bo Zong 伯宗 was of opinion that this was not to be looked upon as a prodigy.

62 洪水滔天懷山襄陵, a reminiscence of *Shangshu* (*Yaodian* 堯典) Part I, 11 (Legge, *Classics* Vol. III, Part I, p. 24).

63 Ed. A. and C.: 若輩者之時乎, Ed. B.: 術乎.

64 It existed already at that early period.

65 See p. II.455.

66 A similar category is believed to attract a similar and to repel a dissimilar one.

67 The common version is that Zeng Zi's 曾子 mother bit her finger, where-upon he felt a pain in his finger too. Cf. *Mayers' Manual* No. 739 and Giles, *Bibl. Dict.* No. 2022, also the *Shangyulu* 商語錄.

68 Kangxi's 康熙 Dictionary quotes this passage.

69 The dictionaries do not know such a man, but *Huainanzi* XVI, 1v. refers to the story here related, saying 老母行歌而動申喜情之至. Consequently Shen Xi 申喜 cannot have lived later than the 2nd cent. BCE. The commentary adds that Shen Xi was a native of Chu 楚. In his youth, he had lost his mother. Once he heard a begging woman sing in the street. The voice impressed him so much, that he went out and recognised his mother.

70 卓茂. Zhuo Mao, a distinguished scholar and excellent official who by Guang Wu Di 光武帝 was ennobled as marquis and died in 28 CE See Giles, *Bibl. Dict.* No. 411.

71 A place in Henan.

72 Under the reign of Ping Di 平帝, 1–5 CE, twenty districts of Henan province were infested by locusts, and only 密縣 Mixian where Zhuo 卓 was magistrate was spared.

73 閩虻. The first character must here mean an insect, a meaning not found in the dictionaries. 閩 stands for 蟁 "a mosquito" which is declared to be equivalent to 蚊. The combination 蚊蝱 "mosquitoes and gadflies" is common. Cf. Chalmers, *Structure of Chinese Characters* p. 93, the *Zhengzitong* 正字通 under 蟁 and Giles, *Dict.* No. 7788.

74 A paragon of integrity.

CHAPTER 20
Wrong Notions about Happiness
Fuxu 福虛

(*Lunheng* Book VI, Chap. i)

1   487–430 BCE.

2   Astrologer at the court of Duke Jing 景 of Song 宋 (515–451 BCE) who venerated him like a god.

3   The planet Mars (cf. p. II.466).

4   The "Great Diviner" of Qi 齊, on whom *vid.* p. II.471.

5   This fact is mentioned in the *Shiji* 史記 chap. 38, p. 14v. The siege took place from 595–594 BCE. The whole story seems to be a quotation from *Liezi* 列子 VIII, 6v. or from *Huainanzi* 淮南子 XVIII, 6 who narrate it with almost the same words.

6   Hua Yuan 華元 was the general of Song 宋, Zi Fan 子反 that of Chu 楚. Both armies being equally exhausted by famine, the siege was raised.

7   According to *Liezi* and *Huainanzi* the two blind men were, in fact, saved from death by their blindness. *Liezi loc. cit.* adds that over half of the defenders of the city wall were killed, and *Huainanzi* says that all except the two blind men were massacred by the besiegers. Wang Chong follows the *Shiji* in his narrative of the salvation of the city.

8   6th cent. BCE.

9   Died 279 BCE.

10   This day is still now regarded as very unlucky in many respects, although it be the Great Summer Festival or the Dragon Boat Festival. On the reasons cf. De Groot, *Les Fêtes annuelles a Émoui.* Vol. I, p. 320.

11   A quotation from the *Shiji*, chap. 75, p. 2v. [QP see correction at Ch. 68 n. 21]

12   A scholar of the Han 漢 time.

13   Demons and spirits who reward the virtuous, and punish the perverse, play an important part in the doctrine of Mo Di 墨子. (Cf. Faber, *Micius*, Elberfeld 1877, p. 91.)

14   The parallel passage in Ch. 7 speaks of nineteen extra years, with which the duke was rewarded.

15   658–619 BCE.

16   634–626 BCE.

17   The Mu in the Duke of Qin's 秦 name = 穆 does not mean: error and disorder, it signifies: majestic, grand, admirable. But this Mu is often replaced by the character 繆, which has the bad meaning given by Wang Chong. I presume that in the original text of the *Lunheng* the latter character was used, whereas we now read the other. In the parallel passage Ch. 7 繆公 is actually written, and so it is in the *Shiji* chap. 5, p. 9v. et seq.

18   The *Shiji* knows nothing of such a miracle. Duke Mu 穆 was a great warrior as was Duke Wen 文, but the latter's rule is described by Sima Qian 司馬遷 as very enlightened and beneficial. (Cf. on Duke Mu: Chavannes, *Mem. Hist.* Vol. II, p. 25–45, and on Duke Wen. Vol. IV, p. 291–308.)

CHAPTER 21

Wrong Notions on Unhappiness
Huoxu 禍虛

(*Lunheng* Book VI, Chap. ii)

1   A disciple of Confucius.

2   One of the most famous disciples of Confucius, whose name has been connected with the authorship of the Great Learning.

3   Bu Shang 卜商 was the name of Zi Xia 子夏. Zi Xia is his style.

4   A small river in the province of Shandong 山東, flowing into the Si 泗.

5   Presumably the western course of the Yellow River.

6   Quoted from the *Liji* 禮記, Tangong 檀弓 I (cf. Legge's translation, *Sacred Books of the East* Vol. XXVII, p. 135).

7   Quotation of *Analects* VI, 8.

8   Bo Niu 伯牛, who was suffering from leprosy.

9   The favourite disciple of Confucius, whose name was Yan Hui 顔回.

10   The *Zuozhuan* 左氏傳, Book XII Duke Ai 哀 15th year, relates that Zi Lu 子路 was killed in a revolution in Wei 衛, struck with spears, no mention

being made of his having been hacked to pieces (cf. Legge, *Chunqiu* 春秋 Pt. II, p. 842). This is related, however, in the *Liji*, Tangong 檀弓 I (Legge, *Sacred Books* Vol. XXVII, p. 123) and by *Huainanzi* 淮南子 VII, 13v.

11 King Zhaoxiang 昭襄 of Qin 秦 305–249 BCE.

12 A famous general of the Qin State who by treachery annihilated the army of Zhao 趙. *Vid.* p. I.95.

13 In Shanxi 山西.

14 Bai Qi 白起 had fallen into disfavour with his liege upon refusing to lead another campaign against Zhao.

15 209–207 BCE.

16 A general of Ershi Huangdi's 二世皇帝 father, Qin Shi Huangdi 秦始皇, who fought successfully against the Xiongnu 匈奴, and constructed the Great Wall as a rampart of defence against their incursions.

17 The Manchurian province of Fengtian 奉天.

18 A city in Gansu 甘肅 at the western extremity of the Great Wall.

19 Quoted from the *Shiji* 史記 chap. 88, p. 5.

20 Remarks of Sima Qian 司馬遷 to *Shiji* chap. 88, p. 5v.

21 The earth is here treated like an animated being, and its wounding by digging out ditches for the earth-works requisite for the Great Wall, and by piercing mountains, is considered a crime. But provided that Meng Tian 蒙恬 suffered the punishment of his guilt, then another difficulty arises. Why did Heaven allow Earth to be thus maltreated, why did it punish innocent Earth? Wang Chong's solution is very simple. Heaven neither rewards nor punishes. Its working is spontaneous, unpremeditated, and purposeless. Meng Tian's death is nothing but an unfelicitous accident.

22 For his intercession in favour of the defeated general Li Ling 李陵 the Emperor Wu Di 武帝 condemned Sima Qian to castration, which penalty was inflicted upon him in a warm room serving for that purpose. (Cf. Chavannes, *Mem. Hist.* Vol. I, p. XL.)

23 *Shiji* chap. 61, p. 3v. Bo Yi 伯夷 (12th cent. BCE) and his elder brother Shu Qi 叔齊 were sons of the Prince of Guzhu 孤竹 in modern Zhili 直隸. Their father wished to make the younger brother Shu Qi 叔齊 his heir, but he refused to deprive his elder brother of his birth-right, who, on his part, would not ascend the throne against his father's will. Both left their country to wander about in the mountains, where at last they died of cold and hunger. They are regarded as models of virtue.

24 Died 125 BCE.

25 The Han 漢 dynasty. The Former Han dynasty reigned from 206 BCE–25 CE, the Later Han dynasty from 25–220 CE.

26 A Turkish tribe.

27 A general term for non-Chinese tribes in the north.

28 District in Gansu 甘肅.

29 Tribes in the West of China.

30 A quotation from *Shiji* chap. 109, p. 6, the biography of General Li 李.

31 A favourite and a general of Han Wu Di 漢武帝, died 106 BCE.

32 A Chinese does not take exception to the incongruity of the equation: $100 : 1 = 10 : 1$. The meaning is plain: a small percentage of survivors, and a great many dying.

33 Prime Minister of Qin Shi Huangdi and a great scholar. He studied together with Han Feizi 韓非子 under the philosopher Xun Zi 荀子.

34 A Daoist philosopher, son of a duke of the Han 韓 State.

35 By his intrigues Li Si 李斯 had induced the King of Qin 秦 to imprison Han Feizi 韓非子. He then sent him poison, with which Han Feizi committed suicide. *Vid. Shiji* chap. 63, p. 11v., Biography of Han Feizi.

36 Li Si 李斯 fell a victim to the intrigues of the powerful eunuch Zhao Gao 趙高. The *Shiji* chap. 87, p. 20v., Biography of Li Si, relates that he was cut asunder at the waist on the market place. At all events he was executed in an atrocious way. The tearing to pieces by carts driven in opposite directions is a punishment several times mentioned in the *Chunqiu.*

37 Shang Yang 商鞅 is Wei Yang 衛鞅, Prince of Shang 商, died 338 BCE. In the service of the Qin 秦 State he defeated an army of Wei 魏, commanded by Prince Ang 卬, whom he treacherously seized, and assassinated at a meeting, to which he had invited him as an old friend. According to the *Shiji*, chap. 68, p. 9, Biography of Prince Shang 商, he lost his life in battle against his former master, and his corpse was torn to pieces by carts like Li Si.

38 The culprit being bound to the carts, which then were driven in different directions.

39 Why does Heaven punish the innocent through the guilty? If Han Feizi and Ang had sinned in secret, Heaven would have been unjust towards those they had wronged, and so on.

40 A high officer, who had gone into exile to avoid the tyrannous rule of Zhou Xin 紂辛 1122 BCE, and subsequently joined Wen Wang 文王.

41 Ning Qi 寗戚 lived in the 7th cent. BCE.

42 Cf. p. I.120.

CHAPTER 22
On Dragons
Longxu 龍虛
(*Lunheng* Book VI, Chap. iii)

1 A minister in Jin 晉, 6th cent. BCE.
2 Quoted from the *Zuozhuan* 左氏傳, Duke Xiang 襄 21st year (Legge, *Classics* Vol. V, Pt. II, p. 491). The mother of Shu Xiang 叔向 spoke these words in a figurative sense, with reference to Shu Xiang's half-brother, and his beautiful mother, a concubine of her husband. Cf. p. II.680–81.
3 A parallel passage, worded a little differently, occurs in Xunzi 荀子.
4 This fact is recorded in the *Lüshi chunqiu* 呂氏春秋 and in *Huainanzi* 淮南子 VII, 8v. *Vid.* also *Lunheng, Yixu* 異虛 (Ch. 18).
5 The Yellow Sea, east of China.
6 This story is narrated in the *Hanshi waizhuan* 韓詩外傳 150 BCE and the *Bowuzhi* 博物志, where the hero is called Zai Qiu Xin 菑丘訢 however.
7 The "Mountain and Sea Classic," the oldest geographical work of the 4th or the 3rd cent. BCE.
8 The Daoist philosopher Shen Dao 慎到 of the 5th cent. BCE, of whose works only fragments are left.
9 Cf. p. I.235.
10 Zhou Xin 紂辛, the last emperor of the Shang 商 dynasty.
11 Ivory chopsticks are very common in China now, and no luxury.
12 Viscount Ji 箕, one of the foremost nobles under Zhou Xin 紂辛, 12th cent. BCE.
13 Dragon liver and unborn leopard would seem to have been considered great delicacies.
14 The historical period comprised by the Chunqiu 春秋 (Spring and Autumn) between 722 and 481 BCE.
15 A principality in Shanxi 山西.
16 A feudal lord under Duke Zhao 昭 of Jin 晉 in Shanxi 山西, 530–524 BCE, whose successors became marquises, and at last kings of Wei 魏.
17 The grand historiographer.

18 The family names Huan Long and Yu Long, 豢龍, 御龍, which literally mean Dragon Keeper and Master of the Dragons, have probably given rise to this queer story.

19 The *Lunheng* calls the man Shu Song 叔宋. In the *Zuozhuan* 左氏傳 his name is Shu An 叔安.

20 A small State.

21 The Emperor Kong Jia 孔甲 1879–1848 BCE.

22 Tao Tang 陶唐 was the princedom of the Emperor Yao 堯 in Shanxi 山西, whose descendants took their clan name therefrom.

23 A noble who flourished under the Shang dynasty.

24 The modern Lushanxian 魯山縣 in Henan 河南.

25 This conversation between Viscount Xian 獻 and Cai Mo 蔡墨 on the rearing of dragons in ancient times is literally culled from the *Zuozhuan*, Duke Zhao 昭 29th year. Cf. Legge, *Chunqiu* 春秋 Pt. II, p. 731.

26 *Yijing* 易經 Book I, Qian 乾 hexagram (No. 1). See also Ch. 41 n. 3.

27 A scholar of the 2nd cent. BCE. See p. I.42.

28 A native of the Jin 晉 State, 5th and 6th cent. BCE. He twice made an attempt upon the life of Viscount Xiang 襄 of Zhao 趙 to avenge the death of his master, the Earl of Zhi 知, whom Xiang had slain. Both attempts failed. The second time he disguised himself in the way described here.

29 A disciple of Confucius.

30 A kind of monkey in western China.

31 This probably means that monkeys have an excellent memory.

32 Magpies are believed to know, whether the next year will be very stormy, for in that case they build their nests near the ground. Moreover, they announce future joy, hence their popular name "birds of joy."

33 A quotation from the Biography of Lao Zi 老子 in the *Shiji* 史記 chap. 63, p. 2v.

CHAPTER 23

On Thunder and Lightning
Leixu 雷虛

(*Lunheng* Book VI, Chap. iv)

1　The same force destroys the tree, the house, and the man.

2　The dragon is accounted a sacred animal.

3　*Yijing* 易經 Book V, Zhen 震 Hexagram (No. 51).

4　The mother of the Emperor Gao Zu 高祖. Cf. p. I.124.

5　Heaven as a spirit was just then engendering Han Gao Zu 漢高祖 the Son of Heaven.

6　In the case of joy as well as of anger.

7　*Analects* XIX, 19. The criminal judge Yang Fu 楊阜 having consulted the philosopher Zeng Zi 曾子 on the duties of his office, the latter advised him to pity the offenders, whose misdeeds were perhaps a consequence of bad administration.

8　This passage is not to be found in our text of the *Shangshu* 尚書.

9　The first wife of Han Gao Zu, who usurped the imperial power, and reigned under her own name against all custom from 187–179 BCE. Her son, the Emperor Hui Di 惠帝, whose nominal reign lasted from 194–187 BCE, was nothing but a puppet in her hands. Lü Hou 呂后 was a fiend in human shape, who had always some poison ready for her enemies. One of her first acts, after she came to power, was to wreak her vengeance on her rival, Lady Qi 戚, a concubine of Han Gao Zu, who had attempted to have her own son made heir-apparent in place of Hui Di, the son of Lü Hou. Hui Di, a very kind-hearted, but weak sovereign did all in his power to shield his half-brother from the wrath of his mother, who poisoned him all the same.

10　This story is abridged from the *Shiji* 史記 chap. 9, p. 3.

11　A city in Zhejiang 浙江.

12　Names of constellations.

13　In China the regular executions take place in autumn.

14　It destroys the guilty on the spot, and does not delay judgment until autumn.

15   *A deductio ad absurdum* from a Chinese point of view, for the holy emperors, Yao 堯, Shun 舜, and the like, were perfect, and could not have omitted to punish serious misdeeds.

16   This seems to be an old adage.

17   Neither the *Liji* 禮記 nor the *Zhouli* 周禮 contains such a passage, as far as I could make out. On the old sacrificial bronze vases, called *zun* 尊 = goblets, clouds and thunders *i.e.* coiled up clouds were represented. The thunder ornament is the Chinese Meander. Specimens of these goblets can be seen in the *Bogutulu* 博古圖錄 chap. 7.

18   The "Plan" appeared to the Emperor Huang Di 黃帝 in the Yellow River. A big fish carried it on its back. Huang Di received the Plan, which consisted of a combination of symbolical lines and diagrams like the *Bagua* 八卦.

19   The "Scroll" was carried by a dragon-horse, which rose from the waters of the Luo 洛, a tributary of the Yellow River, at Fu Xi's 伏羲 time. From the mystic signs on this "Scroll" the emperor is reported to have derived the Eight Diagrams and the first system of written characters, which took the place of the knotted cords, quipos, then in use.

20   767–721 BCE.

21   764–746 BCE.

22   Quoted from *Analects* X, 16.

23   Quoted from the *Liji* Book VI Yuzao 玉藻 (Legge, *Sacred Books* Vol. XXVIII, p. 5).

24   Confucius in the passage quoted from the *Analects*.

25   Quoted from *Xunzi* 荀子.

CHAPTER 24
Daoist Untruths
Daoxu 道虛

(*Lunheng* Book VII, Chap. i)

1　The following story is taken from the *Shiji* 史記, chap. 28, p. 28 v., where an official relates it to Han Wu Di 漢武帝. Cf. Chavannes, *Mem. Hist.* Vol. III, p. 488.

2　In Shanxi 山西 Province, near Puzhoufu 蒲州府.

3　This mountain lies in Shanxi 陝西, near Xianfu 西安府.

4　The context requires 鼎胡 "Tripod beard," but we read 湖 instead of 胡. A place, called 鼎湖 "Tripod lake" actually exists in Henan 河南 (Playfair, *Cities and Towns* No. 7329). This name has perhaps been the origin of the legend, as Wang Chong suggests (cf. above p. I.166). In ancient times only the phonetic part of a character was often written, and the radical left out. Thus 胡 could stand for 鬍 "beard" as well as for 湖 "lake." Our text has 胡 鬋 the "beard."

5　Some commentators hold that the name Wuhao 烏號 = Raven's Cry refers to the lament of the people, others that it was the name of a tree well fit for the fabrication of bows.

6　Huang Di 黃帝, Zhuan Xu 顓頊, Ku 嚳, Yao 堯, and Shun 舜. According to other writers the Five Emperors are: Tai Hao 太昊, Yan Di 炎帝, Huang Di, Shao Hao 少昊, and Zhuan Xu.

7　*Shiji* chap. 28, p. 30v. When Qin Shi Huangdi 秦始皇 had sacrificed on the tomb of Huang Di upon Mount Qiao 橋, he asked, how Huang Di could be an immortal, and yet be buried there. Then somebody replied that Huang Di had ascended to heaven as a genius, and that only his garments and cap were left and interred.

8　The fundamental principle of Daoism. The Daoists have always claimed Huang Di as one of theirs. Hence the legend of his ascension to heaven.

9　This seems to me a fancy etymology. *Huang* 黃 is "yellow," but never means "to pacify." The "Yellow Emperor" was called yellow from the colour of the earth over which he ruled. Thus the name is generally explained, whether correctly is doubtful.

10   Some say that this mountain is situated in the province of Gansu 甘肅, others more eastward in the province of Shanxi 陝西. *Vid. Shiji* 史記 chap. 1, p. 8.

11   China's most sacred mountain in Shandong 山東.

12   Daoism inculcates contemplation and quietism, and abhors an active life.

13   Only he who possesses *Dao* 道, becomes immortal, and can ascend to heaven. If the model emperors Yao and Shun did not attain to *Dao*, why should Huang Di, provided that he worked as hard as Yao and Shun.

14   The hill-sacrifice, 封禪 was not performed, unless the empire enjoyed peace, and peace could not be secured without hard work. Hard work precluded a Daoist life, and without *Dao*, Huang Di could not ascend on high.

15   The text says "Tripod lake." Cf. above p. I.258.

16   In the province of Zhejiang 浙江.

17   This etymology is given by Sima Qian 司馬遷, *Shiji* 史記 chap. 2, p. 26.

18   Liu An 劉安, Prince of Huainan 淮南, commonly known as Huai Nan Zi 淮南子, a Daoist philosopher and alchemist of the 2nd cent. BCE. He was a prince of the imperial family of the Han 漢 emperors. His principality was situated in Anhui 安徽.

19   The elements of which the bodies of all creatures are composed cannot be transformed, therefore those creatures cannot change their nature.

20   These metamorphoses are mentioned in ancient works, and believed by the Chinese up to the present day. Cf. p. I.106–107.

21   140–86 BCE.

22   The modern Yazhoufu 雅州府.

23   An old kingdom in Sichuan 四川.

24   One of the Nine Provinces, into which Yu 禹 divided the Empire, comprising Shanxi 陝西 and Gansu 甘肅.

25   The eight principal Daoist associates of Huai Nan Zi, one of which was Wu Bei 伍被 [QP: Original has Wei Pu/Wei Bu, but given context this seems simply a transposition for Wu Bei]

26   The following story is taken from *Huainanzi*.

27   A traveller of the 3rd cent. BCE.

28   This expression can mean the Gobi.

29   The "Great North" and the "Dark Gate" are Daoist fancy names.

30   It is interesting to note the name Mongol 蒙穀 here. The last character is written 古 now. The Mongols were already known to the Chinese under

their actual name in the second century BCE, when they were living in the north of China.

31 To wit the four quarters, above and below.

32 This is probably the name of a genius.

33 According to the belief of the Daoists there are nine superposed stages or spheres of the heavens.

34 In the "Water Classic" 水經注 Xiang Man Du 項曼都 is called Xiang Ning Du 項寧都.

35 The modern Puzhoufu in Shanxi 山西.

36 A circuit comprising the southern part of Shanxi 山西.

37 A famous doctor, who cannot have lived later than the 4th cent. BCE, for he is mentioned in *Liezi* 列子.

38 A parallel passage of this story occurs in the *Lüshi chunqiu* 呂氏春秋.

39 That is what the Daoists say of themselves.

40 140–85 BCE.

41 A district in Henan 河南. The name of the marquis was Tian Fen 田蚡.

42 The *Shiji* says the tenth year.

43 Duke Huan 桓 of Qi 齊 reigned from 683–641 BCE. The 15th year of his reign was 669 BCE.

44 This story of Li Shao Jun 李少君 is quoted from the *Shiji* chap. 28, p. 21.

45 Why 200 years? Li Shao Jun would have known the nonagenarian's grandfather, if he was about ninety years old himself.

46 The interval is upwards of 500 years.

47 A magician of the 6th cent. BCE, son of King Ling 靈 of the Zhou 周 dynasty. He is reported to have been seen riding on a white crane through the air as an immortal.

48 The Chinese Methuselah, who is believed to have lived over 800 years, and to have been a great grandson of the legendary Emperor Zhuan Xu 2514 BCE.

49 *Viz.* received by man at his birth, when Heaven endows him with a body and the vital fluid.

50 This the Daoists say of their fundamental principle. "*Dao* is without beginning, without end," says *Zhuangzi* 莊子 chap. 17, p. 13, and thus the Daoists which have become one with *Dao*, are immortal.

CHAPTER 25

Exaggerations

Yuzeng 語增

(*Lunheng* Book VII, Chap. ii)

1   Yu 禹 and Xie 契 were both ministers of Yao 堯 and Shun 舜. Yu became emperor afterwards.

2   *Shangshu* 尚書 Part V, Bk. XIV, 5 (Legge, *Classics* Vol. III, Pt. II, p. 455). The passage has been variously explained.

3   *Analects* VIII, 18.

4   The last emperors of the Xia 夏 dynasty.

5   Quoted from the *Shangshu* Part V, Bk. XV, 7 (Legge, *Classics* Vol. III, Pt. II, p. 468).

6   Died 244 BCE. Wu Ji 無忌 was a famous general of the Wei 魏 State, who inflicted some crushing defeats upon the armies of Qin 秦. For some time he succeeded in checking the encroachments of Qin. It was not, until his later years, that he retired from public life, and gave himself up to debauchery.

7   The *Shiji* 史記 chap. 3, p. 10 likewise ascribes superhuman forces and extraordinary natural endowments to the last ruler of the Xia dynasty.

8   Fei Lian 蜚廉 and E Lai 惡來 were two clever, but wicked counsellors of King Zhou 紂. In the *Shiji* chap. 3, p. 11v. Fei Lian is called Fei Zhong [QP: no characters given, possibly 費中 or 費仲]

9   The Zhou 周 dynasty which overthrew the Shang 商 or Yin 殷 dynasty. The name of King Zhou Xin 紂辛 of the Shang dynasty has the same sound, but is quite a different character.

10   According to the *Shiji* and the *Shangshu* King Zhou 紂 fled, when his troops had been routed by Wu Wang 武王, and burned himself, dressed in his royal robes, in the palace. He was not caught by Wu Wang.

11   Cf. p. I.143.

12   Cf. p. I.124.

13   Wu Wang had large, staring sheep's eyes.

14   Cf. p. I.136.

15 The wife of Han Gao Zu 漢高祖.

16 Cf. p. I.124.

17 The Han 漢 dynasty.

18 The Zhou 周 dynasty.

19 Tai Gong Wang 太公王, the counsellor of Wu Wang, laid the plans of the campaign against the Yin dynasty.

20 This plain was situated in Henan 河南.

21 This is the title of the 3rd Book of the 5th Part of the *Shangshu*. (Cf. Legge, *Classics* Vol. III, Pt. II, p. 315.)

22 With which the soldiers were pounding their rice.

23 Meng Ben 孟賁 and Xia Yu 夏育 are both famous for their gigantic strength. The one could tear off the horns, the other the tail from a living ox. Both lived in the Zhou epoch.

24 The legendary rulers accomplished everything by their virtues.

25 *Analects* XIX, 20. In our text of the *Lunyu* 論語 these words are not spoken by Confucius himself, but by his disciple Zi Gong 子貢.

26 A good man avoids the society of disreputable people, for every wickedness is put to their account, even if they be innocent. Thus King Zhou 紂 has been better than his name, which has become a by-word for every crime. Cf. p. II.583.

27 *Mencius* Book VII, Pt. II, chap. 3. The most humane was Wu Wang.

28 In the estimation of the Confucianists Mencius is only a Worthy, not a Sage like Confucius.

29 Wang Mang 王莽 the usurper reigned from 9 to 23 CE.

30 Bi Gan 比干 was a relative of Zhou 紂. When he remonstrated with him upon his excesses, Zhou caused him to be disembowelled.

31 1–6 CE.

32 A city in southern Henan.

33 A terrace near Chang'anfu 長安府, where Wang Mang 王莽 made his last stand.

34 A feudal prince of gigantic size said to have lived under the Emperor Yu, who put him to death. Cf. *Hanfeizi* 韓非子 chap. 19, p. 11v.

35 Di 狄 is a general name for northern barbarians. The *Shangshu, Hongfan* 洪範, 五行, speaks of a Di measuring over 50 feet, Gu Liang 穀梁 of three Di brothers, of which one was so enormous, that his body covered 9 Mu 畝.

36 *I.e.* "Announcement about wine."

37 Cf. p. II.461.

38 The shooting-feasts referred to are the competitions of archery, held in

ancient times at the royal court, at the feudal courts, and at the meetings in the country. A banquet was connected with these festivities. Cf. Legge, *The Li Ki* (*Sacred Books of the East* Vol. XXVII) p. 57.

39 This wine-lake is mentioned in the *Shiji* chap. 3, p. 10v.

40 Quoted from the *Shiji* chap. 3, p. 11.

41 A royal carriage ornamented with deer.

42 Dan 旦, Duke of Zhou 周公, a younger brother of Wu Wang.

43 Kang Shu 康叔 was the first Prince of the Wei 衛 State (Henan), which he governed until 1077 BCE.

44 Cf. *Shangshu* Part V, Book X, 11 (Legge, *loc. cit.*, p. 408).

45 Zhou Gong 周公.

46 The sacrificial tripod is the emblem of royalty. The three chief ministers are likened to its three feet.

47 The Emperor Yu.

48 Quotation from the *Shangshu*, Yi Ji 益稷 Pt. II, Bk. IV, 8 (Legge, *Classics* Vol. III, Pt. I, p. 85). Modern commentators and Legge explain 五服 as "five land tenures," Wang Chong as the Five State Robes worn by the Emperor and the officials, which are mentioned a few paragraphs before our passage (Legge, *loc. cit.*, p. 80).

49 The *Shijing* 詩經 and the *Shangshu*.

50 213 BCE.

51 Near Xi'anfu 西安府 in Shanxi 陝西.

52 An official title.

53 The abolition of feudalism was much disliked by the Literati.

54 The text says, the "discussions of the hundred authors," which means the writers on philosophy and science.

55 Various translations of this last passage have been proposed. Cf. Chavannes, *Mem. Hist.* Vol. II, p. 181 Note 2.

   The foregoing narration is abridged from *Shiji* chap. 6, p. 21v et seq. Our text speaks of 467 scholars, whereas the *Shiji* mentions but 460 odd, and it uses the word 坑 "to throw into a pit" instead of the vaguer term 阬. So perhaps Wang Chong has not culled from the *Shiji*, but both have used the same older source.

56 A State in Zhili 直隸.

57 In 227 BCE Jing Ke 荊軻 made an unsuccessful attempt on Qin Shi Huangdi's 秦始皇 life, who at that time was still King of Qin 秦. It was not before 221 BCE that, having vanquished all the rival States, he assumed the imperial title.

58 All the ascendants and descendants from the great-great-grandfather to

the great-great-grandson.

59 A mountain in the province of Shanxi 陝西.
60 Quoted from *Shiji* chap. 6, p.24.
61 A circuit or province comprising the south of Zhili.
62 A quotation from *Shiji* chap. 6, p. 25v. Cf. p. II.662.
63 The *Shiji* does not mention it.

CHAPTER 26
Exaggerations of the Literati
Ruzeng 儒增
(*Lunheng* Book VIII, Chap. i)

1   Cheng 成 was the successor of King Wu Wang 武王. He reigned from 1115–1078 BCE, and was succeeded by Kang 康 1078–1052 BCE.
2   Cf. *Shiji* 史記 chap. 4, p. 17.
3   A place in Henan 河南.
4   The aboriginal Miao 三苗 tribes which exist still to-day.
5   Shun 舜 banished Gong Gong 共工, Huan Dou 驩兜, the Prince of the San Miao 三苗 and Gun 鯀. Cf. *Mencius* V, Pt. II, 3 and *Shangshu* 尚書 Pt. II, I, 12.
6   The Huai 淮, Yi 夷, and Rong 戎 were non-Chinese tribes; Xu 徐 is the name of one of the Nine Provinces of Yu 禹, in modern Shandong 山東.
7   A minister of the Chu 楚 State in the Zhou 周 epoch.
8   This must be a misprint, for no duke of this name is known. The *Lüshi chunqiu* 呂氏春秋, which mentions the story, speaks of Duke Yi 懿 of Wei 衛, 667–659 BCE.
9   The northern barbarians.
10 Xiong Qu Zi 熊渠子 lived during the Zhou dynasty.
11 This story is told in the *Xinxu* 新序 of Liu Xiang 劉向.
12 Cf. above p. I.287.
13 A general of Han Wu Di 漢武帝, cf. p. I.234.

14 The *Zuozhuan* 左氏傳, Duke Cheng 成 16th year (Legge, *Classics* Vol. V, Pt. I, p. 397) informs us that in a battle fought by the Marquis of Jin 晉 against King Gong 共 of Chu 楚 in 574 BCE. Yi Qi 錡 of Lü 呂, an archer of Jin 晉, shot at King Gong 共 of Chu 楚 and hit him in the eye. The king thereupon ordered his own archer, Yang You Ji 養由基, to revenge him, handing him two arrows. With the first arrow Yang You Ji killed Yi Qi 錡.

    According to this account it was not the Marquis of Jin who was hit in the eye, but the King of Chu, and not Yang You Ji who shot the arrow, but Yi of Lü.

15 The force of a bow, a cross-bow, or a ballista is measured by the weight required to draw them.

    One stone or one picul in ancient times amounted to 120 pounds.

16 A celebrated mechanic of the Lu 魯 State, who lived contemporaneously with Confucius. Lu Ban 魯般 is his sobriquet, his proper name being Gong Shu Zi 公輸子. He has become the tutelary god of artisans.

17 The philosopher Mo Di 墨翟 has been credited with mechanical skill, erroneously I presume.

18 A State in northern Henan.

19 A State comprising the southern part of Henan.

20 Cf. p. I.98.

21 "When the Master was in Qi 齊, he heard the Shao 韶 music, and for three months he did not know the taste of flesh," so engrossed was he was this music, that he did not taste what he ate (Legge, *Analects* p. 199; *Analects* VII, 13).

22 The emissaries of a high officer of Song 宋 tried to kill Confucius by pulling down the tree under which he was practising ceremonies. Cf. Legge, *Analects* p. 202 Note 22.

23 A city in southern Shandong 山東.

24 A territory in Chen 陳.

25 A princedom in Shandong.

26 *Analects* XIV, 14.

27 Gongshu Wenzi 公叔文子 was a high officer in the State of Wei 衛, and Gongming Jia 公明賈 would seem to have been his disciple.

28 658–619 BCE.

29 626–619 BCE.

30 Western barbarians.

31 A dangerous defile in the district of Yongning 永寧, Henan.

32 According to the *Chunqiu* 春秋, Duke Xi 僖 33rd year, the army of Qin 秦 was defeated at Yao 崤 in 626 BCE. The *Zuozhuan* 左氏傳 narrates

the campaign in detail, and relates that the three officers were first taken prisoners, but afterwards released by the intercession of the mother of the Duke of Jin 晉, who was a princess of the ducal house of Qin.

33   Cf. p. I.228.

34   These four princes are known as the "Four Heroes," living at the end of the Zhou epoch, during the time of the "Contending States," the 3rd century BCE.

35   Gao Chai 高柴 or Gao Zigao 高子羔, was a disciple of Confucius, noted for his filial piety.

36   Quotation from the *Liji* 禮記, Tan Gong 檀弓 Sect. I, II, 14.

37   He 和 of Jing 荊 *i.e.* of Chu, known as Bian He 卞和 *viz.* He 和 of the Bian 卞 district. Cf. p. II.472.

38   Posthumous title of the Shang 商 Emperor Wu Ding 武丁. See p. I.109.

39   Quoted from the *Shangshu*, Wu Yi 無逸 Pt. V, Bk. XV, 5 (Legge, *Classics* Vol. III, Pt. II p. 466).

40   Duke Mu 繆 of Qin, 658–619 BCE.

41   A famous sword forged by Mo Ye 莫邪 and Gan Jiang 干將, in later times a term for a good blade in general. Cf. p. I.115.

42   The *Shiji* chap. 86, p. 16v. gives us a graphic description of the assault of Jing Ke 荊軻 on Shi Huangdi 始皇帝. When at a reception the envoy of Yan 燕 presented a map to the king, the latter caught sight of the dagger, which Jing Ke 荊軻 had concealed. Then Jing Ke "with his left hand grasped the sleeve of the King of Qin, and with his right hand the dagger, and was going to strike the king, but, before he touched his body, the king frightened, retreated, and rose, tearing off his sleeve. He tried to draw his sword, but the sword was very long, and while engaged with the scabbard, he was so excited, and the sword was so hard, that he could not draw it out at the moment. Jing Ke chased the king, who ran round a pillar. The assembled officers were thunderstruck. They all rose in a body, but were so much taken by surprise, that they completely lost their heads. By the rules of Qin the officers, waiting upon the king in the palace hall, were not allowed to carry the smallest weapon with them. The armed guards were all stationed below the hall, but, without a special order, they were not permitted to walk up. At the critical moment there was no time to summon the soldiers below. This is the reason, why Jing Ke could pursue the king, and that his attendants, though startled, did not strike the assailant. They all seized him with their hands, however, and the royal physician Xia Wu Ju 夏無且 flung his medicine bag, which he was presenting, against him. While the King of Qin was thus fleeing round the pillar, all were alarmed, but did not know what to do.

The attendants only shouted, 'Push your sword backwards, King! Push your sword backwards!' The king then drew his sword, and hit Jing Ke, cutting his left leg. Jing Ke maimed then lifted his dagger and thrust it at the king, but missed him, and instead hit the copper pillar. Then the King of Qin dealt him another blow, and thus Jing Ke received eight wounds. Seeing that his scheme had failed, he leant against the pillar. Weeping, he squatted down, and said .... At that moment the attendants came forward, and killed Jing Ke."

43   Two swords wrought by the noted sword-cutler Gan Jiang 干將 for He Lu 闔廬, King of Wu 吳 513–494 BCE. Moye 莫邪 was the name of his wife. The Ganjiang sword was regarded as the male, the Moye as the female sword.

44   An author of the 2nd century BCE.

45   Quotation from the *Shangshu*, Wuyi 毋佚 Pt. V, Bk. XV, 1 (Legge, *Classics* Vol. III, Pt. II, p. 464).

46   Abridged from the *Zuozhuan*, Duke Xuan 宣 3rd year.—From the Xia 夏 dynasty these tripods came down to the Shang 商 and the Zhou dynasties, and in 605 BCE were still in existence.

47   A people in the southern part of Guangdong 廣東 province, near the Annanese frontier.

48   The Wo 倭, an old name for the Japanese, which Chinese authors have explained to mean "Pygmies."

49   The virtue of the Emperor Yu 禹.

50   A sacrificial vessel used during the Xia 夏 dynasty.

51   314–255 BCE.

52   305–249 BCE. The full name of this king is Zhaoxiang 昭襄.

53   Cf. the parallel passage in *Shiji* chap. 4, p. 39 where, however, not Nan Wang 赧王, but the Prince of the Eastern Zhou 周 submits to Qin 秦 and cedes his territory.

54   In 255 BCE. *Vid. Shiji* chap. 28, p. 8.

55   The eastern part of Shandong under the Qin dynasty.

56   A city in Jiangsu 江蘇, the modern Xuzhoufu 徐州府.

57   A river in Shandong.

58   Quotation from the *Shiji* chap. 6, p. 18.

59   Taiqiu 太邱 was a place in the Yongcheng 永城 district, Henan.

60   Pengcheng 彭城 does not lie on the Si 泗 River, but on another small river.

61   In 221 BCE. Then the tripods would have been lost in 250 BCE.

62   *Viz.* the Zhou dynasty.

63   179–156 BCE.

64   A place in Shanxi 山西, in the present Wanquanxian 万泉縣.

65   Quotation from the *Shiji* chap. 28, p. 20.

CHAPTER 27
Literary Exaggerations
Yizeng 藝增

(*Lunheng* Book VIII, Chap. ii)

1   Here Wang Chong himself commits the fault which he lays at other people's door. All Orientals like big numbers, which have become quite a special feature of the Chinese language, in which a hundred, a thousand, or ten thousand merely serve to express many.

2   Cf. Ch. 8 n. 3 and 4.

3   We foreigners cannot admit this.

4   This statement is open to criticism: all the classical texts have undergone some alterations in course of time.

5   *Shangshu* 尚書 Part I, chap. I, 2, *Yaodian* 堯典 (Legge, *Classics* Vol. III, Part I, p. 17) Wang Chong writes 萬國 like the *Shiji* 史記. The *Shangshu* has 萬邦.

6   荒服, 戎服, 要服.

7   The utmost limits of the habitable land.

8   穿胸, 儋耳, 焦僥, 跂踵. All these semi-fabulous tribes are in the *Taiping yulan* 太平御覽 ranked among the southern barbarians. The Chuanxiong 穿胸 seem to have received their name from a peculiar sacklike costume merely covering their breasts. The Dan'er 儋耳 were in the habit of disforming their ears, that they hang down upon their shoulders. The Jiaojiao 焦僥 = Pigmies are often mentioned in Chinese literature. *Liezi* 列子 gives them a height of 1 foot 5 inches, in the *Kongzi jiayu* 孔子家語 Confucius describes them as 3 feet high. According to the *Houhanshu* 後漢書 they live in the surroundings of Yongchangfu 永昌府 in Yunnan 雲南 and measure 3 feet. About 110 CE three thousand of them submitted to the Han 漢 and sent as tribute ivory and zebus. They live in caverns and are dreaded by birds and beasts. For Bazhong 跂踵, who are nowhere else mentioned, we had better read Qizhong 跂踵, a tribe said to walk on tiptoe.

9   *Shijing* 詩經 Part III, Book II, Ode V, 2 (Legge, *Classics* Vol. IV, Part II, p. 482).

10 Legge *loc. cit.*, p. 481, Note says that there is no evidence to whom the Ode is addressed. Some hold that it is King Cheng 成.

11 The ancestor of the Zhou 周 dynasty and Lord of Agriculture.

12 The original fief of the Zhou in Shanxi 陝西, with which they were invested by Shun 舜 2255–2206 BCE.

13 827–782 BCE.

14 Wang Chong is mistaken here; calculating is not his strong point. One couple after about 42 generations may well have tens of thousands of descendants.

15 *Shijing* Part II, Book III, Ode X, 2 (Legge, *Classics* Vol. IV, Part II, p. 297).

16 More than 60 000 Li p. I.379.

17 *Shijing* Part III, Book III, Ode IV, 3 (Legge, *Classics* Vol. IV, Part II, p. 530). Already Mencius remarked that this passage must not be taken literally (Legge, *Classics* Vol. II, p. 353).

18 The 兩 of Ed. A, of course, must be 雨.

19 Diagram Feng 豐 No. 55. Legge, *Yijing* 易經, *Sacred Books* Vol. XVI, p. 186.

20 *Shangshu* Part II, Book III, 5 (Legge, *Classics* Vol. III, Part I, p. 73). Legge gives a different interpretation of the passage: "Let him not have the various officers cumberers of their places," which does not agree with Wang Chong's explanation.

21 *Shijing* Part III, Bk. I, Ode I (Legge, *Classics* Vol. IV, Part II, p. 429).

22 *Analects* VIII, 19.

23 *Vid.* p. I.218.

24 The meaning of this question would rather seem to be that the peasant scorned the idea of Yao's 堯 excellence and therefore disdainfully asked about it. Cf. Ch. 60 n. 20.

25 The *Hanshu* 漢書 chap. 99 says with almost the same words 堯舜之世比屋可封.

26 *Analects* XI, 24, where, however, the place is called Bi 費 and not Hou 郈. Cf. the quotations in p. I.322, p. I.409 and p. II.812 with the reading Bi.

27 Which is an exaggeration; men like the ignoramus would have to be excluded.

28 Like the husbandman referred to.

29 That there were people like the man playing with earth ignoring Yao's 堯 virtue.

30 A minister to the Emperor Zhou 紂. Cf. Ch. 71 n. 6.

31 *Shangshu* Part IV, Book X, 4 (Legge, *Classics* Vol. III, Part I, p. 271).

32 Famous politician of the 4th cent. BCE. See Ch. 11 n. 7.

33 Capital of Qi 齊, the present Qingzhoufu 青州府 in Shandong 山東.
34 Quotation from the Biography of Su Qin 蘇秦 in the *Shiji* chap. 69, p. 12v.
35 Chapter of the *Shangshu*, cf. Ch. 25 n. 21.
36 *Eod.* Ch. 25 n. 22.
37 Repeated almost literally from p. I.378.
38 25–57 CE.
39 Place in Henan 河南.
40 179–157 BCE.
41 Punishments were unnecessary, all the people following the good example of their virtuous ruler.
42 The latter half of this sentence is quoted from the *Analects* XIX, 20.

CHAPTER 28

Criticisms on Confucius
Wen Kong 問孔

(*Lunheng* Book IX, Chap. i)

1 Yan Hui 顏回 and Min Zi Qian 閔子騫, two prominent disciples of Confucius.
2 The minister of Shun 舜.
3 The discussions of the two wise men before Shun are to be found in the *Shangshu* 尚書, Gao Yao Mo 皐陶謨.
4 Cf. *Analects* XVII, 4.
5 Meng Yi Zi 孟懿子 was the chief of one of three powerful families in Lu 魯.
6 A disciple of Confucius.
7 *I.e.* Meng Yi Zi.
8 *Analects* II, 5.—The citations from the *Analects* are quoted from Legge's translation, but here and there modified so as to suit the text, for Wang Chong often understands a passage quite differently from Legge and his authorities.
9 *Analects* II, 6.

10   *Analects* III, 1.

11   *Analects* III, 6. This sacrifice was a privilege of the sovereign.

12   So that he might have used him as his mouth-piece as in the case of Meng Yi Zi.

13   He was not afraid of Meng Yi Zi.

14   *Analects* IV, 5.

15   Wang Chong thus interprets the passage, which gives no sense. I should say that he misunderstood Confucius, for every difficulty is removed, if we take the words to mean what Legge translates: "if it cannot be obtained" *viz.* "if it is not possible to act in the aforesaid manner" instead of "if they cannot be obtained."

16   *Analects* V, 1.

17   Confucius gave Nan Rong 南容 the daughter of his elder brother to wife.

18   *Analects* V, 1.

19   Wang Chong's objections are again far-fetched and groundless. The words of Confucius imply that Gong Ye Chang's 公冶長 character was so excellent and above suspicion, that Confucius world not doubt him, even if he were condemned by the world and treated like a criminal, and therefore he made him his son-in-law.

20   *Analects* V, 8.

21   *Analects* XI, 10.

22   *Analects* VI, 9.

23   *Analects* II, 9.

24   *Analects* VI, 5.

25   *Analects* V, 9.

26   The four classes into which the ten principal disciples of Confucius were divided according to their special abilities: virtue, eloquence, administrative talents, and literary acquirements. Zai Wo 宰我 belongs to the second class of the able speakers together with Zi Gong 子貢. Cf. *Analects* XI, 2.

27   *Analects* VIII, 10.

28   This is professedly the aim of the "*Chunqiu* 春秋" or "Spring and Autumn" Record, the only classical work, of which Confucius claims the authorship.

29   *Analects* V, 9.

30   Zai Wo could no more be made responsible for his bodily weakness, than for his death.

31   *Analects* XIII, 15 and XVIII, 10.

32   A minister of the Chu 楚 State.

33　*Analects* V, 18. The following words of Confucius are omitted in our *Analects*.

34　This battle took place in 632 BCE. It is described in the *Zuozhuan* 左氏傳 Book V, 27 (Duke Xi 僖 27th year).

35　*Analects* IV, 7.

36　Duke Ai 哀 of Lu 魯, 494–468 BCE.

37　*Analects* VI, 2.

38　*Analects* VI, 8.

39　Wang Chong understands by fate something material, not a decree. Cf. Ch. 6 and 12.

40　Leprosy. Cf. p. I.231.

41　Fate is a pure substance pervading the body, which cannot excite a foul disease like leprosy.

42　The entire polemic is against the expression "short fate" used by Confucius, who takes fate in the usual acceptation of decree, or appointment of heaven. Wang Chong from his materialistic point of view argues, that fate is always complete and pure, and that there can be no long or short one. The premature death of Yan Hui 顏回 and the disease of Bo Niu 伯牛 are not fate at all.

43　The head of the Ji 季 family in Lu.

44　*Analects* XI, 6.

45　*Analects* XII, 18.

46　*Analects* VI, 26.

47　A most disreputable woman, guilty of incest with her half-brother, Prince Zhao 朝 of Song 宋. The commentators take great pains to whitewash Confucius, who called upon this unworthy princess. What induced her to invite the Sage, and him to accept the invitation, is not known. Various conjectures have been put forward.

48　Cf. p. I.95.

49　Cf. p. I.94–95.

50　*Shangshu*, Yi Ji 益稷, Pt. II, Bk. IV, 1 (Legge, *Classics* Vol. III, Pt. I, p. 84).

51　Yao's 堯 son.

52　*Shangshu loc. cit.*

53　*Analects* IX, 8.

54　On the Plan of the Yellow River *vid.* Ch. 23 n. 18.

55　In the case of Confucius.

56　Cf. p. I.101.

57　The time when the lucky omens become visible.

58　The steps to secure a wise government and perfect peace, which must have been successful, ere the phœnix and the Plan will come forward.

59 Wishing to behold those auspicious portents, Confucius ought first to have instituted an excellent administration, as minister of the reigning sovereign. He sees the result, but overlooks the causes.

60 The Han 漢 emperor whose reign lasted from 179–156 BCE.

61 In the *Shiji*.

62 *Analects* IX, 13.

63 *Analects* III, 5.

64 *Analects* XIII, 3.

65 The disciple Gao Zigao 高子羔.

66 A city in Shandong 山東.

67 *Analects* XI, 24.

68 Zi Gong.

69 We must translate here "receive," and not "acquiesce," as Legge does, relying on the commentators. "Acquiesce" gives no sense here, as can be seen by comparing Hutchinson's translation, *China Review* Vol. VII, p. 169. Moreover, "receive" is in accordance with Wang Chong's system. Throughout his work he speaks of "receiving the fate." Hutchinson has felt, that "receive" is the proper word here—*vid.* his note to p. 170 *loc. cit.*—but is overawed by Legge and the commentators. We must bear in mind that Wang Chong very frequently puts another construction on the words of the Sage than other commentators.

70 *Analects* XI, 18.

71 Cf. p. I.95.

72 Cf. above p. I.320.

73 *Analects* XI, 8.

74 These four friends were: Yan Yuan 顏淵, Zi Gong, Zi Zhang 子張, and Zi Lu 子路, all his disciples.

75 As a Worthy, a degree of excellence next to sagehood, he would have assisted Confucius in his brilliant career.

76 In externals *viz.* the osseous structure and the physiognomy of an individual his fate becomes manifest. Cf. Ch. 11. But fate by no means corresponds to talents and virtue.

77 Quotation from the *Liji* 禮記, Tan Gong 檀弓 (Legge's transl. Vol. I, p. 136).

78 *Analects* XI, 9.

79 The father of Yan Yuan.

80 *Analects* XI, 7.

81 *Loc. cit.*

82 *Analects* XV, 8.

83　*Analects* XII, 7.

84　Cf. p. I.226.

85　A disciple of Confucius.

86　*Analects* XIII, 9.

87　A disciple of Confucius in Wei 衛, with whom he lodged. After Confucius' return to Lu, he sent the messenger to make friendly inquiries.

88　*Analects* XIV, 26.

89　This may have been the view of the old commentators at Wang Chong's time. Zhu Xi 朱熹, on the contrary, holds that the reply of the messenger was admirable, and that the laconic utterance of Confucius contains a praise, not a reproach.

90　See Ch. 28 n.28.

91　Cf. above p. I.315.

92　A high officer in the service of the Zhao 趙 family in the Jin 晉 State, who took possession of Zhongmu 中牟, a city in Henan 河南, in the Zhangde 彰德 prefecture, for himself.

93　*Analects* XVII, 7.

94　Cf. *Huainanzi* 淮南子 XVI, 13 who adds that Mo Di 墨子, who condemned music, would not enter into a city named "Morning Song."

95　*Analects* VII, 15.

96　Legge and some commentators take the words 而不食 in a passive sense "How could I be hung up and not be eaten?" *i.e.* "not be employed."

97　A city in Shandong.

98　Gong Shan Fu Rao 公山弗擾 and Yang Huo 陽貨 combined were holding their liege, Prince Huan 桓 of Ji 季, imprisoned, and trying to arrogate the supreme power of the State of Lu.

99　*Analects* XVII, 5.

100　The eastern Zhou 周 dynasty 770–255 BCE owes its name to its capital Luoyi 洛邑, where it had removed from Haojing 鎬京 in the west (Shanxi 陝西). The commencement of the Eastern Zhou, prior to the civil wars, was felicitous.

101　*Analects* XVII, 1.

CHAPTER 29
Strictures on Han Feizi 韓非子
Fei Han 非韓

(*Lunheng* Book X, Chap. i)

1   On the Daoist philosopher Han Feizi 韓非子 see p. I.235.
2   In chap. 19, no. 49, p. 1 of Han Feizi's work. The chapter is entitled the: "Five kinds of voracious grubs."
3   An ancient coin or a monetary unit whose value is doubtful.
4   Cf. *Hanfeizi* XIII, 5v.
5   *Analects* III, 17.
6   Cf. Ch. 21 n. 23.
7   The posthumous designation of Zhan Huo 展獲, 6th and 7th cent. BCE, who was magistrate of the Liuxia 柳下 district in Lu 魯 and famous for his virtue.
8   Qin 秦 desisted from its invasion of Wei 魏 in 399 BCE, because the Wei State was so flourishing under the Marquis Wen 文, who honoured the Worthies and Literati. *Vid. Shiji* 史記 chap. 44, p. 3v.
9   Cf. p. I.236–37. Tai Gong 太公 was the first Duke of Qi 齊.
10 *Hanfeizi* XIII, 5 speaks only of Kuang Jue 狂譎 being put to death by Tai Gong 太公, not of Hua Shi 華士.
11 See Ch. 41 n. 1.
12 Cf. Ch. 8 n. 32.
13 The same as Zhang Liang 張良, the helpmate of Han Gao Zu's 漢高祖. Cf. p. II.665.
14 Four recluses, who during the troubles attending the overthrow of the Qin 秦 dynasty had taken refuge into the mountains near Xi'anfu 西安府.
15 From *Hanfeizi* chap. 19, p. 2v. we learn that Yan 偃 was the sovereign of a small State covering 500 square li in Handong 漢東 (Hubei 湖北). King Wen 文 of Chu 楚, 688–675 BCE, fearing the growing power of the virtuous Yan—Han Feizi speaks of 36 States which were allied to him—destroyed the Xu 徐 State. *Huainanzi* 淮南子 XIII, 14v. also refers to Yan and mentions that 32 States were his allies.

16　A legendary hermit of the time of the Emperor Yao 堯, reported to have lived in a nest in a tree.

17　Yao's principality.

18　In 481 BCE Chen Heng 陳恆 alias Tian Chengzi 田成子 murdered the sovereign of Qi, a descendant of Tai Gong. The Chen 陳 family had assumed the name Tian 田 in Qi. Cf. *Shiji* 史記 chap. 32, p. 24v. and chap. 36, p. 7.

19　*Vid. Hanfeizi* XIII, 5.

20　Cf. p. I.282.

21　*Analects* XV, 24.

22　The depravity of the people cannot have been as great as Han Feizi presumed, for otherwise the progress made during the three dynasties: Xia 夏, Shang 商, and Zhou 周 could not have been accomplished.

23　1001–946 BCE.

24　A legendary person said to have lived at the time of the Emperor Huang Di 黃帝. He rebelled against the latter, and was defeated. Some say that he was a prince, who terrorised the people, others that he was a minister of Huang Di.

25　Quoted with some slight alterations from *Huainanzi* chap. 16, p. 1.

26　408–375 BCE.

27　His full name is Kong Zi Si 孔子思 or Kong Ji 孔伋, the grandson of Confucius, to whom the Zhongyong 中庸, the "Doctrine of the Mean" is ascribed.

28　*Hanfeizi* XVI, 5. The text slightly differs.

29　Zi Chan 子產 is the style of Gongsun Qiao 公孫僑, a famous minister of the Zheng 鄭 State, 581–521 BCE, who compiled a penal code.

30　*Loc. cit.*, p. 5v.

31　*Hanfeizi* XVI, 1.

32　During the 6th cent. BCE the Ji 季 family, a side branch of the ducal house of Lu 魯, engrossed the power in Lu and almost superseded the reigning princes. Confucius openly condemned their usurpation. Cf. p. I.311.

33　See above p. I.338.

34　*Hanfeizi loc. cit.*

35　*Analects* XVII, 12.

36　*Hanfeizi* XIX, 4.

CHAPTER 30
Censures on Mencius
Ci Meng 刺孟
(*Lunheng* Book X, Chap. ii)

1   *Mencius* I, Pt. I, 1. For the quotations from *Mencius* I adopt Legge's renderings, as far as possible.

2   This interview took place in 335 BCE. Liang 梁 was the capital of the Wei 魏 State, the modern Kaifengfu 開封府.

3   *Yijing* 易經 Bk. I, I, 2.

4   *Yijing* Bk. I, V,1.

5   *Yijing* Bk. I, I, 1. Legge's translation (*Sacred Books of the East* Vol. XVI), p. 57 and 67.

6   *Shangshu* 尚書 Pt. V, Bk. XXX, 6.

7   An officer of Qi 齊.

8   A *zhong* 鍾 is an ancient measure. As to its capacity opinions differ. 100 000 *zhong* of rice was the customary allowance of a minister in a feudal State.

9   A disciple of Mencius, his full name being Chen Zhen 陳臻. See below.

10 *Mencius* II, Pt. II,10.

11 See above p. I.311.

12 The same as Chen Zi 陳子.

13 One *yi* 鎰 was about 24 taels.

14 Double silver "worth twice as much as the ordinary" (Legge).

15 A small principality in the south of Shandong 山東.

16 *Mencius* II, Pt. II, 3.

17 Peng Geng 彭更 was a disciple of Mencius.

18 *Mencius* III, Pt. II, 4.

19 *Mencius* II, Pt. II, 8.

20 A high officer of Qi 齊.

21 Zi Kuai 子噲, King of Yan 燕, a silly man, had ceded his throne to his minister Zi Zhi 子之, hoping that the latter would decline the offer, but he unexpectedly accepted, and Zi Kuai lost his throne. During the troubles caused in Yan by Zi Kuai's son seeking to recover the kingdom, the Qi State made an unsuccessful attempt to conquer Yan. Shen Tong 沈同

had asked Mencius' advice about an invasion of Yan.

22　A man entrusted by Heaven with the execution of its designs.

23　The one Yan is Qi, which was not better than Yan, and therefore not fit to punish Yan as Heaven's delegate.

24　*Mencius* II, Pt. I, 2.

25　A disciple of Mencius.

26　*Mencius* II, Pt. II, 12.

27　The King of Qi wished Mencius to call on him at court, informing him, that he intended waiting upon Mencius himself, but had got a cold, and could not go out. Mencius knew this to be a pretence, and therefore declined to go to court on the pretence that he was unwell likewise. Cf. *Mencius* II, Pt. II, 2. The king and the philosopher were both too jealous of their dignity to get along well.

28　A small place in Qi, where Mencius halted, expecting to be called back.

29　An officer of Qi, with whom Mencius stayed, while the king was waiting for him, at the former occasion.

30　A disciple of Mencius.

31　*Mencius* I, Pt. II, 16.

32　*Mencius* II, Pt. II, 13.

33　A follower of Mencius.

34　Wang Chong omits Di Zhi 帝摯, who followed his father Di Ku 帝嚳. Owing to his dissolute life, he was dethroned, and his brother Yao 堯 was elected in his place.

35　Those are rather round numbers. According to the common chronology Yu 禹 reigned from 2205–2197 BCE, Tang 湯, the founder of the Shang 商 dynasty from 1766–1753 BCE, and the Zhou 周 dynasty commenced in 1122 BCE. Wu Wang's 武王 reign lasted from 1122–1115 BCE, Cheng Wang's 成王 from 1115–1078 BCE. All these rulers are regarded by the Chinese as true emperors. The interval between Yu and Tang is about 400 years, that between Tang and Wen Wang 文王 about 600 years. It is difficult to understand why Wang Chong in both cases speaks of a thousand years. The remark of Mencius that every five hundred years a true sovereign arises, comes much nearer the truth.

36　About 800 years in fact after the usual chronology. The Bamboo Annals reduce this space to about 700 years.

37　*Mencius* III, Pt. II, 4.

38　A quotation from *Analects* V, 4, where Confucius condemns such smartness of speech.—Wang Chong is much smarter here than Mencius. The arguments of Mencius are quite right, and Wang Chong only takes exception at the example adduced by him, which indeed is not very lucky.

39 *Mencius* III, Pt. II, 10.

40 A grandee of the State of Qi.

41 A recluse.

42 A poor place in modern Jinanfu 濟南府 (Shandong 山東).

43 The exemplar of purity cf. Ch. 21 n. 23 and below p. I.333.

44 Cf. p. I.102.

45 See above Ch. 30 n. 8.

46 This seems not to have been the idea of Mencius. The tertium compara-
    tionis is not the purity of the earth-worm, but its independence and self-
    sufficiency. Having its earth to eat and some muddy water to drink, it has
    no further needs, as man has, who is never quite independent of others.
    Unless he break off all intercourse with his fellow-creatures, he cannot
    avoid all pollution. Thus the commentators and Legge understand the
    passage. Wang Chong's interpretation is forced.

47 The Zhou dynasty which Bo Yi 伯夷 regarded as usurpers of the throne
    of the legitimate emperors of the house of Shang.

48 A mountain in Shanxi 陝西.

49 *Mencius* VII, Pt. I, 2.

50 Legge understands this passage differently.

51 Wang Chong denotes by natural destiny something different from what
    Mencius expresses by it, which explains his polemic. Wang Chong's
    natural destiny is not influenced by human actions, whereas the natural,
    right, or correct destiny of Mencius is the upshot of proper conduct. Cf.
    p. I.101.

52 *Vid.* p. I.234.

53 Cf. p. I.230.

54 On Yan Yuan 顏淵 and Bo Niu 伯牛 see p. I.231.

55 Cf. Ch. 25 n. 30.

56 Zi Xu 子胥 or Wu Zixu 伍子胥, the same as Wu Yuan 伍員 p. I.103.

57 Cf. p. I.231.

58 *Vid.* p. I.225–26.

59 *Mencius* I, Pt. II, 16.

60 During a tempest the Xia 夏 Emperor Kong Jia 孔甲, 1879–1848 BCE,
    sought shelter in a cottage. The landlord imagined that the visit of the
    son of heaven was a lucky augury for his son, and that no misfortune
    would befall him in future. Yet this son, later on, doing carpenter's work,
    accidentally broke his axe, and cut off his two legs. He then became a
    doorkeeper, the only office for which he was still fit (*Lüshi chunqiu* 呂氏
    春秋).

CHAPTER 31

On Heaven

Tantian 談天

(*Lunheng* Book XI, Chap. i)

1　In *Huainanzi* 淮南子. Cf. p. II.845–46.
2　A legendary being of prehistoric times.
3　A mythical emperor.
4　The Buzhou 不周 Mountain forms part of the Kunlun 崑崙, which latter is also called "Pillar of Heaven" (Tianzhu 天柱).
5　The sister of the mythical Emperor Fu Xi 伏羲.
6　To wit from east to west.
7　The ocean is in the east of China.
8　Cf. *Liezi* 列子 V, 5v.; where this old tradition is told with almost the same words.
9　The Five Sacred Mountains of China: Taishan 太山 in Shandong 山東, Hengshan 衡山 in Hunan 湖南, Huashan 華山 in Shanxi 陝西, Hengshan 恆山 in Zhili 直隷, and Songshan 嵩山 in Henan 河南.
10　These are still believed to have been preceded by a dynasty of sovereigns of Heaven, and of sovereigns of Earth, all fabulous beings.
11　Supposing heaven to be a spirit or a human-like living being.
12　A scholar of the 4th cent. BCE who wrote on cosmogony and geography. See Ch. 19.
13　The well known chapter of the *Shangshu* 尚書.
14　Literally the "Red Region."
15　The "Divine Circuit."
16　Minor Seas. [Editor's note: aka Pihai 裨海.]
17　Yinghai 瀛海.
18　Cf. p. I.111.
19　The Four Seas supposed to surround the habitable land *i.e.* China.
20　The Four Sacred Mountains: Taishan, Hengshan 衡山, Huashan and Hengshan 恆山 in the East, South, West, and North of ancient China. The Songshan 嵩山 in the Centre is omitted. See above p. I.358.

21 The Daoist philosopher Huai Nan Zi 淮南子 cf. p. I.261.

22 Chap. IV of Huai Nan Zi's work.

23 The "Mountain Book" = *Shanjing* 山經 forms the first five chapters of the "Mountain and Sea Classic" = *Shanhaijing* 山海經, which tradition ascribes to Yu 禹 and his minister Yi 益, but it is probably not earlier than the 4th or the 3rd cent. BCE.

24 *Shiji* 史記 chap. 123, p. 19v.

25 This book is now lost.

26 The *Shiji* has 2,500 Li.

27 玉泉 and 華池. The *Shiji* writes: "the Sweet Wine Spring and the Jasper Lake": 醴泉 and 瑤池.

28 Zhang Qian 張騫 started on his famous expedition in 122 BCE.

29 These subjects are treated in the chapter entitled the "Tribute of Yu."

30 The *Shiji* writes: The *Shanhaijing*.

31 Zhi = 鄭 must be a misprint, for such a character is not to be found in the dictionaries. We ought to read Mao = 鄮. Yin 鄞 and Mao were two districts of the Guiji 會稽 circuit comprising Zhejiang 浙江 and parts of Anhui 安徽 and Fujian 福建 under the Han 漢 dynasty. Yin was in the south-east of Mao, both situated in the present Ningbo 寧波 prefecture. (Cf. Kangxi's 康熙 Dict.)

32 Zou Yan's 鄒衍 assertion.

33 *I.e.* the habitable land or China.

34 Luoyang 洛陽 is considered the centre of the world *i.e.* China.

35 Wang Chong is a better theorist than arithmetician. The square of 100,000 is 10,000 millions, not 1 million. Wang Chong supposes the earth to be an equilateral, rectangular square.

36 The same mistake. The square of 5,000 is 25 millions. 25 million square Li, about 8 million square kilometer is approximately the area of the Eighteen Provinces or China Proper.

37 225,000 square Li (225 millions), which number is based on Zou Yan's hypothesis that there are nine continents as large as China.

38 Wang Chong has calculated a million square Li (10,000 millions). The area of our Earth measures about 510 million square kilometers, not 2,500 millions (= 10,000 million square Li) as results from Wang Chong's calculation.

39 *Huainanzi* says 50,000 Li.

CHAPTER 32

On the Sun

Shuori 說日

(*Lunheng* **Book XI, Chap. ii**)

1   Night is here taken as something positive, something like a black veil, or dark air, not as the absence of light, which does not cause the disappearance of the sun, but is its consequence.

2   The dark fluid of night.

3   According to Chinese symbolism the *Yin* 陰 principle of darkness corresponds to the north.

4   Literally: Dongjing 東井, the "Eastern Well," and Qianniu 牽牛, the "Herdsman."

5   至. The two solstices.

6   分. The two equinoxes.

7   This cyclical sign denotes ENE¾N on the compass and corresponds to Gemini.

8   Xu 戌 = WNW¾N and Aquarius.

9   Turning round with the pole.

10   The sun turning round the pole in Gemini and never disappearing.

11   The north is *Yin*, which is synonymous with female, here the female organ.

12   *Viz.* by heaven knocking against it in its rotation.

13   The Nine Streams regulated by Yu 禹. See Mayers Pt. II, No. 267.

14   See above p. I.361. On p. I.368 Wang Chong says that our world lies in the south-east of the universe.

15   The sun sets in the west and passes through the north, before he rises again in the east.

16   To people living in the east of the universe *i.e.* below the farthest eastern limit reached by the sun in his course, the sun would appear to rise in the north, to culminate in the east, and to set in the south.

17   The context requires that we should read 屬 blended instead of 望 look out of the text.

18   The light becomes invisible for those who look after him.

19   The great distance makes the sun invisible.

20   Because the sun and the moon, which are supposed to be attached to heaven and revolving with it, rise on the southern hemisphere, and go down on the northern.

21   *I.e.* China.

22   In Mongolia.

23   This problem is already enunciated by Lie Zi 列子 V, 9 who makes two lads expose it to Confucius. They ask the Sage to decide between the two antagonistic views, but he is unable to give a satisfactory reply.

24   Wang Chong seems to think that daylight is distinct from the light of the sun.

25   Fusang 扶桑 has been identified with Sakhalin.

26   Xiliu 細柳 must be the Mongolian Desert.

27   At the equinoxes. See above p. I.364–65.

28   *Vid.* above p. I.365.

29   From right to left, facing the polar star which remains motionless and round which heaven revolves from east to west (cf. p. I.372).

30   Their own movement being from west to east, opposite to that of heaven.

31   The Qilin 麒麟, by Europeans usually called unicorn, whose prototype seems to have been the giraffe. The giraffe gallops like the fastest horse. The swiftest horses are likewise said to make 1,000 Li a day.

32   *Yijing* 易經, 30th diagram (Li 離), Legge's transl. p. 237.—Our text slightly differs. It adds "and the stars," and writes "fruits" instead of "grains."

33   Again the misleading symbolism. The moon represents the female principle, *Yin*, to which water corresponds, whence the naïve deduction is made that the moon is water.

34   The Chinese expression is "to consume," "to eat" (食 or 蝕). In the popular belief the sun at an eclipse is being devoured by the "heavenly dog," an idea perhaps derived from India. In Wang Chong's time it must not yet have been current, for otherwise he would most likely not have omitted to mention and controvert it.

35   Wang Chong here speaks of a partial eclipse. That the shadow of the moon in most cases covers only part of the sun cannot invalidate the right view, which Wang Chong rejects on insufficient grounds.

36   *Chunqiu* 春秋, Duke Xi 僖 16th year (Legge, *Classics* Vol. V, Pt. I, p. 170).

37   Tanggu 湯谷.

38   *Shanhaijing* 山海經 chap. 9, p. 1 v.

39 According to other accounts Yao 堯 ordered his minister Yi 益, a famous archer, to shoot at the suns, of which he destroyed nine.

40 The appearance of ten suns is mentioned in many ancient works: in *Zhuangzi* 莊子, the Lisao 離騷, the "Bamboo Annals," the *Zuozhuan* 左氏傳, etc.

41 The ten cyclical signs.

42 The Five Elements are considered to be the substances of the Five Planets, which have been named after them: Metal Star (Venus), Wood Star (Jupiter), etc.

43 Cf. p. I.111.

44 Presumably a coral-tree in the Persian Sea is meant.

45 The Chinese imagine that pearls or the produce of fish, not of shells or oysters.

46 If they were of the same stuff as our sun, *viz.* fire, they would have been extinguished in water, and have burned the wood of the Fusang 扶桑 tree. Since they did not do that, they cannot have been real suns like ours.

47 The one sun in the upper branches of the Fusang tree must have risen prior to the nine others still lingering in the lower branches.

48 As far as the nine suns are concerned, which were still below the horizon.

49 Cf. *Chunqiu* (Legge, *Classics* Vol. V, Pt. I, p. 79). The seventh year of Duke Zhuang 莊 of Lu 魯 is 686 BCE.

50 A quotation from Gong Yang's 公羊 commentary to the *Chunqiu*.

51 Had the distance of those meteors not been more than one foot from the surface of the earth, they would inevitably have collided with the elevations of the earth, such as mountains, buildings, etc. Therefore Confucius omitted the remark of the original text.

52 The meteors never measure a hundred Li.

53 *Yijing* 易經, 55th diagram (Feng 豐), Legge's transl. p. 336.

54 A constellation.

55 Quoted from the *Chunqiu* (Legge, *Classics* Vol. V, Pt. I, p. 170). The event took place in 643 BCE.

56 Gong Yang's 公羊 Commentary, Duke Xi 僖 31st year.

57 The highest peak in Shandong 山東.

58 *Shangshu* 尚書, *Hongfan* 洪範, Pt. V, Bk. IV, 38 (Legge, *Classics* Vol. III, Pt. II, p. 342).

59 *Shijing* 詩經 Pt. II, Bk. VIII, Ode VIII (Legge, *Classics* Vol. IV, Pt. II, p. 422).

CHAPTER 33
On the Cunning and Artful
Daning 答佞
(*Lunheng* Book XI, Chap. iii)

1   Their original nature is essentially the same, but develops differently. Cf. p. I.154–55.

2   Properly speaking these Nine Virtues are eighteen. According to the *Shangshu* 尚書 Part II, Book III, 3 (Legge, *Classics* Vol. III, Part I, p. 71) they are: "Affability combined with dignity; mildness combined with firmness; bluntness combined with respectfulness; aptness for government combined with reverence; docility combined with boldness; straightforwardness combined with gentleness; easiness combined with discrimination; vigour combined with sincerity; and valour combined with righteousness."

3   Ed. C. correctly writes 欺惑, ed. A. and B. have 期惑.

4   材相什百.

5   是是非非.

6   All the three editions here write: 佞人問曰. I think that 佞人 is superfluous and should be dropped.

7   All editions have 善中大佞, which should be 惡中, unless Wang Chong wishes to designate those impostors who have sneaked among the virtuous, but that would be somewhat forced.

8   Too small to be punished.

9   Too great to be pardoned. The passage is quoted from the *Shangshu* Part II, Book II, 12 (Legge, *Classics* Vol. III, Part I, p. 59).

10 A fundamental principle of all penal law, based on the difference of *dolus* and *culpa*.

11 See Ch. 11 n. 7.

12 Yan 燕, Zhao 趙, Han 韓, Wei 魏, Qi 齊, and Chu 楚.

13 See Ch. 43 n. 26.

14 三秦, the three kingdoms into which the State of Qin 秦 was divided by Xiang Yu 項羽 in 206 BCE, *viz.* 雍塞翟 Yong, Sai, and Di. Since Wang

Chong here speaks of the 4th cent. BCE, the time of Su Qin 蘇秦 and Zhang Yi 張儀, when the Three Qin did not yet exist, and since by their creation Qin did not become more powerful, but broke up, I suppose that 三秦 here is a misprint for 三晉 San Jin, the Three Jin States: Han 韓, Wei 魏, and Zhao 趙, into which the once powerful State of Jin split in 453 BCE, thus enabling Qin to come to the front.

15 *Shiji* 史記 chap. 69.

16 *Shiji* chap. 70.

17 The time of the contending States 戰國, beginning in 480 BCE.

18 See Ch. 12 n. 3.

19 *Vid.* p. I.162.

20 Elsewhere Wang Chong says that all these things are the outcome of fate alone.

21 Wang Chong apparently sees in the two politicians Zhang Yi 張儀 and Su Qin 蘇秦 cunning schemers, but not Worthies or virtuous men. The Chinese still cling to the idea that moral laws hold good for politics also, and have not yet accepted the phantom of political morality, another name for the right of the strongest. They call a liar a liar, even though he has been a great statesman who did all his misdeeds for the welfare of his country. Thus most Europeans admire Qin Shi Huangdi 秦始皇, but every Chinese detests him.

22 覺佞, probably the title of a lost chapter of the *Lunheng*.

23 Ed. A. and C.: 不毀於將將. One 將 suffices as in Ed. B.

24 So says the one who seeks to frustrate the promotion of *X* by raising all kinds of fictitious difficulties.

25 從橫 political intriguing, forming and breaking alliances.

26 An ascetic philosopher of the 4th cent. BCE.

27 Abridged from *Shiji* chap. 70, p. 2r.

28 Their exalted positions have many dangers, and they easily come to fall.

29 A vassal of Yao 堯 who resigned his fief, when Yu 禹 became emperor, and took to agriculture. Yu is reported to have visited and questioned him on his fields. See *Zhuangzi* 莊子 V, 4v. (Giles, *Chuang Tse* p. 142). Cf. Ch. 1 n. 19.

30 An appellative of Chen Zhong Zi 陳仲子, a scholar of Qi 齊, mentioned by Mencius. Cf. p. I.352. 於陵子 Wu Ling Zi is reputed the author of a short philosophical treatise in 12 paragraphs, contained in the 子書百家 *Zishu baijia* Vol. 51. According to 劉向 Liu Xiang he wrote a work in 12 chapters 十二篇 (*Peiwen yunfu* 佩文韻府 chap. 25). From the last paragraph of the work still extant we learn that he abandoned his post as

minister of Chu 楚 to water other people's garden. At all events he was a rather extravagant recluse.

31   Wang Zhong Zi 王仲子 or Wang Liang 王良, famous for his learning and excellent character, lived in the time of Guang Wu Di 光武帝, 25–57 CE. He declined the high offices conferred upon him owing to sickness.

32   A place in Yanzhoufu 兗州府, Shandong 山東.

33   The *Lidai mingxian lienü shixingpu* 歷代名賢列女氏姓譜 calls the man: 索廬 Suolu and informs us that Jun Yang 君陽 was his style, and that he was a native of 東郡 Dongjun, not of Dongdu 東都. The *Shangyulu* 商語錄 again writes 索羅 Suoluo. As his name both biographical dictionaries give 放 Fang. Suolu Fang 索廬放 was appointed governor of Luoyang 洛陽 in 30 CE. Twice he resigned owing to bad health. The second time in 55 CE he did not obey the summons of the Emperor Guang Wu Di, who then sent a sedan-chair for him, and after the audience made him a grant of 2000 bushels of rice.

34   A territory in Henan 河南.

35   Cf. Ch. 80 n. 90.

36   The minister of works under Yao, subsequently punished by Shun 舜 (*Shangshu* Part II, Book I, 12, Legge, *Classics* Vol. III, Part I, p. 39).

37   *Analects* V, 4.

38   Only socialists would agree to this.

39   *Analects* XI, 16.

40   The disciple of Confucius, Qiu 求 is pronounced to have been cunning owing to his having taken care of the interests of a nobleman instead of working for the people, a somewhat radical view, but collectors of taxes never have been popular. In the New Testament they are all decried as sinners.

CHAPTER 34
Weighing of Talents
Chengcai 程材

(*Lunheng* Book XII, Chap. i)

1   The masses not only in China, but in other countries as well view everything from the practical side. What is a man worth *i.e.*, how much does he earn, is the usual question of an American. They admire and affect wealth and power, and think very little of learning.

2   將.

3   If these indictments of Wang Chong are just and not dictated by his offended amour-propre owing to his inability to advance in the official career, officialdom in the Han 漢 time must have been different from what it is now, for at present the majority are scholars well versed in literature, but not in business.

4   將相.

5   A remark very characteristic of Wang Chong's time.

6   毗戲.

7   These are the opportunists among the scholars.

8   These uncompromising characters stick to their principles, but do not get on in life.

9   This sort of young firebrands and utopists would reform everything, but they do it with inadequate means, and soon are crushed under the inert masses they are attempting to stop.

10 According to our modern view, this is just what a future official should do. Literature alone, which up to very recent times was the only study of all the candidates, does not suffice. A literary education can be nothing more than a basis for future special studies.

11 This is not true. With virtue and literature alone a country cannot be governed. This requires practical knowledge and experience, of which the typical Literati are destitute, and which they disdain to acquire.

12 In Shandong 山東.

13 An ancient name of Guidefu 歸德府 in Henan 河南.

14   As a rule perhaps, but there are many students so unpractical and only at home in the high spheres of pure thought, that just their great learning and idealism makes them absolutely unfit for business.

15   Erasing knives, see Ch. 35 n. 27.

16   See Ch. 85 n. 7.

17   法家.

18   法令之家. The writers on law form one of the Nine Schools into which Liu Xin 劉歆 7 BCE divided the then existing philosophical literature. These writers are not jurists in the modern acceptation of the word, but rather authors philosophising on the nature of law, rewards and punishments, government, and political economy. The Catalogue in the *Hanshu* 漢書 mentions only ten works of this class. The *Zishu baijia* 子書百家 gives six works. The most celebrated so-called jurists are Guan Zhong 管仲, Yan Zi 晏子, Shang Yang 商鞅, and Han Feizi 韓非子, all well known to, and several times mentioned by, Wang Chong, who has a special dislike for the criminalists Shang Yang and Han Feizi. Cf. Vol. I, chap. 29 *Strictures on Han Feizi* 韓非子.

19   皆出其中. Ed. A. and C. write 其忠, which is less good.

20   The last clause from "if they wish…" seems to be a gloss which ought to be expunged, since it spoils the meaning: officials being of equal talents with scholars, instead of devoting themselves to business, ought to study general principles.

21   A high officer of strong character at the court of the Han 漢 Emperor Wen Di 文帝, 179–157 BCE.

22   *Shiji* 史記 chap. 122. Both officers together enacted several laws, hence Sima Qian's 司馬遷 aversion, who like our philosopher had a strong inclination towards Daoism and in his introduction to the above chapter approvingly quotes chap. 57 of the *Daodejing* 道德經: 法令滋章盜賊多有 "The more laws and edicts, the more robbers and thieves."

23   The new capital of the Zhou 周 dynasty in Henan.

24   大匠.

25   摑經.

26   Ed. B.: 計胸中之穎出溢十萬文. Ed. A. and C. write: 出穎十萬文. Wang Chong is bragging somewhat here. Even in the best Chinese authors, let alone ordinary scholars, we do not discover ingenious thoughts by thousands.

27   The recital of the Chinese Classics is more a chanting than a reading.

28   This is greatly exaggerated.

29　Bribery and corruption seem to have been the canker of Chinese officials at all time.

30　The military spirit of the Chinese in the Han time was greater than it is now, for they were then just emerging from feudalism.

31　A place in Jiangsu 江蘇.

32　The *Shixingpu* 氏姓譜 calls him 宗均 Zong Jun (T. 叔庠 Shu Xiang). The 犀 of our text is probably a misprint. He died in 76 CE.

33　A place in Henan.

CHAPTER 35
The Valuation of Knowledge
Liangzhi 量知
(*Lunheng* Book XII, Chap. ii)

1　Ch. 34.

2　賻禮. The custom of sending presents to the relations of the deceased as a contribution to the funeral expenses, is very old and already mentioned in the *Liji* 禮記 (Cf. Legge, *Sacred Books* Vol. XXVIII, p. 140 seq.). The *Yupian* 玉篇 523 CE defines 賻 as 以財助喪也. In ancient times these presents usually were *in natura*, at present they are mostly in money. I did not find any allusion to this custom in De Groot's great work, *The Religious System of China*.

3　Wang Chong shares the mistake of most Chinese philosophers and of many westerners too, believing that virtue is a necessary correlate of learning. Virtue may be acquired without study, and many scholars are without it.

4　尸位素飡, phrase quoted from the *Hanshu* 漢書 (*Peiwen yunfu* 佩文韻府). These personators of the dead were relatives of the deceased who had to represent the departed soul when sacrifice was offered to it. They were treated with great respect, and refreshments were presented to them.

This custom, several times mentioned in the *Shijing* 詩經 and the *Liji*, was abolished after the Zhou 周 dynasty.

5   有骨無肉脂腴不足 quoted in the *Peiwen yunfu* chap. 7a. The meaning is that such passionate speakers are imbued with the right feelings, but want elegance, and therefore are not held in esteem.

6   I did not succeed in tracing this passage in the *Liji*, and fail to see how a remonstrance can be construed as a flattery.

7   Of men who might offer their advice, which they dare not for fear that they might be suspected of flattery.

8   They are indebted to the high officers for the emoluments they receive from them.

9   Ordinary officials without classical learning do not rank higher than menials and artisans.

10   An unjust reproach, for experience in business is not to be disdained.

11   蒸.

12   Still now-a-days torches are often made of hemp-hard.

13   The fire on the hearth produced by ordinary fire-wood. It goes without saying that scholars are likened to the twigs of hemp, shedding a brilliant light by their intelligence, whereas officials are no more than trunks of trees.

14   All these are emblematic figures mentioned in the *Shangshu* 尚書 Part II, Book IV, 4 (Legge, *Classics* Vol. III, Part I, p. 80). In ancient times they were partly depicted and partly embroidered on official robes, so that painted silk and silk embroideries must already have been known before the Zhou 周 dynasty, perhaps 2000 years BCE.

15   切瑳琢磨. These different manufactures, which still to-day are so very characteristic for China, *viz.* the working of bone and ivory, of jade and jewels, are worthy of note. The four words are from the *Shijing* (Legge, *Classics* Vol. IV, Part I, p. 91).

16   孫武, commonly called Sunzi 孫子, a celebrated general in the service of He Lu 闔廬, to whom a well-known work on the art of war is ascribed.

17   A King of Wu 吳 of the 6th cent. BCE, on whom cf. Ch. 8 n. 29.

18   Officials are compared with such ignorant leaders.

19   穀.

20   粟.

21   飯.

22   米. The variety of names for rice in its different stages—there are still others referring to its quality—show the great importance it has for China.

23   Mining and metallurgy were practised long before the Han 漢 dynasty.

The *Shangshu* (*Yugong* 禹貢) speaks of gold, silver, and copper, the last being the metal *par excellence*. The *Zhouli* 周禮 informs us that tin was mined. From the 7th cent. BCE a tax was levied on salt and iron, and we have a treatise on these two metals the *Yantielun* 鹽鐵論 of the 1st cent. BCE.

24 牒.

25 筆. The same character later on served to designate a pencil or a brush made of hair and invented in the 3rd cent. BCE. The style originally was a bamboo pencil dipped into lacquer to write on the wooden or bamboo tablets then in use.

26 板.

27 奏牘. On ancient Chinese books before the invention of paper, the erasing knife, and the style or pencil see the remarkable paper of Ed. Chavannes, *Les Livres chinois avant l'invention du papier* (*Journal Asiatique*, Janvier–Fevrier 1905).

28 采.

29 The colour of mourning is a greyish white, the colour of undyed stuffs; whereas red is the colour of joy and good augury.

30 Documents written on wooden tablets which are carved and polished.

31 Wang Chong confounds scribes and officials.

32 In auditing accounts.

33 經藝.

34 Chief minister of Zheng 鄭.

35 Celebrated statesman. Cf. Ch. 63 n. 21.

36 Allusion to the *Zuozhuan* 左氏傳, Duke Xiang 襄 31st year, where Zi Chan 子產 dissuades Zi Pi 子皮 from making Yin He 尹何 commandant of a city owing to his being too young and unexperienced. His words are: 今吾子愛人則以政. 猶未能操刀而使割也. (Legge, *Classics* Vol. V, Part II, p. 562.)

37 Cf. p. I.322.

CHAPTER 36
Admitting Shortcomings
Xieduan 謝短

(*Lunheng* Book XII, Chap. iii)

1 Ch. 34.
2 Ch. 35.
3 It is a curious fact that in the Han 漢 time already there were specialists studying only one book or one author just as we have our Goethe, Shakespeare and Dante critics.
4 The doctrine of Confucius of course.
5 Ed. A. and C. have 訓, B: 誂 "to answer."
6 Ed. A. and C. have 訓, B: 誂 "to answer."
7 南面為師.
8 陸沈.
9 The emperors Yu 禹, Tang 湯, and Wen Wang 文王, founders of the Xia 夏, Shang 商, and Zhou 周 dynasties, often mentioned in the Classics.
10 Yin 殷 or Shang dynasty.
11 年, the expression for a year now in use.
12 The downfall of the Xia and Shang dynasties is said to have been brought about by the wickedness of the last emperors Jie 桀 and Zhou 紂. The last rulers of the Zhou 周 dynasty were not depraved, but weak, and so their house fell an easy prey to the attacks of powerful Qin 秦.
13 This is doubtful. Sima Qian 司馬遷 makes the Emperor Zhuan Xu 顓頊 their ancestor, Sima Zhen 司馬貞, the Emperor Shao Hao 少昊. *Vid.* Chavannes, *Mem. Hist.* Vol. II, p. 1, Note 3.
14 These questions are answered in p. II.812 and p. I.283 seq.
15 Chronology is not the strong point of Chinese scholars. Han Gao Zu 漢高祖 reigned from 206–195 BCE. The *Lunheng* was written about 80 CE.
16 Wang Chong speaks of these omens in Ch. 57–60.
17 Gao Zu 高祖 had to fight many battles against rival generals, his most powerful rival being Xiang Yu 項羽, who nearly defeated him. It was only by chance that he and not the latter ascended the throne of the Qin 秦.

18 The collections of bamboo and wooden tablets forming books measured two feet four inches or three feet of the Zhou 周 measure in case of the Classics. Other works of less importance were much smaller, only about one foot long, therefore called 尺籍. But even the *Analects* originally did not exceed one foot. Cf. p. II.818.

19 尺籍.

20 短書.

21 Cf. Ch. 81 n. 40.

22 As a book on divination the *Yijing* 易經 was preserved from destruction. See Legge, *Sacred Books* Vol. XVI, Introduction p. 2.

23 The answers to all these questions are to be found in p. II.810 seq.

24 Chao Cuo 鼂錯, cf. p. II.812–13.

25 The double question is indicated by the two finals ....乎 ... 也, a mode of expression not seldom used in the *Lunheng*.

26 This problem is ventilated in p. II.817.

27 *Loc. cit.*, Ch. 81 n. 35.

28 Cf. Ch. 8 n. 33.

29 According to Wylie, *Notes* p. 5 they were concealed in the house of Confucius.

30 The Catalogue in the *Hanshu* 漢書 mentions seventeen chapters. Cf. Legge, *Classics* Vol. XXVII, Introduction p. 3.

31 1078–1053 BCE.

32 Cheng Wang 成王, 1115–1079 BCE, succeeded Wu Wang 武王, 1122–1116 BCE.

33 Both were wise and virtuous rulers.

34 Legge holds that the *Shijing* 詩經 is a fragment of various collections of odes made during the early reigns of the kings of Zhou 周. The oldest pieces were composed during the Shang dynasty, the youngest go down to the 6th cent. BCE. (Legge, *Classics* Vol. IV, Part I, Prolegomena pp. 27 and 82 seq.)

35 詩言志, 歌詠言, *Shangshu* 尚書 Part II, Book I, 24 (Legge, *Classics* Vol. III, Part I, p. 48) where, however, 永 is written in lieu of 詠. Legge takes 詩 to mean "poetry" and accordingly translates, "Poetry is the expression of earnest thought; singing is the prolonged utterance of that expression." The 詠 of our text seems a better reading than 永.

36 Wang Chong's rendering 詩 by *Shijing* is very doubtful, and his surmise that the *Shijing* existed already at Shun's 舜 time very precarious.

37 Something seems to be wrong in the text here, perhaps we should read "we have a book of Odes," for in Wang Chong's time there were several

editions. The Odes were nearly all recovered in the Han 漢 time, having been preserved in the memory of the scholars more than the other Classics.

38   493–466 BCE. Confucius returned to Lu 魯 in 484 BCE after having passed five to six years in Wei 衛 without taking office. What he did during this time, and how he was treated by the reigning duke we do not know. There is a blank in his history just at this time. Cf. Legge, *Classics* Vol. I, Prolegomena p. 83.

39   Duke Chu 出公, 492–481 BCE.

40   史記, the chronicle of Lu 魯.

41   It was the name of the chronicle of Lu before Confucius edited it. See p. II.819 and Legge, *Classics* Vol. V, Part I, Prolegomena p. 8.

42   法律之家. Cf. Ch. 34 n. 18.

43   九章, The "Nine Statutes" forming the Penal Code of the Han dynasty.

44   五刑. Branding, cutting off the nose, cutting off the feet, castration, and execution.

45   Xiao He 蕭何 assisted Liu Bang 劉邦, the later Han Gao Zu 漢高祖, in his struggle for the throne. He also drew up a Penal Code for the Qian Han 前漢 dynasty. Died 193 BCE. Cf. Giles, *Bibl. Dict.* No. 702.

46   179–157 BCE.

47   Chunyu De 淳于德 had no sons, but five daughters.

48   肉刑 *viz.* branding, cutting off the nose, and cutting off the feet.

49   This episode is told with all the details in the *Shiji* 史記 chap. 10, p. 12v (Chavannes, *Mem. Hist.* Vol. II, p. 474), and in the *Hanshu* chap. 23, p. 12v., where the officer is called Chunyu Yi 湻于意 and 淳于公.

50   象刑. Cf. Chavannes *loc. cit.*

51   We read in the *Hanshu loc. cit.* p. 11r. that under the Zhou dynasty there were nine kinds of punishments 九刑, the five of Yu 禹 and in addition: banishment, fining, whipping, and flogging, and that the Qin 秦 dynasty was conspicuous by its cruelty. Han Gao Zu first hoped to get on with three statutes 三章 providing capital punishment for murder, and talion for bodily injury and theft. These punishments proving insufficient, Xiao He 蕭何 on the basis of the Penal Code of the Qin 秦 dynasty drew up the Nine Statutes in question.

52   *Zhongyong* 中庸 chap. XXVII, 3.

53   禮.

54   律.

55   Ed. B.: 昏禮, A. and C.: 經禮 which gives no sense.

56　盜律.

57　Feudality was abolished by the Qin dynasty, and the feudal lords replaced by functionaries.

58　The joined field system fell into desuetude in the Zhou time already, when land taxes were introduced.

59　更一月. This refers to the obligatory military service during the Zhou epoch, which lasted one month every year. After one month of service it was other people's turn to serve.

60　儒. I suppose that 徭 should be written, for *ru* 儒 gives no sense. The *corvées*, especially military service, lasted from the 23rd to the 56th year under the Han dynasty. Cf. my paper "Das chinesische Finanz- und Steuerwesen" in the *Mitt. d. Sem. f. Orient. Sprachen* Vol. III, 1900, p. 187.

61　臚.

62　Cf. p. II.750.

63　See p. II.759.

64　See p. II.745.

65　Cf. p. II.672. The custom of painting tigers on the door-screens to frighten away demons is practised to the present day. *Vid.* De Groot, *Fêtes annuelles d'Émoui* Vol. II, p. 608.

66　The Chinese titles are: 尉史, 令史, 長史. The meaning of this very concise sentence is very doubtful.

67　A designation for the minister of revenue and the minister of works together.

68　They seem to have been granted for military achievements during the Han time (*Pianzileibian* 駢字類編).

69　簪裊 (Chavannes writes 梟), 上造 are two of the twenty ranks of officials in vogue during the Qin and Han dynasties. Zanniao 簪裊 literally means a horse adorned with a silken harness. The officers of this rank were entitled to ride such horses. The original meaning of *shangzao* 上造 is not clear (Cf. Chavannes, *Mem. Hist.* Vol. II, pp. 528, 529).

70　Ed. A. and C.: 玉杖, B. has: 王杖. Both readings are possible. The staves which in the Zhou dynasty were presented to old men by order of the emperor, were called 王杖 "imperial staves" (*Le Tscheou-li* par *Ed. Biot* Vol. II, p. 394).

71　According to the *Houhanshu* 後漢書 in mid-autumn all the old men of seventy years received a "jade staff," one foot long, adorned with a pigeon at one end, implying the wish that they might eat their food with the same ease as pigeons do. The *Fengsutong* 風俗通 assigns another reason for this old custom: Han Gao Zu, pursued by his adversary Xiang Yu 項羽, concealed himself in the rushes. Pigeons cooing above him, his pursuers did not think that a man was hidden there, and he escaped. After his accession, he had pigeon staves made in remembrance of this adventure to support the old. (*Peiwen yunfu* 佩文韻府 chap. 52). A picture of the handle of such a "pigeon-staff," taken from the *Xiqing gujian* 西清古鑑, will be found in B. Laufer's paper, *The Bird Chariot in China and Europe*, reprinted from the Boas Anniversary Volume, 1906, p. 419. The entry in Giles' Dict. No. 2267 to the effect that the figure of a pigeon was engraved on the staff, should be rectified.

72 The drum is beaten to mark the five night-watches every two hours from 7 p.m. to 5 a.m., and from ancient times the hours are determined by the water-clock. It was in use in the Zhou epoch, and a special officer had charge of the clepsydra (*Le Tscheou-li* Vol. II, p. 201). For day and night a stalk was marked with a hundred divisions, of which about 58 would have to be allotted to day-time and 42 to night. Wang Chong says that day has 60 divisions. In the Han time 48 different stalks, corresponding to the varying lengths of day and night, were used. In 5 BCE one hundred and twenty divisions were introduced for day and night, of which 60 would be allotted to each at the equinoxes.

73 The *Houhanshu* says that in primitive times men lived in caverns and wild places, dressing in furs and covering their heads with skins. In later ages the Sages noticed that birds and beasts had horns, crests, and beards, in imitation whereof they invented bonnets and caps with ribbons. (Kangxi's 康熙 Dict.).

74 Ed. C.: 城廓, A. and B.: 郭.

75 Cf. p. II.573.

CHAPTER 37

The Display of Energy
Xiaoli 效力

(*Lunheng* Book XIII, Chap. i)

1 Ch. 34.

2 Ch. 35.

3 The well known philosopher. Cf. Ch. 42 n. 31.

4 梓材 "The Timber of the Tse Tree" a chapter of the *Shangshu* 尚書. In our text this quotation is not to be found. The Chinese words are: 彊人有王開賢. 厥率化民.

5 One Classic does not suffice.

6 A circuit in Henan 河南.

7 王甲某子.

8 Cf. p. I.411.

9 The Xia 夏 and Shang 商 dynasties.

10 The typical conceit of a Chinese scholar.

11 Quotation from *Analects* VIII, 7.

12 I do not see why a distinction is made between Zeng Zi 曾子 and other scholars. Was Zeng Zi not learned, and are the scholars not virtuous?

13 The same as Gu Yong 谷永 and Tang Lin 唐林 p. II.839.

14 This must refer to the Classics, for it is not known that Confucius revised other books besides.

15 See p. I.381.

16 A "Samson" of the feudal age. Giles, Dict. No. 2334.

17 A great writer. Cf. Ch. 22 n. 27.

18 Cf. *Shiji* 史記 chap. 5, p. 26v. (Chavannes, *Mem. Hist.* Vol. II, p. 76). The death of King Wu 武 took place in 307 BCE. He was very strong himself and fond of strong men like Meng Yue 孟說. After the king's death, the latter and all his relations were executed.

19 Yan Yuan 顏淵 = Yan Hui 顏囘, the disciple of Confucius.

20 勉自什伯. The last character stands for 佰.

21 Scholars not finding the necessary support retire from public life to become recluses and hermits.

22 Cf. Ch. 55 n. 35.

23 Ed. B.: 滂沛之流. Ed. A. and C.: 滂沛不流.

24 A strong man in the Shang dynasty.

25 See Ch. 25 n. 23.

26 Ed. A. has the misprint 鉤. A *jun* 鈞 in the Han 漢 time was equal to 30 pounds or catties.

27 The chief is compared with a mountain unable to hold a big stone, the scholar: Only great men are qualified to appreciate great men and keep them in their service.

28 Others may recommend them, but then their promotion is not of long duration. Ere long, they will get into conflict with their employers and abandon their posts.

29 Cf. Ch. 10 n. 1.

30 See Ch. 10 n. 2.

31 See Ch. 6 n. 19.

32 *Vid.* Ch. 83 n. 15 and 16.

33 Such an officer was 吳起 Wu Qi of Wei 衛, who as chancellor organised the administration of Chu 楚, and vanquished all her rivals.

34 The Zhao 趙 State flourished under 肥義 Fei Yi as minister, who was put to death in 295 BCE.

35 It was for this reason that King Hui 惠 of Wei 魏 in 336 BCE summoned Mencius and other Sages to his court.

36 Shen Buhai 申不害, a native of Luoyang 洛陽, became minister under Prince Zhao 昭 of Han 韓 and died in 337BCE. He is known as Shen Zi 申子 and a Daoist author. The *Shiji* devotes some lines to him in chap. 63, which treats of Lao Zi 老子, Zhuang Zi 莊子, and Han Feizi 韓非子.

37 It is not clear which these three devices were; the *Pianzileibian* 駢字類編 quotes this passage, the *Peiwen yunfu* 佩文韻府 refers to Huai Nan Zi 淮南子. Shen Buhai reorganised the administration, sought the friendship of other States, strengthened the military power of Han 韓, and reformed the criminal law.

38 礚. Ed. A.: 磕. This meaning is wanting in the dictionaries.

39 Living in different elements, they cannot unite or have any intercourse.

40 Cf. Ch. 26 n. 43.

41 Very soft things. The tissues of Lu 魯 in Shandong 山東 must have been exceptionally fine.

42　Very soft things. The tissues of Lu in Shandong must have been exceptionally fine.

43　There must be some force, in default of which the best weapons are useless.

44　See Ch. 26 n. 15.

45　Cf. Ch. 3 n. 20.

46　Xiang Yu 項羽, the rival of Han Gao Zu 漢高祖, was omnipotent in the Chu State.

47　樊酈 better known under the name of Fan Kuai 樊噲, originally a dog-butcher, who was raised to high honours by Han Gao Zu 漢高祖.

48　See Ch. 36 n. 51.

49　Cf. Ch. 8 n. 33.

50　See Ch. 36 n. 51.

51　Both *Liezi* 列子 VIII, 6r. and *Huainanzi* 淮南子 XII, 4r. relate this same fact in almost identical words, but they speak of the gate of the capital. The *Lüshi chunqiu* 呂氏春秋 also has a reference to it.

CHAPTER *38*
On Intelligence
Bietong 別通
(*Lunheng* Book XIII, Chap. ii)

1　Even to-day the Chinese do not use their silks and curios for decorating their poorly furnished rooms, but keep their treasures in trunks and boxes, whence they are seldom removed, to be shown to some good friend.

2　百家.

3　Cf. p. I.425.

4　The Han 漢 took over the bulk of the administration of the Qin 秦 dynasty, for which purpose Xiao He 蕭何 collected their official papers.

5　宮商.

6　癰 *yong*. Kangxi 康熙 quotes this passage and suggests that this character may be a variant of 癰 = 癕 "carbuncles" or extuberances *viz.* in the nose.

7　In China of course.

8　Ed. A. and C.: 西川, Ed. B.: 西州. According to the *Taiping yulan* 太平御覽 chap. 165 Xizhou 西州 would be identical with Gaochang 高昌 or Karakhodjo in Turkestan. Rock-salt is mentioned as a produce of this country, brought as tribute to China under the Liang 梁 dynasty (*Taiping yulan* chap. 865, p. 6r.). But perhaps Wang Chong refers to a Xizhou 西州 in Sichuan 四川 (Playfair No. 2619, 4°), which province was famous for its salt-wells already in the Han 漢 time. See *Taiping yulan* chap. 189, p. 1v., where a passage from the *Hanshu* 漢書 is quoted.

9　法令之家.

10　See Ch. 36 n. 3.

11　*Analects* IX, 10.

12　The Styx of the Chinese.

13　140–87 BCE.

14　This fact is mentioned in the *Zuozhuan* 左氏傳, Duke Xiang 襄 27th and 28th year (Legge, *Classics* Vol. V, Part II, pp. 532 and 542).

15　King Ling 靈 of Chu 楚 executed Qing Feng 慶封, who had fled to Wu 吳 in 537 BCE. See *Chunqiu* 春秋, Duke Zhao 昭, 4th year. According to the *Zuozhuan* King Ling reproached Qing Feng with having murdered his ruler. So his ignorance was not the direct cause of his death.

16　This rule is set forth in the *Liji* 禮記, Jiaotesheng 郊特牲 (Legge, *Sacred Books* Vol. XXVII, p. 425).

17　Ed. A. and C.: 集糅, B.: 雜糅 which is better.

18　甘酒醴不酤飴蜜. 未為能知味也. In Ed. B.: 密 should be replaced by 蜜. The meaning is somewhat obscure. I take it to be that it is not sufficient to sugar common wine to have the taste of sweet wine, which is a special quality. Sugar symbolises the learning of one school, sweet wine, that of all combined.

19　通.

20　達.

21　通

22　無道, literally "no road."

23　It is impossible to bring out the full meaning of this paragraph in English. In Chinese the principal words pointed out in Notes 1–3 have all a double meaning: to communicate, to connect, a road on one side and on the other: intelligent, clever, principle. The general purport is that intelligence, and good principles cannot be dispensed with just as good roads and communications are necessary.

24　*Analects* XIX, 23 (Legge, *Classics* Vol. I, p. 347).

25 Even the natives of the colonies had assumed Chinese dress and Chinese civilisation.

26 These must have been paintings in fresco, perhaps of a similar kind as those recently unearthed in Turkestan.

27 A virgin living in the "southern forest," skilled in swordplay and recommended to the King of Yue 越 by Fan Li 范蠡 (5th cent. BCE). She became the instructor of the king's best soldiers. I cannot explain why a place in Shandong 山東 is coupled with her name here. Was she invited there too?

28 A place in Shandong.

29 山海經. This book has most likely not the age ascribed to it by Chinese critics and is not older than the 4th cent. BCE.

30 Capital of the Jin 晉 State. Cf. Ch. 11 n. 31.

31 Historian of the Jin State, 6th cent. BCE.

32 商瞿 styled Zi Mu 子木 a disciple of Confucius.

33 取書來. This phrase shows that the peculiar use of the auxiliary verb 來, generally believed to be a characteristic feature of the vernacular, had commenced already in the Han 漢 time. 書 may also mean the *Shangshu* 尚書 here.

34 Quoted from *Analects* XVII, 22.

35 The 未 of Ed. A. must be corrected into 末.

36 A magician on whom see p. I.270–271.

37 翼少君 generally known as 李少君 Li Shao Jun, his style being 雲翼 Yun Yi. Cf. p. I.268 seq.

38 The Chinese regard divination as a science for which the *Yijing* 易經 is the standard work.

39 p. II.725 Wang Chong speaks of three hundred and sixty naked creatures.

40 猶吾大夫高子也. This might be an allusion to *Analects* V, 18: 猶吾大夫崔子也 "They are like our high officer Cui" *i.e.*, as bad. 高 is either a misprint or another reading of the *Analects*.

41 The modern Fengxiangfu 鳳翔府 in Shanxi 陝西.

42 In the province of Guangxi 廣西.

43 In Laizhoufu 萊州府, Shandong.

44 The three persons named seem to be contemporaries of Wang Chong.

45 Prince Zhao 昭 of Yan 燕, who employed Zou Yan 鄒衍 and treated him with great consideration.

46 I suppose that 東城 should be written, a district in Fengyangfu 鳳陽府, Anhui 安徽, during the Han time.

47 奇律. Cf. Couvreur's Dict.

48 A district likewise in Fengyangfu, Anhui.

49 Cf. Ch. 35.
50 The Han emperor, 58–76 CE.
51 移中監. Ed A. and C. write 移 instead of 杪. The expression occurs in the biography of Su Wu 蘇武 in the *Qianhanshu* 前漢書 (Couvreur).
52 隨牒.
53 木旁多文字 = 移.
54 See above p. I.433.
55 Jia Kui 賈逵, eminent scholar, 30–101 CE, who together with the historian Ban Gu 班固 was appointed historiographer.
56 Cf. p. II.839.
57 A scholar who left a collection of poetry in 28 chapters. With Ban Gu and Jia Kui he was attached to the Imperial Library and entrusted with editorial work.
58 The philosopher, cf. Ch. 13 n. 15.

CHAPTER *39*

On Preeminence
Chaoqi 超奇

(*Lunheng* Book XIII, Chap. iii)

1 The Chinese have always bestowed great care on their state papers, so that reports to the throne pass for literary productions and are often collected and edited.
2 The chronicle of Lu 魯.
3 We find nothing of all this in the *Chunqiu* 春秋, which are but very dry chronological tables, but the Chinese interpret them in such an artificial way, according to their preconceived ideas, that they discover the deepest meanings in the plainest words, where an unprejudiced reader sees nothing but the statement of simple facts.
4 All authors of the Han 漢 period often mentioned by Wang Chong.
5 儒生.

6   通人.

7   文人.

8   鴻儒.

9   Gigantic savages said to have come to China.

10 They possess only an elementary learning, knowing how to read and write, but the Classics are too high for them.

11 Cf. Ch. 37 n. 13.

12 Ed. B: 說書於牘奏之士. Ed. A and C read 上 for 士, which would not agree with Wang Chong's appreciation of memorialists whom he places above mere commentators.

13 See Ch. 13 n. 17.

14 Ch. 13 n. 18 and 21.

15 Cf. p. II.845.

16 This is evidently wrong. A critic must not be superior to those he criticises. They are in most cases much above him.

17 p. II.836 Wang Chong seems to assign the first place among the writers of the Han time to Sima Qian 司馬子長 and Yang Zi Yun 揚子雲, not to Huan Jun Shan 桓君山.

18 This distinction is rather arbitrary. The *Chunqiu* treats as much of ministers and high officers as of princes, and the records of other writers embrace the doings of princes as well.

19 One of the Three Heroes at the beginning of the Han dynasty, who died in 178 BCE. Called upon to distribute the sacrificial meats at the altar to the spirits of the land, he did it with such impartiality, that the elders wished he might manage the empire, which, later on, he really did.

20 The text writes Shu Sun Ao 叔孫敖, which must be corrected. Sunshu Ao was a minister of Chu 楚 in the 6th cent. BCE. We read in *Huainanzi* 淮南子 that, when he diverted the waters of the Qisi 期思 river, to water the wilds of Yulou 雩婁, King Zhuang 莊 knew that he would be a good prime minister. See also Ch. 20 n. 8.

21 Ed. A: 銛 for 銛.

22 Cf. Ch. 83 n. 15.

23 A politician of the 3rd cent. BCE at the court of Prince Xiao Cheng 孝成 of Zhao 趙.

24 The *Yushi chunqiu* 虞氏春秋 in 15 books.

25 We are ignorant of all further circumstances.

26 See Ch. 13 n. 18.

27 Ch. 83 n. 11.

28 The well-known *Lüshi chunqiu* 呂氏春秋.

29 See above p. II.441.

30 A scholar of the 2nd cent. BCE who gained the sobriquet the Wisdom-Bag. He advised the emperor to get rid of the feudal princes. A work of his in 31 books is mentioned in the *Hanshu* 漢書 chap. 30, among the treatises on law.

31 陳說.

32 On Gu Yong 谷永 and Tang Lin 唐林 see Ch. 83 n. 54.

33 宜言.

34 切議.

35 His full name is 魯仲連 Lu Zhong Lian, a wandering philosopher of the Qi 齊 State. When about 238 BCE a general of Yan 燕 was beleaguered in Liaocheng 聊城, a city in Shandong 山東 originally belonging to Qi, by an army of this State, Lu Zhong Lian 魯仲連 shot a letter bound to an arrow and addressed to the general into the surrounded city. This letter pointing out to the general his helpless condition induced him to commit suicide.

36 See Ch. 85 n. 11.

37 The afore-mentioned Tang Lin 唐林 and Gu Yong 谷永.

38 Cf. Ch. 83 n. 49.

39 A famous writer of the 4th cent. BCE often mentioned by Wang Chong. The Prince of Yan 燕 treated him with great consideration and had a special palace built for him.

40 *I.e.*, 嚴忌 Yan Ji, a scholar who wrote poetry in irregular verse, 2nd cent. BCE. His original name was 莊 Zhuang, which he changed because the character, being the name of an emperor, had become taboo.

41 This man seems to be identical with the Wu Jun Gao 吳君高 mentioned in connexion with Zhou Chang Sheng 周長生 as an elegant writer in Ch. 83 n. 49.

42 宛. In Ch. 26 n. 47 and 48 we find the statement that white pheasants were offered by the Yuechang 越常 people and odoriferous plants by the Japanese.

43 Yongzhou 雍州, Jingzhou 荊州, and Yangzhou 楊州 are three of the Nine Provinces of Yu 禹. Yongzhou corresponds to modern Shanxi 陝西 and Gansu 甘肅, Jingzhou comprised Hunan 湖南, Hubei 湖北, Guangxi 廣西, and parts of Sichuan 四川, Guizhou 貴州 and Guangdong 廣東, and Yangzhou is the modern Zhejiang 浙江, Fujian 福建, and Jiangxi 江西.

44 *Analects* IX, 5. Legge and others here translate 文 by "truth," whereas Wang Chong takes it in the sense given in the translation.

45 A contemporary of Song Yu 宋玉. The *Hanshu* chap. 30 mentions his poems in 4 books.

46 Another poet of Chu, nephew of the famous Qu Yuan 屈原. According to the *Hanshu loc. cit.* he wrote 16 books of poetry, now incorporated into the 楚辭 "Elegies of Chu."

47 Ed. B: 未論列者, Ed. A and C: 未論.

48 According to the ancient division of Yu.

49 Two of the Five Sacred Mountains, situated in Shanxi 陝西 and Shan-dong.

50 In the *Chunqiu* the chronology is based on the reigns of the dukes of Lu 魯 *i.e.*, on their first years, which are specially noted. This is not done because these dukes were much superior to the sovereigns of the other States, but because this work is the chronicle of Lu. Thus Zhou Chang Sheng 周長生 is mentioned as a primus inter pares.

51 Ed. B: 實事之人, Ed. A and C write 何事 which gives no sense.

52 See Ch. 84 n. 15.

53 Meng Jian 孟堅 is the designation of the historian Ban Gu 班固.

54 Between there two model princes and the two States of Lu and Wei 衛 there was no great difference.

55 The Han dynasty is like a fertile land with many trees full of blossoms and fruit, its able scholars, and like a clear sky on which twinkle its stars, many famous writers.

56 Cf. p. I.86.

CHAPTER 40
Apparent Backwardness
Zhuangliu 狀留

(*Lunheng* **Book XIV, Chap. i**)

1   Owing to this supposed supernatural nature they are used for divining purposes.
2   Ed. A. has 汙 instead of 汗.
3   A famous horse trainer, see Ch. 65 n. 1.
4   The well known charioteer.
5   That depends on circumstances.
6   This is no reason.
7   Cf. Ch. 38 n. 36.
8   See Ch. 54 n. 7.
9   This seems to have been the vice of Chinese officials from time immemorial.
10   See p. I.195.
11   All good things require time, therefore the progress of able scholars is slower than that of common officials. The former are like the hard-wood trees, big vessels, or precious merchandise, the latter correspond to the maple and varnish trees, the paper-mulberry, fruit and vegetables. They advance very quickly, but the stuff they are made of is not very valuable.
12   They are heavier and of greater moment.
13   The text is not very clear. The simile is illustrated by the next clause, where unprincipled governors are likened to a wild current and a strong gale.
14   *I.e.*, fair and honest.
15   Strong men.
16   Swiftness alone, in our case a quick promotion, is not a sign of superiority.
17   The sacred unicorn is not as quick as the worthless locusts.
18   It is sent as a tribute, and does not arrive of its own accord.
19   The four sacred animals are outrun by many ordinary ones.
20   The surname of Tai Gong 太公. Ch. 64 n. 101.
21   Famous character of the 7th cent. BCE p. I.293.
22   Very old people whose white hair has already become yellowish.

23　See Ch. 26 n. 43.

24　Great haste is not always an advantage, for it may spoil everything.

25　Ordinary functionaries, of course, are compared to withered organisms. Being much lighter than those full of sap *viz.* men of learning, they are much more easily moved about.

26　Like peasants with their bags of grain, students with their learning betake themselves to town, but the high officers do not care to admit them, so that their learning is of no practical use to them.

CHAPTER 41

On Heat and Cold
Hanwen 寒温

(*Lunheng* Book XIV, Chap. ii)

1　Yan 燕, Zhao 趙, Han 韓, Wei 魏, Qi 齊 and Chu 楚, which in 332 BCE made an offensive and defensive alliance to check the encroachments of the Qin 秦 State, but by and by the latter overpowered and absorbed them all.

2　According to ancient natural philosophy. Consequently temperature cannot be the result of the feelings of the sovereign.

3　A quotation from *Huainanzi* 淮南子 III, 2, with a slight variation of the text.

4　Therefore during a drought clay figures of dragons are set up and worshipped to attract the rain. Cf. Ch. 47.

5　*Viz.* with the body.

6　Cf. Ch. 3 n. 22.

7　An attraction between joy and heat, anger and cold.

8　Qin Shi Huangdi 秦始皇.

9　When Zou Yan 鄒衍, a scholar of the 4th cent. BCE, had been put into prison upon a trumped up charge, he looked up to heaven and wept. All of a sudden snow began to fall, although it was midsummer. See also p. II.471.

10 A class of scholars, often mentioned in the *Lunheng*, who seem to have devoted themselves to the study of natural phenomena and calamities, such as heat and cold, inundations, droughts, famines, etc. to which, however, they did not ascribe natural, but moral causes, misled by the pseudo-science of the *Yijing* 易經 and similar works.

11 Of which the Chinese distinguish 24, beginning with *lichun* 立春 "commencement of spring." They count from the days on which the sun enters the first and fifteenth degree of one of the zodiacal signs.

12 They are all natural phenomena.

13 *Shangshu* 尚書, *Hongfan* 洪範 Pt. V, Bk. IV, 31 (Legge, *Classics* Vol. III, Pt. II, p. 340).

14 Jing Fang 京房, a metaphysician of the 1st cent. BCE, who spent much labour on the elucidation of the *Yijing*.

15 Marked by broken and unbroken lines.

16 The 25th hexagram of the *Yijing*.

17 Quotation from the *Yijing*, 1st diagram (Qian 乾). Cf. p. II.559-60 and II.467.

CHAPTER 42

On Reprimands

Qiangao 譴告

(*Lunheng* Book XIV, Chap. iii)

1 836–826 BCE.

2 Who explain natural phenomena by transcendent causes.

3 The grandfather of Wen Wang 文王, the founder of the Zhou 周 dynasty.

4 Cf. p. I.144.

5 The first and the second of the five ancient notes of the Chinese gamut.

6 *Shangshu* 尚書 Part V, Bk. X, 2 (Legge, *Classics* Vol. III, Pt. II, p. 399) cf. Ch. 25.

7 The Qi 齊 State in Shandong 山東.

8 Yan Ying 晏嬰, an official of Qi, noted for his thrifty habits, died 493 BCE.

9   So small was the offering.

10   A younger brother of Zhou Gong 周公, the first Duke of Wei 衛.

11   A son of Zhou Gong and his successor in the dukedom of Lu 魯.

12   A minister of Wu Wang 武王.

13   The lofty pine and the low Rottlera tree are emblems of father and son.

14   The 3rd diagram.

15   The 58th diagram.

16   In the terminology of the *Yijing* 易經.

17   Filth in a metaphorical sense.

18   The first advice of course. Bad odour can be removed by its contrary, perfumes, but not by more stench.

19   A Worthy of the 5th century BCE (Giles, *Biogr. Dict.* N. 678).

20   Another famous character of old (Giles, *Biogr. Dict.* N. 2088). Giles gives another version of the peculiarities of the two gentlemen regarding their belts. Cf. Ch. 8.

21   612–589 BCE.

22   658–619 BCE.

23   The music of these two States was considered licentious, and most objectionable.

24   In the *Shangshu*, Lüxing 呂刑 Pt. V, Bk. XXVII, 5 (Legge, *Classics* Vol. III, Pt. II, p. 593) King Mu 穆 uses these words with reference to Huang Di 黃帝, who in this manner repressed the lawlessness of the Miaozi 苗子.

25   *Shangshu*, Yi Ji 益稷 Pt. II, Bk. IV, 1.

26   *Shangshu*, Wu Yi 無逸 Pt. V, Bk. XV, 13 (Legge, *Classics* Vol. III, Pt. II, p. 471).

27   Xiao Wu 孝武帝 = Han Wu Di 漢武帝, 140–86 BCE.

28   A distinguished scholar and poet.

29   The Emperor Han Wu Di was infatuated with alchemy, and the magical arts taught by the Daoists.

30   Xiao Cheng 孝成帝 = Han Cheng Di 漢成帝, 32–6 BCE.

31   The philosopher Yang Xiong 揚雄, a philosopher of note of the Confucian school, 53 BCE–18 CE.

32   A celebrated palace near Xi'anfu 西安府 (Chang'an 長安) originally founded by Qin Shi Huangdi 秦始皇.

33   Two high officers of the 2nd cent. BCE. Cf. Ch. 65.

34   Cf. p. I.144.

35   Aborigines in modern Jiangsu 江蘇.

36   In 100 BCE Su Wu 蘇武 was sent as envoy to the Xiongnu 匈奴, who kept him prisoner for about nineteen years. Though the Xiongnu made every endeavour to win him over to their cause, he never threw off his

allegiance to the Han 漢, wherefore he is praised as a paragon of loyalty.

37 Only a barbarian would button his coat on the left side, a Chinaman will button it on the right.

38 A famous general of the 2nd cent. BCE, who subjugated the southern barbarians, and subsequently became their king. (Cf. Ch. 8.)

39 Aborigines in Canton province.

40 Cf. Ch. 8.

41 Two brothers of Zhou Gong and of Wu Wang, who attempted to deprive their nephew Cheng Wang 成王 of the throne, but their rebellion was put down by Zhou Gong.

42 A new law was enacted in the 4th year of the Emperor Xuan Di 宣帝 (70 CE), by which descendants concealing their ascendants, and wives hiding their husbands guilty of a crime, were to be acquitted, whereas ascendants and husbands doing the same for their sons and wives, had to suffer capital punishment. Descendants were no doubt under a moral obligation to help their ascendants under any circumstances, but the same moral law did not exist for ascendants towards their sons. (Cf. *Qianhanshu* 前漢書 chap. 8, p. 11.)

43 Which begins in November.

44 In 34 BCE Gu Zi Yun 谷子雲 = Gu Yong 谷永 attributed an eclipse and an earth-quake to the excessive favour shown by the emperor to the ladies of his seraglio. He wrote many memorials against the abuses of the palace.

45 Cf. p. II.461.

46 The planet Mercury.

47 The stars Beta, Delta, Pi, and Nun, in the head of Scorpio.

48 The stars Antares, Sigma, and Tau, in the heart of Scorpio.

49 Cf. p. I.83.

50 A Daoist rhyme; quoted from the *Lüshi chunqiu* 呂氏春秋. See also *Huainanzi* 淮南子 XVII, 1v: "He who hears the sounding sound is deaf, but he who hears the soundless sound is quick at hearing."

51 The Daoists despise the natural organs: the eye, the ear, the mouth, and pretend to see with a spiritual eye, to hear with a spiritual ear, etc.

52 *Yijing* 易經, 1st diagram (Qian 乾).

53 The son of Dan Fu 亶父 (cf. p. II.460).

54 We now speak of the Five Classics: *Yijing, Shangshu, Shijing* 詩經, *Liji* 禮記, and *Chunqiu* 春秋. During the Han period the "Book of Music" was added, ranking as the fifth Classic before the *Chunqiu*, bringing up the number to six.

55 *Shangshu, Shundian* 舜典 Pt. II, Bk. I, 2 (Legge, *Classics*, Vol. III, Pt. I,

p. 32) According to the commentators this passage means that Shun 舜 received the empire from Yao 堯 before the shrine of the latter's ancestor, who thus might be regarded as the donor.

56　*Vid.* p. I.146–47.

57　We read in the *Shangshu, Hongfan* 洪範 Pt. V, Bk. IV, 3 (Legge, *Classics* Vol. III, Pt. II, p. 323) "Gun 鯀 dammed up the inundating waters, and thereby threw into disorder the arrangement of the Five Elements. God was thereby roused to anger."

CHAPTER 43
Phenomenal Changes
Biandong 變動

(*Lunheng* Book XV, Chap. i)

1　In Ch. 42, which in the *Lunheng* precedes Ch. 43.

2　A famous charioteer (cf. p. I.101).

3　A one-legged bird said to portend rain.

4　Cheerfulness, anger, grief, joy, love, and hatred. It is more common to speak of Seven Passions. They are the same as those given above, but joy is replaced by fear, and desire is added.

5　*Shiji* 史記 chap. 27, p. 34v. The "Celestial Governors" are the sun, the moon, and the planets. The passage referred to here speaks of 8 winds, however, and their attributes are different from those given by Wang Chong.

6　Heaven could not purposely act against the laws of nature, by which the vegetation grows in spring, and fades in winter.

7　Cf. p. II.466 and *Shiji* chap. 27, p. 27v.

8　546–488 BCE.

9　We learn from *Huainanzi* 淮南子 XII, 22r quoted in *Lunheng* IV, 13 (*Bianxu* 變虛 Ch. 17) that Yan Zi 晏子 told the Great Diviner that the earth-quake would take place, because the "Hook" star was between the constellations of the "House" and the "Heart," whereupon the Great Diviner confessed to the duke that the earth would shake, but that it would not be his doing (cf. p. II.466).

10   *I.e.* man. The ancient Chinese foot was much smaller than the one now in use.

11   Cf. Ch. 41.

12   On officer of the Qi 齊 State, who was slain in a battle against the Ju 莒 State (cf. *Mencius* Book VI, Pt. II chap. 6).

13   The "Elegies of Chu 楚" comprising the *Lisao* 離騷 and some other poems of Qu Yuan 屈原 and his contemporaries, all plaintive pieces referring to Qu Yuan's disgrace.

14   King Huai 懷 of Chu 327–294 BCE, King Qing Xiang 頃襄 294–261 BCE. Qu Yuan committed suicide in 294 BCE.

15   King Wu 武 reigned from 739–688 BCE. His predecessor is called Xiong Xuan 熊眴 (756–739 BCE) in the *Shiji* 史記, not Li 厲.

16   Bian He 卞和 was taken for an impostor, and first sentenced to have his left foot cut off. When he presented the stone, a second time, his right foot was cut off. At last the genuineness of the jade-stone was discovered.

17   Cf. p. I.236.

18   A eunuch, who together with Li Si 李斯 caused the death of Fu Su 扶蘇, eldest son of Qin Shi Huangdi 秦始皇, and under Hu Hai 胡亥 usurped all power. In 207 BCE he was assassinated by order of Zi Ying 子嬰, son of Fu Su 扶蘇.

19   Cf. p. I.232–33.

20   The grandfather of Meng Tian 蒙恬, also a general of Shi Huangdi 始皇帝.

21   Cf. p. I.95 and p. I.232.

22   The chapter on Punishments in the *Shangshu* 尚書, now entitled Lüxing 呂刑.

23   *Shangshu*, Lüxing 呂刑, Pt. V, Bk. XXVII, 4 (Legge, *Classics* Vol. III, Pt. II, p. 592).

24   The Zhou 周 epoch. The Zhou calendar began with the 11th month, the Qin 秦 calendar with the 10th. In 104 BCE Han Wu Di 漢武帝 corrected the calendar, and made the year commence with the 1st month, so the Zhou were 2 months ahead with their months.

25   A native of Wei 魏 of humble origin, who first served under Xu Jia 須賈, and accompanied him on a mission to the court of King Xiang 襄 of Qi 齊 (696–683 BCE). This prince appreciating Fan Ju 范雎 for his great dialectical skill, sent him some presents. Xu Jia presuming that Fan Ju had betrayed some State secrets of Wei, denounced his servant to the premier of Wei, Wei Qi 魏齊, who had him beaten almost to death. Fan Ju was then

wrapped in a mat, and thrown into a privy, where the drunken guests uri-
nated upon him. Still he managed to escape, and later on became minister
in Qin.

26 Also a native of the Wei State from a poor family, who played a very important political rôle in Qin and Wei. In his youth, he was suspected in
Chu of having stolen a valuable gem, and severely beaten. Died 310 BCE.

27 *Shiji* chap. 79 and 70.

28 Prince Dan 丹 of Yan 燕 was detained as a hostage in the Qin State. Its
sovereign promised with an oath to set him free, when the sun returned
to the meridian, and Heaven rained grain, when the crows got white
heads, and the horses, horns, and when the wooden elephants, decorating the kitchen door, got legs of flesh. Heaven helped the prince, and
brought about these wonders, when Dan 丹 was released, or, as others
say, he made his escape in 230 BCE. The story is narrated in *Lunheng*
(*Ganxu* 感虛 Ch. 19).

29 The same is said of Xin Yuan Ping 新垣平 (*Shiji* chap. 28 p. 19v).

30 A city in Henan 河南.

31 456–424 BCE.

32 A faithful servant of the Emperor Han Wu Di 漢武帝, who appointed
him Regent for his minor son, Zhao Di 昭帝. He died in 68 BCE. His
family was mixed up in a palace intrigue aiming at the deposition of the
reigning emperor, which was discovered, when all the members of his
family were exterminated.

33 Instead of Qi 杞, an old feudal State in Henan 河南, we ought probably to
read 齊, the name of the Qi 齊 State in Shandong 山東, of which Qi Liang
杞梁 was a native.

34 We learn from the *Zuozhuan* 左氏傳, Duke Xiang 襄 23rd year (550 BCE)
(Legge, *Classics* Vol. V, Pt. II, p. 504) and from the *Liji* 禮記, Tan Gong 檀
弓 Pt. III, 1 (Legge, *Sacred Books* Vol. XXVII, p. 188) that, when the bier
of Qi Liang was brought home to Qi 齊, the Marquis of Qi, Zhuang 莊,
sent an officer to present his condolences, but the widow declined them,
because the road was not the proper place to accept condolences. The
marquis then sent them to her house. The "Prince of Lu 魯" of our text is
probably a misprint, for why should the Prince of Lu condole in Qi?

35 The *Lienüzhuan* 列女傳 relates that Qi Liang's wife cried seven days over
her husband's corpse under the city wall, until it collapsed, and then died
by jumping into a river.

36 Cf. Ch. 25 and 26.

37 Cf. p. II.473.

38   Yu Rang 豫讓, a native of the Jin 晉 State, who made an unsuccessful attempt on the life of Viscount Xiang 襄 of Zhao 趙, who had killed his master, Earl Zhi 知. *Vid.* Ch. 22.

39   A minister of Zhao.

40   A place in the prefecture of Shundefu 順德府 (Zhili 直隸).

41   This attempt on the life of Han Gao Zu 漢高祖 in 199 BCE was frustrated.

42   The star Cor Hydra, mentioned in the *Shangshu* 尚書 (cf. Legge, *Classics* Vol. III, Pt. I, p. 19.)

43   The "Tail" is a constellation consisting of nine stars in the tail of Scorpio, the 6th of the 28 Solar Mansions.

CHAPTER 44
[Attracting Consequences]
Zhaozhi 招致

(*Lunheng* Book XV, Chap. ii)

1   [QP note on lost chapter: still lost at present time of publication, 2023.]

CHAPTER 45
On the Rain Sacrifice
Mingyu 明雩
(*Lunheng* Book XV, Chap. iii)

1   The *Taiping yulan* 太平御覽 chap. 11, p. 2v. quotes this passage but in a different form. The rule, here expressed, refers only to the time of general peace: 太平之時,五日一風,十日一雨.

2   A minister of Yue 越, cf. p. I.141.

3   子 = Aries, right north. Cf. the passage *Shiji* 史記 chap. 129, p. 3v.

4   According to Fan Li 范蠡, floods and droughts depend on the position of the planet Jupiter, whereas the phenomenalists believe these phenomena to be caused by the conduct of the sovereign. The passage of the *Shiji* seems defective.

5   大雩.

6   Cf. Ch. 32 n. 58 and 59.

7   Three ways for the sun and the moon passing this constellation. They either continue their course, without deviating from the original direction, or they turn to the left or the right. Revert they cannot, else there might be four ways.

8   Certain regions of the sky are supposed to correspond to certain countries on the earth. The moon, wandering through the sky, is not connected with any places of our planet, and a sign for the whole world.

9   The *Peiwen yunfu* 佩文韻府 quotes this passage, chap. 66a, under 雨具.

10   407–377 BCE.

11   Sorcerers are believed to be filled with the *Yang* 陽 fluid. Cf. Ch. 65 n. 29.

12   Culled from the *Liji* 禮記 (*Tangong* 檀弓 p. 80), Legge, *Sacred Books* Vol. XXVII, p. 201, where three days instead of five is written.

13   In the *Chunqiu* 春秋 the great rain sacrifice is frequently mentioned.

14   Only a son or a grandson may sacrifice to his ancestors.

15   Therefore Dong Zhongshu 董仲舒 raised a hill for his sacrifice. A sacrifice from the low earth would be as unacceptable to Heaven as an offering from collateral descendants to a deceased.

16 Cf. p. I.381.

17 Cf. Ch. 9 n. 33.

18 Cf. p. I.390.

19 See Ch. 55 n. 4.

20 Ed. B: 召和醫藥者, ed. A and C: 召毉和藥者.

21 A garment of the deceased is used, that the soul may slip into it and return. This custom is very old. The three Rituals: *Liji*, *Yili* 儀禮, and *Zhouli* 周禮 give minute prescriptions about it. They are found in De Groot, *Religious System* Vol. I, p. 243 seq. in a special chapter "Calling back the soul of the dead."

22 鄸 Cf. Ch. 60 n. 22.

23 物. Our text of the *Shangshu* 尚書 has 勿.

24 Quoted from the *Shangshu* Part V, Book XIX, 16–17 (Legge, *Classics* Vol. III, Part II, p. 518). To the first part of this clause Legge gives quite a different interpretation: "And let us never allow others to come between us and them. Yea, in our every word and speech let us be thinking ...."

25 827–782 BCE.

26 76–83 CE.

27 According to the *Chunqiu* 春秋 Lu 魯 had to suffer great dryness in the second and in the tenth year of Duke Wen 文 *i.e.*, in 625 and 617 BCE.

28 A scholar and officer of Lu.

29 Legge translates: "enjoy the breeze among the rain altars." See Note 9.

30 Legge: "and return home singing."

31 *Analects* XI, 25, VII. Cf. p. II.759. I had to remodel my translation of the first volume, borrowed from Legge, in order to agree with Wang Chong's comments.

32 冠者童子雩祭樂人也.

33 Legge has "to wash," adding in his notes that this word 浴 is used with reference to a custom of washing the hands and clothes at some stream, to drive away evil influences.

34 Wang Chong here writes 詠而饋, apparently indentifying 歸 and 饋.

35 Cf. Ch. 43 n. 24.

36 *Zuozhuan* 左氏傳 to Duke Huan 桓 5th year. See also p. II.759.

37 Legge puts quite a different construction upon the words of Zuo Qiu Ming 左邱明 *loc. cit.* See *Classics* Vol. V, Part I, p. 46, Note 7.

38 Cf. *Analects* XII, 21.

39 A strange argument.

40 Ed. A 苔 for 答.

41 Jewels and brocade are offered in sacrifice, and bells and drums sounded.

The *Liji, Yueling* 月令, p. 50v. (Legge, *Sacred Books* Vol. XXVII, p. 274) states that the instruments of music are employed at the great summer sacrifice for rain.

42　博士之官.

43　Wang Chong seems to imply that he acts like the scholars of great learning, that his criticisms do not exceed the right measure, but are necessary to bring out the truth.

44　Our author, obviously, claims to be such a disciple.

CHAPTER 46
Gentle Drums
Shungu 順鼓
(*Lunheng* Book XV, Chap. iv)

1　Quoted from the *Chunqiu* 春秋, Duke Zhuang 莊 25th year.

2　I suppose that *Yin* 陰 should be written here, for at times of great floods the *Yin*, and not the *Yang* 陽 fluid preponderates. See below p. II.494 seq.

3　繆螯 [QP: for 螯 original has 夂 rather than the 攵 variant, somewhat akin to 螯]. Williams writes the last character 鰲 [QP: for 鰲 original has a variant with 幺 atop 幸], *Kangxi* 康熙 and Couvreur 鰲, Giles 鰲 [QP: for 鰲 original has a variant with 幺 atop 辛 akin to 鰲 but 辛 rather than 幸].

4　It would be improper to hurt the sacred body of Earth, by attacking the spirits of the land, merely for the sake of the various things injured by an inundation. Neither Heaven nor Earth are materially affected by floods.

5　Cf. p. I.381.

6　Heaven is *Yang* and Earth is *Yin* and so far the kindred of water which is *Yin* also.

7　Mountains and water of course, the parents and the progeny of rain as Wang Chong puts it.

8　Therefore earth and water should not be interchanged, nor earth be made responsible for inundations.

9　See p. II.565 seq.

10 For more details on this peculiar custom see Ch. 49.

11 Cf. p. II.499 and *Huainanzi* 淮南子 III, 2r.: 陽燧見日則燃而為火,方諸見月則津而為水.

12 Cf. p. II.479.

13 See p. I.373.

14 Cf. p. I.130.

15 尚書大傳, so ed. C. Ed. A writes 太傳, ed. B 天傳. It is a work written by Fu Sheng 伏勝, the preserver of the *Shangshu* 尚書 of the 2nd and 3rd cent. BCE. Cf. Ch. 81 n. 2, and Giles, *Bibl. Dict.* No. 599. According to Zhang Zhidong's 張之洞 Bibliography the work is still in existence.

16 天公.

17 人公.

18 地公.

19 三公. This expression usually denotes the three chief ministers of the Zhou 周 dynasty: 太師 Grand Tutor, 太傅 Grand Assistant, and 太保 Grand Protector, mentioned in the *Shangshu* Part V, Book XX, 5 (Legge, *Classics* Vol. III, Part II, p. 527). The titles given to them in the *Shangshu dazhuan* 尚書大傳: minister of Heaven, of Men, and of Earth, seem not to occur elsewhere; the *Peiwen yunfu* 佩文韻府 ignores them. They bear some resemblance to the 天官 "officer of Heaven" and the 地官 "officer of Earth" of the *Zhouli* 周禮, who have been identified with the 冢宰 "prime minister" and the 司徒 "minister of Instruction" of the *Shangshu*. Cf. Legge, *loc. cit.* p. 528, Notes 7 and 8.

20 In his commentary to the above quoted passage of the *Chunqiu* 春秋, Gongyang 公羊 says that the ceremony was correct.

21 春秋説, apparently a work on the *Chunqiu*, but not enumerated in the Catalogue of the *Houhanshu* 後漢書.

22 Gongyang *loc. cit.* refers to this custom and gives a similar explanation as here given.

23 Ed. A and C: 若, ed. B: 猶.

24 Cf. p. I.248–49.

25 The struggle between Xiang Yu 項羽 who had made himself King of Chu 楚 and Liu Bang 劉邦, the later Han Gao Zu 漢高祖.

26 水病.

27 See below p. II.496.

28 The suggestion that Nü Wa 女媧 should be sacrificed to.

29 攻, the same word which in the foregoing discussions is used in the sense of attacking.

30 *Analects* XI, 16. Cf. p. I.392.

31 The objection that 攻 should be taken in the sense of "attack" in the passage of the *Analects*, as it must be understood in regard to the struggles of the Six States.

32 The word 攻, used concerning the high water sacrifice, cannot be explained by scolding or reproving.

33 Men are mean, compared with the spirits of the land, whom they are supposed to attack.

34 Now gongs are used for the same purpose.

35 This custom is mentioned in the above quoted passage of the *Chunqiu*.

36 筊. Neither *Kangxi* 康熙 nor the *Zhengzitong* 正字通 know this character. It is perhaps a misprint for 筊, a fife or a shrill pipe used to exhort people to work, as the dictionaries say.

37 In 506 BCE.

38 A grandson of a ruler of Chu 楚. See Giles, *Bibl. Dict.* No. 1697.

39 間步 which is paraphrased by: 步行而伺間隙以去.

40 Quotation from the *Liji* 禮記. Cf. Ch. 11 n. 25.

41 Therefore Yao's 堯 not immolating does not tell against the later custom.

42 Cf. p. I.357.

CHAPTER 47
A Last Word on Dragons
Luanlong 亂龍

(*Lunheng* Book XVI, Chap. i)

1 This chapter is not to the credit of our author, who here shows himself as credulous and unjudicious as those of his countrymen whose superstitions he likes to expose.

2 See Ch. 22 n. 25.

3 A contemporary of Confucius of the name of Zi Gao 子高, mentioned in *Zhuangzi* 莊子 (Giles' translation p. 45). She 葉 was a district of Chu 楚.

4 The duke was so fond of dragons, that, in his residence, he had many

dragon ornaments carved. The heavenly dragon, hearing of it, once made its appearance, looking through the window and dragging its tail through the hall. By this unexpected aspect the duke was frightened out of his wits. 孔子集語 *Kongzi jiyu* I, 2v. quoting 申子 Shen Zi.

5   Cf. Ch. 41 n. 3.

6   p. I.241 seq.

7   Cf. Ch. 23 n. 17.

8   頓牟. See on amber the learned paper of B. Laufer, Historical Jottings on Amber in Asia (Memoirs of the American Anthropological Association Vol. I, Part 3, 1907) who refers to this passage as the first literary mention of amber in China. The words quoted by Laufer p. 218, Note 3: "*dunmou* 頓牟 is identical with *hupo* 琥珀 = amber" does not occur in the *Lunheng* 論衡, and must be a gloss.

9   磁石.

10   Son of Liu Xiang 劉向, more generally known under the name of Liu Xin 劉歆, a celebrated scholar like his father. He lived in the 1st cent. BCE and CE and was a protege of Wang Mang 王莽. His studies included the *Yijing* 易經 and occult arts.

11   Quoted from *Huainanzi* 淮南子 III, 2r.

12   伎道之家.

13   *Vid.* p. II.491.

14   Cf. p. I.116.

15   See p. II.793.

16   The *Peiwen yunfu* 佩文韻府 quotes this passage but slightly altered.

17   It is strange that a man as critical as Wang Chong should believe such a story.

18   Cf. *Shangshu* 尚書 Part II, Book I, 2 (Legge, *Classics* Vol. III, Part I, p. 32).

19   Cf. p. I.295 seq.

20   In p. I.295–96 Wang Chong denies that these tripods had any supernatural forces.

21   磁石鉤.

22   The purport of this somewhat misty argument seems to be that a clay image must suffice for clouds and rain, just as images and omens are correlates of spirits.

23   Cf. Ch. 65 n. 16.

24   Cf. Ch. 26 n. 16 and 17, and *Huainanzi* 淮南子 XI, 14v.

25   A general of Han Jing Di 漢景帝, who in 142 BCE made an attack upon the Xiongnu 匈奴. He was a man of great courage and a stern character, who received the sobriquet 蒼鷹 "Grey Eagle." When he died a figure of

wood, resembling him, was carved and placed in view of the Xiongnu at Yanmen 雁門. They shot at it, but, being too much afraid, did not hit it. This is the simple version of the *Shiji* 史記 (*Peiwen yunfu*), favourably contrasting with Wang Chong's mysticism.

26 Jin Mi Di 金日磾, styled Weng Shu 翁叔, the son of Xiu Chu 休屠, a khan of the Xiongnu, was first made a government slave and afterwards raised to high honours, when he received a Chinese name. He died 86 BCE. See Giles, *Bibl. Dict.* No. 382.

27 The words of the text 休屠王閼提 give no sense. In the biography of Jin Mi Di 金日磾, *Hanshu* 漢書 chap. 68, p. 21r. the last two words are written 閼氏, the family name of the mother of Jin Mi Di, which should be inserted for the spurious 閼提.

28 A disciple of Confucius. Cf. p. II.517.

29 p. II.558.

30 The so called "spring ox" 春牛 already mentioned in the *Liji* 禮記. It used to be carried in procession during the last month of the year, to see the cold air off: 出土牛以送寒氣. This custom is still practised in many parts of China. See De Groot, *Fêtes a Emoui* p. 92 seq.

31 Cf. Ch. 75 n. 4.

32 They were used at funerals in ancient and modern times. The dead are supposed to make use of them. See *Liji, Tangong* 檀弓, p. 52r. (Legge, *Sacred Books* Vol. XXVII, p. 173) and also p. II.767.

33 This competition of archery was a great ceremony described in the *Liji, Yili* 儀禮, and *Zhouli* 周禮. The latter work also speaks of the various targets, but the wild beasts allotted to the emperor and his officers are different from those here given (Cf. Biot, Tscheou Li p. 138).

34 諸侯.

35 This explanation is mere fancy. Since the emperor took part in the shooting, one might as well say that the ceremony was meant as a warning for the emperor that he would be shot like a bear, in case he proved to be unprincipled.

36 So it is with dragons. They did not attract clouds and rain, as long as they were domesticated and always there, but their sudden and unexpected arrival has this effect. The clouds are touched, so to say, and then drop their tears.

CHAPTER 48

The Tiger Trouble
Zaohu 遭虎

(*Lunheng* Book XVI, Chap. ii)

1   功曹.
2   A hard judgment indeed.
3   The tiger represents the masculine principle *Yang* 陽.
4   Cf. Ch. 42 n. 48.
5   Cf. Ch. 14 n. 2.
6   A lady of the seraglio of Han Yuan Di 漢元帝, 1st cent. BCE, who once faced a bear that had escaped from its cage.
7   See Ch. 80 n. 82.
8   Government as a whole could be bad, even though the local officials were good.
9   The three noble families, Meng 孟, Shu 叔, and Ji 季 which in the time of Confucius were the real rulers of Lu 魯, the reigning duke being more or less dependent upon them.
10   The catching of fish is what Wang Chong denotes by "destruction in the water," and the hunting of animals what he calls the "fluid, *i.e.* destructive, on the hills."
11   Remaining in their own places, where the destructive fluid of mountain forests *viz.* tigers do not intrude, people would be safe.
12   Cf. Ch. 7 n. 3.
13   蜼玃.
14   閩虽. Cf. Ch. 19 n. 73.
15   The barbarians living towards the four Quarters of China.
16   The savages in the south and the west, here meaning savages in general.
17   Provided that there be always a correspondence between the doings of tigers and high commissioners.
18   The *Hanshu* 漢書 relates that, when the kings of Guangling 廣陵 and Yan 燕 were going to stir up an insurrection, rats were observed dancing in their palaces. Even with us rats are credited with some kind of prescience,

for we say that rats leave a ship which is going to be wrecked.

19 For this reason they are visited by tigers.

20 Fate is looked upon as something material of which there may be greater or smaller quantities.

21 Cf. p. I.196.

22 Cf. Ch. 51 n. 36.

23 King Huai 懷 of Liang 梁 in Henan 河南 was a son of the Emperor Wen Di 文帝. He died in 169 BCE.

24 A place in Shandong 山東.

25 A celebrated official of the 2nd and 1st cent. BCE.

26 The modern Dingzhou 定州 in Zhili 直隸.

27 Originally a poor scholar, later on a privy councillor of the Emperor Han Wu Di 漢武帝, who died in 121 BCE.

28 The present Laizhoufu 萊州府 in the province of Shandong.

29 A circuit in Jiangsu 江蘇 and Anhui 安徽.

CHAPTER 49

Remarks on Insects
Shangchong 商蟲

(*Lunheng* Book XVI, Chap. iii)

1 In 594 BCE Duke Xuan 宣 introduced a new tithing system. Cf. *Chunqiu* 春秋, Duke Xuan 15th year. Zuo Qiu Ming 左邱明 condemns this measure as contrary to rule. The locusts are regarded by Wang Chong as a retribution for this unjust mode of taxation.

2 55 CE.

3 The present Tai'anzhou 泰安州 in Shandong 山東.

4 A circuit comprising the modern Kaifengfu 開封府 in Henan 河南.

5 Henanfu 河南府.

6 Therefore the locusts could not be considered a punishment for unjust taxation.

7   For those offences for which the insects are supposed to have made their appearance.

8   This explanation is forced and certainly erroneous. It would be to the point, if the character 風 designated some insects, and not wind, for to whom would the two components "all" and "insects" suggest the idea of wind? The explanation given by Wieger, Rudiments 12, Leçons etymologiques p. 77 is not satisfactory either. He submits that the ancient character was composed of 日 sun, 丿 movement, and 凡 expansion, and that this combination suggests the atmospheric currents produced by the action of the sunbeams. I suppose that in the character 凡 is the phonetic, and 虫 the radical. 虫 is a crawling animal, a reptile, and describes the crawling, the undulating of the currents of air. Some ancient forms of 風 are formed of 巛, a current, instead of 虫, a reptile, and from the antique form *fig. A* we infer that 日 and 丿, occurring in other characters, were originally connected, *fig. B*, and are nothing else than a viper with a big head, a synonym for 虫 a reptile = *fig. C*.

A   *B*   *C*

9   A method still followed to the present day.

10   A recluse of the Zhou 周 epoch, celebrated for his purity. Zi Gong 子貢 is said to have blamed him for living in a country the government of which he condemned, and under a prince whom he despised. Bao Jiao 鮑焦 took these words so much to heart, that he withered up into dead wood.

11   Another hermit. Cf. Ch. 30 n. 41.

12   蝸疽. My translation is a conjecture. Perhaps the latter character "an ulcer" is spurious.

13   I have omitted translating 蠍, some insect or reptile not mentioned in the dictionaries.

14   When a man passes through marshes, leeches may stick to his feet, and suck his blood.

15   蠕 for which the dictionaries only give the meaning "to wriggle." Here it must be a substantive.

16   *Shijing* 詩經 Part II, Book VII, Ode V (Legge, *Classics* Vol IV, Part II, p. 394)

17   This story is narrated in the biography of the King of Changyi 昌邑, *Qianhanshu* 前漢書, chap. 63, p. 18r. The king was a grandson of the Emperor Han Wu Di 漢武帝.

CHAPTER 50
Arguments on Ominous Creatures
Jiangrui 講瑞
(*Lunheng* Book XVI, Chap. iv)

1   The last paragraph of the *Chunqiu* 春秋, Duke Ai 哀 14th year, merely mentions the capture of a *lin* [ǫꟼ 麟 or 驎]. That it was a deer with one horn is recorded in the "Family Sayings" of Confucius. See Legge's transl. Vol. II, p. 834, Note.

2   73–48 BCE.

3   Cf. p. I.135.

4   The usurper.

5   A political adventurer, cf. p. II.473-74.

6   An enlightened sovereign, cf. p. I.229.

7   Disciple of Confucius.

8   Cf. p. I.135.

9   Huan Tan 桓譚 = Huan Jun Shan 桓君山 lived in the 1st cent. BCE and CE. He was a man of wide learning. Of his works the "Xinlun 新論" "New Reflections" have been preserved.

10 The Confucian philosopher, cf. p. I.155 [ǫꟼ dubious ref. see index].

11 Shao Zheng Mao 少正卯, a high officer of Lu 魯, was later on executed by Confucius for high treason, when Confucius was assistant-minister (*Shiji* 史記 chap. 47, p. 9v.). Some say that Shaozheng 少正 is the official title and Mao 卯 the cognomen. Shaozheng might mean a sub-director, or an assistant-judge. (Cf. *Huainanzi* 淮南子 XIII, 22 comm.) See also Chavannes, *Mem. Hist.* Vol. V, p. 326, Note 7.

12 Cf. Ch. 25 n. 35.

13 Acridotheres cristatellus.

14 *Vid.* p. II.516.

15 *Shangshu* 尚書, *Yiji* 益稷 Pt. II, Bk. IV, 9 (Legge, *Classics* Vol. III, Pt. I, p. 88).

16 This must be the name of an ancient work.

17 73–48 BCE.

18 A locality in Shanxi 陝西 province.

19   The princes of Xin Ling 信陵 and of Meng Chang 孟嘗, cf. Ch. 26.

20   *Vid.* p. I.138–39.

21   A celebrated commander, who gained many brilliant victories over the Xiongnu 匈奴. Died 117 BCE.

22   Cf. p. I.234.

23   25–58 CE.

24   32–6 BCE.

25   6 BCE–1 CE.

26   530–515 BCE.

27   9 BCE–23 CE.

28   In modern Anhui 安徽.

29   A propitious bird which appeared to Wu Wang 武王, cf. p. I.143.

30   The felicitous plant, "*mingjia*" 蓂莢, was found in the court-yard of the Emperor Yao 堯. With the waxing moon it grew one now leaf every day, with the waning moon one leaf dropped every day.

31   越常. In Ch. 26 we read Yueshang 越裳, which were a people near the Annanese frontier.

32   See above p. II.517.

33   Zhang Tang 張湯 lived at the beginning of the 1st cent. CE. *Vid.* Ch. 56.

34   Zeng Zi 曾子, the well known disciple of Confucius, cf. p. I.230.

35   Cf. Ch. 24 n. 20.

36   *I.e.* "Yellow Stone."

37   The favourite consort of the Emperor You Wang 幽王, 781–771 BCE.

38   On this legend, see p. I.164–65.

39   Fan Wenzi 范文子 and Zhonghang Zhaozi 中行昭子, cf. p. II.657.

40   The mother of Xie 契, the ancestor of the Yin 殷 dynasty swallowed an egg dropped by a swallow, and thereupon conceived. Cf. p. I.162.

41   The mother of Great Yu 禹 is said to have conceived after having eaten pearl-barley. See p. I.162.

42   *Vid.* p. I.162.

43   There is no chapter on omens, "Ruiming 瑞命," in the *Liji* 禮記 now.

44   A similar passage occurs in the Hanshi waizhuan 韓詩外傳 (*Taiping yulan* 太平御覽) 2nd cent. BCE.

45   *Shijing* 詩經 Pt. III, Bk. II, Ode VIII (Legge, *Classics* Vol. IV, Pt. II, p. 494).

46   China possesses several varieties of hornless deer.

47   A tribe in Annan.

48   Cf. p. II.472.

49   Style of the reign of the Emperor Ming Di 明帝, 58–76 CE.

50   Styles of the Emperor Zhang Di 章帝, 84–87 and 87–89 CE.

51　This chapter must have been written prior to 84 CE, so that the auspicious reign of the Emperor Zhang Di could not yet be referred to. The author made this addition later i.e. after 89 CE, for it was not before this year that the emperor received his posthumous title Xiao Zhang Di 孝章帝.

52　By the Five Birds perhaps the Five Phœnixes "Wu Feng 五鳳," five different kinds of phœnixes, which differ by their colours, are meant. The "Feng 鳳" is red, the "Yuanchu 鵷鶵" yellow, the "Luan 鸞" blue, the "Yuezhuo 鸑鷟" purple, and the "Gu 鵠" white. Whereas "Feng" and "Luan" are still used as names for the phœnix, one understands by "Yuan chu" a kind of peacock or pheasant, by "Yuezhuo" a kind of duck, and by "Gu" the snowgoose or swan.

CHAPTER 51
Thoughts on Omens
Zhirui 指瑞

(*Lunheng* Book XVII, Chap. i)

1　See Ch. 50.

2　Here again our author falls into his old error of exaggerating analogies. Two things may well be similar without agreeing in every feature. A sage animal must not necessarily adopt human ways, but might practise its sagehood in its own manner.

3　Their names are given in p. I.135.

4　Cf. Ch. 6 n. 28.

5　See Ch. 5 n. 12.

6　As has been said above, the phœnix and the unicorn are supposed to make their appearance in China, when there is a wise ruler, and the State is well governed. But then they must have intercourse with men, to learn what is going on among them.

7　See p. II.522–23.

8   All titles of the reign 年號 of the Han 漢 Emperor Xuan Di 宣帝, 73–49
    BCE *viz.* 五鳳 57 BCE, 神爵 61 BCE, 甘露 53 BCE, 黃龍 49 BCE. Perhaps
    just these names have given rise to all the fables about the appearance of
    there omens under the said emperor's reign.

9   A degree less than a Sage, cf. Ch. 80.

10 Duke Ai 哀, 14th year, the last paragraph of the *Chunqiu* 春秋.

11 Quotation from the 孔子家語 *Kongzi jiayu*, the "Family Sayings of Con-
    fucius" chap. 4, p. 8v., perhaps from the original work which existed prior
    to the Christian era, but the quotation agrees with the later work written
    in the 3rd century CE and generally regarded as spurious.

12 Duke Ai 哀, mentioned above in Note 5.

13 In the "Family Sayings" Confucius, upon being asked why he wept, says,
    "The lin comes only when there is an intelligent king. Now it has appeared
    when it is not the time for it to do so, and it has been injured. This is why
    I was so much affected." (Legge, *Classics* Vol. V, Part II, p. 834.) This reply
    seems to intimate that the times were so bad, that a unicorn arriving by
    mistake lost its life. The badness of the time and the consequent death of
    the sage animal elicited the tears of the Sage.

14 This passage is cited in the *Peiwen yunfu* 佩文韻府.

15 Again a wrong analogy.

16 That this conclusion is likewise wrong needs no proof.

17 The original fluid, the source of every life in the world. See p. II.576.

18 Cf. p. I.126.

19 That must be in the year 6 BCE, for Cheng Di 成帝 reigned from 32–6 BCE
    and Ai Di 哀帝 from 6 BCE to 1 CE.

20 See p. I.167 and II.522.

21 Propitious animals said to have appeared to Wen Wang 文王 and Wu
    Wang 武王. Cf. p. I.143.

22 See p. I.320.

23 A work of Fu Sheng 伏生, 3rd cent. BCE, who preserved the *Shangshu* 尚
    書. Cf. p. II.810.

24 Cf. *Shangshu*, Preface, 29 (Legge, *Classics* Vol. III, Part I, p. 7) and *Shiji* 史
    記 chap. 3, p. 9r. (Chavannes, *Mem. Hist.* Vol. I, p. 196) where Zu Yi 祖乙
    is called Zu Ji 祖己. Both texts differ in that Zu Ji gives another explana-
    tion of the arrival of the pheasant.

25 See p. II.527 — 五趾 has been translated by "five feet," but it might also
    mean "five toes" in one hoof, as the commentator of the *Hanshu* 漢書
    explains the expression 五蹄 in that work.

26 In p. II.527 I have translated 謁者 by "censor." It is better to render it

by "gentleman usher." (Cf. Chavannes, *Mem. Hist.* Vol. II, p. 516) In the *Hanshu*, Zhong Jun 終軍 is also called a 給事中, which means a censor.

27　The Chinese button their coats on the right side.

28　As the Chinese do.

29　Aborigines in Zhejiang 浙江.

30　All the above is quoted almost literally from the biography of Zhong Jun 終軍 in the *Hanshu* chap. 64b, p. 4v. seq.

31　According to ancient symbolism.

32　The old dynasties had each there own element with a corresponding colour by which they were believed to reign. All there ideas have sprung from the mystic theory about the elements. See Ch. 59 n. 34 and Appendix.

33　Cf. p. I.196.

34　A famous author of the 2nd cent. BCE. See Ch. 3 n. 16.

35　In Hunan 湖南, already a circuit under the Qin 秦 dynasty.

36　This incident has been described by Jia Yi 賈誼 himself in his celebrated poem in irregular verse 鵩鳥賦, of which we have a partial translation by W. A. P. Martin, Chinese Legends and other Poems, 1894, p. 32. The translator points out the remarkable parallels of this poem with the Raven of Edgar Allan Poe. The words of our text are culled from Jia Yi's poem, notably the oracle: 服鳥入室主人當去, where the poet writes 野鳥 and inserts a 兮 after 室. He tells us in the preface that he was living in exile as tutor to the Prince of Changsha 長沙. The ill omen had troubled him, for the place was low and damp, and he thought that he would not have long to live. In order to soothe his feelings, he composed the poem. The 西京雜記 *Xijing zaji*, quoted in the *Pianzileibian* 駢字類編 chap. 209, informs us that it was the popular belief in Changsha that the chief of the house visited by a screeching-owl was going to die. We have a similar superstition in Europe. In Germany the screeching-owl is a bird of ill omen likewise, whence its name "Toteneule."

37　Divination would give certain results, but they would not come to pass, there being no person fit to be affected by the omens thus playfully obtained.

38　A mountain in Shanxi 山西.

39　The child became unlucky. For further details *vid.* Ch. 16 n. 88.

CHAPTER 52
Auguries Verified
Shiying 是應
(*Lunheng* Book XVII, Chap. ii)

1   On these omens see p. II.522–23.

2   景星.

3   莲脯.

4   蓂莢.

5   屈軼.

6   山出車澤出舟. A parallel passage of the *Liji* 禮記 IV, 64r. (Legge, *Sacred Books* Vol. XXVII, p. 392) reads: 山出器車河出馬圖, which is its first part Legge supposes to allude to some unknown legend.

7   Quotation from *Liji* III, 31r. (Legge, *Sacred Books* Vol. XXVII, p. 244) where we read 斑白 in lieu of the 頒白 of our text also used in a parallel passage of *Mencius* I Part I, 7 (24). We further learn from the *Liji* that in ancient times men took the right side, and women the left side of the roads.

8   Quoted from a passage in Dong Zhongshu 董仲舒 referring to the time of universal peace, mentioned in the *Peiwen yunfu* 佩文韻府.

9   There must be some harmony, some sympathy between these phenomena and certain events.

10 The *Liji* does not speak of different roads, but of different sides of the roads.

11 Quoted from the *Diwang shiji* 帝王世紀 (*Peiwen yunfu*). The chief authority of the *Taiping yulan* 太平御覽 chap. 873 informs us that these "meat fans" grow like lotus, have many leaves and very thin stalks. Not only do they cool food and drinks, but also drive away or kill flies and other insects. They appeared in the times of Yao 堯 and Shun 舜.

12 冰室. The use of ice and of ice-houses is very old in China. The *Liji* alludes to it several times. (Cf. Legge, *Sacred Books* Vol. XXVII, p. 261 and 308, Vol. XXVIII, p. 423.)

13 Cf. Ch. 43 n. 28.

14　The five vows of the King of Qin 秦 who promised to liberate Prince Dan 丹 in case the afore-mentioned miracles took place.

15　莢.

16　The same description is given by the historian Ban Gu 班固 in his 白虎通 *Baihutong* (*Peiwen yunfu*). Another writer relates that this plant had round leaves and was multicoloured. He makes these leaves grow and drop instead of the capsules. In a short month of 29 days one leave shrinks, but does not fall. (*Taiping yulan* chap. 873.)

17　日曆, expression used by Ban Gu who seems to have believed in the monthly plant.

18　The name expressed by the sexagenary cycle, the usual way of counting days.

19　It would require a simple calculation, of which Chinese scholars are not fond. To find out the date, the difference of the remaining capsules with fifteen must be added to fifteen.

20　堂.

21　戶牖間.

22　扆.

23　See the plan of the imperial palace in Couvreur's dictionary p. 173 under 堂.

24　史官.

25　日月星辰: the sun, the moon, the stars, and the zodiacal signs, cf. *Shangshu* 尚書 as quoted below.

26　Cf. *Shangshu* Part I, chap. II, 3 (Legge, *Classics* Vol. III, Part I, p. 18).

27　The 博物志 *Bowuzhi* (*Kangxi's* 康熙 Dict.) says: 堯時有草生於庭佞人至則屈而指之 "In the time of Yao 堯 there grew a plant in the court, which when a cunning person approached curbed itself and pointed at him." Couvreur omits to translate the pointing.

28　The *Shangshu*.

29　*Shangshu* (Gao Yao Mo 皋陶謨) Part II, Book III, 2 (Legge, *Classics* Vol. III, Part I, p. 70), where the two clauses are transposed: 惟帝其難之,知人則哲.

30　Supposing this plant to be more than a mere freak of fancy I should suggest that the Mimosa pudica has been the archetype. The Chinese name as well as the nature of this peculiar plant seem to countenance such a supposition. 軼 may be used as a synonym for 迭 "repeatedly," the compound 屈軼 therefore might denote a plant repeatedly bending down and contracting itself. That is what the Mimosa does when touched. The feathered, digitated leaves first close, then bend down. After a while, they rise and open again. That may have been the pointing.

31   Mr. Yao Bao Ming, Chinese teacher at the Orientalische Seminar, Berlin, has assured me that some worms have this peculiarity that, though turned round, they will always creep in one direction. When he was first told he did not believe it, but found by experience that it was an undeniable fact. I could not convince him of his error.

32   Yao 堯.

33   觟䚦 Xiezhi, more commonly written 獬豸. For the first character also 獬 occurs, and for the latter 觟 or 廌. *Kangxi* 康熙 quotes this passage. The figure of this fabulous animal is used as official embroidery of censors and Taotais. The name seems to be first mentioned in the *Zuozhuan* 左氏傳 in connexion with a cap worn by southerners. Sima Xiangru 司馬相如, 2nd cent. BCE alludes to the animal in a poem. We learn from the *Houhanshu* 後漢書 that it was hunted in the kingdom of Chu 楚, where the aforesaid caps were first worn. The *Shuowen* 說文 says it was like an ox, the *Guangbowuzhi* 廣博物志 that it existed in the time of Yao and that its hair was woven into a curtain or a tent for the emperor (*Pianzileibian* 駢字類編 chap. 211).

34   狌狌.

35   Cf. p. I.244.

36   師尚父 a surname of 呂尚 Lü Shang (p. II.667). Cf. Chavannes, *Mem. Hist.* Vol. I, p. 225, Note 3.

37   In a corresponding passage of the *Shiji* 史記 chap. 32, p. 3r. (Chavannes, *Mem. Hist.* Vol. IV, p. 37) these two words are replaced by 蒼兕 "green rhinoceros" which Sima Zhen 司馬貞 explains as the title of boat-officers and not the name of any monster. Cf. Chavannes as quoted in Note 3.

38   尚書中候, a work on the *Shangshu*, in 5 chapters, still existing and mentioned by Zhang Zhidong 張之洞 in his bibliography.

39   軫. The *Taiping yulan* quoting the same passage from the *Shangshu zhonghou* 尚書中候 says in Crater 翼.

40   Chavannes, *Mem. Hist.* Vol. III, p. 675 takes it for a meteor. The Baihutong 白虎通 (*Peiwen yunfu*) declares it to be a big star shining even, when there is no moonshine, and enabling people to work at night. The *Shiji* chap. 27, p. 32r. (Chavannes, *Mem. Hist.* Vol. III, p. 392) says that it appears when the sky is clear. It is the star of virtue, has no constant form, and becomes visible in a State endowed with wisdom. Elsewhere it is stated by the same writer that the "brilliant star" appeared in the time of Huang Di 黃帝 shaped like a crescent, 半月, shining so vividly that one could work at night. The last fact is corroborated by another author,

who adds that this star shines during new moon to assist the moon, and it comes for a wise ruler. It is formed of the clear essence of heaven. 文子 Wen Zi concurs with this mystic view, saying that when sincere feelings fill the heart, the fluid affects heaven, so that the "brilliant star" appears. (*Taiping yulan* chap. 7.)

It is doubtful whether we have to do with a real star of great brilliancy or with some meteorological phenomenon.

41 *Shijing* 詩經 Part II, Book V, Ode IX, 6 (Legge, *Classics* Vol. IV, Part II, p. 356).

42 啓明.

43 長庚.

44 Of course they are both the planet Venus.

45 The well known dictionary of classical terms ascribed to the disciple of Confucius, Zi Xia 子夏, 5th cent. BCE.

46 So far quoted from the *Erya* 爾雅 chap. 9.

47 Edit. A and C correctly write 景星, edit. B has 景景. This passage is not to be found in our text of the *Erya*. Something like the words cited by Wang Chong: 四氣和為景星 may originally have stood in this place, for the 文選 *Wenxuan* about 530 CE likewise quotes from the *Erya*: 四氣和為通正. See *Erya zhengyi* 爾雅正義 chap. 9, p. 6.

48 甘露時降,萬物以嘉. Our text of the *Erya* writes 甘雨 "Sweet rain" instead of "sweet dew."

49 This clause is wanting in the modern text of the *Erya*, but incorporated in the old commentary. The *Liji* 禮記 (Liyun 禮運) Legge, *Sacred Books* Vol. XXVII, p. 392 does not support Wang Chong's view. There we read: 天降膏露,地出醴泉 "Heaven sent down its fattening dews; Earth sent forth its 'wine springs.'" Legge, *loc. cit.* gives a very reasonable explanation, that the phrase means nothing but that the dews were abundant and the springs delicious.

50 *Erya* chap. 13.

51 瀸.

52 檻泉. The *Erya* has 濫泉.

53 沃泉.

54 This clause now forms part of the old commentary, but not of the text of the *Erya*.

CHAPTER 53

Periods of Government
Zhiqi 治期

(*Lunheng* Book XVII, Chap. iii)

1   Wang Chong's view that fate is not affected by human activity is as one-sided as that which he impugns *viz.* that virtue can do everything. Human energy is but one of the many circumstances co-operating in what we call fate, but a very important one which cannot be neglected.

2   In former times Chinese officials were paid in grain instead of money, a system not quite abolished even at present.

3   Up to the present day, the Emperor feels himself responsible for the happiness of his State and looks upon an unlucky war or other misfortunes as punishments inflicted upon him by Heaven for his sins. On the other side, he and the manes of his ancestors get the credit for all success.

4   Needles for acupuncture, not for sewing, for there is no cutting in Chinese medicine.

5   A celebrated physician of the 5th cent. BCE. Cf. Ch. 64 n. 13 and Giles, *Biogr. Dict.* No. 396.

6   *Analects* XIV, 38.

7   *Shijing* 詩經 III, Bk. III, Ode IV, 3 (Legge, *Classics* Vol. IV, Part II, p. 530).

8   King Xuan 宣 of the Zhou 周 dynasty, 827–781 BCE.

9   Cf. p. II.564.

10   Wang Chong here anticipates the theory of many modern historians who ascribe great political changes not to the preponderating influence of some individuals, the great men of history, but to the economical conditions of the people.

11   Edition B erroneously writes 溫病 which must be 瘟病 as Ed. A and C have it.

12   In p. I.375 Wang Chong says that, on an average, an eclipse of the sun occurs every 41 or 42 months and of the moon every 180 days.

13   See p. II.475–76.

14   Cf. p. I.95.

15 Neither of these two statements will be unreservedly admitted: The prices, to a great extent, depend on the harvest, and the welfare of a State, on the moral qualities of its citizens, although there may be still other causes at work.

CHAPTER 54
Spontaneity
Ziran 自然

(*Lunheng* **Book XVIII, Chap. i**)

1 Who feeds the silkworms.

2 Inaction does not mean motionlessness, but spontaneous action without any aim or purpose. It is more or less mechanical, and not inspired by a conscious spirit.

3 Duke Huan 桓 of Qi 齊, 683–641 BCE.

4 Duke Huan's famous minister. Cf. p. I.123.

5 One of the counsellors and supporters of Han Gao Zu 漢高祖, died 190 BCE. On his laisser faire policy, *vid.* his biography in the *Shiji* 史記 chap. 54.

6 A State in Henan 河南.

7 A minister of the Emperor Wu Di 武帝, like Cao Can 曹參 a follower of the doctrine of inaction inculcated by Lao Zi 老子. His policy of governing consisted in letting things alone.

8 A disciple of Confucius, cf. Ch. 28. The Daoists also claim him as one of theirs. *Zhuangzi* 莊子, chap. XXV, 33, informs us that "when Qu Bo Yu 蘧伯玉 reached his sixtieth year, he changed his opinions. What he had previously regarded as right, he now came to regard as wrong," *i.e.* from a Confucianist he became a Daoist, and as such upheld the principle of quietism.

9 *Vid.* Ch. 23.

10 Huang Shi 黃石公, cf. Ch. 50.

11   From this mysterious book Zhang Liang 張良 is believed to have derived his plans consolidating the power of the Han 漢 dynasty.

12   Tang Shu 唐叔, the younger Prince of Tang 唐, was a son of King Wu Wang 武王 and younger brother of King Cheng 成 (1115–1078 BCE). He became the founder of the princely house of Jin 晉. Cf. *Shiji* 史記 chap. 39 p. 1v where the character of his palm is likewise referred to.

13   Cheng Ji 成季 was a younger son of Duke Huan 桓 of Lu 魯 (711–693 BCE). We read in the *Shiji* chap. 33 p. 13v the story of his having been born with the character You 友 in his hand.

14   A daughter of Duke Wu 武 of Song 宋 (765–747 BCE) who became married to Duke Hui 惠 of Lu 魯. Cf. Ch. 23.

15   In his remarks added to the biography of Zhang Liang 張良 (*Shiji* 史記 chap. 55 p. 13) Sima Qian 司馬遷 says that many scholars deny the existence of ghosts, but that the story of the yellow stone is very strange.

16   Cf. Ch. 64.

17   We find this same story in *Liezi* 列子 VIII, 2 and in *Huainanzi* 淮南子 XX, 2, but both authors ascribe the words put in the mouth of Confucius here to Lie Zi 列子. Huai Nan Zi 淮南子 makes the mulberry-leaf to be made of ivory, Lie Zi, of jade.

18   The apparition of the lady was evoked by the court magician Shao Weng 少翁 in 121 BCE. (Cf. *Shiji* 史記 chap. 28 p. 23.)

19   *Yijing* 易經, *Jici* 繫辭 II (Legge's transl. p. 383).

20   *Analects* VIII, 19.

21   *Analects* VIII, 18.

22   *Shangshu* 尚書, *Duoshi* 多士, Pt. V, Bk. XIV, 5 (Legge, *Classics* Vol. III, Pt. II, p. 455).

23   All other commentators take the "supreme ruler" as a synonym for God, and I think that they are right, and that Wang Chong's interpretation is forced for the purpose of supporting his theory.

24   Cf. p. II.467.

25   Cf. Ch. 21 n. 37.

26   "The fish forget each other in the rivers and lakes," says *Huainanzi* 淮南子 II, 4r.

27   Both were in a state of blissful forgetfulness and purposelessness. The passage is quoted from *Huainanzi* XI, 5r.

28   A Daoist philosopher, disciple of Lao Zi.

29   Reprimands tell against the system by which they are required, perfect virtue pervading the universe necessitates no recriminations, for all are filled with it as with generous wine.

30 This argument is quite Daoist and borrowed from the *Daodejing* 道德經, chap. XXXVIII.

31 The five leading feudal princes during the later Zhou 周 epoch, to wit: Duke Huan 桓 of Qi 齊 D. 643 BCE, Duke Wen 文 of Jin 晉 D. 628 BCE, Duke Xiang 襄 of Song 宋 D. 637 BCE, King Zhuang 莊 of Chu 楚 D. 591 BCE, and Duke Mu 穆 of Qin 秦 D. 621 BCE.

32 And it is likewise filled with the spontaneous fluid.

33 Qin Zhang 琴張, styled Zi Kai 子開, a disciple of Confucius.

34 *Analects* IX, 6.

35 In the preceding chapters of the *Lunheng*.

CHAPTER 55
Sympathetic Emotions
Ganlei 感類

(*Lunheng* Book XVIII, Chap. ii)

1 This is not in accordance with Wang Chong's system advocating spontaneity and must be taken merely hypothetically as one of two possibilities, either ... or.

2 Sages have many affinities with Heaven which manifests itself by them. Therefore Heaven being agitated, they are agitated too.

3 Wang Chong goes on to prove that all these apprehensions and self-reproaches are baseless.

4 No such passage is to be found in our text of the *Shangshu* 尚書, but in the *Diwang shiji* 帝王世紀 of the 3rd cent. CE quoted in the *Taiping yulan* 太平御覽 chap. 83, p. 2r. we read, "After Tang 湯 had destroyed Jie 桀 there was a great drought for seven years, so that the Luo 洛 dried up. He ordered tripods to be brought and thus prayed to the Mountains and Rivers: 'Have my desires been dissolute? Have I caused pain to the people? Has there been bribery? Have calumniators been predominant? Has there been too much building of palaces? Has the society of women

been sought too much? What is the cause of this absolute want of rain?' The historiographer of Yin 殷 divined and said that a man ought to be sacrificed. 'It is for the people that I pray for rain,' replied Tang. 'If a man is to be immolated I wish to be the one.' Then he fasted, cut his hair, and pared his nails to take the place of the victim. At an altar in a mulberry grove he prayed, 'I, the young man, have come and dare to offer myself as a black victim. I here declare before august Heaven and Earth, if the ten thousand regions have any sins, may they fall upon my person, and if I have any guilt, may it not involve the ten thousand regions. May not the imprudence of one single man induce God and the Spirits to injure the life of the people.' He had not yet finished these words, when a mighty rain poured down over several thousand miles."

Here Tang impeaches himself with six, not with five faults. Only the words in Italics occur in the *Shangshu, Tanggao* 湯誥, with some variations. The gist of the above quotation is also given by Legge, *Classics* Vol. III, Part I, p. 190, Concluding Note.

5   With the object of attracting rain. Cf. Ch. 47.

6   金縢 Part V, Book VI of the *Shangshu*.

7   Quotation from *Shangshu* Part V, Book VI, 16 (Legge, *Classics* Vol. III, Part II, p. 359).

8   This is in accordance with the *Shiji* 史記 chap. 33, p. 6r. (Chavannes, *Mem. Hist.* Vol. IV, p. 100, Note 1), but not with the *Shangshu*, where the Duke of Zhou 周公 is supposed to be banished, but still alive.

9   Territories in modern Henan 河南 which were given as fiefs to the two younger brothers of Wu Wang 武王, who spread the reports about the Duke of Zhou. Cf. *Shiji* chap. 4, p. 15v. (Chavannes, *Mem. Hist.* Vol. I, p. 245, Note 2).

10 The *Shangshu* only says that for two years Zhou Gong 周公 resided in the East. According to the *Shiji loc. cit.* the calumnies had no effect.

11 See *Shangshu loc. cit.* Book VI, 18.

12 *Analects* VII, 9.

13 The *Liji* 禮記.

14 Days designated by these cyclical signs in the calendar.

15 Cf. *Shiji* chap. 28, p. 11v. (Chavannes, *Mem. Hist.* Vol. III, p. 439) and Ch. 24 n. 14.

16 See p. I.124.

17 Quoted from *Huainanzi* 淮南子 VIII, 6v. Yao's 堯 assistant Yi 羿 bound the storm, which must be conceived as the storm-god, Fengbo 風伯.

18 Quoted from *Shangshu* Part II, Book I, chap. 3 (Legge, *Classics* Vol. III,

Part I, p. 32).

19　See above p. II.565.

20　For this story see p. II.462 where all the details are given.

21　As is related in the *Shangshu loc. cit.*

22　A man celebrated for his strength. Cf. Ch. 8 n. 32.

23　See p. I.380.

24　*Shangshu* Part V, Book VI, 16 and 18. (Legge, *Classics* Vol. III, Part II, p. 359). All the three editions write, 王乃得周公死自以為功. In the *Shangshu* 死 is replaced by 所.

25　A place said to have been situated in Puzhoufu 蒲州府 (Shanxi 山西).

26　Cf. *Shangshu* Part IV, Book V, 9 (Legge, *Classics* Vol. III, Part I, p. 203) and *Shiji* chap. 3, p. 6r. (Chavannes, *Mem. Hist.* Vol. I, p. 189).

27　*Shangshu* Part V, Book XVI, 7 (Legge, *Classics* Vol. III, Part II, p. 477).

28　百兩篇.

29　A scholar of the 1st cent. BCE. *Vid.* p. II.811.

30　See *Shangshu loc. cit.* Book VI, 19, where we have a different reading: 天乃雨 "Heaven sent down rain" instead of 天止雨 "Heaven stopped the rain," of our text, which latter is preferable.

31　Cf. p. I.109, where the same story is told of the Shang 商 Emperor Gao Zong 高宗 = Wu Ding 武丁, 1324–1266 BCE and Ch. 18 n. 4 where it is likewise ascribed to Gao Zong. Tai Wu 太戊 reigned from 1637–1563 BCE. According to the *Shiji* chap. 3, p. 7r. (Chavannes, *Mem. Hist.* Vol. I, p. 190) this prodigy happened under Tai Wu, not Gao Zong.

32　See Ch. 7 n. 12 and p. I.187.

33　An argument merely used rhetorically to combat the view that thunder and rain stopped before King Cheng 成 had repented, for Wang Chong holds that Heaven never acts on purpose.

34　追王, expression quoted from the *Zhongyong* 中庸 XVIII, 3 (Legge, *Classics* Vol. I, p. 401). The three persons raised to royal dignity after their death are the father and the ancestors of the founder of the Zhou 周 dynasty. A similar practice has been followed by later dynasties, the reigning Manchu dynasty included.

35　A range of mountains in the north of Sichuan 四川.

36　The Ancestral King, King Ji 季, and King Wen 文王, mentioned above.

37　White pheasants and aromatic plants were presented as tribute to the Duke of Zhou by the Yueshang 越裳 and the Japanese. Cf. p. I.295.

38　This episode is found in the *Liji* 禮記 Book II, Sect. I, Part I, 18 (Legge, *Liji* Vol. I, p. 128).

39　Zeng Zi 曾子 was not directly responsible for the mat, the *soi-disant* too great honour was conferred upon him by the chief of the Ji 季 family, just as the excessive funeral rites were performed by King Cheng 成 for Zhou Gong.

40   Quoted from *Analects* IX, 11.

41   It was improper for a nobleman to offer a sacrifice reserved for the king.

42   A man of Lu 魯 who once asked Confucius about ceremonies.

43   Quotation from *Analects* III, 6. There is a great discrepancy in Legge's translation, who takes 曾 for a particle, whereas Wang Chong explains it as a name *viz.* that of Confucius' disciple Zeng Zi.

44   Cf. p. II.467.

45   See p. I.95.

46   See Ch. 4 n. 11.

47   Only the dream of Wu Wang 武王 is mentioned in the *Liji*, not that of Wen Wang 文王.

48   齡 *ling*. This explanation is also taken from the *Liji loc. cit.*

49   Famous minister of Duke Huan 桓 of Qi 齊, 7th cent. BCE.

50   *i.e.*, we would be savages, following their customs.

51   Quotation from *Analects* XIV, 18.

52   The name of an extravagant tower built by Guan Zhong 管仲.

53   Cf. *Analects* III, 22.

54   See above Ch. 55 n. 43.

55   The inventor of writing, cf. Ch. 84 n. 12.

56   The inventor of carriages, cf. Ch. 84 n. 13 [QP dubious ref. see index].

57   In 636 BCE after nineteen years of exile.

58   麋墨. I could not find any reference to this in the *Zuozhuan* 左氏傳 or the *Shiji*, nor do the encyclopedias know a man of the name of Mi Mo 麋墨. Both words are family names, and Mi 麋 is also an old State in Hubei 湖北 and Hunan 湖南. If we take Mo 墨 to be the surname of the person, Mi 麋 might be his country. The two historical works only inform us that Fan 犯 proposed leaving his nephew, but was reconciled. *Zuozhuan*, Duke Xi 僖 24th year.

59   A minister in Song 宋.

60   The steward of Hua Chen's 華臣 nephew.

61   The gist of this account is contained in the *Zuozhuan*, Duke Xiang 襄 17th year (Legge, *Classics* Vol. V, Part II, p. 473), but the two versions differ in some details. In the Classic the Master of the Left does not menace Hua Chen 華臣 and even intercedes for him with the duke. Nothing is said about his climbing over a wall.

62   *Vid.* p. I.255 seq.

63 Like Tang 湯 who overthrew the Xia 夏 and Wen Wang who destroyed the Shang 商 dynasty, both reputed great Sages.

64 1191–1155 BCE.

65 Yi 乙 hung up a sack filled with blood and shooting at it, declared that he was shooting at Heaven.

66 Two rivers in Shanxi 陝西.

67 The passage seems to be culled from the *Shiji* chap. 3, p. 10r. (Chavannes, *Mem. Hist.* Vol. I, p. 198) where, however, the flogging of the Earth is not mentioned.

68 An author of the Han 漢 time, cf. p. II.843.

69 洪範稽疑 a chapter of the *Shangshu* Part V, Book IV, 20 (Legge, *Classics* Vol. III, Part II, p. 334) where different methods of solving doubts are given.

CHAPTER 56
The Equality of the Ages
Qishi 齊世

(*Lunheng* Book XVIII, Chap. iii)

1 This seems to have been the rule under the Zhou 周 dynasty. Cf. *Liji* 禮記, *Neize* 內則 Sect. II (Legge, *Sacred Books* Vol. XXVII, p. 478).

2 The complexion is yellowish, the lips are red, the teeth white, the hair black, and the veins are bluish.

3 Cf. p. I.279.

4 A contemporary of Confucius, famous for his beauty (cf. *Analects* VI, 14), but of a perverse character. He committed incest with his half-sister Nan Zi 南子, the wife of Duke Ling 靈 of Wei 衛.

5 The Chinese Methuselah.

6 The fourth wife of Huang Di 黃帝, an intelligent, but very ill-favoured woman.

7 9–23 CE.

8 25–56 CE.

9   A circuit in Anhui 安徽.

10 *Yijing* 易經, *Jici* 繫辭 II (Legge's translation p. 385).

11 The most ancient mythical emperor.

12 Does that mean that the pre-historic Chinese lived in a state of matriarchate or in polyandry like the Tibetans? We find the same notice in *Zhuangzi* 莊子 chap. 29, p. 22 v.

13 The Zhou dynasty.

14 *Analects* III, 14.

15 2205–1766 BCE.

16 1766–1122 BCE.

17 1122–249 BCE.

18 People like to contrast, even though there be little difference between the things thus contrasted.

19 A faithful minister of Duke Yi 懿 of Wei 衛. Cf. p. I.288.

20 When in 546 BCE Zhuang 莊, Duke of Qi 齊, was murdered, Bu Zhan 不占 drove to his palace and on hearing the affray, died of fright.

21 A place in Shandong 山東.

22 A circuit in Anhui province.

23 A city in Zhejiang 浙江.

24 These two works of the philosopher Yang Zi Yun 揚子雲 have come down to us. The more celebrated of the two is the *Fayan* 法言, the *Taixuan* 太玄, *soi-disant* an elucidation of the *Yijing*, is very obscure.

25 *Analects* VIII, 19.

26 When Zhou 紂 was defeated, he burned himself on the "Deer Terrace." Afterwards Wu Wang 武王 shot three arrows at the corpse, struck at it with his sword, and with his battle-axe severed the head from the body. Cf. *Shiji* 史記 chap. 4, p. 11.

27 *Analects* XIX, 20.

28 The degenerate son of virtuous Yao 堯.

29 Aboriginal tribes, against which Shun 舜 had to fight. *Vid.* I.287.

30 The hatred of the scholars of the Han 漢 time towards Qin Shi Huangdi 秦始皇 was still fresher and therefore more intense than their aversion to Jie 桀 and Zhou 紂.

31 Cf. p. II.516.

32 Cf. p. II.528.

33 Cf. p. II.522.

34 The Emperor Cheng 成 reigned from 1115 to 1078 BCE, Kang 康 from 1078 to 1052 BCE.

35 The Emperor Zhang Di 章帝, 76–89 CE, who succeeded Ming Di 明帝.

Under his reign the *Lunheng* seems to have been written. *Vid.* Ch. 50 n. 51.

36　The reigns of these three first sovereigns of the later Han dynasty were prosperous indeed.

CHAPTER 57

Praise of the Han Dynasty
Xuan Han 宣漢

(*Lunheng* Book XIX, Chap. i)

1　*Viz.* to bring about universal peace.

2　Cf. Ch. 28 n. 53.

3　*Analects* XIV, 45.

4　Ed. A and C have: 時哉, B better: 時或.

5　景星, Cf. p. II.544 seq.

6　As the Emperor Di Ku 帝嚳 had, p. I.135.

7　We read *loc. cit.* that the eyebrows of Yao 堯 had eight colours, not that he had eight eyebrows.

8　乂安. Ed A has the misprint 又安.

9　Ed. A: 鳥 for 烏.

10　Cf. Ch. 12 n. 1.

11　Ed. A has the misprint 大理 which should be 大虵. About the event see Ch. 64 n. 80.

12　Ed. B and C: 兔, Ed. A: 鬼.

13　*I.e.*, it would be foolish. The story here alluded to of a peasant of Song 宋 who having seen a hare running against the trunk of a tree and breaking its crown, fancied this to be an easy way of catching hares, and therefore settled down near the tree in wait for one, has been told by Han Feizi 韓非子 XIX, 1v. See Petillon, *Allusions* p. 175.

14　Ed. B and C: 間世儒, Ed. A: 匹世儒.

15　*Analects* XIII, 12.

16　From 206 to 179 BCE.

17 Quoted in an abridged form from the biography of Jia Yi 賈誼 in the *Shiji* 史記 chap. 84, p. 8r.

18 The *Lunheng* was written in 82 or 83 CE. Cf. p. II.598, I.7, [and II.1176].

19 From Han Gao Zu 漢高祖 down to Zhang Di 章帝, under whom the *Lunheng* was completed, there are ten emperors altogether, the Empress Lü Hou 呂后 excepted.

20 In 5 CE Ru Zi Ying 孺子嬰, 6–8 CE, was a child and reigned only nominally till in 9 CE Wang Mang 王莽 snatched the empire from him.

21 In 25 CE.

22 See p. II.597.

23 64 BCE.

24 The modern Binzhou 邠州 in Shanxi 陝西.

25 62 BCE.

26 An Annanese tribe. See Ch. 50 n. 47.

27 60 BCE.

28 58 BCE.

29 East of Xi'anfu 西安府 in Shanxi 陝西, the modern Xianningxian 咸寧縣.

30 55 BCE.

31 The 子谷 of our text should be changed into 于谷 as in the *Hanshu* 漢書 whence this passage seems to be cited.

32 The *Hanshu* has 十刻 instead of 十日 "ten odd quarters of an hour" *i.e.,* about two hours and a half.

33 53 BCE.

34 A place in Shanxi 陝西. Cf. Ch. 50 n. 18.

35 All these portents are mentioned in the *Hanshu* chap. 8, p. 21v. seq. also.

36 58–75 CE.

37 Zhang Di 章帝, 76–88 CE.

38 The States Qi 齊 and Lu 魯 are of about equal importance, and so are Chu 楚 and Song 宋.

39 二尺四寸 said of the length of the tablets. Cf. p. II.818.

40 Apart from the *Shiji* 史記 of Sima Qian 司馬遷 who describes only the beginning of the Han 漢 period, the history of the Former Han dynasty was written in the *Qianhanshu* 前漢書 by Ban Gu 班固 and that of the After Han in the *Houhanshu* 後漢書 by Fan Ye 范曄, but though much esteemed, their works have not been raised to the rank of classics.

41 Ban Gu wrote two poems descriptive of the eastern and western capitals of the Han.

42 Figuratively for the border lands of China with their people.

43 Cf. p. II.599.
44 鄯善, a people south of the Lop Nor, said to be identical with the Loulan 樓蘭 between Hami and Turfan.
45 哀牢, a people in Yunnan 雲南, in the present prefecture of Yongchang 永昌.

CHAPTER 58

Further Remarks on the State
Huiguo 恢國

(*Lunheng* Book XIX, Chap. ii)

1   *Analects* IX, 10.
2   On p. II.585.
3   The capital of Huang Di 黃帝 in Zhili 直隸.
4   On Danshui 丹水 and the You Miao 有苗 see Ch. 26 n. 3 and 4.
5   鬼方. An allusion to the *Yijing* 易經, 63rd hexagram (Legge, *Sacred Books* Vol. XVI, p. 205). The "devil country" or "demon region" means the barbarous hordes in the north of China.
6   See p. II.565.
7   陳豨, as the name is written in the *Shiji* 史記. Ed. B has: 狶. Chen Xi 陳豨 was a counsellor to the King of Zhao 趙. He caused an insurrection against Gao Zu 高祖 in 197 BCE and was decapitated in 196. Cf. Chavannes, *Mem. Hist.* Vol. II, p. 393 seq. and 399.
8   Cf. Ch. 63 n. 67.
9   Chao Cuo 鼂錯 eked on five States to rebel against the Han 漢. The plot failed, and Chao Cuo was put to death by order of the emperor in 154 BCE. Cf. Chavannes *loc. cit.* p. 499 and 509.
10 The acceptance of the Chinese calendar has always been regarded as a sign of submission.
11 A fact mentioned in the *Shiji* (Chavannes, *Mem. Hist.* Vol. I, p. 226).
12 This inference is wrong, of course, for we do not know whether the power

of Qin 秦 and Xiang Yu 項羽 was, each of them, equal to that of Jie 桀 or Zhou 紂.

13 Cf. Ch. 21 n. 23 and Ch. 30 n. 47 and 48.

14 Who killed their rightful lieges.

15 三郊 lit. the "three zones" round the capital. Cf. Couvreur Dict.

16 A district in Shanxi 陝西.

17 This passage is quoted in the *Taiping yulan* 太平御覽 chap. 985, p. 3v., but the text differs. There the boy does not eat the cinnabar, but smears his body with it. See also p. I.277–78 where the corresponding passage, which owing to the conciseness of the text was mistranslated, must be corrected. Dan Jiao 丹教 is not a name.

18 Quoted in the *Peiwen yunfu* 佩文韻府.

19 武成 chapter of the *Shangshu* 尚書, see Ch. 25 n. 21 and 22.

20 *I.e.* Wang Mang 王莽 who assumed the title the "New Emperor."

21 A district in the Yingzhou 潁州 prefecture of Anhui 安徽.

22 In 23 CE.

23 Cf. Chavannes, *Mem. Hist.* Vol. I, p. 235.

24 The story is related by Mencius Book I, Part I, chap. VII, 4 (Legge, *Classics* Vol. II, p. 139).

25 In the year 596 BCE the capital of Zheng 鄭 was taken by Chu 楚 after a long siege. Then the scene alluded to took place. The narrative is found in the *Zuozhuan* 左氏傳, Duke Xuan 宣, 12th year.

26 See Ch. 15 n. 14 to 17.

27 Generally known as Liu Xuan 劉玄, a cousin to Guang Wu Di 光武帝.

28 The place where Wen Wang 文王, the father of Wu Wang 武王, was imprisoned by order of King Zhou 紂.

29 The last emperor of the Former Han dynasty.

30 An author, see Ch. 83 n. 49.

31 See p. I.124 seq.

32 A solar mansion corresponding to Gemini.

33 See p. I.126.

34 Cf. *loc. cit.* p. I.126, where the reading Chongling 舂陵 (ed. B.) must be corrected into Chunling 春陵.

35 On these various miracles compare p. I.162 seq.

36 Cf. p. II.534.

37 See p. II.588–89.

38 See p. II.603.

39 Zhang Di 章帝.

40 76–77 CE.

41 In the prefecture of Yongzhou 雍州, Hunan 湖南.

42 More details on these eight dragons are given on p. II.606.

43 All these portents are faithfully chronicled in the *Houhanshu* 後漢書 chap. 3, p. 6r. seq., only in the numbers and the years there are slight differences.

44 p. I.143.

45 By the usurper Wang Mang 王莽 who ousted the Former Han dynasty.

46 The aborigines of Sichuan 四川.

47 越常. In p. I.295 where the same statement is made Wang Chong writes the name 越裳.

48 The two Zhou 周 emperors reigning from 878–828 BCE (Li 厲) and from 781 to 771 BCE (You 幽).

49 He left the old capital Haojing 鎬京 in Shanxi 陝西, and took up his residence farther eastward in Luoyi 洛邑 (Henan 河南).

50 The savages from the four quarters.

51 In 1 CE.

52 They could not converse with the Chinese through one interpreter, finding nobody who could understand their language and Chinese, and therefore required one more to translate their speech into a language from which it could be rendered into Chinese.

53 Tribes in the West of China.

54 Of these tribes only the Liang Yuan 良願 are mentioned in the *Hanshu* 漢書, Biography of Wang Mang (*Peiwen yunfu* 佩文韻府).

55 A place in Gansu 甘肅.

56 The geographical part of the *Suishu* 隋書 (quoted in the *Peiwen yunfu*) informs us that the circuit of the "Western Sea" 西海郡 includes the old city of Fusi 伏俟城, wherever that may be, and embraces the kingdom of Tuyuhun 吐谷渾. There is the stone grotto of Xi Wang Mu 西王母 and the salt lake Kukunor. Chavannes, *Documents sur les Tou Kiue (Turcs) Occidentaux* p. 372 likewise places Tuyuhun on the banks of this lake. The *Xiyuzhuan* 西域傳, on the other side, states that Tiaozhi 條支, which I take to be Syria, is conterminous with Xihai 西海, and that there are big birds whose eggs are like jugs (ostriches). It is impossible that the Han 漢 carried their conquests so far.

57 Cf. Ch. 12 n. 5 and 6.

58 See *Analects* IX, 13 and Ch. 28 n. 62.

59   關頭, an expression not found elsewhere.

60   Two ancient States in Sichuan 四川.

61   The modern Chuxiongfu 楚雄府 in Yunnan 雲南.

62   The present Guilinfu 桂林府, Guangxi 廣西.

63   Gong Yang 公羊, Duke Zhuang 莊 32nd year.

64   The King of Guangling 廣陵 committed suicide in 67 CE, the King of Chu 楚 in 70 CE. See *Houhanshu* 後漢書 chap. 2, p. 13v. and p. 16v.

65   Ed. A and B: 海 for 悔.

66   Ed. A writes: 貴餘, Ed. C: 屋餘 and Ed. B: 胥餘.

67   陰氏, the family of Yin Jiang 隱彊.

68   The son of the last emperor of the Yin 殷 dynasty, also called Lu Fu 祿父. See Chavannes, *Mem. Hist.* Vol. I, p. 207, Note 4. But here two different persons seem to be meant.

69   The Yin dynasty.

70   On the banishment of these four criminals see the *Shangshu* Part II, Book I, 12 (Legge, *Classics* Vol. III, Part I, p. 39) and Chavannes, *Mem. Hist.* Vol. I, p. 67.

71   Cf. Ch. 17 n. 27.

72   This seems to refer to an earthquake which happened in Wang Chong's time.

73   See p. I.195.

74   Cf. p. II.566.

75   Cf. Ch. 80 n. 27. Perhaps the 黿微 there is merely a misprint for 微病.

76   76 CE.

CHAPTER 59
Ominous Signs Investigated
Yanfu 驗符

(*Lunheng* Book XIX, Chap. iii)

1   68 CE.

2   The Huan 皖 district corresponding to the prefecture of Anqing 安慶, the capital of the province of Anhui 安徽.

3   Now Luzhoufu 廬州府, 120 Li west of the present Lujiangxian 廬江縣.

4   竿繡. Ed. A has the misprint 年繡.

5   This *soi-disant* lucky augury is shortly mentioned in the *Houhanshu* 後漢書 chap. 2, p. 14r. where the lake in which the gold was found is called 漠湖 Chaohu, a lake in Hefeixian 合肥縣 (Anhui) now famous for its gold-fish. As further portents which appeared in the same year are enumerated: a unicorn, a white pheasant, a wine spring, and auspicious grain.

6   Extraordinary only for persons prejudiced and desirous to discover omens at all costs.

7   No. The event was very simple and harmless and only construed into a miracle. Small boys, whose testimony is not worth much, saw some vessel in the water, which they first took for a wine amphora, then for something else. When they stirred up the water it disappeared for some time, but at last they succeeded in raising it.

8   The history of these tripods, the insignia of imperial power, is related in p. I.295 seq. Wang Chong here assumes that they were made of gold, the general opinion is that they were made of bronze or copper.

9   In Dalifu 大理府, Yunnan 雲南.

10   The twenty-fourth part of a Tael or a $^1/_{24}$ ounce. In many Chinese rivers gold is found, but in such small quantities as mentioned here, so that the washing does not pay.

11   It is needless to say that under all the other dynasties gold was found as well.

12   The yellow metal = gold, the white metal = silver, and the red metal = copper. Cf. *Shangshu* 尚書, *Yugong* 禹貢 (Legge, *Classics* Vol. III, Part I, p. 110, Note 43).

13   See p. II.557 and II.525.

14   In 78 CE.

15   Cf. Ch. 58 n. 41. Quanling 泉陵 lies north of the modern Linglingxian 零
陵縣 in Hunan 湖南. The *Houhanshu* 後漢書 chap. 3, p. 6r. speaks only
of Lingling 零陵, whence in the 3rd year of the Emperor Zhang Di's 章帝
reign purple boletus was sent as a present.

16   上計. These seem to have been comptrollers or revenue officers.

17   Northwest of the present Xiangyuanxian 湘源縣 in Guangxi 廣西. The
Houhanshu loc. cit. mentions only these three places.

18   In Guilinfu 桂林府, Guangxi.

19   Under the Han 漢 dynasty a part of the Lingling circuit in Hunan 湖南.

20   The *Houhanshu loc. cit.* merely reports that in the 5th year of the emperor
(80 CE) purple boletus was sent from Lingling.

21   The main river of the province of Hunan which falls into the Dongting 洞
庭 Lake.

22   All the editions here write 十六丈 160 feet. I suppose that 尺 should
be written, for else the sequel that the dragons were bigger than horses
would give no sense.

23   The *Houhanshu* contents itself with the short statement that eight yellow
dragons were seen in Quanling. A commentator adds that the two big
dragons playing in the Xiang 湘 were of the size of horses and had horns,
and that the six young ones were as big as colts, but hornless.

24   A city in Xuzhoufu 徐州府, Jiangsu 江蘇. Cf. p. I.297.

25   On this function see Chavannes, *Mem. Hist.* Vol. II, p. 526.

26   *I.e.*, as a genuine phœnix, and a lucky omen.

27   In Xuan Di's 宣帝 time, 73–49 BCE the capital was Chang'an 長安 in
Shanxi 陝西.

28   The distance from the capital.

29   The whole empire is, as it were, the emperor's home, wherefore it is unnecessary to calculate the distance of cities from the capital.

30   In 165 BCE. For further details on Gongsun Chen 公孫臣 cf. Chavannes,
Mem. Hist. Vol. II, p. 479.

31   30 Li north from Qin'anxian 秦安縣 in the province of Gansu 甘肅.

32   The colour of earth, according to Chinese ideas, is yellow like that of the
yellow dragons which are supposed to have indicated it.

33   Earth being the fifth of the Five Elements in the series of the *Shangshu* 尚
書: water, fire, metal, wood, earth, its number is five.

34   The colour of the Xia 夏 dynasty was black. In war they used black horses
and for sacrifices black victims. The Yin 殷 dynasty adopted white as its

colour, and the Zhou 周 dynasty red. See *Liji* 禮記, Legge *Sacred Books* Vol. XXVII, p. 125. The Qin 秦 dynasty again selected black (Chavannes *Mem. Hist.* Vol. II, p. 130). The colour of the present Manchu dynasty is yellow again.

35　Again the shallow symbolism. Sweetness is the taste corresponding to earth.

36　Cf. p. I.197.

37　乾坤 the names of the first and the last of the Eight Diagrams from which the other six, the children, were evolved.

38　*Analects* VI, 21.

39　Earth is placed in the centre, whereas the four other elements correspond to the four cardinal points.

40　Personal name of the "Yellow Emperor" Huang Di 黃帝.

41　The green dragon is the animal of the East, the scarlet bird that of the South, the white tiger that of the West, and the black tortoise that of the North.

42　There is a supposed correspondence between the centre, earth, yellow, sweet, the heart, and Huang Di. See Appendix to Couvreur's Dictionary.

CHAPTER 60
The Necessity of Eulogies
Xusong 須頌

(*Lunheng* Book XX, Chap. i)

1　Quoted from the *Shangshu* 尚書, *Yaodian* 堯典 1 (Legge, *Classics* Vol. III, Part I, p. 15).

2　The words following the above passage are generally regarded as forming part of the original merely edited by Confucius. But we find nearly the same words: 聰明文思 in the Preface to the *Shangshu* which is attributed to Confucius.

3　In 483 BCE when Confucius was already 69 years of age.

4   Quotation from the *Analects* IX, 14.

5   Various explanations of the term *shang* 尚 in *Shangshu* have been proposed by Chinese critics. It is said to mean the "highest" *i.e.*, the most venerable book or the book of the "highest antiquity" (cf. Legge, *loc. cit.* Note). Wang Chong here takes it to signify the book treating of sovereigns.

6   制.

7   作.

8   A noble of the Wei 衛 State, 5th cent. BCE, who took a leading part in a revolution in Wei, which cost Zi Lu 子路 his life. The tripod with the inscription was conferred upon him by the duke. The encomiastic inscription, eulogising the ancestors of the recipient, is given in the *Liji* 禮記, *Jitong* 祭統 p. 66r. (Legge, *Sacred Books* Vol. XXVIII, p. 252).

9   A circuit in Anhui 安徽.

10   Huang Ba 黃霸 was first thrown into prison by the emperor, but then reinstated and highly honoured. He died in 51 BCE. See Giles, *Bibl. Dict.* No. 865.

11   A minister of Shun 舜 and director of State music. Cf. p. I.183.

12   827–782 BCE.

13   The Duke of Shao 邵, Wu Wang's 武王 brother.

14   *Shijing* 詩經, Part I, Book II, Ode V (Legge, *Classics* Vol. IV, Part I, p. 26).

15   These 40 odes form Part IV of the *Shijing*. The term 頌 eulogy is given a different meaning by modern commentators *viz.* "songs for the ancestral temple" or "sacrificial odes." See Legge, *Shijing* Part II, p. 569, Notes.

16   Ch. 57.

17   Ch. 58.

18   *Analects* VIII, 19.

19   Cf. p. I.218. Legge in his Prolegomena to the *Shijing* p. 13 adduces the words of the peasant as the "song of the peasants in the time of Yao 堯."

20   I think that the question of the peasant has not this purport. He only means to say that he does not care for Yao in the least. In the "song of the peasants" this idea is more clearly brought out: 帝力于我何有哉.

21   Rivers in Henan 河南 and Shandong 山東.

22   鄷廣. Wang Chong here and elsewhere uses 鄷 in the sense of 豐.

23   Cf. p. II.591.

24   五三, or as they are called below: 三五.

25   五三, or as they are called below: 三五.

26   On posthumous titles see p. I.229, p. II.642.

27 宣 means "to expand, to propagate" scl. civilisation, consequently Xuan Wang 宣王 is the Civilising King.

28 堯 signifies "high, eminent, lofty."

29 The people are the pedestrians, the rulers, those riding in the State-cart, and their panegyrists are compared to the adornments of this cart.

30 In the *Shiji* 史記.

31 73 BCE–1 CE. The work alluded to was perhaps the Yang Xiong fu shi-erpian 揚雄賦十二篇 mentioned in the Catalogue of the *Hanshu* 漢書 chap. 30, p. 32v.

32 Ch. 56 and 57–59.

33 We do not appreciate panegyrists and their bombastic and coloured descriptions, but want true historians.

34 See the reproductions and translations of Qin 秦 inscriptions in Chavannes, *Mem. Hist.* Vol. II, p. 544 seq.

35 Books IV-VIII of the *Lunheng* (Chinese text).

36 能聖.

37 實聖. Both chapters are lost.

38 Ch. 53.

39 76 CE.

40 Cf. p. II.601.

41 Ch. 45 and 46.

42 Wang Chong probably refers to some place in Zhejiang 浙江 province of which he was a native.

43 計吏. This seems to have been an official charged with the annual revision of the archives.

CHAPTER 61

Lost Texts
Yiwen 佚文

(*Lunheng* Book XX, Chap. ii)

1   Ed. A and C write 300 books (pien).
2   Cf. Ch. 81 n. 10 and Ch. 83 n. 2.
3   郎吏.
4   See p. II.811.
5   *Analects* VIII, 20.
6   This passage is very doubtful, and my translation not much more than a guess.
7   Alias Yang Zhong 楊終, a native of Chengdufu 成都府 in Sichuan 四川, possessing great literary talents.
8   Cf. Ch. 60 n. 43.
9   A tribe in Yunnan 雲南, see Ch. 57 n. 45.
10   58–75 CE.
11   Yang Zi Shan 楊子山 was attached to the library.
12   140–87 BCE.
13   Liu Xin 劉歆, 1st cent. BCE and CE, son of the famous Liu Xiang 劉向, an author like his father and protege of Wang Mang 王莽.
14   周易程傳 *Zhouyi chengzhuan* 1883, chap. 7, p. 12r.
15   58–75 CE.
16   An eminent scholar, 30–101 CE, who together with the historian Ban Gu 班固 was appointed historiographer.
17   A savant who by Xiao Ming Di 孝明帝 was given a post at the Imperial Library, where, conjointly with Ban Gu and Jia Kui 賈逵, he supervised the edition of books. He wrote himself 28 chapters of various poetry and died young.
18   See above Ch. 61 n. 7.
19   Hou Feng 侯諷 seems to be unknown to other writers. The *Peiwen yunfu* 佩文韻府 merely quotes this passage.
20   140–87 BCE.

21 The well known scholar and poet. Cf. Ch. 42 n. 28.

22 32–7 BCE.

23 On the last two named scholars see Ch. 50 n. 9 and 10.

24 *Vid.* Ch. 85 n. 27.

25 Ch. 13 n. 18.

26 That is, "may he live ten thousand years."

27 候氣變者.

28 Ed. A: 生.

29 Diagram Ge 革, No. 49. Legge, *Sacred Books* Vol. XVI, p. 168, Nos. 5 and 6.

30 Diagram Bi 賁, No. 22. Legge, *loc. cit.* p. 231, No. 4.

31 The 22nd of the Twenty-eight Solar Mansions, consisting of eight stars in Gemini.

32 Cf. p. I.124.

33 This supposition is incompatible with Wang Chong's principle of spontaneity which he proclaims for Heaven. He sometimes falls back into the inveterate ideas of his countrymen which he combats elsewhere.

34 p. II.810.

35 The son of Qin Shi Huangdi 秦始皇 lost the throne, and his family was destroyed.

36 On the Five ancient Punishments in use under the Zhou 周 and Han 漢 dynasties see p. I.414–15. Li Si 李斯 was torn to pieces by carts. See p. I.236.

37 194–188 BCE, and 156–141 BCE.

38 48–33 BCE, and 32–7 BCE.

39 9–22 CE.

40 In 25 CE.

41 58–75 CE.

42 In 76 CE.

43 According to tradition which has not yet been historically tested, this period would last from 2357 to 2205 BCE.

44 It is more than doubtful whether there have been books at all at that time.

45 1766–1123, and 1122–255 BCE.

46 Whether the Han had any books dating as far back as the Yin 殷 dynasty is open to doubt.

47 206 BCE.

48 This brightness of the sky and the stars is regarded as a lucky augury.

49 Cf. Ch. 39 n. 44.

50 And we are glad of it.

51 上書.

52 奏記.

53 At present these terms are not restricted in this way, and I doubt whether they really were so in the Han time.

54 The reasoning of this paragraph is not very convincing.

55 *Analects* VIII, 20.

56 Cf. p. II.671 and I.119.

57 Lu Jia 陸賈.

58 Ed. A alone has the spurious reading: 女固 for 在國.

59 Cf. Ch. 13 n. 7.

60 聞知之者. Ed. A and C read: 惡知之者, which is less good.

61 This work embodies the philosophical views of Yang Zi Yun 揚子雲 = Yang Xiong 揚雄, emphasising the value of the *Analects*, whereas his *Taix-uanjing* 太玄經 is especially devoted to the elucidation of the *Yijing* 易經.

62 Ban Biao 班彪, the teacher of Wang Chong and father to Ban Gu.

63 The text reads: 文集於禮, which gives no sense. In accordance with the foregoing: 筆集成文 I would suggest to write: 文集於筆.

64 *Analects* II, 2.

CHAPTER 62

On Death

Lunsi 論死

(*Lunheng* Book XX, Chap. iii)

1 歸

2 伸

3 The Six Domestic Animals are: the horse, the ox, the goat, the pig, the dog, and the fowl.

4 Cf. Ch. 7.

5 A series of mythical rulers of remotest antiquity.

6 The Five Virtues are: Benevolence, Justice, Propriety, Knowledge, and Truth; the Five Organs: the Heart, the Liver, the Stomach, the Lungs, and the Kidneys.

7　No dictionary gives this meaning for *tian* 殄, which usually means "to exterminate, to cut off, to cease." But it cannot be anything else here. The Chinese of to-day will likewise call a faint "death," or "small death," *xiaosi* 小死.

8　A place in Lu 魯 (Shandong 山東).

9　A quotation abridged from the *Liji* 禮記, *Tangong* 檀弓. Cf. Legge, *Liji* 禮記 Vol. I, p. 123. Modern commentators explain the passage quite differently. The dictum of Confucius would mean that the ancients did not repair tombs, because they built them so well, that they could not collapse. Wang Chong's interpretation is more natural.

10　Cf. Ch. 8.

11　Those who used its body as food.

12　His spirit.

CHAPTER 63

False Reports about the Dead
Siwei 死偽

(*Lunheng* Book XXI, Chap. i)

1　827–781 BCE.

2　The story is given a little more in detail in the Zhou Chunqiu 周春秋, which adds that the king broke his spine (cf. Chavannes, *Mem. Hist.* Vol. I, p. 278, Note 2) and also by Mo Di 墨子 chap. 8, p. 2.

3　In the *Lunheng* Bk. IV, p. 5 (*Shuxu* 書虛 Ch. 16) he is called Viscount Jian 簡 of Zhao 趙, the same who is mentioned in Ch. 64.

4　On their fates cf. p. I.102–103 and Ch. 25.

5　A brother of the duke, who had been driven into death by court intrigues.

6　The "Lower Capital" of Jin 晉 *i.e.* Quwo 曲沃 in modern Pingyangfu 平陽府 (Shanxi 山西).

7　The personal name of Duke Hui 惠.

8　Quotation from the *Zuozhuan* 左氏傳, Duke Xi 僖 10th year (649 BCE, Legge, *Classics* Vol. V, Pt. I, p. 157).

9　In Shanxi 山西.

10　A wife of Duke Xian 獻 of Jin 晉, who, in order to secure the throne for her own son, removed the heir-apparent, Shen Sheng 申生.

11　The spirits of the father, the grandfather, and the great-grandfather of King Wu 武 and his younger brother Dan 旦, Duke of Zhou 周公.

12　Quoted in an abridged form from *Shangshu* 尚書, *Jinteng* 金縢, Pt. V, Bk. VI, 1 seq. (Legge, *Classics* Vol. III, Pt. II, p. 351 seq.).

13　An officer of the Jin 晉 State.

14　As was customary. Thus far the story, with some additions and omissions, has been culled from the *Zuozhuan*, Duke Xiang 襄 19th year (553 BCE).

15　670–624 BCE.

16　Quotation from the *Zuozhuan* Duke Wen 文 1st year (625 BCE) (Legge, *Classics* Vol. V, Pt. I, p. 230).

17　*Ling* 靈 might mean: animated, alive, a spirit, but it has many other significations besides, as: intelligent, ingenious, clever, which might well be used as a posthumous title.

18　This 成 would mean: the completer, the perfect one.

19　Li 厲 is in fact not a proper honorary epithet, its sense being: oppressive, cruel, malicious, ugly, terrible.

20　According to the *Zuozhuan* in 542 BCE.

21　Zi Chan 子產 is the style of the celebrated statesman Gongsun Qiao 公孫僑 of Zheng 鄭 581–521 BCE.

22　Duke Mu 穆 of Zheng 626–604 BCE.

23　Quotation from the *Zuozhuan*, Duke Zhao 昭 7th year (534 BCE) (Legge, *Classics* Vol. V, Pt. II, p. 618).

24　603–575 BCE.

25　Near Xi'anfu 西安府 in Shanxi 陝西.

26　In the Pingyang 平陽 prefecture (Shanxi 山西).

27　Aboriginal, non-Chinese tribes.

28　The Di 翟 had dethroned him, and conquered his territory.

29　Wei Ke's 魏顆 father.

30　Quotation from the *Zuozhuan*, Duke Xuan 宣 15th year (593 BCE).

31　Cf. p. II.557.

32　25–57 CE.

33　In Shanxi 山西.

34　The father of Wen Wang 文王.

35　546–488 BCE.

36　The Great Diviner of Qi 齊 (cf. p. II.471) and reputed author of the *Yanzi Chunqiu* 晏子春秋.

37 The founder of the Shang 商 dynasty, 1766–1753 BCE.

38 Tang's 湯 prime minister.

39 All four were sovereigns of the Shang dynasty. Tai Jia 太甲 reigned from 1753–1720 BCE, Wu Ding 武丁 1324–1265 BCE, and Zu Yi 祖乙 1525–1506 BCE.

40 The dukes of Song 宋 derived their descent from the sovereigns of the Shang dynasty.

41 Quoted from Yan Zi's 晏子 *Chunqiu* 春秋 (*Taiping yulan* 太平御覽) with some variations.

42 *Vid.* p. II.642–643.

43 His name was Ping 平 (556–530 BCE).

44 Prime minister of Jin 晉.

45 The father of the Emperor Yu 禹.

46 South of Yizhou 沂州 in Shandong 山東.

47 The Xia 夏 dynasty.

48 Xia, Shang, and Zhou 周.

49 Allied to the reigning house of Zhou.

50 Quoted from the *Zuozhuan*, Duke Zhao 昭 7th year (534 BCE) (Legge, *Classics* Vol. V, Pt. II p. 617).

51 Cf. Ch. 7.

52 Like other dreams. The visions have mostly a symbolical meaning, and must not be semblances of real beings.

53 They would be evoked by his remembrance, but not be real.

54 The Daoist philosopher Huai Nan Zi 淮南子.

55 *Vid.* Ch. 24.

56 With regard to the metamorphose of Gun 鯀.

57 Han Gao Zu 漢高祖, 206–194 BCE.

58 Cf. Ch. 65.

59 Uncle of the Emperor Han Wu Di 漢武帝.

60 District in Henan 河南.

61 Commander-in-chief under the Emperor Jing Di 景帝, 156–140 BCE, who was supplanted by Tian Fen 田蚡.

62 We learn from the *Qianhanshu* 前漢書, chap. 52, p. 12, Biography of Guan Fu 灌夫, that Tian Fen 田蚡 felt pain all over the body, as if he were flogged, and cried for mercy. The emperor sent his visionist to look at him, who reported that the ghosts of Guan Fu and Dou Ying 竇嬰 were holding him, and beating him to death.

63 The present Chenzhou 陳州 in Henan 河南.

64 Cf. Ch. 32.

65   Cf. Ch. 26.

66   Cf. p. I.102–103.

67   Peng Yue 彭越, King of Liang 梁, was executed by order of Han Gao Zu 漢高祖 in 196 BCE, when he had revolted against the emperor. All his relations to the third degree were put to death along with him. *Vid. Shiji* 史記 chap. 8, p. 33v.

68   An epithet often given to Qin Shi Huangdi 秦始皇 and Wang Mang 王莽, both equally detested by the Literati.

69   48–32 BCE.

70   In Caozhoufu 曹州府 (Shandong 山東).

71   946–934 BCE.

72   Near Xi'anfu 西安府, where the tumulus of the mighty emperor is still visible.

73   209–206 BCE.

CHAPTER 64
Spook Stories
Jiyao 紀妖

(*Lunheng* Book XXII, Chap. i)

1   533–499 BCE.

2   On the border of the provinces Zhili 直隸 and Shandong 山東.

3   556–530 BCE.

4   施夷 The *Shiji* 史記 chap. 24, p. 39 v. calls it the "Shihui terrace," 施惠, which was situated on the Fen 汾 river in Shanxi 山西.

5   Cf. *Shiji* chap. 4, p. 11 and Ch. 38.

6   I am not quite certain, whether G, C, and A major are a correct rendering of Chinese *qing* (clear) *shang, zhi* and *jue* 清商, 徵, 角. In the *Memoires concernant les Chinois* Vol. VI, p. 115 these notes are identified with sol, ut, and la. At any rate *qing* (clear) 清 and its correlate *zhuo* (obscure) 濁

would be appropriate terms to designate sharp and flat notes.—The parallel passage of the *Shiji* omits to specify the airs, as is done here.

7　The sacred Mount Tai 太山 is in the East, in Shandong, not in the West.

8　Some say that it is the spirit of wood. It is described as a bird with one wing, always carrying fire in its mouth, and portending fire in the house where it appears. According to the *Shanhaijing* 山海經 it would be a bird like a crane, but with one leg, a green plumage adorned with red, and a white beak.

9　A legendary person said by some to have been a minister of Huang Di 黃帝. Cf. Ch. 29.

10　All the details about the assembly of ghosts are omitted in the *Shiji*.

11　The same story, illustrative of the magical force of music, is told in a parallel passage of the *Shiji*, chap. 24, on music, p. 39 seq. Since the text of the *Lunheng* is fuller, I presume that Wang Chong did not quote the *Shiji*, but had an older source, probably the same, from which the *Shiji* has copied.

12　516–457 BCE.

13　Bian Que 扁鵲 is the honorary appellative of Qin Yueren 秦越人, a celebrated physician who travelled from State to State.

14　A minister of Viscount Jian 簡.

15　658–620 BCE.

16　Officers of Qin 秦.

17　675–651 BCE.

18　634–627 BCE.

19　626–620 BCE.

20　A defile in Henan 河南.

21　On the battle of Yao 崤 which took place in 626 BCE. Cf. *Zuozhuan* 左氏傳 Duke Xi 僖, 33rd year. The weakness of Duke Xiang 襄 consisted in releasing his prisoners at the request of his mother, a princess of Qin 秦, which was deeply resented by his officers. *Vid.* Ch. 26.

22　Northern barbarians. A Di 翟 dog was probably a huge Mongolian dog, resembling a St. Bernard, much bigger than the common Chinese dog.

23　We ought to read "seven generations" as the *Shiji* does. The characters for seven and ten can be easily confounded. Jian's 簡 sickness took place in 500 BCE under the reign of Duke Ding 定 of Jin 晉. From Duke Ding to the end of the Jin State, which in 375 broke up into the three marquisates of Wei 魏, Zhao 趙, and Han 韓, there are only seven rulers, Ding included. Viscount Jian 簡 was a vassal of Duke Ding and ancestor of the later marquises and kings of Zhao.

24 Ying 嬴 was the family name of the viscounts of Zhao.

25 This does not mean the people of the royal domain of Zhou 周, but the people of Wei 衛 (Henan 河南), whose princes were descended from a side branch of the royal house, their ancestor being Kang Shu 康叔, a younger brother of the Emperor Wu Wang 武王. After the extinction of Jin, the Marquis Cheng 成 of Zhao conquered seventy-three towns from Wei.

26 It should be "of the seventh generation," for King Wu Ling 武靈, who was married to Meng Yao 孟姚, was a descendant of Viscount Jian in the seventh degree.

27 Dai 代 and Zhi 知.

28 So far the story has been quoted from the *Shiji*, chap. 43, p. 7 seq.

29 *Comp.* p. I.137–38.

30 Another name for Mount Heng 恆山 in Datongfu 大同府 in North Shanxi 山西.

31 A Di 翟 State occupying the confines of North Shanxi 山西 and Mongolia.

32 Cf. *Shiji*, chap. 43, p. 11v.

33 An earldom in the south of the Jin 晉 State.

34 Name of a mountain in Gansu 甘肅 and of an aboriginal tribe (Rong 戎) settled there.

35 It must be "seven generations."

36 Wu Ling's 武靈 reign lasted from 325–299 BCE.

37 In the *Shiji*, chap. 43, p. 19. Wu Qing 吳慶 is called Wu Guang 吳廣. He was a descendant of Shun 舜.

38 The passage seems to be corrupt. The *Shiji* says "Wu Guang through his wife introduced (to the king) his beautiful daughter Ying Meng Yao 嬴孟姚." First a palace girl, Meng Yao 孟姚, some years later, was raised to the rank of a queen. See on this passage Chavannes, *Mem. Hist.* Vol. V, p. 68 Note 7.

39 Originally a part of Jin, in the modern Dingzhou 定州 of Zhili 直隸 province.

40 These Hu 胡 tribes were settled in the northern provinces: Zhili, Shanxi 山西, Shanxi 陝西, and Gansu.

41 The stars, considered as the officials of God, the Ruler of Heaven, and as divinities.

42 A nobleman of the Lu 魯 State of the 6th cent. BCE.

43 This dream is narrated in the *Zuozhuan* 左氏傳, Duke Zhao 昭 4th year (537 BCE).

44   In 456 BCE (cf. above p. II.658).

45   *I.e.* the viscounts of Han 韓 and Wei 魏, who together with those of Zhao had usurped the power in Jin.

46   Near Taiyuanfu 太原府 in Shanxi 山西.

47   The *Shiji* calls this place Wangze 王澤, which was situated in Jiangzhou 絳州 (Shanxi 山西).

48   The personal name of Viscount Xiang 襄 (cf. p. II.658).

49   A mountain in Yong'anxian 永安縣 (Shanxi 山西) Hedong 河東 circuit.

50   The reading of the *Shiji*: "Marquis of Shanyang 山陽 (name of city) and Envoy of Heaven" seems preferable.

51   A subdivision of the Hu tribes, probably Mongols.

52   A tributary of the Huanghe 黃河.

53   One "*pan*" 板 block is said to measure 8 feet. The *Shiji*, chap. 43, p. 13, writes: 版.

54   So far the narration has been culled with some omissions and alterations from the *Shiji*, chap. 43, p. 12 v. seq.

55   When the Xia 夏 dynasty had begun to decline, two divine dragons made their appearance in the imperial palace, and said that they were two princes of Bao 褒. Cf. *Shiji*, chap. 4, p. 25 (Chavannes, *Mem.Hist.* Vol. I, p. 281) which quotes the *Guoyu* 國語.

56   211 BCE.

57   A place at the bend of the Yellow River in Shanxi 陝西.

58   A town half-way between Dongguan 東關 and Xi'anfu 西安府.

59   The Hao Lake 鎬池 was near Xi'anfu, the capital of Qin Shi Huangdi 秦始皇, who is meant by the prince of the lake.

60   219 BCE.

61   The foregoing are extracts from the *Shiji*, chap. 6, p. 24v. seq.

62   On the south coast of Shandong 山東.

63   勞成山. The *Shiji* writes Rongcheng 榮成山 (*loc. cit.* p. 28). The Laoshan 勞山 and the Chengshan 成山 are two high mountain ranges in Jimo 即墨 (Jiaozhou 膠州) reaching to the sea. The *Dushi fangyu jiyao* 讀史方輿紀要, chap. 36 rejects the reading Rongcheng 榮成山. The mountains must have been on the sea-shore, north of Langye 琅邪 and south of Zhifu 之罘, for this was the way taken by the emperor, as results from *Lunheng* Bk. IV, 9 (*Shuxu* 書虛, Ch. 16) and Bk. XXVI, 1 (*Shizhi* 實知 Ch. 78).

64   The Zhifu 之罘 Promontory, forming the harbour of the treaty-port Zhifu.

65   According to the *Shiji* the emperor shot those big fishes with a repeating

cross-bow (*liannu*) 連弩, (on which cf. my article on the Chinese Cross-bow in *Verhandlungen der Berliner Gesellschaft für Anthropologie* 1896, p. 272).

66   In the Jinanfu 濟南府 prefecture, Shandong.

67   In Shundefu 順德府 (Zhili).

68   As though under a spell or a charm, which is the supernatural.

69   Later Duke Wen 文 of Jin, 634–627 BCE.

70   Banished from Jin, he lived for many years in other States.

71   This happened in Wei [QP: character not specified, assume 魏], whose prince had treated him discourteously.

72   Cf. *Zuozhuan*, Duke Xi 僖 23rd year, where the incident is told, though with other words.

73   Called Zi Fan 子反 in the *Zuozhuan*.

74   An official of Qi 齊, who delivered his country from the invading army of Yan 燕, in the 3rd cent. BCE.

75   City in Shandong, near Jiaozhou 膠州.

76   Tian Dan 田單 used a similar stratagem as Hannibal. During the night he fantastically dressed 1000 oxen, tied sharp blades to the horns and greased rushes to their tails, and lighting these rushes let them loose against the enemy, who were taken by surprise and completely beaten by the men of Yan 燕 following in the rear. *Vid.* the biography of Tian Dan in the *Shiji*, chap. 82, p. 3.

77   Therefore the death of the dragon implies the end of the emperor.

78   泗上. The *Shiji* chap. 8, p. 2v. writes Sishui 泗水, which was a district in the present Yanzhoufu 兗州府 (Shandong).

79   A mountain near Qin Shi Huangdi's 秦始皇 mausoleum in Shanxi 山西, which was built by convicts.

80   The story is quoted from the *Shiji*, chap. 8, p. 5. It is meant as a prophecy of the overthrow of the Qin 秦 dynasty by that of Han 漢. The Qin used metal, to which the white colour corresponded, as the symbol of their power, whereas the Han relied on fire, which has a red colour. According to Chinese symbolism fire overcomes metal, ergo the Qin were doomed to be overpowered by the Han.

81   The Five Planets which from ancient times were worshipped as deities. The Red Emperor is Mars, the White Emperor Venus.

82   699–694 BCE.

83   Duke Li 厲 had been forced to quit his country.

84   Cf. *Zuozhuan*, Duke Zhuang 莊 14th year. The snake inside the city was killed.

85   *Vid.* above p. II.661.

86   The *Zuozhuan*, Duke Zhao 昭 19th year (522 BCE) relates: "There were
     great floods in Zheng 鄭; and some dragons fought in the pool of Wei
     洧, outside the Shi gate 時門. The people asked leave to sacrifice to them;
     but Zi Chan 子產 refused it, saying, 'If we are fighting, the dragons do
     not look at us; when dragons are fighting, why should we look at them?'"
     (Legge, *Classics* Vol. V, Pt. II, p. 675).

87   Zhang Liang 張良 had engaged a bravo to deal the blow with an iron club
     or mallet weighing 120 pounds.

88   In the modern Peizhou 邳州 of Jiangsu 江蘇 province.

89   Instead of Si 泗 the *Shiji* writes: "yi" 圯, the "bridge."

90   In Dong'e 東阿 district (Shandong).

91   The helpmate of Wen Wang 文王, who had been invested with the mar-
     quisate of Qi 齊 in Shandong (cf. p. I.236–37).

92   The story is quoted from Zhang Liang's 張良 Biography in the *Shiji*, chap.
     55, p. 1 v, but somewhat abridged.

93   A simple soldier who in 209 BCE brought about an insurrection against
     Ershi Huangdi 二世皇帝, and assumed the title of a King of Chu 楚.

94   Liu Bang 劉邦 = Gao Zu 高祖, at that time still governor of Pei 沛 in
     Jiangsu.

95   556–531 BCE.

96   A city in modern Taiyuanfu 太原府 (Shanxi 山西).

97   *Zuozhuan*, Duke Zhao 8th year (Legge, *Classics* Vol. V, Pt. II, p. 622).

98   Circuit comprising the northern part of Henan 河南, north of Kaifengfu
     開封府.

99   See above p. II.661.

100 Cf. p. II.557.

101 The surname of Tai Gong 太公, Wen Wang's 文王 associate, who later on
     became Prince of Qi 齊.

102 The personal name of Wu Wang 武王.

103 Cf. p. I.255.

CHAPTER 65
All about Ghosts
Dinggui 訂鬼

(*Lunheng* Book XXII, Chap. ii)

1   A somewhat legendary character, mentioned by Zhuang Zi 莊子 chap. 9, p. 1.

2   For more details on this famous cook or butcher see *Zhuangzi* 莊子 chap. 3, p. 1.

3   We might translate mental fluid, for here the mental functions of the vital fluid are referred to, which is the bearer of life as well as the originator of mind, animus and anima.

4   See p. II.650.

5   The stars.

6   The constellations.

7   This seems to refer to the animals connected with the twelve cyclical signs (cf. p. I.159). A man born under one of these signs is supposed to have been imbued with the same essence as the corresponding animal has.

8   Their views are too fantastic, as can be seen from their works.

9   A legendary ruler of the 26th cent. BCE.

10 According to the "Water Classic" a river in the south-east of China.

11 This passage is not to be found in our *Liji* 禮記. According to the *Peiwen yunfu* 佩文韻府 it is contained in the *Soushenji* 搜神記 (4th cent. CE).

12 The signs *jia* 甲 and *yi* 乙.

13 In his commentary to the *Chunqiu* 春秋, the *Zuozhuan* 左氏傳.

14 Four wicked princes were cast out by Shun 舜 into the four distant regions. winch were believed to be inhabited by devils. *Zuozhuan*, Duke Wen 文 18th year (Legge, *Classic* Vol. V, Pt. I, p. 283).

15 Cf. *Shanhaijing* 山海經 XII, 1.

16 According to the *Fengsutong* 風俗通 of the 2nd cent. CE this story is narrated in the *Huangdishu* 黃帝書, the Book of Huang Di 黃帝. On New-Year's Eve the pictures of Shen Shu 神荼 and Yu Lü 鬱壘 are still at present pasted on the doorways as a talisman against evil spirits.

17　A legendary personage.

18　Two places in the Qi 齊 State, in Shandong 山東.

19　Prince Peng Sheng 彭生 was a half-brother of Duke Xiang 襄 of Qi, who employed him to murder his brother-in-law, the Duke of Lu 魯. The people of Qi put Peng Sheng to death. Cf. *Zuozhuan*, Duke Huan 桓 18th year (693 BCE).

20　Quoted from the *Zuozhuan*, Duke Zhuang 莊 8th year, corresponding to 685 BCE.

21　熒惑.

22　*Shangshu* 尚書, *Hongfan* 洪範 Pt. V, Bk. IV, 5 and 6 (Legge, *Classics* Vol. III, Pt. II, p. 325 and 326).

23　All weird things are manifestations of the *Yang* 陽, the solar fluid, which is fiery.

24　The *Yang* principle is male.

25　The Chinese believe that popular songs and sayings foretelling future events, of which they have collections, are supernatural inspirations or revelations. Hence they bring them into connection with ghosts or supernatural beings. Wang Chong falls back on the *Yang* principle as the origin of those quaint ditties.

26　The *Yin* 陰 fluid is the rain.

27　The sun is eclipsed by the moon, which belongs to the *Yin* fluid.

28　659–626 BCE.

29　The South is the land of the sun, the *Yang* principle.

30　The foregoing futile speculations are based on the gratuitous analogies, in which Chinese natural philosophers, starting from the *Yijing* 易經, indulge.

31　Heir-apparent to Duke Xian 獻 of the Jin 晉 State, by whom he was put to death in 654 BCE. We learn from the *Zuozhuan*, 10th year of Duke Xi 僖, that in 649 BCE the ghost of the murdered prince appeared to an officer of Jin, and spoke to him. He told him that in seven days he would have a new interview with him through a wizard, and that he would take his revenge on Duke Hui 惠 of Jin. Cf. p. II.637.

32　The Earl of Du 杜 had been unjustly put to death by King Xuan 宣 of the Zhou 周 dynasty, 826–780 BCE. According to a legend the ghost of the murdered man appeared to the king while hunting. He was dressed in red, and carried a red bow and red arrows. One of these arrows he shot through the king's heart, who died on the spot. Cf. Chavannes, *Mem. Hist.* Vol. I, p. 278 Note 2. *Vid.* also p. II.636.

33　See p. II.636.

34　By which Ye Gu 夜姑 of Song 宋 was killed. Cf. Ch. 76.

35　The thoughts of ghosts, uttered through the mouth of boys, singing queer songs, or mysteriously written on stones.

36　Cf. p. II.653.

37　See above p. II.673.

38　Duke Jian 簡 of Yan 燕, 503–491 BCE (p. II.636, Ch. 63) speaks of Duke Jian 簡 of Zhao 趙 and *Lunheng* Bk. IV, p. 5 (Ch. 16) of Viscount Jian 簡 of Zhao 趙.

39　See Ch. 76.

40　Duke Hui 惠 of Jin 晉, 649–635 BCE. In 644 the duke was taken prisoner by Qin 秦.

41　Cf. p. II.642.

42　Wei Ke 魏顆 was a commander of the forces of Jin in the 6th cent. BCE, with which he worsted those of the Qin State, and took their strongest man, Du Hui 杜回, prisoner. He was supported during the battle by an old man twisting the grass in such a way as to impede the movements of his enemies. This old man was the spirit of the father of a concubine of Wei Ke's father, whom he had saved from death. Out of gratitude for the kindness shown to his daughter the spirit thus contributed to his victory and to the capture of Du Hui. Cf. p. II.644–45.

43　*Vid. Shiji* 史記 chap. 9, p. 8v. The Empress Lü Hou 呂后 was bitten by a grey dog, which suddenly vanished. The diviners declared it to have been the phantom of Ru Yi 如意, Prince of Zhao 趙, whom Lü Hou had assassinated. Lü Hou died of the bite.

44　Tian Fen 田蚡, Marquis of Wu'an 武安, a minister of the Emperor Han Wu Di 漢武帝 had in 140 BCE caused the death of his predecessor and rival Dou Ying 竇嬰. The ghost of the latter appeared to him, when he was about to die. The general Guan Fu's 灌夫 death was likewise the work of Tian Fen. Cf. p. II.650.

CHAPTER 66

On Poison

Yandu 言毒

(*Lunheng* Book XXIII, Chap. i)

1   Huguang 湖廣 and Zhejiang 浙江.

2   Hubei 湖北.

3   The country south of the Yangzi 江, now the provinces Jiangsu 江蘇, Jiangxi 江西, and Anhui 安徽.

4   Cf. p. II.636.

5   *Kangxi* 康熙 quotes this passage, but does not say what kind of a fish the "*duoshu*" 鮥鮛 is. It may be a variety of the *shu* [QP: 鮛 or 鮇], which seems to be a kind of sturgeon.

6   Cf. *Shangshu* 尚書 (*Hongfan* 洪範) Pt. V, Bk. IV, 5–6.

7   Another instance of Chinese symbolism, which they mistake for science.

8   Cf. p. II.460.

9   A place in Henan 河南 celebrated for its foundries. *Vid.* p. I.115.

10   *Zhen* 鴆 = secretary falcon has become a synonym for poison.

11   The fifth and the sixth of the Twelve Branches (Duodenary Cycle of symbols).

12   The "Green Dragon" is the quadrant or the division of the 28 solar mansions occupying the east of the sky. The "Fire Star" is the Planet Mars. Mars in the quadrant of the "Green Dragon" forebodes war *i.e.* poison; nothing but inane symbolism. (Cf. *Shiji* 史記 chap. 27, p. 6v.)

13   The country north of the Yangzi, now the northern parts of the provinces Jiangsu and Anhui.

14   Which hang down likewise.

15   Which are soft and extensible.—To such ineptitudes even the most elevated Chinese minds are led by their craze of symbolisation.

16   The mischief done by the tongue in speaking, which is not only compared to, but identified with poison.

17   *Shangshu* (*Hongfan*) Pt. V, Bk. IV, 34.

18   Cf. p. II.674 and above p. II.679.

19 A half-brother of Shu Xiang 叔向. His mother was a concubine of Shu Xiang's father.

20 An officer of Jin 晉.

21 Being an exceptional woman by her beauty, she would give birth to an extraordinary son—a dragon, and it would be dangerous for an ordinary man like her son Shu Xiang to be a blood relation of such an extraordinary person, since fate likes to strike the exalted.

22 Quoted from the *Zuozhuan* 左氏傳, Duke Xiang 襄, 21st year (551 BCE).

23 Two noblemen of Jin, cf. p. II.640.

24 A powerful, but unworthy officer in Lu 魯.

25 *Shijing* 詩經 Pt. II, Bk. VII, Ode V.

26 Modern commentators explain the expression 四國 as meaning "the four quarters of the empire."

CHAPTER 67
Simplicity of Funerals
Bozang 薄葬
(*Lunheng* Book XXIII, Chap. ii)

1 These arguments of the Mohists are refuted in Ch. 62.

2 This is Wang Chong's opinion at least.

3 Cf. Ch. 63 n. 2.

4 A practice still prevailing in our time.

5 殉葬.

6 璵璠. Ed. A writes 與.

7 We learn from the "Family Sayings" that, when a member of the Ji 季 family had died, they were going to put cat's-eyes into his coffin, as is customary for princes, and to bestow pearls and jade upon him. Confucius, just then governor of Zhongdu 中都, hearing of it, ascended the steps and interfered saying, "To inter a man with precious stones is like exposing a corpse in the open plain, and thus affording people an opportunity of

gratifying their wicked designs." Jiayu 家語 IX, 16r.

   On the old custom of filling the mouths of deceased princes with jade and other precious objects see De Groot, *Religious System* Vol. I, p. 269 seq.

8   They could afford to put precious things into the grave.

9   Or the diviner Xian 巫咸, who lived under the Yin 殷 dynasty and is mentioned in the Preface of the *Shangshu* 尚書. Cf. Chavannes, *Mem. Hist.* Vol. I, p. 191, Note 1.

10   In Hades.

11   Therefore they treat them, as if they were still alive and together with the living.

12   Two prominent disciples of Confucius.

13   Cf. *Liji* 禮記, Tangong 檀弓 p. 52r. (Legge, *Sacred Books* Vol. XXVII, p. 173).

14   This was not likely, for, historically speaking, human sacrifices precede, but do not follow the use of dummies buried together with the dead.

15   Real vessels are, likewise, antecedent to the so called "spirit vessels," made of straw or clay, and merely symbolical and commemorative of an ancient custom that had fallen into desuetude.

16   The State became impoverished by extravagant funerals.

17   Cf. p. I.385–86.

18   De Groot in his *Religious System* Vol. II, p. 659 speaks at great length of the reaction against expensive funerals, but does not mention Wang Chong as an advocate of economy. He calls attention to two chapters of the *Lüshi chunqiu* 呂氏春秋, recommending simplicity in burials, and to the disquisitions of Wang Fu [QP: most probably 王符] of the 2nd cent. CE. Later on, Zhu Xi [QP: most probably 朱熹] was in favour of plain funerals, but the exaggerated ideas on filial piety have counteracted all reasonable arguments.

CHAPTER 68

Four Things to be Avoided
Sihui 四諱

(*Lunheng* Book XXIII, Chap. iii)

1   494–468 BCE.

2   Quoted from *Huainanzi* 淮南子 XVIII, 18v.

3   Common people believe in these superstitions.

4   *I.e.,* when a new building is erected in the west for the use of a second master. The other possibility that the new building is destined for the one master to enlarge his dwelling, is not taken into account.

5   The *Fengsutong* 風俗通, quoted in the *Peiwen yunfu* 佩文韻府, gives a similar reason: The west is the seat of the superiors, and a new building in this direction would be hurtful to them.

6   Even a good man may innocently suffer punishment and thus become a convict.

7   開. Our text of the *Analects* reads: 啟.

8   *Analects* VIII, 3.

9   See *Liji* 禮記, Jiyi 祭義 (Legge, *Sacred Books* Vol. XXVIII, p. 229).

10   Cf. p. II.460 and I.144, where Wang Ji 王季 is called "King Ji 季" or Ji Li 季歷.

11   *Vid.* p. I.414–15.

12   扶. This meaning is not found in the dictionaries.

13   木實. Ed. A and B have 水 for 木. 水實 might be equivalent to 水菓 "fresh fruit."

14   The horse, the ox, the goat, the pig, the dog, and the cock.

15   更衣之室, a term strangely corresponding to the German word "toilet" = privy.

16   Most Chinese privies are so horrid, that even Chinese try to avoid them.

17   Chinese varnish is so poisonous, that its smell alone suffices to produce a cutaneous eruption.

18   弦.

19 望.

20 晦.

21 Quotation from the *Shiji* 史記 chap. 75, p. 2r. the biography of Tian Wen 田文. Cf. also p. I.228, where, in line 7, "He replied" should be written for "She replied," and, in line 10, "He rejoined" for "She rejoined."

22 This reason may be in accordance with Wang Chong's system, to us it appears inane.

23 This is Wang Chong's opinion. The belief of his countrymen is that many actions, apart from their qualities, entail misfortune, and solely for this reason are to be shunned.

24 Perhaps the electricity caused the sauce to spoil, as milk becomes sour when the air is charged with electricity. Wang Chong does not know this.

25 The first thunder-storms are in spring. This single case, Wang Chong seems to intimate, was the reason that, subsequently, people always liked to have their bean-sauce ready before the first peal of thunder was heard *viz.* before the beginning of spring.

26 Similar "avoidances" have come down to our own rational times. *E.g.* one must not thank any one for a knife or a pair of scissors, otherwise they would cut the friendship. A young lady avoids cutting a fresh pat of butter, otherwise she is sure not to marry during the year.

27 This rule goes back to Confucius, who in bed, did not lie like a corpse. *Analects* X, 16.

28 This may be an allusion to the frailty of the body or of friendship.

29 A man making such a request would be like one having somebody to bury. The very sensible reasons given for these various customs are Wang Chong's.

30 *Liji*, Quli 曲禮 p. 18r. (Legge, *Sacred Books* Vol. XXVII, p. 80).

CHAPTER 69
False Charges against Time
Lanshi 諷時

(*Lunheng* Book XXIII, Chap. iv)

1   This must not be taken literally. It seems to mean to cause damage or misfortune.

2   The North.

3   The West.

4   East-north-east.

5   South-south-east.

6   厭勝.

7   The element metal corresponds to the west.

8   The element of the east is wood, that of the south where the inimical luminaries are placed, while menacing the family, is fire. Charcoal is a combination of wood and fire.

9   On the collision with the year-star = Jupiter of people moving their residence see Ch. 73.

10 In one case they punish those who collide with them, in the other, those living in quite a different direction *viz.* a quarter to the right or the left of their stand-point.

11 We ought to read *you* 酉, as above, I suppose.

12 Perhaps we should add "and a *yin* 寅 house."

13 A province under the Han 漢 comprising Jiangsu 江蘇, Anhui 安徽, Jiangxi 江西, Fujian 福建, and Zhejiang 浙江.

14 In the west.

15 Tibetan tribes.

16 Jupiter was first supposed to stay in the north, outside of China, now it is placed amidst men, in the interior.

17 The suburban sacrifices were offered to Heaven.

18 統. Three *tong* 統 are one *yuan* 元.

19 These periods may be of Daoist origin. Some reckon a *yuan* 元 at 129,600, others at 24,192,000 years, something like a geological period. The Dao-

ists like the Indians are fond of big numbers. According to one authority 3,276,000 years have elapsed from the creation of the world to 481 BCE.

20 弦.

21 望. Cf. also Ch. 68 n. 18 and 19.

22 The twelve hours of the day are denominated after the twelve cyclical signs *yin* 寅, *mao* 卯, &c., marking that place of the horizon over which the sun stays during each double hour. In the same way, every month of the Chinese calendar is connected with that cyclical sign in which the moon rests during that month. In the course of twelve months the moon has passed through all the twelve constellations or cyclical signs. Wang Chong is not correct in saying that the *yin* and *mao* "times" are added to the twelve months, they are not times in this case, but constellations corresponding to those of our zodiac. The twelve 辰, to which belong *yin* and *mao*, are those places of the firmament through which the sun passes in twelve double hours, and the moon in twelve months. For this reason they are made use of to designate the twelve hours as well as the twelve months. Moreover, the course of the planet Jupiter through these signs of the zodiac, which is completed in 12 years, affords a means of denoting the consecutive years, on which cf. Chavannes, *Mem. Hist.* Vol. III, p. 655 seq.

23 Cf. p. I.232–33.

CHAPTER 70

Slandering of Days

Jiri 譏日

(*Lunheng* Book XXIV, Chap. i)

1 Prosperity and decay are the events and circumstances making people happy or miserable.

2 These seem to be geomantic terms.

3 Both are elements.

4 Digging a grave, and making ditches or tilling a garden.

5 Quoted from the *Chunqiu* 春秋, Duke Xuan 宣 8th year.

6 The Duchess of Lu 魯 was Jing Ying 敬嬴.

7 己丑. Ed. A and B have 巳, ed. C writes 己.

8 Originally the duchess was to be buried on a *jichou* 己丑 day, but the rain prevented it. *Jichou*, being the 26th combination of the cycle of sixty, would have been an even day, and as such in harmony with the uneven day of the death of the duchess. The *gengyin* 庚寅 day, the 27th combination, was an odd day again and not tallying with the odd day of death.

9 The *Zuozhuan* 左氏傳, commenting upon the above quoted passage, states that to delay the interment owing to rain was according to rule. The *Liji* 禮記 (Legge, *Sacred Books* Vol. XXVII, p. 223) informs us that common people did not suspend the interment because of rain, and this rule seems to prevail at present, a rain-fall during a burial being regarded as very propitious. Cf. De Groot, *Religious System* Vol. I, p. 213.

10 *Liji eod.*

11 In adding seven, five, or three, the month of death is included.

12 *I.e.*, it would correspond to the month of death, being even in case the latter was even, and uneven if the latter was.

13 血忌.

14 月殺.

15 In general belief, here only used as an argument, for Wang Chong does not share it. See Ch. 15 and below.

16 Because men do not choose propitious days for eating and drinking.

17 Cf. Ch. 56 n. 6.

18 如以首為最尊。尊則浴亦治面。面亦首也. The second 尊 seems out of place and should be expunged.

19 The Chinese still use wooden combs to-day, a fact illustrated by the character for comb 櫛.

20 Fire, the *Yang* 陽 fluid, the producing force of nature is nobler than water, the *Yin* 陰 fluid, which is regarded as passive or destructive.

21 According to the theory on the Five Elements, elaborated in the Han 漢 epoch, of the Twelve Branches 亥 *hai* and 子 *zi* are related to water, and 寅 *yin* and 卯 *mao*, to wood. Cf. Appendix I p. 467.

22 The prescription cannot be explained by the fanciful theory on the elements and their correlates.

23 We have to insert the answer to the preceding rhetorical question: nobody.

24 Ed. A and B have the misprint: 不擇食 for 日.

25 The Eight Objects of Government, enumerated in the *Shangshu* 尚書, *viz.* food, commodities, sacrifices, works, instruction, jurisdiction,

entertainment of guests, and warfare.

26 Its importance lies not so much in its usefulness—in this respect a coat or a cloak are more important—as in its covering the head, the noblest part of the body.

27 These Nine Gifts 九錫 were symbols of authority, anciently bestowed upon vassals and ministers. They were: a chariot and horses, robes of State, musical instruments, vermilion coloured entrance doors, the right to approach the sovereign by the central path, armed attendants, bows and arrows, battle-axes, and sacrificial wines. Mayers' Manual Pt. II No. 284.

28 The disturbance would be the same, whether the day be auspicious or not.

29 The inventor of writing.

30 These dynasties were celebrated for their music.

31 Some days are shunned out of respect for great men that died on these days, but not because they forebode evil.

32 Here again the text writes 曆曆上. One 曆 is superfluous.

33 Confucius admits the existence of ghosts and spirits, and that they be sacrificed to, but avoids speaking of them and answering any questions about their nature.

34 Quotation from the 孝經 Xiaojing (*Peiwen yunfu* 佩文韻府).

CHAPTER 71
On Divination
Bushi 卜筮

(*Lunheng* Book XXIV, Chap. ii)

1 A gratuitous etymology, of which the Chinese are very fond. *Shi* 蓍 = milfoil and *gui* 龜 = tortoise have nothing whatever to do with *qi* 耆 = old and *jiu* 舊 = aged.

2 From *Zhuangzi* 莊子 chap. 26, p. 4v. it appears that for divining purposes the tortoise shell used to be cut into 72 pieces or divining slips.

3 *Analects* XVII, 19.

4   *Yijing* 易經, *Jici* 繫辭 I (Legge's transl. p. 365).

5   Which he uses in burning the tortoise shell.

6   The minister of Zhou 紂.

7   Cf. *Shangshu* 尚書, *Xi bo kan Li* 西伯戡黎 and *Shiji* 史記 chap. 3 (Cha-vannes, *Mem. Hist.* Vol. I, p. 204).

8   The countrymen of Gao Zu 高祖, who was born in Feng 豐, in the sub-prefecture of Pei 沛 in Jiangsu 江蘇.

9   The *Liji* 禮記 writes Shi Tai Zhong 石駘仲.

10 From his concubines.

11 A feudal lord in Wei 衛, mentioned in the *Zuozhuan* 左氏傳, Duke Zhuang 莊 12th year (681 BCE), as influencing the policy of his native State.

12 So far the story is culled from the *Liji, Tangong* 檀弓 II (Legge, *Sacred Books* Vol. XXVII, p. 181).

13 The Duke of Zhou 周公 had built three altars to his three ancestors, whom he consulted on the fate of his sick brother Wu Wang 武王. He probably had one tortoise for each altar. (Cf. *Shiji* 史記 chap. 33, p. 1v. and p. II.639.)

14 Shusun Zhuangshu 叔孫莊叔 or Shusun Dechen 叔孫得臣. When he died in 603 BCE, he received the posthumous name Zhuang 莊.

15 The same as Shusun Muzi 叔孫穆子 mentioned in Ch. 64. His clan name was Shu Sun 叔孫, Mu 穆 being his posthumous title.

16 The diagram Mingyi 明夷.

17 The diagram Qian 謙. Wang Chong here quotes a passage from the *Zuozhuan*, Duke Zhao 昭 5th year (Legge, *Classics* Vol. V, Pt. II, p. 604) where the expression "encountered" 遇 is used.

18 逢.

19 The last emperor of the Shang 商 dynasty, Zhou Xin 紂辛.

20 Those in power win the people over to their views by showing that the omens are favourable, and that the spirits causing them give their approval.

21 Chapter XIX of Han Feizi's 韓非子 work.

22 Cf. *Shangshu* 尚書, *Hongfan* 洪範, Pt. V, Bk. IV, 20 (Legge, *Classics* Vol. III, Pt. II, p. 334).

23 The Viscount of Chu 楚, who styled himself king.

24 The *Zuozhuan* calls him Zi Fan 子犯.

25 Quotation from the *Zuozhuan*, Duke Xi 僖 28th year (631 BCE).

26 I surmise from the context that the character 魋 must denote some defor-mity of the tortoise. *Kangxi* 康熙 says in the appendix that the meaning is unknown.

CHAPTER 72
Criticisms on Noxious Influences
Biansui 辨祟

(*Lunheng* Book XXIV, Chap. iii)

1   Not a moral offence, but a disregard of noxious influences.
2   *Shangshu* 尚書, *Hongfan* 洪範 Pt. V, Bk. IV, 23 (Legge, *Classics* Vol. III, Pt. II, p. 335). By another punctuation the commentators bring out another meaning *viz.* that there are seven modes of divination in all, five given by the tortoise and two by milfoil.
3   We must not suppose that Heaven can fear and tremble, for, as Wang Chong tells us over and over again, Heaven is unconscious and inactive. It possesses those qualities ascribed to it only virtually. They become actual and are put into practice by man, who fulfils the commands of Heaven with trembling awe. Its moral feelings are heavenly principles and heavenly emotions. Cf. p. II.467.
4   Two emperors of the Zhou 周 dynasty of bad repute. You Wang 幽王 reigned from 781 to 771 BCE, Li Wang 厲王 from 878 to 828 BCE.
5   Cf. p. I.95.
6   Even in that case there is fate, which includes human activity.
7   Snakes, reptiles, and worms which like man have no scales, fur, or feathers.
8   *Yijing* 易經, 1st diagram (Qian 乾).
9   *Vid.* p. I.95.
10 Cf. p. II.717–18.
11 The *Shiji* 史記 chap. 8, p. 11v., where this passage occurs (Chavannes, *Mem. Hist.* Vol. II, p. 343), speaks of the city of Xiangcheng 襄城 in Henan 河南, whereas Xiang'an 襄安 is situated in Anhui 安徽.
12 Cf. p. I.95.
13 Three cyclical numbers.
14 On a Wangwang 往亡 day one must not go out, and on a Guiji 歸忌 day returning home is disastrous.
15 Wangwang, Guiji, Suipo, and Zhifu 往亡, 歸忌, 歲破, 直符 are technical terms used by geomancers and in calendars to designate certain classes of unlucky days.

CHAPTER 73

Questions about the Year Star
Nansui 難歲

(*Lunheng* **Book XXIV, Chap. iv**)

1   太歲, a fictitious point, also called *suiyin* 歲陰, "the opposite of Jupiter," used for designating the year by means of the cycle of sixty. (See Chavannes, *Mem. Hist.* Vol. III, p. 654). The term *jiazi* 甲子 would correspond to the North = 子. Then Jupiter itself would have its position due south.

2   歲下.

3   歲破.

4   其移東西. Ed. A and C write 後 for 移.

5   179–157 BCE.

6   Cf. Giles, *Bibl. Dict.* No. 105 and Ch. 80 n. 79.

7   We see from this passage that the personification of "Taisui 太歲" is not a recent invention as De Harlez, *Le Livre des Esprits et des Immortels*, p. 134 says. This spirit is venerated at the present day, and seems by some to be regarded as a dangerous spirit of the soil.

8   On the firmament Jupiter describes a curve, not a straight line.

9   The spirits of Heaven dislike crookedness.

10   While crossing the course of Taisui from north to south.

11   四維相之如猶抵觸之如. Ed. A and C replace 之 by 知.

12   子午, the north and the south points.

13   The fog would spread sideways as well as from north to south.

14   The eastern quadrant of heaven.

15   Wang Chong seems to take the Green Dragon for a real dragon of extraordinary dimensions.

16   *I.e.*, not always keeping on one side of Taisui.

17   Equivalent to China.

18   三河: the Huanghe 黃河, the Huai 淮河, and the Luo 洛河.

19   *Shangshu* 尚書 Part V, Book XII, 14 (Legge, *Classics* Vol. III, Part II, p. 428).

20   Cf. p. I.360.

21 Names of the Nine Circuits.

22 In Chinese natural philosophy the North, or cold, overcomes the South, or heat; there is no real breaking.

23 Theoretically opposite directions as well as opposite qualities of things, in short all opposites, knock together and destroy one another.

24 Cf. p. II.745.

25 The eight terms are those of the Eight Diagrams 八卦.

26 *Viz. kun* 坤 and *dui* 兌.

27 The other six diagrams.

28 In one plan of the Eight Diagrams (Mayers' Manual p. 335) *gen* 艮 represents the North-east.

29 The South-west.

30 The South.

31 Why would the approaching of *wu* 午 from *kun* 坤 not be disastrous?

32 E.N.E.

33 W.S.W.

34 Cf. Ch. 69 n. 19.

35 In the term *jiazi* 甲子, *jia* 甲 does not signify any direction. Together with *yi* 乙 it may stand for the east.

36 Because in the east they might collide with Taisui in *jia* 甲, provided it could stay there.

CHAPTER 74

Criticisms on Certain Theories

Jieshu 詰術

(*Lunheng* Book XXV, Chap. i)

1 This would seem to be the cycle of sixty in which the sign *jia* 甲 recurs six times.

2 The two first of the Five Tones or musical notes.

3 The same as the Five Tones.

4   It is difficult to grasp the full meaning of the aforesaid without a commentary.

5   These signs are thought of as spiritual beings also.

6   Streets and alleys not near an inn, which seem not to have been marked like those surrounding an inn.

7   Therefore these stands and bazaars should be treated like dwelling houses *viz.* be marked with *jia* 甲, *yi* 乙, &c.

8   Only market inns, *i.e.*, solid buildings are placed on a level with dwelling houses.

9   Days are counted by means of the two cycles of ten and of twelve combined.

10   支干.

11   Properly speaking, only the Twelve Branches are added to the hours.

12   *Jia* 甲 corresponds to wood, and *zi* 子 to water, two harmonious elements.

13   3–5 a. m.

14   The element of *yin* 寅 and *mao* 卯 is wood like that of *jia* 甲 and *yi* 乙. Consequently there was no antagonism between the signs *jia* 甲, *zi* 子, and *yin* 寅, and yet Zhou 紂 was unlucky.

15   In so far as this and the duodenary cycle are used to determine the days = 日, which originally means "sun."

16   There are not ten suns, but the ten cyclical signs are attached to each ten consecutive days.

17   These twelve constellations 辰, designated by the Twelve Branches, serve to determine the twelve Chinese double-hours, according as the sun, in its daily course, passes through them.

18   The first signs of the denary and of the duodenary cycles.

19   Here we have the same equivocation of days and suns. The notation by the two cycles merely applies to days, not to suns.

20   Probably a diagram, used for divining purposes, similar to that found in calendars.

21   Based on the well known symbolism by reference to the elements.

22   It determines the hours.

23   In the encyclopedias of surnames one of the Five Sounds is attached to each name. I fail to understand how they were determined by the so-called experts. There is another tradition that Huang Di 黄帝 blew the flute to fix the surnames.

24   They are naturally obtained, and it is superfluous artificially to determine their sounds.

25 *Zuozhuan* 左氏傳, Duke Yin 隱 8th year (Legge, *Classics* Vol. V, Part I, p. 25).

26 Cf. p. I.162.

27 See Ch. 54 n. 13.

28 昌, which may mean: prosperous, flourishing, powerful.

29 發 = to expand, to prosper, to advance, to rise.

30 The mother of Confucius is reported to have ascended the Ni hill, 尼丘, before his birth.

31 This was the personal name of Duke Zhao 昭 of Song 宋, 619–611 BCE (See Chavannes, *Mem. Hist.* Vol. IV, p. 241), and it was borne by some other dukes of other States too.

32 The gist of this passage, but not the examples, is derived from the *Zuozhuan*, Duke Huan 桓 6th year (Legge, *Classics* Vol. V, Part I, p. 49).

33 子貢. The latter character has a similar meaning to 賜.

34 子我. The latter sign has the same sense as 予. The expansion is in both cases affected be the addiction of 子.

35 本姓.

36 氏姓.

37 陶 meaning a potter.

38 田 meaning a farmer.

39 上官, a high officer.

40 司馬, a military officer.

41 孟 and 仲, denoting the eldest and the second son of a family.

42 The theory of clan-names exposed in Legge's translation of the *Zuozhuan* p. 26 differs somewhat.

43 *Liji* 禮記, *Quli* 曲禮 (Legge, *Sacred Books* Vol. XXVII, p. 78).

44 Which they forbid *loc. cit.* See also Ch. 16 n. 67.

45 *Analects* VI, 15.

46 Cf. p. II.750 and 1.516.

47 徵羽, the fourth and the fifth tones corresponding to the south = fire and the north = water. Fire and water would injure metal and earth, the elements of *gong* 宮 and *shang* 商.

48 角 corresponding to wood.

49 Metal = white being destroyed by fire = the south.

50 Earth = yellow not being injured by fire = the south.

51 According to the theory of the Chinese physicists, metal is connected with the west, and wood with the east.

CHAPTER 75
On Exorcism
Jiechu 解除

(*Lunheng* Book XXV, Chap. ii)

1 In addition to the Blue Dragon and White Tiger Wang Chong mentions the 太歲 Taisui, 登明 Dengming and 從魁 Zongkui as such spirits. Cf. *Lunheng*, Ch. 73 (*Nansui* 難歲).
2 The Blue Dragon and the White Tiger are also names of the eastern and western quadrant of the solar mansions. Comp. p. I.159 and p. I.240–41.
3 Cf. p. II.671.
4 The image of the departed, who as master dwells in the ancestral hall.
5 No figures are used at the sacrifices to those deities.
6 A nobleman, related to the ducal house of Jin 晉, of the 5th cent. BCE. The Zhonghang 中行 family possessed large domains in Jin.

CHAPTER 76
Sacrifices to the Departed
Siyi 祀義

(*Lunheng* Book XXV, Chap. iii)

1 Ancient Chinese feet, which are much smaller than the modern.
2 Large kinds of rice and millet.
3 The Five Sacrifices of the house often mentioned in the *Liji* 禮記.
4 Feng Bo 風伯, the Prince of the Wind, Yu Shi 雨師, the Master of Rain,

and Lei Gong 雷公, the Thunderer. Their sacrifices are determined in the Zhou 周 ritual.

5 Duke Bao 鮑 alias Wen 文 of Song 宋, 609–588 BCE. His death is chronicled in the *Chunqiu* 春秋, Duke Cheng 成 2nd year.

6 The Hu 胡 in the north, and the Yue 南越 in the south of China.

7 *Yijing* 易經, 63rd diagram (Jiji 既濟), Legge's translation p. 206.

CHAPTER 77

Sacrifices

Jiyi 祭意

(*Lunheng* Book XXV, Chap. iv)

1 The mountains and rivers of their territory.

2 The five genii of the house to whom the Five Sacrifices were offered. See further on.

3 Cf. *Liji* 禮記, *Quli* 曲禮 (Legge, *Sacred Books* Vol. XXVII, p. 116).

4 *Shangshu* 尚書, *Shundian* 舜典 Pt. II, Bk. I, 6 (Legge, *Classics* Vol. III, Pt. I, p. 33).

5 Huang Di 黃帝, Di Ku 帝嚳 and Zhuan Xu 顓頊 are mythical emperors. Di Ku is said to have been the father of Yao 堯.

6 Gun 鯀, the father of Yu 禹.

7 Ming 冥 was a descendant of Xie 契, who was a son of Di Ku.

8 Ji 稷 = Hou Ji 后稷, the ancestor of the Zhou 周 dynasty.

9 The four sacrifices here mentioned were presented by the sovereigns of the ancient dynasties to the founders of their dynasties, their ancestors, and predecessors.

10 Quotation from the *Liji, Jifa* 祭法 (Law of sacrifices). The commentators, whom Legge follows in his translation (*Sacred Books* Vol. XXVIII, p. 201), read much between the lines, which appears rather problematic.

11 What the "Six Honoured Ones" are, is disputed. Some say: water, fire, wind, thunder, hills, and lakes; others explain the term as signifying: the sun, the moon, the stars, rivers, seas, and mountains.

12   The Spirit of the Land or the Soil.

13   The Spirit of Grain.

14   Qi 棄, the first ancestor of the Zhou 周 dynasty, venerates as the Spirit of Grain under the title Hou Ji 后稷 "Lord of the Grain." On his miraculous birth *vid.* p. I.121.

15   By other authors Qi is not identified with the legendary Emperor Shao Hao 少昊, whose birth was miraculous also. His mother was caused to conceive by a huge star like a rainbow (*Taiping yulan* 太平御覽).

16   According to the commentary of the *Liji* these were not uncles, but sons of Shao Hao.

17   The names of these deities or deified men correspond to their functions: 勾芒 Gou Mang = "Curling fronds and spikelets," 蓐收 Ru Shou = "Sprouts gathered," and 玄冥 Xuan Ming = "Dark and obscure." According to the *Liji* (*Yueling* 月令) these three deities were secondary spirits, each presiding over three months of spring, autumn, and winter. Some say that Xuan Ming was a water spirit. As the spirit of summer 祝融 Zhu Rong, who is related to fire, is venerated. There being a fixed relation between the four seasons, the four cardinal points, and the Five Elements we have the following equations:

    Gou Mang, Genius of Spring, the east, and wood.

    Zhu Rong, Genius of Summer, the south, and fire.

    Ru Shou, Genius of Autumn, the west, and metal.

    Xuan Ming, Genius of Winter, the north, and water.

    I suppose that in the clause "who could master metal, fire and wood" we ought to read water in lieu of fire, for the gods there enumerated are those of wood, metal and water. The spirit of fire follows in the next clause.

    In the *Liji*, Hou Tu 后土, the Lord of the Soil is made to correspond to the middle of the four seasons—in default of a fifth season—to the centre, and to earth. (Cf. Legge, *Sacred Books* Vol. XXVII, p. 281 Note.) Thus we have:

    Hou Tu, Genius of Mid-year, the centre, and earth.

    These Five Spirits are called the Wu Shen 五神. They were worshipped during the Zhou 周 dynasty and are mentioned in ancient works (*Liji*, *Zuozhuan* 左氏傳, *Huainanzi* 淮南子).

18   Another name of Shao Hao, who was lord of Qiongsang 窮桑.

19   A legendary emperor.

20   Cf. Ch. 77 n.17.

21   See p. I.358.

22　Personal name of the Emperor Shen Nong 神農, who was lord of Lie Shan 烈山.

23　Quotation from the *Zuozhuan* 左氏傳, Duke Zhao 昭 29th year (Legge's transl. Vol. II, p. 729). [QP Note from the 1907 Addenda has been incorporated. The addenda reads: The text of the *Zuozhuan* confirms my suggestion (Ch. 77 n.17) that we ought to read: "who could master metal, water, and wood," replacing "fire" by "water," for the Classic speaks of metal, wood, and water. It describes the Five Spirits as officers of the five elementary principles, assigning the proper element to each. I have translated 四叔 by "four uncles." Legge's rendering "four men" is better, 叔 may mean a gentleman or a squire (cf. Williams' Dictionary).]

24　The *Liji* in the current edition writes: Li Shan 厲山.

25　The *Liji* has: Nong 農.

26　*Liji, Jifa* 祭法 (end).

27　Dynastic appellation of Shen Nong.

28　The fourth star in Ursa major.

29　The discontented and mischievous spirits of former sovereigns without children, who must be propitiated.

30　Quotation from the *Liji, Jifa* (Legge, *loc. cit.* p. 206).

31　In 203 BCE.

32　The constellation Tiantian 天田 "Heavenly field" in Virgo.

33　According to the *Shiji* 史記 chap. 28 (Chavannes Vol. III, p. 453) Han Gao Zu 漢高祖 instituted these sacrifices in the 9th and 10th years of his reign.

34　*Analects* XI, 25, VII.

35　River in the south-east of Shandong 山東.

36　Gao Zu 高祖.

37　明星 the "Bright star" is generally regarded as another name of Venus. Cf. *Shiji* chap. 27, p. 22.

38　Thus Jupiter, which rules over spring only, could not well be sacrificed to at the rain sacrifice in autumn.

39　A chapter of the *Liji*.

40　Cf. Legge's translation of the *Liji* (*Sacred Books* Vol. XXVII, p. 251 and 283).

41　The Dragon Star occurs in the *Zuozhuan*, Duke Xiang 襄 28th year, as the star of Song 宋 and Zheng 鄭. The commentary explains it as a synonym of Jupiter.

42　The Ming Star 明星 = Venus governs the west and autumn, whereas Jupiter reigns in the east and in spring.

43　About the prognostics furnished by the stars.

44 Quoted from the *Liji*, *Jifa* (Legge, *loc. cit.* p. 208).

45 Quotation from the *Liji*, *Tangong* 檀弓 (Legge, *loc. cit.* p. 196).

46 Ji Zha 季札, fourth son of King Shou Meng 壽夢 of Wu 吳, who died in 561 BCE.

47 A territory in Jiangsu 江蘇, the appanage of Prince Ji Zi 季子.

48 A State in Anhui 安徽.

49 He was on an embassy to Lu 魯, Qi 齊, Zheng 鄭, Wei 衛 and Jin 晉, and passed through Xu 徐 in 544 BCE.

50 See a parallel passage in the *Shiji* chap. 31, p. 9v.

51 *Analects* X, 8, X.

52 This is not quite true. The *Liji*, the *Zuozhuan*, and the *Shiji* treat of ghosts and spirits in many places, as we have seen.

CHAPTER 78

The Real Nature of Knowledge
Shizhi 實知

(*Lunheng* Book XXVI, Chap. i)

1 聖人.

2 賢.

3 See Ch. 15 n. 11.

4 In the Yangzhou 楊州 prefecture, Jiangsu 江蘇.

5 See p. II.836.

6 子 Zi was the family name of the Yin 殷 dynasty. Wei Zi 微子, the Viscount of Wei 微, a clansman of the last emperor of the Yin dynasty, was made Prince of Song 宋. He is believed to have been the ancestor of Confucius. Cf. Chavannes, *Mem. Hist.* Vol. V, p. 284 seq. In the *Liji* 禮記 (Legge, *Sacred Books* Vol. XXVII, p. 139) Confucius says himself, "I am a man of Yin."

7 Cf. Ch. 15 n. 36.

8 The Plan of the Yellow River containing the Eight Diagrams revealed to

Huang Di 黃帝, see Ch. 23 n. 18.

9　King of Wu 吳, a nephew of Han Gao Zu 漢高祖.

10　This great rebellion broke out in 54 BCE. See *Shiji* 史記 chap. 11, p. 2r. (Chavannes, *Mem. Hist.* Vol. II, p. 498).

11　As given in the *Shiji* chap. 6, p. 26v. from which the following narrative is abridged.

12　The 1st of November 211 BCE (Chavannes, *Mem. Hist.* Vol. II, p. 184).

13　九嶷. The *Shiji* writes 九疑山.

14　Ed. A. and B. have both a full stop after Jieke 藉柯, thus agreeing with Chavannes' punctuation (*Mem. Hist.* Vol. II, p. 185, Note 2). For 藉柯 the *Shiji* has 籍柯.

15　梅渚 evidently the correct reading for the 海渚 of the *Shiji*, which Chavannes *loc. cit.* Note 3 justly regards as corrupt. Meizhu 梅渚 lies in the Jianping 建平 district of Anhui 安徽, which is conterminous with Danyangxian 丹陽縣 in Jiangsu 江蘇.

16　陝, the *Shiji* has 狹.

17　勞成山 Cf. Ch. 64 n. 63.

18　See Ch. 64 n. 67.

19　推原往驗以處來· 賢者亦能·Ed. B. writes: 以處來事者亦能·

20　Cf. p. I.241.

21　The dummies had taken the place of living persons who were thus buried symbolically. Burying them alive would have been a relapse into the primitive custom. Cf. Ch. 67.

22　In 237 BCE.

23　嚴襄 a misprint for 莊襄 Zhuang Xiang, King of Qin 秦, 249–246 BCE.

24　This King of Qin reigned only three days in 250 BCE.

25　*I.e.,* Xiao Wen Wang 孝文王.

26　East of Xi'anfu 西安府, Shanxi 陝西.

27　King Yan Xiang 嚴襄, who had been adopted by Queen Hua Yang 華陽后. His real mother, the Queen-Dowager Xia Taihou 夏太后, was originally a concubine.

28　297 BCE, the *Shiji* chap. 5 adduces the 7th year = 300 BCE.

29　樗里子, a member of the royal house.

30　Near Xi'anfu.

31　In the Song 嵩 district of Henan 河南 province.

32　Non-Chinese tribes in the west.

33　晉 Jin and 秦 Qin combined invited the Rong 戎 to change their residence.

34　In Guazhou 瓜州, Gansu 甘肅.

35 Abridged from the *Zuozhuan* 左氏傳, Duke Xi 僖 22nd year, whence we learn that the Rong emigrated to Yichuan 伊川 in 638 BCE. Xin You 辛有 predicted it, when King Ping 平 of Zhou 周, to avoid the incursions of the Rong, transferred his capital from Chang'an 長安 to Luoyi 洛邑 in 770 BCE. Consequently the hundred years of Xin You are only a round number. The *Zuozhuan* adds that Xin You foresaw the event from the fact that in Yichuan the rules of ceremony were already lost. Wearing long or dishevelled hair is a sign of barbarity, therefore barbarians might well occupy the land.

36 The friend of Han Gao Zu 漢高祖. Cf. Ch. 3 n. 20.

37 They were as superstitious as the old Romans.

38 Unknowable at first sight, not altogether.

39 項託. Cf. *Huainanzi* 淮南子 XIX, 13v. The *Shiji* 史記 chap.71, p. 9v where the same thing is told of this precocious lad, writes the second character 橐. See also Giles, *Biogr. Dict.* No. 696, where we read that Xiang Tuo 項託 was merely qualified to be the teacher of the Sage.

40 *Analects* XVI, 9.

41 9–22 CE.

42 In Shandong 山東.

43 Ceremonial, music, archery, charioteering, writing, mathematics.

44 魏都. I suppose that the capital of Wei 魏 = Daliang 大梁, the modern Kaifengfu 開封府, is thus designated.

45 Even a Sage could not know the erroneousness of such suppositions. Pure thought alone does not provide true knowledge, there must be experience besides and reasoning by analogy.

46 The two former and the two latter were disciples of Confucius.

47 *Analects* II, 23.

48 *Analects* IX, 22.

49 A native of the Chu 楚 State in the Zhou 周 epoch.

50 A small State held by wild tribes, south of Jiaozhou 膠州, of which Ge Lu 葛盧 was the chief.

51 This story is told in the *Zuozhuan*, Duke Xi 僖 29th year.

52 Region in the province of Sichuan 四川.

53 The *Peiwen yunfu* 佩文韻府 cites this passage, but calls the person 漢陽翁仲 Hanyang Wengzhong *i.e.*, Wengzhong 翁仲 of Hanyang 漢陽. I could not find any farther information on the man.

54 Here and elsewhere Wang Chong uses 輒 simply for 則 "then." This use seems to be quite common as I found it in many other authors. Our dictionaries omit it.

55 宣室. Williams and Giles translate this word by "imperial palace," which is much too vague, Couvreur by "chancery," quoting two passages referring to the Tang 唐 time. Originally it must have been a hall where the emperor used to sacrifice and pray to his ancestors for happiness. But other business was transacted there also. We read in the biography of Jia Yi 賈誼, *Shiji* chap. 84, p. 14r. that Jia Yi 賈誼 was received there by the Emperor Xiao Wen Di 孝文帝: 賈生徵見孝文帝方受釐坐宣室上因感鬼神事而問鬼神之本. The commentator remarks that the 宣室 was the principal room in front of the Weiyang 未央 palace. The *Peiwen yunfu* quotes two more passages from the *Hanshu* 漢書: 上帝幸宣室齋居而決事 and 夫宣室者先帝之正處也非法度之正不得入焉.

56 Cf. p. II.468–69.

57 Wang Chong means to say that Huang Di 黃帝 at his birth was as developed as a child of two years, so that his ability to talk would not be so marvellous. He only forgets to tell us how Huang Di could learn speaking, while in his mother's womb.

58 See Ch. 16.

59 *Analects* XIX, 22.

60 *Analects* II, 4.

61 Their wisdom is not supernatural.

62 Cf. Ch. 22 n. 30 to 32, and *Huainanzi* XIII, 14r.

63 See p. II.579–80.

64 *Analects* XV, 30.

65 There are things plain and intelligible by reflexion, others require instruction to be understood, and many remain incomprehensible in spite of learning, baffling all our endeavours.

CHAPTER 79
The Knowledge of Truth
Zhishi 知實
(*Lunheng* Book XXVI, Chap. ii)

1   有諸. These words are wanting in the *Analects*.
2   The *Analects* have 其然. Our text repeats 豈其然乎.
3   *Analects* XIV, 14.
4   *Analects* I, 10.
5   The *Yuanjian leihan* 淵鑑類函 chap. 268, 8v. quotes this passage from the 彙苑 *Huiyuan*.
6   This incident is told, though somewhat differently, in the "Family Sayings" quoted by the *Peiwen yunfu* 佩文韻府. There Yan Yuan 顏淵 simply eats the rice. Confucius desires to have some for an oblation, when Yan Yuan explains why he ate it, and that, owing to the impurity, it was unfit for an offering.
7   A State in the modern Kaifengfu 開封府 in Henan 河南.
8   Confucius was mistaken for Yang Hu 陽虎, an enemy of the people of Kuang 匡, and therefore kept prisoner five days. See Legge, *Classics* Vol. I, p. 217, Note 5.
9   *Analects* XI, 22.
10   Cf. Ch. 14 n. 11. Yang Huo 陽貨 is also called Yang Hu.
11   Wang Chong: 饋, *Analects*: 歸.
12   *Analects* XVII, 1.
13   *Analects* XVIII, 6.
14   五甫. The *Liji* 禮記 writes 五父.
15   鄒曼甫. The *Liji*: 耶曼父.
16   This episode is found in the *Liji*, *Tangong* 檀弓, II, 5r. (Legge, *Sacred Books* Vol. XXVII, p. 124), but the text differs. Chinese critics take it for apocryphal.
17   Quoted from the *Liji* 禮記 *eod.* 4r. (Legge p. 123). See also Ch. 62 n. 17.
18   *Analects* III, 15.

19　Allusion to *Analects* XVI, 10.

20　Ed. A and C write 生人 in lieu of 主人.

21　Cf. p. I.291.

22　*Analects* IX, 14.

23　Cf. Ch. 50 n. 1.

24　Note the interesting character 毉 for 醫, which shows that in ancient times physicians were taken for a kind of sorcerers. 巫.

25　The parallel passage, p. I.244–45, says "those flying" 飛者, which is better. The prototype in the *Shiji* 史記 reads as follow, "I know that birds can fly, that fish can swim, and that beasts can run. Those running may be ensnared, those swimming may be caught with a line, and those flying be shot with an arrow."

26　*I.e.* they did not disparage.

27　*Analects* XI, 4.

28　The father and the brother of Shun 舜.

29　Cf. p. I.120–21.

30　See Ch. 71 n. 13.

31　An official from Qi 齊.

32　The *Peiwen yunfu* 佩文韻府 chap. 91, p. 5v. under 授玉 quotes this story.

33　*Mencius* II, Part II, 9. Our test seems somewhat shortened.

34　Cf. Ch. 8 n. 10 and 1.408.

35　See Ch. 3 n. 4.

36　685–643 BCE.

37　A State in the present Yizhoufu 沂州府, Shandong 山東.

38　A famous controversialist and ready wit of the Qi 齊 State of the 4th cent. BCE. He was the son-in-law of the King of Qi. A sketch of his life is contained in the *Shiji* 史記 chap. 126.

39　370–334 BCE.

40　Ed. B and C have 淳于生, ed. A: 髡子生.

41　Dragon was the name for a horse eight feet high (*Erya* 爾雅).

42　538 BCE in the principality of Shen 申. This meeting is referred to in the *Zuozhuan* 左氏傳, Duke Zhao 昭, 4th year and in the *Shiji* chap. 40, p. 10v. (Chavannes, *Mem. Hist.* Vol. IV, p. 358).

43　The *Zuozhuan* writes Cao 曹 instead of Song 宋, the *Shiji* replaces Zhu 邾 by Jin 晉.

44　Cf. Ch. 59 n. 30.

45　The style Huanglong 黃龍 "Yellow Dragon" under the Emperor Xuan Di 宣帝, 49–48 BCE.

46　故, the *Analects* have 固.

47 *Analects* IX, 6.
48 將者且也
49 *Analects* II, 4.
50 295–277 BCE.
51 This is not true: Sagehood, the highest degree of wisdom and virtue, is in-born and cannot be learned. An intelligent man may increase his knowl-edge by study and do good work, but he will never become a genius.
52 *Mencius* II, Part I, 2 (19).
53 Mencius writes Min Zi 閔子.
54 *Mencius* II, Part I, 2 (20).
55 Our text has 巳, *Mencius:* 止.
56 *Mencius* II, Part I, 2 (22).
57 *Mencius* VII, Part II, 15.
58 Disciple of Confucius. Ch. 11 n. 55.

CHAPTER *80*
A Definition of Worthies
Dingxian 定賢
(*Lunheng* **Book XXVII, Chap. i**)

1 Yao 堯 inquired in open court whom he might employ. First Gun 鯀 and Gong Gong 共工 were recommended to him, but not thought well quali-fied. At last Shun 舜 was mentioned to him. See *Shangshu* 尚書 Part I, 10 (Legge, *Classics* Vol. III, Part I, p. 23).
2 Title of the chief ministers of which Gun and Gong Gong were two. Cf. Chavannes, *Mem. Hist.* Vol. I, p. 50, Note 1.
3 378–343 BCE.
4 In Shandong 山東, near Jiaozhou 膠州.
5 In the Tai'an 泰安 prefecture of Shandong.
6 This story is told in full in the *Shiji* 史記 chap. 46, p. 7v. (Chavannes, *Mem. Hist.* Vol. V, p. 243). In addition to the governor of E 阿, all the sycophants

about him were thrown into a cauldron and boiled.

7 *Analects* XIII, 24.
8 About these men see Ch. 11 n. 55.
9 Cf. p. I.234.
10 Ch. 50 n. 21.
11 A noble in Qi 齊, whose descendants, later on, became dukes of Qi. He died about 460 BCE.
12 He came to the throne in 496 BCE.
13 On Mount Guiji 會稽 he had been surrounded by the King of Wu 吳, and had to sue for peace.
14 See above Ch. 80 n. 8.
15 The noise thus made probably served to produce the crow.
16 Cf. the biography of Meng Chang 孟嘗 in the *Shiji* chap. 75, p. 4v.
17 See p. I.116.
18 Cf. Ch. 47.
19 殿下.
20 The Five Notes of the Chinese musical scale.
21 The drum plays an important part in Chinese music.
22 五服.
23 The teacher has to inculcate them.
24 五采.
25 Quotation from the *Liji* 禮記, *Xueji* 學記 (Legge, *Sacred Books* Vol. XX-VIII, p. 90), but with slight alterations.
26 The Daoists despise external merit.
27 麑微. This expression is nowhere explained, the Appendix to the *Peiwen yunfu* 佩文韻府 merely cites this passage. 微 means an ulcer on the legs, but what is a "hare ulcer"? From the opposition to 篤劇 we may infer that it is some small disease, perhaps only an excoriation, which the Germans call "wolf."
28 吾丘. Ed. C: 吾邱. The *Hanshu* 漢書 has the first reading.
29 State in Shanxi 山西.
30 Han Wu Di 漢武帝, 140–87 BCE.
31 A circuit in northern Henan 河南.
32 Shou Wang 壽王 filled both posts, that of a 都尉 *duwei*, military governor and of a 太守 *taishou*, civil governor.
33 輻湊並至. The *Hanshu* 漢書 writes fuller: 知略輻湊.
34 The income of a military governor was of 2000 piculs and that of a civil one the same amount.
35 So far the text literally agrees with the biography of Shou Wang 壽王 in

the *Qianhanshu* 前漢書 chap. 64a, p. 13v.

36 Cf. p. II.473.

37 One 鎰 *yi* of gold equal to 20 ounces.

38 For a more detailed account see p. I.293–94.

39 His second attempt to assassinate the Viscount Xiang 襄 of Zhao 趙 having failed, he asked permission to pass his sword through the cloak of the viscount, which was granted him. Having thus revenged his master, Earl Zhi 知, symbolically, he committed suicide. See also Ch. 22 n. 28.

40 King Ping 平 of Chu 楚, who had put to death the father and elder brother of Wu Zixu 伍子胥 (Wu Yuan 伍員). The latter fled to Wu 吳, inveighed the prince of this State to an expedition against Chu, which was vanquished. As victor Wu Zixu caused the grave of King Ping to be opened and his corpse to be publicly flogged.

41 Cf. p. II.665.

42 Guan Long Feng 關龍逢, a minister of Jie Gui 桀癸, who remonstrated with him and therefore was put to death.

43 For having dared to object to the excesses of Zhou 紂, the last emperor of the Yin 殷 dynasty, Bi Gan 比干 had a similar fate as Guan Long Feng. Cf. Ch. 25 n. 30.

44 The ancestor of the Zhou 周 dynasty.

45 Minister of Shun 舜.

46 Minister of Shun.

47 Tang 唐 and Yu 虞 were the territories of Yao 堯 and Shun 舜.

48 Allusion to *Analects* X, 18.

49 An officer of Qi 齊, 6th century BCE, who died 493 BCE.

50 These sentiments savour a good deal of Daoism.

51 On a small sheet of water one knows exactly the course one has taken, but not on the ocean where east and west become uncertain.

52 Great virtue becomes visible by contrast and shines forth when there is wickedness all around.

53 Cf. *Analects* XI, 5. Nan Rong 南容, to whom Confucius married the daughter of his elder brother. He used to repeat the lines of the *Shijing* 詩經 "A flaw in a white sceptre-stone may be ground away; but for a flaw in speech nothing can be done." See Legge, *Classics* Vol. I, p. 238, Note 5.

54 Cf. *Analects* V, I. To Gong Ye Chang 公冶長 Confucius gave his daughter to wife.

55 See Ch. 85 n. 9.

56 Ch. 26 n. 19.

57 See Ch. 21 n. 23.

58 The grandfather of Wen Wang 文王, founder of the Zhou 周 dynasty, who removed his capital in consequence of the constant raids of barbarian tribes.

59 Virtues, as it were, are luxuries; to practise them, people must at least be provided with the necessities of life. The state of morality, to a great extent, depends on purely economical conditions.

60 I only found one Yuan Chang 袁敞 whom Wang Chong may have in view, a contemporary of his who, during the reign of He Di 和帝, 89–105 CE, was appointed general.

61 The same as the Kunlun 崑崙. The Yellow River is believed to have its source in Mount Kun 崑. See also p. I.361.

62 Old name of the Poyang 鄱陽 Lake.

63 Now capital of Jiangxi 江西 Province.

64 Allusion to *Analects* VI, 9.

65 Cf. p. I.146.

66 Two hermits of Chu met by Confucius. See *Analects* XVIII, 6.

67 Cf. Ch. 33 n. 30 and p. I.352.

68 The philosophy of Confucius, and in a still higher degree that of Mo Di 墨子, propounds altruism, the Daoism, indifference and self-cultivation.

69 Worthies in the Confucian sense.

70 War chariots by the number of which the military power of a State was gauged.

71 See above p. II.797 and I.244–45.

72 A minister of Zhao 趙 who intended to assassinate Han Gao Zu 漢高祖. This plan was discovered, and Guan Gao 貫高 with all his accomplices and relations to the third degree, were executed. Cf. p. II.475 and *Shiji* chap. 8, p. 32r. (Chavannes, *Mem. Hist.* Vol. II, p. 391 and 392).

73 Virtue and self-sacrifice are easier for persons with a strong constitution than for weak ones. They have more courage and feel bodily pain much less.

74 A hard word, but true, even of many of our philologists.

75 One of the Three Heroes to whom the accession of the Han 漢 dynasty is due. See Ch. 78 n. 36.

76 An old adage which was used by Fan Li 范蠡, minister of Yue 越, 5th cent BCE. Cf. p. I.141, and also by Han Xin 韓信, when he was seized and arraigned for high-treason. Wang Chong here writes: 高鳥死良弓藏狡兔得良犬烹. In the *Shiji* chap. 41 p. 7r. we read: 蜚鳥盡○○○○○死走狗烹 and in *Shiji* chap. 92, p. 16r. the phrase is turned: 狡兔死良狗烹高鳥盡良弓藏. Still another variant is found in *Hanfeizi* 韓非子 XVII, 3r.

77 Cf. Ch. 8 n. 33.

78 Han Xin's 韓信 plan to seize the Empress Lü Hou 呂后 and the heir-apparent having been divulged, he was decapitated, and his whole family exterminated in 196 BCE.

79 A high officer of Wen Di 文帝, 179–157 BCE.

80 Both were raised to the rank of marquis.

81 See Ch. 34 n. 18.

82 Confucius met this woman near the Taishan 太山, while proceeding to Qi 齊. He sent Zi Lu 子路 to question her, and was told that formerly her husband's father had been devoured by a tiger, then her husband, and last her son. Confucius then said to his disciples, "Remember this my children. Oppressive government is more terrible than tigers." *Liji* (Legge, *Sacred Books* Vol. XXVII, p. 190) and the Family Sayings of Confucius, 孔子家語 IX, 4v, where Zi Gong 子貢 takes the place of Zi Lu 子路.

83 A distinguished scholar and poet of the 2nd cent. BCE.

84 The philosopher Yang Xiong 揚雄. Elsewhere (p. II.863 and p. II.845) Wang Chong deals more generously with him.

85 See above Ch. 80 n. 66.

86 Perfect purity is not required to be a Worthy. Zi Lu was one in spite of his covetousness.

87 On the contrary. Confucius commends him and calls him a Worthy. See *Analects* VII, 14 and XVI, 12.

88 Quoted almost literally from *Huainanzi* XVIII, 17r. Another parallel passage is furnished by Lie Zi 列子 IV, 4v, but its wording is somewhat different and fuller, so that it may have been the archetype for *Huainanzi*. There the questioner is Zi Xia 子夏, who inquires about four disciples, adding Zi Zhang 子張.

89 *Mencius* Book VII, Part II, 37.

90 Quoted from the *Shangshu* 尚書 Part II, Book III, 2; but transposed (Legge, *Classics* Vol. III, Part I, p. 70).

91 Cf. Ch. 50 n. 11.

92 See Ch. 85 n. 30.

93 Cf. Ch. 85 n. 93 and *Zuozhuan*, Duke Ding 定 8th year (Legge, *Classics* Vol. V, Part II, p. 769 seq.).

94 If, according to the opinion of Guan Zi 管子, the words of a superior man attract so many people, that they fill rooms and halls, then the effect produced on the hearers would be a criterion of truth. In that case the utterances of all the people ought to fill the whole world to be trustworthy. That is impossible, consequently the principle of Guan Zi cannot be right.

95　See Ch. 83 n. 42.

96　One of the Three Heroes of the Han time, cf. Ch. 11 n. 9. On one occasion, being appointed by the village elders to distribute sacrificial meats at the local altar, he performed this duty with such impartiality, that the elders wished he might manage the affairs of the empire in a similar manner.

CHAPTER 81

Statements Corrected
Zhengshuo 正說

(*Lunheng* Book XXVIII, Chap. i)

1　The Five King or ancient Classics: *Yijing* 易經, *Shijing* 詩經, *Shangshu* 尚書, *Liji* 禮記, and *Chunqiu* 春秋.

2　A scholar of great learning.

3　The capital of Shandong 山東.

4　The *Shiji* 史記 chap. 121, p. 8 says "in a wall."

5　156–141 BCE.

6　73–49 BCE.

7　A city in Huaiqingfu 懷慶府 (Henan 河南).

8　In 156 BCE.

9　A son of the Emperor Jing Di 景帝, who in 154 BCE was made Prince of Lu 魯.

10　In addition to these hundred chapters of the *Shangshu*, a *Li(ji)* in 300 chapters, a *Chunqiu* in 300 chapters and a *Lunyu* 論語 in 21 chapters were brought to light. Cf. *Lunheng* XX, 4v. (*Yiwen* 佚文 Ch. 61).

11　32–7 BCE.

12　A place in Huai'anfu 淮安府 (Jiangsu 江蘇).

13　詩書.

14　Zi Lu 子路 and Zi Gao 子羔 were both disciples of Confucius.

15　A place in Shandong.

16　*Analects* XI, 24.

17 On the burning of the books cf. p. I.283.

18 This is a misprint. It was the 34th year (213 BCE). See the *Shiji* chap. 6, p. 21v. and p. I.283.

19 An official title under the Qin 秦 and Han 漢 dynasties.

20 A noble of the State of Qi 齊, who in 481 BCE put to death the reigning sovereign Duke Jian 簡, and usurped the government of the State with the title of chief minister.

21 The chiefs of the six powerful families in Jin 晉 who struggled for supremacy. Three of these families were destroyed during these struggles, the remaining three: Zhao 趙, Han 韓 and Wei 魏 in 403 BCE divided the Jin State among them.

22 Writers on philosophy and science.

23 There are 28 stellar mansions in all, 7 for each quadrant.

24 The twelve dukes of Lu 魯, whose history is given in the *Chunqiu*.

25 This translation is mere guess. 赤制 might mean "rule for the new-born." According to Chinese ideas pregnancy lasts 7–9 months or 210–270 days, whereas we reckon 182–300 days. The mean number would be 240 or 241 days. The dictionaries do not explain the expression.

26 These Five Timekeepers of the *Hongfan* 洪範 chapter are: the year, the month, the day, the stars, and the dates of the calendar. *Shangshu, Hongfan*, Pt. V, Bk. IV, 8 (Legge, *Classics* Vol. III, Pt. II, p. 327).

27 This would seem a misprint. Duke Yin 隱 of Lu 魯 reigned from 721–711 BCE *i.e.* 10 years, not 50.

28 The chapter of the *Shangshu* entitled "*Hongfan.*"

29 The Emperor Shen Nong 神農.

30 The *Yijing* 易經 of the Zhou 周 Dynasty, the only one which has come down to us.

31 We learn from the *Diwang shiji* 帝王世紀 (3rd cent. CE) that Fu Xi 伏羲 made the Eight Diagrams, and that Shen Nong increased them to sixty-four. Huang Di 黃帝, Yao 堯, and Shun 舜 took them over, expanded them, and distinguished two *Yijing*s. The Xia 夏 dynasty adopted that of Shen Nong, and called it *Lianshan* 連山, the Yin 殷 dynasty took the version of Huang Di, and called it *Guizang* 歸藏. Wen Wang 文王 expanded the sixty-four diagrams, composed the six broken and unbroken lines of which they were formed, and called it *Zhouyi* 周易.

    Others think that Lianshan 連山 is another name of Fu Xi, and Guizang 歸藏 a designation of Huang Di.

32 The tradition about the Plan of the River and the Scroll of the Luo 洛 is very old. We find traces of it in the *Yijing*, the *Liji*, the *Shangshu*, and the

Analects. Cf. Legge's translation of the *Yijing*, p. 14.

33   The author of the *Zuozhuan* 左氏傳.

34   *Analects* II, 23, 2.

35   The Six Institutions or departments of the Zhou: administration, instruction, rites, police, jurisdiction, and public welfare. Cf. *Zhouli* 周禮, Bk. II, *Tianguan* 天官. (Biot's translation, Vol. I, p.20.)

36   Now known as the *Zhouli*.

37   Under the Xia dynasty the foot had ten inches, under the Yin nine, under the Zhou eight. Now it has ten inches again. The foot of the Zhou time measured but about 20 cm., whereas the modern foot is equal to 35 cm.

38   By Prince Gong 共. *Vid.* above p. II.811.

39   It is not plain which rivers are meant. They must have been at the frontier of the two conterminous States. There was the Ji 濟 River, which in Qi 齊 was called the Ji 濟 of Qi 齊, and in Lu 魯 the Ji 濟 of Lu 魯.

40   86–74 BCE.

41   73–49 BCE.

42   The massive Li 隸 characters were invented during the Han 漢 time and form the link between the ancient seal characters and the modern form of script.

43   A place in Hubei 湖北 province.

44   *Analects = Lunyu* 論語.

45   Our text of the *Lunyu* consists of twenty books. In the Han time there were two editions of the Classic, one of Lu 魯 in twenty books and one of Qi 齊 in twenty-two.

46   *Mencius* Bk. IV, Pt. II, chap. 21.

47   The meaning of the names of these old chronicles, Cheng 乘 and Taowu 檮杌, is as obscure as that of the *Chunqiu*.

48   710–693 BCE.

49   *Chunqiu* II, 17, 8.

50   *I.e.* the day of the sexagenary cycle, for the day of the month is mentioned.

51   Two other commentaries to the *Chunqiu*, less important than the *Zuozhuan*.

52   Tang 唐 was situated in Baodingfu 保定府 (Zhili 直隸).

53   In Shanxi 山西.

54   In Kaifengfu 開封府 (Henan 河南).

55   Cheng Tang 成湯, the founder of the Yin (Shang 商) dynasty.

56   A principality in Henan.

57   The kingdom of Zhou 周 in Shanxi 陝西.

58   The kingdom of Qin 秦 in Shanxi 陝西.

59   In Shanxi 陝西.
60   Principality in Nanyangfu 南陽府 (Henan).
61   The president of all the nobles of the empire.
62   *Shangshu, Yaodian* 堯典, Pt. I, Bk. III, 12 (Legge, *Classics* Vol. III, Pt. I, p. 26).
63   *Shangshu, Shundian* 舜典, Pt. II, Bk. I, 2 (Legge, *Classics* Vol. III, Pt. I, p. 31).
64   大麓.
65   Minister of Crime under Shun 舜.

CHAPTER 82

On Literary Work
Shujie 書解

(*Lunheng* Book XXVIII, Chap. ii)

1   A statement contradicted by facts.
2   This reminds us of *Analects* IX, 21: 苗而不秀者,有矣夫.秀而不實者,有
     矣夫. The flowers, of course, are compared with literary productions, and
     the fruit with the author's character.
3   See Ch. 61 n. 14.
4   Cf. *Liji* 禮記 (Legge, *Sacred Books* Vol. XXVII, p. 128) and p. II.570.
5   The expression 文 means writings as well as ornaments.
6   蚡蜦, *i.e.*, its colour is black and yellowish.
7   Signs, looking like Chinese characters, which are made use of for divina-
     tion.
8   Letters and virtue, in Wang Chong's opinion, are always combined.
9   文.
10   理.
11   Again mere symbolism which the old philosophers took for science.
12   See p. II.557.
13   *Vid. loc. cit.*
14   *Analects* XII, 8, where Ji Zi Cheng 棘子成 is introduced saying: "In a
     superior man it is only the substantial qualities (質 = character) which

are wanted; — why should we seek for ornamental accomplishments (文 = literary productions)?"

15 文儒.

16 世儒.

17 博士.

18 In many respects, these remarks apply still to our own times. Originality and genius but seldom qualify a man for a professorship. To obtain this it is much safer to keep in the beaten tracks, holding sound views *viz.* those just in vogue, and to show a fair mediocrity, as any superiority is calculated to offend the amour-propre of "ordinary scholars."

19 Zhou Gong 周公 is believed to be the author of the *Zhouli* 周禮, the Rites of the Zhou 周 dynasty.

20 They are creations, classical works.

21 詩家.

22 Shen Gong 申公 lived in the 2nd and 3rd cent. BCE. His edition of the *Shijing* 詩經 is known as the *Lushi* 魯詩, the *Shijing* of Lu 魯.

23 A scholar of the 2nd cent. BCE, born in Qiancheng 千乘 in Shandong 山東. He was a pupil of the famous Fu Sheng 伏生 and is generally known as 歐陽生 Ouyang Sheng.

24 This seems to be Gongsun Hong 公孫弘, who died 121 BCE. The *Shiji* 史記, however, does not mention him as a commentator of the *Shangshu* 尚書, but couples his name with that of an expositor of the *Shijing*.

25 書家.

26 Notices on these three scholars are given in the *Shiji* chap. 121.

27 Allusion to the *Shangshu*, Part V, Book XV, 10 (Legge, *Classics* Vol. III, Part II, p. 469).

28 *Huainanzi* 淮南子 XIII, 9r. uses these words with regard to the Emperor Yu 禹, substituting 捉 for 握 and adding that during one meal he had to rise ten times. The *Shiji* chap. 33, p. 3v. (Chavannes, *Mem. Hist.* Vol. IV, p. 93) refers them to Zhou Gong 周公. While washing his head, Zhou Gong usually was disturbed by visitors three times.

29 Great poet. See Ch. 42 n. 28.

30 子虛賦. This poem so fascinated the Emperor Han Wu Di 漢武帝, that he summoned Sima Xiangru 司馬相如 to Court (Giles, *Bibl. Dict.* No. 1753).

31 中郎, a title of certain officials of the imperial household.

32 Cf. p. II.572.

33 See Ch. 83 n. 15.

34 Cf. Ch. 37 n. 32.

35 兩有無所睹. The first character 兩 is evidently wrong and should be replaced by 而.

36 The *Lüshi chunqiu* 呂氏春秋, Ch. 83 n. 11.

37 Lü Buwei 呂不韋 was banished to Sichuan 四川 for his intrigues with the queen dowager and on suspicion of high-treason.

38 Cf. p. I.263.

39 See Ch. 21 n. 35.

40 It is a useless attempt to deny this inferiority or awkwardness of men of genius in business. A great plus of mental power in one direction is usually counterbalanced by a minus in another.

41 Ch. 26 n. 43.

42 一旦二也 must be corrected into 一且二也.

43 蚈, which the dictionaries only know as denoting the whirring of insects or the name of an insect. Here it seems to mean to make the bow-string whir *i.e.*, to pull it, which is usually expressed by 弸. Unless it be a misprint, 蚈 here must be a synonym of 弸.

44 A disciple of Confucius, Fu Bu Qi 宓不齊 (T. 子賤) who was governor of Shanfu 單父 in Shandong and has become celebrated for his administration.

45 We have a work, going by Guan Zi's 管子 name, in 24 chapters, and a *Yanzi chunqiu* in 8 chapters, 晏子春秋.

46 Shang Yang 商鞅 as well as the two afore-mentioned persons rank as "jurists." See Ch. 34 n. 18.

47 Yu Qing 虞卿, politician at the court of King Xiao Cheng 孝成 of Zhao 趙, 265–245 BCE who wrote a work entitled *Yushi chunqiu* 虞氏春秋.

48 The family of the Empress Lü Hou 呂后.

49 The family of Han Gao Zu 漢高祖.

50 The Empress Lü Hou attempted to supersede the house of Liu 劉 by her own family, but did not succeed.

51 It has been maintained that they did not write those books ascribed to them, but merely lent their names.

52 Cf. Ch. 85 n. 11.

53 P. I.86.

54 The State of Han 韓 might have won the supremacy instead of Qin 秦.

55 蕞殘.

56 蕞殘滿車不成為道. 玉屑滿篋不成為寶.

57 Cf. p. II.810.

58 See p. II.811.

59 諸子尺書.

60 Cf. Ch. 16 n. 83.
61 From which the Classics are compiled.
62 This cannot, as a rule, be said of the Classics which without commentaries are hardly intelligible.

CHAPTER 83

Critical Remarks on Various Books

Anshu 案書

(*Lunheng* Book XXIX, Chap. i)

1 Mo Di 墨翟, the philosopher of universal love, a younger contemporary of Confucius, 5th or 4th cent. BCE. Cf. E. Faber, *Lehre des Philosophen Micius*, Elberfeld 1877 (Extracts from his works).
2 In the opinion of most Chinese critics the *Chunqiu* 春秋, as we have it, has not been preserved, but was reconstructed from the *Zuozhuan* 左氏傳 or from the other commentaries. This view is supported by what Wang Chong says here. See on this question Legge, *Prolegomena* to his translation of the *Chunqiu*, p. 16 seq.
3 Cf. above p. II.811 and 1.456.
4 Gongyang 公羊 and Guliang 穀梁 are the surnames, Gao 高 and Zhi 賨 the personal names.
5 Hu Mu's 胡母 commentary is not mentioned in the Catalogue of the *Hanshu* 漢書.
6 To wit the *Liji* 禮記 and the *Shiji* 史記.
7 Liu Zi Zheng 劉子政 = Liu Xiang 劉向, 80–9 BCE, was an admirer of the commentary of Guliang 穀梁, whereas his son Liu Xin 劉歆 stood up for the *Zuozhuan* 左氏傳.
8 25–57 CE.
9 Fan Shu 范叔 alias Fan Sheng 范升.

10 Fan Shu in his report to the throne had attacked the *Zuozhuan* on fourteen points.

11 An important work on antique lore composed under the patronage of Prince Lü Buwei 呂不韋 in the 3rd cent. BCE.

12 Works relating marvellous stories.

13 Cf. my paper on the Chinese Sophists, *Journal of the China Branch of the R. As. Soc.*, Shanghai 1899, p. 29 and appendix containing a translation of the remains of this philosopher.

14 Cf. p. I.360.

15 Wei Yang 衛鞅, Prince of Shang 商, a great reformer of the civil and military administration of the Qin 秦 State, which he raised to great power. Died 338 BCE.

16 One of the most celebrated statesmen of antiquity, who died in 645 BCE.

17 A speculative work which passes under the title of Guanzi 管子. The one still in existence is perhaps a later forgery.

18 Sima Qian 司馬遷 extols Guan Zhong 管仲 (*Shiji* 史記 chap. 62, p. 2v) and finds fault with Shang Yang 商鞅 (*Shiji* 史記 chap. 68, p.9), although, in Wang Chong's opinion, their deeds and their theories are very similar. It must be noted, however, that Shang Yang's criminal laws were very cruel. Wang Chong, who is to a certain extent imbued with Daoist ideas, feels a natural aversion to all forms of government, and to legislation in particular.

19 A place in Jiangsu 江蘇.

20 *Shiji* chap. 13.

21 *Shiji* chap. 3.

22 Second wife of the Emperor Ku 嚳.

23 The first ancestor of the Yin 殷 dynasty.

24 *Shiji* chap. 3, p. 1.

25 *Shiji* chap. 4, p. 1.

26 First wife of the Emperor Ku 嚳.

27 Hou Ji 后稷 = "Lord of the Soil," the ancestor of the Zhou 周 dynasty.

28 *Xinyu* 新語. The work still exists.

29 Lu Jia 陸賈 lived in the 2nd cent. BCE at the beginning of the Han 漢 dynasty. Twice he was sent as envoy to the southern Yue 南越. Cf. p. I.119.

30 An author of the 2nd cent. BCE. He wrote the *Chunqiu fanlu* 春秋繁露, the "Rich Dew of the Spring and Autumn," which has come down to us.

31 Cf. p. II.640.

32 Cf. p. II.647.

33 The philosopher Yang Xiong 揚雄. Cf. p. II.671.

34 The largest affluent of the Yangzi 江.

35 Both tributaries of the Yellow River in Gansu 甘肅 and Shanxi 陝西, which joined together, fall into the Huang He 黃河 near its elbow in Shanxi 陝西.

36 *Vid.* p. II.647.

37 *Analects* VIII, 15.

38 The music-master of Lu 魯.

39 The first Ode of the *Shijing* 詩經.

40 Cf. the great number of such collections enumerated in the Catalogue of the *Hanshu* 漢書, chap. 30.

41 Quotation from *Mencius* III, Pt. I, 1 (Legge, *Classics* Vol. II, p. 110).

42 Huan Jun Shan 桓君山 = Huan Tan 桓譚, a great scholar of the 1st cent. BCE and CE. People admired his large library. He incurred the displeasure of Guang Wu Di 光武帝, whom he rebuked for his belief in books of fate, and was sentenced to banishment.

43 Four chapters of Han Feizi's 韓非子 work, forming Ch. 15 and 16, Nos. 36–39.

44 *Yantielun* 鹽鐵論, a treatise on questions of national economy.

45 Huan Kuan 桓寬, also called Zhen Shan Zi 貞山子, lived in the 1st cent. BCE.

46 Xinlun 新論.

47 A region in Anhui 安徽.

48 A city in Zhejiang 浙江.

49 Nothing is known of these authors or their writings. The cyclopedias do not even mention their names.

50 A place in Jiangsu 江蘇.

51 The historian Ban Gu 班固, author of the *Hanshu* 漢書 "History of the Former Han Dynasty," who died 92 CE.

52 Who wrote the famous poem *Lisao* 離騷 cf. p. II.472.

53 Jia Yi 賈誼.

54 Gu Yong 谷永 lived in the 1st cent. BCE. As censor he remonstrated against the abuses of the court, and presented over forty memorials upon divine portents.

55 Liu Zi Zheng 劉子政 = Liu Xiang 劉向, 80–9 BCE, is a celebrated writer of the Han time, who did much for the preservation of ancient literature. Besides he wrote works on government and poetry.

56 Wang Chong's prediction has not proved true. The authors of his time, whom he praises so much, are all forgotten, Ban Gu alone excepted.

57 At the court of the Emperor Cheng Di 成帝 32–7 BCE.

58 In the *Catalogue of Literature*, forming chapter 30 of the *Hanshu*, Liu Xin 劉歆 divided the then existing body of literature under 7 heads: Classics, works on the six arts, philosophy, poetry, military science, divination, and medicine. Owing to the decline of the healing art under the Han 漢 dynasty, the last division was dropped, and no titles of medical books are given. There remained but the six divisions, mentioned in the text. Under these divisions were comprised 38 subdivisions with 596 authors, whose names and works are given in the Catalogue. Their writings contain 13,269 chapters or books.

CHAPTER 84
Replies in Self-Defense
Duizuo 對作
(*Lunheng* Book XXIX, Chap. ii)

1   The philosopher Xun Zi 荀子: Sun Qing 孫卿, cf. Ch. 13.
2   *Vid.* Ch. 83 and the Catalogue of Literature, *Hanshu* 漢書 chap. 30.
3   The philosophers of egoism and altruism, both combated by Mencius.
4   The philosopher Han Feizi 韓非子 was the son of a duke of the Han 韓 State in Shanxi 山西.
5   An allusion to an event in the life of Lu Jia 陸賈, narrated in his biography, *Shiji* 史記 chap. 97 p. 7. When Lu Jia had returned from his successful mission to the King of Yue 越, whom he induced to acknowledge the suzerainty of the Han 漢, Gao Zu 高祖 conferred a high rank upon him. Subsequently, when relating his adventures, Lu Jia would always refer to poetry and history. The emperor displeased with these utterances, told him that he had won his laurels on horseback, why must he make such a fuss about literature. Then Lu Jia showed him, how former conquerors had lost the empire again, if they had not consolidated their power by the arts of peace. This conversation with the emperor lead to the composition of a series of memorials, in which Lu Jia developed his ideas about

government. This collection of memorials received the title "New Words," *Xinyu* 新語, cf. Ch. 83.

6   Princes and nobles.

7   *Mencius* Bk. III, Pt. II, chap. IX, I.

8   Vermilion is regarded as a primary colour, and much liked, purple as secondary, and not much esteemed.

9   Cf. p. I.97.

10   The favourite disciple of Confucius, who died very young, cf. Ch. 28.

11   Another of Wang Chong's works, which has been lost.

12   *Lunheng* 論衡 Ch. 16–24, 25–27, 62 and 65 (cf. p. I.52 seq. and p. I.62 seq.).

13   The *Shiji*.

14   The *Xinxu* 新序.

15   Ban Shu Pi 班叔皮 = Ban Biao 班彪, the father of the historian Ban Gu 班固. He also was devoted to the study of history, and intended to continue the *Shiji*, which was finally done by his son.

16   Cf. Ch. 83.

17   *Jianlun* 檢論.

18   Cf. Ch. 83.

19   A mythical personage.

20   Another legendary person, who is said to have been a descendant of Huang Di 黃帝 and director of chariots under Yu 禹.

21   *Vid.* Ch. 81, where Wang Chong maintains that Fu Xi 伏羲 did not make the diagrams, but received them in a supernatural way.

22   The first year of the Emperor Zhang Di 章帝: 76 CE.

23   An old name for Henan 河南.

24   A circuit in Anhui 安徽.

25   A place in Henan.

26   A report for the emperor, which Wang Chong, not being of sufficiently high rank, could not present directly.

27   The official chronicles of these two States. (Cf. Ch. 81.)

28   A term employed for the first year of a sovereign, also denoting the original fluid of nature.

29   The "Classic of Music."

30   Cf. p. II.472.

31   China.

32   Cf. Ch. 31.

33   *Vid.* Ch. 31.

34   Cf. Ch. 32.

35   A city in Henan. We learn from the *Lunheng* V, 6v. (*Ganxu* 感虛 Ch. 19) that this battle was fought by Duke Xiang 襄 of Lu 魯 against Han 韓. This prince reigned from 572 BCE to 541 BCE. *Huainanzi* 淮南子 VI, 1v., however, from whom this passage is quoted, speaks of the Duke of Lu-yang 魯陽 and the commentary remarks that this was a grandson of King Ping 平 of Chu 楚 (528 BCE–515 BCE), called Luyang Wenzi 魯陽文子 in the *Guoyu* 國語.

36   A legendary hermit of Yao's 堯 time. (Cf. Ch. 29.)

37   Cf. p. I.62 and p. I.63 [Ch. 62 and 65].

38   *Lunheng* Ch. 62 and 63.

39   The tyrant Jie 桀 is reported to have built the first brick houses (*Diwang shiji* 帝王世紀).

40   The ten dynasties of the fabulous age of Chinese history together with the Five Emperors and their houses, whom Chinese fancy has credited with the invention of all the fundamental institutions of civilisation, such as house building, dress making, writing, etc.

41   The Odes of the *Shijing* 詩經.

42   "Equality of the ages."

43   Contained in Books XVIII and XIX, Ch. 56–59.

44   Wang Chong eulogises the emperors of his own time, and places them on a level with the model sovereigns of antiquity.

CHAPTER 85
Autobiography
Ziji 自紀

(*Lunheng* Book XXX, Chap. i)

1   In Shaoxingfu 紹興府 (Zhejiang 浙江).

2   Under the Han 漢 dynasty Guiji 會稽 comprises Zhejiang 浙江, the South of Anhui 安徽, and the North of Fujian 福建.

3   In Damingfu 大名府 (Zhili 直隸).

4   A circuit comprising parts of Zhili and Henan 河南.

5   In the Hangzhou 杭州 prefecture of Zhejiang.

6   27 CE.

7   A prefecture or a circuit—of which there were 36 during the Han 漢 epoch—was divided into 5 regions: the centre and four quarters. Each region was superintended by a chief secretary of the prefect, who had the jurisdiction over his region.

8   A disciple of Confucius, whom the master esteemed very much.

9   Shi Zi Yu 史子魚 — Shi Yu 史魚, a high officer in Wei 衛. When Duke Ling 靈 of Wei 衛 (533–492 BCE) did not employ Qu Bo Yu 蘧伯玉, Shi Zi Yu 史子魚 remonstrated with the duke, but in vain. Soon afterwards he fell sick. Feeling his end coming, he told his son to place his corpse under the window, without performing the usual funeral rites, because he did not deserve them, not having been able to convince the duke of what was right. When the duke paid his condolence, the son informed him of what his father had said. The duke repented, and then appointed Qu Bo Yu. When Confucius heard of this, he exclaimed: "How upright was Shi Zi Yu, who still as a corpse admonished his sovereign." Qu Bo Yu was of a different turn of mind. Confucius said of him that, when bad government prevailed, he could roll his principles up, and keep them in his breast. (*Analects* XV, 6.)

10 One *zhong* 鍾 = 4 pecks.

11 Zou Yang 鄒陽 lived under the reign of Jing Di 景帝 (156–141 BCE). At the court of King Xiao 孝 of Liang 梁 he was denounced by Yang Sheng 羊勝 and others, and thrown into prison, but by a memorial, which from his confinement he sent to the king, he obtained his release, and was reinstated into all his honours.

12 It is not certain where this Mount Li 歷山 was situated. Various places are assigned to it.

13 *Jisujieyi* 譏俗節義.

14 Parts of the *Shangshu* 尚書.

15 The minor odes of the *Shijing* 詩經.

16 A politician of the 4th cent. BCE. (Cf. Ch. 83.)

17 *Vid.* Ch. 21 n. 37.

18 Duke Xiao 孝 of Qin 秦, 361–337 BCE.

19 This adventure is related by Huai Nan Zi 淮南子 (quoted in the *Peiwen yunfu* 佩文韻府) likewise, who adds that the horse of Confucius was retained by the peasants, because it had eaten their corn.

20 A minister of Shun 舜.

21 Yi Di 儀狄, the inventor of wine, who presented the first cup to Great Yu 禹.

22 Yi Ya 易牙, the famous cook of Duke Huan 桓 of Qi 齊, 7th cent. BCE. (Cf. *Mencius*, Bk. VI, Pt. I, chap. 7, Legge, *Classics* Vol. II, p. 281.)

23 The matron-saint of a village.

24 An old State in Anhui.

25 *Zhengwu* 政務.

26 The Golden Age.

27 According to the *Shiji* 史記 chap. 63 p. 11v (Biography of Han Feizi 韓非子) the emperor said: "Alas! If I could see this man, I would be willing to live and die with him!"

28 Han Feizi was sent as envoy from his native State (Han 韓) to Qin Shi Huangdi 秦始皇, who first appreciated him very much and wished to appoint him to some high post. By the intrigues of Li Si 李斯, however, he was induced to imprison him, and to condemn him to death. The emperor afterwards repented, and cancelled the death warrant, but is was too late, for meanwhile Han Feizi had taken poison. (Cf. p. I.235.)

29 Cf. Ch. 13.

30 The philosopher Guan Zhong 管仲.

31 In Zheng 鄭 licentious music, but not the serious songs of the Book of Odes were appreciated.

32 The five leaders of the empire, the most powerful princes during the 7th cent. BCE to wit: Duke Huan 桓 of Qi 齊, Duke Wen 文 of Jin 晉, Duke Xiang 襄 of Song 宋, Duke Zhuang 莊 of Chu 楚, and Duke Mu 穆 of Qin 秦. They were more bent on conquest than interested in the moral laws expounded in the Canons of Yao 堯 and Shun 舜 in the *Shangshu* 尚書.

33 The chiefs of two noble families in Lu 魯, contemporaries of Confucius.

34 *Vid.* p. II.853.

35 Cf. p. II.845–46.

36 Duke Wen 文 placed the tablet of his deceased father above that of his uncle in the ancestral temple. The latter, Duke Min 閔, was a younger brother of Duke Xi 僖, but he preceded in reign. For more details *vid.* *Zuozhuan* 左氏傳, Duke Wen 文 2nd year.

37 The music-master of the Duke of Jin 晉 (cf. Ch. 64).

38 Lü Buwei 呂不韋, the author of the *Lüshi chunqiu* 呂氏春秋.

39 It is related of Lü Buwei that he placed a copy of his work in the market place and offered a reward of a thousand *jin* 金 to any one who could alter one character in it. The same is not known of Huai Nan Zi 淮南子.

40 Both were princes.

41 *Vid.* p. II.845.

42 Like Yao 堯 (cf. Ch. 11).

43 As Shun 舜 had (*loc. cit.*).

44 Tai Gong Wang 太公王 is the full appellative of Wen Wang's 文王 minister, usually called Tai Gong 太公, on whom cf. Ch. 25.

45 Cf. p. I.42 and Ch. 83.

46 When forced to leave Qi 齊. (*Vid. Mencius* Bk. V, Pt II, chap. I, 4, Legge, *Classics* Vol. II, p. 247.)

47 Cf. Ch. 26.

48 Xian 憲 = Yuan Si 原思, a disciple of Confucius, noted for his contempt of worldly advantages. Made governor of a town, he declined his official allowance (*Analects* VI, 3) Zhuang Zi 莊子 makes him live in a mud hut. He contrasts him with Ci 賜, another follower of Confucius, who came driving up to his door in a fine chariot and in a white robe lined with purple.

49 Ci 賜 = Duanmu Ci 端木賜 or Zi Gong 子貢, a disciple of Confucius, who became a high official, and very wealthy (*vid.* Ch. 8 and 28). He was a swell, just the reverse of Xian 憲.

50 The Chinese are in awe of, but do not like wonders, miracles, monsters, in short all that is against the regular course of nature. So they are prejudiced against Wang Chong, because he is a *homo novus*. Not being a descendant from a literary or a noble family, he should not attempt to rise above the average of his fellow-citizen.

51 The source of the Feng 灃, an affluent of the Wei 渭 in Shanxi 陝西 is well known. I presume that for "Feng river" 灃水 we ought to read "Wine Spring" 醴泉. The phonetic element for Feng 灃 and Li 醴 "Wine" is very similar, and the Wine Springs are often mentioned as auspicious omens in connection with phœnixes, unicorns, and auspicious grain.

52 Minister of Tang 湯, the founder of the Shang 商 dynasty.

53 Cf. p. II.860–61.

54 Yu's 禹 father.

55 Gu Sou 瞽瞍, Shun's 舜 father.

56 A disciple of Confucius, who suffered from leprosy (cf. Ch. 28).

57 Another disciple of Confucius, a relation of Bo Niu 伯牛, both belonging to the Ran 冉 clan.

58 Yan Hui's 顏回 father.

59 Cf. p. I.42 and Ch. 83.

60 86 CE.

61 Under the Han 漢 a circuit comprising parts of Jiangsu 江蘇 and Anhui.

62 A circuit in Anhui.

63 Another circuit in Anhui.

64 A very large province under the Han dynasty, comprising nearly the whole territory of the modern provinces of Jiangsu, Anhui, Jiangxi 江西, Fujian 福建, and Zhejiang 浙江.

65 88 CE.

66 The cyclical years *gengyin* 庚寅: 90 CE and *xinmao* 辛卯: 91 CE.

67 *Yangxingshu* 養性書.

APPENDIX I

The Theory of the Five Elements and the Classifications Based Thereon

1 禹曰、於帝念哉、德惟善政、政在養民、水火金木土穀、惟修、正德利用厚生、惟和、九功惟敘、九敘惟歌、戒之用休、董之用威、勸之以九歌、俾勿壞。

2 Shun 舜, thus apostrophised by Yu 禹.

3 帝曰、俞、地平天成、六府三事允治、萬世永賴、時乃功。

4 The "Counsels of the Great Yu," Yu being the founder of the Xia 夏 dynasty.

5 夏書曰、戒之用休、董之用威、勸之以九歌、勿使壞、九功之德、皆可歌也、謂之九歌、六府三事、謂之九功、水火金木土穀、謂之六府、正德、利用、厚生、謂之三事。

6 有扈氏、威侮五行、怠棄三正、天用勦絕其命、今予惟恭行天之罰。

7 箕子乃言曰、我聞在昔、鯀陻洪水、汨陳其五行、帝乃震怒、不畀洪範九疇。

8 一五行、一曰水、二曰火、三曰木、四曰金、五曰土、水曰潤下、火曰炎上、木曰曲直、金曰從革、土爰稼穡、潤下作鹹、炎上作苦、曲直作酸、從革作辛、稼穡作甘。

9 曰休徵、曰肅、時雨若、曰乂、時暘若、曰哲、時燠若、曰謀、時寒若、曰聖、時風若、曰咎徵、曰狂、恆雨若、曰僭、恆暘若、曰豫、恆燠若、曰急、恆寒若、曰蒙、恆風若。

　　曰、王省惟歲、卿士惟月、師尹惟日。歲月日、時無易、百穀用成、乂用明、俊民用章、家用平康。日月歲、時旣易、百穀用不成、乂用昏不明、俊民用微、家用不寧。

10 簡子曰、敢問何謂禮。對曰、吉也聞諸先大夫子產、曰、夫禮、天之經也、地之義也、民之行也、天地之經、而民實則之、則天之明、因地之性、生其六氣、用其五行、氣爲五味、發爲五色、章爲五聲。

11 民有好惡、喜怒、哀樂、生於六氣、是故、審則宜類、以制六志。

12 先王之濟五味、和五聲也、以平其心、成其政也、聲亦如味。

13 水勝火

14 火勝金

15 水、火之牡也。

16 火、水妃也。

17 丙子若壬午作乎、水火所以合也。

18 子水位也

19 五行一黑位水、二赤位火、三蒼位木、四白位金、五黃位土。

20 故人者、其天地之德、陰陽之交、鬼神之會、五行之秀氣也。

21 播五行於四時。

22 五行之動、迭相竭也、五行四時十二月、還相爲本。

23 The two first of the ten cyclical signs.

24 This number is said to refer to the vernal element wood. The Five Elements are counted in the sequence of their creation (see above, p. III.867): water, fire, wood, metal, earth. Now the last only is given its natural number 5. All the other elements have their number in the series plus 5.

25 One of the five sacrifices of the house. Cf. p. II.750. The correspondence of these offerings with the seasons and elements is obvious. The door symbolises the opening of the year and the display of the energies of nature. The outer door, or the gate, is the counterpart of the inner door and therefore connected with the autumn sacrifice. The sacrifice to the hearth goes well with fire, that to the inner court with earth or the centre, and that of the well with water. Our text of the *Liji* 禮記 reads "path" 行 for 井 "well." (Cf. Legge, *loc. cit.* p. 297, Note 1.) I follow Wang Chong p. II.750.

26 The eastern part of the Hall of Distinction, where the emperor went on the first day of the month. Qingyang 青陽 means "green and bright."

27 定下因地利、制以五行、左木、右金、前火、後水、中土、營軍陳土、不失其宜、五度旣正、無事不舉。

28 帝曰、寒、暑、燥、濕、風、火、在人合之、奈何、其於萬物、何以生化。

29 南方生熱、熱生火、火生苦、苦生心、心生血、血生脾、其在天爲熱、在
    地爲火、在體爲脈、在氣爲息、在藏爲心、其性爲暑、其德爲顯、其用
    爲躁、其色爲赤、其化爲茂、其蟲羽、其政爲明、其令鬱蒸、其變炎爍、其
    眚燔炳、其味爲苦、其志爲喜、喜傷心、恐勝喜、熱傷氣、寒勝熱、苦傷
    氣、鹹勝苦。

30 Lacuna in the text.

31 北方生寒、寒生水、水生鹹、鹹生腎、腎生骨髓、髓生肝、其在天爲寒、在
    地爲水、在體爲骨、在氣爲堅、在藏爲腎、其性爲凜、其德爲寒、其用
    爲○其色爲黑、其化爲肅、其蟲鱗、其政爲靜、其令○○其變凝冽、其
    眚冰雹、其味爲鹹、其志爲恐、恐傷腎、思勝恐、寒傷血、燥勝寒、鹹傷
    血、甘勝鹹。

32 五氣更立、各有所先、非其位則邪、當其位則正。

33 散明謐勁靜

34 怒喜思憂恐. The 5 impulses partly correspond to the 6 impulses of the
    Zuozhuan 左氏傳. See above p. III.870.

35 筋脈肉皮毛骨

36 The Six Fluids of the *Zuozhuan* 左氏傳, not expressly mentioned, would
    be different, if the commentators are right. Cf. p. III.870. But they practi-
    cally agree with the Five Fluids of the *Shangshu* 尚書: rain, sunshine, heat,
    cold, and wind (see above, p. III.867), leaving aside fire.

37 陰陽者、天地之大理也、四時者、陰陽之大經也、刑德者、四時之合也、
    刑德合於時、則生福、詭則生禍。

38 As will be seen in the following, rewards are in accordance with spring
    and summer, punishments with autumn and winter. From time imme-
    morial capital punishment in China has been meted out in autumn and
    winter, so that the Chinese have come to consider this the natural course
    of nature.

39 In the chapter on the Five Elements, XIV, 16v. seq. In the preceding one
    on the Four Seasons, XIV, p. 8v. he still adheres to the theory of the Four
    Seasons, stating that earth, the element of the centre, helps the Four Sea-
    sons 輔四時.

40 土日月星辰

41 See below Appendix I n. 50.

42 冬三月、以壬癸之日發五政、一政曰、論孤獨、恤長者、二政曰、善順陰、
    修神祀、賦爵祿、授備位、三政曰、效會計、毋發山川之藏、四政曰、捕
    姦遁、得盜賊者有賞、五政曰、禁遷徙、止流民、圉分異、五政苟時、冬
    事不過、所求必得、所惡必伏. *Guanzi* 管子 XIV, 11 r.

43 The Chinese probably discovered some analogies between these measures

and winter, and for that reason prescribed them: There is some similarity between the desolateness of winter and destitute persons. Winter, being the end of the year, may be compared with old and aged persons. We ourselves personify it by an old man, and spring by a young boy. In winter the *Yin* 陰 principle is at its height, and incorporeal spirits belong to it. Accounts use to be settled at the end of the year. The hidden treasures of mountains and rivers 藏 must not be moved, because hiding and torpidity is the nature of winter. The forces of nature do not move, hence the moving about of the people is prohibited. Criminals, as we have seen, are called to account in autumn and winter.

44 故春凋秋榮冬雷夏有霜雪、此皆氣之賊也。刑德易節失次、則賊氣遬至、賊氣遬至、則國多菑殃、是故聖王務時而寄政焉、作教而寄武、作祀而寄德焉、此三者聖王所以合於天地之行也。

45 The *Yang* 陽 is warm and thus may be symbolised by warmth of heart, benevolence and rewards. *Yin* is cold and has an analogy in cold-hearted severity and punishments.

46 An eclipse of the sun, the chief representative of the *Yang*, means that rewards have been incomplete.

47 The moon again represents the *Yin* fluid and punishments. Its partly annihilation shows that punishments have been insufficient.

48 Wind is the fluid of spring, the characteristic feature of which is productiveness. Fighting for brightness must signify that wind chasing the clouds attempts to obscure the brightness of the sun, which now and then breaks through the clouds.

49 日掌陽、月掌陰、星掌和、陽爲德、陰爲刑、和爲事、是故日食、則失德之國惡之、月食、則失刑之國惡之、彗星見、則失和之國惡之、風與日爭明、則失生之國惡之、是故聖王、日食、則修德、月食、則修刑、彗星見、則修和、風與日爭明、則修生、此四者、聖王所以免於天地之誅也。
Guanzi XIV, 11 v.

50 This is the cyclical sign of the day beginning the period of 72 days assigned to the element wood. Here we have a key to the understanding of the pairs of cyclical signs joined to each element in the *Liji* 禮記, the meaning of which was not clear to Legge. The days of spring are *jia* 甲 and *yi* 乙 (cf. p. III.872) means nothing else than that the first and the second days of this season bear these signs, being in the sexagenary cycle *jiazi* 甲子 and *yichou* 乙丑. Summer begins when we arrive at the sign *bingzi* 丙子, after having passed through the entire cycle of 60, adding 12, *i.e.*, after 72 days. The second day of summer or of the element fire is a

dingchou 丁丑 day, so that the *Liji* may say that the days of summer are *bing* 丙 and *ding* 丁, &c. Of course, the assigning of three full months to each season by the *Liji* is not in keeping with these cyclical signs, which can only be applied to seasons of 72 days.

51　Spring is the time of growth, but not of destruction.

52　According to a commentator this is the season of ease and indulgence.

53　A drought is a consequence of too much heat symbolised by hurried and hasty actions.

54　By building the element earth is disturbed.

55　This again would mean a disturbance of the metal hidden in the mountains.

56　睹甲子、木行御、天子不賦不賜賞、而大斬伐傷、君危不殺、太子危、家人夫人死、不然則長子死、七十二日而畢。睹丙子、火行御、天子敬行急政、旱札、苗死民厲、七十二日而畢。睹戊子、土行御、天子修宮室、築臺榭、君危、外築城郭、臣死、七十二日而畢。睹庚子、金行御、天子攻山擊石、有兵作戰而敗士死、喪執政、七十二日而畢。睹壬子、水行御、天子決塞、動大水、王后夫人薨、不然則羽卵者段、毛胎者膿脃婦銷弃、草木根本不美、七十二日而畢也。 *Guanzi* XIV, 18v. (*Shizi quanshu* 十子全書).

57　The utterance of the *Yijing* 易經 are very obscure and I doubt whether they really refer to the elements.

58　A work dating from the 3rd cent. CE. I doubt whether this chapter 五帝 treating of the Five Elements really goes back to Confucius, since he is made to say that he was informed about the elements by Lao Zi 老子.

59　If we speak of the green earth we regard its coat, the green vegetation, as part of it.

60　That is to say, they have not conceived the idea of the elements, but ascribe the single ones to the four quarters like the Chinese: Wind belongs to the North, water to the West, fire to the South, and earth to the East.

61　關尹子, a Daoist author, but the work bearing his name, is believed to be a production of the Tang 唐 or the following minor dynasties, 618–960 CE.

62　升者爲火、降者爲水、欲升而不能升者爲木、欲降而不能降者爲金。

63　水之平也、火之銳也、土之圓也、木之曲直也、金之方也、此其以形言也。 In another chapter the same author gives 尖圓方直曲 as the shapes of the elements. 直 "straight" seems to stand for "level," and 曲 "crooked" alone for "straight and crooked," the shape of wood.

64　董仲舒春秋繁露、五行相生○天地之氣、合而爲一、分爲陰陽、判爲四時、列爲五行。(*Han Wei congshu* 漢魏叢書).

65 班固白虎通、五行○　火者陽也、尊故上、水者陰也、卑故下、木者少陽、
　　金者少陰。

66 子華子、北宮意問○陽中之陽者火是也、陰中之陰者水是也、陽中之
　　陰者木是也、陰中之陽者金是也、土居二氣之中間、以治四維、在陰
　　而陰、在陽而陽。

67 北方陰極、而生寒、寒生水、南方陽極而生熱、熱生火、東方陽動以散
　　而生風、風生木、西方陰止以收而生燥、燥生金、中央陰陽交而生濕、
　　濕生土。(*Zishu baijia* 子書百家).

68 朱子全書○　天一生水、地二生火、天三生木、地四生金。　(*Tushu ji-cheng* 圖書集成).

69 易經、繫辭上傳○　天一地二天三地四天五地六天七地八天九地十。

70 水至陰也、必待天一加之、而後生者、陰不得陽、則終不得而成也。火
　　至陽也、必待地二加之、而後生者、陽不得陰、則無所得而見也。五行
　　皆然、莫不生於陰陽之相加、陽加陰、則爲水爲木爲土、陰加陽、則爲
　　火爲金。

71 陽變陰合、初生水火、水火氣也。流動閃鑠、其體尚虛、其成形猶未定。
　　次生木金、則確然有定形矣、水火初是自生、木金則資於土。

72 乾冷成土、濕冷成水……濕熱成氣……乾熱成火。

73 性理會通、五行、周子曰○質則陰陽交錯凝合而成、氣則陰陽兩端循
　　環不已。

74 蔡氏曰、五行在天、則爲五氣、雨暘燠寒風也。在地、則爲五質、水木火
　　金地。天之五氣、雨暘質也。地之五質、水火氣也。

75 章潢圖書編、五行氣質○質根於地、氣運於天……生之者氣、成之者
　　質。

76 性理會通、膚語○水火氣多而質少、故生成居先。金木質多而氣少、
　　故生成居後。土氣質均當、後水火、而先金木。

77 水氣陽而質陰、陰之性滋、故水生木。火氣陰而質陽、陽之性烈、故火
　　不生金。土也者、氣陽而質陰者也、故接火之陽而生金之陰。

78 春生、夏長、秋收、冬藏。*Guanzi* XIV, 8v. has nearly the same attributes:
　　一春嬴育、夏養長、秋聚收、冬閉藏。

79 木者春生之性、農之本也○　火者夏成長○　土者夏中成熟百重○金
　　者秋殺氣之始也○水者冬藏至陰也○

80 歲星、熒惑、鎮星、太白、辰星。

81 熒惑、曰南方火、主夏.

82 金史、五行志序○　五行之精氣、在天爲五緯、在地爲五材、在人爲五
　　常及五事。

83 王文祿、補衍五德主運篇○每仰觀五星、初昏卽見五色、朗然不亂、
　　是五行之精也。

84 Bouche-Leclerq, *Astrologie Grecque*, p. 314.

85 See the list of living beings 五行動物屬圖 in the 性理會通.

86 宋儲泳、論劉向災異五行志○五行者、人身之五官也、氣應五臟。

87 南唐、譚子化書、五行相濟相伐○ 五常者、五行也、仁發生之謂也、故君于木、義救難之謂也、故君于金、禮明白之謂也、故君于火、智變通之謂也、故君于水、信慤然之謂也、故君于土。

88 五行人體性情圖

89 *Huainanzi* 淮南子 III, 3v.: 蒼龍、朱鳥、白虎、元武、黃龍。

90 The translation "Blue Dragon" must be changed into "Green Dragon."

91 *Baihutong* 白虎通 II, 2v.: 青龍、鳥離、鸞、白虎、玄武。

92 戴廷槐五行統論 contained in the 性理會通.

93 辰戌丑未

94 天一生水、地六成之、地二生火、天七成之、天三生木、地八成之、地四生金、天九成之、天五生土、地十成之。*loc. cit.*

95 土生數五、成數十、但言五者、土以生爲本。

96 周子太極圖○以質而語其生之序、則曰水火木金土、以氣而語其行之序、則曰木火土金水。

97 朱子語類○取其天地始生之序。

98 木勝土、土勝水、水勝火、火勝金、金勝木。

99 春秋繁露、五行相生○比相生而間相勝也。

100 黃帝索問、寶命全形論○木得金而伐、火得水而滅、土得木而達、金得火而缺、水得土而絕。

101 關尹子、二柱篇○ 木之爲物、鑽之得火、絞之得水、金之爲物、擊之得火、鎔之得水。

102 章潢圖書編、五行氣質○ 土得水則柔、得火則剛。金得火則流、得水則止。木得水則長、得火則消。火得木則生、得水則死。水得金則寒、得火則煖。

103 儲泳祛疑說、五行體象生克之性○火生於木、而焚木。金生於土、而鋤土…木克土、而土養木。土克水、而水澤土。

104 戴廷槐、五行統論○ 有母必能生子、子必能爲母報讎之義焉。

105 朱子語類○金爲氣之母、天體乾金也。

106 木生于亥、壯于卯、死于未、三辰皆木也。火生于寅、壯于午、死于戌、三辰皆火也、&c.

107 *Huainanzi* 淮南子 IV, 9r.: 木壯水老火生金囚土死、火壯木老土生水囚金死、&c.

108 黃帝經, the *Huangdi suwen* 黃帝素問 is meant.

109 明孫昭、系包考○ 五行十二變曰生曰浴曰官曰臣曰君曰委曰病曰死曰藏曰止曰渾曰育。

110 *Loc. cit.* 其論五行、一曰水、其系包在巳、其胎在午、其養在未、其生在申、其沐浴在酉、其冠帶在戌、其臨官在亥、其帝旺在子、其衰老在丑、其病在寅、其死在卯、其墓在辰。

111 Cf. Legge's translation p. 280 and 281, Note 1.

112 See *Liji* 禮記, Legge's translation p. 225 and *Lunheng* p. II.758.

113 Metal is supposed to meet with the other four elements or to collide with them, as the text says. That merely signifies that, in consequence of the preponderance of these unseasonable elements, autumn changes its character and, in its temperature, resembles spring, summer, or winter. In the next clause winter is supposed to undergo similar changes. The consequences of these irregularities of the seasons are, most of them, taken from experience and not contradicted by facts.

114 春秋繁露、治亂五行○　水干金、則魚不爲。木干金、則草木再生。火干金、則草木秋榮。土干金、五穀不成。木干火、冬蟄不藏。土干水、則蟄蟲冬出。火干水則星墜。金干水、則冬大寒。*Dong Zhongshu* 董仲舒 XIV, 1 r.

115 *Loc. cit.* 五行變救○木有變、春凋秋榮、秋大水、春多雨、此繇役衆、賦斂重、百姓貧窮、叛去道、多饑人、救之者省繇役、薄賦斂、出倉穀、賑困窮矣。火有變、冬温夏寒、此王者不明、善者不賞、惡者不紲、不肖在位、賢者伏匿、則寒暑失序、而民疾疫、救之者舉賢良、賞有功、封有德。*Dong Zhongshu* XIV, lv.

APPENDIX II

The Cycle of the Twelve Animals

1 Le Cycle Turc des douze animaux in *T'oung-pao*, Serie II, Vol. VII, Nr. 1 (1906).

2 F. Hirth, *Nachworte zur Inschrift des Tonjukuk* 1899, p. 121 (W. Radloff, *Die alttürkischen Inschriften der Mongolei*).

3 Schuyler, *Turkestan* Vol. I, p. 333.

4 G. Schlegel, *Uranographie Chinoise*, Leiden 1875, Vol. I, p. 558 seq.

5 L. de Saussure, Les origines de l'astronomie chinoise E. Le cycle des douze animaux (*T'oung-pao*, Serie 2, XI, 1910, p. 583 seq.).

6 See Chavannes, *Mem. Hist.*, Vol. III, p. 654 seq.

7   爾雅正義 chap. 9, p. 11 seq.

8   F. K. Ginzel, *Handbuch der Mathematischen und Technischen Chronologie*, Leipzig 1906, Vol. I, p. 324, Note 1.

9   *Loc. cit.* p. 369. I do not understand what Ginzel means by saying that the cycle of Jupiter was used by the Chinese for astrology only, whereas in India the calendar was based on it (p. 493). From the "Bamboo Annals" onward it is the basis of Chinese chronology, all years being denoted by the sexagesimal cycle, a combination of the duodenary and the denary.

10 Epochae celebriores Astronomis, Historicis, Chronologis, Chataiorum, Syro-Graecorum, Arabum, Persarum, Chorasmiorum usitatae ex traditione Ulug Beigi re-censuit J. Gravius, London 1650.

11 و ترکان بر دور دوازده کانه مذکور اختصار نمایند و قید تاریخ ایشان مارا معلوم نیست
Ulugh Beg p. 50.

12 He wrote about 1444 CE in Transoxiania.

13 L. Ideler, *Über die Zeitrechnung der Chinesen*, Berlin 1839, p. 80.

14 H. Vambery, *Das Türkenvolk*, Leipzig 1885, p. 47 seq.

15 Cf. Chavannes p. 53, Note 6.

16 E. Sieg and W. Siegling, *Tocharisch, die Sprache der Indoskythen* (Sitzungsberichte der Kgl. Preuß. Akad. der Wissenschaften Vol. XXXIX 1908, p. 915 seq.).

17 O. Franke, *Beiträge zur Kenntnis der Türkvölker und Skythen Zentralasiens* (Abh. der Kgl. Preuß. Akad. der Wissenschaften 1904) p. 46 seq.

18 Chavannes p. 53, Note 6 and K. Foy, *Azerbajğanische Studien* (Mitt. des Sem. f. orient. Sprachen, II. Abt. 1905) p. 234, Note 4.

    The *i* in *lui* or *lüi* is a remnant of the nasal *ng*. The Mongols also call the dragon *luu* (*loo*), cf. Foy *loc. cit.*

    Hirth's view that *lüi* would be Chinese *lei* (thunder) p. 119 seems to me untenable.

19 و نزد منجمان خطا و ایغور از نیم شبست تا نیم شب دیکر   p. 4.

20 و منجمان خطا و ایغور شبانروزرا یکبار بدوازده قسم کنند و هر یکرا
چاغ کویند و هر چاغیرا نامیست بدین ترتیب   p. 6.

21 و هر چاغیرا بهشت قسم کنند و هر یکرا که کویند   p. 8.

22 حکماء خطا و ترکستان روزها و سالهارا دوری نهاده اند که بر دوازده
می کردد چنانچه اقسام شبانروزرا بهمان نامها که مذکور شده   p. 42.

23 Albiruni, *The chronology of ancient nations*, translated by E. Sachau, p. 83.

24 *Suishu* 隋書 chap. 1, p. 15v. and 16r. 突厥阿波可汗遣使貢方物○突厥沙鉢略可汗遣使貢方物。

25 *Eod.* p. 17r. and v. 大將軍韓僧壽破突厥於雞頭山、上柱國李充破突厥於河北山○突厥入長城○上柱國李充破突厥於馬邑。

26　*Eod.* p. 19r. and v. 突厥寇邊○衛王爽破突厥於白道○突厥遣使來朝
　　○行軍總管李晃破突厥於摩那渡口○行軍元帥竇榮定破突厥及吐谷
　　渾於涼州○突厥遣使請和。

27　P. 21r. and v. 班新曆○突厥蘇尼部男女萬餘人來降○突厥可汗阿史
　　那玷率其屬來降○宴突厥高麗吐谷渾使者於大興殿。

28　P. 22v. 遣上大將軍元契使于突厥阿波可汗○突厥沙鉢略上表稱臣○
　　沙鉢略可汗遣子庫含眞特勒來朝。

29　可賀敦

30　*Suishu* 隋書 chap. 84, p. 8v. seq.

31　*Suishu* chap. 1, p. 23r. 班曆於突厥。

32　(書法) 頒歷外夷始此。

33　The Nine Mansions 九宮 into which the compass is divided. Why they
　　are thus attributed to males and females, and what the intercalary month
　　means perhaps Chinese horoscopists can tell.

34　光緒三十年甲辰火　一歲龍男六宮女九宮○光緒二十九年癸卯金　二
　　歲兔男七宮女八宮閏五月.

35　On this expression 疇人 see Chavannes, *Mem. Hist.*, Vol. III, p. 326, Note
　　5. One commentator explains it as "those knowing the stars" another as
　　"experts in chronology."

36　幽厲之後、周室微、陪臣執政、史不記時、君不告朔、故疇人子弟分散、
　　或在諸夏、或在夷狄、

37　L. Ideler, *Über die Zeitrechnung der Chinesen*, Berlin 1839, p. 83.

38　*Eod.* p. 85.

39　*Eod.* p. 88.

40　*Eod.* p. 89.

41　Chavannes p. 94.

42　De Saussure p. 638.

APPENDIX III

On Some Implements Mentioned by Wang Chong

1   扇自關而東謂之箑、自關而西謂之扇。

2   Cf. the explanation given by Wieger, *Leçons etymologiques* p. 196: 扇以戶 以羽、會意。門兩傍如羽也。

3   管子四時篇○夏以內丁之日發五政、三日合禁扇去笠. Cf. above, p. III.885.

4   抱朴子外篇○風不輟、則扇不用、日不出、則燭不息。

5   淮南子人間訓○譬猶失火而鑿池、披裘而用箑。

6   春秋繁露○故以龍致雨、以扇逐暑。

7   See my translation in "Bluethen Chinesischer Dichtung," 1899 p. 11.

8   竹扇賦.

9   Pfizmaier in his "Denkwürdigkeiten von chinesischen Werkzeugen und Geräten" (*Journal of the Wiener Akademie der Wissenschaften 1872*, Vol. 72 p. 247–322) mistranslates this expression 蒲葵 (Livistona) or 葵 by mallow. Mallows cannot be used for fans.

10   語林○葛巾白羽扇指麾三軍、三軍皆隨其進止。

11   西京雜記

12   宋書明恭王皇后傳

13   南史臨川王宏傳

14   南齊書

15   See the 陔餘叢考 chap. 33 p. 13 seq. under 摺扇

16   高麗國宣和六年九月遣使李資德金富轍至本朝、謝恩私覿之物有松扇三盒、摺疊扇二隻。

17   高麗白松扇、展之廣尺餘、合之止兩指。

18   洛陽人家端午贈遺辟瘟扇。

19   玉海○漢尙方竹扇。

20   西京雜記○漢制天子夏設羽扇冬繒扇。

21   宋朝會要○漢武帝時、王侯不得用雉扇、公以下用團扇。

22   晉中興書○安帝義熙元年禁絹扇及樗蒲。

23   西京雜記○長安巧工丁緩作七輪扇連七輪大皆徑丈相連續一人運之則滿堂寒顫。

24 古奇器錄○王元寶家有一皮扇子製作甚質每暑月燕客即以此扇置於坐前使新水灑之則颯然風生巡酒之間客有寒色遂命撤去明皇會命中使取視愛而不受曰此龍皮扇子也。

25 箕子歎曰彼爲象箸必爲玉桮。

26 荀子解蔽篇○從山上望木者十仞之木若箸。

27 淮南子齊俗訓○糟丘生乎象箸。

28 漢書周亞夫傳○召亞夫賜食、獨置大胾、無切肉、又不置箸、亞夫心不平、顧謂、尙席取箸。Cf. Giles, *Biogr. Dict.* No. 462.

29 犀辟毒箸

30 后驕逸、體微病、輒不自飲食、須帝持匕箸。

31 禮記曲禮○飯黍毋以箸。

32 羹之有菜者用梜、其無菜者不用梜。

33 掌以夫遂取明火于日、以鑒取明水于月。

34 陽燧釋名○火鏡也。以銅鑄成。其面凹。摩熱向日、以艾承之、則得火。周禮司烜氏以火燧取明火于日是矣。

35 考工記云。銅錫相半、謂之鑑燧之劑。是火爲燧、水爲鑑。

36 搜神記云○五月丙午日午時鑄爲陽燧、十一月壬子日子時鑄爲陰燧。

37 陽燧見日、則燃而爲火。方諸見月則津而爲水。

38 內則。子事父母、左佩金燧、右佩木燧。

Finding List

Between 1907, 1911 Editions and QP Edition
[Last two columns indicate *Lunheng* book division and QP chapter number]

Part I

A. Biographical

1	Autobiography—*Ziji* 自紀	Bk. XXX, Ch. i	85
2	Replies in Self-Defense—*Duizuo* 對作	Bk. XXIX, Ch. ii	84

B. Metaphysical [see also Part II A]

3	Spontaneity—*Ziran* 自然	Bk. XVIII, Ch. i	54
4	The Nature of Things—*Wushi* 物勢	Bk. III, Ch. v	14
5	Phenomenal Changes—*Biandong* 變動	Bk. XV, Ch. i	43
6	On Reprimands—*Qiangao* 譴告	Bk. XIV, Ch. iii	42
7	Heaven's Original Gift—*Chubing* 初禀	Bk. III, Ch. iii	12
8	What Is Meant by Destiny?—*Mingyi* 命義	Bk. II, Ch. ii	6
9	On Destiny and Fortune—*Minglu* 命祿	Bk. I, Ch. iii	3
10	On Chance and Luck—*Xing'ou* 幸偶	Bk. II, Ch. i	5

11   Wrong Notions about Happiness—*Fuxu*
     福虛   Bk. VI, Ch. i   20

12   Wrong Notions on Unhappiness—*Huoxu*
     禍虛   Bk. VI, Ch. ii   21

13   Auspicious Portents—*Jiyan* 吉驗   Bk. II, Ch. v   9

14   On Divination—*Bushi* 卜筮   Bk. XXIV, Ch. ii   71

15   On Death—*Lunsi* 論死   Bk. XX, Ch. iii   62

16   False Reports about the Dead—*Siwei* 死偽   Bk. XXI, Ch. i   63

17   Spook Stories—*Jiyao* 紀妖   Bk. XXII, Ch. i   64

18   All About Ghosts—*Dinggui* 訂鬼   Bk. XXII, Ch. ii   65

C. Physical

19   On Heaven—*Tantian* 談天   Bk. XI, Ch. i   31

20   On the Sun—*Shuori* 說日   Bk. XI, Ch. ii   32

21   On Heat and Cold—*Hanwen* 寒溫   Bk. XIV, Ch. ii   41

22   On Thunder and Lightning—*Leixu* 雷虛   Bk. VI, Ch. iv   23

23   On Poison—*Yandu* 言毒   Bk. XXIII, Ch. i   66

24   On Anthroposcopy—*Guxiang* 骨相   Bk. III, Ch. ii   11

25   Long Life and Vital Fluid—*Qishou* 氣壽   Bk. I, Ch. iv   4

26   Miracles—*Qiguai* 奇怪   Bk. III, Ch. vi   15

27   Unfounded Assertions—*Wuxing* 無形   Bk. II, Ch. iii   7

28   Daoist Untruths—*Daoxu* 道虛   Bk. VII, Ch. i   24

29   On Dragons—*Longxu* 龍虛   Bk. VI, Ch. iii   22

30   Arguments on Ominous Creatures—*Jiangrui*
     講瑞   Bk. XVI, Ch. iv   50

D. Ethical [see also Part II B]

31   The Forming of Characters—*Shuaixing* 率性   Bk. II, Ch. iv   8

32   On Original Nature—*Benxing* 本性   Bk. III, Ch. iv   13

E. Critique—philosophical, literary and historical
[see also Part II C]

33	Criticisms on Confucius—*Wen Kong* 問孔	Bk. IX, Ch. i	28
34	Censures on Mencius—*Ci Meng* 刺孟	Bk. X, Ch. ii	30
35	Strictures on Han Feizi—*Fei Han* 非韓	Bk. X, Ch. i	29
36	Statements Corrected—*Zhengshuo* 正說	Bk. XXVIII, Ch. i	81
37	Critical Remarks on Various Books—*Anshu* 案書	Bk. XXIX, Ch. i	83
38	The Equality of the Ages—*Qishi* 齊世	Bk. XVIII, Ch. iii	56
39	Exaggerations—*Yuzeng* 語增	Bk. VII, Ch. ii	25
40	Exaggerations of the Literati—*Ruzeng* 儒增	Bk. VIII, Ch. i	26

F. Folklore and religion *[see also Part II D]*

41	Sacrifices to the Departed—*Siyi* 祀義	Bk. XXV, Ch. iii	76
42	Sacrifices—*Jiyi* 祭意	Bk. XXV, Ch. iv	77
43	Criticisms on Noxious Influences—*Biansui* 辨祟	Bk. XXIV, Ch. iii	72
44	On Exorcism—*Jiechu* 解除	Bk. XXV, Ch. ii	75

Part II

A. Metaphysical *[see also Part I B]*

1	Coincidences—*Ouhui* 偶會	Bk. III, Ch. i	10
2	Periods of Government—*Zhiqi* 治期	Bk. XVII, Ch. iii	53
3	Sympathetic Emotions—*Ganlei* 感類	Bk. XVIII, Ch. ii	55

B. Ethical *[see also Part I D]*

4	Success and Luck—*Fengyu* 逢遇	Bk. I, Ch. i	1
5	Annoyances and Vexations—*Leihai* 累害	Bk. I, Ch. ii	2
6	On the Cunning and Artful—*Daning* 答佞	Bk. XI, Ch. iii	33
7	Weighing of Talents—*Chengcai* 程材	Bk. XII, Ch. i	34
8	The Valuation of Knowledge—*Liangzhi* 量知	Bk. XII, Ch. ii	35
9	Admitting Shortcomings—*Xieduan* 謝短	Bk. XII, Ch. iii	36
10	The Display of Energy—*Xiaoli* 效力	Bk. XIII, Ch. i	37
11	On Intelligence—*Bietong* 別通	Bk. XIII , Ch. ii	38
12	Apparent Backwardness—*Zhuangliu* 狀留	Bk. XIV, Ch. i	40
13	The Real Nature of Knowledge—*Shizhi* 實知	Bk. XXVI, Ch. i	78
14	A Definition of Worthies—*Dingxian* 定賢	Bk. XXVII, Ch. i	80

C. Critique *[see also Part I E]*

15	Fictitious Phenomena—*Bianxu* 變虛	Bk. IV, Ch. ii	17
16	Fictitious Prodigies—*Yixu* 異虛	Bk. V, Ch. i	18
17	Fictitious Influences—*Ganxu* 感虛	Bk. V, Ch. ii	19
18	Praise of the Han Dynasty—*Xuan Han* 宣漢	Bk. XIX, Ch. i	57
19	Further Remarks on the State—*Huiguo* 恢國	Bk. XIX, Ch. ii	58
20	Ominous Signs Investigated—*Yanfu* 驗符	Bk. XIX, Ch. iii	59
21	The Necessity of Eulogies—*Xusong* 須頌	Bk. XX, Ch. i	60
22	On Literary Work—*Shujie* 書解	Bk. XXVIII, Ch. ii	82
23	Falsehoods in Books—*Shuxu* 書虛	Bk. IV, Ch. i	16
24	Literary Exaggerations—*Yizeng* 藝增	Bk. VIII, Ch. ii	27
25	Lost Texts—*Yiwen* 佚文	Bk. XX, Ch. ii	61
26	The Knowledge of Truth—*Zhishi* 知實	Bk. XXVI, Ch. ii	79
27	On Preeminence—*Chaoqi* 超奇	Bk. XIII, Ch. iii	39

D. Folklore and religion *[see also Part I F]*

28	Thoughts on Omens—*Zhirui* 指瑞	Bk. XVII, Ch. i	51
29	Auguries Verified—*Shiying* 是應	Bk. XVII, Ch. ii	52
30	On the Rain Sacrifice—*Mingyu* 明雩	Bk. XV, Ch. iii	45
31	Gentle Drums—*Shungu* 順鼓	Bk. XV, Ch. iv	46
32	A Last Word on Dragons—*Luanlong* 亂龍	Bk. XVI, Ch. i	47
33	The Tiger Trouble—*Zaohu* 遭虎	Bk. XVI, Ch. ii	48
34	Remarks on Insects—*Shangchong* 商蟲	Bk. XVI, Ch. iii	49
35	Simplicity of Funerals—*Bozang* 薄葬	Bk. XXIII, Ch. ii	67
36	Four Things to be Avoided—*Sihui* 四諱	Bk. XXIII, Ch. iii	68
37	False Charges against Time—*Lanshi* 䦧時	Bk. XXIII, Ch. iv	69
38	Slandering of Days—*Jiri* 譏日	Bk. XXIV, Ch. i	70
39	Questions about the Year Star—*Nansui* 難歲	Bk. XXIV, Ch. iv	73
40	Criticisms on Certain Theories—*Jieshu* 詰術	Bk. XXV, Ch. i	74
[lost]	[Attracting Consequences]—*Zhaozhi* 招致	Bk. XV, Ch. ii	44

Quotations

The numbers in brackets refer to the pages or notes of the translation. L. means Legge's translation of the Classics and of the *Yijing* and the *Liji* in the Sacred Books *viz.* Vols. XVI, XXVII, XXVIII.

Latin figures serve to designate the books of a work and Arabic, the page, except in the *Analects* where they denote the number of the chapter.

Analects

I, 10 (Ch79 n4).

II, 2 (Ch61 n64); II, 4 (Ch78 n60, Ch79 n49); II, 5 (Ch28 n8); II, 6 (Ch28 n9); II, 9 (Ch28 n23); II, 19 (Ch13 n11); II, 23 (Ch78 n47); II, 23, 2 (Ch81 n34).

III, 1 (Ch28 n10); III, 5 (Ch28 n63); III, 6 (Ch28 n11, Ch55 n43); III 14 (Ch56 n14); III, 15 (Ch79 n18), III, 17 (Ch29 n5), III, 22 (Ch55 n53).

IV, 5 (Ch13 n22, Ch28 n14); IV, 7 (Ch28 n35).

V, 1 (Ch28 nn16, 18, Ch80 n54); V, 4 (Ch30 n38, Ch33 n37); V, 8 (Ch28 n20); V, 9 (Ch28 nn25, 29); V, 18 (Ch28 n33, Ch38 n40); V, 27 (Ch16 n75).

VI, 2 (Ch28 n37); VI, 5 (Ch28 n24); VI, 6 (Ch85 n48); VI, 8 (Ch5 n1, Ch21 n7, Ch28 n38); VI, 9 (Ch28 n22, Ch80 n64); VI, 12 (Ch12 n48); VI, 14 (Ch56 n4); VI, 15 (Ch74 n45); VI, 17 (Ch5 n2); VI, 19 (p38); VI, 21 (Ch59 n38); VI, 26 (Ch28 n46).

VII, 9 (Ch55 n12); VII, 13 (Ch26 n21); VII, 14 (Ch80 n87); VII, 15 (Ch28 n95); VII, 34 (Ch19 n43).

VIII, 3 (Ch68 n8); VIII, 7 (Ch37 n11); VIII, 10 (Ch28 n27);

VIII, 12 (Ch12 n26); VIII, 15 (Ch83 n37); VIII, 18 (Ch25 n3); VIII, 18 (Ch54 n21); VIII, 19, (Ch27 n22, Ch54 n20, Ch56 n25, Ch60 n18); VIII, 20 (Ch61 nn5, 55).

IX, 5 (Ch39 n44); IX, 6 (Ch54 n34); IX, 6 (Ch79 n47); IX, 8 (Ch28 n53); IX, 10 (Ch38 n11, Ch58 n1); IX, 11 (Ch55 n40); IX, 13 (Ch28 n62, Ch58 n58); IX, 14 (Ch60 n4, Ch79 n22); IX, 21 (Ch82 n2); IX, 22 (Ch78 n48).

X, 8, 10 (Ch77 n51); X, 16 (Ch23 n22, Ch68 n27); X, 18 (Ch80 n48).

XI, 4 (Ch79 n27); XI, 7 (Ch28 n80); XI, 8 (Ch10 n17, Ch77 n34); XI, 9 (Ch28 n78); XI, 16 (Ch33 n39, Ch46 n30); XI, 18 (Ch28 n7); XI, 22 (Ch79 n9); XI, 24 (Ch27 n26, Ch28 n67, Ch81 n16); XI, 25, 7 (Ch45 n31, Ch77 n34).

XII, 5 (p26, Ch6 n3); XII, 7 (Ch28 n83); XII, 8 (Ch82 n14); XII, 18 (Ch28 n45); XII, 21 (Ch45 n38).

XIII, 3 (Ch28 n64); XIII, 9 (Ch28 n86); XIII, 12 (Ch57 n15); XIII, 15 (Ch28 n31); XIII, 24 (Ch80 n7).

XIV, 14 (Ch26 n26, Ch79 n3); XIV, 18 (Ch55 n51); XIV, 26 (Ch28 n88); XIV, 38 (Ch10 n39, Ch53 n6); XIV, 45 (Ch57 n3).

XV, 1 (Ch5 n12); XV, 6 (Ch85 n9); XV, 8 (Ch28 n82); XV, 24 (Ch29 n21); XV, 30 (Ch78 n64).

XVI, 9 (Ch78 n40); XVI, 10 (Ch79 n19).

XVII, 1 (Ch14 n11, Ch28 n101, Ch79 n12); XVII, 2 (Ch13 n12); XVII, 3 (Ch13 n13); XVII, 4 (Ch28 n4); XVII, 5 (Ch28 n99); XVII, 6 (I, 283); XVII 7 (Ch28 n93); XVII, 12 (Ch29 n35); XVII, 19 (Ch71 n3); XVII, 22 (Ch38 n34).

XIX, 19 (Ch23 n7); XIX, 20 (Ch25 n25, Ch27 n42, Ch56 n27); XIX, 22 (Ch78 n59); XIX, 23 (Ch38 n24).

Shujing/Shangshu

L. I, p. 15 (Ch60 n1).
L. I, p. 17 (Ch27 n5).
L. I, p. 24 (Ch19 n62).
L. I, p. 25 (Ch4 n6).
L. I, p. 26 (Ch81 n62).
L. I, p. 31 (Ch81 n63).
L. I, p. 32 (Ch42 n55, Ch55

n18).
L. I, p. 33 (Ch77 n4).
L. I, p. 47 (Ch16 n86).
L. I, p. 48 (Ch36 n35).
L. I, p. 49 (Ch19 n40).
L. I, p. 51 (Ch4 n9).
L. I, p. 59 (Ch33 n9).

L. I, p. 70 (Ch52 n29, Ch80 n90).
L. I, p. 71 (Ch33 n2).
L. I, p. 73 (Ch27 n20).
L. I, p. 80 (Ch35 n14).
L. I, p. 84 (Ch28 n50).
L. I, p. 85 (Ch25 n48).
L. I, p. 88 (Ch50 n15).
L. I, p. 108 (Ch16 n34).
L. I, p. 113 (Ch16 n51).
L. I, p. 127 (Ch8 n17).
L. I, p. 271 (Ch27 n31).
L. II, p. 315 (Ch25 n21).
L. II, p. 330 (Ch8 n1).
L. II, p. 340 (Ch41 n13).
L. II, p. 342 (Ch32 n58).
L. II, p. 351 (Ch63 n12).

L. II, p. 359 (Ch55 nn7, 24).
L. II, p. 385 (Ch12 n23).
L. II, p. 399 (Ch42 n6).
L. II, p. 428 (Ch73 n19).
L. II, p. 455 (Ch25 n2, Ch54 n22).
L. II, p. 464 (Ch26 n45).
L. II, p. 466 (Ch26 n39).
L. II, p. 468 (Ch25 n5)
L. II, p. 469 (Ch82 n27).
L. II, p. 471 (Ch42 n26).
L. II, p. 477 (Ch55 n27).
L. II, p. 518 (Ch45 n24).
L. II, p. 592 (Ch43 n23).
L. II, p. 593 (Ch42 n24).
L. II, p. 629 (Ch30 n6).

Shiji

Chap. 3 p. 1 (Ch83 n24); chap. 3 p. 10r. (Ch55 n67); chap. 3 p. 11 (Ch25 n40).
Chap. 4 p. 1 (Ch83 n25); chap. 4 p. 39 (Ch26 n53).
Chap. 6 p. 6 (Ch11 n47); chap. 6 p. 18 (Ch26 n58); chap. 6 p. 21v (Ch25 n55); chap. 6 p. 24 (Ch25 n60); chap. 6 p. 24v (Ch64 n61); chap. 6 p. 25v. (Ch25 n62); chap. 6 p. 26v. (Ch78 n11).
Chap. 8 (Ch3 n19); Chap. 8 p. 1 v. (I, 178); chap. 8 p. 2 (Ch11 n12); chap. 8 p. 5 (Ch64 n80); chap. 8 p. 11v. (Ch72 n11); chap. 8 p. 35v. (Ch3 n19).
Chap. 24 p. 39 (Ch64 n11).
Chap. 28 p. 20 (Ch26 n65); chap. 28 p. 21 (Ch24 n44).
Chap. 31 p. 9v. (Ch77 n50).
Chap. 33 p. 3v. (Ch82 n28).
Chap. 40 p. 11 (Ch9 n25).
Chap. 41 p. 6v. (Ch11 n42); chap. 41 p. 7r. (Ch80 n76).
Chap. 43 p. 7 (Ch64 n28); chap. 43 p. 11 (Ch64 n32); chap. 43 p. 12 (Ch64 n54); chap. 43 p. 19 (Ch64 n37).
Chap. 47 p. 12v. (Ch11 n54).
Chap. 55 p. 1v. (Ch64 n92).
Chap. 57 p. 6v (Ch11 n35).
Chap. 61 p. 3v. (Ch21 n23).
Chap. 63 p. 2v. (Ch22 n33).
Chap. 69 p. 12v. (Ch27 n34).
Chap. 70 p. 2r. (Ch33 n27).
Chap. 75 p. 2r (Ch68 n21); chap. 75 p. 2v. (Ch20 n11).
Chap. 83 p. 9v. (Ch19 n20).

Chap. 84 p. 6r. (Ch2 n13).
Chap. 86 end (Ch19 n24).
Chap. 88 p. 5 (Ch21 n19).
Chap. 91 p. 1 (Ch11 n27).
Chap. 92 p. 16r. (Ch80 n76).

Chap. 109 p. 6 (Ch21 n30).
Chap. 111 p. 1v. (Ch11 n29).
Chap. 123 p. 9v. (Ch9 n11).
Chap. 129 p. 3v. (Ch45 n3).

Chunqiu

Huan, 17th year (Ch81 n49).
Zhuang, 2nd year (Ch16 n70).
Zhuang, 7th year (Ch32 n49).

Zhuang, 25th year (Ch46 n1).
Xi, 16th year (Ch32 n55).

Zuozhuan

Ai, 9th year (App.I n13).
Ai, 9th year (App.I n18).
Huan, 5th year (Ch45 n36).
Huan, 6th year (Ch74 n32)
Zhuang, 8th year (Ch65 n20).
Xi, 10th year (Ch63 n8).
Xi, 22nd year (Ch78 n35).
Xi, 28th year (Ch71 n25).
Xi, 29th year (Ch78 n51).
Wen, 1st year (Ch63 n16).
Wen, 18th year (Ch65 n14).
Xuan, 3rd year (Ch26 n46).
Xuan, 15th year (Ch63 n30).
Xiang, 19th year (Ch63 n14).
Xiang, 21st year (Ch22 n2).
Xiang, 21st year (Ch66 n22).
Xiang, 31st year (Ch35 n36).

Zhao, 4th year (Ch64 n43).
Zhao, 5th year (Ch71 n17).
Zhao, 7th year (Ch63 n23).
Zhao, 7th year (Ch63 n50).
Zhao, 8th year (Ch64 n97).
Zhao, 9th year (App.I n16).
Zhao, 13th year (Ch9 n25).
Zhao, 17th year (App.I n15).
Zhao, 19th year (Ch64 n86).
Zhao, 20th year, (App.I n12).
Zhao, 25th year (Ch10 n19).
Zhao, 25th year (Ch10 n20).
Zhao, 26th year (Ch17 n14).
Zhao, 29th year (Ch22 n25).
Zhao, 29th year (Ch77 n23)
Zhao, 31st year (App.I n14).
Yin, 8th year (Ch74 n25)

Mencius

Bk. I, Pt. I, 1 (Ch30 n1).
Bk. I, Pt. II, 16 (Ch30 n31).
Bk. I, Pt. II, 16 (Ch30 n59).

Bk. II, Pt. I, 2 (Ch30 n24).
Bk. II, Pt. I, 2 (19) (Ch79 n52).
Bk. II, Pt. I, 2 (20) (Ch79 n54).

Bk. II, Pt. I, 2 (22) (Ch79 n56).

Bk. II, Pt. II, 3 (Ch30 n16).

Bk. II, Pt. II, 8 (Ch30 n19).

Bk. II, Pt. II , 9 (Ch79 n33).

Bk. II, Pt. II, 10 (Ch30 n10).

Bk. II, Pt. II, 12 (Ch30 n26).

Bk. II, Pt. II, 13 (Ch30 n32).

Bk. III, Pt. I, 1 (Ch83 n41).

Bk. III, Pt. II, 4 (Ch30 n18).

Bk. III, Pt. II, 4 (Ch30 n37).

Bk. III, Pt. II, 9(1) (Ch84 n7).

Bk. III, Pt. II, 10 (Ch30 n39).

Bk. IV, Pt. I, 15 (Ch13 n7).

Bk. IV, Pt. II, 21 (Ch81 n46).

Bk. VI, Pt. I, 2 (Ch13 n9).

Bk. VII, Pt. I, 2 (Ch30 n49).

Bk. VII, Pt. I, 3 (Ch6 n15).

Bk. VII, Pt. II, 3 (Ch25 n27).

Bk. VII, Pt. II, 15 (Ch79 n57).

Bk. VII, Pt. II , 37 (Ch80 n89).

Huainanzi

II , 4 r. (Ch54 n26).

III, 2 (Ch41 n3).

III, 2r. (Ch47 n11).

III, 3v. (App.I n89).

IV, 9r. (App.I n107).

VI, 1v. (Ch19 n8).

VI, 1v. (Ch19 n9).

VI, 1v. (Ch84 n35).

VI, 2r. (Ch19 n27).

VII, 8v. (Ch18 n35).

VIII, 5r. (Ch18 n30).

VIII, 5r. (Ch19 n47).

VIII, 5r. (Ch19 n53).

VIII, 6v. (Ch55 n17).

XI, 5r. (Ch54 n27).

XII, 4r. (Ch37 n51).

XII, 11v. (Ch17 n7).

XII, 11v. (Ch7 n12).

XII, 22r. (Ch17 n27).

XIII, 9r. (Ch82 n28).

XIII, 14r. (Ch78 n62).

XVI, 1 (Ch29 n25).

XVI, 1v. (Ch19 n37).

XVI, 1v. (Ch19 n69).

XVI, 13 (Ch28 n94).

XVII, 25v. (Ch8 n3).

XVIII, 6 (Ch20 n5).

XVIII, 17r. (Ch80 n88).

XVIII, 18v. (Ch68 n2).

XVIII, 19r. (Ch1 n21).

XX, 2 (Ch54 n17).

Liji

L. I, p. 80 (Ch68 n30).

L. I, p. 84 (Ch7 n1).

L. I, p. 123 (Ch62 n9).

L. I, p. 123 (Ch79 n17).

L. I, p. 128 (Ch55 n38).

L. I, p. 135 (Ch21 n6).

L. I, p. 136 (Ch26 n36).

L. I, p. 136 (Ch28 n77).

L. I, p. 181 (Ch71 n12).

L. I, p. 201 (Ch45 n12).

L. I, p. 208 (Ch77 n44).

L. I, p. 244 (Ch52 n7).

L. I, p. 260 (Ch6 n21).
L. I, p. 310 (Ch6 n21).
L. I, p. 344 (Ch4 n11).
L. II, p. 5 (Ch23 n23).
L. II, p. 5 (Ch47 n40).

L. II, p. 90 (Ch80 n25).
L. II, p. 201 (Ch77 n10).
L. II, p. 206 (Ch77 n30).
L. II, p. 208 (Ch77 n26).
L. II, p. 208 (Ch77 n44).

Shijing

Pt. I, Bk. IV, Ode IX, 2 (Ch8 n2); (Ch13 n14).
Pt. II, Bk. III, Ode X, 2 (Ch27 n15).
Pt. II, Bk. V, Ode III, 2 (Ch16 n15).
Pt. II, Bk. V, Ode IX, 6 (Ch52 n41).
Pt. II, Bk. VII, Ode V (Ch49, n16); (Ch66 n25).
Pt. II, Bk. VIII, Ode VIII (Ch32 n59).
Pt. III, Bk. I, Ode I (Ch27 n21).

Pt. III, Bk. I, Ode II (Ch17 n12).
Pt. III, Bk. I, Ode VII, 1 (Ch12 n24).
Pt. III, Bk. II, Ode I, 2 (Ch15 n8).
Pt. III, Bk. II, Ode V, 2 (Ch27 n9).
Pt. III, Bk. II, Ode VIII (Ch50 n45).
Pt. III, Bk. III, Ode IV, 3 (Ch27 n17).
Pt. III, Bk. III, Ode IV, 3 (Ch53 n7).
Pt. IV, Bk. III, Ode II (Ch8 n18).

Yijing

1st diagram (Ch12 n25, Ch22 n26, Ch30 n5, Ch41 n17, Ch42 n52, Ch72 n8).
5th diagram, L. p. 67 (Ch32 n53).
22nd diagram, L. p. 231 (Ch61 n30).
30th diagram, L. p. 237 (Ch32 n32).
49th diagram, L. p. 168 (Ch61 n29).
55th diagram, L. p. 186 (Ch27 n19).
55th diagram, L. p. 336 (Ch32 n53).
63rd diagram, L. p. 205 (Ch58 n5).
63rd diagram, L. p. 206 (Ch76 n7).

Jice II, L. p. 383 (Ch54 n19). Jice II, L. p. 385 (Ch56 n10).

Chap. I p. 7v. (Chin. text) (Ch19 n44).

Han Feizi

XIII, 5 (Ch29 n10).
XIII, 5 (Ch29 n19).
XIII, 5v. (Ch29 n4).
XVI, 1 (Ch29 n31).

XVI, 1 (Ch29 n34).
XVI, 5 (Ch29 n28).
XIX, 4 (Ch29 n36).

Liezi

IV, 4v. (Ch80 n88).
V, 5v. (Ch31 n8).
VIII, 2 (Ch54 n17).

VIII, 6r. (Ch38 n51).
VIII, 6v. (Ch20 n5).

Zhongyong

Chap. XV (Ch5 n4).

Chap. XVIII, 3 (Ch55 n34).

Gongyang

Zhuang, 7th year (Ch32 n50).

Xi, 31st year (Ch32 n56).

Erya

Chap. 9 p. 6 (Ch52 n47).

Kongzi jiayu

Chap. 4, p. 8v. (Ch51 n11).

Shanhaijing

Chap. 9, p. 1v. (Ch32 n38).

Lüshi chunqiu

VI, 2v. (Ch16 n88)

Qianhanshu

Chap. 8, p. 21v. (Ch57 n35).
Chap. 64a, p. 13v. (Ch80 n35).
Chap. 68 p. 21r. (Ch47 n27).

Chinese Works Quoted

1. My translation of the Lunheng 論衡 is based on the text contained in the 子書百家, 110 vols., printed in Wuchang 武昌, 1875. The text agrees with that of the *Han Wei congshu* 漢魏叢書, it is clearer than that of the latter work in my possession, but not punctuated as the *Han Wei congshu* 漢魏叢書 is.

2. I quote the Classics from Legge's translation. For the *Liji* 禮記 and the *Yijing* 易經, of which Legge does not give the Chinese text, I have used the *Liji Chenshi jishuo* 禮記陳氏集說, 10 vols., printed in Nanjing 南京, 1893, and the *Yijing benyi* 易經本義, 2 vols., by Zhu Xi 朱熹, printed in Nanjing 南京 in the same year.

3. The Dynastic Histories:—the *Shiji* 史記, the two *Hanshu* 漢書, the *Suishu* 隋書, and the *Jiu-Tangshu* 舊唐書 are quoted from the *Ershisi shi* 二十四史, Shanghai 上海 edition 1894.

4. For the Philosophers:—*Zhuangzi* 莊子, *Liezi* 列子, *Hanfeizi* 韓非子, *Huainanzi* 淮南子, and *Xunzi* 荀子 the *Shizi quanshu* 十子全書, 24 vols., printed in Suzhou 蘇州 1804, has been used.

5. *Mozi* 墨子, the *Shanhaijing* 山海經, and the *Lüshi chunqiu* 呂氏春秋 are quoted from the *Zishu baijia* 子書百家 (see above).

Besides I have made use of the:—

6. *Taiping yulan* 太平御覽, 120 vols., edited by Bao Chongcheng 鮑崇城 in 1812.

7. *Qinding siku quanshu zongmu* 欽定四庫全書總目, 100 vols., Guangdong 廣東 reprint of 1868.

8. *Lidai ming xian lie nü shi xing pu* 歷代名賢列女氏姓譜, 144 vols., by Xiao Zhihan 蕭智漢 1792.

9. *Shumu dawen* 書目答問, 2 vols., by Zhang Zhidong 張之洞, printed in Shanghai 上海 in 1895.

Additional Note to
the 1907 Edition

As my readers will have seen from the Preface, I originally proposed to make a selection of Wang Chong's Essays, and to translate only 44, *i.e.* the philosophical ones, being in my opinion the more important. Some of the leading sinologues having pointed out to me the desirability of having a complete version of Wang Chong's work, I now have changed my mind, and am going to translate the essays left out likewise. They will, later on, be published as "Lun-Hêng, Part II, Miscellaneous Essays," in contradistinction to the present volume, which I now call "Lun-Hêng, Part I, Philosophical Essays of Wang Ch'ung." The whole work will also appear, later on, in the "Mitteilungen des Seminars für Orientalische Sprachen," probably in 5 parts. The first was already published last year, under the title "Selected Essays of the Philosopher Wang Ch'ung." I am very much indebted to Geheimrat SACHAU, Director of the Seminar für Orientalische Sprachen, for kindly having undertaken the publishing of this voluminous work.

Berlin, April 1907.
A. FORKE.

Postscript to the 1911 Edition

This second volume of the *Lunheng* contains the 40 chapters omitted in Vol. 1 [Arabic numbers replace the original roman numbers to the volumes to distinguish them from the QP edition,] and referred to in the Additional Note p. III.1175. The version of Wang Chong's work is now complete, only the sequence of the chapters differs from the original edition [QP: reinstated in this 3 vol. ed. See Publisher's Note I.vii *seq.* See also the Fiding List p. III.1159 *seq.* for sequence of the 1907 and 1911 editions]. A Comparative Table of the Chinese Text and the Translation on p. I.^{48} *seq.* will enable the reader in possession of the original to find each chapter of the translation without difficulty.

As the time of the publication of the *Lunheng* I gave the years 76–84 CE [p. I.7.] A passage on [p. II.598] of this volume allows of a still narrower limitation. Wang Chong there speaks of the sixth year of the Emperor Zhang Di 章帝 = 81 CE. Consequently the *Lunheng* must have been written after 81 and prior to 84 CE, *viz.* in 82 or 83 CE.

It has been noticed that the *Lunheng* originally contained more than a hundred chapters, whereas we now only possess 84, and of one the mere title. From the present volume we learn the names of three more lost chapters: [*Juening*] 覺佞 "Recognising the Cunning" (Ch. 33 n. 22), probably in the style of the existing chapter 33 "On the Cunning and Artful," [*Nengsheng*] 能聖 "How to Become a Sage," and [*Shisheng*] 實聖 "True Sagehood" (Ch. 60 n. 36 and 37), most likely propounding similar views to those contained in chapters 78 "The Real Nature of Knowledge" and 79 "The Knowledge of Truth."

In the Introduction to Vol. 1, p. I.8–9, I mentioned a separate edition of the *Lunheng* printed under the Ming 明 dynasty which I had not seen, and of which I was ignorant whether it was still to be found in the book-shops, since my efforts to buy one had been unsuccessful. In the meantime I was fortunate enough to obtain a copy of this edition, which I regard as the best of the three current editions, and for this reason have used it as the basis of the second volume of my translation.

This Ming edition referred to by Zhang Zhidong 張之洞 in his bibliography (Ed. B) was prepared by a certain *jinshi* 進士, Liu Guangdou (Hui Ji, Ren Wei) 劉光斗 (T. 暉吉, 訒韋) of Jinling 晉陵 = Changzhoufu 常州府 in Jiangsu 江蘇, together with his friends, all fervent admirers of Wang Chong, most likely in 1626 CE. Each of them has written a preface, so that we have five altogether. Two of these prefaces are dated 1626.

Liu Guangdou informs us that in course of time the text of the *Lunheng* had been disfigured by misprints and errata sometimes completely altering the sense. Searching into the libraries and spending much money, his friend Yan Guangbiao (Zi Yi) 閻光表 (子儀), a native of Qiantang 錢塘 in Zhejiang 浙江, at last succeeded in hunting up a good edition of Yang Wenchang 楊文昌, a *jinshi* of the Song 宋 time. This Song edition was first revised by Liu Guangdou, afterwards by Yan Guangbiao and his friends Ma Yuan (Ren Bo) 馬元 (T. 仁伯) and Shi Zhuang (Kang Fu) 施莊 (T. 康夫). Yan Guangbiao finally fixed the text and edited it at his own expense. His preface dates from his "Hall of Frozen Perfume," whence this edition is designated as 凝香閣藏板 on the title-page.

My copy seems to be the original edition, and a red stamp on the title-page to contain the name of Yan 閻 (Guangbiao 光表). Another red impression states that the blocks of this edition are kept in the office of the owner, and that any unauthorised reprint will be pursued to a thousand Li's distance: 本衙藏板翻刻千里必究.

I have denoted the edition of the *Han Wei congshu* 漢魏叢書 as Ed. A, the Ming edition as Ed. B, and the edition contained in the *Zishu baijia* 子書百家 as Ed. C. In my notes to Vol. 2, I have frequently pointed out differences in the three editions, which after all are not very great. In regard to correctness of the text Ed. B ranks first, then follows Ed. C, and Ed. A comes last. Whenever there is any divergence, Ed. A and C mostly agree, but Ed. C avoids the apparent misprints of which

Ed. A has a great many. This remark refers to my own edition of the *Han Wei congshu* which is not very good. In the newly acquired copy of the Royal Library in Berlin many mistakes have been corrected. Ed. C would seem to be a revised reprint of Ed. A. Ed. B is much more independent, and in most cases gives the best reading.

Wang Chong is very fond of quoting the Classics and other old authors, notably the *Analects*, the *Shangshu* 尚書, and the *Shiji* 史記. Since not only his reading often differs from the now authorised text, but his explanations also not seldom disagree with those of modern commentators, I thought it worth while preparing a list of all the quotations I was able to trace, which may be useful for a critique of the old texts.

Index

Index

Acupuncture 針 *zhen*, I 115, II 495, III Ch53 n4.

Ai 哀, Duke of Lu 魯, I 317–18, 414, II 690, 708, 857, III Ch16 n85, Ch28 n36, Ch51 n12.

Ai 哀, Duke of Wei 衛, I 288.

Ai Di 哀帝, Han 漢 Emperor, II 522, 534, 613, III Ch51 n19.

Ailao 哀牢, people in Yunnan 雲南, II 591, 599, 618.

Altar(s) of the land 社 *she*, II 430, 486, 490, 495, 694.

Alternation of nature and culture, prosperity and decay, II 549, 579.

Altruism 讓 *rang*, grows from opulence; strife, from indigence, II 550, 800, 801.

Amber 頓牟 *dunmou*, takes up straws, II 499, 500.

Amulets and charms 蘭服牙身 *lan fu ya shen*, boys wear jadestones, girls pearls, I 295.

Analects = *Lunyu* 論語, the "Utterances of Confucius," I 147, 250, 256, 291, 303, 309–10, 327, III 759, 837, 849; their origin and original size, III 818.

Ancestral tablet 主 *zhu* of wood, one foot two inches long, II 503.

Ancestral worship, minister of 秩宗卿 *zhi zong qing* = 宗正 *zongzheng*, I 183.

Ancient characters 古文 *guwen*, II 811, 818.

Ang 卬, Prince of Wei 魏, treacherously killed by Wei Yang 衛鞅, I 236, III Ch21 nn37, 39.

Angels, III 880, informing the Spirit of Heaven of human misdeeds, I 252, a fallen angel 斥仙 *chixian*, I 266.

Angling 釣 *diao*, II 603, 667, with wooden fish, II 502.

Animals, are creatures like man, II 455–56, the killing of animals is wicked, II 455.

Annanese, 越 *yue*, II 753, III 915, Ch26 n47, Ch50 n31, Ch57 n26, mahout, I 161.

Annan 日南 *Rinan*, kingdom, the South of the Sun, I 362, II 444, 600.

Annoyances and vexations 累害 *leihai*. There are three annoyances and three vexations, I 79 seq.

Anthroposcopy and physiognomy, 骨相 *guxiang*, I 135 seq.

Anti-alcoholic memorial, I 5.

Antidotes, I 11, 225, II 580, 678, III 907.

Antiquarians know how to determine the age of old swords, I 270.

Antiquity, II 584, 590, 612, 615, 618, 723, 737, 775, 819, 838, overestimated by scholars and artists, II 580–81, Sages of, II 789.

Ao 昇, strong man in the Shang 商 epoch, I 422–23.

Apparitions 妖 *yao*, either ghosts shaped like men, or men behaving like ghosts, II 662–63, 672–73, 678–79, 681, 752, III Ch54 n18.

Aquila, Qianniu 牽牛 = Herdsman, constellation reached by the sun in winter, I 365.

Archæologists 古文家 *guwenjia*, II 565.

Archery 射 *she*, II 795, III Ch25 n38, Ch26 n14, Ch78 n43, competition of, II 503, III Ch32 n39, Ch47 n33.

Arithmeticians 九九之人 *jiujiuzhiren*, honoured by Duke Huan 桓 of Qi 齊, I 183, Wang Chong, III Ch31 n35.

Army 軍 *jun*, 4,000 men, divided into 2 divisions 師 *shi*, I 117, 138, 277, 335, II 647, 704, 814, III 881.

Ascension to heaven, I 265–66, of Huang Di 黃帝, I 258, III Ch24 n8, of Huai Nan Zi 淮 南子, I 261–63, by the soul, II 660.

Astrologers 史官 *shiguan*, regulated the calendar and fixed the days, II 541, astrologer of Lu 魯史 *lushi*, II 690–91, Zi Wei 子韋, III Ch7 n12.

Auguries, I 196, 202–3, 216, 320, II 509, 534, 538, 551, 587, 588, 591, 598, 608, 615, 645, 662, 707–8, 711, 718, 724, 729, 764, 769. *See also* Omens

Auspicious grain 嘉禾 *jiahe*, I 167, 201, II 523–24, 538, 863, III Ch59 n5, Ch85 n51; a felicitous omen, II 589, 597–98.

Aversions and dislikes different with different people, II 696.

Avoidances 諱 *hui*, things that must be avoided, otherwise they entail misfortune, II 690 seq., avoidances of inauspicious days, II 706 seq.

Ba 巴, concubine of King Gong 共 of Chu 楚, I 123.

Ba 巴, ancient State in Sichuan 四 川, II 600.

Ba Chu 霸出, giant, II 578.

Bagongzhuan 八公之傳, "Memoir of the Eight Companions" of Huainanzi 淮南子, I 263.

Bai Gui 白圭, rich man, I 86.

Bai Li Xi 百里奚, official of Qin 秦, I 293, II 451.

Bai Qi 白起, famous general of Qin 秦, I 99, 232, 235, III Ch21 n14.

Bai Yi Bing 白乙丙, officer of Qin 秦, I 291.

Baihai 稗海, Minor Seas, I 360.

Baishui 白水, district in Shanxi 陝 西, II 595.

Bactria, 大夏 *Daxia*, I 361, III 875.

Baling 霸陵, bridge, II 730.

Ballista 弩 *nu*, of ten stones, I 289, pulled with a windlass 車 *ju*, I 294; of five stones, I 425.

Bamboo and silk 竹帛 *zhubo*, i.e. tablets and scrolls used for writing, I 169, 432, 433, II 444, 611, 614, 824, 842.

Ban Gu 班固, historian, II 436, 591, 611, 613, 614, 616, 619, 839, III 887, 890–91, 894, 901, 907, 927, Ch38 nn55, 57, Ch39 n53, Ch52 nn16, 17, Ch57 nn40, 41, Ch61 nn16, 17, 62, Ch83 nn51, 56, Ch84 n15.

Ban Meng Jian 班孟堅 = Ban Gu 班固, II 445.

Ban Shu Pi 班叔皮 = Ban Biao 班彪, father of Ban Gu 班固, II 445, 623, 843, III Ch84 n15.

Bao 褒, princes of the Xia 夏 epoch, II 661.

Bao 褒, princes of, I 197.

Bao 鮑, Duke of Song 宋, II 752.

Bao Jiao 鮑焦, recluse of the Zhou 周 epoch, II 512.

Bao Shu Ya 鮑叔牙, bosom friend of Guan Zhong 管仲, I 77, 123, 146, III Ch1 n29, Ch9 n20, Ch12 nn15, 16.

Bao Si 褒姒, Empress, I 129, 197, III Ch18 n11, her supernatural birth, I 165, II 525.

Bazhong 跋踵, fabulous tribe, I 300, III Ch27 n8.

Beauty, engendered by a magical force, vicious and depraved, II 681.

Beckoning to the departed to return 以衣招復 *yi yi zhao fu*, II 483.

Bei Ren Wu Ze 北人無擇, contemporary of Shun 舜, I 73, III Ch1 n18.

Beiqiu 貝丘, place in Shandong 山東, II 674.

Ben Guang 賁光, official under Guang Wu Di 光武帝, I 306–7.

Bi 費, city in Shandong 山東, I 291, 322, 330, 409, II 812, III Ch27 n26.

Bi 濞, King of Wu 吳, II 765.

Bi Gan 比干, kinsman of, and killed by, the tyrant Zhou Xin 紂辛, I 129, 182, 279, 356, II 616, 637, 644, 686, 797, III Ch16 n77, Ch25 n30, Ch80 n43.

Bi Xi 佛肸, high officer in Jin 晉, I 328–29, 330.

Bian He 卞和, of Chu 楚 and the jade stone, II 472, 845, 857, III Ch26 n37, Ch43 n16.

Bian Que 扁鵲, celebrated physician, I 87, 431, II 548, 601, 656, 687, 795, III Ch64 n13.

Bifang 畢方, fabulous bird, II 654.

Big-bellied persons 簍篠 *quchu*, are often deceitful, I 81.

Bin 邠, city in Shanxi 陝西, I 144, III Ch12 n4.

Bird 鳥 *niao*, star, II 475, 552.

Births, supernatural, I 163, II 834–5.

Black Tortoise 玄武 *Xuanwu*, the northern quadrant of solar mansions, I 159, 240, III 901.

Blue Dragon 倉龍 *Canglong*, the eastern quadrant of solar mansions, I 159, 240, II 745, III Ch75 nn1, 2, App.I n90.

Bo Cheng Zi Gao 伯成子高, vassal of Yao 堯 and Shun 舜, I 73,

390–91, III Ch1 n19.

Bo Qi 伯奇, knew how to endure hardships, I 172, 211.

Bo Qin 伯禽, son of the Duke of Zhou 周, II 461.

Bo Le 伯樂, famous horse trainer, II 448, 668.

Bo Lu 伯魯, Prince of Zhao 趙, I 134.

Bo Niu 伯牛, disciple of Confucius, his sickness, I 95, 102, 231, 317, 356, II 863, III Ch21 n8, Ch28 n42, Ch30 n54, Ch85 n57.

Bo Pi 帛喜, minister in Wu 吳, I 72.

Bo Ya 伯牙, famous lute-player, I 81, III Ch8 n24, Ch19 n37.

Bo Yi 伯翳, ancestor of the Qin 秦 dynasty, I 163.

Bo Yi 伯益, assistant of Yu 禹, I 73.

Bo Yi 伯夷, famous for his integrity, I 73, 113, 170, 233, 333, 336, 353, II 514, 777, 788–89, 799, 800, 805, 862, III Ch1 n17, Ch30 n47, and his brother Shu Qi 伯夷叔齊, II 521, 594, III Ch8 n7, Ch21 n23.

Bo Yi 伯夷, minister under the Emperor Shun 舜, I 183, 184.

Bo Yi 伯益, baron Yi 益, the forester of Shun 舜, I 218–19.

Bo You 伯有, minister of Zheng 鄭, II 642, 676.

Bo Yu 伯魚, son of Confucius, II 524.

Bo Yu 伯余, inventor of clothes, II 846.

Bo Zong 伯宗, officer of the Jin 晉, I 219, 220, III Ch19 n61.

Bohai 勃海, place in Shandong 山東, II 769.

Boletus, see Purple Boletus.

Book of Prophecies 讖書 *Chenshu*, ascribed to Confucius, I 163, 185, II 766, 836.

Books of the various philosophers 諸子尺書 *Zhuzi chi shu*, one foot long, II 830.

Boqin 柏寢, hall of Duke Huan 桓 of Qi 齊, I 269.

Boren 柏人, place in Zhili 直隸, II 475.

Brilliant Star 景星 *jingxing*, II 538 seq., 586, III Ch52 n40.

Brocades 錦 *jin*, II 487, 804, III Ch45 n41, woven in Xiang 襄 by the people, I 397, their manufacture requires exceptional skill, I 400, 404, 406.

Bronze vase of the year 669 BCE with inscription, I 269.

Bu Zhan 不占, officer of Qi 齊, II 580, III Ch56 n20.

Bureaucrats 隨牒 *suidie*, I 394, 396, 401, 402, 436.

Burning glasses 陽遂/陽燧 *yangsui*, I 115–16, II 499–500, 738, 793, III 932 seq.

Burning of the Books by Qin Shi Huangdi 秦始皇, I 283, 412–13, 414, II 638, 811–12.

Buzhou 不周, mountain in the Kunlun 崑崙, I 357, 359, II 496, 845, III Ch31 n4.

Cai 蔡, State, territory in Henan 河南, I 72, 81, 209, 210, II 531, 565, 594, 799, 861, III Ch2 n19, Ch5 n12.

Cai 蔡, Prince of, brother of Wu Wang 武王, II 600.

Cai Bo Xie 蔡伯偕, governor, I 435.

Cai Mo 蔡墨, historiographer of

Wei 魏, historian of the Jin 晉 State, I 241, 433, II 869, III Ch22 n25.

Cai Shen 蔡沈, disciple of Zhu Xi 朱熹, III 893.

Cai Shu Du 蔡叔度, brother of Zhou Gong 周公, II 464.

Cai Ze 蔡澤, minister of Qin 秦, native of Yan 燕, I 86, 141, III Ch3 n13.

Calendars 歷 *li*, for burials, II 707, for sacrifices, II 708–9, for bathing, II 710–11, for building, II 711–12, a great variety of spirits mentioned in the calendars, II 712–13.

Calumniation 毀謗 *huibang*, different kinds of, I 80–82, 388, 389; 讒 *chan*, I 383.

Cang Jie 蒼頡, minister of Huang Di 黃帝, inventor of writing, I 136, 166, 200, 216, 417, 436, II 496, 511, 573, 574, 673, 712, 843, 846, III Ch15 n36.

Cangguang 倉光, monster with nine heads living in rivers, II 544.

Cangwu 蒼梧, place in Henan 河南, Ningyuan 寧遠 district, I 131, 173–75.

Cangwu Wang 蒼梧王, Emperor of the Liu Song 劉宋 dynasty, III 927.

Cannibalism, in times of dearth, I 235.

Cao Can 曹參, minister of Han Gao Zu 漢高祖, II 556, III Ch54 n7.

Carts 車 *che*, creeping plants flying about led to their construction, II 573.

Cascade 沃泉 *woquan*, II 545.

Cassia 桂 *gui*, used as medicine, II 512.

Cat's-eyes 璵璠 *yufan*, put into a coffin, II 685.

Ceremonies originate from a want of loyalty, II 561.

Chai 柴, region in Shandong 山東, I 126.

Chan 產, private gentleman, I 435.

Chan Zi 纏子, Mohist of the Han 漢 time, I 228–29.

Chance 幸 *xing*, definition, I 94 seq., 105.

Chang 昌, personal name of Wen Wang 文王, I 144, II 739.

Chang 常, mountain in Shanxi 山西, II 658.

Chang 昌門, gate of the capital of Wu 吳, II 773.

Chang Ju 長沮, hermit of the time of Confucius, II 779, 800, 804.

Chang'an 長安, capital under the Han 漢 dynasty, I 125, 415, II 596, 930, III Ch42 n32, Ch59 n27, Ch78 n35.

Changes 易 *yi* = *Yijing* 易經, II 831.

Changle 長樂, palace, II 516, 589, 768.

Changping 長平, city in Shanxi 山西, I 99–100, 104, 208, 232, II 473, 475, 476, 727.

Changsha 長沙, circuit in Hunan 湖南, II 509, 536, III Ch51 n36.

Changyan 昌衍, place in Lu 魯, II 771.

Changyi 昌邑, place in Shandong 山東, II 509, 514, III Ch49 n17.

Chao Cuo 鼂錯, politician of the 2nd cent. BCE, received the Shangshu 尚書 from its hiding place, II 443, 594, 811, 813, 830, III Ch36 n24, Ch58 n9.

Chao Wu 朝吳, officer of Cai 蔡, I 81.

Chaos 溟涬濛澒 *ming xing meng hong*, I 359.

Character 性 *xing* and natural gifts 才 *cai* determine human intelligence and conduct, I 84, transformed by instruction and the influence of virtue, I 117, depend on the quantity of the original fluid, I 118.

Character 質性 *zhixing*, transformed by good and evil practice, I 401–2.

Charms 厭勝 *yasheng*, used to paralyse evil influences, II 700.

Chen 陳, family in Wei 魏, murdered its sovereign, I 337.

Chen 陳, State, in southern Henan 河南, I 72, 81, 100, 191, 209, 210, 291, II 475, 531, 552, 580, 799, 861.

Chen Jia 陳賈, officer of Qi 齊, II 783.

Chen Jue 陳爵, boy in Lujiang 廬江 (Anhui 安徽), II 603–4.

Chen Ping 陳平, very poor, but fine looking, I 136.

Chen Ping 陳平, one of the Three Heroes of the Han 漢 time, II 442, 809.

Chen Ping Zhong 陳平仲, writer, II 613.

Chen She 陳涉, King of Chu 楚, II 666.

Chen Ting 陳挺, boy in Lujiang 廬江 (Anhui 安徽), II 603.

Chen Xi 陳豨, high officer of the 2nd cent. BCE, II 594, III Ch58 n7.

Chen Yuan 陳元, admirer of the *Zuozhuan* 左氏傳, II 833.

Chen Zhen 陳臻 = Chen Zi 陳子, I 345, III Ch30 n9.

Chen Zhong Zi 陳仲子, recluse/ hermit, I 352–55, II 512, III Ch33 n30.

Chen Zi 陳子, disciple of Mencius, I 345, III Ch30 n12.

Chen Zi Hui 陳子迴, scholar, II 839.

Chen Zi Qin 陳子禽, disciple of Confucius, II 778.

Chen Zi Yu 陳子瑀, prefect, I 402.

Cheng 成, King of Chu 楚, I 202, II 641–42, 720.

Cheng 成, King of Zhou 周 = Cheng Wang 成王, I 85, 112, 196, 287, 349, 414, II 463, 467, 484, 491, 565–75, 584, 590, 591, 594, 599, 601, III Ch3 n5, Ch27 n10, Ch54 n12, Ch55 nn33, 39.

Cheng 乘, chronicle of the Jin 晉 State, II 819, 844.

Cheng Di 成帝, Han 漢 Emperor, I 137, II 522, 534, 618–19, 620, III 927, Ch42 n30, Ch51 n19, Ch83 n57.

Cheng Gong 程躬, private official, II 604.

Cheng Ji You 成季友, son of Duke Huan 桓 of Lu 魯, II 557, 667, 824.

Cheng Liang 程量, admirer of Guan Zhong 管仲, II 572.

Cheng Tang 成湯, founder of the Shang 商 dynasty, I 72, 104, 198, II 535, 600, 612, III Ch1 n5, Ch81 n55.

Cheng Ying Qi 程嬰齊, adherent of Zhao Shuo 趙朔, I 124.

Chengji 成紀, place in Gansu 甘肅, II 607.

Chengpu 城濮, place, I 202.

Chenliu 陳留, place in Henan 河南, I 82, 126, 217, 402, 419, II 511.

Chenshu 讖書, "Book of Prophecies," I 163, II 836.

Chi Song 赤松, magician, I 109.

Chi You 蚩尤, legendary person, I 339, II 455, 473, 654.

Chixian 赤縣, China, I 360, 362, II 732.

Chong Er 重耳, Prince of Jin 晉, I 136, II 663, III Ch11 n6.

Chong Lan 充蘭, petty officer, I 126, 145.

Chong Yu 充虞, follower of Mencius, I 349.

Chongling 春陵, city in Henan 河南, I 127, III Ch58 n34.

Chongshan 崇山, place in Hunan 湖南, I 175.

Chopsticks 箸 *zhu*, I 208, III 931–32, Ch22 n11; of ivory 象箸 *xiangzhu*, considered a great luxury under the Shang 商 dynasty, I 241; made under Zhou 紂, II 767; not solid, II 699.

Chronicle of Yu, 禹本紀 *Yubenji*, I 361.

Chu 楚, State in Hubei 湖北 and Hunan 湖南, I 103, 116, 123, 128, 183, 202, 223, 251, 287, 288, 292, 316, 336, 424, 430, II 444, 459, 462, 472, 475, 493, 495–96, 498, 500, 509, 528, 552, 565, 590, 594, 596, 600, 620, 641, 677, 680, 720, 786, 819, 844, 845, III Ch1 n22, Ch2 n17, Ch6 n19, Ch8 nn14, 27, Ch10 n3, Ch11 n7, Ch18 n38, Ch19 n69, Ch20 n6, Ch26 nn7, 14, Ch28 n32, Ch29 n15, Ch33 nn12, 30, Ch37 n33, Ch38 n15, Ch39 n20, Ch41 n1, Ch43 n13, Ch46 nn25, 38, Ch47 n3, Ch52 n33, Ch54 n31, Ch57 n38, Ch58 nn25, 64, Ch64 n93, Ch71 n23, Ch78 n49, Ch80 n40, Ch84 n35, Ch85 n32.

Chu Li Zi 樗里子, kinsman of the royal house of Qin 秦, II 768.

Chuan Yi 傳毅, scholar, II 839.

Chuanxiong 穿胸, fabulous tribe with covered breasts, I 300, III Ch27 n8.

Chuci 楚辭, "Elegies of Chu 楚," II 472.

Chujiu 杵臼, personal name of Duke Zhao 昭 of Song 宋, II 739.

Chun Shen 春申, Prince of, I 292, II 792.

Chunling 春陵, place in Henan 河南, II 597, III Ch58 n34.

Chunqiu 春秋, epoch, 722-481 BCE, I 99, 326, II 491, 567, 769, III Ch22 n14.

Chunqiu 春秋, the "Spring and Autumn" Chronicle of Confucius, I 181, 294, 306, 315, 378, 379, 381, 399, 414, 420, II 439, 440, 441–42, 445, 480, 485–86, 488, 489, 490, 492, 494, 498, 516, 531, 575, 590, 600, 617, 618, 672, 708, 713, 765, 781, 795, 808–9,

814–16, 818, 819, 822, 825, 826, 833, 835, 838, 840–41, 844–45, III Ch28 n28, Ch39 nn3, 18, 50, Ch42 n54, Ch45 nn13, 27, Ch46 n21, Ch81 nn1, 10, 24, 47, 51, Ch83 n2.

Chunqiu 春秋 = *Lüshi chunqiu* 呂氏春秋, work of Lü Buwei 呂不韋, II 828.

Chunqiu 春秋 = *Yushi chunqiu* 虞氏春秋, II 442.

Chunqiu fanlu 春秋繁露, III 890, 910, 927, Ch83 n30.

Chunyu Cang 淳于倉, governor, II 769.

Chunyu De 淳于德, official of Han Wen Di 漢文帝, I 414, III Ch36 n47.

Chunyu Kun 淳于髡, native of the Qi 齊 State, II 785–86.

Chunyu Yue 淳于越, officer of Qin 秦, I 283–84, II 812.

Ci 賜 = Zi Gong 子貢, disciple of Confucius, I 114, 322–23, 332, II 740, 783, 862, III Ch85 nn48, 49.

Cinnabar 丹 *dan*, a boy turned red eating cinnabar, II 595–96, III Ch58 n17; honey and cinnabar cure, II 678.

Clay figures 土象人 *tuxiangren* and clay ox 土牛 *tuniu*, used at the beginning of spring, II 503.

Clepsydra, I 416, III Ch36 n72.

Cockfight 鬥雞 *douji*, I 129, III Ch10 n19.

Coins 錢 *qian*, golden, II 603–4.

Coincidences 偶會 *ouhui*, I 128 seq.

Colours of dynasties, II 535.

Comet 彗星 *huixing*, to be averted by prayer, I 187–88, comet proceeded from Chu 楚, I 202–3, when a whale dies, a comet appears, II 499.

Commerce resorted to by lazy agriculturists, I 235.

Confucianists 儒生 *rusheng* 儒家 *rujia*, II 683, 684, believe in destiny, I 99, oppose the principle of spontaneity, II 563, 844, regard Confucius as their master, II 833.

Confucius, 孔子 *Kongzi*, short of provisions, I 72, and Mo Di, 孔墨, I 80, 82, 397, 432, II 581, 838, 840, 857, 861, 863, found guilty, I 81, felt sad, I 82, as wise as Confucius, I 84, on life and death, I 86, on Yan Hui's 顏回 death, I 94–95, on good fortune, I 95, passing the city gate of Lu 魯, I 96, inferior to Shun 舜, I 98, his disciples, I 113–14, at the death of Yan Yuan 顏淵 and Zi Lu 子路, I 129, on the impeachment of Zi Lu 子路, I 133, II 548, his arms turning backwards, I 135, II 518, prognosticated for Tan Tai Zi Yu 澹臺子羽, I 141, in Zheng 鄭, I 141–42, on people above and below the average, I 151, the Nestor in wisdom and virtue, I 152, as a boy playing with sacrificial vessels, I 152, afraid of Yang Hu 陽虎, I 160, II 682, naturally born, I 166, playing the flute, I 167, on Mount Tai 太山, I 171, buried on the shores of

the Si 泗 river, I 178, 179, II
655, his descendants should
be appointed, I 178–79, he
met with rebuffs, I 179, an
honest man like Confucius,
I 182, endangered in Chen
陳 and Cai 蔡, I 209–10,
II 531, 799, and prayer, I
214–15, seriously ill, I 225,
on a white calf, I 226, and
Bo Niu 伯牛, I 231, did not
become an emperor, I 234,
on dragons, I 240, on Lao Zi
老子 being like a dragon, I
245, deeply impressed by a
thunderstorm, I 256, on Yao
堯 and Shun 舜, I 276, II
559, could drink a hundred
gallons, I 279, wandering
about, I 291, 423, on Gao Zi
高子, I 292, on Yao 堯, I 303,
II 582, 610, and the appointment of Zi Gao 子羔, I 304,
Criticisms on Confucius, I
308 seq., on the appointment
of Zi Gao 子羔, I 322, 409, II
812, on a sacrificial sheep, I
332, on the three dynasties,
I 339, a Sage, I 350, II 724,
did not become an emperor,
I 356, on meteors, I 378, 380,
on cunning, I 392, wrote
the *Chunqiu* 春秋, I 306,
399, 414, 420, II 575, 808–9,
814–15, 825, 826, 838, on filial piety and brotherly love,
I 400, wrote the definitions
of the *Yijing* 易經, I 412, the
Rites of Zhou 周 established
before his time, I 413, the
strongest man in the Zhou
周 epoch, I 420, revised the

Classics, I 420, possessed of
wonderful strength, I 421,
could lift the bar of a gate, I
426, asking about Gongshu
Wenzi 公叔文子, I 423,
his school took up the Five
Canons, I 429, his teachings
illustrated by the ancestral
temple, I 431–32, his love of
study at the point of death,
I 434, edited the *Odes* and
composed the *Chunqiu* 春秋,
II 439, wrote the *Chunqiu* 春
秋, II 440, 441–42, 492, on
the writings of Wen Wang
文王, II 444, his knowledge,
II 460, foreseeing rain, II
479, 482, and Zeng Xi 曾晳,
II 485, on the rain sacrifice,
II 488, on Qiu 求, II 494,
resembled You Ruo 有若, II
502, and the tiger trouble,
II 506, a holy man, II 517,
resembling You Ruo 有
若, II 517, compared with
Zi Gong 子貢, II 518–19,
and Shao Zheng Mao 少正
卯, II 519, 807, no unicorn
appeared during his time,
II 522, unlike his father and
his son, II 524, and the dead
unicorn, II 531–32, a Sage
without the royal dignity, II
532, born towards the end of
the Zhou 周 dynasty, II 534,
on the phœnix, II 534, on a
carved mulberry-leaf, II 558,
his blissful forgetfulness, II
561, his abilities in various
arts, II 563, did not cry and
sing on the same day, II 566,
his sickness, II 570, on Guan

Zhong 管仲, II 573, dur-
ing a thunderstorm, II 574,
on the Zhou 周 epoch, II
578–79, on Zhou's 紂 wick-
edness, II 583, on rendering
people happy, II 585, on
the phœnix, II 585–86, on a
true emperor, II 587–88, the
profoundness of his doc-
trine, II 593, on the knowing
and the benevolent, II 608,
editor of the *Shangshu* 尚書,
II 609, on Yao 堯, II 610–11,
illustrated three ways of
amassing merit, II 616, his
house demolished, II 617, on
the difficulty of finding talents, II 618, on the writings
of Wen Wang 文王, II 621,
on the ancient dynasties, II
622, burying his mother, II
630, against extravagance of
funerals, II 684–86, on spirit
vessels, II 687, on the body
received from the parents, II
693, his intellect very acute,
II 708, on building houses, II
713, on divination, II 714, on
Heaven's speaking, II 716, on
an omen, II 720, on destiny,
II 724, called Qiu 丘, II 739,
on passing through the door,
II 741, and his dog, II 761,
on the sacrifice to Earth, II
762, his cognizance of Qin
Shi Huangdi 秦始皇 and
Dong Zhongshu 董仲舒,
II 765, ignored his descent,
II 765 seq., sighed because
dummies were buried in Lu
魯, II 767, on different classes on men, II 769, taught

by Xiang Tuo 項託, II 769,
773, on the dynasty after the
Zhou 周, II 770, on youth,
II 770, knew the rhinopithecus, II 772, on study, II 773,
and his equals are Sages, II
775, on learning, II 776, on
Gongshu Wen 公叔文, II
777, a Sage, II 778, 808, his
information how obtained,
II 778, witnessing Yan Yuan
顏淵 stealthily eating, II 778,
surrounded in Kuang 匡, II
779, thought that Yan Yuan
顏淵 had died, II 779, did
not wish to see Yang Huo 陽
貨, II 779, passing by Chang
Ju 長沮 and Jie Ni 桀溺, II
779, burying his parents,
II 779–80, asked about the
grand temple, II 780, knew
the Five Canons, II 780, was
not prescient, II 781, arrang-
ing the *Shijing* 詩經, II 781,
produced the *Chunqiu* 春秋,
revised the *Shijing* 詩經 and
the *Shangshu* 尚書, II 781,
Confucius and the unicorn,
II 782, he saw Lao Zi 老子,
II 782, on Min Zi Qian 閔子
騫, II 782, on Zi Gong's 子貢
commercial transactions, II
783–84, he noticed every-
thing, II 784, not yet a Sage,
II 787, his gradual development, II 787, disclaimed to
be a Sage, II 788, how he
would take office, II 789, not
equalled by Yi Yin 伊尹, Bo
Yi 伯夷, and Liu Xia Hui 柳
下惠, II 789, on character,
II 791, his principles on the

recognising of Worthies, II 792, his sorrow for the world, II 801, placed Zi Gong 子貢 below Yan Yuan 顏淵, II 803, disapproves of Bo Yi 伯夷, II 805, on Yan Yuan 顏淵, Zi Gong 子貢 and Zi Lu 子路, II 805, knew how to use his faculties, II 805, on the good people of the villages, II 805, qualified to become an emperor, II 808, did not become an emperor, II 809, his school demolished, II 811, transmitted the *Shangshu* 尚書, II 811, 813, on Rites, II 817, and the *Analects*, II 818, his house pierced, II 818, ambiguity not to his mind, II 819–20, the Classics and the school of Confucius, II 830, a *Zuozhuan* 左氏傳 found in his house, II 833, did not speak of strange things, II 833, his works finished by Dong Zhongshu 董仲舒, II 836–37, on the music-master Zhi 摯, II 837, on poetry, II 845, avoided all pomp, II 846, spoke of destiny, II 851, as official had no aversions, II 852, lost a horse, II 853, eating a peach, II 857, his works not read, II 857, nobody more talented, II 861, his hardships, II 861, Confucius and Mo Di 墨子 noble of themselves, but of low rank, II 861, both Sages, II 863.

Contingencies 遭 *zao*, I 27, 49, III Ch6 n31, definition, I 104–5, contingencies and chance agree or disagree with destiny, II 463.

Cook, in Song 宋, famous for butchery, II 668.

Corporal punishments 肉刑 *rouxing*, abolished by Han Wen Di 漢文帝, I 415.

Correspondencies, A major, wood, wind, and rain, I 213, II 710–11, 741.

Corvées 傜 *yao* (for 儒 *ru*), from the twenty-third year, I 416, III Ch36 n60.

Corvus, 軫 *zhen*, constellation, II 544.

Cow, may give birth to a horse, II 563.

Creation, I 359–60.

Cricket and chrysalis no emblem of immortality, I 108–9, 266, 270.

Cries of a new-born child indicative of the length of its life, I 91.

Cross-bow 弩 *nu*, I 289, 371, 424, II 744, III Ch26 n15, Ch64 n65.

Crows 烏 *niao* / 烏 *wu*, I 379, weeding the grave of Yu 禹, I 131, 174, red crow an augury of Wu Wang 武王, I 143, 277, II 523, 526, 534, 535.

Cunning and artful 佞 *ning*, I 382 seq.

Cutting and carving 切瑳琢磨 *qie cuo zhuo mo* of bone, ivory, jade, and jewels, I 407.

Da Nao 大撓, minister of Huang Di 黃帝, III 918.

Dai 戴, brother of Chen Zhong Zi 陳仲子, I 353.

Dai 代, King of, the later Emperor Han Wen Di 漢文帝, I 87.

Dai 代, aboriginal State north of Shanxi 山西, II 657, 658, III Ch64 n27.

Daizong 岱宗 = Taishan 太山, sacred mountain in Shandong 山東, II 444.

Daliang 大梁 = Kaifengfu 開封府, I 141, III Ch27 n44.

Dan 旦, personal name of the Duke of Zhou 周公, II 639.

Dan 旦, King of Yan 燕, I 430.

Dan 丹, Prince of Yan 燕, I 52, 185, 209–10, 284, II 474, 540, 846, III Ch19 n24, Ch43 n28, Ch52 n14.

Dan Fu 亶父, grandfather of Wen Wang 文王, I 144, II 460, 799, III Ch42 n53.

Dan Jiao 丹教, boy, I 277, III Ch58 n17.

Dan Zhu 丹朱, son of Yao 堯, I 103, 117, 150, 152, 319, II 463, 524, 583.

Dan'er 儋耳, fabulous tribe with hanging ears, I 300, III Ch27 n8.

Danshui 丹水, place in Henan 河南, I 286, II 593, III Ch58 n4.

Dantu 丹徒, place in Jiangsu 江蘇, I 176.

Danyang 丹陽, circuit in Jiangsu 江蘇 and Anhui 安徽, II 509, 766, 863.

Dao 道, fundamental principle of Daoism, I 86–87, 109, 111, 228, 259 seq., III Ch24 n13, Ch24 n50.

Daoism, I 261, II 563, 670, 762, 828, III Ch24 nn8, 12, Ch34 n22, Ch80 nn50, 68.

Daoists, 道人 daoren, I 258 seq., II 794, said to have become genii, I 109, make artificial gems, I 115, exhibiting tricks at the court of Huai Nan Zi 淮南子, I 261, drinking the elixir of life and eating purple boletus, I 265, cannot be drowned nor burned, I 267, living on air and regulating their breath to become immortal, I 272–73, take medicines with a view to prolong life, I 273, made an artificial figure of the deceased wife of Han Wu Di 漢武帝, II 502–3, argue on spontaneity, II 554–55, 558–59, made an artificial apparition of Lady Wang 王, II 558, possess real virtue *i.e.* inaction and quietism, II 561, studying the art of immortality, II 762, not Worthies, II 801.

Days and nights, their different lengths how caused, I 365.

Dazhuan 大傳, ancient work, II 520.

Dead people 死人 *siren*, cannot be resuscitated by sacrifices, are hidden from our view, dissolved and belonging to another sphere, II 684–85, the service of the dead analogous to that of the living, II 708–9.

Death 死 *si*, II 625 seq., human life and death depend on the length of the span, 196, correlate of birth, I 274, premature how caused, I 131–32, regarded as the greatest evil, II 551.

Denary cycle 甲乙 *jiayi*, II 736 seq., corresponding spirits, II 737.

Deng Tong 鄧通, favourite of the Emperor Han Wen Di 漢文帝, I 139–40, III Ch11 n36.

Deng Xi 鄧析, sophist, I 81, III Ch2 n25.

Dengming 登明, one of the Twelve Spirits of the cardinal points, II 733, III Ch75 n1.

Destinies 命 *ming* may be connected by chances and coincidences, I 129.

Destiny 命 *ming*, I 83 seq., 99 seq., determines life and death, rank and wealth, I 83, not influenced by virtue or knowledge, I 84, destiny of a State stronger than that of individuals, I 100, connected with the stars, I 100, natural 正 *zheng*, concomitant 隨 *sui*, adverse 遭 *zao*, I 101–2, received at the time of conception, I 102, does not agree with natural disposition, good or bad character, I 102, natural destiny according to Mencius' view, I 355–56, destiny depends on Heaven, II 723.

Devil country 鬼方 *guifang*, barbarous hordes in the north of China, II 593, III Ch58 n5.

Di 翟, northern barbarians, II 645, 656–59.

Di 狄, northern barbarians, I 199, 200, 217, 279, 288, 300, II 439, 511, 519, 572, 591, 599.

Di Ku 帝嚳, mythical emperor, I 135, 166, 349, II 751, 756, 760, 773, III Ch11 n1, Ch30 n34, Ch57 n6, Ch77 nn5–6.

Di Yi 帝乙, Emperor of the Shang 商 dynasty, II 574–75.

Dian 點, name of Zeng Xi 曾晳, II 485–86.

Ding 定, Duke of Jin 晉, III Ch64 n3.

Ding 定, Duke of Lu 魯, II 808.

Ding 丁, Duke of Song 宋, I 183–84.

Ding Bo 丁伯, enemy of Wang Chong's 王充 family, II 849.

Ding Bo Yu 丁伯玉, elegant writer, I 436.

Ding Hou 丁后, wife of the Emperor Gong Wang 共王, II 651–52.

Dinghu 鼎湖, place in Henan 河南, I 166, 258, 260.

Dingtao 定陶, place in Shandong 山東, II 651.

Dipper 斗 *dou*, constellation, I 379, II 813, III Ch10 n24.

Diseases have natural causes, II 725.

Distance, its effect on vision, I 306–6, 367, 371–72, 378–79.

Distillation 熾釀 *chiniang*, II 844, of spirits for sacrifices with fragrant grass, I 201.

District cities 縣邑 *xianyi*, exceeding ten thousand, I 174.

Divination 卜 *bu* / 卜筮 *bushi*, II 714 seq., by tortoise shells, straws, and diagrams, I 208–9, II 783, by diagrams 卦 *gua*, I 434, divination for a State and an individual, II 622, diviners employed in case of sickness, II 686, by tortoise shell and milfoil, II 714, by shells and by diagrams, II 719–20.

Divine splendour 神光 *shenguang*, a felicitous sign, II 588–89, a brilliant fluid 光氣 *guangqi* shining over Han Gao Zu 漢高祖, II 597, supernatural glamour, II 598.

Dong 董, dragon-keeper, I 242.

Dong Anyu 董安于, minister of Viscount Jian 簡 of Zhao 趙, I 118, II 462, 656.

Dong Fu 董父, I 241, 242.

Dong Jiang 東匠, of Zheng 鄭, murdered by his wife, I 340.

Dong Ming 東明, King of Fuyu 夫餘 in Korea, I 122.

Dong Wuxin 董無心, Confucianist of the Han 漢 time, I 228.

Dong Zhongshou 董仲綬, magistrate, I 435.

Dong Zhongshu 董仲舒, author of the Han 漢 epoch, I 153, 294–95, 399, 421, 433, 435, 436, II 440, 444, 480, 486, 488, 492, 503–4, 619, 765–66, 795, 836–37, 841, 860, III 887, 890, 894, 904, 905, 910, 912, 927, Ch3 n9, his rain sacrifice, I 243, II 494, 496–97, 498, 565, 567, 639–40, 793, 835–36, 837, III Ch45 n15.

Dongcheng 東成, place, I 435.

Dongdu 東都, city, probably Luoyang 洛陽, I 391, III Ch33 n33.

Dongguan 東莞, place, I 126.

Dongguan 東關, place in Shanxi 陝西, II 662, III 926, Ch64 n58.

Dongguo Ya 東郭牙, high officer of the Ju 莒 State, II 784–85, 787.

Dongjun 東郡, circuit in northern

Henan 河南, I 284, II 666, 795–96, III Ch33 n33.

Dongfan 東番, place, II 838.

Dongfang Shuo 東方朔, Daoist magician, I 270–71, 434, II 449.

Donghai 東海, place in Jiangsu 江蘇, I 402, II 568, 618, 811, 834.

Donglai 東萊, place in Shandong 山東, I 435, II 509.

Dongli 洞歷, work of Zhou Chang Sheng 周長生, II 444, 838–39.

Dongming 東冥, mountain, I 183.

Dongxia 東下, place, I 115.

Dou 竇, Empress-Dowager, wife of Han Wen Di 漢文帝, I 125.

Dou Guang Guo 竇廣國, brother of the Empress-Dowager Dou 竇, I 356.

Dou Ying 竇嬰, general, II 463, 650, 670, 676, III Ch63 n62, Ch65 n44.

Dragons 龍 *long*, reptiles that undergo transformations, I 109, 238 seq., as portents, I 129, two dragons in the court of Xia 夏 from whose saliva Bao Si 褒姒 was born, I 164–65, auspicious animals, I 167, a yellow dragon carried the boat of Yu 禹, I 202, 239, dragons in midsummer rise on clouds and rain, I 218, they were domesticated under Yao 堯 and Shun 舜, I 218, live in the water, I 239, like fish and reptiles, I 239, represented with a horse's head and a snake's tail, I 240, mount the clouds, and are like earthworms and ants,

I 241, not intelligent, I 241, dragon liver and unborn leopard, I 241, reptiles that can be domesticated and eaten, I 241–42, attract the clouds and the rain, I 242–43, II 455, ride on the clouds, I 243, contract and expand their bodies, can become visible and invisible, I 244, can transform themselves, I 244, rising to heaven, I 246–47, fetched by Heaven during a tempest, I 285, 351, found in the deepest water, I 428, appeared in the suburbs of Jiang 絳, I 433, divine dragon, II 451, the dragon appears in the second month, II 486, clouds follow the dragon, II 498, clay dragon of Dong Zhongshu 董仲舒 put up at the rain sacrifice, II 498 seq., 565, yellow dragons under Xiao Xuan Di 孝宣帝, II 531, a yellow dragon appeared, II 589, a dragon appeared above Gao Zu's 高祖 mother, II 597, 620, Yao's 堯 mother moved by a red dragon, II 597, eight dragons appeared under Ming Di 明帝, II 598, 606 seq., the dragon is the animal of the eastern region, II 608, require clouds and rain to soar to heaven, II 613, dragon-liver a delicacy, II 767, Lao Zi 老子 like a dragon, II 782, yellow dragon appearing under Xiao Wen Di's 孝文帝

reign, II 786, a clay dragon could attract rain, II 793, have ornaments on their scales, II 824.

Dragon horse 龍馬 *longma*, a horse 8 feet high, II 786, III Ch23 n19.

Dragon Star 龍星 *longxing*, II 759–60, III Ch77 n41.

Dreams and visions 夢 *meng*, their nature doubtful, II 634, 648, direct dreams, II 659–60, interpretation of dreams, II 659, 721.

Drums 鼓 *gu*, beaten in time of high water, II 496 seq.

Du 杜, Marquis of, killed by King Xuan 宣 of Zhou 周, appeared as a ghost, I 177, II 636, 675, 679, 682, III Ch65 n32.

Du Fu 杜撫, poet of the Han 漢 time, II 591, 611.

Du Hui 杜回, strong man of Qin 秦, II 645, 676, III Ch65 n42.

Duan Gan Mu 段干木, scholar of Wei 魏, I 333–34, 335, 336.

Duling 杜陵, place in Shanxi 陝西, II 589, 768.

Dummies 偶人 *ouren*, I 428, II 452, 558, interred in Lu 魯, II 688, 767, mud carts and straw figures symbolise life, II 503, dummies to serve the corpses, II 684, III Ch67 n14, Ch78 n21.

Dun 頓, territory in Henan 河南, I 291.

Dunmou 頓牟, city in Henan 河南, II 474.

Duodenary cycle 子丑 *zichou*, II 738 seq.

Dushuo 度朔, fabulous mountain,
II 501, 672.
Dwarfs, used as actors, II 578.

E 阿, place in Shandong 山東, II
791.
E Lai 惡來, minister of King Zhou
紂, I 276–77, III Ch25 n8.
Eagles transformed into pigeons
and vice versa, II 525.
Earth 土 *tu*, the ruling element of
the Han 漢 dynasty, II 605,
607 seq., 786, its colour
is yellow, its position the
centre, II 608, stronger than
water, II 490, 496.
Earth 地 *di*, governs the growing of
things, I 217, has an inundation, I 302, size of its area, I
362, does not move, I 372,
high in the north-west and
low in the south-east, I 373,
injuring the body of Earth,
II 707, the Spirit of Earth
disturbed by the turning up
of the soil, II 712, has a body
like man, II 715, has many
marks and lines, II 824.
Earthquake 地動 *didong*, predicted
from the stars, I 193, II 466,
471, 601.
East 東 *dong*, is benevolent, II 608.
Eastern well 東井 *dongjing*, solar
mansion = Gemini, II 597,
620, III Ch32 n4.
Eclipses 蝕 *shi*, II 675, 819, III 886,
912, Ch32 nn34, 35, Ch42
n44, Ch65 n27, App.I n46,
how caused, I 374 seq., every
42 months there is an eclipse
of the sun, and every 56
months, one of the moon, II
551–52, III Ch53 n12, at an
eclipse of the sun drums are
beaten and animals immo-
lated at the altars of the land,
II 495.
Eight degrees of nobility 八級 *baji*
in the Han 漢 time, I 416.
Eight Diagrams 八卦 *bagua*,
invented by Fu Xi 伏羲, ex-
panded by Wen Wang 文王,
I 412, II 578, 816, 843, III
914, Ch23 n19, Ch59 n37,
Ch73 nn25, 28.
Eight Objects of Government 八政
bazheng, food, commodities,
sacrifices, works, instruction,
jurisdiction, entertainment
of guests, warfare, II 711.
Elementary books 小學之書 *xiao-
xue zhi shu*, I 436.
Elephants 象, tilling the grave of
Shun 舜, I 131, 174.
Elixir of life 金玉之精 *jinyu zhi
jing*, made of gold and gems,
drunk by Daoists, I 265.
Embroidery 刺繡 *cixiu*, made in
Qi 齊 from generation to
generation, I 397, extraordinary skill required for this
handicraft, I 404, different
kinds of silk embroidery and
the method of embroidering,
I 406.
Emperor, ruler and king 皇帝王
huangdi wang, different de-
grees of sagehood, I 73.
Emperors, their investiture by
Heaven, I 145–46.
Energy, human, doubled by fear, I
289–90.
Energy of men of talent, I 418 seq.
Engineer 大匠 *dajiang*, I 400.

Envy 嫉 *ji* of people of exceptional abilities, I 81–82.

Equanimity of the wise who placidly await their fate, I 84–85, 87–88.

Equinoxes, vernal and autumnal 分 *fen*, I 365, 370.

Er Fu 貳負, some strange being, I 433, 436.

Ershi Huangdi 二世皇帝, son of the Emperor Qin Shi Huangdi 秦始皇, I 232, 277, 400, II 596, 652, III Ch15 n15, Ch21 n16, Ch64 n93.

Erya 爾雅, dictionary of classical expressions, II 545–46, III 917, Ch52 nn46–50, 52, 54.

Exaggerations, why people are fond of them, II 842.

Executions are wicked, II 455.

Exorcism 解除 *jiechu*, II 743 seq.

Fa 發, personal name of Wu Wang 武王, II 667, 739.

Fan 范, family name, I 242.

Fan 樊, Lady, of Chu 楚, II 462.

Fan 汎, grandfather of Wang Chong 王充, II 848.

Fan 犯, kinsman of Duke Wen 文 of Jin 晉, II 573, III Ch55 n58.

Fan Chi 樊遲, disciple of Confucius, I 310, 311, II 486.

Fan Ju 范睢, native of Wei 魏, almost beaten to death, I 86, II 473–74, III Ch3 n13, Ch43 n25.

Fan Kuai 樊噲, partisan of Han Gao Zu 漢高祖, I 125, III Ch37 n47.

Fan Li 范蠡, minister of Yue 越, I 141, II 478, III Ch3 n4, Ch38 n27, Ch45 n4, Ch80 n76.

Fan Li 樊酈 = Fan Kuai 樊噲, partisan of Han Gao Zu 漢高祖, I 425.

Fan Shu 范叔, attacked the *Zuozhuan* 左氏傳, II 833, III Ch83 nn9–10.

Fan Wenzi 范文子, minister of Jin 晉, II 657, III Ch50 n39.

Fan Xuan Zi 范宣子, officer of Jin 晉, II 640, 681.

Fan Zeng 范增, counsellor of Xiang Yu 項羽, I 124, III Ch9 n36.

Fang 防, place in Shandong 山東, II 630, 779.

Fangfeng 防風, Prince of, Goliath, I 279, II 578.

Fang Yu Gong 方與公, native of Zhao 趙, II 786.

Fankui 范魁, place, II 656.

Fanling 范陵, place, II 768.

Fanquan 阪泉, place where Yan Di 炎帝 was vanquished by Huang Di 黃帝, I 116.

Fans 扇 *shan*, III 926 seq., used in winter, I 75, 萐, used in summer to cause wind, II 540.

Fate, 命 *ming*, see Destiny, I 144, is obtained spontaneously, not by any effort, I 88, fate of long life, I 90, 317, a spontaneous principle holding sway over happiness and misfortune, I 128, works spontaneously, I 132, preventing grain from growing, I 132, fate and Heaven allowed Confucius and Mencius to be slandered, I 133, becomes the mind internally and the body externally, I 144, when a dynasty perishes, or a man expires, their fate is fulfilled, I 196, fate exhausted and time out of gear, II 508, virtue has no influence upon fate, II 547, 549, fate regulating the length of life is a very subtle essence, II 571, heavenly fate, II 598, its quantity, II 598, wealth and honour are fate, II 790, to avoid injury is chance and a propitious fate, II 799.

Favourites 幸 *xing* of emperors, liked for their beauty, I 74, 佞倖 *ningxing*, they have a pleasant appearance, II 790.

Fayan 法言, work of Yang Xiong 揚雄/Yang Zi Yun 揚子雲, II 582, 623, 826, III Ch56 n24.

Fayue 伐閱, extraordinary merit, I 416.

Fei Lian 蜚廉, minister of King Zhou 紂, I 276–77, III Ch25 n8.

Felicitous plant 蓂莢 *mingjia*, II 523, III Ch50 n30.

Female fluid 女氣 *nüqi*, supposed to remove ulcers, I 184.

Fen 賁, tortoise with three legs, II 543.

Fen 汾, river in Shanxi 山西, II 661, III Ch64 n4.

Feng 豐, place in Jiangsu 江蘇, I 100, 133, II 717, 727.

Feng 灃水, river in Shanxi 陝西, II 863.

Feng 馮婦, courageous lady, II 506.

Feng Bo 風伯, Wind God, II 760, III Ch76 n4.

Fenyin 汾陰, place in Shanxi 山西, I 298.

Ferghana, 宛 *yuan*, II 444, III Ch9 n8.

Fever 虐 *nüe*, II 678, III 907; cured with pills causing perspiration, II 456–57; *see also* Ghost of Fever.

Fifteen dynasties 十五家 *shiwu jia* at the beginning of history, II 846–47.

Fifth month child supposed to kill its parents, I 228.

Fire, 火 *huo*, I 81, 90, 95, 98, 100, 104–5, 107, 115–16, 117, 121, 126, 127, 130, 132, 145, 156 seq., 190, 204–5, 207, 210, 217, 243, 255–56, 261, 267, 268, 289, 295, 311, 318, 343, 364, 368, 369, 370, 372–73, 376–77, 399, 406, 407, 413, 416, 422, II 451, 454, 462, 465, 472, 478, 493, 499, 507, 534, 539, 577, 579, 596, 628, 629, 630, 634, 635, 651–52, 662, 674, 678, 679–80, 681, 700, 704–5, 710, 717, 738, 757, 758, 775, 793, 801, 812, 813, 858, III 865 seq., 924, 933–34, fire is the solar fluid, I 33, has its place in the south; the summer air corresponds to it, II 733, 742, fire injures metal, II 741, III 870. *See also* God of Fire.

Fishes and turtles are metamorphosed from snakes and reptiles, I 107, 122, 235, 387, 428, 525, fishes and birds are related, both can fly and are oviparous, II 679.

Five Birds 五鳥 *wuniao*, II 528, III Ch50 n52.

Five Canons (Classics) 五經 *wujing*:—*Yijing* 易經, *Shijing*

詩經, *Shangshu* 尚書, *Liji* 禮記, and *Chunqiu* 春秋, I 399, 411, 412–15, 421, 429, 434, II 620, 621, 780, 810, 811, 812, 822.

Five classes of literature 五文 *wuwen*:—Classics and Arts, records, essays, memorials, descriptions of virtuous actions, II 621–22.

Five Colours 五采 *wucai*, black, red, green, white, yellow, III 871, 889, 896, 924, corresponding to the Five Elements, II 794, III 870, 871, 872, 874, 893, 925.

Five degrees of mourning 五服 *wufu*:—for parents, grandparents, brothers and sisters, uncles and aunts, distant relatives, II 794.

Five Elements 五行 *wuxing*:—metal, wood, water, fire, and earth, I 376, II 500, 635, III 865 seq., Ch14 n3, Ch59 n33, Ch70 n21, their fluids different, I 157 seq., II 490, either affect or overcome each other, I 220, II 490, employed as amulets, II 700, 707, their antagonism modified by their quantity, II 704, 710, their correspondences, II 710, 737, 739–40 741–42.

Five Emperors 五帝 *wudi*:—Huang Di 黃帝, Zhuan Xu 顓頊, Ku 嚳, Yao 堯 and Shun 舜, I 278, II 517, 528, 562, 859, 863, III 868, 869, 871, 872, 874, 876, 896, 911, Ch16 n63, Ch24 n6, Ch84 n40.

Five Emperors and Three Rulers

五帝三王 *wudi sanwang*:—Huang Di 黃帝, Zhuan Xu 顓頊, Ku 嚳, Yao 堯, Shun 舜, and Yu 禹, Tang 湯, and Wen Wang 文王, I 101, 168, 179, 189, 260, 278, 320, II 517, 584, 585, 589–90, 597, 602, 612, 614, 751, 774, 834, 837.

Five Grains 五穀 *wugu*:—hemp, millet, rice, wheat, and beans, I 118, 200, 303, 386, II 473, 511–12, 539, 546, 550, 552, 739, 796, 824, III 874, 912.

Five Lakes 五湖 *wuhu* = Taihu 太湖 in Jiangsu 江蘇, I 117, III Ch8 n30.

Five Leading Princes 伍伯 *wubo*:—Duke Huan 桓 of Qi 齊, Duke Wen 文 of Jin 晉, Duke Xiang 襄 of Song 宋, Duke Zhuang 莊 of Chu 楚, and Duke Mu 穆 of Qin 秦, II 562, 857.

Five Monarchs 五代 *wudai*:—Yao 堯, Shun 舜, Yu 禹, Tang 湯, Wen Wang 文王, and Wu Wang 武王, II 595, 598.

Five Mountains 五嶽 *wuyue*, sacred:—Taishan 太山, Hengshan 衡山, Huashan 華山, Hengshan 恆山, and Songshan 嵩山, I 358.

Five Organs (intestines) 五藏 *wuzang*:—the heart, the liver, the stomach, the lungs, and the kidneys, I 158, III 898, Ch8 n37, Ch62 n6, the necessary substratum of the Five Virtues, I 118, II 628, regulating the Vital Fluid, I 288.

Five Planetary Emperors 五帝 wudi, II 664.

Five Planets 五星 wuxing:—Venus, Jupiter, Mercury, Mars, and Saturn, I 376, II 544, 597, III 872, 895, Ch64 n81, are made of the substance of the Five Elements, I 380, III 884, 895 seq., Ch32 n42.

Five presidents of the board of works 五司空 wusikong, II 602.

Five Punishments 五刑 wuxing of the Emperor Yu 禹—branding, cutting off the nose, cutting off the feet, castration, and execution, II 620.

Five Qualities 五常 wuchang:—benevolence, justice, propriety, knowledge, and truth, I 118, 155, III Ch8 n37.

Five relationships 五品 wupin, sovereign and subject, father and son, elder brother and jounger, husband and wife, friend and friend, II 492.

Five Rulers 五帝 wudi = Five Emperors:—Huang Di 黃帝, Zhuan Xu 顓頊, Ku 嚳, Yao 堯, and Shun 舜, II 550, 551.

Five Sacrifices 五祀 wusi of the house, the outer and inner doors, the well, the hearth, and the inner court, II 741, 751, 757, 758, III 869, 874, 910–11, Ch76 n3, Ch77 n2, App.I n25.

Five Sages 五聖 wusheng, Yao 堯, Shun 舜, Yu 禹, Tang 湯, and Wen Wang 文王, I 197, III Ch18 n14.

Five Secretaries 五曹 wucao, super-intending the 5 regions into which, under the Han 漢, a circuit or prefecture was divided, I 398.

Five Sounds 五音 wuyin, II 741–42, III 870, 874, 890, 893, Ch74 n23, five notes of the musical scale, II 736, 794, experts of the Five Sounds, II 739, system of, II 740, five sounds corresponding to the Five Elements, II 741 seq.

Five State Robes 五服 wufu, worn under the reign of the Emperor Yu 禹, I 282–83, III Ch25 n48.

Five Timekeepers 五紀 wuji of the Shangshu 尚書:—the year, month, day, stars, and dates of calendar, II 815, III Ch81 n26.

Five Tones 五聲 wusheng, the five musical notes = Five Sounds, II 737, III Ch74 nn2, 3.

Five Virtues 五常 wuchang:—benevolence, justice, propriety, knowledge, and truth, I 158, 215, 302, 434, II 542, 579, 628, III 896, 898–99, Ch62 n6; see also Five Qualities.

Flatulence, its causes, III 884.

Fluid, see Vital Fluid and Primogenial Fluid.

Fluid-eaters 食氣者 shiqizhe, Daoists living on air to obtain immortality, I 272–73.

Flying fish, I 244.

Fortune-tellers 相工 xianggong and their methods, I 135 seq.

Fortune-telling 占射 zhanshe, I 434, diviners, II 620, there are methods for this science which is not supernatural, II 772–73.

Founders melting metal, I 255.

Fountain 檻泉 *kanquan*, II 451, 545.

Four branches of literature 四科 *sike*, composition, thought, classical, and historical literature, II 446.

Four classes of the disciples of Confucius 四科 *sike*, I 114, 314–15, 316, III Ch8 n9, Ch28 n26.

Four Grey Beards 四皓 *sihao*, recluses at the beginning of the Han 漢 epoch, I 335.

Four kinds of savages 四夷 *siyi*, II 508, 599.

Four Quadrants (Constellations) 四星 *sixing*.—Blue Dragon, White Tiger, Scarlet Bird, and Black Tortoise, III 901, 919, Ch14 n7.

Four Sacred Mountains 四嶽 *siyue*, Hengshan 恆山, Huashan 華山, Hengshan 恆山 (in Shanxi 山西), and Taishan 太山, I 173, III Ch16 n20, Ch31 n20.

Four Seas 四海 *sihai*, the border lands of China, I 173, 240, 303, 360, II 595, 795, 845, III Ch31 n19.

Four Seas and Four Mountains 四海, 四山 *sihai sishan*, forming the limits of ancient China, I 360.

Four stars 四星 *sixing*, the sun, the moon, the stars, the zodiacal signs, I 159.

Fragrant grass 暢草 *changcao*, auspicious plant, I 200–1.

Frogs become quails, I 107, 261, II 525.

Fu 甫, Marquis of, minister of King Mu 穆, I 339.

Fu 傅, Marquis of Yin Jiang 隱彊, II 600.

Fu Chai 夫差, King of Wu 吳, I 72, 128, 175, 176, III Ch1 n4, Ch10 n4.

Fu Hou 傅后, wife of the Emperor Yuan Di 元帝, II 651, 652.

Fu Ning 傅寧, woman, II 605.

Fu Qing 扶卿, disciple of Kong Anguo 孔安國, II 818.

Fu Sheng 伏生, scholar who preserved the *Shangshu* 尚書, II 620, 811, 813, 830, III Ch46 n15, Ch51 n23, Ch82 n23.

Fu Su 扶蘇, son of Qin Shi Huangdi 秦始皇, II 472, III Ch43 n18.

Fu Xi 宓戲 or 伏羲, most ancient mythical emperor, I 412, II 494, 578, 734, 816–17, 843, III Ch31 n5, Ch81 n31, Ch84 n21.

Fu Yi 傅毅, scholar, I 436, II 619.

Fu Yue 傅說, minister of Gao Zong 高宗, I 129, III Ch10 n14.

Fu Zi Jian 宓子賤, philosopher, I 149, III Ch13 n2.

Funerals, I 139, 324–25, 403, II 565–66, 567, 694–95, III 930, Ch35 n2, Ch47 n32, Ch55 n39, Ch67 nn16, 18, Ch85 n9, simplicity of 薄葬 *baozang*, II 683 seq., 846, time of funerals, II 708.

Fusang 扶桑, region where the sun rises, I 370–71, 376, 377, III Ch32 n25, a tree, I 377–78, III Ch32 n46.

Fushi 輔氏, place in Shanxi 陝西, II
　　644–45.
Fuxing 甫刑, chapter on Punish-
　　ments in the *Shangshu* 尚書,
　　II 462, 473.
Fuyu 夫餘, State in Liaodong 遼東,
　　I 122.

Gai 該 = Ru Shou 蓐收, Genius of
　　Autumn, II 757.
Ganjiang 干將, famous sword, I
　　294, 424, II 451, 828, III
　　Ch26 n43.
Ganquan 甘泉, palace near
　　Chang'an 長安, II 463, 502.
Gao 郜, city in Qi 齊, I 181.
Gao Huangdi 高皇帝 = Gao Zu 高
　　祖, II 649.
Gao Jianli 高漸麗, native of Yan 燕
　　and friend of Jing Ke 荊軻, I
　　185, III Ch16 n104.
Gao Yao 皋陶, minister of Shun 舜,
　　I 72, 73, 135, 142, 309, 386,
　　414, II 517, 518, 542, 543,
　　797, 821, 853.
Gao Zi 告子, philosopher, oppo-
　　nent of Mencius, I 151–52.
Gao Zi 高子, officer, I 435.
Gao Zigao 高子羔, disciple of Con-
　　fucius, I 292–93, III Ch26
　　n35, Ch28 n65.
Gao Zong 高宗 = Wu Ding 武丁,
　　Emperor of the Shang 商
　　dynasty, I 93, 109–10, 129,
　　188, 195–96, 198, 199, 205,
　　292, II 490, 535, 593, 601,
　　III Ch4 n14, Ch7 n10, Ch10
　　nn13–14, Ch55 n31.
Gao Zu 高祖 = Han Gao Zu 漢高
　　祖, I 87, 100, 124–25, 133,
　　136, 145, 146, 163, 164, 165,
　　167, 277, 335, 412, 413, 414,

425, II 446, 475, 566, 590,
　　591, 594, 595, 596–97, 613,
　　619–20, 650, 664–65, 666,
　　717, 727, 759, 765, 794, 829,
　　841, III 922, Ch3 n23, Ch9
　　nn35, 38, Ch11 nn9, 14,
　　Ch15 n13, Ch23 n4, Ch36
　　n17, Ch58 n7, Ch64 n94,
　　Ch71 n8, Ch77 n36, Ch84
　　n5.
Gaolaisi jilu 高來禩記錄, work on
　　illustrious men, I 386.
Ge 蓋, Prince of Qi 齊, I 353.
Ge Lu 葛盧, chief of the Jie 介 State,
　　I 199, II 771–72, III Ch78
　　n50.
Gemini, 東井 *dongjing*, "Eastern
　　Well," constellation reached
　　by the sun in summer, I
　　365–66, III 899, Ch32 nn7,
　　10, Ch58 n32, Ch61 n31.
Gems and pearls, made artificially
　　by the Daoists, I 115–16.
Genii 仙人 *xianren*, I 260, 261,
　　265–66, 271, II 599, III 869,
　　871, represented with feath-
　　ers and wings, I 111, 254, so
　　light that they can fly like
　　wild geese, I 239.
Geomancers 占射事者 *zhan-
　　sheshizhe*, II 728, III Ch72
　　n15.
Ghosts 鬼 *gui*, are believed to ap-
　　pear to dying persons and
　　to kill them, I 130, ghosts of
　　two women causing a storm,
　　I 178, cried at the invention
　　of writing, I 200, 216, ghosts
　　and spirits agreed with Shen
　　Nong 神農, I 218, know
　　what is secret, I 252, wor-
　　shipped as though they were

men, II 486, the dead do not become ghosts and have no consciousness, II 625, diffuse and invisible, II 626, a name of the passive principle, II 626, ghosts are not the essence of the dead, II 626 seq., 668 seq., ghosts are visions of sick people, II 668, 669, seen by madmen, II 669, apparitions of the fluid of sickness, II 670, made of the stellar fluid, II 670, ghosts the essence of old creatures, II 670, ghosts living in men, II 670, the spirits of cyclical signs, II 671, creatures like men:—flying corpses 飛尸 *feishi*, crawling demons 走凶 *zouxiong*, goblins 魅 *mei*, devils 魑 *chi*, II 672, kingdom of the Ghosts 鬼國 *guiguo*, II 672, wicked ghosts 萬鬼 *wangui*, II 672, ghosts apparitions in human shape, II 673, are the Yang 陽 fluid, therefore red, burning and able to abscond, II 674, devils are supernatural apparitions produced by the sun, II 678, ghosts are burning poison and have a red colour, II 679, the Mohists hold that men after death become ghosts, possess knowledge, assume a shape, and injure people, II 683, ghosts and spirits call the sinners to account, II 701, ghosts are the essences of dead men, II 708, in reality there are no ghosts, II 709, the sway of ghosts and spirits, II 711–12, expulsion of ghosts, II 743, sick people see ghosts, II 745, ghosts and spirits more ethereal than immortals, II 762, insensible of joy and anger, II 762–63, ghosts and spirits speak to man through the mouths of sorcerers, II 774.

Ghost of Fever 虐鬼 *nüegui*, son of Zhuan Xu 顓頊, II 671, 745.

Giants 大人 *daren* devour Pigmies, 小人 *xiaoren*, II 508.

Gilt and silvered vessels 金銀塗飾 *jinyin tushi*, I 432.

Gobi, 流沙 *liusha*, "Flying sand," western limit of the earth, I 362, III Ch24 n28.

God = Shang Di 上帝, I 146, 229, II 572, 637, 731, III 867, Ch7 n14, Ch15 nn6, 20, Ch19 n41, Ch42 n57, Ch54 n23, Ch55 n4, Ch64 n41, public spirit, who does not trouble about private grievances, I 109, 165, 242, II 638, 656 seq., supreme being, I 187, Tang 湯 implored God, I 214.

Gold and gems 金玉 *jinyu*, choicest omens, II 605.

Golden Age, its praise unfounded, II 576 seq.

Gong 共, King of Chu 楚 and his five sons, I 123.

Gong 共, Prince of Lu 魯, II 811, 833.

Gong 恭, Prince of Lu 魯, II 617.

Gong Gong 共工, legendary being, chief minister of Yao 堯, I 357, 358–59, II 496, 601,

758, 791, 845, III 869, Ch26
n5, Ch80 nn1, 2.

Gong Shan Fu Rao 公山弗擾, noble
of Lu 魯, I 330, III Ch28
n98.

Gong Sui 龔遂, official, II 509, 514.

Gong Wang 共王, Zhou 周 Em-
peror, II 651.

Gong Ye = Gong Ye Chang 公冶長,
son-in-law of Confucius, II
799.

Gong Ye Chang 公冶長, son-in-law
of Confucius, I 312–13, III
Ch28 n19, Ch80 n54.

Gongbo Liao 公伯寮, relative of the
ducal house of Lu 魯, I 82,
133, II 548.

Gongming Jia 公明賈, disciple of
Gongshu Wen 公叔文, I 291,
II 777–78, III Ch26 n27.

Gongshu Wen 公叔文 = Gongshu
Wenzi 公叔文子, officer of
the Wei 衛 State, II 777.

Gongshu Wenzi 公叔文子, officer
of Wei 衛, I 291, III Ch26
n27.

Gongsun 公孫 = Gongsun Hong
公孫弘, scholiast of the
Shangshu 尚書, II 826.

Gongsun Chen 公孫臣, scholar of
the 2nd cent. BCE, II 607,
786, III Ch59 n30.

Gongsun Chou 公孫丑, disciple of
Mencius, I 347.

Gongsun Duan 公孫段, officer of
Zheng 鄭, II 642–43, 644,
676.

Gongsun Hong 公孫弘, councillor
of Han Wu Di 漢武帝, II
509, III Ch82 n24.

Gongsun Long 公孫龍, sophist, II
834.

Gongsun Nizi 公孫尼子, philosopher, disciple of Confucius, I
149, 154, III Ch13 n2.

Gongsun Shu 公孫述, Han 漢 general, I 199.

Gongsun Zhi 公孫支, officer of Qin
秦, II 656.

Gongyang 公羊 = Gongyang Gao
公羊高, commentator of the
Chunqiu 春秋, I 181, II 485,
492, 819, 835, III Ch16 n69,
Ch46 nn20, 22, Ch83 n4.

Gongyang Gao 公羊高, II 833.

Gou 緱氏, some person, I 221.

Gou Jian 勾踐, King of Yue 越, I
117, II 792, III Ch11 n40.

Gou Long 勾龍 = Hou Tu 后土,
Lord of the Soil, II 758, III
869.

Gou Mang 勾芒, Genius of Spring,
II 757, III 869, 873, 874,
Ch77 n17.

Government, must be based on
virtue, not on criminal law,
I 338, by not governing, II
557.

Grand Annalist 太史公 *Taishigong*
= Sima Qian 司馬遷, the
author of the *Shiji* 史記, I 87,
96, 210, 233, 259, 270, 361,
386, 400, II 444, 445, 521,
557, 623, 772, 802, 804, 826,
833, 834, 843, 846, III 872.

Great Diviner 太卜 *Taibu* = Great
Diviner of Qi 齊太卜, I 193,
226, II 471, III Ch43 n9.

Great Diviner of Qi, 齊太卜 *Qi
Taibu*, I 193, II 471, III Ch20
n4, Ch63 n36.

Great Plan 洪範 = Hongfan, chapter of the *Shangshu* 尚書, II
575, III 867.

Great Wall 長城 *Changcheng*, built by Meng Tian 蒙恬, I 232, II 703, III 922, Ch21 nn16, 18, 21.

Green Dragon 青龍 *qinglong*, the eastern quadrant of Heaven, II 680, 731, III 873, 901, 919, Ch59 n41, Ch66 n12, Ch73 n15, App.I n90. *See also* Blue Dragon.

Gu Bu Zi Qing 姑布子卿 (high officer in Zhou 周), physiognomist, I 138, 144, II 657.

Gu Sou 瞽瞍, unfeeling father of great Shun 舜, I 121, II 524, 782, 797, III Ch85 n55.

Gu Yong 谷永 = Gu Zi Yun 谷子雲, essayist, II 443, 839, 845, III Ch37 n13, Ch39 nn32, 37, Ch42 n44, Ch83 n54.

Gu Zi Yun 谷子雲 = Gu Yong 谷永, essayist, I 420, 436, II 440, 443, 466, III Ch42 n44.

Guan 管, territory in Henan 河南, II 565, 594.

Guan 管, Prince of, brother of Wu Wang 武王, II 600.

Guan Fu 灌夫, general of the 2nd cent. BCE, II 463, 650, 670, 676, III Ch63 n62, Ch65 n44.

Guan Gao 貫高, minister of Zhao 趙, attempted to murder Han Gao Zu 漢高祖, I 208, II 475, 801, III Ch80 n72.

Guan Long Feng 關龍逢, minister to the last emperor of the Xia 夏 dynasty, I 129, 182, III Ch80 nn42.

Guan Shu 管叔 = Guan Shu Xian 管叔鮮, brother of Zhou Gong 周公, II 783.

Guan Shu Xian 管叔鮮 = Guan Shu 管叔, II 464.

Guan Zhong 管仲, famous minister of Duke Huan 桓 of Qi 齊, I 85, 123, 146, 182, 184, 275, 423–24, II 555–56, 572–73, 784–85, 800, 827, 828, 834, III Ch1 n29, Ch9 n20, Ch12 nn15, 16, 17, Ch34 n18, Ch55 n52, Ch83 n18, Ch85 n30.

Guan Zi 管子 = Guan Zhong 管仲, minister of Qi 齊, statesman and writer, II 808, 856, III 884–85, 895, 901, 910, 912, Ch80 n94, Ch82 n45.

Guang Guo 廣國 = Dou Guang Guo 竇廣國, younger brother of the Empress-Dowager Dou 竇, I 125–26.

Guang Wen Bo 廣文伯, official, I 126.

Guang Wu Di 光武帝, Han 漢 Emperor, I 126, 127, 148, 167, 306–7, II 522, 534, 584, 588–89, 590, 591, 594, 595, 596, 597, 599, 613, 621, 645, 833, 846, III Ch9 nn51, 54, Ch19 n70, Ch33 nn31, 33, Ch58 n27, Ch83 n42.

Guanghan 廣漢, region in Sichuan 四川, I 126, II 771.

Guangling 廣陵, kingdom in Jiangsu 江蘇, I 178, II 600, 839, III Ch16 n55, Ch48 n18, Ch58 n64.

Guanjin 觀津, place in Henan 河南, I 125, III Ch9 n42.

Guanju 關雎, first Ode of the Shijing 詩經, II 837.

Gucheng 穀城, mountain in Shandong 山東, II 666.

Gufen 姑棼, place in Shandong 山東, II 674.

Gui Gu Zi 鬼谷子, philosopher of the 4th cent. BCE, I 389–90, II 481.

Guiji 歸忌, unlucky day, II 727, III Ch72 nn14, 15.

Guiji 會稽, circuit and city in Zhejiang 浙江, I 131, 173–75, 176, 185, 251, 361, II 443, 444, 445, 509, 581, 766, 793, 838, 848, III Ch16 nn17, 26, 34, Ch31 n31, Ch85 n2.

Guiji 會稽, mountain, I 260, II 614, III Ch80 n13.

Guizang 歸藏, name of an edition of the *Yijing* 易經, I 412–13, II 816–17, III Ch81 n31.

Guliang 穀梁, commentator of the *Chunqiu* 春秋, I 181, II 485, 819, III Ch83 nn4, 7.

Guliang Zhi 穀梁寔 = Guliang 穀梁, II 833.

Gun 鯀, father of great Yu 禹 and chief minister of Yao 堯, I 107, 116, 167, II 524, 601, 647–49, 756, 760, 791, 863, III 867, Ch8 n22, Ch26 n5, Ch42 n57, Ch63 n56, Ch77 n6, Ch80 nn1, 2.

Guo Lu 郭路, scholar, I 421.

Guoyu 國語, work of Zuo Qiu Ming 左邱明, II 833–34, III Ch15 n22, Ch64 n55, Ch85 n35.

Habit and its affects on arts and handicraftswork, I 397.

Hailing 海陵, place in Jiangsu 江蘇, I 175.

Halo (aureole) 光氣 *guangqi*, I 120, 208–9, II 475–76.

Han 漢, dynasty, 202 BCE–220 CE, I 86, 108, 198, 234, 270, 306, 399, 411, 428, 432, II 440, 445, 464, 487, 502, 521, 556, 557, 585, 593, 604, 610, 611, 617, 765, 786, 804, 818, 820, 830, 841, 864, III 927, Ch6 n8, Ch7 n5, Ch8 n49, Ch10 n42, Ch11 n9, Ch12 n12, Ch13 nn2, 15, Ch16 n27, Ch18 n26, Ch21 n25, Ch24 n18, Ch25 n17, Ch27 n8, Ch28 n60, Ch31 n31, Ch34 n21, Ch35 n23, Ch38 n4, Ch42 n36, Ch51 n8, Ch54 n11, Ch58 nn9, 56, Ch59 n19, Ch61 n36, Ch64 n80, Ch69 n13, Ch80 n75, Ch81 n19, Ch83 nn29, 58, Ch84 n5, Ch85 nn2, 61.

Han 漢, epoch, I 183, 210, 419, II 453, 499, 581, 825, 833, 836, 845, III 887, 919, Ch9 n9, Ch20 n12, Ch34 n3, Ch36 nn3, 37, Ch37 n26, Ch38 nn8, 33, Ch39 n4, Ch55 n68, Ch56 n30, Ch57 n40, Ch70 n21, Ch81 n42, Ch85 n7.

Han 漢, affluent of the Yangzi 江, I 177, 242, II 804, 836.

Han 漢, people, I 277, II 597, 809.

Han 漢, territory of the Han 漢 dynasty in Shanxi 陝西, I 119, 133, 176, 425, II 493, 614, 620, 651.

Han 韓, State, territory in Shanxi 山西, I 97, 184–85, 206, II 638, 660, 841, III Ch11 n7, Ch16 n97, Ch21 n34, Ch33 nn12, 14, Ch37 nn36, 37, Ch41 n1, Ch64 nn23, 45, Ch81 n21, Ch82 n54, Ch84 nn4, 35, Ch85 n28.

Han Anguo 韓安國, counsellor of Han Wu Di 漢武帝, I 134, 139, III Ch10 n44, Ch11 n38.

Han Feizi 韓非子, Daoist philosopher, I 242, II 619, 620, 828, 829, 839, 856, III Ch2 n18, Ch21 nn33, 35, 39, Ch34 n18, Ch37 n36, Ch57 n13, Ch71 n21, Ch83 n43, Ch84 n4, Ch85 n28, assassinated by Li Si 李斯, I 236, on dragons, I 241, II 522, on style, I 327, 331 seq., II 838, disparages divination, II 720, the bulk of his work, II 841, 860.

Han Gao Zu 漢高祖, founder of the Han 漢 dynasty, I 146, 208, 249, 335, II 664, III 876, Ch3 n20, Ch5 n5, Ch6 n10, Ch8 n33, Ch11 nn10, 12, Ch12 nn21, 22, Ch23 nn5, 9, Ch25 n15, Ch29 n13, Ch36 nn15, 45, 51, Ch36 n71, Ch37 nn46, 47, Ch43 n41, Ch46 n25, Ch54 n5, Ch57 n19, Ch63 n57, Ch63 n67, Ch77 n33, Ch78 nn9, 36, Ch80 n72, Ch82 n49.

Han Jue 韓厥, official in Jin 晉, I 124.

Han Man 汗漫, genius, I 264.

Han Wen Di 漢文帝, Han 漢 Emperor, II 597, III Ch3 n25, Ch11 n32.

Han Wu Di 漢武帝, see Wu Di 武帝, I 268, III 929, Ch9 n51, Ch21 n31, Ch24 n1, Ch26 n13, Ch42 nn27, 29, Ch43 nn24, 32, Ch48 n27, Ch49 n17, Ch63 n59, Ch65 n44, Ch80 n30, Ch82 n30.

Han Xin 韓信, helpmate of Han Gao Zu 漢高祖, I 87, 133, 136, 425, II 768, 800, 802–3, III Ch80 nn76, 78.

Han Xuan Zi 韓宣子, minister of Jin 晉, II 647.

Han Zao Xin 韓蚤信, father of Han Feizi 韓非子, II 829.

Hangzhou 杭州 Bore, I 178, III Ch16 n56.

Hanzhong 漢中, in Shanxi 陝西, II 820.

Happiness 福 *fu*, definition of happiness and misfortune, I 79, luck has its time and cannot be prayed for (運氣 *yunqi*), II 482, good and bad luck can be ascertained, II 509, good and bad luck happen by chance, II 515, not the result of virtue, II 549, happiness and misfortune not depending on goodness or badness, II 552.

Happiness 福 *fu* and fortune 祿 *lu* not connected with wisdom and intelligence, I 85, 223 seq., 230 seq., not given by Heaven as a reward, I 223.

Hao 鎬池, lake near Xi'anfu 西安府, II 662.

Hare 兔 *tu*, conceives by licking the pubescence of plants, and the leveret issues from its mouth, I 163, in the moon, I 373–74.

He 和 of Jing 荊 = Bian He 卞和, I 292, III Ch26 n37.

He 和, astronomer of Yao 堯, II 541.

He 合, officer in Song 宋, II 573.

He Lu 闔廬, King of Wu 吳, I 117,

407, III Ch26 n43, Ch35
n16.

Heart 心 *xin*, constellation, I 186,
188, 190 seq., II 466, 475,
569, 601, 661, a good heart
alone distinguishes between
right and wrong, I 188, those
who have a good heart speak
good words, and good words
are accompanied by good actions, I 188, II 806, the constellation Heart corresponds
to Song 宋, I 191, is like a
ball or an egg, I 436, governs
the members and the senses
and is not governed by them,
II 470–71, becomes visible in
summer; is a heavenly sign
of dragons, II 506, the heart
of a Sage is bright, that of a
Worthy well-principled, II
807.

Hearth 竈 *zao*, sacrifice to, II 751,
757, III 874, 911, App.I n25,
God of the Hearth, II 758.

Heat and cold 寒温 *hanwen*, II 453
seq., coinciding with joy and
anger, I 249, not influenced
by the sovereign, II 453.

Heaven 天 *tian*, wealth and honour
come from Heaven, I 98
seq., 319, its ways difficult to
know, I 132, Heaven's decree,
I 143, 145 seq., 322, II 783,
787, Heaven is spontane-
ous, I 146, human qualities
ascribed to it, I 146–47,
emits its fluid into Earth, I
166, Heaven rewards virtue,
I 179, Spirit of Heaven, I
179, Heaven hears what men
say, I 187 seq., has a body
like Earth, and does not hear
man, I 189, Heaven and man
have the same law, I 191,
Heaven raining grain, an ill
omen, I 200, distance be-
tween Heaven and man sev-
eral ten thousand Li, I 204,
a certain sympathy between
Heaven and man, I 206, a
storm expressive of Heaven's
anger, I 206, to affect Heaven
a person should concentrate
his mind, I 206, Heaven not
to be moved by the human
mind, I 208, Heaven raining
grain, I 209, 216, Heaven
could not help Tang 湯, Wen
Wang 文王, and Confu-
cius, I 209, Heaven rained
hoar-frost for Zou Yan 鄒
衍, I 211, felt no sympathy
for Shen Sheng 申生 and
Wu Zixu 伍子胥, I 211, sent
down rain at the prayer of
Tang 湯, I 214, Heaven em-
ployed God and the spirits to
injure people, I 214, Heaven
confines itself to emitting its
fluid, I 217, Heaven's anger,
I 246 seq., the dark blue sky,
I 248, Heaven humanised, I
248–49, all beings to Heaven
like children, I 250, Heaven
does not write, I 255, sends
down a drought, I 302,
minister of Heaven, I 347,
Mencius on Heaven, I 348–
49, Heaven's ways difficult
to understand, I 357 seq.,
II 671, the pure elements
formed heaven, the impure
ones earth, I 359, heaven

is not air, but has a body, I 363, its distance from earth, I 363, its circumference 365 degrees, I 363, not raised in summer, nor depressed in winter, I 366, not high in the south, nor low in the north, I 366, not shaped like a reclining umbrella, I 367, looks like a bowl turned upside down, I 367, is as level as earth, I 368, heaven makes a circumvolution of 365 degrees = 730,000 Li every day, I 371, heaven's movement the spontaneous emission of fluid, I 373, its distance from earth upwards of 60,000 Li, I 379, Heaven invested the Han 漢, I 412, Heaven filled with the primogenial fluid, II 445, its principle spontaneity, II 457, does not reprimand a sovereign, nor kill malefactors, II 465, Heaven's spontaneity and inaction preclude wisdom and sensations, II 466, Heaven does not speak, II 467, the words of the wise are the words of Heaven, II 467, anthropomorphisms of the *Shijing* 詩 經 and the *Shangshu* 尚書, II 467, the heart of Heaven in the bosom of the Sages, II 467, affects things, but is not affected by them, II 468, is the master of man and things, II 468, 470, its fluid forms the shapeless empyrean, II 472, not moved by the sighs of ten thousand people, II 472, does not pay heed to human actions, II 479, either a spirit or clouds and rain, II 481, its ears and eyes far away, II 481, Heaven's anger, II 492, to understand the mind of Heaven one starts from human thoughts, II 493, the fluid of Heaven in disharmony, II 497, the principle of Heaven is spontaneity, II 499, 515, Heaven and time, II 549, success and discomfiture emanate from Heaven, II 552, emits its fluid everywhere, but acts spontaneously, II 554, has neither mouth nor eyes, II 555, its fluid is:—placid, tranquil, desireless, inactive, and unbusied 恬澹無欲無 爲無事 *tiandan wuyu wuwei wushi*, II 555, its principle spontaneity, II 556, and inactive, II 560, does not speak nor act, II 562, reprimands contrary to its nature, II 563, Heaven responded with rain to Tang 湯 inculpating himself during a drought, II 564, sent a thunder-storm, manifesting its anger, II 565, 566, Heaven indignant at Qin's 秦 destruction of literature, II 566, moved its terrors, to display the virtue of the Duke of Zhou 周公, II 568, Confucius would not impose upon Heaven, II 570, Heaven took several years from Wen Wang 文王, adding them to Wu Wang's

武王 span, II 571, Heaven intimating its disapproval by thunder and rain, II 574, its principle inaction, II 574, destroying depraved persons by a thunderbolt, II 574–75, Heaven does not reprimand, II 575, the Heaven of antiquity is the Heaven of to-day, II 576, Guang Wu Di 光武帝 received Heaven's decree, II 595, Heaven helped the Han 漢 with thunder and rain, II 596, Heaven's command, II 600–1, its signs, II 620, 623, Heaven does not speak nor hear, its nature is non-interference, II 658, 716, Heaven not following the excentricity of the year-star, II 701, does not eat men, II 702, laws of Heaven, II 705, hard to know, II 712–13, the spirits of Heaven, II 713, its body, II 715, Heaven the master of the hundred spirits, II 724, virtues are its principles, II 724, Heaven is a body like the Earth, II 750, Heaven has endowed Confucius, II 787, even Heaven may be induced to respond by tricks, II 793, Heaven has celestial signs, II 824.

Heaven and Earth 天地 *tiandi*, like a great furnace filled with *Yang* 陽 (fire) and *Yin* 陰 (water), I 111, 164, 255, do not create man on purpose, I 156–57, their fluids mixing, things grow naturally and spontaneously, I 157, are like husband and wife, I 166, 248, II 555, 560, the nature of Heaven and Earth corresponds to the doings of birds and beasts, I 175, the nature of Heaven and Earth remained the same, I 177, sound affecting Heaven and Earth, I 213, Heaven and Earth knew Confucius to be faultless, I 214, a Sage displays virtue like Heaven and Earth, I 215, inundations and droughts of Heaven and Earth, I 215, Heaven and Earth produced the Plan and the Scroll, I 216, agreed with Shen Nong 神農, I 218, the effects of virtue said to affect Heaven and Earth, I 220, believed to punish the wicked, I 230, father and mother of mankind, I 248, are both bodies, I 262, were not born and do not die, I 274, King Xuan 宣 serving Heaven and Earth, I 300, contain air, I 359, act in spontaneous harmony, I 381, the fluids of Heaven and Earth, I 430, their nature is spontaneity, II 455, the great man equals them in virtue, II 467, Heaven and Earth honoured by the sovereign like father and mother, II 489, 494, sacrifices to Heaven and Earth neglected, II 492, their fixed periods rule over calamities, II 549, by the fusion of their fluids all things are produced, II 554, are inactive, II 559, cannot act, are devoid of knowledge, II 562–63, conjointly produce all things, II 577, set in order, II 627, spirits of Heaven and Earth, II 700, nature of Heaven and Earth, II 704, cannot be interrogated by diviners, II 714, do not respond, II 716; have a body, II 716, in man the mind of Heaven and Earth reach their highest development, II 726, Heaven and Earth do not hurt mankind, II 734, their size many ten thousand Li, II 750, the emperor treats Heaven like his father and Earth like his mother, II 757, Confucius could not talk to them, II 784.

Heavenly fluid 天氣 *tianqi*, I 101, 108, 127, 145, 157, II 458, 468, 469, 470, 471, 473, 476, 552, 559, 676, produces thunder and rain, II 574, 733, it may be influenced by ordinary people, II 590, 793.

Heavenly officials 百官 *baiguan*, the stars, I 101, II 658.

Hebei 河北, in Shanxi 山西, I 127, II 645, III 922.

Hedong 河東, a circuit in Shanxi 山西, I 126, 265, 266, III Ch64 n49.

Henan 河南, Henanfu 河南府, II 511, III 889, 926, Ch2 n32, Ch5 n12, Ch6 n9, Ch8 n13, Ch8 nn41, 43, 45, Ch9 nn33, 40, 42, 44, 56, Ch11 nn22, 51, Ch12 nn29, 30, Ch16 nn29, 88, 96, Ch18 n36, Ch19 nn6, 51, 71, 72, Ch22 n24, Ch24 nn4, 41, Ch25 nn20, 32, 43, Ch26 nn3, 18, 19, 31, 59, Ch27 n39, Ch28 n92, Ch31 n9, Ch33 n34, Ch34 nn13, 23, 33, Ch37 n6, Ch43 nn30, 33, Ch48 n23, Ch49 nn4, 5, Ch54 n6, Ch55 n9, Ch58 n49, Ch60 n21, Ch63 nn60, 63, Ch64 nn20, 25, 98, Ch66 n9, Ch72 n11, Ch78 n31, Ch79 n7, Ch80 n31, Ch81 nn7, 54, 56, 60, Ch84 nn23, 25, 35, Ch85 n4.

Henei 河內, city in Henan 河南, I 413, II 811.

Heng 恆 = Hengshan 恆山, mountain in Shanxi 山西, I 173, III Ch16 n20, Ch31 nn9, 20, Ch64 n30.

Hengshan 衡山, mountain in Hunan 湖南, III Ch16 n20, Ch31 nn9, 20.

Hero quelling fire 厭火丈夫 *yanhuo zhengfu*, I 416.

Hesperus, 長庚 *changgeng*, II 544.

Hill sacrifice 封禪 *fengshan*, I 258, 升封 *shengfeng*, I 174, II 588.

Homeopathetic treatment 以類治之 *yilei zhizhi*; cold cured by cold, and fever by fire, II 678.

Hong Ru 閎孺, minion, I 96.

Hong Yan 弘演, loyal official of Duke Yi 懿 of Wei 衛, I 288, II 580, 581.

Hongfan 洪範 / 鴻范, Flood Regulation, chapter of the *Shangshu* 尚書, I 207, II 457, 458, 467, 674, 720, 815, III 867–68, Ch25 n35, Ch42 n57, Ch81 nn26, 28.

Hongnong 弘農, city in Henan 河南, I 148.

Hook Star 鈎星 *Gouxing* = Mercury, I 193, II 466, 471, 601, III Ch43 n9.

Hot Water Abyss, I 376, 377–78, 380. See also Tanggu 湯谷.

Hou 邸, place, I 304, III Ch27 n26.

Hou Feng 侯諷, writer of the Han 漢 time, II 619, III Ch61 n19.

Hou Ji 后稷, Lord of Agriculture, I 121, 122, 144, 162, 164, 166, 167, 301, 411, II 512, 597, III Ch15 nn6, 7, Ch77 nn8, 14, Ch83 n27.

Hou Pu Zi 侯鋪子, adherent of Han Feizi 韓非子, II 839.

Hou Tu 后土, Lord of the Soil, II 589, 758, III 869, 874, Ch77 n17.

House 房星 *fangxing*, constellation, II 466, 471, 475, 479, 491, 601, III Ch43 n9.

Hu 胡, aboriginal tribes in the North, I 234, II 593, 658, 747, 765, III Ch64 n40, Ch76 n6.

Hu Ba 瓠芭, famous lute-player, I 213, III Ch8 n24, Ch19 n37.

Hu Hai 胡亥 = Ershi Huangdi 二世皇帝, I 163, II 765, III Ch43 n18.

Hu Mu 胡母, commentator of the Chunqiu 春秋, II 833, III Ch83 n5.

Hu Tu 狐突, officer of Jin 晉, II 637–38.

Hua 滑, mountain, II 646.

Hua 華, sacred mountain in Shanxi 陝西, II 444, III Ch16 n20, Ch31 n9.

Hua Chen 華臣, minister in Song 宋, II 573–74, III Ch55 nn60, 61.

Hua Shi 華士, scholar of Qi 齊, I 334, 336, III Ch29 n10.

Hua Wu 華吳, officer in Song 宋, II 573.

Hua Yang 華陽, Princess of, II 462.

Hua Yang 華陽后, consort of King Xiao Wen Wang 孝文王 of Qin 秦, II 767, III Ch78 n27.

Hua Yuan 華元, general of Song 宋, I 226, III Ch20 n6.

Huai 淮, river in Henan 河南 and Anhui 安徽, I 239, II 611.

Huai 淮, aboriginal tribes, I 287.

Huai 懷, King of Chu 楚, I 128, II 472.

Huai 懷, King of Liang 梁, II 509.

Huai Nan 淮南 = Huai Nan Zi 淮南子, Prince of Huainan 淮南 famous Daoist philosopher and author, I 261, 263, 265, 268, 361, 362, II 649, 828, 829, 845, 858, III 887, Ch1 n22, Ch24 nn18, 25, Ch31 nn21, 22, Ch37 n37, Ch54 n17, Ch63 n54, Ch85 nn19, 39, on fate, I 86, 263, 376–77.

Huainan 淮南, princedom in Anhui 安徽, I 261, 360, III Ch3 n17.

Huaiyang 淮陽, State in Henan 河南, II 556, 650.

Huan 桓, Duke of Qi 齊, I 123, 180–83, 184, 236, 269, 275, 423, II 555–56, 572, 784, 827, 863, III Ch1 n29, Ch3 n6, Ch9 n19, Ch16 n80, Ch24 n43, Ch54 nn3, 31, Ch55 n49, Ch85 nn22, 32.

Huan 桓, Duke of Qin 秦, II 644.

Huan 桓, Duke of Lu 魯, II 819, III Ch54 n13.

Huan 皖, marquisate in Anhui 安徽, II 603, Ch59 n2.

Huan Dou 驩兜, minister of Yao 堯, I 391, II 601, III Ch26 n5.

Huan Jun Shan 桓君山, scholar of the Han 漢 time, II 439, 440–41, 442, 499, 504, 518, 619, 809, 837–38, 843, 863, III Ch39 n17, Ch50 n9, Ch83 n42.

Huan Kuan 桓寬, writer of the 1st cent. BCE, III 838, Ch83 n45.

Huan Long 豢龍, dragon-keeper under Shun 舜, I 241–42, III Ch22 n18.

Huan Tan 桓譚 = Huan Jun Shan 桓君山, scholar, II 841, III Ch50 n9, Ch83 n42.

Huang Ba 黃霸, high officer, II 610, III Ch60 n10.

Huang Ci Gong 黃次公, minister of Han Xuan Di 漢宣帝, I 132, 137–38, III Ch11 n21.

Huang Di 黃帝, legendary emperor, I 75, 104, 116, 120, 135, 136, 166, 168, 239, 258–61, 268, 428, II 444, 516, 560, 593, 597, 613, 654, 672, 751, 756, 760, 773, 801, 834–35, 864, III 874, 881, 909, 918, Ch1 n26, Ch8 n21, Ch11 n1, Ch15 n30, Ch16 n12, Ch23 n18, Ch24 nn6, 7, 8, 13, 14, Ch29 n24, Ch42 n24, Ch52 n40, Ch56 n6, Ch58 n3, Ch59 nn40, 42, Ch64 n9, Ch65 n16, Ch74 n23, Ch77 n5, Ch78 nn8, 57, Ch81 n31, Ch84 n20, the school of

Huang Di 黃帝 and Lao Zi 老子 arguing on spontaneity, II 460, both inactive, II 559, 563, Huang Di 黃帝 and Lao Zi 老子, II 843.

Huang Shi 黃石公, Mr. Yellow Stone, II 525, III Ch54 n10.

Huayin 華陰, place in Shanxi 陝西, II 662, 663.

Hui 惠, Duke of Jin 晉, II 637–38, 676, III Ch63 n7, Ch65 nn31, 40.

Hui 惠, Duke of Lu 魯, I 255, II 667, 824, III Ch54 n14.

Hui 惠, King of Chu 楚, I 223.

Hui 惠, King of Liang 梁 = Wei 魏, I 344–45, II 785–86, III Ch37 n35.

Hui 惠, of Liuxia 柳下, II 789.

Hui Di 惠帝, Han 漢 Emperor, I 251, II 620, III Ch5 n5, Ch23 n9.

Human Emperors 人皇 *renhuang*, mythical rulers of remotest antiquity, I 359, II 627.

Hunchbacks 戚施 *qishi*, II 578, are full of envy, I 81.

Hundred spirits 百神 *baishen*, hundred ghosts, I 501, various kinds of spirits, I 218–19, II 724, 735, 746.

Huo 霍, mountain in Henan 河南, I 173.

Huo Guang 霍光, regent for Han Zhao Di 漢昭帝, II 474.

Huo Qubing 霍去病, Han 漢 general, II 521, 792.

Huotai 霍太, mountain in Shanxi 山西, II 661.

Hyades, 畢 *Bi*, when the moon approaches them, it rains, I 381, II 479–80, 482, 491.

Ice-houses 冰室 *bingshi*, II 539, III Ch52 n12.

Ignorance, blissful of primitive times, II 561.

Immortality, I 111, 274, aimed at by Daoists, I 260, 261–62, 268–69, 271, II 762, drug of 仙藥 *xianyao*, I 261.

Inaction 無爲 *wuwei*, I 146, 460, 466, 555, 557, 559, 560, 561, 574, 804, III Ch54 n7.

Incest 亂骨肉 *liangurou*, I 180, 淫 *yin*, I 181.

Incidents 偶 *ou*, definition, I 105.

Indicator 屈軼 *quyi*, miraculous plant, II 538 seq.

Inner apartment 內 *nei* of the wealthy, filled with boxes, I 427.

Inscriptions, on tripods 鼎銘 *dingming*, II 610, 611–12, 662, III Ch60 n8, on stone by Li Si 李斯, II 614, III Ch60 n34, on stone, II 667, 766, of the Orkhon, III 920, Turkish, III 922, 925.

Insects 蟲 *chong*, eating grain likened to officers, II 491–92, 510 seq., produced by the fluid of wind, II 511, depend on warm and damp weather, II 513.

Interpreters 譯 *yi*, I 195, II 599, 719, required by savage tribes, sometimes two, I 189, II 600, III Ch18 n3, Ch58 n52.

Intoxication, the virtuous believed not to become intoxicated, I 280.

Intuitive knowledge 不學自知 *buxuezizhi*, is impossible, II 769, 786 seq.

Japanese, 倭人 *woren*, I 295, II 599, III 915, 925, 929, Ch26 n48, Ch39 n42, Ch55 n37.

Jaundice 癉疾 *danbing*, II 493.

Ji 稷 = Hou Ji 后稷, Lord Ji 稷, god of cereals, ancestor of the Zhou 周 dynasty, I 72, 85, 152, 386, II 756, 757, 797, 834–35, III Ch77 n8.

Ji 稷, territory in Shanxi 山西, II 644.

Ji 季, family in Lu 魯, II 494, 509, 536, 570, 857, III Ch14 n11, Ch28 n43, Ch29 n32, Ch48 n9.

Ji 季 = Ji Li 季歷, son of Dan Fu 亶父, I 460, III Ch55 nn36, 39, Ch67 n7, Ch68 n10.

Ji 姬, surname of the Zhou 周 dynasty, I 162, 166, II 739.

Ji 濟, river in Shandong 山東, II 611, III Ch81 n39.

Ji An 汲黯, statesman under Han Wu Di 漢武帝, II 449, 556.

Ji Huan Zi 季桓子, Prince Huan 桓 of Ji 季, I 330, III Ch28 n98.

Ji Li 季歷, son of Dan Fu 亶父, I 144, III Ch12 n5, Ch68 n10.

Ji Ru 籍孺, favourite of Hui Di 惠帝, I 74.

Ji Sun 季孫, nobleman in Lu 魯, I 133, II 548, 570.

Ji Zi 箕子, noble under Zhou Xin 紂辛, I 72, 129, 241, 242, II 767.

Ji Zi 季子, Prince of Wu 吳, I 169–71, II 761, III Ch77 n47.

Ji Zi Cheng 棘子成, officer of Wei 衛, II 824, III Ch82 n14.

Jia 嘉, King of Yan 燕, I 185.

Jia Kui 賈逵, scholar of the 1st cent. CE, I 436, II 619, III Ch38 nn55, 57, Ch61 n17.

Jia Yi 賈誼, poet and scholar under Han Wen Di 漢文帝, I 509, 536, 588, 607, 616, 839, III Ch51 n36, Ch57 n17, Ch78 n55, Ch83 n53, on destiny, I 86–87.

Jian 漸, name of terrace near Chang'an 長安, I 279.

Jian 簡, Viscount of Zhao 趙, I 134, 138, 165, 177, II 557, 636, 656, III Ch63 n3, Ch64 nn14, 23, Ch65 n38.

Jian 簡, Duke of Yan 燕, II 676, III Ch65 n38, Ch81 n20.

Jian Di 簡狄, mother of Xie 契, II 834.

Jiang 絳, principality in Shanxi 山西, capital of Jin 晉, I 139, 241, 433.

Jiang 姜 = Wen Jiang 文姜, duchess of Lu 魯, I 181.

Jiang Yuan 姜原, mother of Hou Ji 后稷, I 164, 166, II 834, III Ch15 nn6, 31.

Jiangbei 江北, north of the Yangzi 江, II 680.

Jiangcheng 江乘, place in Jiangsu 江蘇, II 766.

Jiangdu 江都, place in Jiangsu 江蘇, II 765.

Jiangnan 江南, south of the Yangzi 江, II 678, 680.

Jianlun 檢論, "Critical Reflections," work of Zou Yan 鄒衍, II 843 III Ch84 n17.

Jianzhang 建章, name of a palace of the Han 漢 emperors, I 138, 234.

Jiaojiao 焦僥/僬僥, Pigmies, I 300, III Ch27 n8.

Jibei 濟北, place in Shandong 山東, II 666.

Jie 桀 = Jie Gui 桀癸, last Emperor of the Xia 夏 dynasty, I 71, 113, 182, 411, II 582, 846, III Ch1 n2, Ch10 n8, Ch84 n39.

Jie 介, native State south of Jiaozhou 膠州, I 199, II 771.

Jie and Zhou 桀紂, I 113, 128–29, 163, 181, 182, 190, 205, 229, 275, 297, 411, II 547, 550, 575, 582, 583, 594, 596, 644, 724, 746, 797, III Ch36 n12, Ch56 n30, Ch58 n12.

Jie Gui 桀癸, tyrant, last Emperor of the Xia 夏 dynasty, III Ch80 n42.

Jie Ni 桀溺, hermit of the time of Confucius, II 779, 800, 804.

Jie Ru 藉孺, minion, I 96, III Ch1 n24.

Jieke 藉柯, place, II 766, III Ch78 n14.

Jieshi 碣石, mountain in Zhili 直隸, I 131.

Jimo 卽墨, city in Shandong 山東, II 663, 791, III Ch64 n63.

Jimo 籍墨, technical expression, I 416.

Jin 金, old coins, I 85, 115, 145, 331, II 522, 859, III Ch85 n39.

Jin 金, name of Dongfang Shuo 東方朔, I 270.

Jin 晉, State, in Shanxi 山西, I 96, 124, 136, 165, 202, 212, 219, 229, 289, 291, II 517, 525, 557, 573, 637, 640, 643, 644, 647, 653, 663, 666, 667, 676, 720, 748, 768, 819, 824, 835, 844, III 929, Ch6 n22, Ch7 n16, Ch9 n26, Ch11 nn6, 31, Ch13 n5, Ch18 n39, Ch19 nn31, 60, Ch22 nn1, 16, 28, Ch26 nn14, 32, Ch28 n92,

Ch38 n30, Ch43 n38, Ch54 nn12, 31, Ch63 nn6, 10, 13, 44, Ch64 nn23, 33, Ch65 nn31, 40, Ch66 n20, Ch75 n6, Ch77 n49, Ch79 n43, Ch81 n21, Ch85 nn32, 37.

Jin Wengshu 金翁叔, Xiongnu 匈奴 Prince, II 502.

Jin Zhuan 靳專, native of Guiji 會稽, I 251.

Jinan 濟南, city in Shandong 山東, II 811.

Jincheng 金城, city in Gansu 甘肅, II 599.

Jing 涇, river in Shanxi 陝西, tributary of the Huanghe 黃河, II 574, 836.

Jing 荊, mountain in Shanxi 陝西, I 258.

Jing 荊, King of Guangling 廣陵, II 600.

Jing 景, Duke of Song 宋, I 109, 186, 188, 207, II 569, III Ch19 n17, Ch20 n2.

Jing 景, Duke of Jin 晉, I 219.

Jing 景, Duke of Qi 齊, I 187, 193, II 471, 646, 778.

Jing Chou 景丑, officer of Qi 齊, I 348.

Jing Ci Fei 荊次非, I 239.

Jing Di 景帝, Han 漢 Emperor, I 125, 139, II 620, 765, 811, III Ch9 nn39, 43, Ch63 n61, Ch81 n9, Ch85 n11.

Jing Fang 京房, commentator of the *Yijing* 易經, II 458, III Ch42 n14.

Jing He 荊和 = He 和 of Jing 荊, wept tears of blood, I 292.

Jing Ke 荊軻, attempted to assassinate Qin Shi Huangdi 秦始皇, I 185, 208, 284-85, 293-94, 475, 796-97, III Ch16 n103, Ch25 n57, Ch26 n42.

Jing Zi 景子, Viscount Jing 景 of Zhao 趙, II 643.

Jingzhou 荊州, place in Hubei 湖北, II 818.

Jingzhou 荊州, ancient province, II 732, III Ch39 n43.

Jinyang 晉陽, city in Shanxi 山西, II 661.

Jisujieyi 譏俗節義, "Censures on Morals," work of Wang Chong 王充, II 852, 853, 854, III Ch85 n13.

Jiu 摎, general of Qin 秦, I 296, 297.

Jiu Fan 咎犯, officer of Jin 晉, I 202-3, II 663, 721.

Jiujiang 九江, circuit in Anhui 安徽, II 863, III Ch11 n26.

Jiuyi 九嶷, place, II 766.

Jiuzhen 九眞, tribe in Annan, II 526, 589.

Jiyang 濟陽, in Shandong 山東, I 126.

Jiyang 濟陽, palace, I 126, 145, 167, II 522, 534.

Jizhou 冀州, one of the Nine Provinces of Yu 禹, I 175, II 732.

Joined field system 井田 *jingtian*, I 415, III Ch36 n58.

Ju 莒, State in Shandong 山東, II 784, III Ch43 n12.

Juan 涓, music-master of Wei 衛, II 653-54.

Jun Shang 君上, personal name of the Emperor Cheng Di 成帝, I 137.

Jun Xian 君賢, father of Chen Jue 陳爵, II 604.

Jupiter, 歲星 *suixing*, star, II 475-76, 478, 544, 552, 700

seq., 729 seq., 759–60, III 877–78, 880, 884, 895–96, 917–18, 919, Ch32 n42, Ch45 n4, Ch69 nn9, 16, 22, Ch73 nn1, 8, Ch77 nn38, 41, 42, App.II n9.

Jurists 法家 *fajia* or 法令之家 *faling zhi jia*, I 399, 429, 法律之家 *falü zhi jia*, I 414.

Kang 康, King of Zhou 周, I 93, 286, 414, I 584, 590, III Ch26 n1, Ch56 n34.

Kang 康, King of Chu 楚, I 123.

Kang Shu 康叔, brother of Zhou Gong 周公, I 146, 282, II 461, III Ch25 n43, Ch64 n25.

Kang Zi 康子 = Ji Kang 季康, head of the Ji 季 family in Lu 魯, I 318.

Killing animals, *see* animals.

Killing people to follow the deceased into their graves 殉葬 *xunzang*, II 684.

Knives for erasing and pencils for writing 刀筆 *daobi*, I 398, 400, 406.

Kong Anguo 孔安國, grandson of Confucius, II 818.

Kong Jia 孔甲, Emperor of the Xia 夏 dynasty, I 183–84, 242, 356, II 537, III Ch22 n21, Ch30 n60.

Kong Kui 孔悝, noble of the Wei 衛 State, 5th cent. BCE, II 610.

Kongtong 空同, mountain and aborigines in Gansu 甘肅, II 658.

Ku 嚳 = Di Ku 帝嚳, mythical emperor, I 167, II 773, III Ch24 n6, Ch83 nn22, 26.

Kuang 曠, music-master, I 172, 212, II 567, 654, 666, 858, III Ch19 n37.

Kuang 匡, State in Henan 河南, II 779, III Ch79 n8.

Kuang Jue 狂譎, scholar of Qi 齊, I 334, 336, III Ch29 n10.

Kuang Zhang Zi 匡章子, high officer of the Qi 齊 State, I 352–53.

Kuang Zhi Gui 匡稚圭, savant, I 86.

Kuhanzhen 窟含眞, III 923.

Kui 夔, director of State music under Shun 舜, I 183–84, II 610, III Ch16 n85.

Kui 魁, constellation of Ursa major, I 130.

Kuiqiu 葵丘, place in Shandong 山東, I 182.

Kun 崑 = Kunlun 崑崙, mountain in Turkestan, II 800, III Ch80 n61.

Kun Mo 昆莫, King of the Wusun 烏孫, I 121–22, III Ch9 n11.

Kunlun 崑崙, mountain in Turkestan, the gate of Heaven, I 197, 218–19, 263, 361, 422, III Ch31 n4, Ch80 n61.

Kunyang 昆陽, city in Henan 河南, I 279, II 596.

Ladle turning southward (magnetic needle?) 司南之杓 *sinan zhi shao*, II 542.

Land division in Wei 魏, I 118.

Land tax 租 *zu*, in the Han 漢 time, I 415, 賦 *fu*, I 416.

Language, different in ancient and modern times and in different parts of the empire, II 856.

Langye 琅邪, south coast of Shandong 山東, I 185, 296, II 581, 614, 662, 766, III Ch64 n63.

Lanling 蘭陵, place in Shandong 山東, I 391.

Lao 牢 = Qin Zhang 琴張, disciple of Confucius, II 563.

Lao and Cheng 勞成, mountains of the Shandong 山東 coast, I 185, II 662, 766, III Ch64 n3, Ch78 n17.

Lao Zi 老子, lived over 200 years, I 93, dragon, I 245, 782, his theory to prolong life by quietism and dispassionateness, I 271, founder of Daoism, II 460, 559, 563, 782, 801, 843, III Ch4 n13, Ch37 n36, Ch54 nn7, 28, App.I n58, obtained long life through the spontaneous fluid, II 555, Lao Zi 老子 and Wen Zi 文子 like Heaven and Earth, II 561.

Learned men 通人, well versed in literature, I 394, II 439.

Learning 學知, its superiority, I 403 seq.

Lei Gong 雷公, Thunderer, I 253, II 760, III Ch76 n4.

Lelang 樂浪, ancient State, II 600.

Lengdao 冷道, district in Henan 河南, II 606.

Li 禮 = Dadaili 大戴禮, Ritual of the Senior Dai 戴, I 103.

Li 鯉, son of Confucius, I 325.

Li 厲, King of Zhou 周, I 129, 197, II 599, 612, 642, 724, III 924, Ch18 n9, Ch43 n15, Ch58 n48, Ch63 n19.

Li 厲, Duke of Zheng 鄭, II 665, III Ch64 n83.

Li 厲, King of Chu 楚, II 472.

Li 犁, Marquis of, II 645.

Li 犁 = Zhu Rong 祝融, God of Fire, II 758, 869.

Li 驪, mountain = Lishan 驪山, II 664.

Li 李, consort of the Han 漢 Emperor Wu Di 武帝, II 502.

Li Dui 李兌, II 852.

Li Ji 驪姬, wife of Duke Xian 獻 of Jin 晉, II 638.

Li Ji Gong 李季公, prefect, I 435.

Li Fu 李父, companion of Han Yuan Di 漢元帝, I 126.

Li Guang 李廣, general of Han Gao Zu 漢高祖, I 234, 289, 290.

Li Ling 李陵, general of Han Gao Zu 漢高祖, I 233, III Ch21 n22.

Li Lou 離婁 = Li Zhu 離朱, I 172.

Li Si 李斯, prime minister of Qin Shi Huangdi 秦始皇, I 284, II 472, 614, 829, 839, III Ch21 n35, Ch43 n18, Ch 61 n36, Ch85 n28, torn to pieces by carts, I 236, III Ch21 nn36, 37, caused the Burning of the Books, I 283, II 620, 638–39, 811, 812, 830.

Li Shao Jun 李少君, Daoist magician, I 268–71, III Ch24 nn44, 45, Ch38 n37.

Li Wen Bo 禮文伯, official, II 509.

Li Zhu 離朱, man of very keen sight, I 171–72, III Ch16 n13.

Li Zizhang 李子長, official, II 500.

Liang 梁 = Liangshan 梁山, mountain in Shanxi 陝西, I 219, 284.

Liang 梁 = Kaifengfu 開封府, capital of the Wei 魏 State, I 344, III Ch30 n2.

Liang 梁, Wei 魏 State in Henan 河南, I 72, II 443, 509, 785, 829, III Ch48 n23, Ch63 n67, Ch85 n11.

Liang Qiao 良橋, tribe, II 599.

Liang Yuan 良願, tribe, II 599, III Ch58 n54.

Liangzhou 梁州, one of the Nine Provinces, II 732, III 922.

Lianshan 連山, name of an edition of the *Yijing* 易經, I 412–13, II 816–17, III Ch81 n31.

Liao 飂, State, I 241.

Liaodong 遼東, ancient State in Manchuria, I 232, II 600, III Ch9 n14.

Library, imperial 蘭臺 *lantai*, II 436, 618, 621, III Ch61 n11.

Lie 列, Marquis of Han 韓, I 184.

Lie Shan 烈山 = Shen Nong 神農, II 758, 816, III Ch77 n22.

Life 生 *sheng*, its proper length a hundred years, I 91, II 577, Daoists endeavour to pro-long life by quietism and dis-passionateness, I 271; long life, the shortest 70 years, medium 80 years, longest 90 years, II 815.

Life and death 死生 *sisheng* depend on Destiny, I 99 seq.

Liji 禮記, "Book of Rites," I 107, 110, 254, 256, 405, 413, II 486, 525–26, 671, 699, 708, 713, 753, 756, 758–59, 762, 811, 813, 817, 833, III 866, 872, 873, 874, 881, 882, 884, 885, 893, 897, 898, 899, 900, 901, 902, 903, 904, 910, 911–12, 930, 932, 933, Ch6 n21, Ch7 n18, Ch10 n24, Ch16 n67, Ch21 n10, Ch23 n17, Ch35 nn2, 4, 6, Ch42 n54, Ch45 n21, Ch47 nn30, 33, Ch50 n43, Ch52 nn6, 7, 10, 12, Ch52 n49, Ch55 nn13, 38, 47, Ch65 n11, Ch70 nn9, 10, Ch71 n9, Ch74 n43, Ch76 n3, Ch77 nn16, 17, 24, 25,26, 39, 52, Ch78 n6, Ch79 nn14–17, Ch80 nn25, 82, Ch81 nn1, 32, Ch82 n4, Ch83 n6, App.I nn25, 50, 112.

Lin Fang 林放, man of Lu 魯, II 570.

Lin Hu 林胡, barbarians, II 661.

Ling 靈, King of Chu 楚, I 123, 430, II 641, 786, III Ch38 n15.

Ling 靈, Duke of Wei 衛, I 182, 318, II 653, III Ch56 n4, Ch85 n9.

Ling 靈星, star/constellation, I 416, II 486, 759.

Ling 陵, river, I 176.

Lingling 零陵, place in Henan 河南, II 598, 605–7, III Ch59 nn15, 19, 20.

Linhuai 臨淮, place in Anhui 安徽, II 581, 838.

Lintao 臨洮, city in Gansu 甘肅, I 232.

Linzi 臨菑, capital of Qi 齊, I 305.

Lisao 離騷, poem of Qu Yuan 屈原, II 472, 839, III Ch32 n40, Ch43 n13, Ch83 n52.

Lishan 歷山, mountain, II 852, III Ch85 n12.

Lishan 驪山, mountain in Shanxi 陝西, II 652, 664.

Literati 儒 *ru*, I 86, 92, 135, 149, 156, 162, 167, 173, 178, 204, 258, 261, 263, 265, 266, 283, 284, 286 seq., 303, 309, 312,

330, 331–33, 357, 359, 363, 364, 371, 372, 373–74, 381, 388, 394, 397, 399, 402, 410, 412, 414, 419, II 465, 517, 519, 520, 525, 530, 531, 532, 538, 540, 541, 542, 545, 560, 565, 578, 580, 585, 592, 598, 613, 615, 638, 731, 732, 759, 760, 764, 810, 812, 834, III Ch25 n53, Ch29 n8, Ch34 n11, Ch63 n68; despise the Han 漢 time, studying only the Classics, I 590, blind and dumb, I 611, literary men receive their writings from Heaven, I 621, have no original ideas and resemble simple artisans, II 802.

Literature, light 短書 *duanshu*, I 135, 169, 243, 244.

Liu 劉, Duke, ancestor of the Zhou 周 dynasty, I 144.

Liu 劉, family name of the Han 漢 dynasty, II 829.

Liu 劉媼, mother of Han Gao Zu 漢高祖, I 124, 144–45, 163, 249, II 566.

Liu 留, Marquis of = Zhang Liang 張良, II 665, 666, 824.

Liu An 劉安, Prince of = Huai Nan Zi 淮南子, I 263, 265, 360, II 649, III Ch24 n18.

Liu Chang 劉長, father of Liu An 劉安, I 263.

Liu Chun 劉春, Daoist, I 251.

Liu Kun 劉琨, native of Henan 河南, 1st cent. BCE, I 148.

Liu Lei 劉累, dragon-rearer, under the Emperor Kong Jia 孔甲, I 242.

Liu Sheng Gong 劉聖公, cousin to Guang Wu Di 光武帝, II 596.

Liu Xia Hui 柳下惠, Hui 惠 of Liuxia 柳下, famous for his purity of mind, I 113, 171, 333, II 789.

Liu Xiang 劉向, celebrated author of Han 漢 time, II 887, III Ch13 n17, Ch18 n33, Ch26 n11, Ch33 n30, Ch47 n10, Ch61 n13, Ch83 n7, Ch83 n55.

Liu Zi Jun 劉子駿 = Liu Xin 劉歆, son of Liu Xiang 劉向, II 499, 504, 619.

Liu Zi Zheng 劉子政 = Liu Xiang 劉向, famous author, I 152, 153–54, 433, 436, II 439, 440, 683, 684, 802, 825, 833, 839, 843, 846, III Ch83 nn7, 55.

Liyang 歷陽, city in Anhui 安徽, I 99–100, 104, 123, II 552, 727.

Loadstone 磁石 *cishi*, attracts needles, II 499, horse-shoe magnet, II 500.

Locusts 蝗蟲 *huangchong*, I 221–22, II 451, III Ch19 n72, Ch40 n17, Ch49 nn1, 6, measures taken against them, II 491 seq., 511.

Long 龍, minister of Shun 舜, I 183.

Long Feng 龍逢 = Guan Long Feng 關龍逢, minister to the last emperor of the Xia 夏 dynasty, II 797.

Longquan 龍泉, place in Zhejiang 浙江, I 115.

Longxi 隴西, district in Gansu 甘肅, I 234.

Longyuan 龍淵, famous sword, I 294.

Lu 魯, State in Shandong 山東, the country of Confucius, I 86,

96, 107, 129, 133, 136, 165,
171, 181, 196, 206, 255, 291,
306. 311, 339, 341, 348, 380,
414, 424, II 445, 455, 475,
479, 480, 482, 485, 492, 506,
509, 511, 517, 523, 526, 532,
557, 570, 590, 607, 609, 610,
617, 627, 648, 659, 667, 675,
685, 690, 708, 718, 720, 739,
765, 771, 781, 783, 786, 804,
808, 811, 814, 818, 824, 826,
833, 844, 857, III Ch8 n8,
Ch10 n19, Ch14 n11, Ch16
n85, Ch17 n25, Ch18 n23,
Ch26 n16, Ch28 nn5, 36,
Ch29 nn7, 32, Ch32 n49,
Ch36 nn38, 40, Ch37 n41,
Ch39 nn2, 50, Ch42 n11,
Ch43 n34, Ch45 n27, Ch48
n9, Ch50 n11, Ch54 nn13,
14, Ch55 n42, Ch57 n38,
Ch62 n8, Ch64 n42, Ch65
n19, Ch66 n24, Ch70 n6,
Ch77 n49, Ch81 nn9, 24, 27,
39, 45, Ch82 n22, Ch83 n38,
Ch84 n35, Ch85 n33.

Lu Ao 盧敖, traveller, I 263–66.

Lu Ban 魯般, famous mechanic of Lu
魯, I 290, II 501, III Ch26 n16.

Lu Fu 祿父, descendant of the Yin
殷 dynasty, II 600, III Ch 58
n68.

Lu Jia 陸賈, writer and envoy from
the Han 漢 to Zhao Tuo 趙
他, King of Yue 越, I 119,
153, 172, II 440, 442, 446,
464, 619, 620, 622, 683, 684,
686, 825, 829, 835, 841, III
Ch8 n49, Ch61 n57, Ch83
n29, Ch84 n5.

Lu Lian = Lu Zhong Lian 魯仲連,
wandering philosopher of

the Qi 齊 State, II 443.

Lu Qiu Xin 魯邱訢, killed two
water-dragons, I 239, 244.

Luan 欒水, river, II 646.

Luan 鸞, bird inferior to the phœnix, II 521, III Ch50 n52.

Luan Huai Zi 欒懷子, officer of Jin
晉, II 640, 681.

Lucifer, 啓明 *qiming*, II 544.

Luck 祿 *lu*, definition, I 104.

Lugubrious look 凶色 *xiongse*, the
sign of death, I 192, II 551.

Luhun 陸渾, place in Gansu 甘肅,
II 768.

Lujiang 廬江, circuit in Anhui 安
徽, II 603, 604, 863.

Lumbago (sciatica) 腓 *fei* or 邊
bian, said to be caused by
devils flogging the patient, II
678, cured with honey and
cinnabar, II 678.

Lunheng 論衡, the "Disquisitions,"
Wang Chong's 王充 princi-
pal work, I 410, II 504, 598,
611, 612, 613, 615, 624, 841
seq., 853, 854–55, 858, III
901, Ch7 nn9, 12, Ch10 n35,
Ch15 nn22, 36, Ch20 n17,
Ch22 nn4, 19, Ch33 n22,
Ch36 nn15, 25, Ch41 n10,
Ch43 nn1, 9, 28, Ch47 n8,
Ch54 n35, Ch56 n35, Ch57
nn18, 19, Ch60 n35, Ch63
n3, Ch64 nn11, 63, Ch65
n38, Ch75 n1, Ch81 n10,
Ch84 nn12, 35, 38, App.I
n112.

Lunu 盧奴, place in Zhili 直隸, II
509.

Lunyu 論語, the "Analects of Confucius," II 617, 818, III Ch25
n25, Ch81 nn10, 44, 45.

Luo 洛, tributary of the Yellow
    River, I 119, 216, 255, II 557,
    586, 667, 816, 824, III Ch8
    n47, Ch23 n19, Ch55 n4,
    Ch73 n18, Ch81 n32.
Luo 洛 = Luoyi 洛邑, II 731.
Luoguo 躶國, Naked People, visited
    by Yu 禹, I 321, II 592.
Luoyang 洛陽, = Luoyi 洛邑, centre
    of China, I 119, 362, III Ch31
    n34, city on the Luo 洛 in
    Henan 河南, II 651, 660, III
    929, Ch33 n33, Ch37 n36,
    eastern capital of the Zhou 周
    dynasty, II 704.
Luoyi 洛邑, capital of the Zhou 周
    dynasty on the Luo 洛 river
    in Henan 河南, I 400, II 732,
    III Ch28 n100, Ch58 n49,
    Ch78 n35.
Luxian 魯縣, city, I 242.
Luyang 魯陽, city in Henan 河南,
    II 845, III Ch84 n35.
Lü 呂, father of the Empress Lü
    Hou 呂后, I 136.
Lü 呂, clan of the Empress Lü Hou
    呂后, II 829, III Ch3 n23.
Lü Buwei 呂不韋, author of the 3rd
    cent. BCE, 43, II 442, 828,
    829, 873, III Ch82 n37, Ch83
    n11, Ch85 nn38, 39.
Lü Hou 呂后, Empress Lü 呂, wife of
    Han Gao Zu 漢高祖, I 87, 124,
    125, 136, 251, 277, 335, II 597,
    649–50, 676, III Ch3 n23, Ch23
    n9, Ch57 n19, Ch65 n43, Ch80
    n78, Ch82 nn48, 50.
Lü Shang 呂尚, surname of Tai
    Gong 太公, II 451, 667, III
    Ch10 n12, Ch52 n36.
Lü Shi 呂氏 = Lü Buwei 呂不韋, II
    858.

Lü Wang 呂望 = Tai Gong 太公,
    counsellor of King Wu 武,
    I 129.
Lujiang 廬江, place in Anhui 安徽,
    II 603, 604, 863.
Lüshi chunqiu 呂氏春秋, work of
    Lü Buwei 呂不韋, II 833,
    III Ch8 n4, Ch10 n26, Ch16
    nn85, 88, 89, 95, Ch22 n4,
    Ch24 n38, Ch26 n8, Ch37
    n51, Ch39 n28, Ch42 n50,
    Ch67 n18, Ch82 n36, Ch85
    n38.

Madness 狂癡 *kuangchi*, of nature
    I 117, II 466, disturbance of
    the vital force, II 669.
Magician, *see* Sorcerer.
Magpies 乾鵲 *qianque* / 鳱鵲
    ganque, I 160, II 523, 528,
    828, know the future, I 244,
    II 543, 774.
Mainah 鸜鵒 *quyu*, its prophecy,
    I 129, 196, II 509, 519, 527,
    536, III Ch10 n20.
Man 人 *ren*, imbibing the heavenly
    fluid man is born, I 101, nev-
    er metamorphosed, I 108–9,
    noblest of the productions of
    Heaven and Earth / noblest
    of creatures, I 107, 163, 239,
    434, II 451, 514, 736, like
    lice, I 165, endowed with
    a spontaneous mind and a
    uniform disposition, I 151,
    average people and people
    above and below the average,
    I 151, 155, endowed with the
    nature of Heaven and Earth,
    I 155, with the Five Quali-
    ties, I 155, man measures
    seven feet, I 164, 208, 215,

427, II 471, 577, III Ch15 n19, is born by propagation, I 166, born from man and not from earth, I 184, a tiny creature that cannot affect Heaven, I 190, II 471, the great man equals Heaven and Earth in virtue, I 214, II 467, 560, 571, first among naked creatures, I 240, II 511, 725, a creature like others, I 250, not different from other creatures, I 261, his insignificance, when compared with Heaven and Earth, II 468–69, filled with the heavenly fluid, II 470–71, cannot affect Heaven, II 479, man a naked animal, II 508, born from Heaven and Earth and endowed with the heavenly fluid, II 559, why active, II 559, is to be judged by his signs, II 620, before his birth and after death man is part of the primogenial fluid, II 628, he is born and kept alive by the *Yin* 陰 and the *Yang* 陽, II 676, the six domestic animals produce their young like man, II 696, man a pigmy, II 715, the most intelligent of the ten thousand creatures, II 725.

Man Fu 曼甫, neighbour of Confucius, II 779.

Man Qian 曼倩, style of Dongfang Shuo 東方朔, I 270.

Man Yi 蠻夷, savages in the south and in the west, II 508.

Mang and Dang 芒碭, mountains, Han Gao Zu's 漢高祖 hiding place in Henan 河南 and Jiangsu 江蘇, I 124, III Ch9 n33.

Marriage, age of, II 577.

Mars, 熒惑 *yinghuo* or 火星 *Huoxing*, I 109, 130, 186 seq., 207, II 466, 569, 661, 662, 674, III 877–78, 880, 884, 895–96, Ch7 n12, Ch10 n23, Ch19 n17, Ch20 n3, Ch64 n81, Ch66 n12.

Matriarchate, II 578, III Ch56 n12.

Meat fan 蓮脯 *shafu*, wonderful plant, II 538 seq.

Mechanisms:—a flying kite, a wooden carriage and horses, made by Mo Zi 墨子 and Lu Ban 魯般, I 290–91.

Medicine, I 97, II 460, 494, 512, 796–97, III 877, 881, Ch53 n4, Ch83 n58, liquid and pills, I 273–74, II 457, mineral drugs 藥石 *yaoshi*, I 359–60.

Meizhu 梅渚, place in Anhui 安徽, II 766, III Ch78 n15.

Mencius, 孟子 *Meng Zi*, II 840–41, III Ch25 n28, Ch27 n17, Ch33 n30, Ch37 n35, Ch84 n3; distressed, I 72, found culpable, I 81, full of sorrow, I 82, and Duke Ping 平 of Lu 魯, I 86, on destiny, I 102, his mother changed her domicile, I 119, slandered by Zang Cang 臧倉, I 133, on the goodness of human nature, I 150 seq., III Ch13 n8, judged men by the pupils of their eyes, I 150, II 622, on the defeat of the Yin 殷 dynasty, I 278, Censures on

Mencius, I 344 seq., on Guan Shu 管叔 and Zhou Gong 周公, II 783, on the sagehood of the disciples of Confucius, II 788–89, on the different ways of taking office, II 788, on the good people of the villages, II 805, on the *Chunqiu* 春秋, II 819, no controversialist, II 842, spoke of Heaven, II 851, knew an intelligent man by the sparkling of his eyes, II 856.

Meng 蒙, uncle of Wang Chong 王充, II 849.

Meng 孟, noble family in Lu 魯, I 311, II 740, 857, III Ch48 n9.

Meng 孟, ford in Huaiqingfu 懷慶府, Henan 河南, I 205, II 544.

Meng Ao 蒙驁, grandfather of Meng Tian 蒙恬, II 472.

Meng Ben 孟賁, famous for his strength, I 81, 117, 278, 294, 335, 395, II 506, 567, 632, 704, 770, III Ch25 n23.

Meng Chang 孟嘗, Prince of, I 74, 228, 292, II 481, 500, 521, 792, 793, III Ch1 n23, Ch50 n19, Ch80 n16.

Meng Chang Jun 孟嘗君, Lord Mengchang, I 210, III Ch19 n27.

Meng Guan 孟觀, prefect, II 443.

Meng Ming Shi 孟明視, officer in Qin 秦, I 291.

Meng Sun 孟孫 = Meng Yi Zi 孟懿子, I 310.

Meng Tian 蒙恬, general of Qin 秦, builder of the Great Wall, I 232–34, 235, II 472, 703, III Ch21 n21, Ch43 n20.

Meng Wu Bo 孟武伯, scion of the Meng 孟 family in Lu 魯, I 310–11.

Meng Yao 孟姚, wife of King Wu Ling 武靈 of Zhao 趙, II 656, 658, III Ch64 nn26, 38.

Meng Yi Zi 孟懿子, scion of the Meng 孟 family in Lu 魯, I 310–11, III Ch28 nn5, 7, 12, 13.

Meng Yue 孟說, strong man of Qin 秦, I 172, 421, III Ch37 n18.

Meng Zhang 孟章, unselfish official, II 581.

Mercury, 鉤星 = Hook Star, III 877–78, 880, 884, 896, Ch42 n46, foreboding an earthquake, II 471, 475.

Metal 金 *jin*, subdues wood, II 704, connected with the west, II 742.

Meteorologists 候氣變者 *houqi bianzhe*, II 620.

Meteors 星墜 *xingzhui*, I 284, 305 seq., 376, 378, 380, II 661–62, III Ch32 nn51, 52, Ch52 n40.

Mi Mo 麋墨, man in Jin 晉, II 573, III Ch55 n58.

Miao 三苗, the 3 Miao 苗 tribes civilized by Yao 堯 and Shun 舜, I 116, II 601, III Ch26 nn4, 5.

Milfoil 蓍 *shi*, supernatural plant, becomes 700 years old, II 447, knows auguries, II 714 seq., 764, used for divination, II 536, Ch71 n1, Ch72 n2.

Min 閔, disciple of Confucius = Min Zi Qian 閔子騫, I 309, III Ch85 n36.

Min 岷山, mountains in Sichuan 四川, I 422, II 569.

Min Zi Qian 閔子騫, disciple of Confucius, II 687, 782, 788, III Ch28 n1.

Ming 冥, descendant of Xie 契, II 756, 761, III Ch77 n7.

Ming 明星, star, II 759, III Ch77 nn37, 42.

Ming Di 明帝 = Xiao Ming Di 孝明帝, II 584, III Ch50 n49, Ch56 n35.

Mingguang 明光宮, palace, I 430.

Mining and metallurgy, I 407.

Miracles 怪 *guai*, I 162 seq., II 672–73, produced by Heaven for Prince Dan 丹 of Yan 燕, I 209–10, are bound to a certain species, I 217, the miraculous births of Yao 堯, Xie 契, Tang 湯 and Hou Ji 后稷, II 597, the discovery of a vessel filled with gold coins, II 604–5, magical music, when the Classics were discovered in the house of Confucius, II 617, miracles of Zhong Zi 仲子 and Zhang Liang 張良, II 824.

Mo Di 墨子 = Mo Di 墨翟, philosopher, I 80, 82, 397, 398, 432, II 506, 581, 832, 838, 840, 842, 857, 861, 863, III Ch6 n1, Ch8 n4, Ch20 n13, Ch26 n17, Ch28 n94, Ch63 n2, Ch80 n68, Ch83 n1.

Mo Mu 嫫母, ugly wife of Huang Di 黃帝, I 75, II 578, 710.

Mohists, 墨家 *mojia*, followers of Mo Di 墨翟, I 99, 228–29, II 683–85, 688–89, III Ch67 n1; neglect the burials,

but honour the ghosts, II 832–33.

Mongolia, 蒙穀 *menggu*, I 263, III Ch32 n22, Ch64 n31.

Mongols, 胡 *hu*, II 753, III 915, 916, 924, 925, Ch24 n30, Ch64 n51, App.II n18.

Monoceros 鮭鯱 *xiezhi*, goat with one horn butting the guilty, II 543 seq.

Monthly plant 蓂荚 *mingjia*, wonderful plant, I 199, 201, II 538, 540–41, III Ch52 n17.

Moon 月 *yue*, when it fades shells shrink in the sea, I 131, it influences the tides, I 178, when it follows the stars there is wind and rain, I 207, moves 13 degrees = 26,000 Li every day, I 371, a hare and a toad in the moon, I 373, II 491, the moon is water, I 373, approaching the Hyades and the stars, causes wind and rain, I 381, II 480, 491, completes a circumvolution in thirty days, II 480, the essence of all the *Yin* 陰, II 491, when the moon is eclipsed, snails and corn-weevils decrease on earth, II 491, the moon is water, II 499, its splendour overshadowed on the fifteenth, II 616, the first three days of the moon 魄 *po*, II 696, the "crescent" 弦 *xian* on the eighth, the full moon 望 *wang*, "facing" of sun and moon, on the fifteenth, the "dark moon" 晦 *hui* on the thirtieth day of the month, II 696–97, 702–3, moon causing misfortune by consuming some land, II 700 seq..

Moon mirror 方諸 *fangzhu*, attracts the water of the moon, II 491, III 933.

Mou 牟, princedom in Shandong 山東, I 291.

Mountain and Sea Classic 山海經 *Shanhaijing*, ascribed to Yi 益, I 433, III Ch22 n7, Ch31 n23.

Mountain Book, 山經 *Shanjing*, part of the *Shanhaijing* 山海經, I 361, III Ch31 n23.

Moxa 艾 *ai*, used externally as medicine, II 495.

Moye 莫邪, famous sword, I 294, III Ch26 n43.

Mu 穆, King of Zhou 周, I 93, 339, II 462, III Ch1 n9, Ch6 n14, Ch42 n24.

Mu 繆 or Mu 穆, Duke of Qin 秦, I 109, 229, 291, 293, II 462, 638, 656, III Ch21 n18, Ch26 n40, Ch54 n31, Ch85 n32.

Mu 繆, Duke of Lu 魯, I 339, II 480.

Mu 穆, Duke of Zheng 鄭, II 643, III Ch63 n22.

Mu 牧 / Mu 牧野, plain in Henan 河南, where the troops of the Yin 殷 dynasty were defeated, I 277, 305, II 595.

Mu Shu 穆叔, of Lu 魯, son of Zhuang Shu 莊叔, II 718.

Music 樂 *yue*, its power on animals, I 116, plaintive music, I 183, its magical force, I 212–14, II 567, 654–55, 766, gay music, II 617.

Music = Classic of Music, II 831.

Naked People 躶 *luo* / 躶國 *luoguo*, savages, I 174, 189, 300, 321, II 592.

Nan 赧 = Nan Wang 赧王, last sovereign of the Zhou 周 dynasty, I 163, 296.

Nan Gong Da You 南宮大有, diviner, I 137.

Nan Rong 南容, disciple of Confucius, married to his niece, I 313, II 799, III Ch28 n17, Ch80 n53.

Nan Zi 南子, wife of Duke Ling 靈 of Wei 衛, invited Confucius, I 318.

Nanchang 南昌, now capital of Jiangxi 江西, II 800.

Nanyang 南陽, place in Henan 河南, I 221, III Ch81 n60.

Nature 性 *xing*, natural 正 *zheng*, concomitant 隨 *sui*, adverse 遭 *zao*, I 103, human nature affected by its environment, I 113, by instruction, I 118–19, different views on original nature, I 149 seq.

Natural feelings and natural disposition 情性, the basis of human activity, I 149, said to correspond to the *Yin* 陰 and the *Yang* 陽, I 153.

Neng 能, turtle with three legs, II 543.

Ni Kuan 倪寬, secretary of State, received the *Shangshu* 尚書, 2nd cent. BCE, I 134, 140, II 811, III Ch10 n44.

Nie Zheng 聶政, officer in the Han 韓 State, I 184–85, III Ch16 n101.

Nine Continents 九州 *jiuzhou*, I 360, 363, II 732, III Ch31 n37; of which China is one, II 731–32.

Nine Gifts 九錫 *jiuci*, chariot and horses, robes of State, musical instruments, vermilion doors, the right to use the central path, armed attendants, bows and arrows, battle-axes, sacrificial wines, II 711.

Nine Heavens 九垓 *jiugai*, I 264, III Ch24 n33.

Nine Provinces (Circuits) 九州 *jiuzhou* of ancient China = China, I 155, 295, 360, 361, 362, 363, 428, II 444, 479, 731–32, 758, III Ch2 n33, Ch13 n25, Ch16 n29, Ch24 n24, Ch26 n6, Ch39 n43, Ch74 n21.

Nine Relations 九族 *jiuzu*, ascendants and descendants, I 284–85.

Nine Savages 九夷 *jiuyi*, II 599.

Nine Statutes 九章 *jiuzhang*, the Penal Code of the Han 漢 dynasty, I 414–15, III Ch36 nn43, 51.

Nine Streams 九川 *jiuchuan*, I 367, III Ch32 n13.

Nine Tribes 九牧 *jiumu* of the time of Yu 禹, I 321, II 605.

Nine Tripods 九鼎 *jiuding*, of the Zhou 周 dynasty, auspicious, I 295–96, their history, I 296, made of gold, II 605, disappeared, II 650.

Nine Virtues 九德 *jiude*:—affability, mildness, bluntness, aptness for government, docility, straightforwardness, easiness, vigour, valour, I 383–85, III Ch33 n2.

Nine Wild Tribes of the East 九夷 *jiuyi*, I 321.

Ning Qi 審戚, privy councillor of Duke Huan 桓 of Qi 齊, 7th cent. BCE, I 183, 236, III Ch21 n41.

Niu Ai 牛哀, Duke of Lu 魯, changed into a tiger, I 107, 165, II 507, 627, 648.

Niu Que 牛缺, I 96–97.

Notes, musical, II 461, 654–55.

Noxious influences 祟 *chong*, II 500, 722 seq., 748.

Nü Wa 女媧, sister of Fu Xi 伏羲, I 357, 358–60, II 494, 496–97, III Ch46 n28.

Nursing of children, I 91.

Odes of the *Shijing* 詩經, 詩, I 414, 430, II 439, 609, 624, III Ch84 n41, Ch85 n15.

Omens (Portents) 驗 *yan*, I 120 seq., different kinds, I 120, II 715–16, lucky and unlucky auguries, I 188, 197, 208–9, II 769, of the mulberry and paper-mulberry, I 195 seq., II 569, during the Han 漢 epoch, I 320, 328–29, correspond to something good, II 524–25, happen spontaneously, II 524–25, large and small ones, II 534, presages not the commands of Heaven, II 536–37, auguries formed of a strange fluid, II 538, under Ming Di 明帝, II 584, under Guang Wu Di 光武帝, II 584, omens of universal peace not always the same, II 586 seq., 597, auspicious omens of the Han 漢, II 604–5, lucky omens follow an excellent man, II 608, omens of the Han 漢 time, II 613, 615, 620, shaped like man, II 661, indicate future happiness or misfortune, II 673, the lucky meet with lucky omens by chance, II 717–18, omens and signs are always true, II 721, omens of Zhou Gong 周公, II 783.

Ominous creatures 瑞物 *ruiwu*, have no species, are born by accident, II 522, from a propitious fluid, II 523.

One thousand seven hundred and ninety-three feudal States in the Zhou 周 time, I 300.

Original fluid 元氣 *yuanqi*, man endowed with it, II 445, resides only in living organisms, II 451, a child filled with it, II 695, 697, it is the finest essence between Heaven and Earth, II 695. *See also* Primogenial fluid

Orion and its sword, 參伐 *canfa*, II 506.

Orphan of Zhao 趙 趙孤, I 124, III Ch10 n45.

Ouyang 歐陽 = Ouyang Sheng 歐陽生, scholiast of the *Shangshu* 尚書, II 826, III Ch82 n23.

Paintings 圖畫 *tuhua*, popular legends the subjects of paintings, I 177, of portraits on walls, I 432, pictures of Nü Wa 女媧, II 496, pictures of dragons, II 500, paintings of tigers on doors, II 501, portraits of King Xiu Chu 休屠 and his wife, II 502, pictures of bears and elks painted on targets, II 503, pictures of their produce made by distant countries, II 605, portraits of Han 漢 officers under Xuan Di 宣帝, II 611.

Palmisters 察掌理者 *chazhanglizhe*, II 620.

Pang Shao Du 龐少都, scholar, I 419.

Pang Xian 龐捆, I 339, 341–42.

Parrots 鸚鵡 *yingwu*, can talk, I 244, II 439, 543.

Peach wood figure 桃象人 *taoxiangren*, warding off demons, I 416, II 501.

Pearls, I 295, 394, II 439, 577, III Ch8 n19, Ch67 n7; genuine ones in fishes, I 377, II 854, III Ch32 n45, and shells, I 115–16.

Pearl-tree in the farthest southwest 珠樹 *zhushu*, I 377.

Pei 沛, ancient State in Anhui 安徽, II 523.

Pei 沛, prefecture in Jiangsu 江蘇, I 100, 133, II 666, 717, 727, III Ch6 n8, Ch10 n42, Ch64 n94, Ch71 n8.

Penal Code 律 *lü* of the Han 漢 period, I 415, III Ch36 n43; drafted by Xiao He 蕭何, I 425, III Ch36 nn45, 51.

Peng 彭, city in Jiangsu 江蘇, II 606.

Peng Geng 彭更, disciple of Mencius, I 346, 351–52, III Ch30 n17.

Peng Sheng 彭生, Prince of Qi 齊, II 674, III Ch65 n19.

Peng Yue 彭越, King of Liang 梁, was pickled, I 176, II 594, 651, III Ch63 n67.

Peng Zu 彭祖, the Chinese Methusaleh, I 273, II 578.

Pengcheng 彭城, city in Jiangsu 江蘇, I 296, 297, II 606, III Ch26 n60.

Pengli 彭蠡, old name of the Poyang 鄱陽 lake, I 175, II 800.

Perfect man, I 147, 316, 428.

Personators of the dead 尸位 *shiwei*, I 404–5, III Ch35 n4.

Phantoms 妖 *yao* consist of the solar fluid, II 673, emit poison, II 675, 676.

Phenomenal changes 變 *bian*, are not brought about by government, I 186 seq., II 551, strange phenomenon on the sky, I 192, phenomenal changes in heaven spontaneously respond to prognostics, I 209, drought is a phenomenon of heat, I 215, locusts not entering the territory of a wise official, I 221, calamitous changes during the age of a Sage, II 615.

Phenomenalists 變家 *bianjia* or 變復之家 *bianfu zhi jia*, scholars who explained calamities and other natural phenomena by moral causes, I 190, 212, 219, II 456, 458, 460, 466, 467, 478–79, 482, 485, 505, 507, 510, 511, 513, III Ch45 n4.

Phœnix 鳳凰 *fenghuang*, II 516 seq.; did not come at Confucius's time, I 179, 320, II 534, 585, less light-winged than swallows, II 451, a holy bird, huge with a variegated plumage, II 516, accompanied by thousands of birds, II 520, phœnix and unicorn signs of universal peace, II 521, as big as a horse; 5 feet high, II 522–23, phœnix and unicorn appear for a holy emperor, II 530, kind-hearted and sage animals, II 530, in the time of Xuan Di 宣帝, II 531 seq., in the time of Yao 堯 and Shun 舜, II 531, 586, 587 seq., phœnix and unicorn, II 538, at the birth of Guang Wu Di 光武帝, II 597, in the times of Huang Di 黃帝, Yao 堯 and Shun 舜, II 597–98, of Wen Di 文帝, Wu Di 武帝, Xuan Di 宣帝, II 597–98, 606–7, the plumage of the phœnix has five colours, II 824.

Physicists 伎道之家 *jidao zhi jia*, II 499, 737, 738, III Ch74 n51.

Physiognomies 相 *xiang*, indicative of the future, I 131, of wealth and honour, I 133–34, the physiognomies of sage rulers must not be similar, II 586.

Physiognomist 相 *xiang*, I 195, II 658, III Ch11 n49, Ch12 n9; have divided human features into more than seventy classes, II 855.

Physiognomy, *see* Anthroposcopy.

Pictures, *see* Paintings.

Pigmies 小人 *xiaoren*, I 300, II 715, III Ch27 n8, devoured by Giants, II 508.

Pillar of Heaven 天柱 *tianzhu* = Kunlun 崑崙, I 357–58, 359, II 496, 845, III Ch31 n4.

Ping 平, Duke of Jin 晉, I 212–14, II 653, 666, III Ch63 n43.

Ping 平, Duke of Lu 魯, I 86, 133, 348, III Ch10 n40.

Ping 平, King of Chu 楚, II 797, III Ch80 n40, Ch85 n35.

Ping 平, King of Zhou 周, II 599, III Ch78 n35.

Ping 平, terrace, I 185, II 766.

Ping Di 平帝, Han 漢 Emperor, I 279, II 588, 596, 598, 599, 613, III Ch19 n72.

Ping Yuan 平原, Prince of, I 292, II 792.

Pingyuan 平原, place in Shandong 山東, I 185, II 662, 766.

Plan of the Yellow River 河圖 *hetu*, I 179, 216, 255, 320, II 534, 557, 585–87, 667, 765, 816, 824.

Pleiades, 昴 *mao*, see Venus, I 208, II 475; not visible when Mars comes forth, I 130.

Plum, may grow on a cherry-tree, II 563.

Poison 毒 *du*, II 677 seq., the hot air of the sun, II 677, bad men filled with a poisonous fluid, II 679, poison of glib-tongued people, II 682.

Polar star 極星 *jixing*, I 366, 斗極 *douji*, I 368.

Pole of heaven 天極 *tianji*, I 361, 362, 366.

Political intriguing 從橫 *zongheng*, I 390.

Poll tax 頭錢 *touqian*, from the seventh year, I 416.

Polygamy, its drawbacks, I 104.

Portents, *see* Omens.

Posthumous titles 謚 *shi*, I 229, 258–59, II 612, 623, 641–42, III Ch7 n8, Ch26 n38, Ch29 n7, Ch50 n51, Ch60 n26, Ch63 n17, Ch71 nn14, 15.

Prayer 禱 *dao*, that of Tang 湯, I 214, Confucius on prayer, I 214, 215.

Pregnant women, what they are to avoid, while with child, I 103–4.

Prescience 先知 *xianzhi*, not possessed by Sages, II 777 seq.

Prescription (recipe) 方 *fang*, II 794.

Primitive life, II 579, happy without virtue and knowledge, II 561–62.

Primogenial fluid 元氣 *yuanqi*, genuine and harmonious, all people filled with it, II 576–77, vague, diffuse, and unconscious, the human fluid a part of it, II 628–29.

Primordial generation of fish and grass, II 524.

Privies 更衣之室 *gengyi zhi shi*, II 696.

Prodigy, *see* Omen.

Prophecy books 讖記 *chenji*, II 766–67.

Propriety and righteousness upheld against Han Feizi 韓非子, I 332 seq.

Pu 濮, river in Shandong 山東, II 653, 675.

Puban 蒲坂, the modern Puzhoufu 蒲州府 in Shanxi 山西, I 126, 265.

Public instruction and criminal law what for, I 117.

Punishments meted out in autumn and winter, I 87, 252, II 455.

Purity 清 *qing*, different degrees of, I 73, may be polluted, I 80.

Purple boletus 紫芝 *zizhi*, felicitous

plant, I 145, eaten by Daoists, I 265; a lucky omen, II
589, 605, III Ch59 nn15, 20.

Qi 杞, State in Henan 河南, II 474,
III Ch43 n33.

Qi 戚, Lady, concubine of Han Gao
Zu 漢高祖, massacred by the
Empress Lü Hou 呂后, I 251,
III Ch23 n9.

Qi 齊, State in Shandong 山東, I 72,
75, 86, 116, 123, 141, 180,
187–88, 193, 196, 228, 236,
266, 269, 275, 283, 291, 292,
305, 334, 345, 346, 348, 397,
430, II 455, 461, 466, 471,
500, 509, 536, 570, 590, 596,
640, 646, 657, 663, 667, 674,
688, 697, 767, 778, 784, 791,
792, 798, 818, 834, III Ch1
n22, Ch3 nn4, 6, Ch6 n29,
Ch8 n27, Ch10 n20, Ch11
n7, Ch16 n8, Ch17 n10,
Ch19 n26, Ch20 n4, Ch24
n43, Ch26 n21, Ch27 n33,
Ch29 n9, Ch30 nn7, 20, Ch33
nn12, 30, Ch39 n35, Ch41
n1, Ch42 n7, Ch43 nn12, 25,
33, Ch43 n34, Ch54 nn3, 31,
Ch55 n49, Ch56 n20, Ch57
n38, Ch63 n36, Ch64 nn74,
91, 101, Ch65 n18, Ch77 n49,
Ch79 nn31, 38, Ch80 nn11,
49, 82, Ch81 nn20, 39, 45,
Ch85 nn22, 32, 46.

Qi 啟, successor of the Emperor Yu
禹, II 467, III 866.

Qi 棄 = Hou Ji 后稷, I 144, II 757,
758, III Ch77 n14.

Qi Diao Kai 漆雕開, philosopher,
disciple of Confucius, I 149,
III Ch13 nn1, 2.

Qi Ji 棄疾, Prince of Chu 楚, I 123.

Qi Liang 杞梁, officer of Qi 齊, I
210–11, II 471, 474–75, 481,
III Ch43 nn33, 34.

Qi Sheng 祁勝, made a rebellion in
Jin 晉, in the 6th cent. BCE,
I 150.

Qiancheng 千乘, place in Shandong
山東, II 826, III Ch82 n23.

Qiang 羌, Tibetan tribes in the west
of China, I 234, II 599, 701.

Qiang Rong 羌戎, western barbarians, I 291.

Qiantang 錢唐, city in Zhejiang 浙
江, I 176–77, II 766, 848, III
Ch16 n52.

Qiantang 錢塘, river, I 176–77, III
Ch2 n25, Ch16 n56.

Qiao 橋, mountain in Gansu 甘
肅 or Shanxi 陝西, where
Huang Di 黃帝 was buried, I
259, III Ch24 n7.

Qiao Zhong 橋種, tribe, II 599.

Qin 秦, State in Shanxi 陝西, I 74,
86, 99, 108, 109, 116, 124,
133, 136, 141, 146, 172, 185,
208, 209, 232, 277, 284, 291,
293, 333, 385, II 442, 455,
462, 473, 474, 475, 495, 500,
561, 570, 575, 596, 614, 638,
644–45, 647, 656, 727, 768,
793, 796, 811, 820, 834, 852,
III Ch3 n13, Ch8 n28, Ch11
n7, Ch15 n10, Ch19 n24,
Ch21 nn11, 35, 37, Ch25 nn6,
57, Ch26 nn32, 53, Ch29 n8,
Ch33 n14, Ch36 nn12, 17,
Ch41 n1, Ch52 n14, Ch54
n31, Ch58 n12, Ch64 nn16,
21, Ch65 n40, Ch78 n23,
Ch81 n58, Ch82 n54, Ch83
n15, Ch85 nn18, 32.

Qin 秦, dynasty, 249-206 BCE, I
    163, 296, 400, 411, 428, II
    557, 594, 619, 620, 703, 764,
    820, 827, 864, III 876, Ch11
    n45, Ch12 n21, Ch29 n14,
    Ch36 n51, Ch38 n4, Ch51
    n35, Ch59 n34, Ch60 n34,
    Ch64 n80, Ch81 n19.
Qin 秦 epoch, I 380, 419, II 567,
    581, 650, III Ch43 n24.
Qin Shi Huangdi 秦始皇, founder
    of the Qin 秦 dynasty, read-
    ing Han Feizi 韓非子, I 124,
    125, 141, 178, 185, 284, 296,
    297, II 566, 588, 597, 614,
    619, 652, 661–62, 663–64,
    665, 666, 765–66, 767, 797,
    856, III Ch8 n49, Ch15 n15,
    Ch16 n103, Ch21 nn16, 33,
    Ch24 n7, Ch25 n57, Ch33
    n21, Ch41 n8, Ch42 n32,
    Ch43 n18, Ch56 n30, Ch61
    n35, Ch63 n68, Ch64 nn59,
    79, Ch85 n28; burned the
    books, I 283, 412, II 620,
    638–39, 812.
Qin Xi 禽息, officer in Qin 秦, I 77,
    smashed his head, I 293, III
    Ch1 n29.
Qing Bu 黥布, King of Huainan 淮
    南, attacked by Han Gao Zu
    漢高祖, I 87, criminal who
    became a prince, I 138, III
    Ch11 n26.
Qing Du 慶都, Yao's 堯 mother, I
    163.
Qing Feng 慶封, high functionary
    of Qi 齊, I 430, III Ch38 n15.
Qinghe 清河, prefecture in Henan
    河南, I 125, III Ch9 n42.
Qinghe 清河, city in Shandong 山
    東, I 137.

Qingqiu 青丘, wild region, II 567.
Qingzhou 青州, one of the Nine
    Provinces of Yu 禹, II 732.
Qiong Sang 窮桑 = Shao Hao 少昊,
    III 869.
Qisi 期思, river, II 442, III Ch39
    n20.
Qiu 丘, name of Confucius, II 739.
Qiu 求 = Ran Qiu 冉求, disciple of
    Confucius, I 392, II 494, III
    Ch33 n40.
Qixian 蘄縣, district in Anhui 安
    徽, II 523.
Qu 曲, river in Jiangsu 江蘇, I 178,
    III Ch16 n55.
Qu Bo Yu 蘧伯玉, disciple of Con-
    fucius, I 327–28, II 557, 799,
    850, III Ch54 n8, Ch85 n9.
Qu Ping 屈平 = Qu Yuan 屈原, I
    102, III Ch6 n19; his death,
    I 103.
Qu Yuan 屈原, famous statesman
    and poet who drowned
    himself, I 128, 176, 424, II
    444, 462, 472, 655, 839, III
    Ch2 n13, Ch6 n19, Ch10 n2,
    Ch16 n40, Ch39 n46, Ch43
    nn13, 14.
Quanling 泉陵, district in Hunan
    湖南, II 605, 606, III Ch59
    nn15, 23.
Qucheng 曲城, place in Shandong
    山東, I 432.
Queli 闕里, place where Confucius
    died, I 98.
Quipos, II 578, III Ch23 n19.

Rain 雨 *yu*, fluid emitted by
    Heaven, I 250, its origin, I
    381, becomes dew and frost,
    I 381, caused by the moon,
    I 381, 479 seq., it rains from

the Taishan 太山, I 381, II 481, portended by insects, by the expansion of chords, and by chronic diseases, II 468–69, rain like tears, II 481–82, when Heaven is going to rain, ants come out, II 515, the Rain God 雨師 *Yu Shi*, II 751, 760.

Rain sacrifice 大雩 *dayu*, I 243, II 478 seq., 498, 499, 502, 565, 567, 615, 674–75, 759–60, 837, III Ch77 n38.

Ran Niu 冉牛, disciple of Confucius, II 788.

Ran You 冉有, disciple of Confucius, I 327.

Rat 鼠病 *shubing*, skin-disease cured by eating a cat, I 225.

Rats 鼠 *shu*, their agitation indicates an extraordinary calamity, II 508.

Raven 三足烏 *sanzuwu*, three-legged, cannot live in the sun, I 373.

Red bird 赤雀 *chique*, red crow, II 534, felicitous omen indicating the investiture of Wen Wang 文王, II 597.

Red Emperor 赤帝 *chidi*, I 124, II 664, 896, III Ch64 n81.

Ren An 任安, governor, II 443.

Rhinopithecus 狌狌 *xingxing*, knows the past, I 244, II 774, 蜼蠼, II 507, 543, 772.

Rites 禮 *li* = *Liji* 禮記, I 413, II 494, 503, 566, 574, 740, 747, 759, 817, 831, III Ch82 n19.

Ritual 禮 *li* of the Han 漢 period, I 415.

Rivers 百川 *baichuan*, like veins and arteries; their flowing forwards and backwards like human respiration, I 177.

Rong 戎, western barbarians, I 287, 300, II 591, 599, 658, 768, III Ch26 n6, Ch64 n34, Ch78 n33.

Ru Shou 蓐收, Genius of Autumn, II 757, III 869, 874, Ch77 n17.

Ru Yi 如意, son of Han Gao Zu 漢高祖, poisoned by Lü Hou 呂后, II 649–50, III Ch65 n43.

Runan 汝南, place in Henan 河南, I 306, II 844.

Ruo 若, river, II 671, 745.

Sacrifices 祭祀 *jisi*, II 749 seq., 756 seq.; before the winter solstice 臘 *la*, I 416, to the Gate, the Door, the Well and the Hearth 門戶井竈 *men hu jing zao*, I 416, to the Spirits of the Land and Grain, Shen Nong, and the Ling Star 杜稷先農靈星 *duji xiannong lingxing*, I 416, to Hou Tu 后土 and Heaven and Earth, II 589, the sacrifices of the Confucianists are merely symbolical, II 683, 708 seq., sacrificing is feeding the ghosts, II 708-9, sacrifices do not bring happiness, II 709, the meaning of sacrifices, II 746–47, 749–50, to Mountains, Gates, and Doors, II 748, of no avail, II 748, of millet, rice-cake, and soup offered to Earth, II 750, presented to Heaven and Earth, Mountains and

Rivers, the Spirits of the Land and Grain, II 750–51, 756, of an ox, II 754, to the Five Genii and the ancestors, II 756, to the Five Emperors and Three Rulers, II 756, to Shang Di 上帝, to the Six Superior Powers, II 756, the imperial, suburban, patriarchal, and ancestral sacrifices, II 756, sacrifices to the Seasons, to Heat and Cold, the Sun, the Moon, the Stars, the Four Cardinal Points, to Water and Drought, II 757, of wood, a calf, a sheep, II 757 seq., motives of sacrifices:—gratitude and ancestor worship, II 757, they are not enjoyed by ghosts or spirits, but merely symbolical, II 761, to Earth, at the meals, II 762.

Sages 聖人 *shengren*, endued with the harmonious fluid, I 93, not imbued with a special fluid, I 166, credited with the gift of prophecy, I 240, produced by Heaven every 500 years, I 349–50, Sages regarded as perfect, II 482, three Sages of the Zhou 周 period, II 590, the feelings of a Sage appear from his utterances, II 619, 823, not supernatural or foreknowing, II 764 seq., not easy to know, II 806, Sages write the classics and Worthies, the commentaries to the classics, II 829–30.

Sage birds and animals, II 527.

Salt 鹽 *yan*, moisture trickling down, I 429, salt-wells in Xizhou 西州, I 429, salt-wagon, II 448, salt-land, II 599.

San Miao 三苗, aboriginal tribes or their chieftain, II 601, III Ch26 n5.

Sanfu 三府, some officers, II 618.

Sangui 三歸, name of a tower, II 573.

Savages, with covered breasts, hanging ears, Pigmies and Bazhong 跋踵, I 300.

Scarlet Bird 朱鳥 *zhuniao*, the southern quadrant of solar mansions, I 143, 145, 146, 147, 159, 240, III 901, 919, Ch59 n41.

Scholars 儒生 *rusheng* and Officials 文吏 *wenli*, their appreciation and their superiority, I 393 seq., 403 seq., both have their shortcomings, I 410 seq., 419–20, scholars ousted by officials, II 447 seq., ordinary 世儒 *shiru*, professors 博士 *boshi*, literary 文儒 *wenru*, II 824–25, scholars able to explain one Classic 儒生 *rusheng*, learned men, well versed in literature 通人 *tongren*, men of letters 文人 *wenren*, eminent scholars composing themselves 鴻儒 *hongru*, II 439 seq.

Schools 庠序 *xiangxu*, founded from olden times, I 332–33.

Screeching owl 鵬鳥 *funiao*, bird of ill omen, II 509, 536.

Screen 扆 *yi*, partition between the door and the window in the palace, I 183.

Scroll of the Luo, 洛書 *luoshu*, I 216, 255, II 557, 586, 667, 816, 824, III Ch81 n32.

Secretary falcon 鴆 *zhen*, poisonous, II 680, III Ch66 n10.

Sensations, how caused by the mental fluid, II 669.

Seven Sacrifices 七祀 *qisi*, performed by the Emperor, II 758.

Seventy odd disciples of Confucius 七十子 *qishi zi*, all Sages, I 94–95, 113, 233, 308–9, 312, III Ch13 n1.

Shanfu 單父, place in Shandong 山東, I 136, III Ch82 n44.

Shangshu 尚書, *Shujing* 書經, "Canon of History," I 146, 183, 198, 213, 250, 288, 294, 300 seq., 319, 322, 344, 361, 381, 391, 413–14, II 458, 479, 480, 520, 535, 544, 564–66, 573, 575, 590, 600, 609, 617–18, 674, 723, 756, 781, 805, 810 seq., 826, 831, 849, III 865 seq., 882, 888, 890, 893, 904, 905, 910, 911, Ch8 n16, Ch16 nn18, 20, 33, Ch19 n10, Ch25 nn10, 21, 35, 49, Ch27 n5, Ch27 n35, Ch28 n3, Ch31 n13, Ch33 n2, Ch35 nn14, 23, Ch36 n35, Ch37 n4, Ch38 n33, Ch42 nn24, 54, 57, Ch43 n22, Ch45 n23, Ch46 nn15, 19, Ch51 n23, Ch52 nn28, 38, Ch55 nn4, 8, 10, 24, 30, 69, Ch58 n19, Ch59 n33, Ch60 nn2, 5, Ch70 n25, Ch81 nn1, 10, 28, 32, Ch82 n24, Ch85 nn14, 32, App.I n36.

Shangzao 上造, honorary title under the Han 漢 dynasty, I 416, III Ch 36 n69.

Shanhaijing 山海經, "Mountain and Sea Classic," ancient geographical work, I 240, 242, 376, 377, 433, II 672, III Ch7 n19, Ch10 n35, Ch31 nn23, 30, Ch64 n8.

Shanshan 鄯善, people south of the Lobnor, II 591, 599.

Shanyin 山陰, river in Zhejiang 浙江, I 176–77, III Ch16 nn43, 52.

Shanyu 單于, title of the chieftain of the Xiongnu 匈奴, I 121.

Shang 商, dynasty, 1766–1122 BCE, I 72, 128, 188, II 592, 595, 739, 758, III Ch1 nn5, 6, 27, Ch7 n8, Ch8 n6, Ch9 n15, Ch10 n13, Ch11 n2, Ch13 n4, Ch22 n10, Ch25 n9, Ch26 nn38, 46, Ch29 n22, Ch30 n35, Ch36 n9, Ch37 n9, Ch55 n31, Ch55 n63, Ch63 n37, Ch71 n19, Ch81 n55, Ch85 n52.

Shang 商 = Bu Shang 卜商, name of Zi Xia 子夏, I 230.

Shang Chen 商臣, son of King Cheng 成 of Chu 楚, II 641.

Shang Di 上帝, God, II 756, III Ch7 n14, Ch19 n41.

Shang Fu 尚父 = Shi Shang Fu 師尚父, II 544.

Shang Jun 商均, son of Shun 舜, I 103, 150, 152, II 524.

Shang Qu 商瞿 = Zi Mu 子木, disciple of Confucius, I 434.

Shang Yang 商鞅 = Wei Yang 衛鞅, Prince of Shang 商, I 74, 236, 424, II 442, 561, 827, 834,

852, III Ch1 n20, Ch21 n37, Ch34 n18, Ch82 n46, Ch83 n18.

Shang Zi 商子, minister of Wu Wang 武王, II 461.

Shanglin 上林, imperial park, II 516, 520, 589.

Shangshu dazhuan 尚書大傳, work on the *Shangshu* 尚書, II 492, III Ch46 n19.

Shangyang 商羊, one-legged bird, portending rain, II 468.

Shangyu 上虞, river in Zhejiang 浙江, I 176, III Ch16 n52.

Shangyuxian 上虞縣 = Shangyu 上虞, city in Zhejiang 浙江, II 848, 849, III Ch16 n43.

Shao 邵, Duke of, brother of Wu Wang 武王, I 93, 112, II 445, 608, 610, III Ch60 n13.

Shao Hao 少昊, legendary emperor, II 757, III 869, 874, Ch24 n6, Ch36 n13, Ch77 nn15, 16, 18.

Shao Zheng Mao 少正卯, scholar in Lu 魯, II 519, 807, III Ch50 n11.

Shaqiu 沙丘, place in Zhili 直隸, I 185, II 662, 764–65, 766.

She 葉, Duke of Chu 楚, II 498, 500.

She Ji 社稷, Spirits of the Land and Grain, II 757.

Shen Bao Xu 申包胥, nobleman of Chu 楚, II 495–96.

Shen Buhai 申不害, minister under Prince Zhao 昭 of Han 韓, I 424, III Ch37 nn36, 37.

Shen Feng 沈酆, prefect, II 605.

Shen Gong 申公, editor of the *Shijing* 詩經, II 826, III Ch82 n22.

Shen Nong 先農 *xiannong*, god of agriculture, I 416, 神農 *shennong*, I 218, II 512, III Ch7 n15, Ch8 n21, Ch77 nn22, 27, Ch81 nn29, 31.

Shen Sheng 申生, Prince of Jin 晉, I 211, II 637–38, 675–76, III Ch63 n10.

Shen Shu and Yu Lü 神荼鬱壘, the door gods, who frighten the ghosts away, II 501, 672, III Ch65 n16.

Shen Tong 沈同, officer of Qi 齊, I 346–47, III Ch30 n21.

Shen Tu Di 申徒狄, drowned himself in the Huanghe 黃河, I 176, III Ch16 n41.

Shen Xi 申喜, native of Chu 楚, I 221, III Ch19 n69.

Shen Zi 慎子, Daoist philosopher, I 241, 242, III Ch37 n36.

Sheng 勝, Marquis of Jiang 絳, I 139.

Shengmu 勝母, village, I 261.

Shenzhou 神州, China, I 360, 362.

Shi Ji 師己, officer of Lu 魯, I 196.

Shi Qi Zi 石祁子, son of Shi Tai 石駘, II 718.

Shi Shang Fu 師尚父 = Lü Shang 呂尚, minister of war of Wen Wang 文王, II 543.

Shi Tai 石駘, nobleman of Wei 衛, II 718.

Shi Wei 豕韋, noble under the Shang 商 dynasty, I 242.

Shi Zi 世子 = Shi Shi 世碩, Confucian philosopher, on human nature, I 149, 154.

Shi Zi 時子, officer of Qi 齊, I 345.

Shi Zi Yu 史子魚, officer of Wei 衛, II 850, III Ch85 n9.

Shi'an 始安, district in Guangxi 廣西, II 606.

Shijing 詩經, "Book of Odes," I 112, 146, 152, 162, 163, 167, 172, 187–88, 288, 300–2, 322, 381, 414, II 467, 479, 480, 514, 526, 544, 548, 600, 610, 611, 624, 682, 781, 812, 813, 826, III Ch15 nn3, 20, Ch25 n49, Ch35 n4, Ch36 nn34, 36, Ch42 n54, Ch60 n15, Ch80 n53, Ch81 n1, Ch82 nn22, 24, Ch83 n39, Ch84 n41, Ch85 n15.

Shiyi 施夷, terrace, II 653.

Shou 首, mountain in Shanxi 山西, whose copper was exploited by Huang Di 黃帝, I 258, 260.

Shou Wang 壽王, official under Han Wu Di 漢武帝, II 795–96, III Ch80 nn32, 35.

Shouling 壽陵, place, II 767.

Shoushan 首山, mountain in Shanxi 山西, II 537.

Shouyang 首陽, mountain in Shanxi 陝西, I 355, II 521, 594.

Shu 叔姬, Lady Shu 叔姬 of Jin 晉, I 150, III Ch13 n5.

Shu 蜀, kingdom in Sichuan 四川, I 263, II 599, 600, 623, 828, III Ch18 n26.

Shu 舒, State in Anhui 安徽, II 853.

Shu An 叔安 = Shu Song 叔宋, I 241, III Ch22 n19.

Shu Hu 叔虎, half-brother of Shu Xiang 叔向, II 681.

Shu Liang He 叔梁紇, father of Confucius, II 524.

Shu Qi 叔齊, brother of Bo Yi 伯夷, famous for his integrity, II 521, 594, III Ch8 n7, Ch21 n23.

Shu Song 叔宋, I 241, III Ch22 n19.

Shu Sun Tong 叔孫通, high official of Han Gao Zu 漢高祖, I 117, 413, 425.

Shu Xiang 叔向, officer in Jin 晉, II 681, III Ch22 n2, Ch66 nn19, 21.

Shun 舜, ancient emperor, I 72, 92, 98, 113, 121, 129, 136, 166, 168, 173–75, 177, 178, 183, 190, 215, 218, 229, 236–37, 242, 260, 275–76, 282, 286–87, 303, 309, 319, 338, 346, 349, 391, II 463, 467, 500, 516, 517, 524, 528, 529, 531, 541, 542, 547, 556, 559–60, 567, 582–84, 585, 586, 590–91, 593, 595, 597, 599, 601, 607, 610, 614, 621, 656, 746, 756, 760, 766, 782–83, 788, 789, 791, 795, 797, 805–6, 820–21, 837, 852, 853, 855, 857, 859, 863, III 889, Ch1 nn17, 18, 19, Ch3 n3, Ch4 n8, Ch6 n24, Ch9 nn1, 2, 5, Ch10 n21, Ch11 nn1, 4, Ch15 nn18, 37, Ch16 nn16, 18, Ch18 n14, Ch19 n52, Ch23 n15, Ch24 nn6, 13, Ch25 n1, Ch26 n5, Ch27 n12, Ch28 nn2, 3, Ch33 n36, Ch36 n36, Ch42 n55, Ch52 n11, Ch56 n29, Ch60 n11, Ch64 n37, Ch65 n14, Ch79 n28, Ch80 nn1, 45–47, Ch81 nn31, 65, Ch85 nn20, 32, 43, 55, App.I n2.

Shusun Muzi 叔孫穆子, nobleman of Lu 魯, II 659, III Ch71 n15.

Si 姒, family name of the Xia 夏 dynasty, I 162, 166, II 739.

Si 泗, river in Shandong 山東, I 136, 178, 230, 296, II 557, 645, 646, 655, 665, III Ch16 n65, Ch21 n4, Ch26 n60.

Si Dai 駟帶, officer of Zheng 鄭, II 642–44, 676.

Sickness expelled at the end of the year 逐疫 *zhuyi*, I 416, II 493.

Sickness not a punishment of Heaven, II 459.

Sight and hearing depending on distance, I 171–72, does not extend beyond ten Li, I 301.

Silk, silk ribbons 綬 *shou*, I 183, manufacture of silk pongees 帛 *bo*, I 200–1, gauze, white and coloured 紗縞 *shazi*, I 401, tissues of Lu 魯, 魯縞 *lugao*, very fine, I 424–25, silk embroidery, II 439, 623, a red silk thread used in combating inundations, II 492–93, red silk denotes heat, II 495.

Sima Qian 司馬遷 / 司馬子長, historian and author of the *Shiji* 史記, I 233, II 440, 474, 613, 825, 836–37, III Ch4 n13, Ch19 n24, Ch20 n18, Ch21 nn20, 22, Ch24 n17, Ch36 n13, Ch39 n17, Ch54 n15, Ch57 n40, Ch83 n18.

Sima Xiangru 司馬相如, scholar and poet of the Han 漢 period, II 463, 613, 619, 804, 826, 827, III Ch52 n33, Ch82 n30.

Sishang 泗上, place in Shandong 山東, II 664.

Six Arts 六藝 *liuyi*:—ceremonial, music, archery, charioteer-ing, writing, mathematics, II 621, 769, III Ch83 n58.

Six Canons (Classics) 六經 *liujing*, the Five Canons and the Classic of Music, I 171, 419, II 590, 831.

Six Departments of Literature 六略 *liulüe*, under the Han 漢 dynasty:—classics, six arts, philosophy, poetry, military science, and divination, II 839, 840.

Six Domestic Animals 六畜 *liuchu*, the horse, the ox, the goat, the pig, the dog, and the fowl, II 627, 695–96, 709, III 919.

Six Honoured Ones 六宗 *liuzong*, II 757, III Ch77 n11.

Six Institutions of the Zhou 周 dynasty 六典 *liudian*:—admin-istration, instruction, rites, police, jurisdiction, public welfare, I 413, II 817–18, III Ch81 n35.

Six Passions 六情 *liuqing*:—cheer-fulness, anger, grief, joy, love, and hatred, II 469, III Ch43 n4.

Six Reigns 六代 *liudai*, probably:—Yao 堯, Shun 舜, Yu 禹, Tang 湯, Wen Wang 文王 and Wu Wang 武王 also called the Five Monarchs, II 612.

Six States 六國 *liuguo*:—Yan 燕, Zhao 趙, Han 韓, Wei 魏, Qi 齊, and Chu 楚, leagued against Qin 秦, I 174, 195, 196, 198, 335, 385, 390, 424, 430, II 453, 480, 493, 494, 552, 570, III Ch11 n7, Ch46 n31.

Sixty-Four Diagrams 六十四卦 *liushisigua*, composed by Wen Wang 文王, I 412, II 578, 816–17, 843–44, III Ch81 n41.

Solstices 至 *zhi* in summer and winter, I 365, 370–71.

Song 誦, father of Wang Chong 王充, II 848.

Song 宋, State, the north-western corner of Jiangsu 江蘇 Province, I 100, 109, 183, 184, 186, 188, 190, 191, 193, 207, 226–27, 255, 257, 266, 291, 297, 316, 338, 345, 376, 380, II 475–76, 522, 552, 557, 558, 559, 569, 573, 578, 590, 646–47, 668, 676, 739, 752, 753, 765, 781, 786, III Ch6 n9, Ch16 n95, Ch19 n17, Ch20 nn2, 6, Ch26 n22, Ch28 n47, Ch54 nn14, 31, Ch55 n59, Ch57 nn13, 38, Ch63 n40, Ch65 n34, Ch74 n31, Ch76 n5, Ch77 n41, Ch78 n6, Ch79 n43, Ch85 n32.

Song Weng Yi 宋翁一, officer of Han Xuan Di 漢宣帝, II 607.

Song Yu 宋玉, poet of Chu 楚, II 444, III Ch39 n45.

Sophists 辯士 *biantu*, poison flowing from their mouths, II 682.

Sorcerers 巫 *wu*, employed in case of misfortune to expel evil influences, I 395, to be burned to obtain rain, II 480, wizards know good and ill luck, II 543, mischievous magician, II 600, filled with the *Yang* 陽 fluid, II 674,

678, live in the South, II 675, can predict fate, II 675, ghosts speak through their mouths, II 774.

Sou 叟 = Gu Sou 瞽瞍, Shun's 舜 father, II 863.

Soul 魂 *hun*, the souls of the dead are dissolved and cannot hear any more, II 641; animal soul 魄 *po* and mind 魂 *hun*, II 643, the soul = vital fluid, II 660, roaming about during a dream, II 660.

Sound, its fluid 音氣 *yinqi*, II 481.

Southern Circuit 南郡 *nanjun* = Dongjun 東郡 in Hubei 湖北, II 678.

Sparrows turn into clams, I 107, 261–62, II 525.

Specialists studying only one Classic, I 411, 412, 419, 429, one Classic does not suffice, I 430, II 439, 440.

Speech and fire have the same essence, II 679–80.

Spirits 神 *shen* / 鬼神 *guishen*, it seems as if the spirits helped the happy and caused the misfortune of the miserable, I 83, 227, Spirit of Heaven, I 179, II 481, called down by sacrifices, I 201, alighting on the Kunlun 崑崙, I 218, believed to punish the guilty, I 230, diffuse and incorporeal, I 239, 253, II 747, can soar, I 239, what is vague and unsubstantial has the nature of a spirit, I 240, spirits Heaven's angels, I 252, useless to immolate to spirits in case of sickness, II 483, spirits of the land attacked, II 491, spirits of the land the chiefs of all *Yin* 陰, II 495, spirits speak to men by images, II 501, their fluid like clouds and rain, II 501, persons that after death come to life again are looked upon as genii, II 599, diffuse and shapeless 恍惚無形 *huanghu wuxing*, II 626, 神 *shen* spirit, a name of the active principle, II 626, 神氣 *shenqi* the spiritual fluid forms man and at death reverts to its original state, II 626; spirits are unconscious; II 631, spirit of the house, II 691, a spirit disposes of good and bad luck, II 691, mischievous spirits, II 691, the spirits of the year and the months, II 691, spirits of Heaven and Earth must have equal minds, II 700, are treated like men, II 702, the mouth and stomach of a spirit must be like those of man, II 703, the Sages do not speak of spirits, II 712, no spirits more powerful than Heaven and Earth, II 733, 734, *jia* 甲, *yi* 乙 are spirits of Heaven and Earth, II 738, clothes, 5-6 inches long, offered to spirits, II 755.

Spirit bird/spiritual birds 神雀 *shenque*, II 521, auspicious portent, II 589, 598, 619.

Spirit of Earth 土神 *tushen*, II 712, 717, 750, III 911; propitiated after the building of a house, II 746-47.

Spirit of Heaven 天神 *tianshen*, I 164, 179, II 481, 563, 717, 730, 731, 750; like a king in his residence, I 239, 251-52, angry, I 248, changing his mind, I 322, 324, reprimanding a sovereign, II 459, impersonated by a man, II 663.

Spirit of Rain 雨師 *yushi*, II 654.

Spirit of Sickness 疫鬼 *yigui*, II 745-46.

Spirit of the Wind 風伯 *fengbo*, II 654.

Spirit Tower 靈臺 *lingtai*, I 201.

Spirit vessels 明器 *mingqi*, buried with the dead, II 687-88, III Ch67 n15.

Spiritism by means of mediums in a trance, II 629.

Spontaneity 自然 *ziran*, II 554 seq.; of fate, I 128, 132-33, and time, I 133, means absence of purpose, II 457-58; the principle of Heaven, II 457-58, 499.

Spontaneous fluid 氣自爲 *qiziwei* / 自然之氣 *ziran zhi qi*, I 143, II 562, 564, 598, III Ch54 n32.

Spontaneous harmony of heaven and earth, when it rains, I 381.

Spook 妖 *yao*, II 653 seq.

Spring and Autumn 春秋 *Chunqiu*, work of Confucius, I 327-28, 414, II 494, 578, 810, 814, 815-16, 819-20, 831, III Ch28 n28.

Spring and Autumn period, 722-480 BCE, I 241, 297, 305, 374, 376, 378, II 474, 479, 490, 519, 520, 522, 526, 536, 565, 644, 707, 708, 814,

III Ch22 n14.

Staff, of jade 玉杖 *yuzhang*, presented to old people, I 416, pigeon-staff 鳩杖 *jiuzhang*, I 416, III Ch36 n71.

Stars 星 *xing*, their effluence 氣 *qi* gives wealth and honour, I 101, of the same essence as the sun and the moon, I 207, are the productions of Heaven, I 217, stars are not round, I 376, their size a hundred Li, I 379, produces and develops things on earth, II 670, are attached to heaven, II 751.

Stoves 鑪 *lu*, used in summer, I 75.

Struggle for existence, I 158 seq.

Style, II 853 seq.

Styles 筆 *bi* and pencils, I 407–8.

Su Bo A 蘇伯阿, Lord Marshall and fortune teller, could tell the future from the currents of wind, I 127, II 597.

Su Qin 蘇秦, statesman of the 4th cent. BCE, I 136, 305, 385–86, 389–90, II 481, 688, 834, 852, III Ch11 n8, Ch27 n34, Ch33 nn14, 21.

Su Wu 蘇武, high officer, went as envoy to the Xiongnu 匈奴, II 436, 464, III Ch38 n51, Ch42 n36.

Su Yong 蘇永, soldier, I 126, 145.

Success 遇 *yu*, depends upon time, I 71, definition of luck = success, I 76–77, earnestness of purpose does not secure it, I 100–1, success of designs is invisible, I 146.

Sui 隨, Marquis of, made artificial pearls, I 115, III Ch8 n19.

Suipo 歲破, unlucky day, II 728.

Sun 日 *ri*, is fire, I 204, 207, 243, 372, 377, ten suns in Yao's 堯 time, I 204–5, 376–78, 380, II 738, 845, III Ch32 n40, Ch74 n16, fluid, I 205, came back at the command of Duke Xiang 襄 of Lu 魯, I 206–7, sun and moon bring about summer and winter, I 207, moves 1 degree = 2,000 Li every day, I 207, 371, 372, II 499, 738, a white halo encircling the sun, I 208, reverts to the meridian, I 209, II 474, 846, motion of the sun and the moon, I 357, 364 seq., takes 16 different courses during a year, not nine, I 366, its different size in the morning and at noon, I 369, sun and moon like ants crawling on a mill-stone are carried along by heaven from east to west, I 371, 372, a three-legged raven in the sun, I 373, sun and moon not round, I 376, encircled by a white halo, when Jing Ke 荊軻 stabbed Shi Huangdi 始皇帝, II 475, traverses several thousand Li in a quarter of an hour, II 616, the sovereign's virtue equalling sun and moon, II 622, solar fluid = heavenly fluid, II 676, the sun came back, II 845.

Sun Qing 孫卿, philosopher of the 3rd cent. BCE, I 152, 153, 155, 436, III Ch84 n1.

Sun-stroke 火流所刺 *huoliu suoci*, the effect of poisonous air, II 678–79.

Sun Wu 孫武, celebrated general and writer on the art of war, 6th cent. BCE, I 407.

Sunshu Ao 孫叔敖, minister of Chu 楚, I 227–28, III Ch39 n20.

Sunyi 孫一, ancestor of Wang Chong 王充, III 848.

Supernatural powers 神靈 *shenling*, I 296, II 536, 715, 766, do not exist, II 772–73.

Surnames, personal names, and styles 姓名字 *xingmingzi*, II 739 seq.

Swearing by Heaven, I 318 seq.

Sweet dew 甘露 *ganlu*, lucky omen, produced by the harmonious fluid, II 523, 529, 531, 538, 539, 545–46, 586, 589, 598, 606, 607, 608, III Ch52 n48.

Sword of honour 佩刀 *peidao*, worn on the right, blade for fighting 舞刀 *wudao*, worn on the left side, I 417, the sword of Han Gao Zu 漢高祖 was three feet long, II 595, swords either pointed or sharp, II 828.

Swords, their manufacture, I 115, famous swords, I 294.

Swordsmen 劍伎之家 *jianji zhi jia*, I 432–33.

Symbolical punishments 象刑 *xiangxing*, of the Han 漢 time, I 414–15, II 693–94.

Sympathy 同氣 *tongqi*, peculiar sympathy between Zeng Zi 曾子 and his mother, I 220–21.

Tablets, tablets joined together form an essay, II 442, tablets in the ancestral temple, one foot two inches long, II 503, of two feet four inches 二尺四寸 *erchi sicun* for the Classics, II 590, joined together for writing, II 823, covered with elegant compositions, II 826.

Tai 邰, city in Shanxi 陝西, I 144.

Tai 邰, fief of the Zhou 周 in Shanxi 陝西, I 301.

Tai Bo 太伯, son of Dan Fu 亶父, I 144, II 460, 464, 599, 680, 694, III Ch12 n5.

Tai Gong 太公, helpmate of Wen Wang 文王, I 73, 236, 277, 334, 336–38, II 595, 667, 719, 721, 767, III Ch10 n12, Ch29 nn9, 10, 18, Ch40 n20, Ch64 n101, Ch85 n44.

Tai Gong 太公, father of Gao Zu 高祖, I 163.

Tai Gong Wang 太公王 = Tai Gong 太公, minister of Wen Wang 文王, II 860, 863, III Ch25 n19, Ch85 n44.

Tai Jia 太甲, Shang 商 Emperor, II 568, 647, III Ch63 n39.

Tai Wang 太王, grandfather of Wen Wang 文王, II 569, 639, 694.

Tai Wu 太戊, Emperor of the Shang 商 dynasty, II 490, 569, III Ch18 n4, Ch55 n31.

Taia 太阿, famous sword, I 115.

Taihua 太華, mountain in the west, I 173.

Tail 尾 *wei*, constellation, II 475–76, 506, 552, III Ch10 n24, Ch43 n43.

Taiqiu 太邱, place in Henan 河南, I 297, III Ch26 n59.

Taishan 太山, circuit in Shandong 山東, II 511

Taishan 太山, Mount Tai 太山, sacred mountain in Shandong 山東, I 171, 174, 260, 311, 368, 379, 381, 405, 420, II 439, 481, 524, 566, 570, 588, 646, 773, 828 = 岱 *dai*, II 444.

Taishan 太山, mountain in the West, II 654.

Taisui 太歲, the opposite of Jupiter, II 729 seq.; which in moving one's residence must be avoided, II 729 seq.

Taiwei 太微, constellation, I 251.

Taixuanjing 太玄經, metaphysical work of Yang Xiong 揚雄 / Yang Zi Yun 揚子雲, II 440, 826, 839, 845, III Ch61 n61.

Talents 才 *cai*, great and small talents do not harmonise, I 72–73, minor talents may please and higher ones be despised, I 74, useless talents, I 75, high and low talents, II 440-41, many brilliant talents in the Han 漢 time, II 440–41, the Han 漢 fertile in literary talents, II 446, talents difficult to find, II 618, from a man's style one may infer his talent, II 619, it does not happen that men of talents have no leisure for literary compositions, II 827, not necessarily awkward in business, II 828.

Tallow candles 脂燭 *zhizhu*, II 595–96.

Tan Tai Zi Yu 澹臺子羽, disciple of Confucius, I 141.

Tang 唐, Yao's 堯 territory, I 121, 152, 336, II 587, 595, 611, 797, 820 = Yao 堯, II 591, 622.

Tang 湯, founder of the Shang 商 dynasty, I 73, 128, 129, 135, 209, 210, 214–16, 349, 411, II 482, 484, 493, 549–51, 564, 565, 568, 582, 594, 595, 597, 646, 757, 761, 786, 794, 820, 864, III Ch11 n2, Ch18 n14, Ch30 n35, Ch36 n9, Ch55 nn4, 63, Ch85 n52.

Tang Ju 唐舉, physiognomist, I 141–42, III Ch11 n50.

Tang Le 唐勒, poet of Chu 楚, II 444.

Tang Lin 唐林 = Tang Zi Gao 唐子高, memorialist, II 839, 845, III Ch37 n13, Ch39 nn32, 37.

Tang Shu Yu 唐叔虞, son of Wu Wang 武王, II 557, 667, 824.

Tang Yang 唐鞅, officer in Song 宋, I 257.

Tang Zi Gao 唐子高 = Tang Lin 唐林, memorialist, I 420, 435, II 440, 443.

Tanggu 湯谷, Hot Water Abyss, whence the sun rises, I 378 seq., III Ch32 n37.

Tangxi 棠溪, place in Henan 河南, I 115, II 680.

Tao Tang 陶唐, family seat and clan of the Emperor Yao 堯, I 242, III Ch22 n22.

Tao Zhu 陶朱, name assumed by Fan Li 范蠡, minister of Yue 越, I 85, II 784.

Taowu 檮杌, history of the Chu 楚 State, II 819, 844, III Ch81 n47.

Taoyang 洮陽, district in Guangxi 廣西, II 606.

Tattooing the body 文身 *wenshen*, I 174, II 599, 694.

Tempest, expression of Heaven's anger, I 238–39, 246–47.

Ten Stems and Twelve Branches 支干 *zhiqian*, cyclical signs, II 737, 738, III 870, 874, 902, 924.

Ten Worthies 十賢 *shixian*, I 197, III Ch18 n15.

Teng 滕, Duke of, I 136.

Territory 地 *di*, of the Yin 殷 and Zhou 周 dynasties measured 5,000 Li, that of the Han 漢 10,000 Li, I 300, 301, 362, 365, II 529, 591, 731, 732.

Testament 遺教戒之書 *yijiaojie zhi shu*, I 433.

Thirty-five kingdoms 三十五國 *sanshiwuguo*, beyond the sea, where plumigerous and feathered tribes live, I 111, 360.

Three Dynasties 三代 *sandai:*—Xia 夏, Yin 殷, and Zhou 周, I 163, 166, 167, II 647, 834, III Ch15 n7; their different systems of government, II 579–80.

Three Emperors 三王 *sanwang* = Three Rulers, I 413, II 526.

Three hundred naked creatures 倮蟲三百 *luochong sanbai*, of which man is the noblest, I 434, II 511.

Three hundred penalties 正刑三百 *zhengxing sanbai*, of the Zhou 周 epoch, I 415.

Three hundred rules of ceremony of the Zhou 周 dynasty 禮三百 *li sanbai*, I 415.

Three hundred scaly animals 三百鱗蟲 *sanbai linchong*, of which the dragon the first, I 240.

Three hundred and sixty naked animals 三百六十倮蟲 *sanbailiushi luochong*, among which man ranks first, II 725, 898, III Ch38 n39.

Three hundred and sixty officers of the Zhou 周 dynasty 周官三百六十 *zhouguan sanbailiushi*, I 413.

Three ministers 三公 *sangong*, of Heaven, Earth, and man, I 116, 282, II 492, III Ch25 n46, Ch46 n19.

Three Mountains disappeared during the Qin 秦 epoch, II 567, 650.

Three Offerings 三祀 *sansi*, made to the Genii of Spring, Autumn, and Winter, II 758.

Three Qin 三秦 *sanqin*, the three kingdoms:—Yong 雍, Sai 塞, and Di 翟, into which Qin 秦 was divided, I 385, III Ch33 n14.

Three Rivers 三河 *sanhe*, the Huanghe 黃河, Huai 淮河, and Luo 洛河, II 731, 732.

Three Rulers 三王 *sanwang:*—Yu 禹, Tang 湯, and Wen Wang 文王, I 278, II 517, 561, 562, 859. See also Five Emperors and Three Rulers.

Three Sacrifices 三祀 *sansi*, of the high dignitaries, II 758, 869.

Three thousand minor paragraphs (on punishments) of the Zhou 周 epoch 科條三千 *ketiao sanqian*, I 415.

Three thousand rules of demeanour

of the Zhou 周, 威儀三千 *weiyi sanqian*, I 415.

Thunder 雷 *lei*, I 246 seq.; the thunder and the dragon attract one another, I 243, thunder how caused, I 243–44, not Heaven's angry voice, I 246, not caused by Heaven's fetching a dragon, I 246–47, represented by drums or as the "Thunderer," I 253, the exploding solar fluid, I 254, fire, I 255, why thunder must be fire, I 255, its effect upon a superior man, II 496, 574, thunder is the heavenly fluid, II 733.

Thunder goblet 雷罇 *leizun*, of the Xia 夏 dynasty, could attract thunder, I 254, 296, II 499, 504.

Thunderer 雷公 *leigong*, the God of Thunder, an athlete with drums and a hammer, I 253–54, III Ch76 n4.

Ti Ying 緹縈, daughter of Chunyu De 淳于德, I 415.

Tian Chang 田常, noble of Qi 齊, II 812.

Tian Chengzi 田成子, noble of Qi 齊, II 792, III Ch29 n18.

Tian Dan 田單, official of Qi 齊, II 663, III Ch64 n76.

Tian Fen 田蚡, minister of Han Wu Di 漢武帝, II 650, III Ch24 n41, Ch63 nn61, 62, Ch65 n44.

Tian Guang 田光, magistrate, II 509.

Tian Qu 田訕, scholar, II 788.

Tian Wen 田文, Prince of Meng Chang 孟嘗 in Qi 齊, son of

Tian Ying 田嬰 of Qi 齊, I 228, II 697.

Tian Ying 田嬰, father of Tian Wen 田文, minister of Qi 齊, I 228, II 697–98.

Tiao 條, principality in Shanxi 山 西, I 87, 139.

Tides follow the phases of the moon, I 178.

Tigers 虎 *hu*, howling attracts the wind, I 243, II 454–55, 498, painted on door screens to frighten away demons, I 416, II 501, sympathetic fluid between wind and the tiger, I 498, the devouring of men by tigers a consequence of the misdeeds of officials, II 505 seq., tigers and wolves are man devouring brutes, II 702, their skin coloured like the mole and the bull-frog, II 824.

Time 時 *shi*, only when there is the proper time a sovereign employs able men, I 72, the right time, I 76–77, II 794–95, propitious or unpropitious, I 84, 85, and fate must be spontaneous, I 133, the subsistence and decay of a State depend on the duration of its time, I 196, definition, I 236–37, time and destiny determine whether a disease may be cured or not, II 548, time governs good and bad luck, II 552, determines happy and unhappy events, II 726.

Time periods 節氣 *jieqi*, 24 solar periods, into which the year is divided, II 456, III Ch41 n11.

Tin 錫 *xi*, how won and worked, I 407.

Toad 蟾蜍 *chanchu*, cannot live in the moon, I 373–74.

Tong 桐, palace, II 568.

Tong 統, period of 1539 years, II 702, 734, III Ch69 n18.

Tortoise 龜 *gui* / 神龜 *shengui*, divine creature living 3,000 years, II 447, less agile than a frog, II 451, tortoise and milfoil consulted, II 483, spiritual, II 522, used for divination, II 536, 639, knows the future, II 764, is wise and carries characters on its back, II 824.

Trance (Faint) 殄 *tian*, II 629.

Tribute of Yu 禹, *Yugong* 禹貢, chapter of the *Shangshu* 尚書, I 115, 360, 361, 376, III Ch8 n16, Ch31 n29.

Tripod 鼎 *ding*, King Wu 武 of Qin 秦 died lifting a tripod, I 172, tripods of Yu 禹, II 500, of Kong Kui 孔悝, had an inscription, II 610.

Tu An Gu 屠岸賈, minister of Jin 晉, who destroyed the whole house of Zhao 趙, I 124, III Ch9 nn27, 28.

Tuoli 橐離, State in northern Korea, I 122.

Tuoping 託平, place in Shanxi 山西, II 661.

Twelve Branches 十二支 *shi'er zhi*, II 737, 738, III 870, 902–3, 908, 909, 917, Ch14 n9, Ch70 n21, Ch74 nn11, 17; and their corresponding animals, III 915.

Twelve constellations 十二辰 *shi'er chen*, II 738, III 908, 917, Ch69 n22, Ch74 n17.

Twelve Holy Men = Twelve Sages 十二聖 *shi'er sheng*, II 517, 518.

Twelve horary characters and their corresponding animals 十二辰之禽 *shi'erchen zhi qin*, I 159, III Ch14 n9.

Twelve-month 齡 *ling* = a year, II 571.

Twelve-Sages 十二聖 *shi'er sheng*, Huang Di 黃帝, Zhuan Xu 顓頊, Di Ku 帝嚳, Yao 堯, Shun 舜, Yu 禹, Tang 湯, Wen Wang 文王, Wu Wang 武王, Zhou Gong 周公, Gao Yao 皋陶, Confucius, I 135, II 785.

Twelve Spirits of the Cardinal Points 十二神 *shi'er shen*, II 733, 745.

Twenty-eight constellations (solar mansions) 二十八宿 *ershiba su* / 二十八舍 *ershiba she*, the resting-places of sun and moon, I 363, III 901, Ch14 n7, Ch61 n31.

Two Sacrifices 二祀 *ersi*, to the Spirit of Fire and the Lord of the Soil, II 758; Two Offerings of ordinary scholars, II 758.

Unconsciousness of the dead, II 628.

Unicorn = Qilin 麒麟, I 371, III Ch32 n31, Ch40 n17, Ch51 nn6, 13, Ch59 n5, Ch85 n51; a felicitous presage, I 198, II 451, 531, 586, 589, 598, 782, like a deer with one horn, a holy animal, II 516, a white unicorn with five feet, II 526, 535, like a deer with two horns, II 526, resembling a stag, II 526, wild animal with joined horns, II 527; a dead one, II 532.

Universal peace 太平 *taiping*, I 92, 93, 174, 199, 200, 214, 260, 295, 300, 304, II 454, 484, 521–22, 525, 529, 533–35, 538, 539, 542, 544, 546, 547, 551, 557, 566, 568, 572, 585 seq., 597, 610, III Ch52 n8, Ch57 n1.

Unpropitious 忌 *ji* years and months, I 132, sites, I 132, II 700 seq., 706 seq.

Varnish, black 墨漆 *moqi*, detestable, II 696.

Venus, 太白 *taibo*, eclipsed the Pleiades, when Jing Ke 荊軻 stabbed Qin Shi Huangdi 秦始皇, I 208, 209, II 475–76, 544, III 877–78, 880, 884, 895–96, Ch32 n42, Ch52 n44, Ch64 n81, Ch77 nn37, 42.

Vermilion grass 朱草 *zhucao*, an auspicious plant, I 145, 199, 201, II 523, produced by the harmonious fluid, II 533–34, 538.

Virtue 德 *de*, the virtuous have the same conduct, I 171, virtue leads to happiness, II 691, the greater a man's virtue, the more brilliant is his literary work, II 823, virtue and letters indispensable to Worthies and Sages, II 824.

Visions of ghosts, caused by pain and fear, II 668–69.

Vital energy 氣力 *qili*, exhausted, I 172, vital force 精氣 *jingqi* disperses by death, II 509, 687.

Vital fluid 氣 *qi*, 精氣 *jingqi* or 氣力 *qili*, copious or scarce, determines the length of life, I 90–91, 109, the length of life depends upon it, I 101, received by men at their birth, forms the constitution, I 106, vanishes at death, I 110, is drawn from food, I 272, the vital force concentrated forms the human being, I 274, man lives by the vital fluid residing in the arteries, II 625, it fills the body as millet and rice a bag, and disperses at death, II 626; blood the vital force of the living, II 627; its seat in the blood, II 628, 629; vital energy maintained by eating and drinking, II 632; vital force within the body and outside the body, II 632; through death the fluid is lost, and the vital spirit 精神 *jingshen* dissolved, II 632–33; after death it is a formless fluid, II 633, the vital spirit of all creatures is extinguished by death, it evaporates and disappears, II 634, causes thought and sensations, II 669, it gives knowledge and speech, II 676.

Vital force = Vital fluid.

Voices of birds and beasts 鳥獸之音 *niaoshou zhi yin* understood by Yang Weng Zhong 楊翁仲, II 771–72.

Wan Shi 萬石, II 562.

Wang 王姬, woman of the time of Han Gao Zu 漢高祖, I 124.

Wang 王夫人, wife of the Emperor Wu Di 武帝, II 558.

Wang Changsun 王長孫, fortune-teller, I 126.

Wang Chong 王充, philosopher, author of the *Lunheng* 論衡, II 848 seq., his ideal, II 862, in Introduction passim.

Wang Gong Zi 王公子, scholar of the time of Huan Jun Shan 桓君山, II 440.

Wang Ji 王季, father of Wen Wang 文王, II 569, 639, 646, 694, III Ch68 n10.

Wang Jian 王翦, general of Qin 秦, I 185.

Wang Liang 王良, famous charioteer, I 72, 81, 101, 113, 338, II 448, 468, III Ch33 n31.

Wang Mang 王莽, the usurper, I 132, 181, 279, II 517, 522–23, 544, 575, 578, 594, 596–97, 619, 621, 651, 769, 820, III Ch25 nn29, 33, Ch47 n10, Ch57 n20, Ch58 nn20, 45, Ch61 n13, Ch63 n68.

Wang Qiao 王喬, Prince of Jin 晉, immortal, I 109.

Wang Shuo 王朔, diviner, I 234.

Wang Yang 王陽, famous teacher, 1st cent. CE, I 147–48.

Wang Zhong Zi 王仲子, scholar of the 1st cent. CE, I 391, III Ch33 n31.

Wang Zi Feng 王子鳳, official, II 509.

Wang Zi Qiao 王子喬, see Wang Qiao 王喬, I 272.

Wangwang 往亡, kind of unlucky day, II 727, III Ch72 nn14, 15.

Wansui 萬歲, palace, II 589.

Water 水 *shui* injuring fire 火 *huo* I 132, II 493, 741, its procreative power, II 431, water and wood belong to the Five Elements, II 710, water less noble than fire, II 710, winter air is cold, corresponds to water, has its position in the north, II 733, 741, 742.

Water sickness 水病 *shuibing*, II 493–94.

Water Spirit 魍魎 *wangliang*, son of Zhuan Xu 顓頊, II 671, 745, III Ch77 n17.

Wealth 富 *fu* appreciated more than intelligence 通 *tong*, I 427–28, wealth and honour are heavenly fate, II 790.

Wei 衛, State in Henan 河南, I 97, 100, 138, 176, 182, 191, 201, 208, 288, 291, 318, 324, 327, 414, II 445, 462, 475, 552, 557, 609, 610, 653, 718, 781, 786, 842, III 922, Ch5 n11, Ch21 n10, Ch25 n43, Ch26 nn8, 27, Ch28 n87, Ch36 n38, Ch39 n54, Ch42 n10, Ch56 nn4, 19, Ch60 n8, Ch64 n25, Ch71 n11, Ch77 n49, Ch85 n9.

Wei 魏, State in Shanxi 山西, I 81, 118, 136, 179, 236, 241, 276, 292, 333, 424, II 660, 788, III Ch2 n20, Ch3 n7, Ch11 n7,

Ch21 n37, Ch22 n16, Ch25 n6, Ch29 n8, Ch30 n2, Ch33 nn12, 14, Ch37 n35, Ch41 n1, Ch43 n25, Ch64 nn23, 45, Ch64 n71, Ch78 n44, Ch81 n21.

Wei 魏郡, circuit, parts of Zhili 直 隸 and Shanxi 山西, I 137, II 848.

Wei 渭, tributary of the Huanghe 黃河, river in Shanxi 陝西, II 574, 836, III Ch85 n51.

Wei 威, King of Qi 齊, II 791.

Wei Ke 魏顆, general of Jin 晉, II 645, 676, III Ch65 n42.

Wei Liao 尉繚, supporter of Qin Shi Huangdi 秦始皇, I 141, III Ch11 n43.

Wei Qi 魏齊, premier of Wei 魏, II 473, III Ch43 n25.

Wei Qing 衛青, general, I 138, 234–35, II 521, 792.

Wei Wu Zi 魏武子, father of Wei Ke 魏顆, II 645.

Wei Zi 微子, Viscount of Wei 微, I 150, III Ch78 n6.

Weidu 魏都, capital of Wei 魏, II 769.

Weinan 渭南, city near Xi'anfu 西 安府, II 768.

Weird ditties/sayings of children 僮謠 *tongyao*, I 129, 196, II 662, 667, 774, III Ch18 n8; due to the influence of Mars, II 674.

Weiyang 未央, palace near Chang'an 長安, II 768.

Weiyu 魏榆, city in Shanxi 山西, II 666.

Wen 文, Duke of Jin 晉, I 96, 97, 202, 229, II 517, 573, 656, 720, III Ch54 n31, Ch64 n69, Ch85 nn32, 36.

Wen 文, Duke of Lu 魯, I 196, II 485, 808, 857.

Wen 文, Marquis of Wei 魏, I 333, III Ch3 n7, Ch5 n7, Ch29 n8.

Wen Cheng 文成, Daoist thaumaturgist, I 271.

Wen Di 文帝, Han 漢 Emperor, I 87, 125, 139, 306, 415, II 588, 605, 607, 608, 730, 803, III Ch9 nn39, 43, Ch11 n36, Ch34 n21, Ch48 n23, Ch80 n79.

Wen Jiang 文姜, duchess of Lu 魯, I 181.

Wen Wang 文王, King Wen 文, founder of the Zhou 周 dynasty, I 75, 93, 104, 135, 143, 166, 167, 187, 209, 236, 279, 286, 295, 302, 349, 387, 411, 412, II 439, 444, 461, 467, 530, 569, 571, 578, 584, 590, 595, 621, 639, 646, 694, 708, 734, 739, 754, 756, 767, 799, 816, 817, 826, 843, III Ch4 n11, Ch11 n2, Ch12 n2, Ch18 n14, Ch21 n40, Ch30 n35, Ch36 n9, Ch42 n3, Ch51 n21, Ch55 nn36, 47, Ch58 n28, Ch63 n34, Ch64 n91, Ch80 n58, Ch81 n31.

Wen Zhi 文摯, famous physician, I 266–68.

Wen Zi 文子, Daoist philosopher, II 561, III Ch52 n40.

Wen Zi 文子, orphan of Zhao 趙, I 124.

Wenchang 文昌, constellation, I 251.

Western Sea 西海郡 *xihaijun*, circuit, II 599, III Ch58 n56.

White Emperor 白帝 *baidi*, II 664–65, 896, III Ch64 n81.

White fish 白魚 *baiyu*, lucky omen
    of Wen Wang 文王, I 143
    seq., II 534 seq.
White pheasants 白雉 *baizhi*, lucky
    augury, I 198–99, 295, II
    444, 523, 535, 570, 589, 591,
    III Ch18 n19, Ch55 n37,
    Ch59 n5, a white and a black
    one, II 498, 598, 599.
White Tiger 白虎 *baihu*, western
    quadrant of solar mansions,
    I 159, 240, II 745, III 901,
    919, Ch59 n41, Ch75 nn1, 2.
Will-o'-the-wisp 燐 *lin*, the blood
    of the slain, II 627, III 897.
Wind 風 *feng*, lucky wind, I 127,
    follows the tiger, I 131, II
    498, wind is air; said by
    some to be the commanding
    voice of Heaven and Earth,
    I 206, foreseen by insects, II
    469, its influence on robbers
    and thieves, and on the mar-
    ket prices, II 469–70; winds
    on New Year's Day portend
    the new year, II 470, an east
    wind causes wine to flow
    over, II 499, a big storm fet-
    tered by Yao 堯, II 567, the
    God of Wind 風伯 *fengbo*, II
    751, 760.
Wine-springs 醴泉 *liquan*, auspi-
    cious portent, II 523, lucky
    omen, II 531, 545, 586, 589,
    produced by the harmonious
    fluid, II 534.
Wizards, see Sorcerers.
Wizards and priests 巫祝 *wuzhu*,
    have no power, II 748.
World, lying in the south-east of the
    universe, I 263, 368.
Worthies 賢 *xian*, have their

imperfections, II 482, their
    influence not sufficient to
    bring about universal peace,
    II 585, one degree less than
    Sages, II 764, 784–85, their
    nature, II 790 seq.
Writing 書 *shu*, invented by Cang
    Jie 蒼頡, I 216, foot-prints
    of birds led to its invention,
    II 573.
Writing tablets of bamboo 牒 *die*, I
    407–8, of wood (boards) 板
    ban, I 407–8.
Wu 武, King of Chu 楚, II 472, III
    Ch43 n15.
Wu 武 = Wu Wang 武王, I 128,
    129, 205, II 467, 568, 569,
    572, 583, 584, 594, 639, 717,
    853, III Ch10 n12, Ch37
    n18, Ch63 n11.
Wu 武, Duke of Song 宋, I 255, III
    Ch54 n14.
Wu 武, King of Qin 秦, I 172, 421.
Wu 武負, elderly lady of the time of
    Han Gao Zu 漢高祖, I 124.
Wu 吳, son of Xun Yan 荀偃 of Jin
    晉, II 640.
Wu 吳, State in Jiangsu 江蘇, I 128,
    144, 170, 171, 174, 175, 176,
    423, II 460, 464, 495, 594,
    599, 651, 680, 694, 765, 773,
    III 928, Ch1 n4, Ch6 n19,
    Ch8 nn14, 29, 31, Ch10 n4,
    Ch12 n6, Ch15 n2, Ch16 n2,
    Ch19 n32, Ch26 n43, Ch35
    n17, Ch38 n15, Ch77 n46,
    Ch78 n9, Ch80 nn13, 40.
Wu Bei 伍被, Daoist, friend of Huai
    Nan Zi 淮南子, I 263, 360,
    III Ch24 n25.
Wu Di 武帝, Han 漢 Emperor, I
    270–71, 435, II 449, 502–3,

516, 520, 526, 527, 535, 558, 590, 598, 608, 617, 619, 795, 811, III Ch9 n43, Ch21 n22, Ch54 n7.

Wu Ding 武丁, Shang 商 Emperor, II 647, III Ch4 n14, Ch7 n8, Ch10 n13, Ch26 n38, Ch55 n31, Ch63 n39.

Wu Geng 武庚, son of the last emperor of the Yin 殷 dynasty, II 600.

Wu Huo 烏獲, strong man of the feudal age, I 421.

Wu Ji 無忌, Prince of Wei 魏, I 81, 276, III Ch25 n6.

Wu Jun Gao 吳君高, writer, I 173–74, II 838, III Ch39 n41.

Wu Jun Shang 吳君商 = Wu Jun Gao 吳君高, elegant writer, II 444.

Wu Li 五利, Daoist magician, I 271.

Wu Ling 武靈, King of Zhao 趙, II 658, III Ch64 n26.

Wu Ling Zi 於陵子, scholar of Qi 齊, I 391, III Ch33 n30.

Wu Qing 吳慶, officer of Zhao 趙, II 658, III Ch64 n37.

Wu Wang 武王, King of the Zhou 周 dynasty, I 73, 75, 93, 143, 145, 146, 147, 166, 167, 205–6, 225, 250, 276–77, 278, 286, 305, 336, 349, 414, 434, II 439, 526, 534, 535–36, 565, 571–72, 582, 590, 591, 594–96, 597, 599, 616, 654, 720, 738, 739, 756, 761, 783, 820, III Ch4 n11, Ch11 nn2, 3, Ch12 n2, Ch25 nn10, 13, 19, 27, 42, Ch26 n1, Ch36 n32, Ch42 nn12, 41, Ch50 n29, Ch51 n21, Ch54 n12, Ch55 nn9, 47, Ch56 n26,

Ch58 n28, Ch64 nn25, 102, Ch71 n13.

Wu Xian 巫咸, diviner, II 687.

Wu Xu 無恤, name of Viscount Xiang 襄 of Zhao 趙, I 134, 138, II 658, 661.

Wu Yan 無鹽, wife of King Xuan 宣 of Qi 齊, I 75, III Ch1 n27.

Wu Yuan 伍員, minister of Wu 吳, 6th cent. BCE, I 72, 102, III Ch6 n19, Ch10 n1, Ch30 n56, Ch80 n40.

Wu Zixu 伍子胥 / Wu Zi Xu 伍子胥 / Zi Xu 子胥 / Wu Yuan 伍員, I 424, II 651, III Ch2 n25, Ch10 nn1, 2, Ch16 nn55, 58, Ch30 n56, Ch80 n40.

Wu'an 武安, Marquis of, I 269, II 650, 676, III Ch65 n44.

Wufu 五甫, region in Shandong 山東, II 779.

Wuling 於陵, place in Shandong 山東, I 352, 353, 354, 355.

Wuqiu 吾丘, place in Shanxi 山西, II 795.

Wusun 烏孫, non-Chinese tribe, I 121.

Wutong 吳通, place on the Ling 陵 river, I 176.

Wuyi 毋佚, chapter of the *Shangshu* 尚書 毋佚, I 294.

Xi 僖, Duke of Lu 魯, I 380, II 675, 771, III Ch85 n36.

Xi 熙 = Xuan Ming 玄冥, God of Winter, II 757, 869.

Xi 曦, astronomer of Yao 堯, II 541.

Xi Menbao 西門豹, Worthy of the 5th cent. BCE, I 118, II 462.

Xi Qi Shu 西乞術, officer of Qin 秦, I 291.

Xi Wang Mu 西王母, Daoist goddess, I 111.

Xi Wang Mu 西王母, tribe (?), II 599, III Ch58 n56.

Xi Zhong 奚仲, inventor of chariots, I 417, II 496, 573–74, 843, 846.

Xia 夏, dynasty, 2205-1766 BCE, I 128, 130, 162, 164, 166, 173, 188, 197, 218, 242, 260, 282, 295, 411, II 499, 537, 568, 579, 590, 593, 599, 605, 647, 712, 739, 756, 758, 797, 816, 820, 835, III Ch1 n2, Ch6 n27, Ch8 n6, Ch15 n9, Ch18 n12, Ch25 n4, Ch26 nn46, 50, Ch29 n22, Ch30 n60, Ch36 n9, Ch37 n9, Ch55 n63, Ch59 n34, Ch63 n47, Ch64 n55, Ch81 n31, App.I n4.

Xia 夏, family seat of Yu 禹 and the Xia 夏 dynasty in Henan 河南, II 820.

Xia Lei 俠累, minister of Han 韓, I 184–85, III Ch16 nn97, 101.

Xia Taihou 夏太后, Queen-Dowager of Qin 秦, II 767, III Ch78 n27.

Xia Wu Ju 夏無且, physician of Qin Shi Huangdi 秦始皇, II 796–97, III Ch26 n42.

Xia Yu 夏育, famous for his strength, I 278, 395, 422, II 770, III Ch25 n23.

Xiaguo 下國, "lower capital" of Jin 晉, II 637.

Xian 獻, Duke of Jin 晉, II 656, III Ch19 n31, Ch63 n10, Ch65 n31.

Xian 獻, Duke of Wei 衛, I 201.

Xian 獻, Viscount of Wei 魏, I 241, II 869, III Ch22 n25.

Xian 憲 = Yuan Si 原思, disciple of Confucius, noted for his love of poverty, II 862, III Ch85 nn48, 49.

Xian Zi 縣子, official in Lu 魯, II 480

Xiang 襄, Duke of Jin 晉, I 291, II 656.

Xiang 襄, Duke of Lu 魯, I 206, III Ch84 n35.

Xiang 襄, Duke of Qi 齊, I 123, II 674, III Ch65 n19.

Xiang 襄, King of Chu 楚, I 181, II 472.

Xiang 襄, Viscount of Zhao 趙, I 138, 208, II 474, 658, 660, 797, III Ch22 n28, Ch43 n38, Ch80 n39.

Xiang 襄 = Zhaoxiang 昭襄, King of Qin 秦, I 232, III Ch11 n50, Ch21 n11, Ch26 n52.

Xiang 襄, ancient name of Guidefu 歸德府 (Henan 河南), I 397.

Xiang 象, Shun's 舜 wicked brother, I 121, II 782.

Xiang 湘, river in Hunan 湖南, I 176, 178, II 606, III Ch16 n40, Ch59 n23.

Xiang 湘, mountain in Hunan 湖南 on the Xiang 湘 river, I 178.

Xiang Bo 項伯, saved Han Gao Zu's 漢高祖 life, I 125.

Xiang Man Du 項曼都, Daoist genius, I 265–66, III Ch24 n34.

Xiang Tuo 項託, teacher of Confucius, II 769–70, 772, 773–74, III Ch78 n39.

Xiang Yu 項羽, rival of Han Gao Zu 漢高祖, I 100, 124–25, 136, 146, 163, 168, 277, 425, II 594, 596, 727, III Ch9 n35, Ch12 n22, Ch33 n14, Ch36 nn17, 71, Ch37 n46, Ch46 n25, Ch58 n12.

Xiang Zhuang 項莊, attempted to kill Han Gao Zu 漢高祖, I 125.

Xiang'an 襄安, city in Anhui 安徽, II 727, III Ch72 n11.

Xianming 咸銘, work of Yuan Wen Shu 袁文術, II 838.

Xianyang 咸陽, city near Xi'anfu 西安府, I 283, II 596, 620, 812.

Xiao 孝, Duke of Qin 秦, I 74, 424, II 827, 852, III Ch85 n18.

Xiao 孝, King of Liang 梁, II 443, III Ch85 n11.

Xiao Cheng Di 孝成帝 = Cheng Di 成帝, Han 漢 Emperor, II 463, 617, 619, 811

Xiao He 蕭何, legislator under Han Gao Zu 漢高祖, I 414–15, 425, 428, II 794, III Ch36 nn45, 51, Ch38 n4.

Xiao Hui 孝惠, Emperor Hui Di 惠帝, son of Gao Zu 高祖 and Lü Hou 呂后, I 74, 136.

Xiao Jing Di 孝景帝 = Jing Di 景帝, Han 漢 Emperor, II 594, 811.

Xiao Ming Di 孝明帝, Han 漢 Emperor, I 436, II 528, 584, 589–90, 591, 598, 600, 601, 613, 614, 618, 619, 621, III Ch61 n17.

Xiao Wen 孝文, King of Qin 秦, II 767, III Ch78 n25.

Xiao Wen Di 孝文帝 = Wen Di 文帝, Han 漢 Emperor, I 74, 297–98, 306–7, 320, 414, II 607, 786, III Ch78 n55.

Xiao Wu 孝武 = Xiao Wu Di 孝武帝, II 463, III Ch42 n27.

Xiao Wu Di 孝武帝 = Wu Di 武帝, Han 漢 Emperor, I 198, 263,

430, II 463, 526, 535, 607, 613, 617, 619, 833, 841.

Xiao Xuan Di 孝宣帝, Han 漢 Emperor, II 516, 520, 524, 526, 529, 531, 533, 589, 590, 591, 607, 610, 811.

Xiao Zhang Di 孝章帝, Han 漢 Emperor, II 528, III Ch50 n51.

Xiapei 下邳, place in Jiangsu 江蘇, II 665, 666.

Xiatai 夏臺, place where Cheng Tang 成湯 was confined, I 104, 209, 210.

Xie 契, minister of Shun 舜, I 85, 274, 386, II 597, 756, 761, 797, 834, III Ch15 nn3, 35, Ch25 n1, Ch50 n40, Ch77 n7.

Xiliu 細柳, region where the sun sets, I 370–71, III Ch32 n26.

Xilu Jun Yang 昔廬君陽, official, I 391.

Xin Huangdi 新皇帝, the "New Emperor" = Wang Mang 王莽, II 596.

Xin Ling 信陵, Prince of, I 292, II 521, 792, III Ch50 n19.

Xin You 辛有, officer of King Ping 平 of Zhou 周, II 768, III Ch78 n35.

Xin Yuan Ping 新垣平, on the Zhou 周 tripods, I 297–98, III Ch43 n29.

Xindu 新都, territory in Henan 河南, II 820.

Xinfeng 新豐, place in Shanxi 陝西, II 521, 589.

Xinlun 新論, "New Reflections," work of Huan Jun Shan 桓君山, II 441, 443, 809, 838, 843, III Ch50 n9, Ch83 n46.

Xinping 新平, place in Shanxi 陝西, II 589.

Xinxu 新序, "New Introduction," work of Liu Xiang 劉向, II 843, III Ch18 n33, Ch26 n11, Ch84 n14.

Xinyu 新語, "New Words," work of Lu Jia 陸賈, II 442, 619, 829, 835, III Ch13 n18, Ch83 n28, Ch84 n5.

Xizhou 西州, place with salt-wells, I 429, III Ch38 n8.

Xuan Yuan 軒轅, personal name of Huang Di 黃帝, II 608.

Xue 薛, small principality in Shandong 山東, I 345.

Xiong Qu Zi 熊渠子, remarkable bow-man, I 288–89, 290, III Ch26 n10.

Xiongnu 匈奴, Turkish tribes, I 121, 139, 234, 368, II 464, 502, 535, 591, 594, 599, 740, III 875, 917, Ch9 nn9, 10, Ch21 n16, Ch42 n36, Ch47 nn25, 26, Ch50 n21.

Xiu 修, God of Winter, II 757.

Xiu Chu 休屠, khan of the Xiongnu 匈奴, II 502, III Ch47 n26.

Xu 徐, small State in Hubei 湖北, I 336.

Xu 徐, State in Anhui 安徽, I 96, 170, II 761.

Xu 徐, one of the Nine Provinces, in Shandong 山東, and its aborigines, I 287.

Xu 許, family related to the royal house of Chu 楚, II 600.

Xu Fu 許負, fortune-teller, I 139–40, 144.

Xu Jia 須賈, officer of Wei 魏, II 473, III Ch43 n25.

Xu Qin 序秦, name of a chapter in

a work of Zi Wei 子韋, I 194.

Xu Shu 許叔, famous for his magnanimity, II 581.

Xu You 許由, hermit, I 73, 170, 336, II 846, III Ch1 n17.

Xu Yue 徐樂, scholar, I 86, II 446, 829.

Xuan 宣, King of Zhou 周, I 177, 300, II 484, 548, 590, 610, 612, 636, 676, 679, III Ch53 n8, Ch65 n32.

Xuan 宣, King of Qi 齊, II 596, III Ch1 n27.

Xuan 宣, Duke of Lu 魯, II 511, III Ch49 n1.

Xuan Di 宣帝, Emperor of the Han 漢 dynasty = Xiao Xuan Di 孝宣帝, I 137, 413, II 520, 523, 526–27, 531, 584, 590, 598, 606, 611, 613, 813, 818, III Ch11 n21, Ch13 n15, Ch42 n42, Ch51 n8, Ch79 n45.

Xuan Ming 玄冥, God of Winter, II 758, 869, 874, III Ch77 n17.

Xuanyuan 軒轅, constellation, I 251.

Xun Yan 荀偃, officer of Jin 晉, II 641.

Xun Zi 荀子 = Sun Qing 孫卿, II 840, III 931, Ch13 n15, Ch19 n37, Ch21 n33, Ch84 n1.

Xuzhou 徐州, one of the Nine Provinces, II 732.

Ya Fu 亞父, title of Fan Zeng 范增, I 125.

Yan 嚴, King of Chu 楚, II 459.

Yan 偃, King of Xu 徐, I 96–97, 336, III Ch29 n15.

Yan 延, music-master of Zhou 紂, II 654.

Yan 燕, State in Zhili 直隸, I 116,
185, 208, 209, 211, 212, 284,
285, 293, 346, 430, 435, II
443, 457, 473, 540, 663, 676,
688, 796, 846, III Ch3 n13,
Ch8 n28, Ch11 nn7, 50,
Ch16 n103, Ch19 n24, Ch26
n42, Ch30 n21, Ch33 n12,
Ch38 n45, Ch39 nn35, 39,
Ch41 n1, Ch43 n28, Ch48
n18, Ch64 nn74, 76, Ch65
n38.

Yan 閼 (for the spurious 焉), family
name of a Xiongnu 匈奴
queen, II 502.

Yan Di 炎帝 = Shen Nong 神農,
god of the Hearth, I 116,
120, II 758, III 874, Ch8 n21,
Ch24 n6.

Yan Fang 顏方, scholar, II 839.

Yan Fu Zi 嚴夫子, poet of the 2nd
cent. BCE, II 444.

Yan Hui 顏囘, disciple of Confucius, I 80, 82, 94–95, 313–14,
317–18, 319, II 524, 582,
843, 863, III Ch6 nn17, 29,
Ch10 n16, Ch21 n9, Ch28
nn1, 42, Ch37 n19.

Yan Lu 顏路, father of Yan Hui 顏
囘, I 325, II 524, 863.

Yan Sheng 衍盛, private officer, II
605.

Yan Weng Zhong 嚴翁仲, famous
bravo in Henan 河南, I 184.

Yan Xiang 嚴襄, misprint for 莊襄,
Zhuang Xiang, King of Qin
秦, II 767, III Ch78 n27.

Yan Ying 晏嬰, officer of Qi 齊, II
785, 828, III Ch6 n29, Ch42
n8.

Yan Yuan 顏淵 = Yan Hui 顏囘,
disciple of Confucius, I 102,
129, 171–72, 231, 233–34,
323–25, 356, 421, 429, II
517, 519, 561, 593, 770, 773,
774, 778, 779, 788, 800, 803,
805, 837, III Ch10 n16, Ch16
n11, Ch28 nn74, 79, Ch30
n54, Ch37 n19, Ch79 n6.

Yan Yue 閻樂, assassin of Hu Hai
胡亥, I 163, II 596.

Yan Zhang 偃章, I 86.

Yan Zi 晏子 = Yan Ying 晏嬰, officer of Qi 齊, I 104, 187,
188, 193, II 461, 466, 601,
646–47, 783, 798, III Ch6
n29, Ch17 n14, Ch34 n18,
Ch43 n9.

Yandao 嚴道, city in Sichuan 四川,
I 263.

Yang 陽, Marquis of, II 661, III
Ch19 n7.

Yang 陽 fluid (principle), an immense fire, I 255, shines like
the sun, prevails in sum-
mer and is scarce in winter,
I 365, its warmth requires
months, II 451, is warm
and genial, II 454, is brightness and warmth, II 458, is
broiling hot, II 465, comes
forth spontaneously, II 469,
560, governs life, II 470, the
hot fluids, II 470, droughts
corresponds to it, II 478, red
corresponds to Yang 陽, II
493, Yang 陽 having reached
its climax, turns into Yin
陰 and vice versa, II 493,
Yin 陰 being strong, Yang
陽 is weak, II 495, Yang 陽
principle vanquished, II 497,
at its cynosure in summer
and autumn, causes rain

and thunderstorms, II 566, becomes the mind, II 643, is fire and as such hot and red, II 674, boys and sorcerers imbued with it, II 674–75; it predominates at the time of a drought, II 675, the Yang 陽 fluid produces the vital spirit, II 676, ornaments originate from the Yang 陽, II 681, in the 5th month Yang 陽 reaches its acme, II 698.

Yang Hu 陽虎 = Yang Huo 陽貨, minister of the Ji 季 family in Lu 魯, I 160, II 682, 779, III Ch14 n11, Ch79 nn8, 10.

Yang Huo 陽貨 = Yang Hu 陽虎, enemy of Confucius, I 330, II 779, III Ch28 n98, Ch79 n10.

Yang Sheng 羊勝, lived under the Former Han 漢 dynasty, II 850–51, III Ch85 n11.

Yang Weng Zhong 楊翁仲, understood the voices of birds and brutes, II 771–72.

Yang Xin 楊信, Princess, I 138.

Yang Xiong 揚雄 = Yang Zi Yun 揚子雲, I 155, II 862, III 926, Ch42 n31, Ch60 n31, Ch61 n61, Ch80 n84, Ch83 n33.

Yang You Ji 養由基, famous archer, I 287–88, 289–90, III Ch26 n14.

Yang Zhong 楊終, scholar, I 436, II 619, 839, III Ch61 n7.

Yang Zhu 楊朱, philosopher of egoism, II 841, 842, III Ch8 n3.

Yang Zi 楊子 = Yang Zhu 楊朱, the philosopher, I 113, 299.

Yang Zi Shan 楊子山, scholar, II 618, III Ch61 n11.

Yang Zi Yun 揚子雲 = Yang Xiong 揚雄, famous philosopher, I 87, 418, 421, II 439, 440–41, 463, 518, 582, 613, 619, 623, 655, 804, 825, 826–27, 836, 839, 845, 859, 863, III Ch39 n17, Ch56 n24, Ch61 n61.

Yangcheng Zizhang 陽成子長, author of the *Yuejing* 樂經, II 440, 441, 845, 859.

Yanghou 陽侯, Marquis of Lingyang 陵陽, I 205, III Ch19 n7.

Yangshe Shiwo 羊舌食我, native of Jin 晉, 6th cent. BCE, I 103, 150, III Ch13 n5.

Yangxia 陽夏, city in Henan 河南, I 137.

Yangxingshu 養性書, "Macrobiotics," work of Wang Chong 王充, II 864, III Ch85 n67.

Yangzhou 楊州, ancient province, II 732, 863, III Ch78 n4.

Yangzi 江, river, I 81, 175–76, 177–78, 202, 239, 422, II 444, 569, 662, 663, 671, 696, 745, 766, III Ch2 n25, Ch66 nn3, 13, Ch83 n34.

Yanhu 掩淲, river in Korea, I 122.

Yanling 延陵, place in Jiangsu 江蘇, I 169–70, II 761.

Yanshiqiu 燕室丘, mountain and cliffs on the river Xiang 湘, II 606.

Yanshou 延壽, palace, II 589.

Yantielun 鹽鐵論, treatise on "Salt and Iron" by Huan Kuan 桓寬, II 838, III Ch35 n23, Ch83 n44.

Yanzhou 兗州, one of the Nine Circuits of Yu 禹, parts of Zhili 直隸 and Shandong 山東, I 82, II 732.

Yao 堯, ancient emperor, I 71, 72, 92, 98, 113, 142, 144, 147, 163, 173, 190, 197, 204–5, 215, 229, 237, 260, 275, 286, 336, 338, 346, 349, 376, 397, 400, II 457, 482, 484, 493, 516, 517, 524, 531, 541, 547, 549, 556, 582, 585, 593, 595, 607, 610–11, 621, 647, 746, 756, 760, 791, 820, 852, III Ch1 nn2, 14, 17, Ch6 n23, Ch7 n4, Ch9 n5, Ch11 n1, Ch13 n16, Ch16 n85, Ch18 n14, Ch22 n22, Ch23 n15, Ch24 n6, Ch25 n1, Ch29 n16, Ch30 n34, Ch32 n39, Ch33 n29, Ch42 n55, Ch50 n30, Ch52 nn11, 27, Ch52 n32, Ch56 n28, Ch57 n7, Ch60 n19, Ch77 n5, Ch80 nn1, 47, Ch81 n31, Ch85 nn32, 42.

Yao 崤, defile in Henan 河南, I 291, II 656, III Ch26 n32, Ch64 n21.

Yaodian 堯典, chapter of the *Shangshu* 尚書, I 173, III Ch16 n18.

Ye 鄴, city in Wei 魏, I 118.

Ye Gu 夜姑, officer of Song 宋, II 676, 752–53, III Ch65 n34.

Year, fluids of, 歲氣 *suiqi*, harmonious or otherwise, II 487.

Year-star 歲 *sui* = Jupiter, causes misfortune by swallowing some land, II 700 seq., a collision with it to be avoided, II 729 seq.

Yellow 黃 *huang*, the colour of the Han 漢 dynasty, II 607.

Yellow River, 河 *he*, I 81, 148, 176, 197, 205, 216, 242, 255, 320, 361, 422, II 444, 456, 524, 557, 586, 640, 646, 667, 704, 804, 816, 824, 836, III Ch2 n25, Ch7 n6, Ch9 nn47, 57, Ch21 n5, Ch23 nn18, 19, Ch28 n54, Ch64 n57, Ch78 n8, Ch80 n61, Ch83 n35.

Yi 夷, eastern barbarians, I 122, 199, 217, 287, 300, II 508, 511, 572, III 924, Ch26 n6.

Yi 益, minister of Yu 禹, I 111, 360, 377, 433, III Ch19 n52, Ch31 n23, Ch32 n39.

Yi 翳, King of Yue 越, I 89.

Yi 沂, river in Shandong 山東, II 485, 759.

Yi 圯, bridge, II 605, III Ch64 n89.

Yi 鎰 = 20 ounces, I 345, II 796, III Ch30 n13.

Yi Di 夷狄, barbarian tribes, I 380.

Yi Di 儀狄, inventor of wine, II 465, 853, 858, III Ch85 n21.

Yi Li 儀禮, one of the Three Rituals, 413.

Yi Shao Jun 翼少君 = Li Shao Jun 李少君, Daoist magician, I 434.

Yi Wu 夷吾, Prince of Jin 晉, II 637.

Yi Ya 易牙, cook of Duke Huan 桓 of Qi 齊, II 465, 853, 858, III Ch85 n22.

Yi Yin 伊尹, minister of Tang 湯, I 72, 122–23, 129, II 568, 646–47, 788, 789, 863.

Yichuan 伊川, place in Henan 河南, II 768, III Ch78 n35.

Yijing 易經, "Canon of Changes," I 214, 243, 248, 302–3, 344, 359, 372, 412–13, II 458, 467, 498, 504, 559, 560, 578, 619, 620, 716, 718, 723, 726,

754, 810, 811, 813, 816–17,
823, 826, 843, 844, III 887,
891, 892, 894, 903, 914, Ch36
n22, Ch38 n38, Ch41 nn10,
14, 16, Ch42 n16, Ch42 n54,
Ch47 n10, Ch56 n24, Ch58
n5, Ch61 n61, Ch65 n30,
Ch81 nn1, 30, 32, App.I n57.

Yin 殷, dynasty = Shang 商 dynasty,
I 128, 146, 162, 166, 168,
195, 197, 198, 277, 282, 411,
432, II 449, 463, 490, 535,
571, 579, 584, 590, 595, 600,
611, 621, 712, 756, 766, 797,
816, 834, 835, III 931, Ch15
nn7, 9, Ch16 n41, Ch25 n9,
Ch36 n10, Ch50 n40, Ch55
n4, Ch58 n68, Ch59 n34,
Ch61 n46, Ch67 n9, Ch78
n6, Ch80 n43, Ch81 n31,
Ch83 n23.

Yin 殷, epoch, I 419, 424.

Yin 殷, principality of Cheng Tang
成湯 in Henan 河南, II 820.

Yin 殷, State, I 305, II 610, 783.

Yin 鄞, district in Zhejiang 浙江, I
361, III Ch31 n31.

Yin 隱, Duke of Lu 魯, II 708, 815,
III Ch81 n27.

Yin 陰, family, Marquis Fu 傅 of
Yin Jiang 隱彊, II 600.

Yin Fang 尹方, precocious youth, II
769–70, 772, 773–74.

Yin He 尹何, officer of Zheng 鄭, I
409, III Ch35 n36.

Yin Jiang 隱彊, marquisate, II
600–1, III Ch58 n67.

Yin Qi 尹齊, official, II 650–51.

Ying 英, King of Chu 楚, I 251, II
600.

Ying 英, generous official, II 581.

Ying 英, palace in Chu 楚, II 509.

Ying 應, marquisate of Fan Ju 范
雎, I 86.

Ying 嬴, family name of the viscounts of Zhao 趙, II 656,
658, III Ch64 n24.

Yingchuan 潁川, circuit in Anhui
安徽, II 578, 610, 844.

Yinghai 瀛海, the Great Ocean, I
360, III Ch31 n17.

Yiyang 宜陽, city in Henanfu 河南
府, I 125.

Yizhangju 易章句, work of Yuan
Tai Bo 袁太伯, II 838.

Yi zhong jian 栘中監, master of the
horse, I 436.

Yin 陰 fluid (principle), II 469, 560,
abounds in winter, I 130,
clouds and rain are Yin 陰,
I 254–55, is dark, abounds
in winter, and falls short in
summer, I 364–65, corre-
sponds to the North, I 365,
its cold requires months,
II 451, is cold murder, II
454, is rain and cold, II 458,
governs death, II 470, the
cold fluids, II 470, attacked
when it rains without ceas-
ing, II 491, the altars of the
land correspond to Yin 陰,
II 492, water is Yin 陰, II
493, it causes incessant rain,
II 495, predominates during
an eclipse of the sun, II 675,
it produces the bones and
flesh, II 676.

Yin and Yang 陰陽, and good and
evil, I 152, in harmony,
I 156, II 465, 559, their
harmony resulting in the
production of grain, I 200,
violent wind and rain show

that there is a confusion of the Yin 陰 and Yang 陽, I 214, coming into friction produce thunder and lightning, I 254, were not born and do not die, I 274, disorganised, when propriety and righteousness are neglected, I 332, cause the length and the shortness of the days, I 365, 458, when in harmony, wind and rain set in at the proper time, I 386, regulated by man, II 479, floods and droughts are their fluids, II 486, to harmonize the Yin 陰 and Yang 陽, II 486, both thrown into confusion by bad government, II 489, their fluids, II 492, preponderance of Yin 陰 and impotence of Yang 陽, II 495, Yang 陽 is male, Yin 陰 female, II 496, follow their species, II 498, the Yin 陰 creatures appear in winter, the Yang 陽 animals in summer, II 505, all creatures born from the Yin 陰 and the Yang 陽, II 513, disharmony of the Yin 陰 and Yang 陽, II 514, their fluids the fluids of Heaven and Earth, II 525, at variance cause calamitous changes, II 564, the harmonious blending of the Yin 陰 and Yang 陽, II 586, their harmony accompanied by a time of public peace, II 586, 793, crystallise and produce man, who by death is again dissolved into these

fluids, II 630, can injure the good, II 671, the fluid of the Yin 陰 and Yang 陽 reaches a limit after one year, II 734, in harmony, when the government is good, II 835.

Yong 雍 = Ran Yong 冉雍, disciple of Confucius, I 392.

Yong Men Zi 雍門子, famous for his weeping, I 210, II 481, III Ch19 n27.

Yongchang 永昌, circuit in Yunnan 雲南, II 605, III Ch57 n45.

Yongzhou 雍州, one of the Nine Provinces of Yu 禹, comprising Shanxi 陝西 and Gansu 甘肅, I 263, II 444, 732, III Ch39 n43, Ch58 n41.

You 友, Prince of Lu 魯, II 557, 739.

You 幽, King/Emperor of the Zhou 周 dynasty, I 129, 165, 197, II 599, 724, III 924, Ch15 n24, Ch18 n9, Ch58 n48.

You 由 = Zhong You 仲由 styled Zi Lu 子路, disciple of Confucius, II 570.

You Fufeng 右扶風, prefecture in Shanxi 陝西, I 435.

You Miao 有苗, aboriginal tribes, I 287, II 583, 593, III Ch58 n4.

You Ruo 有若, disciple of Confucius, II 502, 517.

Youli 羑里, place where Wen Wang 文王 was imprisoned, I 81, 104, 209–10, II 531, 596, 799, III Ch6 n28.

Yu 禹, ancient emperor, I 72, 73, 111, 115, 120, 142, 162, 163, 173, 197, 202, 215, 219, 239, 260, 275, 296, 309, 319, 349, 360, 376, 386, 397, 400, 411, 414, 433, II 454, 457, 463,

467, 494, 500, 524, 559, 580, 595, 756, 766, 786, 820, 859, III 865, Ch2 n33, Ch7 nn4, 20, 21, Ch8 nn16, 22, Ch10 nn22, 32, Ch11 n1, Ch15 n7, Ch16 n29, Ch18 n14, Ch19 n52, Ch24 n24, Ch25 n1, Ch26 nn6, 49, Ch30 n35, Ch31 n23, Ch32 n13, Ch33 n29, Ch36 nn9, 51, Ch39 n43, Ch50 n41, Ch63 n45, Ch77 n6, Ch82 n28, Ch84 n20, Ch85 n21, App.I n2.

Yu 羽, mountain to which Gun 鯀 was banished, I 107, II 647–48.

Yu 虞, Shun's 舜 territory in Shanxi 山西, I 129–30, II 587, 605, 782, 797, 820 = Shun 舜, II 622.

Yu 予 = Zi Wo 子我, disciple of Confucius, II 740, 770.

Yu Long 御龍, dragon-keeper under the Emperor Kong Jia 孔甲, I 241, 242, III Ch22 n18.

Yu Lü 鬱壘, see Shen Shu 神荼, II 501, 672, III Ch65 n16.

Yu Qing 虞卿, politician of the 3rd cent. BCE, II 442, 828, III Ch82 n47.

Yu Shi 雨師, Rain God, II 760, III Ch76 n4.

Yu Rang 豫讓, would-be assassin of the Viscount of Zhao 趙, I 208, 244, II 797, 801, III Ch43 n38.

Yu Zi 豫子 = Yu Rang 豫讓, II 475.

Yu Zi Da 虞子大, minister, I 126.

Yuan 元, period of 4,617 years, II 702, 734.

Yuan 元, Duke of Song 宋, II 522.

Yuan 元, Princess of Lu 魯, daughter of Han Gao Zu 漢高祖, I 136.

Yuan 元, son of Zeng Zi 曾子, II 823.

Yuan 員, brother to the Marquis Fu 傅 of Yin Jiang 隱彊, II 600.

Yuan 袁, general, II 800.

Yuan Di 元帝, Han 漢 Emperor, I 126, 137, II 620, 651, III Ch9 n54, Ch48 n6.

Yuan Guo 原過, minister of Viscount Xiang 襄 of Zhao 趙, II 661.

Yuan Tai Bo 袁太伯, writer, II 838.

Yuan Wen Shu 袁文術, writer, II 838.

Yuancheng 元城, city in Zhili 直隸, II 848.

Yuansi 元思, work of Zou Bo Qi 鄒伯奇, II 838.

Yuchang 魚腸, famous sword, I 115.

Yue 越, State in Zhejiang 浙江, I 74, 89, 116, 141, 174, 176, 432, II 460, 464, 535, 670, 677, 694, 720, 792, III Ch3 n4, Ch8 nn12, 31, 49, Ch11 n40, Ch15 n2, Ch38 n27, Ch45 n2, Ch80 n76, Ch84 n5.

Yue 南越, southern aborigines in Guangdong 廣東 and Annan, I 119, II 464, 599, 622, 679, 747, III Ch13 n18, Ch76 n6, Ch83 n29.

Yue Zheng Zi 樂正子, disciple of Mencius, I 348, 349.

Yuechang 越嘗 / 越常 = Yueshang 越裳, people in Guangdong 廣東, I 199, II 523, 591, 599, III Ch18 n24, Ch39 n42.

Yuejing 樂經, "Classic of Music," work of Yangcheng Zizhang

陽成子長, II 845.

Yueling 月令, Book III of the *Liji* 禮記, I 103, II 759, III 872, 873, Ch6 n21, Ch10 n24, Ch45 n41, Ch77 n17.

Yueniu 越紐, work of Wu Jun Gao 吳君高, II 838.

Yueshang 越裳, people in Guangdong 廣東, I 295, III Ch50 n31, Ch55 n37.

Yuesui 越巂, ancient State in Yunnan 雲南, II 600.

Yugong 禹貢, the "Tribute of Yu 禹," chapter of the *Shangshu* 尚書, I 175, III Ch8 n16, Ch35 n23, Ch59 n12.

Yuji 餘暨, place in Zhejiang 浙江, I 176.

Yulin 鬱林, old State in Guangxi 廣西, II 600.

Yulin 鬱林, prefecture in Guangxi 廣西, I 435.

Yunmeng 雲夢, place in Hubei 湖北, II 766.

Yuzhou 豫州, one of the Nine Provinces, II 732.

Zai Pi 宰嚭, official in Chu 楚, who slandered Qu Yuan 屈原, I 128.

Zai Wo 宰我, disciple of Confucius, I 314–16, III Ch28 nn26, 30.

Zai Yu 宰予, disciple of Confucius, renowned for his gift of speech, I 142, II 789, III Ch11 n55.

Zang Cang 臧倉, favourite of Duke Ping 平 of Lu 魯, I 82, 86, 133, 348.

Zang Wen Zhong 臧文仲, scholar of Lu 魯, II 485.

Zanniao 簪裊, honorary title under the Han 漢 dynasty, I 416, III Ch36 n69.

Zao Fu 造父, famous charioteer, I 101, 113.

Zhai 翟, slave-girl of Jian 簡, Viscount of Zhao 趙, I 138.

Zhan 詹, native of Qi 齊, II 798.

Zhan He 詹何, native of the Chu 楚 State, II 771–72, 775.

Zhang 漳, river in Henan 河南, I 118.

Zhang 章臺, terrace near Weinan 渭南, II 768.

Zhang Ba 張霸, writer who produced a *Shangshu* 尚書, II 568, 618–19, 811.

Zhang Bo Song 張伯松, contemporary of Yang Xiong Zhang Liang 張良, partisan of Han Gao Zu 漢高祖, II 582.

Zhang Meng Chang 張孟嘗, prefect, I 435.

Zhang Mengtan 張孟談, minister of Viscount Xiang 襄 of Zhao 趙, II 661.

Zhang Qian 張騫, famous traveller, I 361, III Ch31 n28.

Zhang Shang 張商, writer, II 834.

Zhang Shizhi 張釋之, high officer of Han Wen Di 漢文帝, I 400, II 730, 803.

Zhang Tang 張湯, official of the Han 漢 time, I 400, II 804, III Ch50 n33, tall man, II 524, 578.

Zhang Wu 章武, Marquis of, I 125.

Zhang Xiangru 張相如, high officer of Han Wen Di 漢文帝, II 803.

Zhang Yi 張儀, politician, native of Wei 魏 had a double rib, I 136, II 473–74, 517, contemporary of Su Qin 蘇秦,

I 385–86, 389–90, II 481, 834, III Ch33 nn14, 21.

Zhang Zhong Shi 張仲師, giant, II 578.

Zhang Zifang 張子房, see Zhang Liang 張良, I 335.

Zhao 昭, Duke of Han 韓, I 97, III Ch37 n36.

Zhao 昭, Duke of Jin 晉, III Ch22 n16.

Zhao 昭, Duke of Lu 魯, I 129, 196, II 509, 536, III Ch10 n19.

Zhao 昭, Duke of Song 宋, III Ch74 n31.

Zhao 昭, King of Chu 楚, II 495.

Zhao 昭, King of Qin 秦, I 296, II 768, III Ch3 n13.

Zhao 昭, King of Wei 魏, II 788.

Zhao 昭, Prince of Yan 燕, I 435, II 443, III Ch38 n45.

Zhao 朝, Prince of Song 宋, a Paris, II 578, III Ch28 n47.

Zhao 趙, State in Shanxi 山西, I 86, 99, 124, 132, 134, 137, 138, 165, 177, 208, 232, 292, 297, 390, 424, II 442, 473, 474, 557, 636, 643, 649, 656, 660, 727, 772, 786, 795, 852, 857, III Ch10 n45, Ch11 n7, Ch21 n12, Ch22 n28, Ch28 n92, Ch33 nn12, 14, Ch37 n34, Ch39 n23, Ch41 n1, Ch43 n38, Ch58 n7, Ch63 n3, Ch64 n23, Ch65 nn38, 43, Ch80 nn39, 72, Ch81 n21, Ch82 n47.

Zhao Di 昭帝, Han 漢 Emperor, II 818, III Ch43 n32.

Zhao Dun 趙盾, minister of Jin 晉 and deadly enemy of Tu An Gu 屠岸賈, I 124.

Zhao Gao 趙高, eunuch who contrived the death of Fu Su 扶蘇, II 472, III Ch15 n14, Ch21 n36.

Zhao Liang 趙良, II 561.

Zhao Shuo 趙朔, relative of Zhao Dun 趙盾, I 124, III Ch9 nn29, 30.

Zhao Tuo 趙他, King of the southern Yue 南越, I 119, II 464, 622, III Ch8 n49.

Zhao Wu 趙武, the "orphan of Zhao 趙," I 134.

Zhao Yao 趙堯, official, II 786.

Zhao Yu 趙禹, official of the Han 漢 time, I 400.

Zhao Zidu 趙子都, scholar, I 86.

Zhaoge 朝歌, city, I 261.

Zhe 浙江, river in Zhejiang 浙江, I 176, II 766.

Zheng 正君, Lady, aunt of the Emperor Wang Mang 王莽, became empress herself, I 132, 137.

Zheng 鄭, State in Henan 河南, I 100, 141, 191, 291, 340, 409, II 462, 473, 552, 596, 642, 643, 644, 647, 665, 786, 835, 857, III Ch11 n53, Ch29 n29, Ch35 n34, Ch58 n25, Ch63 n21, Ch64 n86, Ch77 nn41, 49, Ch85 n31.

Zheng Ji 鄭季, father of Wei Qing 衛青, I 138.

Zheng Xiu 鄭袖, Queen of Chu 楚, I 81, III Ch2 n18.

Zhengwu 政務, work of Wang Chong 王充, on government, II 843 seq., III Ch85 n25

Zhi 跖 / 蹠, famous robber, I 102, 153, 222, 233, 342, 353, II 514, 521, 862.

Zhi 知, territory in Jin 晉, II 658, 660–61, III Ch22 n28, Ch43 n38, Ch64 n27, Ch80 n39.

Zhi 質阝 / Zhi Xian 質阝縣 = 鄭 Mao, district in Zhejiang 浙江, I 361, III Ch31 n31.

Zhi 職, son of King Cheng 成 of Chu 楚, II 641.

Zhi 摯, music-master of Lu 魯, II 837.

Zhi 穉, father of Lady Zheng 正君, I 137.

Zhi Du 郅都, a general of the 2nd cent. BCE, II 502.

Zhi Sui 質睢, prime-minister in Lu 魯, II 690–91.

Zhifu 直符/眞符, unlucky day, II 728, III Ch72 n15.

Zhifu 之罘, mountain in Shandong 山東, II 662, 766, III Ch64 nn63, 64.

Zhong 種, prefect, I 141.

Zhong 重 = Gou Mang 勾芒, Genius of Spring, II 757, III 869.

Zhong Gong 仲弓, disciple of Confucius, II 863.

Zhong Jun 終軍, censor, officer of Han Wu Di 漢武帝, I 198, II 527, 535, III Ch51 nn26, 30.

Zhong Ren 仲任, style of Wang Chong 王充, II 848.

Zhong Yong 仲雍, son of Dan Fu 亶父, I 144, III Ch12 n5.

Zhong Zi 仲子, daughter of Duke Wu 武 of Song 宋, had writing on her palm, I 255, II 557, 667, 824.

Zhongchang 重常, strange bird, I 433.

Zhonghang Zhaozi 中行昭子, minister of Jin 晉, II 657, III Ch50 n39.

Zhonghang Mizi 中行密子, father of Zhonghang Yin 中行寅, II 748.

Zhonghang Yin 中行寅, nobleman of Jin 晉, II 748.

Zhongli 鍾離, district in Anhui 安徽, I 435.

Zhongmu 中牟, city in Henan 河南, I 328, III Ch28 n92.

Zhongshan 中山, territory in Zhili 直隸, II 658.

Zhongzhou 中州 = Henan 河南, II 844.

Zhou 紂 = Zhou Xin 紂辛, last Emperor of the Shang 商 dynasty, I 72, 113, 128–29, 150, 162, 181, 182, 190, 198, 205, 206, 229, 241, 250, 275 seq., 304–5, 411, II 461, 463, 544, 547, 550, 569, 574–75, 582–83, 594, 595 seq, 644, 654, 673, 675, 717, 719, 721, 724, 738, 746, 754, 767, 797, III 931, Ch10 n10, Ch13 n4, Ch16 n77, Ch25 nn8, 10, 26, 30, Ch27 n30, Ch36 n12, Ch56 nn26, 30, Ch58 nn12, 28, Ch71 n6, Ch74 n14, Ch80 n43.

Zhou 畫, small place in Qi 齊, I 348.

Zhou 周, dynasty, 1122-249 BCE, I 85, 93, 128, 129, 146, 162, 165, 166, 177, 183, 197, 199, 201, 236, 277, 278, 279, 282, 296, 297, 300, 339, 349, 355, 392, 400, 411, 412, 413, 414, 430, 432, II 445, 462, 467, 473, 475, 484, 485, 491, 494, 500, 516, 523, 534, 544, 559, 565, 566, 569–70, 572–73, 580, 583, 584, 587, 593,

594–95, 596–97, 599, 601,
605, 608, 611, 612, 621, 636,
639, 650, 676, 679, 704, 708,
717, 718, 719, 720, 721, 731,
739, 746, 756, 757–58, 759,
770, 783, 808, 817, 825, 826,
834–35, III 868, 917, 926,
Ch3 n5, Ch6 nn14, 28, Ch8
n23, Ch11 nn2, 3, Ch12 n3,
Ch15 nn7, 10, Ch24 n47,
Ch25 nn9, 18, 42, Ch26 n53,
Ch27 n11, Ch28 n100, Ch29
n22, Ch30 n35, Ch34 n23,
Ch35 nn4, 14, Ch36 nn9, 12,
18, 34, Ch42 n3, Ch46 n19,
Ch53 n8, Ch55 n34, Ch56
n1, Ch58 n48, Ch59 n34,
Ch61 n36, Ch63 nn48, 49,
Ch64 n25, Ch65 n32, Ch72
n4, Ch77 nn8, 14, 17, Ch78
n35, Ch80 nn44, 58, Ch81
n30, Ch82 n19, Ch83 n27.
Zhou 周, kingdom of the Zhou 周
dynasty in Shanxi 陝西, II
820, III Ch81 n57.
Zhou 周, people, I 302, 336–37, II
548, 656, 816, 840.
Zhou 周, period, I 76, 149, 174, 199,
295, 300, 363, 419, 436, II
442, 578–79, 600, III 931, Ch8
n32, Ch15 n19, Ch17 n17,
Ch26 n7, Ch43 n24, Ch49
n10, Ch54 n31, Ch78 n49.
Zhou 周, State, I 73, 152, 305, 330,
II 475, 552, 610, 719, 826.
Zhou Bo 周勃, high officer of Han
Wen Di 漢文帝, II 803.
Zhou Chang 周昌, high officer of
Zhao 趙, II 786.
Zhou Chang Sheng 周長生,
scholar/writer, II 838–39, III
Ch39 nn41, 50.
Zhou Fu 周服, native of Quanling
泉陵, II 606.
Zhou Gong 周公, Duke of Zhou 周,
brother of Wu Wang 武王, I
135, 166, 282, 311, 337–38,
349, 439, II 461, 463, 464,
566 seq., 590, 594, 599, 600,
767, 783, 817, 826, III Ch25
n45, Ch42 nn10, 11, 41,
Ch55 nn10, 39, Ch82 nn19,
28.
Zhouli 周禮, "Book of Rites of the
Zhou 周," II 817–18, III 868,
869, 910, 930, 932–34, Ch23
n17, Ch35 n24, Ch45 n21,
Ch46 n19, Ch47 n33, Ch81
n36, Ch82 n19.
Zhou Qingchen 周青臣, major-
domo of Shi Huangdi 始皇
帝, I 283, II 812.
Zhou Ya Fu 周亞夫, general and
chief minister under Han
Wen Di 漢文帝, I 87, 139,
III 931–32, Ch11 n30.
Zhouyi 周易 = Yijing 易經 of the
Zhou 周 dynasty, I 412–13,
II 816, III Ch81 n31.
Zhu 洙, tributary of the Si 泗 in
Shandong 山東, I 231.
Zhu 柱, Spirit of the Grain, II 758.
Zhu 邾, State in Shandong 山東, II
786, III Ch79 n43.
Zhu Fu Yan 主父偃, enemy of
Dong Zhongshu 董仲舒, I
86, II 446, 841, III Ch3 n9.
Zhu Rong 祝融, Genius of Summer
and Fire, II 758, III 869, 874,
Ch77 n17.
Zhuan Xu 顓頊, mythical emperor,
I 135, 166, 357–58, II 496,
517, 671, 745, 756, 758, 761,
845, III 869, 874, Ch11 n1,

Ch24 nn6, 48, Ch36 n13, Ch77 n5.

Zhuang 莊, Duke of Lu 魯, I 181, 305, 378, III Ch32 n49, Ch71 n14.

Zhuang 莊, Duke of Qi 齊, III Ch56 n20.

Zhuang 莊, King of Chu 楚, II 462, 596, III Ch39 n20, Ch55 n31, Ch85 n32.

Zhuang Qiao 莊蹻, robber, I 102, 153.

Zhuang Shu 莊叔, minister of Lu 魯, II 718.

Zhuang Zi Yi 莊子義, phantom, minister of Duke Jian 簡 of Yan 燕, II 675–76.

Zhuang Zi Yi 莊子義, minister of Viscount Jian 簡 of Zhao 趙, I 177, II 636–37, 638.

Zhuang and Yue 莊嶽, two quarters in the capital of Qi 齊, I 117, III Ch8 n27.

Zhuo 卓 = Zhuo Mao 卓茂, official of the 1st cent. CE, I 221, III Ch19 n72.

Zhuolu 涿鹿, place in Zhili 直隸, II 593.

Zhuoyong 著雍, territory, II 640.

Zi 子, family name of the Shang 商 (Yin 殷) dynasty, I 162, 166, II 739.

Zi 子, great officer of Song 宋, ancestor of Confucius, II 765, 766.

Zi Chan 子產 = Gongsun Qiao 公孫僑, famous minister of Zheng 鄭, I 142, 191, 340–41, 409, 433, II 642–43, 644, 647, 649, 665, 786, 828, 835, III 869, Ch29 n29, Ch35 n36, Ch63 n21, Ch64 n86.

Zi Er 子耳, father of Bo You 伯有 of Zheng 鄭, II 643.

Zi Fan 子反, general of Chu 楚, I 74, 227, III Ch1 n22, Ch20 n6, Ch64 n73, Ch71 n24.

Zi Gan 子干, Prince of Chu 楚, I 123.

Zi Gao 子羔 = Gao Zigao 高子羔, disciple of Confucius, I 304, 322, 409, II 812, III Ch47 n3, Ch81 n14.

Zi Gong 子貢, disciple of Confucius, I 74, 86, 142, 244, 313–14, 316, 323, 324, 326, 332, 431, II 506, 518–19, 557, 720, 740, 761, 770, 774, 778, 783–84, 787, 788, 791, 803, 804–5, 824, 853, III Ch8 n10, Ch25 n25, Ch28 nn26, 68, 74, Ch49 n10, Ch80 n82, Ch85 n49.

Zi Jian 子賤, disciple of Confucius, II 828.

Zi Jiu 子糾, Prince of Qi 齊, I 123, III Ch9 n19.

Zi Kuai 子噲, King of Yan 燕, I 346, III Ch30 n21.

Zi Lan 子蘭, official in Wu 吳 who slandered Wu Zixu 伍子胥, I 128.

Zi Liang 子良, grandfather of Bo You 伯有 of Zheng 鄭, II 643, 644.

Zi Lu 子路, disciple of Confucius, I 114, 129, 133, 176, 214–15, 231, 304, 313, 318–19, 322, 328, 329, 330, 356, 409, II 479, 482, 548, 570, 714, 779, 804–5, 812, III Ch21 n10, Ch28 n74, Ch60 n8, Ch80 nn82, 86, Ch81 n14.

Zi Ming 子明, his self-sacrifice, II 581.

Zi Pi 子皮, chief minister of Zheng 鄭, I 409, III Ch35 n36.

Zi Qin 子禽 = Chen Ziqin 陳子禽, II 778.

Zi Shen 梓慎, great officer of Lu 魯, I 191.

Zi Si 子思 = Kong Zi Si 孔子思, grandson of Confucius, I 339–40, 341, 342.

Zi Wei 子韋, astrologer in Song 宋, I 186 seq., 226, II 466, III Ch7 n12, Ch17 n22.

Zi Wei Shulu 子韋書錄, work of Zi Wei 子韋, I 194.

Zi Wen 子文, minister of Chu 楚, I 316–17.

Zi Wo 子我, disciple of Confucius, II 740, 770.

Zi Xi 子皙, officer of Zheng 鄭, II 642, 643, 644.

Zi Xi 子皙, Prince of Chu 楚, I 123.

Zi Xia 子夏, disciple of Confucius, I 99, 101, 230–32, 356, II 788, III Ch6 n11, Ch21 n3, Ch52 n45, Ch80 n88.

Zi Xu 子胥 / Wu Zixu 伍子胥 / Wu Zi Xu 伍子胥 / Wu Yuan 伍員, I 81, 128, 175–78, 211, 356, II 637, 644, III Ch30 n56.

Zi Ying 子嬰, last Emperor of the Qin 秦 dynasty, I 163, II 596, III Ch43 n18.

Zi You 子游, disciple of Confucius, I 309, 311, II 788, III 872.

Zi Yu 子玉, minister of Chu 楚, I 316–17.

Zi Yu 子輿, minister of Qin 秦, II 656.

Zi Yu 子圍, Prince of Chu 楚, I 123.

Zi Zhang 子張, disciple of Confucius, I 316, II 788, III Ch28 n74, Ch80 n88.

Zi Zhao 子招, Prince of Chu 楚, I 123.

Zi Zhi 子之, minister of Yan 燕, I 346, III Ch30 n21.

Zicai 梓材, "The Timber of the Tse Tree," chapter of the *Shangshu* 尚書, I 418.

Zifu Jingbo 子服景伯, great officer of Lu 魯, II 548.

Zifu Libo 子服厲伯, at the court of Duke Mu 繆 of Lu 魯, 4th cent. BCE, I 339–40, 341.

Zigong 紫宮, constellation, I 251.

Zixufu 子虛賦, poem of Sima Xiangru 司馬相如, II 826.

Zeng Can (Shen) 曾參 = Zeng Zi 曾子, I 80, 82.

Zeng Shen 曾參 = Zeng Zi 曾子, II 524, 797.

Zeng Xi 曾皙, father of Zeng Zi 曾子, II 485, 524, 797.

Zeng Zi 曾子, disciple of Confucius, I 211, 220–21, 230–32, 329, 419–20, II 570–71, 582, 687, 693, 770, 823, III Ch19 n29, Ch23 n7, Ch37 n12, Ch50 n34, Ch55 nn39, 43.

Zong Shu Xi 宗叔犀, high officer, I 402.

Zongchuan 酆川, principality, I 242.

Zongkui 從魁, one of the Twelve Spirits of the cardinal points, II 733, III Ch75 n1.

Zongyi 酆夷, family name, I 242.

Zou 鄒, place in Shandong 山東, II 779.

Zou Bo Qi 鄒伯奇, author, II 575, 596, 838, 843.

Zou Yan 鄒衍, scholar of the 4th cent. BCE, I 211–12, 435, 436, II 443, 701, 796, 845,

on the Nine Continents, I
360, II 456, 457, causing a
fall of frost, II 471, causing
the "Cold Valley" to become
warm, II 473, his works, II
834.

Zou Yang 鄒陽, officer of the
2nd cent. BCE, II 443, 829,
850–51, III Ch85 n11.

Zu Ji 祖己, official of Gao Zong 高
宗, I 195–96, 198, 202, 203,
III Ch51 n24.

Zu Yi 祖乙, Shang 商 Emperor, II
647, 717, III Ch63 n39.

Zu Yi 祖乙 [probably a mistake for
祖己], officer of the Emperor
Gao Zong 高宗, II 535, III
Ch51 n24.

Zu Yi 祖伊, minister of the Emper-
or Zhou 紂, I 304, 305.

Zuo Qiu Ming 左邱明, author of
the *Zuozhuan* 左氏傳, I 181,
200, 380, II 618, 672, 817,
833–34, III Ch45 n37, Ch49
n1.

Zuo Wu 左吳, Daoist connected
with Huai Nan Zi 淮南子,
I 360.

Zuozhuan 左氏傳, commentary to
the *Chunqiu* 春秋 "Spring
and Autumn" Classic, I
113, 152, 379, 380, II 618,
818, 819, 833, 834, III 866,
869–71, 882, 893, 900, 902,
905, Ch9 n25, Ch22 n19,
Ch32 n40, Ch52 n33, Ch55
n58, Ch64 n73, Ch65 n13,
Ch70 n9, Ch71 n24, Ch74
n42, Ch77 nn17, 52, Ch78
n35, Ch79 n43, Ch81 nn33,
51, Ch83 nn2, 7, 10, App I
nn34, 36.

Notes

Notes

⤙ *Notes* ⤙

Notes

꩜ *Notes* ꩜

ABOUT QUIRIN PRESS

Established in 2012 Quirin Press is a small independent publisher specializing in:
Asian Studies; Cultural Studies; Poetics; and Aesthetics.

The first titles of the press have concentrated on re-issuing classical works in the field
that have been out of print for some time. These are new editions that update and revise
established titles in line with current scholarship and practices (e.g. the older Wade-
Giles transliteration of Chinese words is updated to the current Pinyin standard).

ARNTZEN Ikkyū & the Crazy Cloud Anthology

A.C. GRAHAM Reason and Spontaneity

MASPERO Methods of "Nourishing the Vital Principle" in the Ancient Daoist Religion

BODMAN Poetics and Prosody in Early Mediaeval China
A Study and Translation of Kūkai's Bunkyō Hifuron

A.C. GRAHAM The Problem of Value

WIXTED Poems on Poetry Revised Edition

A. C. Graham Yin-Yang and the Nature of Correlative Thinking

MIURA & SASAKI ZEN DUST
The History of the Koan and Koan Study in Rinzai (Linji) Zen

MASPERO TAOISM AND CHINESE RELIGION Revised Edition

OWEN The Great Age of Chinese Poetry:
The High Tang Revised Edition

OWEN The Poetry of the Early Tang Revised Edition

For details on any of our present or forthcoming titles visit:
www.QuirinPress.com
and follow us on Twitter @QuirinPress

LUN HENG

The Complete Essays of Wang Chong

王充

論

衡

Translated and annotated by
† ALFRED FORKE

Vol. I

Chapters 1-38

LUNHENG

The Complete Essays of Wang Chong

王充

Translated and annotated by

† ALFRED FORKE

Vol. II

Chapters 39–85

Publisher's Note		vii
Contents		xi
Preface		xv
Introduction		
I	The Life of Wang Chong 王充	1
II	The Works of Wang Chong	6
III	Wang Chong's Philosophy	11
IV	Synoptic Table of Contents of the *Lunheng*	48
1	Success and Luck—*Fengyu* 逢遇	71
2	Annoyances and Vexations—*Leihai* 累害	78
3	On Destiny and Fortune—*Minglu* 命祿	83
4	Long Life and Vital Fluid—*Qishou* 氣壽	90
5	On Chance and Luck—*Xing'ou* 幸偶	94
6	What Is Meant by Destiny?—*Mingyi* 命義	99
7	Unfounded Assertions—*Wuxing* 無形	106
8	The Forming of Characters—*Shuaixing* 率性	112
9	Auspicious Portents—*Jiyan* 吉驗	120
10	Coincidences—*Ouhui* 偶會	128
11	On Anthroposcopy—*Guxiang* 骨相	135
12	Heaven's Original Gift—*Chubing* 初禀	143
13	On Original Nature—*Benxing* 本性	149
14	The Nature of Things—*Wushi* 物勢	156
15	Miracles—*Qiguai* 奇怪	162
16	Falsehoods in Books—*Shuxu* 書虛	169
17	Fictitious Phenomena—*Bianxu* 變虛	186
18	Fictitious Prodigies—*Yixu* 異虛	195
19	Fictitious Influences—*Ganxu* 感虛	204
20	Wrong Notions About Happiness—*Fuxu* 福虛	223
21	Wrong Notions on Unhappiness—*Huoxu* 禍虛	230
22	On Dragons—*Longxu* 龍虛	238
23	On Thunder and Lightning—*Leixu* 雷虛	246
24	Daoist Untruths—*Daoxu* 道虛	258
25	Exaggerations—*Yuzeng* 語增	275
26	Exaggerations of the Literati—*Ruzeng* 儒增	286
27	Literary Exaggerations—*Yizeng* 藝增	299
28	Criticisms on Confucius—*Wen Kong* 問孔	308
29	Strictures on Han Feizi 韓非子—*Fei Han* 非韓	331
30	Censures on Mencius—*Ci Meng* 刺孟	344
31	On Heaven—*Tantian* 談天	357
32	On the Sun—*Shuori* 說日	364
33	On the Cunning and Artful—*Daning* 答佞	382
34	Weighing of Talents—*Chengcai* 程材	393
35	The Valuation of Knowledge—*Liangzhi* 量知	403
36	Admitting Shortcomings—*Xieduan* 謝短	410
37	The Display of Energy—*Xiaoli* 效力	418
38	On Intelligence—*Bietong* 別通	427

39	On Preeminence—*Chaoqi* 超奇	438
40	Apparent Backwardness—*Zhuangliu* 狀留	447
41	On Heat and Cold—*Hanwen* 寒温	453
42	On Reprimands—*Qiangao* 譴告	459
43	Phenomenal Changes—*Biandong* 變動	468
44	[Attracting Consequences] *Zhaozhi* 招致 [lost]	477
45	On the Rain Sacrifice—*Mingyu* 明雩	478
46	Gentle Drums—*Shungu* 順鼓	489
47	A Last Word on Dragons—*Luanlong* 亂龍	498
48	The Tiger Trouble—*Zaohu* 遭虎	505
49	Remarks on Insects—*Shangchong* 商蟲	510
50	Arguments on Ominous Creatures—*Jiangrui* 講瑞	516
51	Thoughts on Omens—*Zhirui* 指瑞	530
52	Auguries Verified—*Shiying* 是應	538
53	Periods of Government—*Zhiqi* 治期	547
54	Spontaneity—*Ziran* 自然	554
55	Sympathetic Emotions—*Ganlei* 感類	564
56	The Equality of the Ages—*Qishi* 齊世	576
57	Praise of the Han Dynasty—*Xuan Han* 宣漢	585
58	Further Remarks on the State—*Huiguo* 恢國	593
59	Ominous Signs Investigated—*Yanfu* 驗符	603
60	The Necessity of Eulogies—*Xusong* 須頌	609
61	Lost Texts—*Yiwen* 佚文	617
62	On Death—*Lunsi* 論死	625
63	False Reports about the Dead—*Siwei* 死偽	636
64	Spook Stories—*Jiyao* 紀妖	653
65	All about Ghosts—*Dinggui* 訂鬼	668
66	On Poison—*Yandu* 言毒	677
67	Simplicity of Funerals—*Bozang* 薄葬	683
68	Four Things to Be Avoided—*Sihui* 四諱	690
69	False Charges against Time—*Lanshi* 䛄時	700
70	Slandering of Days—*Jiri* 譏日	706
71	On Divination—*Bushi* 卜筮	714
72	Criticisms on Noxious Influences—*Biansui* 辨祟	722
73	Questions about the Year Star—*Nansui* 難歲	729
74	Criticisms on Certain Theories—*Jieshu* 詰術	736
75	On Exorcism—*Jiechu* 解除	743
76	Sacrifices to the Departed—*Siyi* 祀義	749
77	Sacrifices—*Jiyi* 祭意	756
78	The Real Nature of Knowledge—*Shizhi* 實知	764
79	The Knowledge of Truth—*Zhishi* 知實	777
80	A Definition of Worthies—*Dingxian* 定賢	790
81	Statements Corrected—*Zhengshuo* 正說	810
82	On Literary Work—*Shujie* 書解	823
83	Critical Remarks on Various Books—*Anshu* 案書	832
84	Replies in Self-Defense—*Duizuo* 對作	840
85	Autobiography—*Ziji* 自紀	848

www.ingramcontent.com/pod-product-compliance
Lightning Source LLC
Chambersburg PA
CBHW050611110726
47899CB00001B/66